Operations Management

PEARSON

We work with leading authors to develop the strongest learning experiences, bringing cutting-edge thinking and best learning practice to a global market. We craft our print and digital resources to do more to help learners not only understand their content, but to see it in action and apply what they learn, whether studying or at work.

Pearson is the world's leading learning company. Our portfolio includes Penguin, Dorling Kindersley, the Financial Times and our educational business, Pearson International. We are also a leading provider of electronic learning programmes and of test development, processing and scoring services to educational institutions, corporations and professional bodies around the world.

We enable our customers to access a wide and expanding range of market-leading content from world-renowned authors and develop their own tailor-made book. You choose the content that meets your needs and Pearson produces a high-quality printed book.

Every day our work helps learning flourish, and wherever learning flourishes, so do people.

To learn more please visit us at: www.pearsoned.co.uk/personalised

Operations Management

Compiled from:

Essentials of Operations Management
First Edition
Nigel Slack, Alistair Brandon-Jones and Robert Johnston

Service Operations Management
Fourth Edition
Robert Johnston, Graham Clark and Michael Shulver

PEARSON

Harlow, England • London • New York • Boston • San Francisco • Toronto • Sydney • Auckland • Singapore • Hong Kong
Tokyo • Seoul • Taipei • New Delhi • Cape Town • Sao Paulo • Mexico City • Madrid • Amsterdam • Munich • Paris • Milan

Pearson Education Limited
Edinburgh Gate
Harlow
Essex CM20 2JE

And associated companies throughout the world

Visit us on the World Wide Web at:
www.pearson.com/uk

© Pearson Education Limited 2014

Compiled from:

Essentials of Operations Management
First Edition
Nigel Slack, Alistair Brandon-Jones and Robert Johnston
ISBN 978-0-273-75242-4
© Nigel Slack, Alistair Brandon-Jones and Robert Johnston 2011

Service Operations Management
Fourth Edition
Robert Johnston, Graham Clark and Michael Shulver
ISBN 978-0-273-74048-3
© Pearson Education Limited 2001, 2012

All rights reserved. No part of this publication may be reproduced, stored in a retrieval system, or transmitted in any form or by any means, electronic, mechanical, photocopying, recording or otherwise, without either the prior written permission of the publisher or a licence permitting restricted copying in the United Kingdom issued by the Licensing Agency Ltd, Saffron House, 6–10 Kirby Street, London EC1N 8TS.

ISBN 978-1-78376-372-6

Printed and bound in Great Britain by Ashford Colour Press, Gosport, Hampshire.

Contents

Chapter 1 Operations Management — 1
Chapter 1 in *Essentials of Operations Management*, First Edition
Nigel Slack, Alistair Brandon-Jones and Robert Johnston

Chapter 2 Introducing Service Operations Management — 25
Chapter 1 in *Service Operations Management*, Fourth Edition
Robert Johnston, Graham Clark and Michael Shulver

Chapter 3 Understanding the Challenges for Operations Managers — 43
Chapter 2 in *Service Operations Management*, Fourth Edition
Robert Johnston, Graham Clark and Michael Shulver

Chapter 4 Operations Strategy — 67
Chapter 2 in *Essentials of Operations Management*, First Edition
Nigel Slack, Alistair Brandon-Jones and Robert Johnston

Chapter 5 Social, Environmental and Economic Performance — 86
Chapter 3 in *Essentials of Operations Management*, First Edition
Nigel Slack, Alistair Brandon-Jones and Robert Johnston

Chapter 6 The Design of Services and Products — 109
Chapter 4 in *Essentials of Operations Management*, First Edition
Nigel Slack, Alistair Brandon-Jones and Robert Johnston

Chapter 7 Process Design — 132
Chapter 5 in *Essentials of Operations Management*, First Edition
Nigel Slack, Alistair Brandon-Jones and Robert Johnston

Chapter 8 Location, Layout and Flow — 160
Chapter 6 in *Essentials of Operations Management*, First Edition
Nigel Slack, Alistair Brandon-Jones and Robert Johnston

Chapter 9 Supply Network Management — 179
Chapter 7 in *Essentials of Operations Management*, First Edition
Nigel Slack, Alistair Brandon-Jones and Robert Johnston

Chapter 10 Capacity Management — 209
Chapter 8 in *Essentials of Operations Management*, First Edition
Nigel Slack, Alistair Brandon-Jones and Robert Johnston

Chapter 11	**Inventory Management**	**238**
	Chapter 9 in *Essentials of Operations Management*, First Edition	
	Nigel Slack, Alistair Brandon-Jones and Robert Johnston	
Chapter 12	**Planning and Control**	**265**
	Chapter 10 in *Essentials of Operations Management*, First Edition	
	Nigel Slack, Alistair Brandon-Jones and Robert Johnston	
Chapter 13	**Lean Synchronization**	**288**
	Chapter 11 in *Essentials of Operations Management*, First Edition	
	Nigel Slack, Alistair Brandon-Jones and Robert Johnston	
	Index	**309**

Chapter 1

Operations management

Key questions

- What is operations management?
- Why is operations management important in all types of organization?
- What is the input–transformation–output process?
- What is the process hierarchy?
- How do operations processes have different characteristics?
- What are the activities of operations management?

Introduction

Operations management is about how organizations design, deliver, and improve services and products for their customers. Everything you wear, eat, sit on, use, read or knock about on the sports field comes to you courtesy of the operations managers who organized its creation. Every book you borrow from the library, every treatment you receive at the hospital, every service you expect in the shops and every lecture you attend at university – all have been created. While the people who supervised their creation may not always be called operations managers, that is what they really are. And that is what this book is concerned with – the tasks, issues and decisions of those operations managers who have made the services and products on which we all depend. This is an introductory chapter, so we will examine what we mean by 'operations management', how operations processes can be found everywhere, how they are all similar yet different, and what it is that operations managers do.

PEARSON myomlab

Check and improve your understanding of this chapter using self-assessment questions and a personalized study plan, audio and video downloads, and an eBook – all at www.myomlab.com.

Operations in practice IKEA[1]

(All chapters start with an 'Operations in practice' example that illustrates some of the issues that will be covered in the chapter.)

Love it or hate it, IKEA is the most successful furniture retailer ever. With 276 stores in 36 countries, it has managed to develop its own special way of selling furniture. The stores' layout means customers often spend two hours in the store – far longer than in rival furniture retailers. IKEA's philosophy goes back to the original business, started in the 1950s in Sweden by Ingvar Kamprad. He built a showroom on the outskirts of Stockholm where land was cheap and simply displayed suppliers' furniture as it would be in a domestic setting. Increasing sales soon allowed IKEA to start ordering its own self-designed products from local manufacturers. However, it was innovation in its operations that dramatically reduced its selling costs. These included the idea of selling furniture as self-assembly flat packs (which reduced production and transport costs) and its 'showroom–warehouse' concept which required customers to pick the furniture up themselves from the warehouse (which reduced retailing costs). Both of these operating principles are still the basis of IKEA's retail operations process today.

Stores are designed to facilitate the smooth flow of customers, from parking, moving through the store itself, to ordering and picking up products. At the entrance to each store large notice-boards provide advice to shoppers. For young children, there is a supervised children's play area, a small cinema, and a parent and baby room so parents can leave their children in the supervised play area for a time. Parents are recalled via the loudspeaker system if the child has any problems. IKEA 'allow customers to make up their minds in their own time' but 'information points' have staff who can help. All furniture carries a ticket with a code number which indicates its location in the warehouse. (For larger items, customers go to the information desks for assistance.) There is also an area where smaller items are displayed, and can be picked directly. Customers then pass through the warehouse where they pick up the items viewed in the showroom. Finally, customers pay at the checkouts, where a ramped conveyor belt moves purchases up to the checkout staff. The exit area has service points and a loading area that allows customers to bring their cars from the car park and load their purchases.

Behind the public face of IKEA's huge stores is a complex worldwide network of suppliers: 1,300 direct suppliers, about 10,000 sub-suppliers, wholesale and transport operations including 26 Distribution Centres. This supply network is vitally important to IKEA. From purchasing raw materials, right through to finished products arriving in its customers' homes, IKEA relies on close partnerships with its suppliers to achieve both ongoing supply efficiency and new product development. However, IKEA closely controls all supply and development activities from IKEA's home town of Älmhult in Sweden.

However, success brings its own problems and some customers became increasingly frustrated with overcrowding and long waiting times. In response IKEA in the UK launched a £150 m programme to 'design out' the bottlenecks. The changes included:

- Clearly marked in-store short cuts allowing customers who just want to visit one area to avoid having to go through all the preceding areas.
- Express checkout tills for customers with a bag only rather than a trolley.
- Extra 'help staff' at key points to help customers.
- Redesign of the car parks, making them easier to navigate.
- Dropping the ban on taking trolleys out to the car parks for loading (originally implemented to stop vehicles being damaged).
- A new warehouse system to stop popular product lines running out during the day.
- More children's play areas.

IKEA spokeswoman Nicki Craddock said: *'We know people love our products but hate our shopping experience. We are being told that by customers every day, so we can't afford not to make changes. We realized a lot of people took offence at being herded like sheep on the long route around stores. Now if you know what you are looking for and just want to get in, grab it and get out, you can.'*

Operations management is a vital part of IKEA's success

IKEA shows how important operations management is for its own success and the success of any type of organization. Of course, IKEA understands its market and its customers. Just as important, it knows that the way it manages the network of operations that design, produce and deliver its products and services must be right for its market. No organization can survive in the long term if it cannot supply its customers effectively. This is essentially what operations management is about – designing, producing and delivering products and services that satisfy market requirements. For any business, it is a vitally important activity. Consider just some of the activities that IKEA's operations managers are involved in.

- Arranging the store's layout to give smooth and effective flow of customers (called process design).
- Designing stylish products that can be flat-packed efficiently (called product design).
- Making sure that all staff can contribute to the company's success (called job design).
- Locating stores of an appropriate size in the most effective place (called supply network design).
- Arranging for the delivery of products to stores (called supply chain management).
- Coping with fluctuations in demand (called capacity management).
- Maintaining cleanliness and safety of storage area (called failure prevention).
- Avoiding running out of products for sale (called inventory management).
- Monitoring and enhancing quality of service to customers (called quality management).
- Continually examining and improving operations practice (called operations improvement).

Importantly, these activities are only a small part of IKEA's total operations management effort. But they do give an indication, first of how operations management should contribute to the businesses success, and second, what would happen if IKEA's operations managers failed to be effective in carrying out any of its activities. Badly designed processes, inappropriate products, poor locations, disaffected staff, empty shelves, or forgetting the importance of continually improving quality, could all turn a previously successful organization into a failing one. Yet, although the relative importance of these activities will vary between different organizations, operations managers in all organizations will be making the same *type* of decision (even if *what* they actually decide is different).

What is operations management?

Operations management
Operations function

Operations management is the activity of managing the resources which create and deliver services and products. The **operations function** is the part of the organization that is responsible for this activity. Every organization has an operations function because every organization produces some type of services and/or products. However, not all types of organization will necessarily call the operations function by this name. (Note that we also use the shorter terms 'the operation' and 'operations' interchangeably with the 'operations function'.) **Operations**

Operations managers

managers are the people who have particular responsibility for managing some, or all, of the resources which comprise the operations function. Again, in some organizations the operations manager could be called by some other name. For example, he or she might be called the 'fleet manager' in a distribution company, the 'administrative manager' in a hospital or the 'store manager' in a supermarket.

Operations in the organization

The operations function is central to the organization because it creates the services and products which are its reason for existing, but it is not the only function. It is, however, one

Three core functions

of the **three core functions** of any organization. These are:

- the marketing (including sales) function – which is responsible for *communicating* the organization's services and products (or more generically, offerings) to its markets in order to generate customer requests for service;

- the service/product development function – which is responsible for developing new and modified offerings in order to generate future customer requests for service;
- the operations function – which is responsible for *fulfilling* customer requests for service through the creation and delivery of services and products.

Support functions

In addition, there are the **support functions** which enable the core functions to operate effectively. These include, for example:

- the accounting and finance function – which provides the information to help economic decision-making and manages the financial resources of the organization;
- the human resources function – which recruits and develops the organization's staff as well as looking after their welfare.

Remember that different organizations will call their various functions by different names and will have a different set of support functions. Almost all organizations, however, will have the three core functions, because all organizations have a fundamental need to sell their services, satisfy their customers and create the means to satisfy customers in the future. Table 1.1 shows the activities of the three core functions for a sample of organizations.

Broad definition of operations

In practice, there is not always a clear division between the three core functions or between core and support functions. This leads to some confusion over where the boundaries of the operations function should be drawn. In this book we use a relatively **broad definition of operations**. We treat much of the product/service development, technical and information systems activities and some of the human resource, marketing and accounting and finance activities as coming within the sphere of operations management. We view the operations function as comprising all the activities necessary for the day-to-day fulfilment of customer requests. This includes sourcing services and products from suppliers and transporting them to customers.

Working effectively with the other parts of the organization is one of the most important responsibilities of operations management. It is a fundamental of modern management that functional boundaries should not hinder efficient internal processes. Figure 1.1 illustrates some of the relationships between operations and some other functions in terms of the flow of information between them. Although it is not comprehensive, it gives an idea of the nature of each relationship.

Table 1.1 The activities of core functions in some organizations

Core functional activities	Internet service provider (ISP)	Fast food chain	International aid charity	Furniture manufacturer
Marketing and sales	Promote services to users and get registrations Sell advertising space	Advertise on TV Devise promotional materials	Develop funding contracts Mail out appeals for donations	Advertise in magazines Determine pricing policy Sell to stores
Product/service development	Devise new services and commission new information content	Design hamburgers, pizzas, etc. Design décor for restaurants	Develop new appeals campaigns Design new assistance programmes	Design new furniture Coordinate with fashionable colours
Operations	Maintain hardware, software and content Implement new links and services	Make burgers, pizzas etc. Serve customers Clear away Maintain equipment	Give service to the beneficiaries of the charity	Make components Assemble furniture

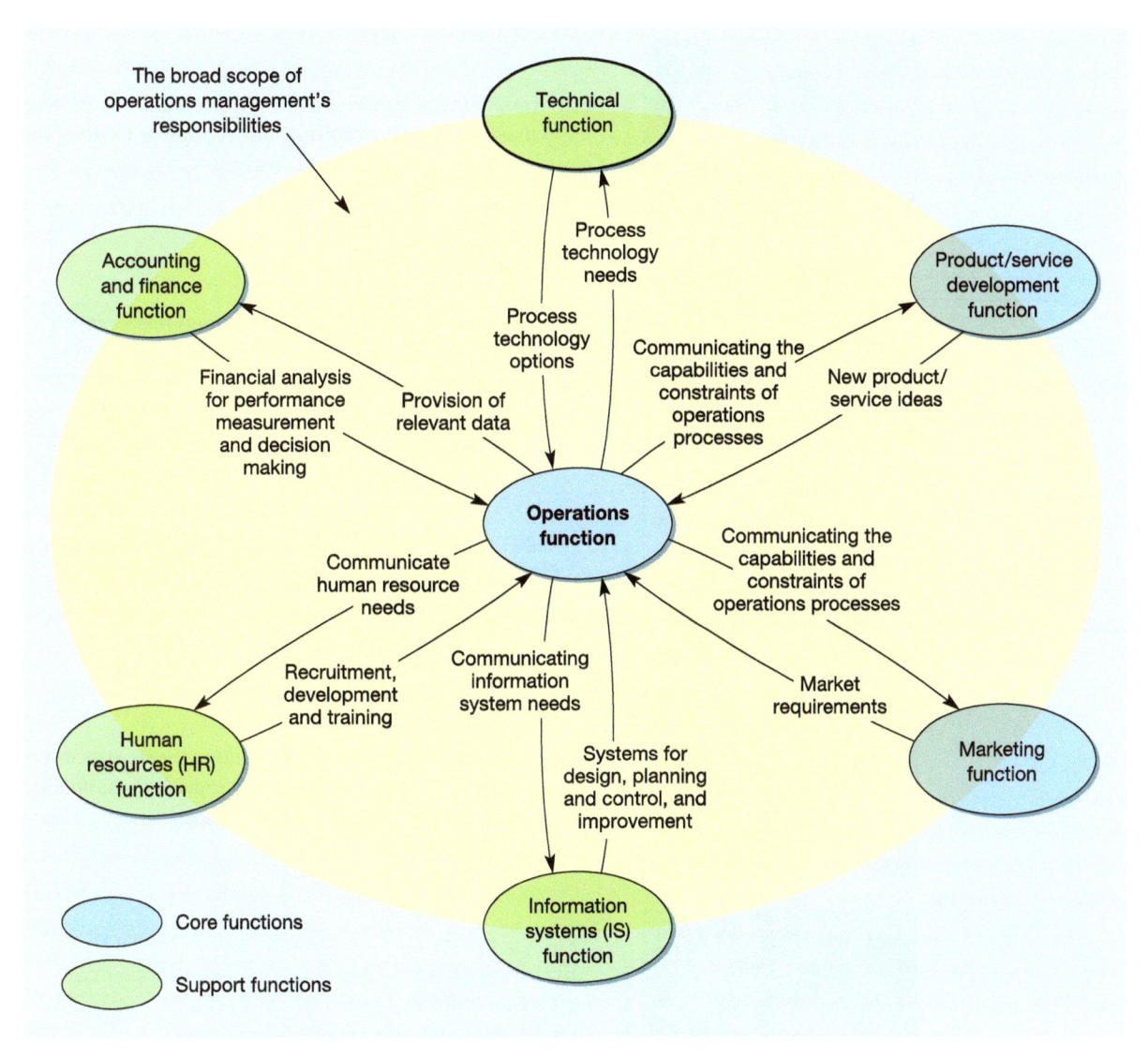

Figure 1.1 The relationship between the operations function and other core and support functions of the organization

Operations management is important in all types of organization

In some types of organization it is relatively easy to visualize the operations function and what it does, even if we have never seen it. For example, most people have seen images of automobile assembly. But what about an advertising agency? We know vaguely what they do – they produce the advertisements that we see in magazines and on television – but what is their operations function? The clue lies in the word 'produce'. Any business that produces something must use resources to do so, and so must have an operations activity. So, the advertising agency and the automobile plant have one important element in common: both have a higher objective – to make a profit from creating and delivering their services or products. Yet not-for-profit organizations also use their resources to produce services, not to make a profit, but to serve society in some way. Look at the following examples of what operations management does in five very different organizations and some common themes emerge.

Physician (general practitioner) – *Operations management uses knowledge to effectively diagnose conditions in order to treat real and perceived patient concerns*

Automobile assembly factory – *Operations management uses machines to efficiently assemble products that satisfy current customer demands*

Management consultant – *Operations management uses people to effectively create the services that will address current and potential client needs*

Disaster relief charity – *Operations management uses our and our partners' resources to speedily provide the supplies and services that relieve community suffering*

Advertising agency – *Operations management uses our staff's knowledge and experience to creatively present ideas that delight clients and address their real needs*

Whatever terminology is used there is a common theme and a common purpose to how we can visualize the operations activity in any type of organization: small or large, manufacturing or service, public or private, profit or not-for-profit. Operations management uses *resources* to *appropriately create outputs* that *fulfil defined market requirements.* See Figure 1.2. However, although the essential nature and purpose of operations management is the same in every type of organization, there are some special issues to consider, particularly in smaller organizations and those whose purpose is to maximize something other than profit.

Operations management in the smaller organization

Irrespective of their size, all companies need to produce and deliver their products and services efficiently and effectively. However, managing operations in a small or medium-size organization has its own set of problems. Large companies may have the resources to dedicate individuals to specialized tasks, but smaller companies often cannot, so people may have to do different jobs as the need arises. Such an informality may allow a quick response as opportunities present themselves. But decision-making can also become confused as **individuals' roles can overlap in small operations**. However, small operations can also have significant advantages; the short case on Acme Whistles illustrates this.

The role of operations management in smaller organizations often overlaps significantly with other functions

Operations management uses...								
resources	to	appropriately	create	outputs	that	fulfil	defined	market	requirements
			produce						
experience			change				potential	citizens'	
people		effectively	sell	ideas		match	perceived	client	dreams
machines		efficiently	assemble	products		satisfy	current	customer	demands
knowledge		creatively	move	services		exceed	emerging	society	needs
partners		etc.	cure	etc.		delight	real	etc.	concerns
etc.			shape			etc.	etc.		etc.
			etc.						

Figure 1.2 Operations management uses resources to appropriately create outputs that fulfil defined market requirements

Short case
Acme Whistles[2]

Acme Whistles can trace its history back to 1870 when Joseph Hudson decided he had the answer to the London Metropolitan Police's request for something to replace the wooden rattles that were used to sound the alarm. So the world's first police whistle was born. Soon Acme grew to be the premier supplier of whistles for police forces around the world. *'In many ways'*, says Simon Topman, owner and Managing Director of the company, *'the company is very much the same as it was in Joseph's day. The machinery is more modern, of course, and we have a wider variety of products, but many of our products are similar to their predecessors. For example, football referees seem to prefer the traditional snail-shaped whistle. So, although we have dramatically improved the performance of the product, our customers want it to look the same. We have also maintained the same manufacturing tradition from those early days. The original owner insisted on personally blowing every single whistle before it left the factory. We still do the same, not by personally blowing them, but by using an air line, so the same tradition of quality has endured.'*

The company's range of whistles has expanded to include sports whistles (they provide the whistles for the soccer World Cup), distress whistles, (silent) dog whistles, novelty whistles, instrumental whistles (used by all of the world's top orchestras), and many more types. *'We are always trying to improve our products'*, says Simon, *'it's a business of constant innovation. Sometimes I think that after 130 years surely there is nothing more to do, but we always find some new feature to incorporate. Of course, managing the operations in a small company is very different to working in a large one. Everyone has much broader jobs; we cannot afford the overheads of having specialist people in specialized roles. But this relative informality has a lot of advantages. It means that we can maintain our philosophy of quality amongst everybody in the company, and it means that we can react very quickly when the market demands it.'* Nor is the company's small size any barrier to its ability to innovate. *'On the contrary'*, says Simon, *'there is something about the culture of the company that is extremely important in fostering innovation. Because we are small we all know each other and we all want to contribute something to the company. It is not uncommon for employees to figure out new ideas for different types of whistle. If an idea looks promising, we will put a small and informal team together to look at it further. It is not unusual for people who have been with us only a few months to start wanting to make innovations. It's as though something happens to them when they walk through the door of the factory that encourages their natural inventiveness.'*

Operations management in not-for-profit organizations

Terms such as *competitive advantage*, *markets* and *business*, which are used in this book, are usually associated with companies in the for-profit sector. Yet operations management is also relevant to organizations whose purpose is not primarily to earn profits. Managing the operations in an animal welfare charity, hospital, research organization or government department is essentially the same as in commercial organizations. **Operations have to take the same decisions** – how to create services and products, invest in technology, contract out some of their activities, devise performance measures, and improve their operations performance and so on. However, the strategic objectives of not-for-profit organizations may be more complex and involve a mixture of political, economic, social and environmental objectives. Nevertheless, the vast majority of the topics covered in this book have relevance to all types of organization, including non-profit, even if some terms may have to be adapted.

> Operations decisions are the same in commercial and not-for-profit organizations

Short case
Oxfam International[3]

Oxfam International is a confederation of 13 like-minded organizations based around the world that, together with partners and allies, work directly with communities seeking to ensure that poor people can improve their lives and livelihoods and have a say in decisions that affect them. With an annual expenditure that exceeds US$700 million, Oxfam International focuses its efforts in several areas, including development work, long-term programmes to eradicate poverty and combat injustice, emergency relief delivering immediate life-saving assistance to people affected by natural disasters or conflict, helping to build their resilience to future disasters, campaigning and raising public awareness of the causes of poverty, encouraging ordinary people to take action for a fairer world, and advocacy and research that pressures decision-makers to change policies and practices that reinforce poverty and injustice.

All of Oxfam International's activities depend on effective and professional operations management. For example, Oxfam's network of charity shops, run by volunteers, is a key source of income. The shops sell donated items and handcrafts from around the world giving small-scale producers fair prices, training, advice and funding. Supply chain management and development is just as central to the running of these shops as it is to the biggest commercial chain of stores. The operations challenges involved in Oxfam's ongoing 'Clean Water' exercise are different but certainly no less important. Around 80 per cent of diseases and over one-third of deaths in the developing world are caused by contaminated water and Oxfam has a particular expertise in providing clean water and sanitation facilities. The better their coordinated efforts of identifying potential projects, working with local communities, providing help and education and helping to provide civil engineering expertise, the more effective Oxfam is at fulfilling its objectives.

More dramatically, Oxfam International's response to emergency situations, providing humanitarian aid where it is needed, must be fast, appropriate and efficient. Whether the disasters are natural or political, they become emergencies when the people involved can no longer cope. In such situations, Oxfam, through its network of staff in local offices, is able to advise on what and where help is needed. Indeed, local teams are often able to provide warnings of impending disasters, giving more time to assess needs and coordinate a multi-agency response. The organization's headquarters in Oxford in the UK provides advice, materials and staff, often deploying emergency support staff on short-term assignments. Shelters, blankets and clothing can be flown out at short notice from the Emergencies Warehouse. Engineers and sanitation equipment can also be provided, including water tanks, latrines, hygiene kits and containers. When an emergency is over, Oxfam continues to work with the affected communities through their local offices to help people rebuild their lives and livelihoods. In an effort to improve the timeliness, effectiveness and appropriateness of its response to emergencies, Oxfam recently adopted a more systematic approach to evaluating the successes and failures of its humanitarian work. Real-time evaluations, which seek to assess and influence emergency response programmes in their early stages, were implemented during the response to floods in Mozambique and

Source: Rex Features

South Asia, the earthquake in Peru, Hurricane Felix in Nicaragua and the conflicts in Uganda. These exercises provided Oxfam's humanitarian teams with the opportunity to gauge the effectiveness of their response, and make crucial adjustments at an early stage if necessary. The evaluations highlighted several potential improvements. For example, it became evident that there was a need to improve preparation ahead of emergencies, as well as the need to develop more effective coordination planning tools. It was also decided that adopting a common working approach with shared standards would improve the effectiveness of their response to emergencies. Oxfam also emphasizes the importance of the role played by local partners in emergencies. They are often closer to, and more in tune with, affected communities, but may require additional support and empowerment to scale up their response and comply with the international humanitarian standards.

The new operations agenda

Modern business pressures have changed the operations agenda

The business environment has a significant impact on what is expected from operations management. In recent years there have been new pressures for which the operations function has needed to develop responses. Table 1.2 lists some of these **business pressures** and the operations responses to them. These operations responses form a major part of a *new agenda* for operations. Parts of this agenda are trends which have always existed but have accelerated, such as globalization and increased cost pressures. Part of the agenda involves seeking ways to exploit new technologies, most notably the Internet. Of course, the list in Table 1.2 is not comprehensive, nor is it universal. But very few businesses will be unaffected by at least some of these concerns. When businesses have to cope with a more challenging environment, they look to their operations function to help them respond.

Table 1.2 Changes in the business environment are shaping a new operations agenda

The business environment is changing . . .	Prompting operations responses . . .
For example,	For example,
• Increased cost-based competition	• Globalization of operations networking
• Higher quality expectations	• Information-based technologies
• Demands for better service	• Internet-based integration of operations activities
• More choice and variety	• Supply chain management
• Rapidly developing technologies	• Customer relationship management
• Frequent new product/service introduction	• Flexible working patterns
• Increased ethical sensitivity	• Mass customization
• Environmental impacts are more transparent	• Fast time-to-market methods
• More legal regulation	• Lean process design
• Greater security awareness	• Environmentally sensitive design
	• Supplier 'partnership' and development
	• Failure analysis
	• Business recovery planning

The input–transformation–output process

Transformation process model
Input resources
Outputs of services and products

All operations create services and products by changing *inputs* into *outputs* using an 'input-transformation-output' process. Figure 1.3 shows this general **transformation process model**. Put simply, operations are processes that take in a set of **input resources** which are used to transform something, or are transformed themselves, into **outputs of services and products**. Although all operations conform to this general input–transformation–output

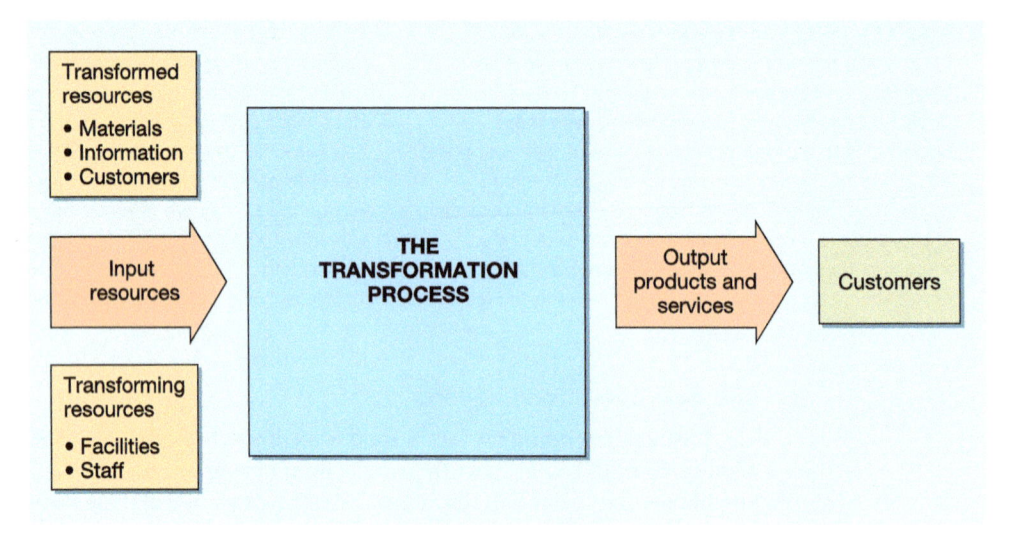

Figure 1.3 All operations are input–transformation–output processes

model, they differ in the nature of their specific inputs and outputs. For example, if you stand far enough away from a hospital or a car plant, they might look very similar, but move closer and clear differences do start to emerge. One is a service operation, creating and delivering services that change the physiological or psychological condition of patients; the other is a manufacturing operation producing products. What is inside each operation will also be different. The motor vehicle plant contains metal-forming machinery and assembly processes, whereas the hospital contains diagnostic, care and therapeutic processes. Perhaps the most important difference between the two operations, however, is the nature of their inputs. The vehicle plant transforms steel, plastic, cloth, tyres and other materials into vehicles. The hospital transforms the customers themselves. The patients form part of the input to, and the output from, the operation. This has important implications for how the operation needs to be managed.

Inputs to the process

One set of inputs to any operation's processes are **transformed resources**. These are the resources that are treated, transformed or converted in the process. They are usually a mixture of the following:

- **Customers** – operations which process customers might change their *physical properties* in a similar way to materials processors: for example, hairdressers or cosmetic surgeons. Some *store* (or more politely *accommodate*) customers: hotels, for example. Airlines, mass rapid transport systems and bus companies transform the *location* of their customers, while hospitals transform their *physiological state*. Some are concerned with transforming their *psychological state*, for example most entertainment services such as music, theatre, television, radio and theme parks.
- **Materials** – operations which process materials could do so to transform their *physical properties* (shape or composition, for example). Most manufacturing operations are like this. Other operations process materials to change their *location* (parcel delivery companies, for example). Some, like retail operations, do so to change the *possession* of the materials. Finally, some operations *store* materials, such as in warehouses.
- **Information** – operations which process information could do so to transform their *informational properties* (that is the purpose or form of the information); accountants do this. Some change the *possession* of the information, for example market research

Table 1.3 Dominant transformed resource inputs of various operations

Predominantly processing inputs of customers	Predominantly processing inputs of materials	Predominantly processing inputs of information
Hairdressers	All manufacturing operations	Accountants
Hotels	Mining companies	Bank headquarters
Hospitals	Retail operations	Market research company
Mass rapid transport	Warehouses	Financial analysts
Theatres	Postal services	News service
Theme parks	Container shipping line	University research unit
Dentists	Trucking companies	Telecoms company

companies sell information. Some *store* the information, for example archives and libraries. Finally, some operations, such as telecommunication companies, change the *location* of the information.

Often one of these is dominant in an operation. For example, a bank devotes part of its energies to producing printed statements of accounts for its customers. In doing so, it is processing **inputs of material**, but no one would claim that a bank is a printer. The bank is also concerned with processing **inputs of customers**. It gives them advice regarding their financial affairs, cashes their cheques, deposits their cash and has direct contact with them. However, most of the bank's activities are concerned with processing **inputs of information** about its customers' financial affairs. As customers, we may be unhappy with badly printed statements and we may be unhappy if we are not treated appropriately in the bank. However, if the bank makes errors in our financial transactions, we suffer in a far more fundamental way. Table 1.3 gives examples of operations with their dominant transformed resources.

Material inputs
Customer inputs

Information inputs

Transforming resources

The other set of inputs to any operations process are **transforming resources**. These are the resources which act upon the transformed resources. There are two types which form the 'building blocks' of all operations:

Facilities
Staff

- **facilities** – the buildings, equipment, plant and process technology of the operation;
- **staff** – the people who operate, maintain, plan and manage the operation. (Note that we use the term 'staff' to describe all the people in the operation, at any level.)

The exact nature of both facilities and staff will differ between operations. To a five-star hotel, its facilities consist mainly of 'low-tech' buildings, furniture and fittings. To a nuclear-powered aircraft carrier, its facilities are 'high-tech' nuclear generators and sophisticated electronic equipment. Staff will also differ between operations. Most staff employed in a factory assembling domestic refrigerators may not need a very high level of technical skill. In contrast, most staff employed by an accounting company are, hopefully, highly skilled in their own particular 'technical' skill (accounting). Yet although skills vary, all staff can make a contribution. An assembly worker who consistently misassembles refrigerators will dissatisfy customers and increase costs just as surely as an accountant who cannot add up. The balance between facilities and staff also varies. A computer chip manufacturing company, such as Intel, will have significant investment in physical facilities. A single chip fabrication plant can cost in excess of $4 billion, so operations managers will spend a lot of their time managing their facilities. Conversely, a management consultancy firm depends largely on the quality of its staff. Here operations management is largely concerned with the development and deployment of consultant skills and knowledge.

Outputs from the process

Some operations create and deliver just services and others just products, but most operations produce a mixture of the two. Figure 1.4 shows a number of operations (including some described as examples in this chapter) positioned in a spectrum from **'pure' product** operations to **'pure' service** operations. Crude oil producers are concerned almost exclusively with the product which comes from their oil wells. So are aluminium smelters, but they might also produce some services such as technical advice. Services produced in these circumstances are called **facilitating services**. To an even greater extent, machine tool manufacturers produce facilitating services such as technical advice and applications engineering. The services produced by a restaurant are an essential part of what the customer is paying for. It is both a manufacturing operation which produces meals and a provider of service in the advice, ambience and service of the food. An information systems provider may produce software 'products', but primarily it is providing a service to its customers, with **facilitating products**. Certainly, a management consultancy, although it produces reports and documents, would see itself primarily as a service provider. Finally, pure services produce no products, a psychotherapy clinic, for example.

Margin notes: 'Pure' products; 'Pure' service; Facilitating services; Facilitating products

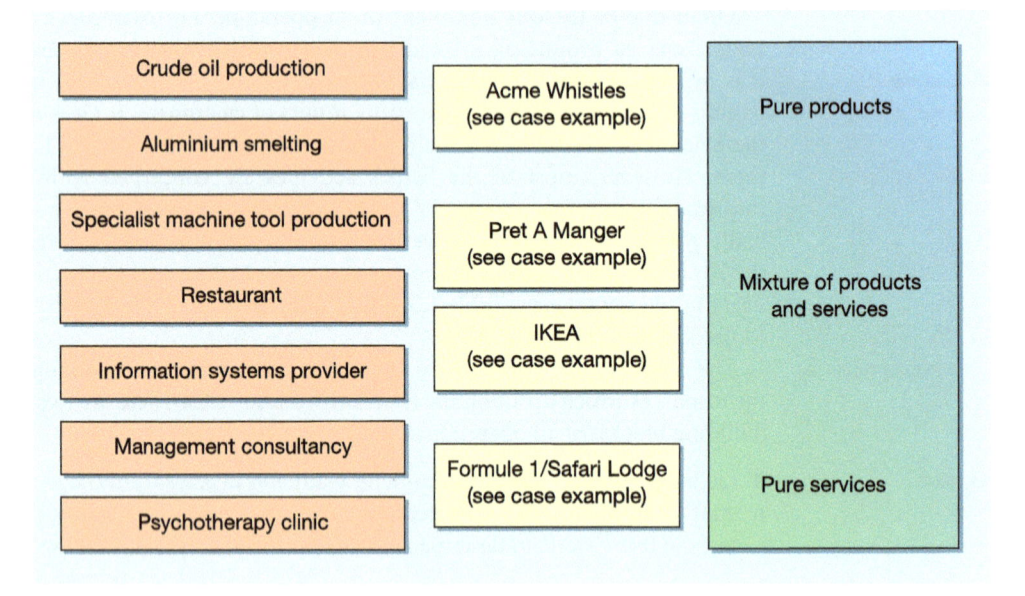

Figure 1.4 The output from most types of operation is a mixture of services and products

Services and products are merging

Increasingly, the distinction between services and products is both difficult to define and not particularly useful. Internet-based retailers, for example, are increasingly 'transporting' a larger proportion of their services into customers' homes. Even official statistics have difficulty in separating services and products. Software sold on a disc is classified as a product. The same software sold over the Internet is a service. Some authorities see the essential purpose of all operations processes as being to 'service customers'. Therefore, they argue, **all operations are service providers** which may create and deliver products as a part of serving their customers.

Margin note: All operations are service providers

Short case
Pret A Manger[4]

Described by the press as having *'revolutionized the concept of sandwich making and eating'*, Pret A Manger opened their first shop in the mid-1980s, in London. Now they have over 130 shops in UK, New York, Hong Kong and Tokyo. They say that their secret is to focus continually on quality – not just of their food, but in every aspect of their operations practice. They go to extraordinary lengths to avoid the chemicals and preservatives common in most 'fast' food, say the company. *'Many food retailers focus on extending the shelf life of their food, but that's of no interest to us. We maintain our edge by selling food that simply can't be beaten for freshness. At the end of the day, we give whatever we haven't sold to charity to help feed those who would otherwise go hungry. When we were just starting out, a big supplier tried to sell us coleslaw that lasted sixteen days. Can you imagine! Salad that lasts sixteen days? There and then we decided Pret would stick to wholesome fresh food – natural stuff. We have not changed that policy.'*

The first Pret A Manger shop had its own kitchen where fresh ingredients were delivered first thing every morning, and food was prepared throughout the day. Every Pret shop since has followed this model. The team members serving on the tills at lunchtime will have been making sandwiches in the kitchen that morning. The company rejected the idea of a huge centralized sandwich factory even though it could significantly reduce costs. Pret also own and manage all their shops directly so that they can ensure consistently high standards in all their shops. *'We are determined never to forget that our hard-working people make all the difference. They are our heart and soul. When they care, our business is sound. If they cease to care, our business goes down the drain. In a retail sector where high staff turnover is normal, we're pleased to say our people are much more likely to stay around! We work hard at building great teams. We take our reward schemes and career opportunities very seriously. We don't work nights (generally), we wear jeans, we party!'* Customer feedback is regarded as being particularly important at Pret. Examining customers' comments for improvement ideas is a key part of weekly management meetings, and of the daily team briefs in each shop.

The processes hierarchy

So far we have discussed operations management, and the input–transformation–output model, at the level of 'the operation'. For example, we have described 'the whistle factory', 'the sandwich shop', 'the disaster relief operation', and so on. Now look *inside* any of these operations. One will see that all operations consist of a collection of processes (though these processes may be called 'units' or 'departments') interconnecting with each other to form a network. Each process acts as a smaller version of the whole operation of which it forms a part, and transformed resources flow between them. In fact within any operation, the mechanisms that actually transform inputs into outputs are these **processes**. A process is 'an arrangement of resources that produce some mixture of products and services'. They are the 'building blocks' of all operations, and they form an 'internal network' within an operation. Each process is, at the same time, an **internal supplier** and an **internal customer** for other processes. This 'internal customer' concept provides a model to analyse the internal activities of an operation. It is also a useful reminder that, by treating internal customers with the same degree of care as external customers, the effectiveness of the whole operation can be improved. Table 1.4 illustrates how a wide range of operations can be described in this way.

Processes

Internal supplier
Internal customer

Table 1.4 Some operations described in terms of their processes

Operation	Some of the operation's inputs	Some of the operation's processes	Some of the operation's outputs
Airline	Aircraft Pilots and air crew Ground crew Passengers and freight	Check passengers in Board passengers Fly passengers and freight around the world Care for passengers	Transported passengers and freight
Department store	Goods for sale Sales staff Information systems Customers	Source and store goods Display goods Give sales advice Sell goods	Customers and goods 'assembled' together
Police	Police officers Computer systems Information systems Public (law-abiding and criminals)	Crime prevention Crime detection Information gathering Detaining suspects	Lawful society, public with a feeling of security
Frozen food manufacturer	Fresh food Operators Processing technology Cold storage facilities	Source raw materials Prepare food Freeze food Pack and freeze food	Frozen food

Within each of these processes is another network of individual units of resource such as individual people and individual items of process technology (machines, computers, storage facilities, etc.). Again, transformed resources flow between each unit of transforming resource. So any business, or operation, is made up of a network of processes and any process is made up of a network of resources. In addition, any business or operation can itself be viewed as part of a greater network of businesses or operations. It will have operations that supply it with the products and services it needs and unless it deals directly with the end-consumer, it will supply customers who themselves may go on to supply their own customers. Moreover, any operation could have several suppliers and several customers and may be in competition with other operations producing similar services to those it produces itself. This network of operations is called the **supply network**. In this way the input–transformation–output model can be used at a number of different 'levels of analysis'. Here we have used the idea to **analyse businesses at three levels**, the process, the operation and the supply network. One could define many different 'levels of analysis': moving upwards from small to larger processes, right up to the huge supply network that describes a whole industry.

This idea is called the **hierarchy of operations** and is illustrated for a business that makes television programmes and DVDs in Figure 1.5. It will have inputs of production, technical and administrative staff, cameras, lighting, sound and recording equipment, and so on. It transforms these into finished programmes, music, videos, etc. At a more macro level, the business itself is part of a whole supply network, acquiring services from creative agencies, casting agencies and studios, liaising with promotion agencies and serving its broadcasting company customers. At a more micro level, within this overall operation there are many individual processes: workshops manufacturing the sets; marketing processes that liaise with potential customers; maintenance and repair processes that care for, modify and design technical equipment; and so on. Each of these individual processes can be represented as a network of yet smaller processes, or even individual units of resource. So, the set manufacturing process could consist of four smaller processes: one that designs the sets, one that constructs them, one that acquires the props, and one that finishes (paints) the set.

> **Critical commentary**
>
> The idea of the internal network of processes is seen by some as being over-simplistic. In reality the relationship between groups and individuals is significantly more complex than that between commercial entities. One cannot treat internal customers and suppliers exactly as we do external customers and suppliers. External customers and suppliers usually operate in a free market. If an organization believes that in the long run it can get a better deal by purchasing goods and services from another supplier, it will do so. Conversely internal customers and suppliers are not in a 'free market'. They cannot usually look outside either to purchase input resources or to sell their output goods and services (although some organizations are moving this way). Rather than take the 'economic' perspective of external commercial relationships, models from organizational behaviour, it is argued, are more appropriate.

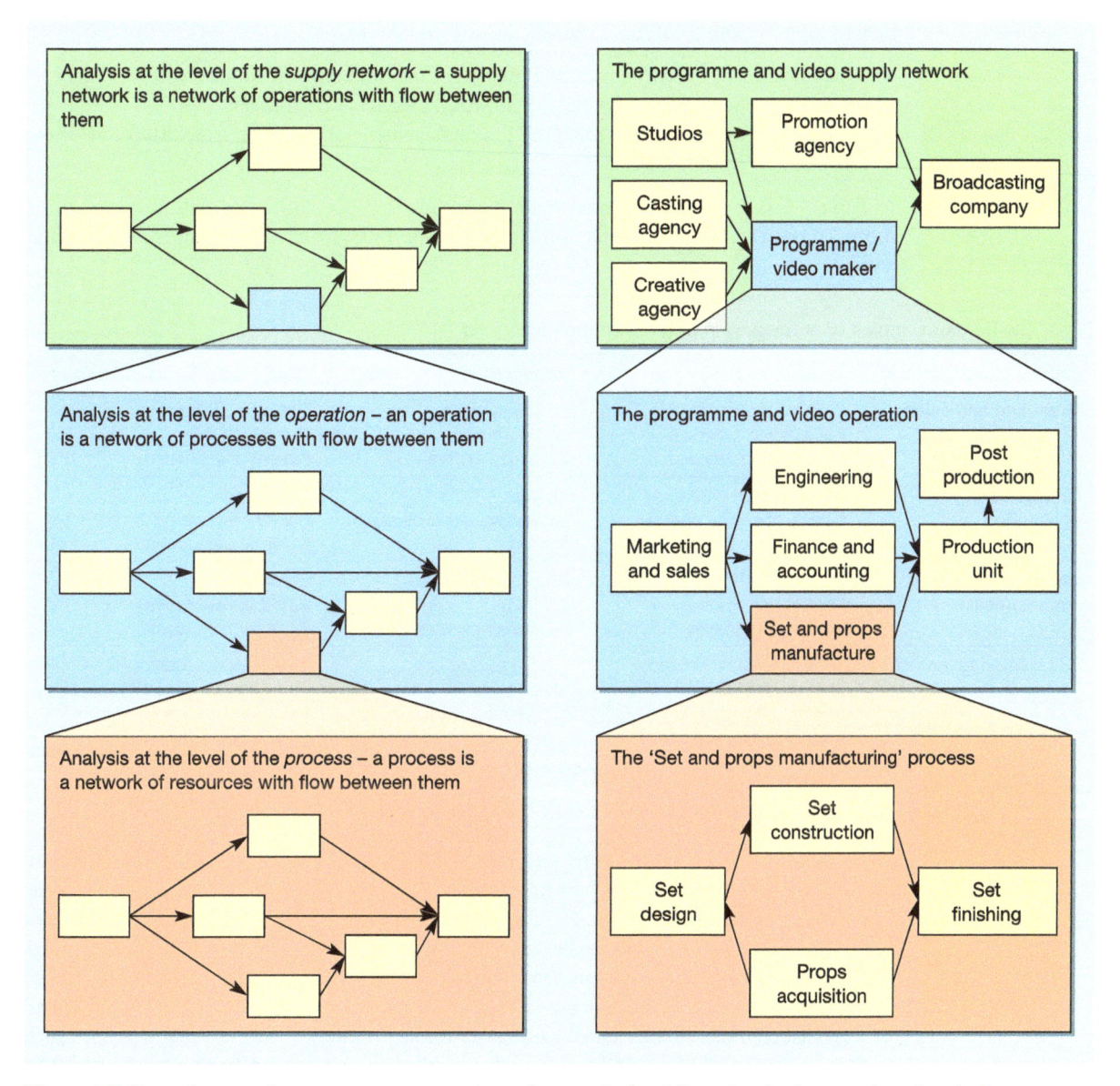

Figure 1.5 Operations and process management requires analysis at three levels: the supply network, the operation, and the process

Operations management is relevant to all parts of the business

All functions manage processes

The example in Figure 1.5 demonstrates that it is not just the operations function that manages processes; **all functions manage processes**. For example, the marketing function will have processes that create forecasts, create advertising campaigns and create marketing plans. These processes also need managing using principles similar to those within the operations function. Each function will have its 'technical' knowledge. In marketing, this is the expertise in designing and shaping marketing plans; in finance, it is the technical knowledge of financial reporting. Yet each will also have a 'process management' role of creating and delivering plans, policies, reports and services. The implications of this are very important. As all managers have some responsibility for managing processes, they are, to some extent, operations managers. They all should want to give good service to their (often internal) customers, and they all will want to do this efficiently. So, **operations management is relevant for all functions**, and all managers should have something to learn from the principles, concepts, approaches and techniques of operations management. It also means that we must distinguish between two meanings of 'operations':

All managers, not just operations managers, manage processes

Operations as a function
- **'Operations' as a function**, meaning the part of the organization which creates and delivers the services and products for the organization's external customers;

Operations as an activity
- **'Operations' as an activity**, meaning the management of the processes within any of the organization's functions.

Table 1.5 illustrates just some of the processes that are contained within some of the more common non-operations functions, the outputs from these processes and their 'customers'.

Table 1.5 Some examples of processes in non-operations functions

Organizational function	Some of its processes	Outputs from its process	Customer(s) for its outputs
Marketing and sales	Planning process Forecasting process Order taking process	Marketing plans Sales forecasts Confirmed orders	Senior management Sales staff, planners, operations Operations, finance
Finance and accounting	Budgeting process Capital approval processes Invoicing processes	Budgets Capital request evaluations Invoices	Everyone Senior management, requesters External customers
Human resources management	Payroll processes Recruitment processes Training processes	Salary statements New hires Trained employees	Employees All other processes All other processes
Information technology	Systems review process Help desk process System implementation project processes	System evaluation Advice Implemented working systems and aftercare	All other processes All other processes All other processes

Business processes

Whenever a business attempts to satisfy its customers' needs it will use many processes, in both its operations and its other functions. Each of these processes will contribute some part to fulfilling customer needs. For example, the television programme and DVD production company, described previously, creates two types of 'product'. Both of these products involve a slightly different mix of processes within the company. The company decides to reorganize its operations so that each product is created from start to finish by a dedicated process that contains all the elements necessary for its production. So customer needs for each product are entirely fulfilled from within what is called an **'end-to-end' business process**. These often cut across conventional organizational boundaries. Reorganizing (or 're-engineering') process boundaries and organizational responsibilities around these business processes is the philosophy behind **business process re-engineering** (BPR).

'End-to-end' business processes

Business process re-engineering

Operations processes have different characteristics

Although all operations processes are similar in that they all transform inputs, they do differ in a number of ways, four of which, known as the four Vs, are particularly important:

Volume
Variety
Variation
Visibility

- The **volume** of their output;
- The **variety** of their output;
- The **variation** in the demand for their output;
- The degree of **visibility** which customers have of the production of their output.

The volume dimension

Let us take a familiar example. The epitome of high-volume hamburger production is McDonald's, which serves millions of burgers around the world every day. Volume has important implications for the way McDonald's operations are organized. The first thing you notice is the **repeatability** of the tasks people are doing and the **systematization** of the work where standard procedures are set down specifying how each part of the job should be carried out. Also, because tasks are systematized and repeated, it is worthwhile developing specialized fryers and ovens. All this gives *low unit costs*. Now consider a small local cafeteria serving a few 'short-order' dishes. The range of items on the menu may be similar to the larger operation, but the volume will be far lower, so the repetition will also be far lower and the number of staff will be lower (possibly only one person) and therefore individual staff are likely to perform a wider range of tasks. This may be more rewarding for the staff, but less open to systematization. Also it is less feasible to invest in specialized equipment. So the cost per burger served is likely to be higher (even if the price is comparable).

Repeatability
Systematization

The variety dimension

A taxi company offers a high-variety service. It is prepared to pick you up from almost anywhere and drop you off almost anywhere. To offer this variety it must be relatively *flexible*. Drivers must have a good knowledge of the area, and communication between the base and the taxis must be effective. However, the cost per kilometre travelled will be higher for a taxi than for a less customized form of transport such as a bus service. Although both provide the same basic service (transportation), the taxi service has a high variety of routes and times to offer its customers, while the bus service has a few well-defined routes, with a set schedule. If all goes to schedule, little, if any, flexibility is required from the operation. All is **standardized** and regular, which results in relatively low costs compared with using a taxi for the same journey.

Standardized

The variation dimension

Consider the demand pattern for a successful summer holiday resort hotel. Not surprisingly, more customers want to stay in summer vacation times than in the middle of winter. At the height of 'the season' the hotel could be full to its capacity. Off-season demand, however, could be a small fraction of its capacity. Such a marked variation in demand means that the operation must change its capacity in some way, for example, by hiring extra staff for the summer. The hotel must try to predict the likely level of demand. If it gets this wrong, it could result in too much or too little capacity. Also, recruitment costs, overtime costs and under-utilization of its rooms all have the effect of increasing the hotel's costs operation compared with a hotel of a similar standard with level demand. A hotel which has relatively level demand can plan its activities well in advance. Staff can be scheduled, food can be bought and rooms can be cleaned in a *routine* and *predictable* manner. This results in a high utilization of resources and unit costs which are likely to be lower than those in hotels with a highly variable demand pattern.

The visibility dimension

Visibility means process exposure

Visibility is a slightly more difficult dimension of operations to envisage. It refers to how much of the operation's activities its customers experience, or how much the operation is **exposed** to its customers. Generally, customer-processing operations are more exposed to their customers than material- or information-processing operations. But even customer-processing operations have some choice as to how visible they wish their operations to be. For example, a retailer could operate as a high-visibility 'bricks and mortar', or a lower-visibility web-based operation. In the 'bricks and mortar', high-visibility operation, customers will directly experience most of its 'value-adding' activities. Customers will have a relatively *short waiting tolerance*, and may walk out if not served in a reasonable time. Customers' perceptions, rather than objective criteria, will also be important. If they perceive that a member of the operation's staff is discourteous to them, they are likely to be dissatisfied (even if the staff member meant no discourtesy), so high-visibility operations require staff with good customer contact skills. Customers could also request goods which clearly would not be sold in such a shop, but because the customers are actually in the operation they can ask what they like! This is called **high received variety**. This makes it difficult for high-visibility operations to achieve high productivity of resources, so they tend to be relatively high-cost operations. Conversely, a web-based retailer, while not a pure low-contact operation, has far lower visibility. Behind its web site it can be more 'factory-like'. The *time lag* between the order being placed and the items ordered by the customer being retrieved and dispatched does not have to be minutes as in the shop, but can be hours or even days. This allows the tasks of finding the items, packing and dispatching them to be *standardized* by staff who need few **customer contact skills**. Also, there can be relatively *high staff utilization*. The web-based organization can also centralize its operation on one (physical) site, whereas the 'bricks and mortar' shop needs many shops close to centres of demand. Therefore, the low-visibility web-based operation will have lower costs than the shop.

High received variety

Customer contact skills

Short case
Two very different hotels

Formule 1

Hotels are high-contact operations – they are staff-intensive and have to cope with a range of customers, each with a variety of needs and expectations. So, how can a highly successful chain of affordable hotels avoid the costs of high customer contact? Formule 1, a subsidiary of the French Accor group, manages to offer outstanding value by adopting two principles not always associated with hotel operations – standardization and an innovative use of technology. Formule 1 hotels are usually located close to the roads, junctions and cities which make them visible and accessible to prospective customers. The hotels themselves are made from state-of-the-art volumetric prefabrications. The prefabricated units are arranged in various configurations to suit the characteristics of each individual site. All rooms are nine square metres in area, and are designed to be attractive, functional, comfortable and soundproof. Most importantly, they are designed to be easy to clean and maintain. All have the same fittings, including a double bed, an additional bunk-type bed, a wash basin, a storage area, a working table with seat, a wardrobe and a television set. The reception of a Formule 1 hotel is staffed only from

6.30 am to 10.00 am and from 5.00 pm to 10.00 pm. Outside these times an automatic machine sells rooms to credit card users, provides access to the hotel, dispenses a security code for the room and even prints a receipt. Technology is also evident in the washrooms. Showers and toilets are automatically cleaned after each use by using nozzles and heating elements to spray the room with a disinfectant solution and dry it before it is used again. To keep things even simpler, Formule 1 hotels do not include a restaurant as they are usually located near existing restaurants. However, a continental breakfast is available, usually between 6.30 am and 10.00 am, and of course on a 'self-service' basis!

Mwagusi Safari Lodge
The Mwagusi Safari Lodge lies within Tanzania's Ruaha National Park, a huge undeveloped wilderness, whose beautiful open landscape is especially good for seeing elephant, buffalo and lion. Nestled into a bank of the Mwagusi Sand River, this small exclusive tented camp overlooks a watering hole in the riverbed. Its ten tents are within thatched bandas (accommodation), each furnished comfortably in the traditional style of the camp. Each banda has an en-suite bathroom with flush toilet and a hot shower. Game viewing can be experienced even from the seclusion of the veranda. The sight of thousands of buffalo flooding the riverbed below the tents and dining room banda is not uncommon, and elephants, giraffes, and wild dogs are frequent uninvited guests to the site. There are two staff for each customer, allowing individual needs and preferences to be met quickly at all times. Guest numbers vary throughout the year, occupancy being low in the rainy season from January to April, and full in the best game viewing period from September to November. There are game drives and walks throughout the area, each selected for customers' individual preferences. Drives are taken in specially adapted open-sided four-wheel-drive vehicles, equipped with reference books, photography equipment, medical kits and all the necessities for a day in the bush. Walking safaris, accompanied by an experienced guide can be customized for every visitor's requirements and abilities. Lunch can be taken communally, so that visitors can discuss their interests with other guides and managers. Dinner is often served under the stars in a secluded corner of the dry riverbed.

Mixed high- and low-visibility processes

Some operations have both high- and low-visibility processes within the same operation. In an airport, for example, some activities are totally 'visible' to its customers such as information desks answering people's queries. These staff operate in what is termed a **front-office** environment. Other parts of the airport have little, if any, customer 'visibility', such as the baggage handlers. These rarely-seen staff perform the vital but low-contact tasks, in the **back-office** part of the operation.

Front office

Back office

The implications of the four Vs of operations processes

All four dimensions have implications for the cost of creating services or products. Put simply, high volume, low variety, low variation and low customer contact all help to keep processing costs down. Conversely, low volume, high variety, high variation and high customer contact generally carry some kind of cost penalty for the operation. This is why the volume dimension is drawn with its 'low' end at the left, unlike the other dimensions, to keep all the 'low cost' implications on the right. To some extent the position of an operation in the **four dimensions** is determined by the demand of the market it is serving. However, most operations have some discretion in moving themselves on the dimensions. Figure 1.6 summarizes the implications of such positioning.

'Four Vs' analysis of processes

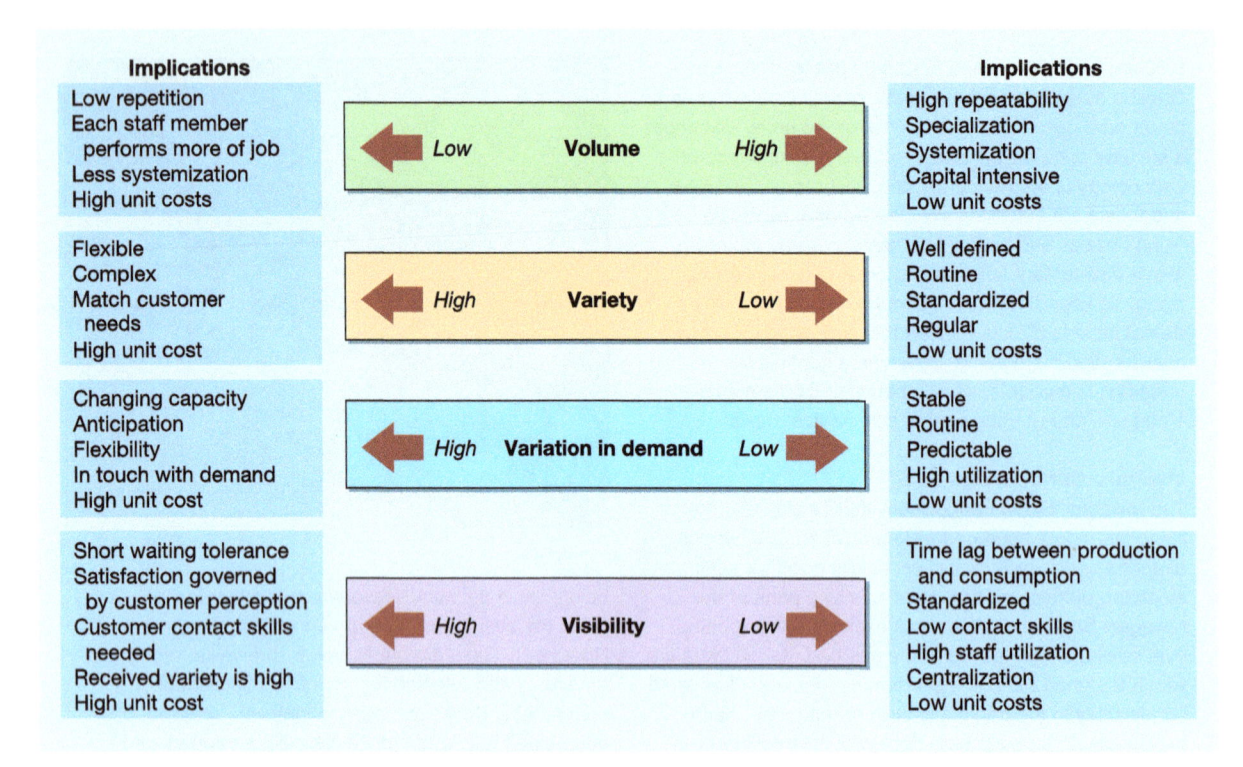

Figure 1.6 A typology of operations

Implications (left)	Dimension	Implications (right)
Low repetition Each staff member performs more of job Less systemization High unit costs	**Low ← Volume → High**	High repeatability Specialization Systemization Capital intensive Low unit costs
Flexible Complex Match customer needs High unit cost	**High ← Variety → Low**	Well defined Routine Standardized Regular Low unit costs
Changing capacity Anticipation Flexibility In touch with demand High unit cost	**High ← Variation in demand → Low**	Stable Routine Predictable High utilization Low unit costs
Short waiting tolerance Satisfaction governed by customer perception Customer contact skills needed Received variety is high High unit cost	**High ← Visibility → Low**	Time lag between production and consumption Standardized Low contact skills High staff utilization Centralization Low unit costs

Worked example

Figure 1.7 illustrates the different positions on the dimensions of the Formule 1 hotel chain and the Mwagusi Safari Lodge (*see* the short case on 'Two very different hotels'). Both provide the same basic service as any other hotel. However, one is of a small, intimate nature with relatively few customers. Its variety of services is almost infinite in the sense that customers can make individual requests in terms of food and entertainment. Variation is high and customer contact, and therefore visibility, is also very high (in order to ascertain customers' requirements and provide for them). All of this is very different from Formule 1, where volume is high (although not as high as in a large city-centre hotel), variety of service is strictly limited, and business and holiday customers use the hotel at different times, which limits variation. Most notably, though, customer contact is kept to a minimum. The Mwagusi Safari Lodge hotel has very high levels of service but provides them at a high cost. Conversely, Formule 1 has arranged its operation in such a way as to minimize its costs.

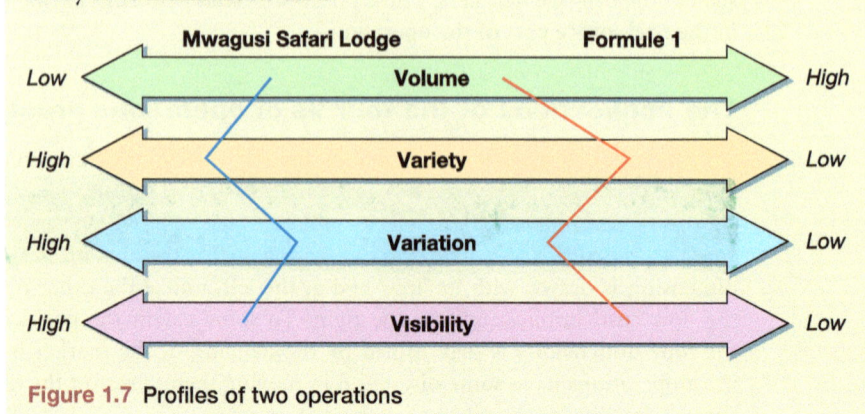

Figure 1.7 Profiles of two operations

The activities of operations management

Operations managers find themselves involved with many different activities within the organization. Many of these are cross-functional, involving managers from other parts of the organization, but other activities are seen as the prime responsibilities of operations managers specifically. These all begin with the letter D.

Directing the overall strategy of the operation. A general understanding of operations and their strategic purpose, together with an appreciation of how operations performance should be assessed is a prerequisite to managing any type of operations. This chapter, together with Chapters 2 and 3, are devoted to this set of activities.

Designing the operation's services, products and processes. Design is the activity of determining the physical form, shape and composition of operations and processes together with the products and services that they produce. Chapters 4–6 deal with these issues.

Delivering to customers. The ongoing creation of services and products must be managed, from choosing and controlling the suppliers of input resources right through to their delivery of products and services to customers. The activities involved in this ongoing delivery are examined in Chapters 7–11.

Developing process performance. Increasingly, it is recognized that for any operation or any process, managers cannot simply routinely deliver services and products in the same way that they always have done. They have a responsibility to develop the capabilities of their processes to improve process performance. These development responsibilities are looked at in Chapters 12 and 13.

The model of operations management

We can now combine two ideas to develop the model of operations management which will be used throughout this book. The first is the input–transformation–output model and the second is the categorization of operations management's activity areas. Figure 1.8 shows how these two ideas go together. The model now shows two interconnected loops of **activities**. The bottom one more or less corresponds to what is usually seen as operations management, and the top one to what is seen as operations strategy. This book concentrates on the former but tries to cover enough of the latter to allow the reader to make strategic sense of the operations manager's job.

Operations activities define operations management and operations strategy

Critical commentary

The central idea in this introductory chapter is that all organizations have operations processes which produce products and services and all these processes are essentially similar. However, some believe that by even trying to characterize processes in this way (perhaps even by calling them 'processes') one loses or distorts their nature, depersonalizes or takes the 'humanity' out of the way in which we think of the organization. This point is often raised in not-for-profit organizations, especially by 'professional' staff. For example the head of one European 'Medical Association' (a doctors' trade union) criticized hospital authorities for expecting a *'sausage factory service based on productivity targets'*.[5] No matter how similar they appear on paper, it is argued, a hospital can never be viewed in the same way as a factory. Even in commercial businesses, professionals, such as creative staff, often express discomfort at their expertise being described as a 'process'.

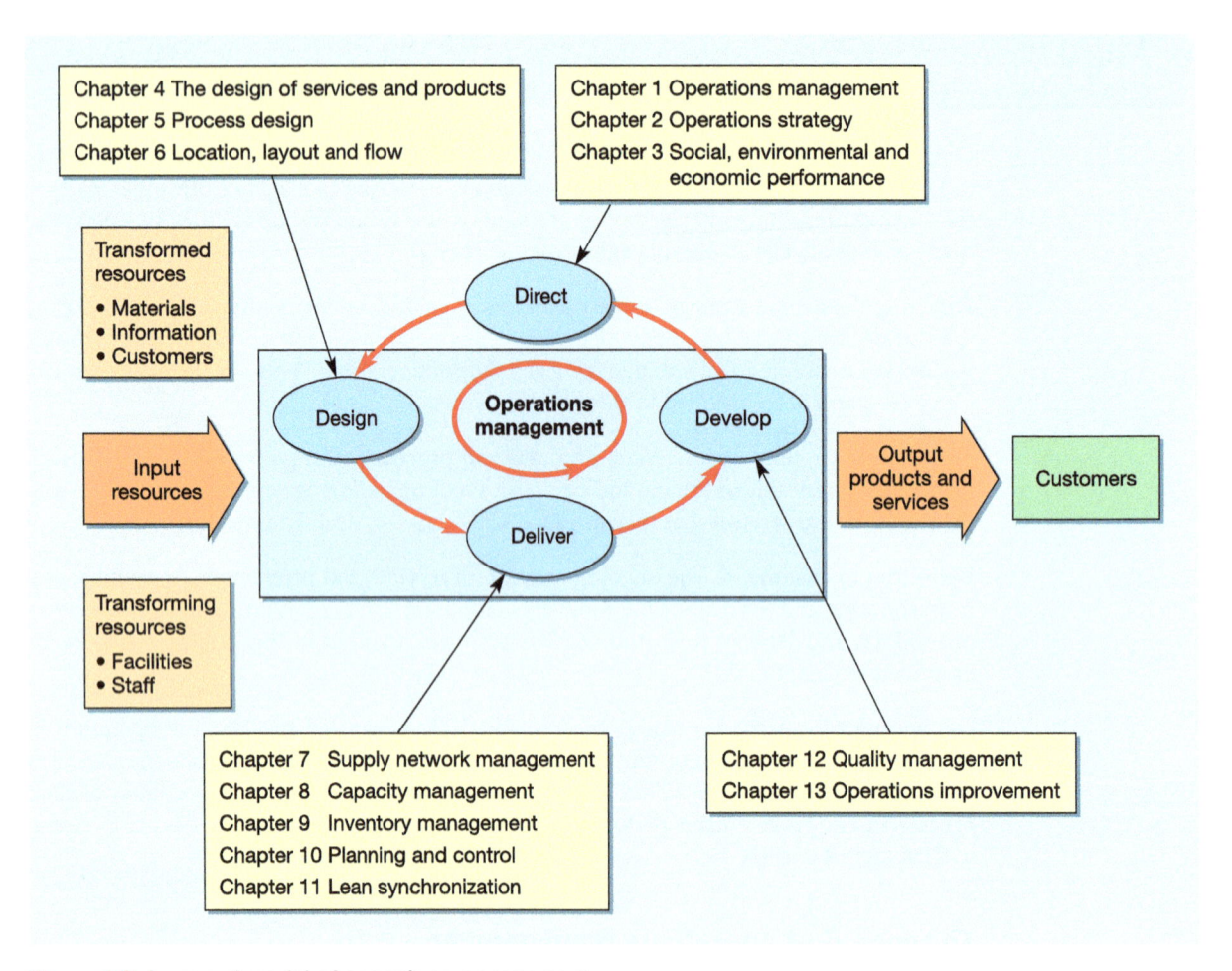

Figure 1.8 A general model of operations management

Summary answers to key questions

Check and improve your understanding of this chapter using self-assessment questions and a personalized study plan, audio and video downloads, and an eBook – all at www.myomlab.com.

➤ What is operations management?

- Operations management is the activity of managing the resources which are devoted to the creation and delivery of services and products. It is one of the core functions of any business, although it may not be called operations management in some industries.
- Operations management is concerned with managing processes. All processes have internal customers and suppliers. As all management functions also have processes, operations management has relevance for all managers.

➤ Why is operations management important in all types of organization?

- Operations management uses the organization's resources to create outputs that fulfil defined market requirements. This is the fundamental activity of any type of enterprise.

- Operations management is increasingly important because today's business environment requires new thinking from operations managers.

➤ What is the input–transformation–output process?

- All operations can be modelled as input–transformation–output processes. They all have inputs of transforming resources, which are usually divided into 'facilities' and 'staff', and transformed resources, which are some mixture of customers, materials and information.
- Few operations create and deliver only services or products. Most produce some mixture of products and services.

➤ What is the process hierarchy?

- All operations are part of a larger supply network which, through the individual contributions of each operation, satisfies end-customer requirements.
- All operations are made up of processes that form a network of internal customer–supplier relationships within the operation.
- End-to-end business processes that satisfy customer needs often cut across functionally based processes.

➤ How do operations processes have different characteristics?

- Operations differ in terms of the volume of their outputs, the variety of outputs, the variation in demand for their outputs, and the degree of visibility they have.
- High volume, low variety, low variation and low customer visibility are usually associated with low cost.

➤ What are the activities of operations management?

- Responsibilities include defining an operations strategy, understanding social, environmental and economic objectives, designing the operation's services, products and processes, delivering to customers, and developing the operation over time.

Learning exercises

These problems and applications will help to improve your analysis of operations. You can find more practice problems as well as worked examples and guided solutions on MyOMLab at www.myomlab.com.

1. Read the short case on Pret A Manger and **(a)** identify the processes in a typical Pret A Manger shop together with their inputs and outputs, **(b)** Pret A Manger also supplies business lunches (of sandwiches and other take-away food). What are the implications for how it manages its processes within the shop? **(c)** What would be the advantages and disadvantages if Pret A Manger introduced 'central kitchens' that made the sandwiches for a number of shops in an area? (As far as we know, they have no plans to do so.)

2. Compare and contrast Acme Whistles and Pret A Manger in terms of the way that they will need to manage their operations.

3 Visit and observe three restaurants, cafés or somewhere that food is served. Compare them in terms of the Volume of demand that they have to cope with, the Variety of menu items they service, the Variation in demand during the day, week and year, and the Visibility you have of the preparation of the food. Think about and discuss the impact of volume, variety, variation and visibility on the day-to-day management of each of the operations and consider how each operation attempts to cope with its volume, variety, variation and visibility.

4 (Advanced) Find a copy of a financial newspaper or magazine (*Financial Times*, *Wall Street Journal*, *Economist*, etc.) and identify one company which is described in the paper that day. Using the list of issues identified in Table 1.1, what do you think would be the *new operations agenda* for that company?

Want to know more?

Chase, R.B., Jacobs, F.R. and Aquilano, N.J. (2004) *Operations Management for Competitive Advantage* (10th edn), McGraw-Hill/Irwin, Boston, MA. There are many good general textbooks on operations management. This was one of the first and is still one of the best, though written very much for an American audience.

Chopra, S., Deshmukh, S., Van Mieghem, J., Zemel, E. and Anupindi, R. (2005) *Managing Business Process Flows: Principles of Operations Management*, Prentice-Hall, Englewood Cliffs, NJ. Takes a 'process' view of operations. Mathematical but rewarding.

Heizer, J. and Render, B. (2006) *Operations Management* (8th edn), Prentice Hall, Englewood Cliffs, NJ. Another good US authored general text on the subject.

Johnston, R. and Clark, G. (2008) *Service Operations Management* (3rd edn), Financial Times-Prentice Hall, Harlow. What can we say! A great treatment of service operations from the same stable as this textbook.

Useful websites

www.opsman.org Useful materials and resources.

www.iomnet.org.uk The Institute of Operations Management site. One of the main professional bodies for the subject.

www.poms.org A US academic society for production and operations management. Academic, but some useful material, including a link to an encyclopaedia of operations management terms.

www.sussex.ac.uk/Users/dt31/TOMI/ One of the longest-established portals for the subject. Useful for academics and students alike.

www.ft.com Useful for researching topics and companies.

www.journaloperationsmanagement.org The home site for the best known operations management journal. A bit academic, but some pages are useful.

Now that you have finished reading this chapter, why not visit MyOMLab at www.myomlab.com where you'll find more learning resources to help you make the most of your studies and get a better grade.

Chapter 1
Introducing service operations management

Chapter objectives

This chapter is about how to understand the role of service operations management and its contribution to organiational success.

- What are services?
- What is 'service'?
- What is service operations management?
- Why is service operations management important?

1.1 Introduction

We all come into contact with service operations and experience their services every single day. We are customers or users of a wide range of commercial and public services, such as childcare services, hospitals, shops, schools, holiday firms, restaurants, television and the internet. Furthermore, many of us are responsible for providing services not only as part of our jobs, in organisations such as those above, but also as part of daily life for our friends and families; providing cooking, cleaning and 'taxi' services, organising holidays and providing emotional support services for example.

It is important to note at the start of this book that service operations covers a far broader field than these 'everyday' services that we buy or receive or the 'personal' services that we provide to each other. They include the services organisations provide to each other such as procurement or consulting services; services inside organisations (internal services) such as information technology (IT) or human relations (HR) support; public services provided by governments (social services, police services or fire and rescue services); and the many and diverse services provided by not-for-profit and voluntary organisations such as faith organisations or international aid organisations (see next section).

The principles we describe in this book apply to all these types of organisations, indeed any organisation that uses resources in order to provide some form of service. In this book we give a detailed coverage of service operations issues and we provide many tools and frameworks that managers can use to understand, assess and improve the performance of their operations. While the development of operations management as a discipline has its roots in production management,[1] this text concentrates on operations issues in service organisations. However, many of the concepts are equally relevant to manufacturing organisations because all manufacturing companies provide services, such as after-sales service and customer training, and internal services such as HR or IT support.

Every single organisation is involved in service and so a knowledge and understanding of service operations management can make a real difference to their success. In this introductory chapter we want to explain its role in delivering organisational success. But first we will introduce some key concepts, starting with what we mean by services.

1.2 What are services?

Services come in many shapes and forms provided by a variety of types of organisations, including business-to-consumer (B2C) services, business-to-business (B2B) services, internal services, public services and not-for-profit and voluntary services.

Business-to-consumer services are services provided by organisations to individuals, examples being financial services (from banks and insurance providers), retail services (from supermarkets and clothes shops), travel services (airlines and bus companies), leisure services (cinemas and gyms), and hospitality services (restaurants and hotels). A subset of B2C services are those organisations which facilitate communication and service provision between customers (sometimes described as customer-to-customer or C2C services); examples are social networks such as Facebook, business networks such as LinkedIn, video-sharing sites such as YouTube, peer-to-peer games such as Farmville and Cafe World, and buying and selling sites such as eBay.

Business-to-business services are services provided between businesses and include consulting, office equipment provision and support, communications, corporate travel services, business insurance, finance and legal services.

Internal services are the many sorts of formal and informal services that people inside organisations provide to each other. The formal ones include internal services such as personnel, IT, HR, payroll or security services. Sometimes organisations subcontract or outsource such services so they become B2B services. Furthermore, almost everyone working in an organisation provides some form of service to other people in the organisation, such as writing reports, arranging meetings, taking part in discussions or providing information. These are informal internal services.

Public services (sometimes referred to as G2C – government-to-consumer) cover the wide range of services provided by local, regional and central governments to their citizens and communities. These include social housing, police, education, welfare and health services.

Not-for-profit and voluntary services include the services provided by non-governmental organisations (NGOs) such as aid organisations like Oxfam, Red Crescent and Médecins sans Frontières. Other not-for-profit and voluntary organisations include faith organisations, charities, trusts, the Scouting Association and the many small voluntary clubs and societies such as sports clubs and photographic societies.

Finally we cannot ignore the wide range of services that customers and users provide for themselves and each other. This includes the personal services we provide to each other, friendship and support services, catering and taxi services.

1.2.1 Customers

It is important to note that all these different organisations often use different terms for their customers. Public services provide services to citizens, the police service has victims and criminals, IT service providers talk about users, hotels have guests and radio stations have listeners. We use the word 'customer' to cover all of these individuals and communities to which organisations deliver service. We also use the word 'customer' to cover all the individuals and departments within organisations who provide each other service (internal customers) and also the external organisations with which they provide services. For example, the police work with social services and the courts to look after vulnerable children. While the child is the recipient, the other organisations need to provide service to each other to help the child.

We will develop the concept of customers further in Chapter 4.

1.3 What is 'service'?

It follows then that 'service' will mean different things depending on the type of service that is being provided. The service provided by your local bar or gym will be quite different to that provided by IBM to its business customers. When we talk to managers it is clear that the word 'service' conjures up many different images. For some it is synonymous with complaints or customer care, for others it is the equivalent of the logistics function, or internal services such as accounting or personnel. For others it means the 10,000-mile check-up to their car. The word 'service' is used to describe around 80 per cent of economic activity in developed nations; it includes the activities of all those organisations listed in the previous section. It is therefore perhaps not surprising that there is, as yet, no single, agreed and comprehensive definition of what a 'service' is.[2]

However, there are the beginnings of an emerging consensus.[3] While a product is a thing, a service is an activity – a process or a set of steps – which involves the treatment of a customer (or user) or something belonging to them, where the customer is also involved, and performs some role in the service process (also referred to as the service delivery process).[4] Defined as such, 'service' is much more than the point of staff–customer interaction – the service encounter, sometimes referred to as customer contact or the moment of truth.

We also find it helpful to consider service from two perspectives, the service provided from the operation's point of view and the service received from the customer's point of view (we will expand this idea into the 'service concept' in Chapter 3). Let us use the example of a hospital to illustrate this (see also Case Example 1.1).

1.3.1 Service – the operation's perspective

A hospital is a very complex service organisation that employs large numbers of staff (or employees – we use the terms interchangeably), from cleaners and porters to highly skilled surgeons. It will care for hundreds of patients each day, through many different specialist departments, each providing a range of treatments. Managing this type of service operation is extremely challenging, not only because they are dealing with life and death situations every hour, but also because of the complexity of the operation. The complexity is in part due to the volumes of patients and the wide range of treatments available, but also due to the fact that, like many service organisations, hospitals comprise many different service operations that must be coordinated and linked together in order to deliver healthcare to their customers. For the hospital, these include reception services, diagnostics, pharmacy, theatres (where operations *on* people are carried out), catering, portering, physiotherapy and so forth. In addition, there are the internal services such as information systems support, human resource services, training and finance.

Each of these service operations uses and manages many input resources, such as nurses, surgeons, drugs, equipment such as defibrillators, scanning and X-ray machines, and facilities such as wards, beds and theatres. One important input is also the customer – the patient who is getting the treatment or the internal member of staff who requires IT support or training services for example. Thus the hospital has many operations that 'process' customers whether they are patients or members of staff. These processes (activities) are the services they provide, such as reception services, diagnostic services, heart transplant surgery, intensive care

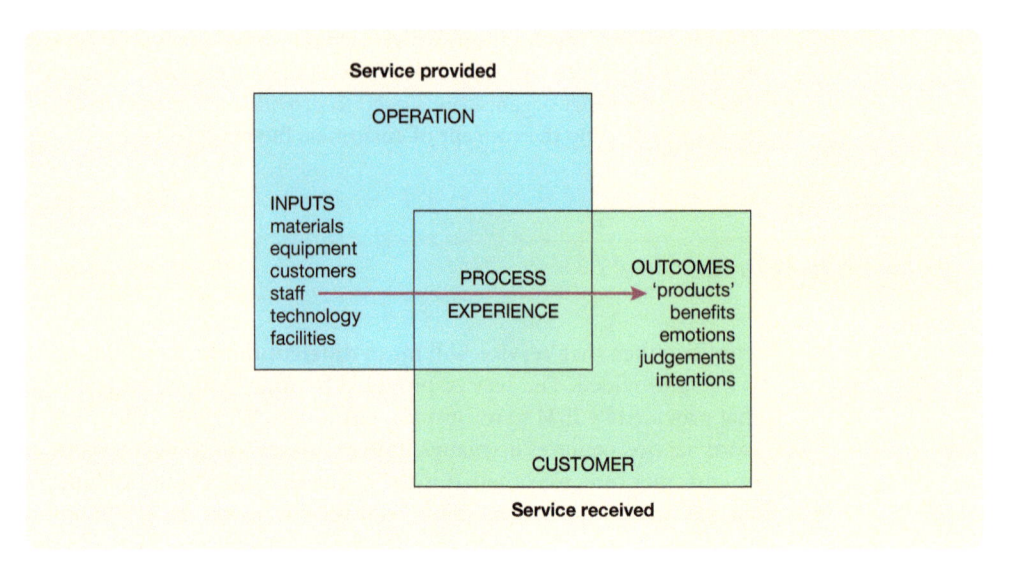

Figure 1.1 Service provided and received

treatment, or staff catering, IT support and training. The outputs of these processes are, hopefully, cured patients, fed staff and more knowledgeable operators, for example.

So from the operation's point of view, **the service provided** is the service process and its outputs which have been designed, created and enacted by the operation using its many input resources, including the customer, where the customer also takes some part in the service process. This involvement may be limited, in the case of pharmacy services for example, or significant, for diagnostic and surgical services for example. Services are therefore 'co-created' or 'co-produced' along with the customer (see Section 1.3.4). Thus the **service provided** occurs, or is enacted, where the operation and the customer meet as represented by the overlap in Figure 1.1.

1.3.2 Service – the customer's perspective

So while a service is the process or activity, from the customer's perspective, sometimes referred to as the customer-dominant logic perspective,[5] the **service received** is their *experience* of the service provided which results in *outcomes* such as 'products', benefits, emotions, judgements and intentions.

The customer experience

The customer experience is the customer's direct and personal interpretation of, and response to, their interaction with and participation in the service process, and its outputs, involving their journey through a series of touch points/steps. An experience is perceived purely from the point of view of an individual customer and is inherently personal, existing only in the customer's mind. Thus, no two people can have the same experience.[6]

Aspects of the customer experience include:

- the degree of personal interaction
- the responsiveness of the service organisation
- the flexibility of customer-facing staff
- customer intimacy
- the ease of access to service personnel or information systems

- the extent to which the customer feels valued by the organisation
- the courtesy and competence of customer-facing staff
- interactions with other customers.

The service outcomes

We use the term service outcomes to describe the results for the customer of the service process and their experience. The key outcomes are 'products', benefits, emotions, judgements and intentions (see Figure 1.1 and Case Example 1.1).

- *'Products'.* One key and important outcome is the 'functional' output of the service provided, 'products' such as the food and drink provided by a restaurant, or the ability of a delegate on a training course to construct a spreadsheet, or the new heart for the heart operation patient.
- *Benefits.* The benefits are important to the customer. This is why they have chosen or used the service provider. The benefits of a service are how the customer perceives they have 'profited' or gained from the service provided, their experience of it and the 'products' provided, i.e. how well their requirements and needs have been met. The patient who has undergone the heart operation will benefit from a longer and more active life. The benefits for students will be better job prospects or higher salaries and/or new capabilities and skills. The benefit of using a firm of consultants may be reduced costs and/or greater commercial success.
- *Emotions.* Experiencing a service results in the customer feeling emotions, of which there are many hundreds, including joy, surprise, love, fear, anger, shame and sadness (see Chapter 7). In a hospital the patient hopefully experiences a well-managed stay, where they feel at ease and assured throughout with minimal pain and inconvenience. A student at a university may have an enjoyable and challenging experience with some memorable lectures and seminars and exciting extra-curricular activities. A senior manager employing a firm of consultants will hopefully feel assured with increased confidence to pursue a particular strategy.[7]
- *Judgements.* Another outcome of the service from a customer's point of view will be their conscious or unconscious assessment of the service provided, their experience and the perceived benefits gained. This results in judgements about fairness (or equity), and, importantly, their perceived value of the service received. (Value (see Chapter 3) is the customer's assessment of the service provided, their experience and the benefits derived weighed against all the costs involved.) These assessments and feelings, conscious or unconscious, will then be rationalised into a feeling of satisfaction or dissatisfaction (an emotion) about the overall service (as well as individual elements of it) (see Chapter 5).[8]
- *Intentions.* These judgements, good, bad or indifferent, will result in intentions, such as the intention to repurchase or not (see Chapter 4), the intention to recommend to others, or the intention to complain or not. These intentions may or may not result in action.

It is important to note that in some cases some of these outcomes may be related and a customer's evaluation of one component may influence their perception of another. A superb learning experience may help the student better understand the material and thus benefit from greater knowledge and confidence. Sometimes they can be contradictory, for example a patient may feel annoyed or disappointed that the outcome of the operation was not a success (i.e. of no benefit for them) but be delighted (highly satisfied) with the way they were treated during their hospital stay (the experience).

The outcomes outlined above are from a customer perspective. There are also important outcomes from the organisation's perspective. Organisational outcomes will be concerned with meeting targets and objectives. A hospital may have clinical targets such as waiting times, number of operations carried out and recovery rates; operational targets such as theatre usage; and financial targets such as adherence to budgets (see Section 1.5). To be successful an operation has to meet both its desired customer outcomes and organisational outcomes. Service operations management plays a vital role in both of these.

Case Example 1.1 Singapore General Hospital

Singapore General Hospital (SGH) is the country's largest acute care tertiary hospital and national referral centre for specialities like haematology, orthopaedic surgery, plastic surgery, renal medicine, nuclear medicine and pathology. With almost 7,000 staff, from clinical and research directors to hospital attendants, covering over 30 clinical specialities the hospital has nearly a million patient encounters a year. Dedicated to providing multidisciplinary medical care and backed by state-of-the-art facilities, SGH offers team-based quality patient care widely acknowledged to be the best in the world. SGH is structured as a private limited company for flexibility of operations, but is a not-for-profit organisation owned by the Government of Singapore.

Source: Corbis/Jonathan Drake/epa

The hospital's mission is to deliver quality care to every patient through comprehensive integrated clinical practice, medical innovation and lifelong learning. It has three pillars supporting the mission statement. The first pillar is service – their number one priority – taking care of patients. The second pillar is education and nurturing the next generations of care-givers, doctors, nurses, physiotherapists, etc. The third pillar is undertaking clinical research to expand its knowledge and skills in medical science.

The hospital has defined its quality commitment as 'best outcome, best experience' for its patients. Best experience is about the way it serves its patients and their families by providing quality healthcare with compassion, respect and integrity. Best outcome is about treating the patient's medical condition as well as they can to achieve the best health benefits for the patient. Lawrence Lim was the Chief Executive who introduced this commitment. He explained:

We want to provide the best outcome by providing the best clinical care. I know people do not wish to come to a hospital, but if they have to, we want to provide them with the best experience possible. This idea was derived and drawn up by the doctors and administrators together and provides a common purpose, mindset and language that permeate the whole hospital. There are three key principles underlying this:

- *assure best outcomes and benefit for the patient (i.e. clinical quality)*
- *create seamless service (i.e. operational quality)*
- *delight with personalised care (i.e. service quality).*

We created a Quality Council comprising doctors and administrators that came together to chart the strategies and programmes for quality in the hospital. They discussed clinical quality, which has to do with getting doctors, nurses, physiotherapists, etc. to produce the best outcome and health benefits for the patient. We also talked about operational quality; that is how we moved a patient around and how we could organise our services around the patient. These activities mainly concerned operational processes, which we then 'engineered' to create a seamless service for the patient. We were also concerned with what we called service quality, which was about the patient's experience; building a relationship with the patients and showing that we cared. From the patients' perspective all these three types of quality, i.e. clinical, operational and service, are intertwined, but we needed to ensure that our staff were focused on all of them too.

We worked with all the different people in the hospital to try to get everybody to think how they could improve the service. We got them to think about communication skills, even grooming, dress and body language. SGH is a government hospital and people's concept of government hospitals was that they are bureaucratic, officious and slow to respond. I told my staff, let's surprise the patient!

1.3.3 Products, services and value

Most, if not all, organisations provide a combination of products (things) and services (activities). A manufacturer of washing machines or cars not only makes the machine – they also provide sales services, and after-sales services such as servicing and repairs. Service organisations such as restaurants 'manufacture' food and the restaurant would be of little value without it. Consultants provide tangible reports, but their main value is their diagnostic and advice services.

Many product-based organisations recognise the value provided by their 'add-on' services. Indeed IBM (see Case Example 1.2) has capitalised on its service provision to create its Global Services division, recognising that only a small part of its value was in hardware and software. Indeed, many product-based organisations see 'service' as a means of differentiating themselves from the competition. Amazon, initially a bookseller and now a global retailer, gained an advantage over traditional booksellers by allowing customers to buy online, store their delivery address and credit card details to allow one-click future purchases, receive suggestions and read reviews, all from their laptop or phone, wherever they might be.

The movement towards thinking in terms of the complete product-service offering, and changing product-based organisations' business models to market and deliver this, is often referred to as servitisation.

One could argue that 'product' versus 'service' is now an old fashioned distinction and the boundaries between them are blurred. What is more important to customers, the product or the service? What is a 'product'? Is Amazon a product or a service organisation? The critical point is not the relative amount of product versus service that an organisation delivers, or whether it sees itself as a product producer or service provider, but where the value is for the customer. Take the example of a car. From a car manufacturer's point of view a vast amount of value (cost) is tied up in the product and paid for by the customer (value-in-exchange).[9] But from most customers' point of view, its value is in its use (value-in-use).[10] Having a car allows us to go where we want, when we want, in relative comfort, listening to what we want to listen to.

Value is created in the experience and the outcomes (in particular the benefits) at the point(s) of consumption.[11] Importantly, the customer is the ultimate judge of value. Value is perceived by the customer over the time we keep the car and we hope that its value-in-use is at least as good as the price we had to pay for it; though we may often not realise this until the car breaks down. We will return to the notion of value in Section 1.5 and Chapter 3.

One important corollary to this is that the customer has a significant role in value creation in services. How we use and maintain the car has an impact on how we value it. How well the staff co-operate with the firm of consultants may well affect their ability to do their job. How well we explain our symptoms to our doctor will not only help them but aid our recovery. The role the customer plays in service delivery is referred to as co-production.

Case Example 1.2 — IBM Global Services

IBM is widely regarded as a successful global service company providing its business customers with solutions to their problems. In 2010 IBM had a turnover of over $99bn with a gross profit of over $46bn. While sales of systems, technology and software accounted for around 40 per cent of revenue, its service division, IBM Global Services, generated 57 per cent of its revenue, accounting for 33 per cent of the organisation's gross profit. IBM's Global Services has expanded rapidly (see Figure 1.2) establishing IBM as a leading global IT service company. In 2007 Global Services was split into two reporting

Source: Pearson Education Ltd/Imagestate/John Foxx Collections

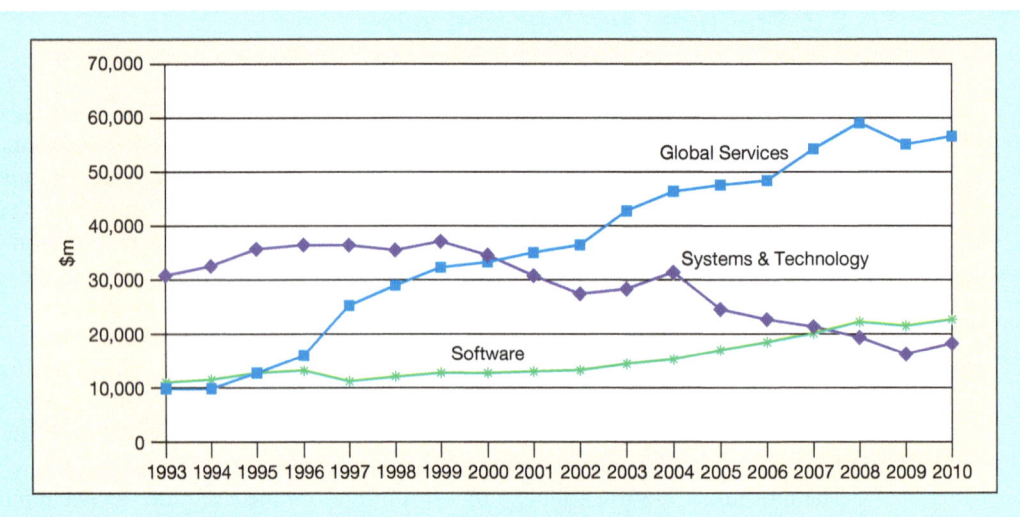

Figure 1.2 IBM Turnover ($ millions) 1993–2010: Global Services, Systems & Technology and Software

divisions: Global Business Services (GBS) and Global Technology Services (GTS). GBS provides professional services (consulting) and application outsourcing services whereas GTS focuses on infrastructure services (computer installation and maintenance services) and business process services.

Brian Sellwood was the general manager of IBM Global Services responsible for delivery, operations and applications management services across Europe, Africa and the Middle East. He described the importance of services:

In today's computing industry it is very difficult to differentiate one supplier from another in terms of their hardware and software. The product itself is no longer, or very rarely, a differentiator. It's what you can offer the customer around that product, and that's invariably service, services such as project management, application implementation, fixing a fault with a machine, how you manage and perform that service. It's about what you do with that product, how you manage that relationship, how you treat the customer, how you respond to their problems and the solutions you can offer your customers to make their businesses stronger and better.

This approach is considerably different to that 15 years ago when IBM was renowned as a product-based company specialising in developing and selling computer hardware and software. It was also making a loss. IBM then set about creating an organisation that was focused on its services and the needs of its customers and not on the company's products. Brian Sellwood explained:

We were not into services; we were a hardware/software product company. The first step was to start understanding what the customer wanted; what they wanted to buy and how they wanted to see it packaged. Having undertaken some market analysis we decided to start very simply with what we had, and package it better, rather than build a whole new set of new services. Over time we realised that what we had was not quite what the customers wanted to buy; they wanted value-add. That meant we had to change and redefine our portfolio. We had to listen to what our customers were asking for and at the same time observe what the competition were doing and try to see where there were gaps in their portfolios and opportunities for us. And this has been a continuous process ever since. This continual refinement of what we are offering to the customer has played a key role in stimulating our growth over the last ten years.

In the early stages we found that customers were looking for help but had not always been able to express that need because there was not always someone willing to listen. In fact there was no shortage of opportunities for us to go and advise customers on how to make better use of their installed equipment. We found customers wanted almost anything and our challenge was to respond appropriately. No two customers were the same and so the challenge was to be able to offer the customers solutions to their specific problems rather than saying we have this solution and that will fit your business. From that beginning we were able, slowly, to add more services, eventually developing a business consulting capability where we could advise on how to use and manage applications more effectively, how to install and help customers install applications, and advise customers on process engineering, supply chain development and business transformation.

1.3.4 Co-production

One of the most important, intriguing and challenging aspects of managing service operations (certainly when compared to manufacturing operations) is that many, though not all, service operations 'process' customers. (Other service operations process things belonging to the customer.) These are sometimes referred to as customer processing operations. The theme park cannot physically give you the rides unless you turn up, the doctor cannot give you an injection unless you are physically in the same place. This means that the customer's experience is an intrinsic part of the operation's process (see Figure 1.1). As a result, the customer sees much of the process and, in many cases, plays a key role in the process itself as well as receiving the service – thus service is a two-way flow. We will develop this idea in Chapter 4.

It is important to note that customers may not see and/or experience the whole of the process; they will only be involved in the 'front office' (the overlapping section in Figure 1.1). The 'back office' contains tasks that are carried out usually unseen by the customers, such as cooking the food in restaurants, or baggage handling at an airport (see Chapter 7).

The part played by customers in the service process is referred to as co-production (or co-creation). (This was an idea that emerged over 40 years ago describing the way citizens could get more involved in public sector services.[12]) We all play a part in many services. We take ourselves around the supermarket shelves, pick the items, take them to the checkout, sometimes scan them ourselves, then pack them and transport them to the car. (Alternatively we could reduce our input and go for home delivery and let the supermarket pick, pack and deliver our goods, though we still have to get involved in ticking the boxes on the order form.) When we visit the doctor with an ailment we are needed to describe the symptoms to them and discuss alternative treatments.

In a restaurant or on a train, for example, we also provide services to other customers. In the restaurant we help provide the ambiance, the gentle buzz of conversation around the room, and our adherence to a formal or informal dress code which helps set the scene (the servicescape). In a train, we keep other seats free of our luggage so that others can sit down, and we refrain from noisy or unruly behaviour. So, besides managing materials, technology, people and processes, service operations managers also have to manage the customer as a resource too (see Chapter 11).[13]

This overlap of the process and the customer's experience, together with the direct involvement of the customer in many services, makes the job of a service operations manager particularly challenging, exciting and, at times, frustrating (see Chapter 2).

1.4 What is service operations management?

Service operations management is the term that is used to cover the activities, decisions and responsibilities of operations managers in service organisations. It is concerned with providing services, and value, to customers or users, ensuring they get the right experiences and the desired outcomes. It involves understanding the needs of the customers, managing the service processes, ensuring the organisation's objectives are met, while also paying attention to the continual improvement of the services. Operations managers are responsible for most of an organisation's assets, for managing most costs and staff and for generating the organisation's revenues. As such, operations management is a central organisational function and one that is critical to organisational success.

Service operations managers are often called operations managers but many other titles are used, such as managing partners in consultancy firms, nursing managers in hospitals, headteachers in schools, fleet managers in transport companies, call centre managers, customer service managers, restaurant managers ... They may be responsible for managing 'front office' operations – the parts of the process that a customer might see, or the 'back office' operations invisible to the customer, or indeed both. The back office operation on the exotic island of Baros in the Maldives (see Case Example 1.3) involves a wide range of activities such as water treatment plants, laundry, catering etc., all hidden from the guests' view. The front office operations include restaurants, accommodation and watersports. Ahmed Jihad is the operations manager with overall responsibility for both the back and front office operations.

All operations managers have a number of things in common:

- They are responsible for the service operation – the configuration of resources and processes that provide service for the customer (see Figure 1.1).
- They are responsible for some of the organisation's resources (we refer to these as inputs – see Figure 1.1), including materials, equipment, staff, technology and facilities. These resources often account for a very large proportion of an organisation's total assets, so service operations managers are responsible for much of an organisation's cost base.
- They are responsible for the organisation's customers (sometimes referred to as clients, users, patients or students, for example) and/or the things belonging to their customers, such as their parcels or orders.
- They are responsible for 'processing' their customers or their parcels or orders. For the managing partner in a consultancy firm this might involve overseeing meetings with clients, data gathering, analysis and report writing. For the nursing manager it might involve overseeing patient admissions, tests, treatment and discharge. (The service process is the set of activities or steps in the provision of the service.)
- They are also responsible for the outputs; the 'products' provided to their customers. The nursing manager delivers (discharges) recovering patients together with their prescriptions for medicines and outpatient appointments. The managing partner delivers the final report and the solution to a problem to the client.
- They are responsible for designing, creating and providing the right experience and outcomes for their customers. The nursing manager will be concerned to ensure the patient feels well cared for and leaves in a better condition than how they came in. The managing partner will want their clients to feel informed, assured and valued, and provide them with some real business benefits.
- They are responsible for delivering value to their customers and also to the organisation. Value to the customers comes from their experiences and the benefits gained. Value for the organisation comes from operations managers keeping to budgets, delivering revenue, reducing costs and delivering the organisation's strategy, for example.
- Service operations managers are responsible for generating most, if not all, of an organisation's revenue/income and managing most of its assets and staff.

Case Example 1.3 Baros, the Maldives

The Republic of the Maldives is a small country lying 700 kilometres south-west of Sri Lanka in the Indian Ocean. It consists of over 1,000 small islands grouped together in atolls. Spread over an area of about 90,000 square kilometres, this country stretches from the equator to 1,000 kilometres north, yet it has a total land mass of less than 470 square kilometres. With its coral reefs, white sandy beaches and a climate of between 28 and 32 degrees it is a holiday paradise and a destination for the affluent traveller.

The tiny island of Baros is a five-star de luxe resort, owned and operated by Universal Resorts which run eight secluded island resorts in the Maldives, Seychelles and Sri Lanka. Baros is just a 25-minute speedboat ride from the island airport which is close to the main island containing the capital Malé. Guests are met in the airport and escorted to the resort's awaiting boat.

There are just 75 luxury villas on the island. Some are beach villas, sheltered and secluded in lush tropical vegetation, with direct access to the beach. Other villas are water villas, built above the water, each with their own private balcony and sea view. All the villas are spacious and air-conditioned. The resort has its own spa, diving and snorkelling centre, gym, bars and three restaurants, including the famous Lighthouse Restaurant.

In charge of all back office and front office operations is Ahmed Jihad, a Maldivian with international experience in hotel management. From the point of view of the guests the place is stunning, peaceful and quiet and their expectations are well met, if not exceeded. Although Baros looks the perfect posting for an operations manager, Mr Jihad explained that there was a lot of hard work behind the scenes.

We have to manage around 275 staff looking after our 100–150 guests. The operation never stops; it is 24 hours a day, 7 days a week. We have to make sure everyone has the energy and the motivation to keep our high standards, every hour, every day. We have to keep the place, all the wooden decks, furniture, the thatched roofs, looking in pristine condition. We also have a significant logistical operation as all our supplies are brought in by air then by boat. There is also a considerable back office operation which our guests don't see, or even think about.

Most of the back office operations are hidden away in the centre of the island overseen by the resort manager and the chief engineer. As there are no utilities to the island the resort has to generate its own electricity, run a desalination water treatment plant, an electricity generating plant and a sewerage treatment plant. It also has to provide all the facilities, including accommodation, for its staff.

Mr Jihad explained:

Baros is the real essence of the Maldives. It has a natural beauty, white sands, reefs, the lagoon, and a high customer profile – people with very high expectations. My main responsibility is the front office operations – to make sure the guests are happy; from airport receiving through their stay here to their departure at the airport. I usually greet the guests and talk to them during their stay. I make sure we have all the right SOPs (standard operating procedures) to create the high standards of this resort and I make sure they are all implemented correctly, from check-in to catering to cleaning. I also oversee the food and beverage operations and the sales and marketing; I check all their materials and provide my ideas. I conduct daily and weekly meetings and briefings with the staff, and with contractors, and oversee the training of staff.

There is no typical day, but if we take yesterday, Monday, for example, I started at 7.30 in the morning. This is one of our very busy days so my key objective was to make sure all the rooms were ready for our incoming guests, make sure reception goes smoothly for them, and that all the facilities they booked are ready for them. I also like to know who the returning guests are. The first thing I did was to check my emails, then I had a breakfast meeting with our chef. I held a meeting with all my departmental managers where we deal with any issues and brief them about the day's activities. This was followed by the general staff meeting at 10.00. I then spent some time talking to guests around the site, followed by a meeting with the Spa Manager at 11.30; we discussed how we can increase utilisation of this facility. This was followed with a similar meeting with the Diving Centre Manager. I then went off to my room, had a shower and freshened up. I had lunch at 1.30. I usually have it with one of my managers; yesterday it was with the HR Manager. We are in the middle of developing our fire and safety training programme so I was checking how it was going and also the new SOPs we had recently put in place. These meetings are important, it gives me time to check things and discuss issues. I then went to my office and signed all the cocktail party invitations for all our guests and the personal welcome letters for our arriving guests; I also checked the special arrangements for the honeymoon guests. Throughout the afternoon I then met the boats bringing in the arriving guests. At 5.30 I went back to my room and had a shower and watched the BBC and CNN for a while. At 7.30 I went back to the office and checked the emails again. I then went over to the Lighthouse to talk to guests, and checked over one of the other restaurants; it's important for the staff to see managers around. I then went to reception to talk about today's (Tuesday's) departures. I had dinner around 9.30 with my chief engineer and the HR manager, again about the fire and safety training. This is quite a big project for us at the moment. I then went back to the office, checked the emails and went to bed at 10.30.

No two days are the same, but every one of them is enjoyable.

1.5 Why is service operations management important?

We hope by now it is becoming clear that service operations managers have an important and responsible role. In essence, service operations managers

- are responsible for managing the design and delivery of services to organisations' customers,
- are responsible for managing most of organisation's resources,
- have a significant impact on the success of an organisation.

The success of service operations managers is not simply about performing a good technical task, such as educating a student, delivering a project on time, or providing a holiday. Good service operations management should lead to better (or more appropriate) services and experiences that are better for the customer, better for the staff and also better for the organisation – the 'triple bottom line'.

1.5.1 Better for the customer

Customers will be satisfied, even delighted if they are provided with the right service, a good experience and the desired outcomes. This delivers value for the customer (for more discussion on value see Chapter 3).

A problem for service managers is that the customer's idea of what represents value may well vary from customer to customer and shift through time, and even from day to day. At the most basic level, the economising customers will think of value as getting more for their money. Other customers may be prepared to pay more in order to receive a higher service specification. Still others will value the psychological value in being able to say that they are able to afford to be customers of high-status services (even though the specification may be no better than a lower priced service). The service operations manager must be aware of the full range of influences on the customer's assessment of value. A key element in this understanding is the relationship between the service brand values as communicated to the customer and the potential mismatch in terms of customer experience.

1.5.2 Better for the staff

Good service operations management and the provision of the right services, experiences and outcomes for the customer will also mean a better experience for the staff:

- Customers will be easier to deal with because they are satisfied and the service and experience meet their needs.
- Because the operation works well and generates the right outcomes there will be fewer problems and therefore less hassle for the staff and fewer (unpleasant) complaints to deal with.
- Customers who are satisfied tend to be more tolerant, so when things go wrong they are much more accepting than they might otherwise have been, again making life easier for the staff.
- A smooth operation and contented customers means things are going well, thus staff are more likely to have pride in both the job they do and the organisation they work for.

1.5.3 Better for the organisation

Delivering the right service and experience through good operations management delivers many organisational benefits:

- Satisfied customers who perceive value from the service are more likely to return and also more likely to provide positive word-of-mouth and recommend the organisation and its services to others, thus generating more revenue (assuming it's a revenue-generating organisation).

- Better service operations management means improved processes which should be cheaper and more efficient, reducing the organisation's costs.
- Increased revenue and/or reduced costs will improve the profitability and/or viability of the organisation.
- Better services may also provide the organisation with a source of competitive advantage.
- Better and more efficient services will enhance the organisation's reputation and brand.
- Delivering the right services and experiences should also enable the organisation to achieve its goals/objectives/mission, supporting the organisation's strategic intent.
- Good service operations management which thinks both reactively and proactively should be able to help shape and develop the organisation's future intent and develop skills and competencies that will support the development of the organisation.

1.5.4 Economic contribution

A final and important contribution, but at a macro level, is the contribution that services, in general, make towards a nation's economy. Service activities are a vital and significant part of most developing and developed economies. In most developed countries services account for in excess of 80 per cent of gross domestic product (GDP), and for over 50 per cent of GDP in developing economies. They also provide employment for a significant number of people. The challenges facing service operations managers throughout the whole range of service organisations – such as financial institutions, government bodies, retailers, wholesalers and personal service providers – need to be taken seriously and managed well to support economic success and development.

We can see that from the standpoint of economic value alone we should pay attention to the service sector, and to service operations in particular as this is where the service, and therefore wealth and value, are created. Services also have an important economic role in non-service organisations. Many manufacturing companies have significant revenue-earning service activities, such as customer support, and also many service activities internal to the organisation, such as payroll, catering, information and IT services etc. Indeed it has been estimated that around 75 per cent of non-service organisations' activities may be directly or indirectly associated with the provision of services.[14]

Service organisations provide employment for the vast majority of the working population in most developed and developing countries. In many economies the service sector is the only area where new jobs are being created, notably in tourism and leisure. Many service organisations, such as hospitality and transportation, are people-intensive, requiring different mixes of skilled and unskilled labour. Other organisations, such as banking and many financial services, are more technology-based.

Finally, we cannot ignore the vast numbers of people employed in the public and voluntary sectors. Managing services such as education, health, fire, police, social services, famine relief organisations, faith organisations and charities requires as much expertise as their private sector counterparts. Governments are increasingly subcontracting many services to the voluntary sector that were previously provided directly by the state. In so doing, governments are applying commercial approaches to supplier assessment, and there is therefore a growing pressure on the voluntary sector to apply improvement methodologies (see Chapter 12). Whatever the type of service organisation, there is no doubt that there is ever-increasing pressure to provide higher levels of 'value for money' with the same or reducing resources.

1.6 Summary

What are services?

- Services are provided by a variety of types of organisations, including business-to-consumer services (B2C), business-to-business services (B2B), internal services, public services and not-for-profit and voluntary services.

What is 'service'?

- A service is an activity – a process or set of steps (unlike a product which is a thing) – which involves the treatment of a customer (or user) or something belonging to them, where the customer is also involved, and performs some role (co-production), in the service process.
- From the operation's point of view, the service provided is the service process and its outputs which have been designed, created and enacted by the operation using its many input resources, including the customer, where the customer also takes some part in the service process.
- From the customer's perspective, the service received is the customer's experience of the service provided and their interaction with it, perceptions of it, and response to it, which results in outcomes such as 'products', benefits, emotions, judgements and intentions.

What is service operations management?

- Service operations management is concerned with the activities, decisions and responsibilities of operations managers in service organisations. It entails providing services, and value, to customers or users, ensuring they get the right experiences and the desired outcomes. It involves understanding the needs of the customers, managing the service processes, ensuring the organisation's objectives are met, while also paying attention to the continual improvement of the services.

Why is service operations management important?

- Service operations managers
  - are responsible for a large proportion of the organisation's assets
  - are responsible for delivering service to the organisation's customers
  - have a significant impact on the success of an organisation.
- Good service operations management, resulting in good services and experiences, will deliver the 'triple bottom line', i.e.
  - better for the customer
  - better for the staff
  - better for the organisation.
- At a macro level services are a critical part of most economies, accounting for a significant proportion of GDP and employment.

1.7 Discussion questions

1. Describe the customer experience and outcomes for a fast-food restaurant, a doctor's surgery and an internet-based fashion clothing retailer. Compare and contrast the services of these three organisations.
2. How do students assess the value of a university course? How does this differ from the organisation's view of value?
3. Think of a time when you recently received poor service. If service operations are so important, why do you think they sometimes deliver poor service?

1.8 Questions for managers

1. Describe your service from both an operational and customer perspective. Assess the mismatches between these perspectives.
2. How is the success of your operation assessed? Is this approach appropriate?
3. How well is the contribution of the operation understood in your organisation and what are the implications?

Suggested further reading

Johnston, Robert (2005), 'Service Operations Management: From the Roots Up', *International Journal of Operations and Production Management* 25 (12) 1298–1308

Johnston, Robert and Xiangyu Kong (2011), 'The Customer Experience: A Road Map for Improvement', *Managing Service Quality* 21 (1) 5–24

Lusch, Robert F., Stephen L. Vargo and Matthew O'Brien (2007), 'Competing through Service: Insights from Service Dominant Logic', *Journal of Retailing* 83 (1) 2–18

Neu, Wayne A. and Stephen W. Brown (2005), 'Forming Successful Business-to-Business Services in Goods-Dominant Firms', *Journal of Service Research* 8 (1) 3–17

Sampson, Scott E. and Craig M. Froehle (2006), 'Foundations and Implications of a Proposed Unified Services Theory', *Production and Operations Management* 15 (2) 329–343

Shaw, Colin, Qaalfa Dibeehi and Steven Walden (2010), *Customer Experience: Future Trends and Insights*, Palgrave Macmillan

Slack, Nigel, Stuart Chambers and Robert Johnston (2010), *Operations Management*, 6th edition, FT Prentice Hall, Harlow

Vargo, Stephen L. and Robert F. Lusch (2004), 'Evolving to a New Dominant Logic of Marketing', *Journal of Marketing* 68 (January) 1–17.

Wong, Amy (2004) 'The Role of Emotions in Service Encounters', *Managing Service Quality* 14 (5) 365–376

Useful web links

A list of many service operations management texts, practitioner books, service journals, videos and links to a site with practitioner papers can be found at:
http://group.wbs.ac.uk/om/teaching/service/materials/

IBM is leading a Service Science, Management, and Engineering (SSME) initiative. Their website provides articles, case studies, materials and references to what some organisations and universities are doing in this emerging discipline:
http://www.ibm.com/university/ssme

The Customer Service Network is an independent UK forum for customer service professionals:
http://www.customernet.com/

The Institute of Customer Service is the UK's professional body for customer service:
http://www.instituteofcustomerservice.com/

Notes

1. For a discussion see Johnston, Robert (2005), 'Service Operations Management: From the Roots Up', *International Journal of Operations and Production Management* 25 (12) 1298–1308 and Johnston, Robert (1994), 'Operations: From Factory to Service Management', *International Journal of Service Industry Management* 5 (1) 49–63

2. See Haywood-Farmer, John, and Jean Nollet (1991), *Services Plus: Effective Service Management*, Morin, Boucherville, Quebec; Sampson, Scott E. and Craig M. Froehle (2006), 'Foundations and Implications of a Proposed Unified Services Theory', *Production and Operations Management* 15 (2) 329–343

3. Johnston, Robert and Xiangyu Kong (2011), 'The Customer Experience: A Road Map for Improvement', *Managing Service Quality* 21 (1) 5–24

4. Sampson, Scott (2005), *Understanding Service Businesses*, 2nd edition, Wiley; Sampson, Scott E. and Craig M. Froehle (2006), 'Foundations and Implications of a Proposed Unified Services Theory', *Production and Operations Management* 15 (2) 329–343

5. Lusch, Robert F., Stephen L. Vargo and Matthew O'Brien (2007), 'Competing through Service: Insights from Service Dominant Logic', *Journal of Retailing* 83 (1) 2–18

6. Pine, II, B. Joseph and James H. Gilmore (1998), 'Welcome to the Experience Economy', *Harvard Business Review* 76 (4) 97–105

7. For more information on the customer experience see Shaw, Colin (2005), *Revolutionize Your Customer Experience*, Palgrave Macmillan, Basingstoke; Pullman, Madeleine E. and Michael A. Gross (2004), 'Ability of Experience Design Elements to Elicit Emotions and Loyalty Behaviors', *Decision Sciences* 35 (3) 551–578; Csikszentmihalyi, Mihaly (2000), 'The Costs and Benefits of Consuming', *Journal of Consumer Research* 27 (2) 267–272; Ding, David Xin, Paul Jen-Hwa Hu, Rohit Verma and Don G. Wardell (2010), 'The Impact of Service System Design and Flow Experience on Customer Satisfaction in Online Financial Services', *Journal of Service Research* 13 (1) 96–110

8 Zomerdijk, Leonieke G. and Christopher A. Voss (2010), 'Service Design for Experience-Centric Services', *Journal of Service Research* 13 (1) 67–82 and Carbone, Lewis P. (2004), *Clued In*, FT Prentice Hall, New Jersey

9 Lusch, Robert F., Stephen L. Vargo and Matthew O'Brien (2007), 'Competing through Service: Insights from Service Dominant Logic', *Journal of Retailing* 83 (1) 2–18

10 Lusch, Robert F., Stephen L. Vargo and Matthew O'Brien (2007), 'Competing through Service: Insights from Service Dominant Logic', *Journal of Retailing* 83 (1) 2–18 and Edvardsson, Bo, Bo Enquist and Robert Johnston (2005), 'Co-creating Customer Value through Hyperreality in the Prepurchase Service Experience', *Journal of Service Research* 8 (2) 149–161

11 Vargo, Stephen. L. and Robert F Lusch (2004), 'The Four Service Marketing Myths – Remnants of a Goods-Based, Manufacturing Model', *Journal of Service Research* 6 (4) 324–335 and Edvardsson, Bo and Jan Olsson (1996), 'Key Concepts for New Service Development', *The Service Industries Journal* 16 (2) 140–164

12 See for example *Brudney, Jeffrey L. and Robert E. England (1983)*, 'Toward a Definition of the Coproduction Concept', *Public Administration Review* 43 (1), 59

13 Johnston, Robert (1989), 'The Customer as Employee', *International Journal of Operations and Production Management* 9 (5) 15–23

14 Quinn, Joseph B. and Christopher E. Gagnon (1986), 'Will Services Follow Manufacturing into Decline?', *Harvard Business Review* 64 (6) 95–103

Chapter 2
Understanding the challenges for operations managers

Chapter objectives

This chapter is about how to understand the key challenges facing service operations managers.

- What are the key strategic challenges faced by service operations managers?
- What are the key tactical challenges faced by service operations managers?
- What are the challenges for different types of services?
- What are the challenges for different types of processes?
- What are the challenges in working with other management functions?
- How can this book help?

2.1 Introduction

From Chapter 1 it should be clear that the key decision areas for operations managers include managing their inputs – materials, staff/employees, technology and their customers and designing, creating and enacting service processes which provide a range of services. They also have to create the right experience for their customers whilst generating the right outcomes for the customer ('products', benefits and emotions) and also creating the right outcomes for the organisation (revenue, cost management, achievement of strategic aims etc.).

In this chapter we want to share with you the main problems and challenges facing service operations managers and introduce the structure of this book to show how to deal with these challenges. While each operation has its own particular demands, there are a number of key challenges faced by most if not all service operations and service operations managers. In the first part of this chapter we want to outline the nature of those challenges; the strategic and the tactical challenges. We will then look at the particular challenges faced by specific types of service operations and the various types of processes found within them. We will also discuss the issues faced by operations managers in working with other management functions such as strategy, marketing and HR. As we describe all these challenges we will point you to the parts of this book that provide ideas and tools to help deal with them. We will conclude with an overview of the structure of the book.

2.2 What are the key strategic challenges faced by service operations managers?

The key strategic challenges faced by most service operations managers include

- Managing tactically and strategically
- Making operations a contributor to strategy as well as an implementer
- Making the business case for service
- Understanding the service concept.

2.2.1 Managing tactically and strategically

Operations managers need to manage both tactically and strategically. Being tactical is about being focused on the short-term, day-to-day activities. Strategy is concerned with the long-term and with the operation's wider contribution to the organisation (see Chapter 1, Section 1.5). You may have noticed that Ahmed Jihad in Case Example 1.3 was bogged down with day-to-day activities and seemed to have little time to deal with the future and with important medium- and longer-term operational issues such as:

- How will the resort need to change to compete with the opening of new high-quality resorts in the Maldives?
- How can it reduce costs to deal with economic slowdown?
- As sustainable tourism is becoming increasingly important what changes will the operation need to make?
- How can the resort deal with rising sea levels over the next twenty years? The highest point in the Maldives is just 2.4 metres (8 feet) above sea level.

The problem for operations managers is that a significant part of the excitement of managing operations is its immediacy. By this we mean the constant challenge of dealing with the needs of a stream of customers, managing the staff and making operational decisions to ensure the delivery of an appropriate quality of service at an appropriate cost. The danger of this immediacy is that it can lead to a short-term focus. Many service operations managers concentrate their time and effort on managing the day-to-day operations for the following reasons:

- The pressure on the operation to deliver its day-to-day services may leave little time for medium-term operational improvement activities or longer-term strategic planning. For example, it is difficult for a headteacher to put time into dealing with solving major underlying problems, such as poor facilities, inadequate funding, high levels of absenteeism etc., when they are heavily involved in trying to find part-time staff to cover for sudden absences, recruiting new staff to vacant posts, processing the many forms and requests that land on the desk each day and also dealing with a constant stream of student behavioural problems.
- Operations managers, because of the nature of the job and often their background, tend to feel more comfortable with the unambiguous and rational nature of many short-term tactical decisions. The more intuitive processes required for strategic thinking are quite different and excuses found to put them to one side. The headteacher is likely to have been promoted through the profession and they may get a 'buzz' and feel more comfortable in dealing with students and the curriculum. They may be less inclined to put time into the 'less exciting' and 'less pressing' tasks of data collection, analysis, report writing and high-level debate and discussion with various parties to try to resolve underlying and longer-term issues.

As a result, the development and strategic aspects of operations management are frequently neglected and a disproportionate amount of time is spent on managing the day-to-day operations. In some organisations this problem is built in by not giving senior operations managers a seat at the boardroom table (or its equivalent). Given they are responsible for most of the organisation's assets, people, costs and revenue, this would seem very short-sighted.

Good operations managers are those who can pay attention to, and create time in their day for, both strategic issues and also managing the day-to-day operations in order to create and sustain a successful organisation (see Chapters 7–14 for managing the day-to-day, tactical issues and Chapters 15–17 for the strategic issues).

2.2.2 Making operations a contributor to strategy as well as an implementer

Operations managers are involved in the 'doing' part of the business. It is the operation and its staff that deliver the service, not its marketers or financial managers, though in a small organisation these roles may be undertaken by the same people. As such operations managers are responsible for the implementation of strategy. As an implementer of strategy operations managers must first of all understand the organisation's strategy. This may be market dominance for a large retailer, or the speedy provision of water and food for an aid agency, or a high level of childcare with strong links into the community for a nursery. This then defines what the operation has to be good at (or how it has to compete for competitive organisations). This might involve delivering service at a low cost with dependability (see Case Example 2.1) or providing a wide range of services or a pleasurable customer experience, for example. This then defines the key decision areas and tasks for the operation, such as minimising costs and implementing lean initiatives, or focusing on speed of delivery and developing supply networks, or continually improving quality and innovating new services (we will develop this further in Chapter 15).

Case Example 2.1 SouthWest Airlines

SouthWest Airlines is a US organisation that many budget airlines have copied in recent years. There are a number of reasons for its continued success but first and foremost SouthWest delivers the concept of low-cost, dependable transportation incredibly well. They understand that what passengers want is not airport to airport transport but rather door to door. They also understand that competition comes in the form of buses and cars rather than other airlines.

In order to deliver this proposition, SouthWest Airlines have focused on cost and dependability as the heart of their operations strategy. Key decision areas were

Source: Southwest airlines

- Using secondary airports (lower cost and less congestion delivering dependability)
- Using short haul flights with no interconnections (dependability)
- Use of one type of plane (lower maintenance and crewing costs)
- Direct booking only (low cost – and greater visibility of demand)
- Choice of routes with potential to grow volume (cost and dependability).

The additional stroke of genius with SouthWest Airlines is that even though this is a high-volume, standardised service, they have managed to create a customer-focused culture with some life to it! As the CEO of SouthWest Airlines, Gary Kelly, stated, 'Our people are our single greatest strength and most enduring long-term competitive advantage'. You only have to go on to YouTube to see some of the antics of cabin crew which go towards creating a friendly service and an incredibly loyal customer base. SouthWest concentrates on building relationships, both internal and external, and this is their leadership focus. It is perhaps no surprise that other low-cost airlines can copy the product but not the experience!

As we can see from Case Example 2.1 operations also have an important proactive role as a major contributor to strategy. For example service operations managers might be able to provide the platform for future competitive advantage. Rather than taking a service concept (see Chapter 3) and designing and running an operation to deliver it, it may be that there are a set of competences in the operation that can be turned to create a strategic advantage. The webcam installed by the nursery (see Case Example 2.2) might provide it with a competitive advantage that may be difficult for less technologically advanced nurseries to provide by, for example, extending it to provide a daily or weekly webcast by the children to their parents.

Thus service operations managers can have a significant contribution into developing strategy (Chapter 15) by knowing what they can, or could, deliver (Chapters 7–11) and by driving change and improvement through the organisation to provide it (Chapters 12–17).

Case Example 2.2 Cybernurseries

The very first webcam was set up by a group of Cambridge University students from the School of Computer Science. They focused it on the faculty coffee machine so that members of staff could see on their desk computer a 'live' picture of the machine, updated every few minutes. This allowed them to check whether or not the coffee jug was empty before they went to use the machine.

Webcams are now everywhere. Anyone with an internet connection can now see some breathtaking and bizarre sights, including the conditions at 3,880 metres on Mount Everest, the view of the top of the ski run at Lake Tahoe, sights in the African bush, views from the Palazzo Senatorio in Rome, weddings at Las Vegas' Little White Chapel, the view from the Trans-Siberian Railway during its 5,700-mile journey from Moscow to Vladivostok, even the contents of a Swedish family's fridge!

Source: Pearson Education Ltd/Jules Selmes

One application has been the use of webcams in nurseries so that anxious parents can use their computer at work or home to 'look in' on their children. Security is tight, with pictures being encrypted and passwords required for access. The pictures parents receive are single frames, updated every minute, but the quality is good enough for parents to check if their child is relaxed, happy and well cared for – and to remind them what life is about!

While parents and grandparents are revelling in this innovation, others are queuing up to condemn it. Some psychologists are concerned that it becomes an on-screen substitute for involvement in a child's upbringing that simply assuages the guilt of working mothers. Other people worry about it fuelling the current paranoia about child safety. However, at a time when childcare is needing an injection of trust and with more and more working parents, cybernurseries could soon be commonplace.

2.2.3 Making the business case for service

Many of the service operations managers we speak to tell us that they totally understand how important service is. At the end of Chapter 1, we summarised why good service, and good operations management, mean making things better for the customer, better for the staff and better for the organisation. (Better for the organisation may mean retaining customers, attracting new customers, entering new markets, increasing revenues, reducing costs, making greater profit or simply meeting budget targets.) Yet when asked to make the case to demonstrate that better service does indeed make things better for the organisation they often fall back on belief and intuition. The nursery manager (see Case Example 2.2) will intuitively know that spending more money on improving the facilities will bring in more customers, thereby increasing revenue, but they may have difficulty persuading the owner to invest without some hard evidence. Making a business case to the financial director, or the equivalent, in order to obtain the resources required to provide a better operation and deliver a better service requires a clear argument providing evidence of the relationship between service and costs and revenues. Such knowledge will also enable the operations manager to understand the impact of any decisions they make on both the service provided and organisational success. We will explain how this can be done in Chapter 17.

2.2.4 Understanding the service concept

Strategically it is important that there is a shared and defined view about the nature of the service that the organisation provides. The service concept defines what the organisation does, what marketing have to sell and what the operations have to deliver. In a product-based organisation this is usually straightforward; the product can be seen and touched. But a service is an activity or process and it is easy for various people inside the organisation to have quite different views about what that process is. Likewise there may also be differing views about what an organisation is 'selling' and what the customer is 'buying'. Some parents may see the nursery as simply a babysitting service; others may see it as a critical educational experience for their offspring. Articulating and communicating the service concept (Chapter 3) is critical for clarifying the organisation's product to all its customers, internal and external, and for ensuring that it can be, and is, delivered (Chapters 7–11).

2.3 What are the key tactical challenges faced by service operations managers?

The key tactical, day-to-day, challenges faced by most service operations managers include:

- Understanding the customer perspective
- Managing multiple customers
- Managing the customer
- Managing in real time
- Co-ordinating different parts of the organisation
- Encouraging improvement and innovation.

2.3.1 Understanding the customer perspective

A key challenge (and sometimes a difficulty) for many managers in service operations is that they see things from an internal, organisational viewpoint, often referred to as

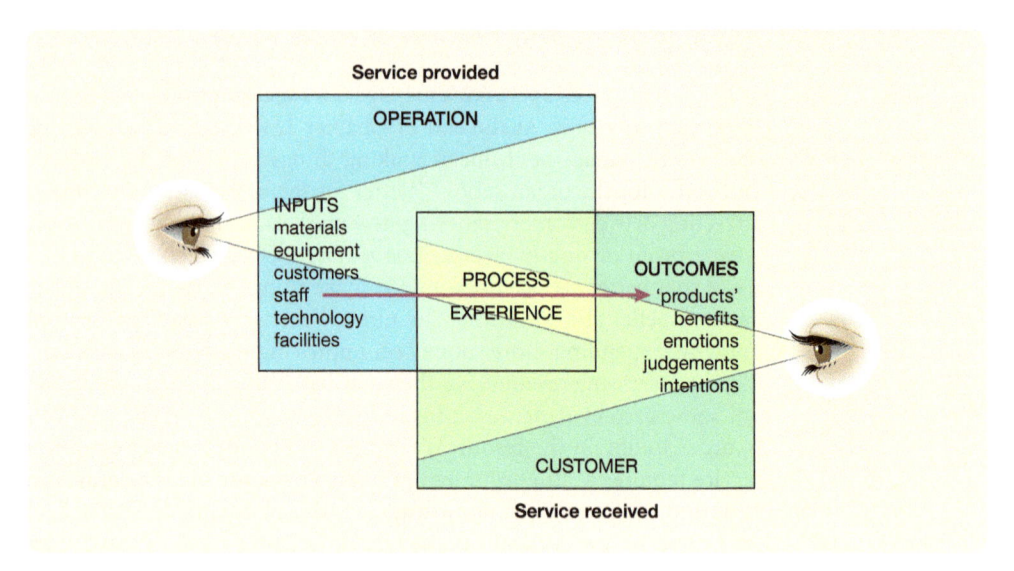

Figure 2.1 Inside-out versus outside-in

'inside-out'.[1] The operation's perspective understands the *service provided*. It focuses on the inputs that have to be managed (including the customer – often seeing them as an 'input' to be processed rather than as a person) and making sure that all the processes are working well. Managers, quite naturally, spend their time worrying about managing their resources and processes, managing capacity, scheduling people, meeting performance targets and financial goals (see Chapters 8–11).

However, the customers will see (the same) things from a very different perspective, 'outside-in' (see Figure 2.1). They are interested in the *service received*, their experience and the outcomes such as how they feel, the 'products' they receive and how they benefit from the service. Customers of the service are less concerned with the management of resources, processes and targets; they want a good experience, they want to have a good outcome and to benefit from the service. The nursery staff may see their key activities as child development and education, whereas the parent (as customer) may see it as an expensive babysitting service while they are at work. These different views may cause some conflicts. For example, when the parent is held up at work they may expect a babysitting service to wait a while for them, whereas a teacher will expect the parent to be on time and make alternative arrangements should they be late. Managing the relationship with the customer (see Chapter 4), managing customer expectations and perceptions (see Chapter 5) and delivering the customer experience (see Chapter 7) are key challenges in managing service operations.

Seeing things from a customer point of view is, surprisingly, unusual in service organisations. Table 2.1 illustrates these two perspectives for three different services, hip replacement surgery, education and consultancy.

Recognising both of these perspectives is important. Operations managers need to manage their operations to create their services; they need to manage their suppliers, people, facilities, process and technology (see Chapters 6 and 8–11), but at the same time they need to recognise how their efforts create value for the customer which in turn creates value for the organisation (see Chapter 1). Indeed some people argue that the customer is the ultimate arbiter of the value an organisation creates and delivers.[2] While value is delivered through the process and the service, it is located in the customer's experience and the outcomes for the customer (see Chapters 1 and 3).[3]

Table 2.1 The operation's and customer's perspectives

Service	The operation's (inside-out) perspective		
	Inputs	Processes	Outputs
Surgery	GP, nurses, surgeon, bed, operating theatre	Diagnosis, operation, aftercare	Hip replacement
Education	Lectures, library, computers, seminar rooms	Timetabling, lectures, exams, marking	Information, slide packs, degrees
Consultancy	Consultants, information, skills, knowledge	Data collection and analysis	Presentations, reports

Service	The customer's (outside-in) perspective		
	Experience	'Products'	Benefits
Surgery	Empathetic and pain-free treatment	A working hip	Greater mobility
Education	Memorable and useful lecturers/seminars	Knowledge, confidence and skills	Better job prospects/capability
Consultancy	Helpful and timely discussions and advice	Solutions	Reduced costs and greater commercial success

We find many organisations today talk about developing a 'customer focus' or becoming 'customer orientated'. A better understanding of the outside-in perspective is a good way to start this process. Cathay Pacific is one organisation that takes an outside-in perspective, focusing on the customer's experience and the emotions they should feel (see Case Example 2.3). In Chapters 4, 7 and 15–17 we explain how this outside-in perspective can be developed.

Case Example 2.3 Cathay Pacific Airways

Cathay Pacific Airways is an international airline based in Hong Kong, offering scheduled passenger and cargo services to over 100 destinations around the world. The airline owns Dragonair and is also a major shareholder in Air Hong Kong, an all-cargo carrier operating in the Asian region. Cathay Pacific and its subsidiaries and associates employ over 25,000 people worldwide, with around 18,600 staff in Hong Kong, making it one of Hong Kong's biggest employers. The airline is a founder member of the **one**world global alliance, whose combined network serves almost 700 destinations in 150 countries worldwide.

Source: Cathay Pacific

> The company's vision is to make Cathay Pacific the most admired airline in the world by:
> - Ensuring safety comes first
> - Providing 'Service Straight from the Heart'
> - Encouraging product leadership
> - Providing rewarding career opportunities.
>
> Angelique Tam was Cathay Pacific's Head of Customer Relations. She explained what was meant by 'Service Straight from the Heart':
>
> *Service Straight from the Heart means that our staff have to be resourceful, and be able to find sensible on the spot solutions. They need to be dynamic and be proactive and find opportunities to excel and serve our customers well. We also expect them to show the highest standards of care and professionalism so they need to be fully committed. We want to create an experience that makes our customers feel welcome, comfortable, appreciated and above all, reassured. This is not as easy as it sounds. We need to be friendly but not overly intimate, caring but not over-attentive, efficient but not mechanical, consistent but with a willingness to be flexible, anticipating but not presumptuous and professional but very approachable.*
>
> Not surprisingly Cathay Pacific has been the recipient of many awards for its service. It was named as Airline of the Year 2009 by Skytrax, and most admired company in Hong Kong by Wall Street Journal Asia in 2010.

2.3.2 Managing multiple customers

Many service organisations do not serve a homogeneous group of customers; they often serve, in different ways, different types of customers. The nursery's customers (see Case Example 2.2) include both the child for whom it is providing an education and social experience, and also the parents for whom it is providing a 'parental substitute' service. There are other customers, sometimes termed stakeholders, such as education authorities and health and safety officials, for whom the nursery provides information and related services. There are also internal customers – the staff – whose welfare and training needs, for example, need to be provided for. Understanding who are the various customers (Chapter 4), understanding their needs and expectations (Chapter 5), developing relationships with them (Chapter 4) and managing the various customers (Chapters 7–9) are key tasks for service operations managers.

2.3.3 Managing the customer

The nature of service means that the operation's process is the customer's experience. In product-based organisations these two are usually distinct. A car manufacturer's processes for building a car are quite separate from their customer's experience of buying and then driving the car. This is not the case in service organisations. In universities, for example, the process of education is inseparable from the educational experience. Likewise the childcare and the childcare experience are inseparable. This provides several particular challenges for service operations managers.

Firstly customers are an input into some of the service operation's processes and they take some part, active or passive, in that process. As a consequence service operations managers not only have to manage their usual inputs and processes, they have to manage the customer as well. In universities we don't only have to deliver the material in a lecture, for example; we also need to manage the student's learning experience by trying to enthuse them and create a passion for our subject and learning (see Chapters 7 and 8).

Secondly the customer's mood, attitude and actions may affect not only their own experience but that of other customers, thereby having a direct bearing on the quality of other people's experiences. The behaviour of students in a lecture (such as talking, coming in late, taking phone calls) or the behaviour of diners in a restaurant (such as talking loudly, swearing or throwing bread rolls) will impact the other customers and affect the quality of their experience.

Thirdly, the experiential nature of services provides particular problems for both specification and indeed control. Some contact centres, for example, use scripts to ensure conformance and clarity, but such scripts lose out on flexibility, development of rapport and maybe also opportunities for cross-selling. The nursery needs clear guidelines and protocols about how to deal with particular issues but each situation may be different; the staff will need to apply some degree of judgement. This requires clarity about the service concept (see Chapter 3), how to deal with and learn from problems (see Chapter 13) and how to set up appropriate measurement and control systems to make sure that staff respond in the 'right' way (see Chapter 9).

So, service operations managers, unlike their manufacturing counterparts, have to manage, so far as is possible, the customer during the service process. This requires careful design of not only the back office processes but those front office processes that handle the customer. The design of these processes must manage the customer through the process with an awareness of the impact on the customer's experience and other customers' experiences. A good design will also take account of how the processes impact on the employees' feelings, as their attitudes will have a significant bearing on service performance (see Chapters 7–11). A key task for the nursery workers is managing the children in their care and recognising that tears or tantrums can easily affect the other children in the group.

The presence of the customer also means that the operation is visible to the customer. In the nursery the facilities and activities are visible not only to the child but also to the parents when dropping off and picking up the child and during the day as they 'drop in' via the web. So the service environment, sometimes referred to as the 'servicescape', needs to be designed to create the right atmosphere for the service to fit with the service concept (Chapter 3). A high-class restaurant, for example, should not have peeling wallpaper and dirty floors. The nursery should smell fresh and look clean with tidy and colourful pictures around the room.

2.3.4 Managing in real time

Because the customer is an input to, and involved in, the process, i.e. the process is their experience, many services happen in real time – they cannot be delayed or put off. A passenger wanting to purchase a ticket for immediate travel may not be willing to return if the agent is busy. Streams of aircraft coming into land cannot easily be put on hold while equipment is serviced or controllers take a break. Children screaming for attention or in danger of hurting themselves in the nursery likewise cannot be ignored. Furthermore, during a service encounter it is not possible to undo what is done or said – things said in the heat of the moment or promises made that cannot be kept. Unlike in manufacturing organisations where it is possible to scrap defective products and remake them, in service there is no 'undo' or 'rewind' button. Smacking a child in the nursery is inexcusable and will not go unnoticed with webcam 'spies' in the room. Managing resources (Chapter 11), managing staff/employees (Chapter 10) and creating an appropriate culture (Chapter 16) are key tasks in managing real time services.

2.3.5 Co-ordinating different parts of the organisation

The service operations manager is responsible for co-ordinating the various parts of the organisation in the delivery of the service; this includes not only understanding the needs of customers (see Chapter 5) but also overseeing the logistics of the supply chain to ensure that all materials and equipment are in the right place at the right time (see Chapter 6) and working closely with the other functions in the organisation (see Section 1.5). A nursery without the right staff and the right materials will not only provide a poor experience for the child but could be potentially dangerous.

2.3.6 Encouraging improvement and innovation

A challenge faced by all service operations managers is how continually to improve and develop their processes and their customers' experiences (Chapters 12–14), ensure that the outcomes are real improvements (Chapter 9) and that there is a culture that is supportive of service and change (Chapters 15 and 16). The challenge for some organisations is how to create a world-class service organisation (Chapter 17).

Improving the operation is about taking what exists and developing it. Innovation, on the other hand, looks for what is not there, i.e. what is new. Innovation therefore usually requires an element of risk; financial risk because innovations require time and money, and often personal risk as the 'champion' for change puts their reputation on the line. Introducing the webcam to the nursery was an innovation that required some expense and no doubt attracted some detractors. Whether it is a success only time will tell. A critical role for service operations managers is to be alert to, and seek out, new ideas but also to have the will, and support, to assess them carefully and follow through if appropriate (see Chapters 12, 13, 14 and 17).

2.4 What are the challenges for different types of services?

Although much of the general theory and practice described in this book applies to all operations, each sector of the service economy (such as financial services, tourism, leisure, charities, government, hospitals, business-to-business services) has its own set of specific challenges. Managing a for-profit consultancy with a small number of high-value clients poses rather different problems to managing an aid agency in a disaster-struck, heavily populated region of a developing country. This section describes some of the differences between the various types of services and outlines some of the particular challenges faced by each sector. In reading this section, it is necessary to be aware that each of these services will also have issues relating to aspects such as:

- The volume of transactions in a given time period. The hypermarket has very different operation challenges from the local grocery store, not least in simply managing the flow of hundreds of customers in the store.
- The mode of service delivery. The retail sector provides a good example of this diversity, with face-to-face service in traditional stores, remote service through mail order, telephone shopping or web-based services.

We will deal with these 'process' differences in the next section. Here we explore some of the key differences in service provision between five broad sectors of the service economy (see Table 2.2):

- business-to-business (B2B) services
- business-to-consumer (B2C) services
- internal services
- public (G2C) services
- not-for-profit services.

It is important to remember that we use the term 'customer' as an all-embracing term that covers users, consumers, internal customers, etc.

Table 2.2 Types of service and their key challenges

	Business-to-business (B2B) services	Business-to-consumer (B2C) services	Internal services	Public services (G2C)	Not-for-profit services
Description	Services provided for businesses	Services provided for individuals	Services provided by internal functions within organisations	Services provided by central or local government	Services provided by non-government organisations (NGOs) or charities
Examples	Maintenance Consultancy Training Catering	Shops Hotels Banks Food	Finance Purchasing IT Personnel	Prisons Hospitals Schools Leisure	Hospices Counselling Faith organisations Aid agencies
Customers	Professionals, who are not necessarily the end users	Individual consumers	Users who have little or no choice of provider; frequently funded by central budget	Citizens who may have little day-to-day choice; funded through taxation with the allocation of resources influenced by political processes	Beneficiaries are self-selecting or chosen recipients; funded through individual and organisational giving
Key challenges	Providing high-quality services to business customers who frequently have high purchasing power	Providing consistent service to a wide variety and high volume of customers	Demonstrating value for money against possible external alternatives	Balancing the various political pressures and providing acceptable public services	Dealing with differences between volunteers, donors and beneficiaries; dealing with emotional and sometimes overwhelming needs

2.4.1 Business-to-business (B2B) services

B2B services are provided by businesses for other businesses or organisations. IBM Global Services, for example (see Chapter 1), provides a range of services to its business customers, including computer installation and maintenance and a range of management consulting services. Other B2B services include outsourced catering services, buildings' maintenance or leasing and supporting equipment, financial services and market research. Some of the challenges for B2B services include:

- Dealing with multiple contacts in the organisation. Consultants may have to work with a wide range of employees in their client organisations and so maintain relationships at different levels in the organisation (Chapter 4).
- Working with a complex set of relationships. The users or recipients of a service will frequently not be the purchasers, and this purchasing group may in turn be different from those who commission or specify the service standards (see Chapter 4).
- B2B relationships may last for a long time. The challenge here is for the relationship not to become too 'cosy', with the customer or supplier being taken for granted (see Chapters 4 and 6).

2.4.2 Business-to-consumer (B2C) services

B2C services are those that individuals purchase for themselves or on behalf of another individual. They range through leisure services such as hotels, restaurants and sports provision, retail services such as shops and supermarkets, financial services such as banks and insurance providers, through to professional services such as lawyers and accountants. The challenges faced by most B2C services include:

- The organisation may deal with many different customers each day. Each has their own special needs and expectations of the service provided and, to make matters more difficult, these may change for the same individual from day to day (see Chapters 4 and 5).
- Because the operation serves so many customers, it faces a major challenge in keeping the experience fresh for the next new customer. It may be the first and only time the customer experiences this service, although the customer may be just one out of hundreds that an individual member of staff sees in a day (see Chapters 7 and 8).
- Many B2C service operations have the added complication of the need for consistency across many points of contact with customers, frequently spread nationally if not globally (see Chapter 9).

2.4.3 Internal services

Most managers are involved in providing and receiving internal service, not just internal services such as personnel, finance, purchasing and IT support, but also the day-to-day service they provide to each other, such as information and support. Indeed the Internal Service Rule highlights the importance of internal service provision: the level of external customer service will never exceed the level of internal customer service. The challenges posed by internal service provision include:

- Getting people within an organisation to recognise the service and the importance of the service they provide to each other, and treat it, assess it, measure it and improve it in just the same way as they deal with external service (see Chapters 3 to 11).
- Demonstrating that the internal services, such as IT and finance, provide at least as good 'value for money' as an external alternative. This is a challenge faced by many IT departments, for example, whose users often feel that they could obtain cheaper equipment more rapidly from the local computer store or via the internet (see Chapters 3 and 6).
- Adapting the service to business needs. If the service provision is effectively a commodity, it can be outsourced (see Chapter 6). Internal service providers must demonstrate their ability to tailor their offerings to the changing business needs in a way that external providers cannot (see Chapter 15).
- Gaining acceptance from their internal customers. Centrally funded services are frequently viewed with suspicion by local operating units and may not receive the co-operation required to carry out their tasks effectively (Chapter 6).

2.4.4 Public services (G2C)

These services are provided by central or local government for the community at large. Funding comes through the various forms of business and individual taxation, which is then largely allocated by policies set by government. Examples include police, prisons, hospitals and education. Specific challenges for public sector services include:

- The provision of 'best-value' services. Public services are under continual scrutiny. As a result, aspects of service operations that might be taken for granted by their private sector colleagues must be carefully justified in these organisations (see Chapter 9).

- Rationing supply of service. Public sector organisations cannot use the pricing mechanism to regulate demand. With essential services, this can be a very sensitive issue. The health service must make policy decisions as to how much resource can be devoted to heart operations, to maternity services, and so on. Expenditure on intensive care units, accident and emergency provision and very expensive drugs is particularly sensitive since lives are at stake, but inevitably there will be times when demand outstrips supply or costs exceed budgets (see Chapter 11).
- Multiple stakeholders. Public services suffer from having many 'customers'. With B2C services it is reasonably clear who the customers are, and if this group is satisfied, generally speaking the organisation should be successful. This is not the case with the public sector, where the recipients of the service, as individuals, have little power to influence. Politicians and service managers themselves may have far more power to decide current priorities (see Chapter 4).
- A confused service concept. The service concept provides direction for the organisation (we devote Chapter 3 to the discussion of the role of the service concept). Some public services are provided for the good of society at large and are not necessarily loved by those who have to deal with them. Prisons, police services and tax collectors may fall into this category.

2.4.5 Not-for-profit services

Charities of various types form the majority of these services. Most engage in a mixture of fund raising, providing information about the cause or issue that concerns them, and some form of social action. An organisation such as Oxfam must gather funds for famine relief and then organise to supply and distribute aid as required (see Case Example 2.4). Challenges for these services include:

- Managing a workforce of volunteers who, though highly motivated, may not always follow the organisation's procedures (see Chapter 10).
- Managing the allocation of resources to ensure that maximum funds flow to the beneficiaries of the organisation, while developing effective processes and people (see Chapters 7 to 11).
- Dealing with differences between the activities that might influence and impress donors, but which might conflict with the requirements of their 'customers' (see Chapter 3).
- Working in a highly emotional area, sometimes being overwhelmed by demand for service (see Chapter 11).

Case Example 2.4 Oxfam International

Oxfam is a major international development, relief and campaigning organisation dedicated to finding lasting solutions to poverty and suffering around the world. It is a confederation of 15 international organisations (country-based Oxfams) working with over 3,000 local partner organisations and alongside communities in 98 countries. It has three main activates: firstly, responding quickly to emergencies providing life-saving assistance to people affected by disasters; secondly, helping people living in poverty take control of their lives. Third, as a part of global movement for change, Oxfam spends time raising public awareness about the causes of poverty and pressing decision makers to change policies and practices to reduce poverty and injustice.

Source: Helen Jones

Each year Oxfam International launches emergency responses when lives, health, and livelihoods are threatened by disasters; natural disasters, such as earthquakes and storms, or political conflicts, such as riots and wars. In 2008–09 it worked on over ten major disaster areas where over 1,500,000 people were affected. The emergency programmes are usually run by Oxfam's regional and country offices. The organisation's headquarters provides advice, materials and staff, deploying emergency support personnel (ESP) on short-term assignments when and where their skills are required. Shelters, blankets and clothing can be flown out at short notice from the emergency warehouses. Engineers and sanitation equipment can also be provided, including water tanks, latrines, hygiene kits and containers such as the 'Oxfam bucket', which is light, easy to carry and transport, and has a sealable lid.

Every emergency is different, with differing security situations, aid needs, logistical problems and access issues. The responses of other agencies, such as governments or other relief agencies, will also be different, depending on the nature and location of the disaster. Oxfam relies on its local team, with support from headquarters as necessary, to assess each situation and decide whether and how the organisation can make a difference. Furthermore, local teams and partners are sometimes able to provide warnings of impending disasters, giving more time to assess need and enable a multi-agency response.

Importantly, when an emergency is over, Oxfam often continues to work with the affected communities through its local offices and partner organisations, to help people rebuild their lives and livelihoods.

With more than one billion people living in poverty across the world, Oxfam, like other aid and development organisations, has no shortage of 'non-emergency' work. Oxfam is recognised as a global expert in water and sanitation. Around 80 per cent of diseases and over one-third of deaths in the developing world are caused by contaminated water, and this can escalate in crises. Oxfam also puts pressure on governments to invest in agriculture and develop policies to help poor people benefit from international trade. It also promotes education and works with communities to provide education opportunities and with governments to train new teachers for poor countries.

All this work comes at a cost. The organisation's total expenditure on programmes in 2009–10 was €596.3 million which has to be raised through its affiliate organisations. Oxfam GB, for example, raised a total of £318 million, from legacies, gifts and donations and through events such as the Trailtrekker team endurance event and a Bookfest. The organisation also sells items donated by the public as well as Fair Trade products – food and handicrafts from around the world, giving small-scale producers fair prices, training, advice and funding support. Orders for items can be made by mail or over the internet through Oxfam GB's online shop, or through its network of 250 charity shops staffed by over 20,000 volunteers.

2.4.6 Different services within a sector

Just as each particular sector has its own set of challenges, there can be significant differences between service operations within sectors. This may relate to the way the organisation has chosen to compete or which customer segments are to be served. Table 2.3 outlines some key

Table 2.3 Comparing airline operations

	Low-cost airline	Full-service airline
Business model	High volume, low cost	Global network, profit made on business travel
Network	Short haul, with no connections to other carriers	Long haul, with connections to global partner airlines
Cabin service	Basic, no food, no frills	Range from economy to first class
Locations	Secondary, low-cost airports	Primary airports to allow interconnections
Volume	Multiple flights per route each day	Range from three flights per day to one flight per week for less popular destinations
Booking system	Direct through own website, and/or own contact centre	Usually through intermediaries (travel agents) or websites

differences between two B2C organisations operating in the same sector: a 'low-cost' airline and a 'full-service' airline.

One of the challenges for service operations managers is to match the style of operations, decisions about processes, people and technology to the overall strategy of the organisation (Chapter 15). To do this, the operations manager must have a clear understanding of how the operations function contributes to the overall success of the organisation (see Chapter 1).

2.4.7 A merging of distinctions

Over the last few years the distinctions between different types of organisations that we have outlined above are starting to disappear: 'Old borderlines are evaporating, old categories are merging. The divisions between commercial, public-sector and non-profit organisations are becoming blurred. All organisations now act on the same stage, and need to justify their place on that stage.'[4] Some non-commercial organisations, public sector organisations and charities, for example, emulate the private sector; they have chief executives, strategic plans, marketing departments and talk about 'customers'. Public organisations, although they do not have competitors, recognise that their customers judge their service against for-profit organisations. Charities and government bodies have money-making arms. The British Council, for example, which promotes British culture around the world, also runs for-profit language schools. Universities, charities and faith organisations talk openly about market share.

On the other hand, some commercial organisations commit themselves to adhere to the principles of corporate social responsibility (CSR). Some appoint board members to check that company decisions support human rights, environmental goals and conservation projects, for example, to demonstrate that the organisation stands for something beyond the usual commercial goals. Sir Richard Branson, who heads up the Virgin group of companies, supports a wide range of non-commercial activities, including supporting AIDS work and wildlife and habitat conservation in Africa. Finding himself in a position of power and influence after working hard to establish a profitable set of companies, he is keen to fulfil his lifelong ambition of 'trying to change the world'. He explains: 'I'd always thought that Virgin should be more than just a money-making machine, and that, as Virgin has the wealth of a small nation, we should use that wealth to tackle social issues . . . Companies do have a responsibility to tackle them.'[5]

2.5 What are the challenges for different types of processes?

From an operations perspective we tend to be less concerned with the type of organisation or the sector in which we are working and more concerned with the types of processes we are managing.

Different processes provide us with different benefits and also different challenges. Extremely flexible processes may be excellent for responding to a wide range of special customer requirements but may be quite costly to maintain. On the other hand, processes suited to delivering high-volume low-cost services are usually not very flexible. A simple example drawn from the hotel industry illustrates the differences:

- A five-star hotel prides itself on providing a wide range of services for its guests. Staff at the reception desk are prepared to spend time dealing with each customer's request and endeavour to answer every question. As a result, each transaction is quite lengthy and the hotel employs extra staff to ensure that the highest levels of service are achieved at all times for guests, who are paying premium prices.

- A budget hotel provides basic, reasonably comfortable accommodation for travellers normally staying for one or two nights. In this case, reception processes are designed to carry out only the basic check-in and payment activities as quickly as possible. Guests are not encouraged to request extra services and the number of receptionists is maintained at the minimum level to keep costs low.

Operational process design is influenced by two key parameters: the volume of transactions to be performed per period per unit, and the variety of tasks to be carried out by a given set of people and processes (we will discuss these in more detail in Chapter 8).

Commodity (high volume and low variety)

The budget hotel reception process is close to the 'commodity' position (high volume and low process variety) in Figure 2.2. Processes here are clearly defined, leaving little room for individual customisation. Many consumer services employ these types of processes, having benefits of consistency as well as economy. Other examples include many contact centre processes and retail activities. We have termed these commodity processes because there is little differentiation between services. They, however, have the benefit of delivering a clear service concept. A customer knows exactly what product and service to expect when purchasing a Big Mac from McDonald's.

Capability (low volume and high variety)

At the other end of the spectrum, we find 'capability' processes. Processes here have much less definition, with each task potentially significantly different from its predecessor. The reception activity in the five-star hotel is probably closer to this position rather than the commodity position of the budget hotel. The service concept is likely to be far less defined than the Big Mac and the 'have-a-nice-day' service that goes with it. In fact, many customers will be buying the ability of the service organisation to work with them to clarify the need or problem to be solved and then to develop a customised solution. Some professional service providers, such as consultants, will work in this way, although larger,

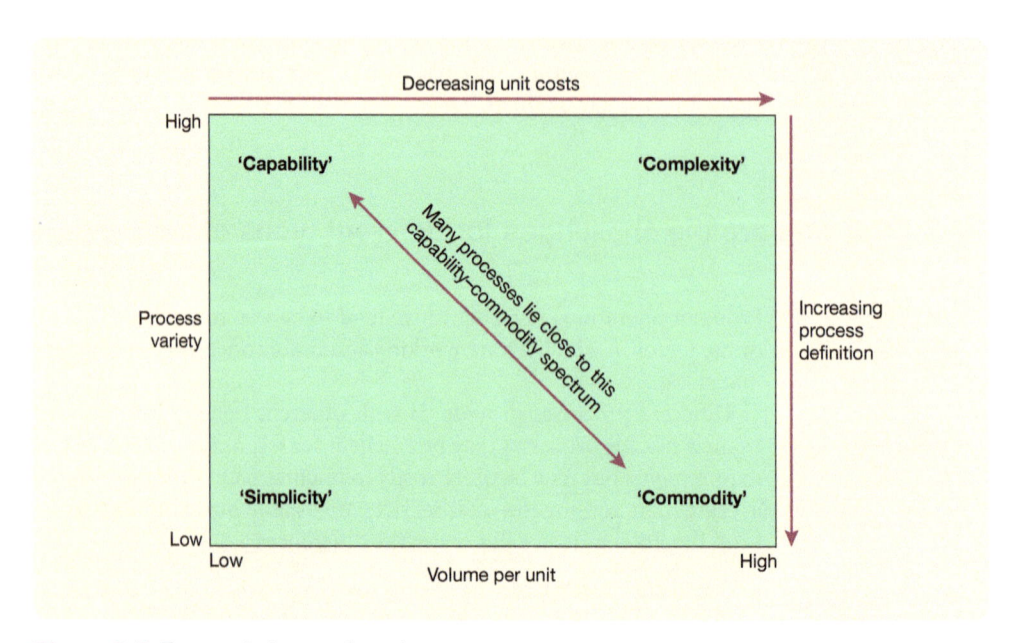

Figure 2.2 Four main types of service processes

Table 2.4 Capability versus commodity processes

	Capability	Commodity
Examples	Luxury hotel Management guru Corporate lawyer Builder of architect-designed luxury homes Aviation insurance broker	Budget hotel chain Software package training provider House conveyancer Garden shed erector Motor insurance provider
Process style	Flexible processes allowing for wide range of experiences and outcomes	Relatively rigid processes focused on narrow range of experiences and outcomes
Service offer	Ability to diagnose customer needs and to develop a customised solution	Ability to provide an economical and consistent service to meet the needs of many customers
What do they do well?	Flexible, innovative and responsive to individual customer needs	Low cost, with consistent quality and often rapid response
Major challenges	Co-ordinating the response of individual employees Maintaining differentiated competencies to justify premium prices Managing productivity Making best use of highly skilled and knowledgeable individuals	Delivering consistently across multi-sites and many providers Employee morale and ownership of process and customer Managing innovation Managing large numbers of staff and customers

global professional service firms often adopt a relatively standardised way of working, implementing pre-packaged solutions, which places them closer to the bottom right corner of Figure 2.2. Table 2.4 summarises some of the key differences between capability and commodity processes. We have provided examples at each end of the capability–commodity spectrum from similar sectors to demonstrate that not all services within a broad sector will employ the same processes. In Chapter 8 we will return to the challenge faced by many services, which is that they must operate in more than one position on this volume–variety matrix.

There are two 'off-diagonal' positions also identified in Figure 2.2: simplicity and complexity.

Simplicity (low volume and low variety)

These include small operations such as microbreweries, and small and specialist consultancies. Some larger organisations may also develop 'simple' operations as start-up services, which then may grow in terms of volume or variety or both (we refer to this as an incubator in Chapter 8).

Complexity (high volume and high variety)

At first sight, this position might seem to be the ideal, providing maximum flexibility for as many customers as possible. In reality, however, providing flexibility for large numbers of customers is invariably expensive, achieved by employing large numbers of highly skilled people and/or high-tech equipment.

One of the challenges for service operations managers is to ensure that the type of process is appropriate to deliver the service concept (see Chapter 3). As service concepts change and evolve, existing processes may become less appropriate for the task in hand. Effective managers will recognise this issue and proactively develop new process designs to meet the future requirements.

2.6 What are the challenges in working with other management functions?

The management of service operations, as we hope is becoming clear, is extremely demanding. However, operations managers cannot do their job in isolation; they require a close working relationship with other internal functions, such as marketing (to ensure what is sold can be delivered), IT (to ensure the equipment and software used by the operation is appropriate and available when needed), HR (to ensure the right people with the right skills are in place) and so on. However, working closely with other management functions poses some particular challenges; indeed for some organisations these internal challenges are some of the most difficult that they face!

- *Too much focus on the day-to-day.* We mentioned earlier that the excitement of managing operations is its immediacy, dealing with the needs of a stream of customers, managing the staff and making the many tactical decisions that are needed to ensure the delivery of an appropriate quality of service at an appropriate cost. As a result operations managers tend to focus on the day-to-day issues. Indeed, this is what many of them are good at; sorting out the day-to-day problems. The perspective of other functions may be concerned with more long-term issues; the board may be focused on strategic decision-making, IT may be investigating new technological opportunities and HR trying to evaluate how changes in regulations may affect pensions. Of course many of these functions are running day-to-day activities as well. IT is keeping the hardware and software going, HR is dealing with staff grievances. These are their 'operational' activities – as all managers are operations managers and deliver service in the short or long term to their internal customers. The point is that operations' focus on the here-and-now can cause tensions with other functions where managers are trying to plan for the longer term. Operations managers are often too tied up to be able to spare the time to become involved.

- *Lack of strategic influence.* Because of the short-term focus of the job, operations tend to attract and recruit people who are good at being reactive and fire-fighting problems as they arise. As a result they tend to lack strategic focus and are naturally less good at dealing with the higher-level and more intuitive processes required for contributing to strategic decision-making. As a result operations managers' influence in the boardroom is sometimes limited and therefore the organisation's understanding of the present and future capability of the operation is not always taken into account.

- *Limited focus on innovation.* Operations managers tend to be rooted in the present, dealing with the day-to-day issues. They tend to be reactionary and conservative, though we prefer to call it being 'rooted in reality'. As a result operations managers are not always willing to open themselves to new ideas and opportunities. Any change usually has often unwelcome and significant operational consequences (see the Case Exercise on Sky Airways at the end of this chapter). Such tensions and differing points of view, however, are ideal ingredients for innovation, so operations managers need to be better at managing the conversations with other functions.

- *Difficulty of making the business case.* Any changes tend to have to be justified in financial terms. Operations managers usually know the cost of any change they want to make, whether it's the purchase of new equipment or the recruitment of new staff; they also intuitively understand the positive impact this will have on customers, staff and sales for example, but these things can be very difficult to demonstrate in concrete enough terms to convince a financial director. This is an important area and in Chapter 17 we will explain how operations managers can make the business case to support their requirements.

2.7 How can this book help?

One of the key purposes of this book is to help you deal with the many challenges that service operations managers face which we have outlined in this chapter. The book is structured into five main parts: Frame, Connect, Deliver, Improve and Implement. The chapters in these parts are focused on how to deal with the various challenges. The single chapter in the Frame part deals with a critical and central issue: how to develop and use the service concept to define and communicate the nature of the business, create organisational alignment, drive innovation and strategic advantage, and design the service. The following parts, Connect, Deliver, Improve and Implement, each contain several chapters with their associated 'how tos', as shown in Figure 2.3.

- How to develop and use the service concept to define and communicate the nature of the business, create organisational alignment, drive innovation and strategic advantage, and design the service

- How to design the customer experience
- How to design the service process
- How to measure, control and manage service operations
- How to motivate people, staff and customers, to deliver great service
- How to manage resources effectively

- How to understand and develop customer relationships
- How to gain insight into customers' expectations and perceptions to create satisfied customers
- How to manage supplier relationships and harness the potential of supply networks

FRAME
CONNECT → DELIVER
IMPLEMENT ← IMPROVE

- How to employ a range of tools to improve service operations
- How to learn from problems to improve an operation and its services
- How to learn from other operations to improve performance

- How to create and implement the service organisation's strategy
- How to understand and influence service culture
- How to build a world-class organisation and deliver excellent service

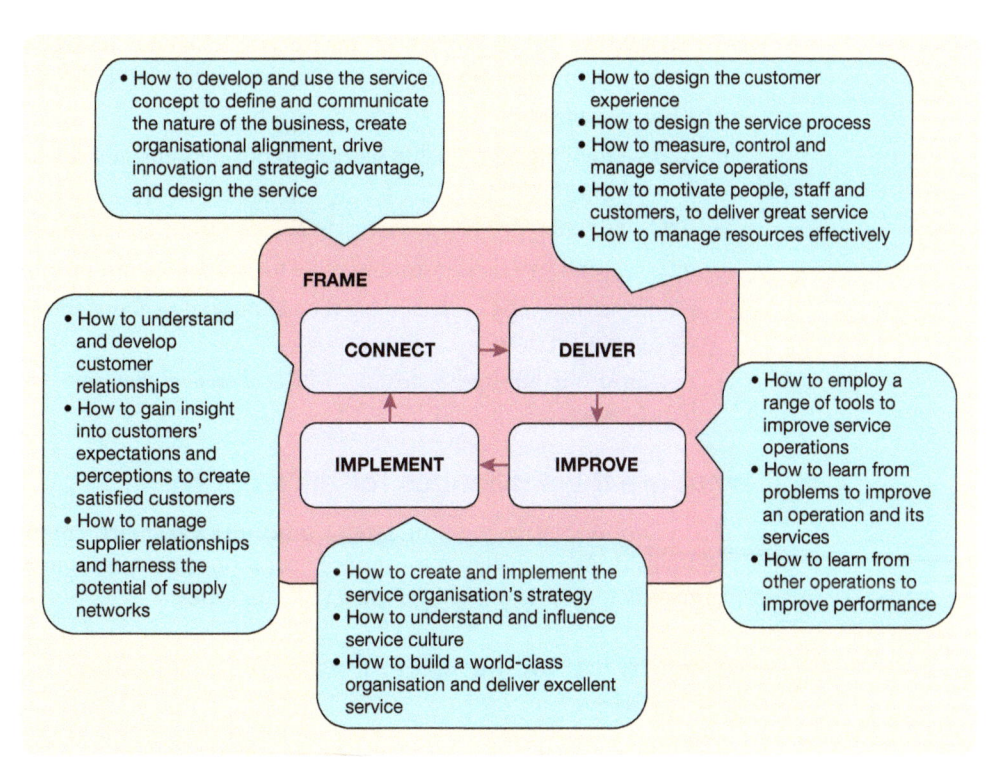

Figure 2.3 The structure of the book

2.8 Summary

What are the key strategic challenges faced by service operations managers?

- Managing tactically and strategically
- Making operations a contributor to strategy as well as an implementer
- Making the business case for service
- Understanding the service concept.

What are the key tactical challenges faced by service operations managers?

- Understanding the customer perspective
- Managing multiple customers
- Managing the customer
- Managing in real time
- Co-ordinating different parts of the organisation
- Encouraging improvement and innovation.

What are the challenges for different types of services?

- There are five broad sectors of the service economy: business-to-business services, business-to-consumer services, internal services, public services and not-for-profit services.
- The key challenges are:
  - B2B – providing high-quality services to business customers who frequently have high purchasing power
  - B2C – providing consistent service to a wide variety and high volume of customers
  - internal services – demonstrating value for money against possible external alternatives
  - public services (G2C) – balancing the various political pressures and providing acceptable public services
  - not-for-profit services – dealing with differences between volunteers, donors and beneficiaries.

What are the challenges for different types of process?

- There are four main types of service processes: capability, commodity, simplicity and complexity. A key challenge for service operations managers is to ensure that the type of process is appropriate to deliver the service concept.

What are the challenges in working with other management functions?

- Too much focus on the day-to-day
- Lack of strategic influence
- Limited focus on innovation
- Difficulty of making the business case.

2.9 Discussion questions

1. What are the similarities and differences in terms of the operational challenges faced by global service organisations such as FedEx, Accenture, Amnesty International and Red Crescent? Use their websites for more information about what the organisations do.
2. Consider your university/college. What do you think are the challenges their course delivery operations face in providing you with good service?
3. What do you think are the challenges faced by multi-site operations (organisations that have many outlets)?

2.10 Questions for managers

1. What are the key tactical and strategic challenges your service operation faces?
2. How would you categorise your service operation? What are the implications?
3. What are the key relationships operations has with other parts of the organisation and how well are they managed?

Case Exercise   Sky Airways

Robert Johnston and Bridgette Sullivan-Taylor, Warwick Business School

Sky Airways is a major European airline with routes predominantly in Europe but offering daily flights to New York, Johannesburg, Mumbai and St Petersburg. At the last meeting of the board of directors the airline's chief executive, Bernie Williamson, expressed concern at the growing number of complaints his airline was receiving. His analysis of the increasing trend revealed a strong link between number of complaints and minutes' delay. This did not surprise him. What did surprise him was the large number of underlying complaints that were, in the main (around 72 per cent), about the on-board catering.

Given his desire to increase RPK (revenue passenger kilometre), which had declined by 5 per cent over the past three years, he was keen to hear ideas from his team as to how they could deal with the problem. This was an opportunity seized upon by Angela Carter-Smith, Sky's recently appointed marketing director. She suggested that the airline should consider moving away from pre-packed and reheated meals in tourist class to the business-class style of service, whereby food is pre-cooked but heated, assembled and served in front of the customers. She explained: 'Many international airlines are attempting to enhance their competitive edge by differentiating their in-flight service offering across their global network.' The food costs, she suggested, would be little different but simply require more time by cabin attendants, which they have on the longer flights. If this proved to be successful on the long hauls, it could then be considered on the short hauls. When Bernie reminded her that they needed to provide an upgraded service for the premium-fare passengers, she added that the answer here was to provide 'culturally sensitive' meals: flying to and from Mumbai, the food should be Indian, while to Johannesburg it should have a distinct African flavour. All eyes then turned to Peter Greenwood, the operations director, who had his head in his hands and was groaning. He promised to 'look into it' and report back at the next meeting.

The next day Peter made time to talk about the rising trend in complaints to Christina Towers, the catering subcontract manager, Justin Maude, a senior cabin attendant, and David Goh, senior gate manager.

Christina Towers explained:

The problem we have, like all other catering companies, is consistency. Although we can specify menus, portions and costs there are inevitably wide variations in quantity and quality loaded at various airports around the world. We have the biggest problems at the furthest destinations. You also put us under pressure to reduce costs, so we only try to load the precise number of meals required in order to reduce wastage and space required. It is not easy making pre-flight predictions about both numbers and choices, and you cannot expect it to be right 100 per cent of the time without substantially increasing the number of meals loaded over and above passenger predictions. It is not cost effective and it is weight prohibitive to load two of every meal option, even for a business-class passenger who would expect, more than anyone else, to receive their first choice. I think we would get fewer complaints if we reduced choice of menus.

Justin Maude added:

You would not believe the difficulties we face in providing something as simple as meals to passengers. We frequently have to explain to passengers, in all the cabins, why they can't have their first choice of meal. This creates a great deal of stress for the crew. There is just no room for more meals on board; the galleys are really tight for space. The biggest problem we have is over passengers who order special meals for religious, dietary or health reasons. I reckon one in five is not loaded on to the aircraft. Sometimes we have passengers on board who ask whether the food contains nuts and we have no idea. We can only offer them water and bread rolls to be safe. I think we should ensure the caterers let us know the contents of every meal and always provide extra vegetarian and kosher meals because passengers don't always remember to pre-book them. Another problem is caused by the last-minute passengers whom you want us to take to fill seats, so we often have to ask for more meals shortly before take-off. I know this causes problems but, unlike a restaurant, during flight there is nowhere to find additional supplies. I think it would help if we could have meals that needed less preparation time and take less space, so we can load more meals in anticipation of an increase in passengers and also load additional special meals, just in case.

David Goh then added his views:

The main problem I have is ten minutes before take-off when we find that the incorrect quantity, quality and meal type are loaded and the crew request extra meals. We often end up delaying a plane and missing a slot while the caterers rush over half a dozen extra meals. We should let the plane go. I am sure not everyone actually wants a meal. They only eat because they are bored. I think we should stop providing meals altogether, certainly on the short hauls. Tourist-class passengers often eat at the airport anyway and we already provide food for business class in the executive lounges.

Peter had not dared raise the idea of changing the methods of service in tourist class and increasing the range and type of meals to business-class passengers. His thoughts turned to how he could explain to the board the difference between what might be desirable and what is deliverable and appropriate.

Questions

1 What problems does Peter Greenwood face?
2 If you were Peter Greenwood, what would you say to the board?

Suggested further reading

Johnston, Robert (2005), 'Service Operations Management: From the Roots Up', *International Journal of Operations and Production Management* 25 (12) 1298–1308

Neu, Wayne A. and Stephen W. Brown (2005), 'Forming Successful Business-to-Business Services in Goods-Dominant Firms', *Journal of Service Research* 8 (1) 3–17

Shaw, Colin, Qaalfa Dibeehi and Steven Walden (2010), *Customer Experience: Future Trends and Insights*, Palgrave Macmillan

Slack, Nigel, Stuart Chambers and Robert Johnston (2010), *Operations Management*, 6th edition, FT Prentice Hall, Harlow

Useful web links

A short paper by Robert Hayes outlining his view of operations challenges:
http://findarticles.com/p/articles/mi_qa3796/is_200204/ai_n9067667/

An interesting piece by Carina Paine Schofield of the Ashridge Public Leadership Centre on key challenges facing public sector leaders:
www.ashridge.org.uk—KeyChallengesFacingPublicSectorLeaders.pdf

A piece on topical service management challenges from CTMA consulting in New Zealand:
www.ctmaworld.com/Challenges.htm

An article on the challenges faced by female service managers at the Diversity in Leadership blog:
www.robturknett.com/diversityinleadership

Currently a topical issue: third sector management challenges discussed at The Australian Review of Public Affairs:
www.australianreview.net—cutcher.html

Notes

1. Shaw, Colin and John Ivens (2002), *Building Great Customer Experiences*, Palgrave, London; Price, Reg and Roderick J. Brodie (2001), 'Transforming a Public Service Organization from Inside Out to Outside In', *Journal of Service Research* 4 (1) 50–59
2. Carbone, Lewis P. (2004), *Clued In*, FT Prentice Hall, New Jersey
3. Edvardsson, Bo and Jan Olsson (1996), 'Key Concepts for New Service Development', *The Service Industries Journal* 16 (2) 140–164
4. Jones, Robert (2001), *The Big Idea*, Harper Collins Business, London
5. Branson, Richard (2003), *Losing My Virginity: The Autobiography*, Virgin Books, London, p. 529

Chapter 2

Operations strategy

Key questions

➤ What is strategy and what is operations strategy?
➤ What is the difference between a 'top-down' and a 'bottom-up' view of operations strategy?
➤ What is the difference between a 'market requirements' and an 'operations resources' view of operations strategy?
➤ How can an operations strategy be put together?

Introduction

No organization can tell exactly what will happen in the future, but all organizations need strategic direction and can benefit from some idea of where they are heading and how they could get there. Once the operations function has understood its role in the business, it needs to formulate a set of general principles which will guide its decision-making. This is the operations strategy of the company. Yet the concept of 'strategy' itself is not straightforward; neither is operations strategy. This chapter considers four perspectives, each of which goes part way to illustrating the forces that shape operations strategy. Figure 2.1 shows where this chapter fits into the overall operations model.

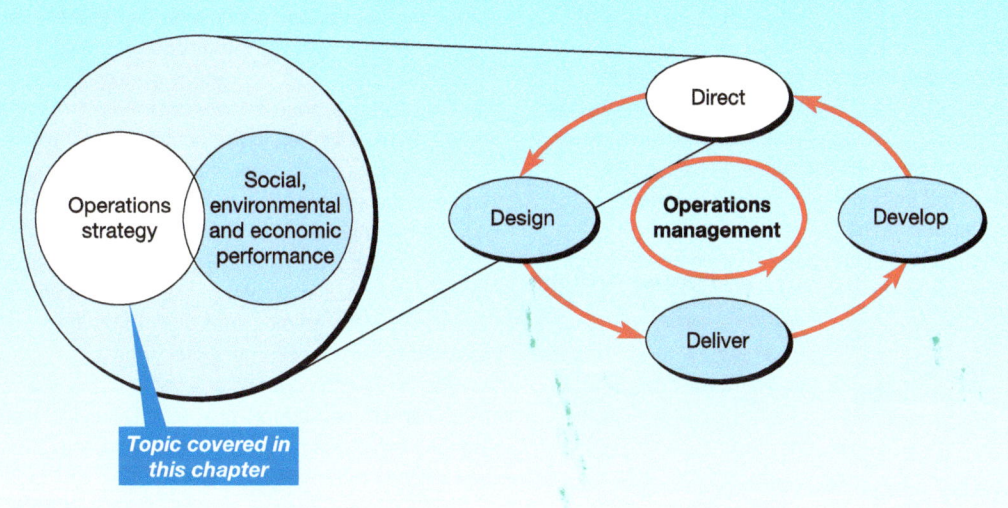

Figure 2.1 This chapter examines operations strategy

Check and improve your understanding of this chapter using self-assessment questions and a personalized study plan, audio and video downloads, and an eBook – all at www.myomlab.com.

Operations in practice: Two operations strategies: Flextronics and Ryanair[1]

The two most important attributes of any operations strategy are first that it aligns operations activities with the strategy of the whole organization, and second that it gives clear guidance. Here are two examples of very different businesses and very different strategies which nonetheless meet both criteria.

Ryanair is today Europe's largest low-cost airline (LCAs) and whatever else can be said about its strategy, it does not suffer from any lack of clarity. It has grown by offering low-cost basic services and has devised an operations strategy which is in line with its market position. The efficiency of the airline's operations supports its low-cost market position. Turnaround time at airports is kept to a minimum. This is achieved partly because there are no meals to be loaded onto the aircraft and partly through improved employee productivity. All the aircraft in the fleet are identical, giving savings through standardization of parts, maintenance and servicing. It also means large orders to a single aircraft supplier and therefore the opportunity to negotiate prices down. Also, because the company often uses secondary airports, landing and service fees are much lower. Finally, the cost of selling its services is reduced where possible.

Ryanair has developed its own low-cost Internet booking service. In addition, the day-to-day experiences of the company's operations managers can also modify and refine these strategic decisions. For example, Ryanair changed its baggage handling contractors at Stansted airport in the UK after problems with misdirecting customers' luggage. The company's policy on customer service is also clear. *'We patterned Ryanair after Southwest Airlines, the most consistently profitable airline in the US'*, says Michael O'Leary, Ryanair's Chief Executive. *'Southwest founder Herb Kelleher created a formula for success that works by flying only one type of airplane, – the 737, using smaller airports, providing no-frills service on-board, selling tickets directly to customers and offering passengers the lowest fares in the market. We have adapted his model for our marketplace and are now setting the low-fare standard for Europe. Our customer service'*, says O'Leary, *'is about the most well defined in the world. We guarantee to give you the lowest air fare. You get a safe flight. You get a normally on-time flight. That's the package. We don't, and won't, give you anything more. Are we going to say sorry for our lack of customer service? Absolutely not. If a plane is cancelled, will we put you up in a hotel overnight? Absolutely not. If a plane is delayed, will we give you a voucher for a restaurant? Absolutely not.'*

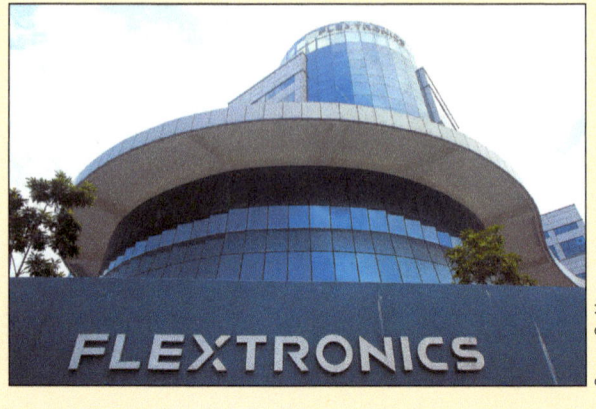

Flextronics is a global company based in Singapore that lies behind such well-known brand names as Nokia and Dell, which are increasingly using electronic manufacturing services (EMS) companies, such as Flextronics, which specialize in providing the outsourced design, engineering, manufacturing and logistics operations for the big brand names. It is amongst the biggest of those EMS suppliers that offer the broadest worldwide capabilities, from design to end-to-end vertically integrated global supply chain services. Flextronics' operations strategy must balance their customers' need for low costs (electronic goods are often sold in a fiercely competitive market) with their need for responsive and flexible service (electronics markets can also be volatile). The company achieves this in a number of ways. Firstly, it has an extensive network of design, manufacturing and logistics facilities in the world's major electronics markets, giving them significant scale and the flexibility to move activities to the most appropriate location to serve customers. Secondly, Flextronics offers vertical integration capabilities that simplify global product development and supply processes, moving a product from its initial design through volume production, test, distribution, and into post-sales service, responsively and efficiently. Finally, Flextronics has developed integrated industrial parks to exploit fully the advantages of their global, large-scale, high-volume capabilities. Positioned in low-cost regions, yet close to all major world markets, Flextronics' industrial parks can significantly reduce the cost of production. Locations include Gdansk in Poland, Hungary, Guadalajara in Mexico, Sorocaba in Brazil, Chennai in India and Shanghai in China. Flextronics' own suppliers are encouraged to locate within these parks, from which products can be produced on-site and shipped directly from the industrial park to customers, greatly reducing freight costs of incoming components and outgoing products. Products not produced on-site can be obtained from Flextronics' network of regional manufacturing facilities located near the industrial parks. Using this strategy, Flextronics says it can provide cost-effective delivery of finished products within 1–2 days of orders.

What is strategy and what is operations strategy?

Strategic decisions

Surprisingly, 'strategy' is not particularly easy to define. Linguistically the word derives from the Greek word '*strategos*' meaning 'leading an army'. Here, by **strategic decisions** we mean those decisions which are widespread in their effect on the organization to which the strategy refers, define the position of the organization relative to its environment, and move the organization closer to its long-term goals. But 'strategy' is more than a single decision; it is the *total pattern of the decisions* and actions that influence the long-term direction of the business. Thinking about strategy in this way helps us to discuss an organization's strategy even when it has not been explicitly stated. Observing the total pattern of decisions gives an indication of the *actual* strategic behaviour.

Operations strategy

Operations strategy concerns the pattern of strategic decisions and actions which set the role, objectives and activities of the operation. The term 'operations strategy' sounds at first like a contradiction. How can 'operations', a subject that is generally concerned with the day-to-day creation and delivery of services and products, be strategic? 'Strategy' is usually regarded as the opposite of those day-to-day routine activities. But '*operations*' is not the same as '*operational*'. 'Operations' are the resources that create services and products. 'Operational' is the opposite of strategic, meaning day-to-day and detailed. So, one can examine both the operational *and* the strategic aspects of operations. It is also conventional to distinguish between the '**content**' and the '**process**' of operations strategy. The *content* of operations strategy is the specific decisions and actions which set the operations' role, objectives and activities. The *process* of operations strategy is the method that is used to make the specific 'content' decisions.

'Operations' is not the same as 'operational'

The content and process of operations strategy

Hayes and Wheelwright's four stages of operations contribution

The four-stage model of operations contribution

The ability of any operation to contribute to business strategy can be judged by considering the organizational aims or aspirations of the operations function. Professors Hayes and Wheelwright of Harvard University[2] developed a **four-stage model** which can be used to evaluate the role and contribution of the operations function. The model traces the progression of the operations function from what is the largely negative role of stage 1 operations to its becoming the central element of competitive strategy in excellent stage 4 operations. Figure 2.2 illustrates the four stages.

Stage 1: Internal neutrality. This is the very poorest level of contribution by the operations function. It is inward-looking and reactive, with very little positive to contribute towards competitive success. Paradoxically, its goal is 'to be ignored' (or to become 'internally neutral') by avoiding making mistakes. At least then it isn't holding the company back in any way.

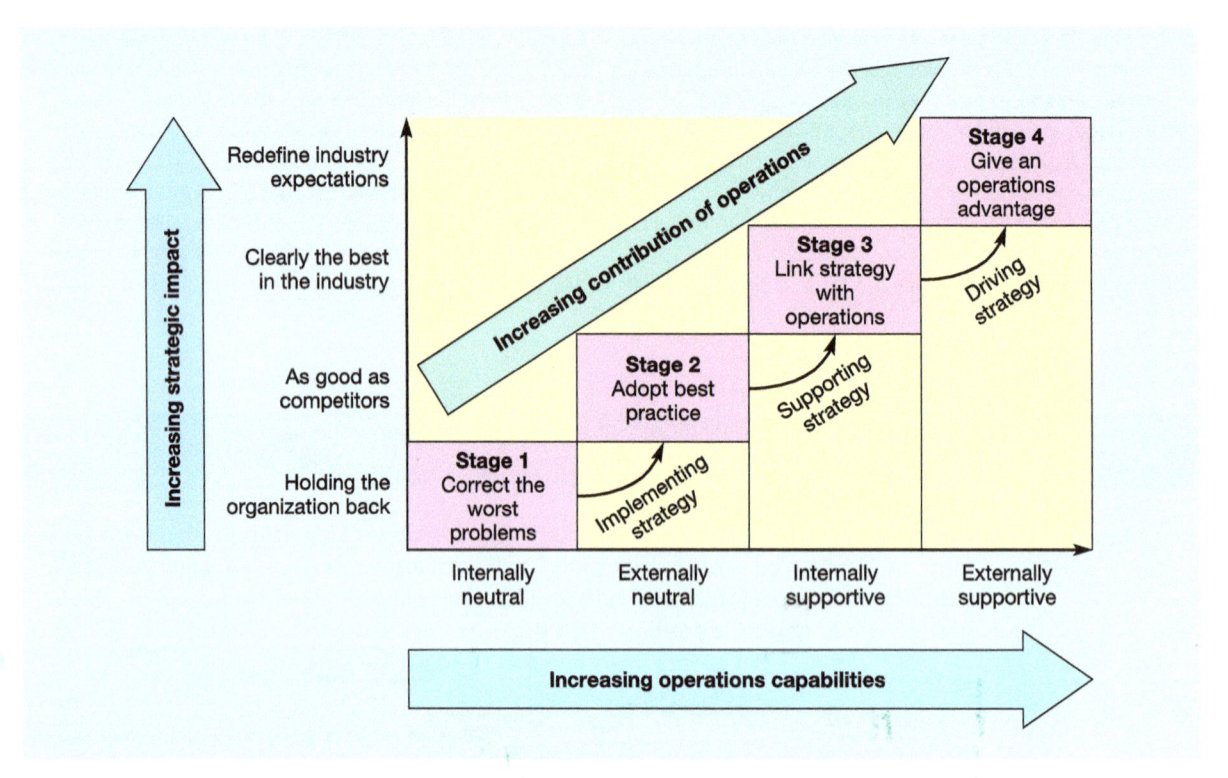

Figure 2.2 The four-stage model of operations contribution

Stage 2: External neutrality. The first step of breaking out of stage 1 is for the operations function to begin comparing itself with similar companies or organizations in the outside market (being 'externally neutral'). This may not immediately take it to the 'first division' of companies in the market, but at least it is measuring itself against its competitors' performance and trying to implement 'best practice'.

Stage 3: Internally supportive. Stage 3 operations are amongst the best in their market. Yet, stage 3 operations still aspire to be clearly and unambiguously the very best in the market. They achieve this by gaining a clear view of the company's competitive or strategic goals and supporting it by developing appropriate operations resources. The operation is trying to be 'internally supportive' by providing a credible operations strategy.

Stage 4: Externally supportive. Yet Hayes and Wheelwright suggest a further stage – stage 4, where the company views the operations function as providing the foundation for its competitive success. Operations looks to the long term. It forecasts likely changes in markets and supply, and it develops the operations-based capabilities which will be required to compete in future market conditions. Stage 4 operations are innovative, creative and proactive and are driving the company's strategy by being 'one step ahead' of competitors – what Hayes and Wheelwright call 'being externally supportive'.

> ### Critical commentary
>
> The idea that operations can have a leading role in determining a company's strategic direction is not universally supported. Both Hayes and Wheelwright's stage 4 of their four-stage model and the concept of operations 'driving' strategy do not only imply that it is possible for operations to take such a leading role, but are explicit in seeing it as a 'good thing'. A more traditional stance taken by some authorities is that the needs of the

> market will always be pre-eminent in shaping a company's strategy. Therefore, operations should devote all their time to understanding the requirements of the market (as defined by the marketing function within the organization) and devote themselves to their main job of ensuring that operations processes can actually deliver what the market requires. Companies can only be successful, they argue, by positioning themselves in the market (through a combination of price, promotion, product design and managing how products and services are delivered to customers) with operations very much in a 'supporting' role. In effect, they say, Hayes and Wheelwright's four-stage model should stop at stage 3. The issue of an 'operations resource' perspective on operations strategy is discussed later in the chapter.

Perspectives on operations strategy

Different authors have slightly different views and definitions of operations strategy. Between them, four 'perspectives' emerge:[3]

Top-down
Bottom-up

Market requirements
Operations resource capabilities

- Operation strategy is a **top-down** reflection of what the whole group or business wants to do.
- Operations strategy is a **bottom-up** activity where operations improvements cumulatively build strategy.
- Operations strategy involves translating **market requirements** into operations decisions.
- Operations strategy involves exploiting the **capabilities of operations resources** in chosen markets.

None of these four perspectives alone gives the full picture of what operations strategy is. But together they provide some idea of the pressures which go to form the content of operations strategy. We will treat each in turn (see Figure 2.3).

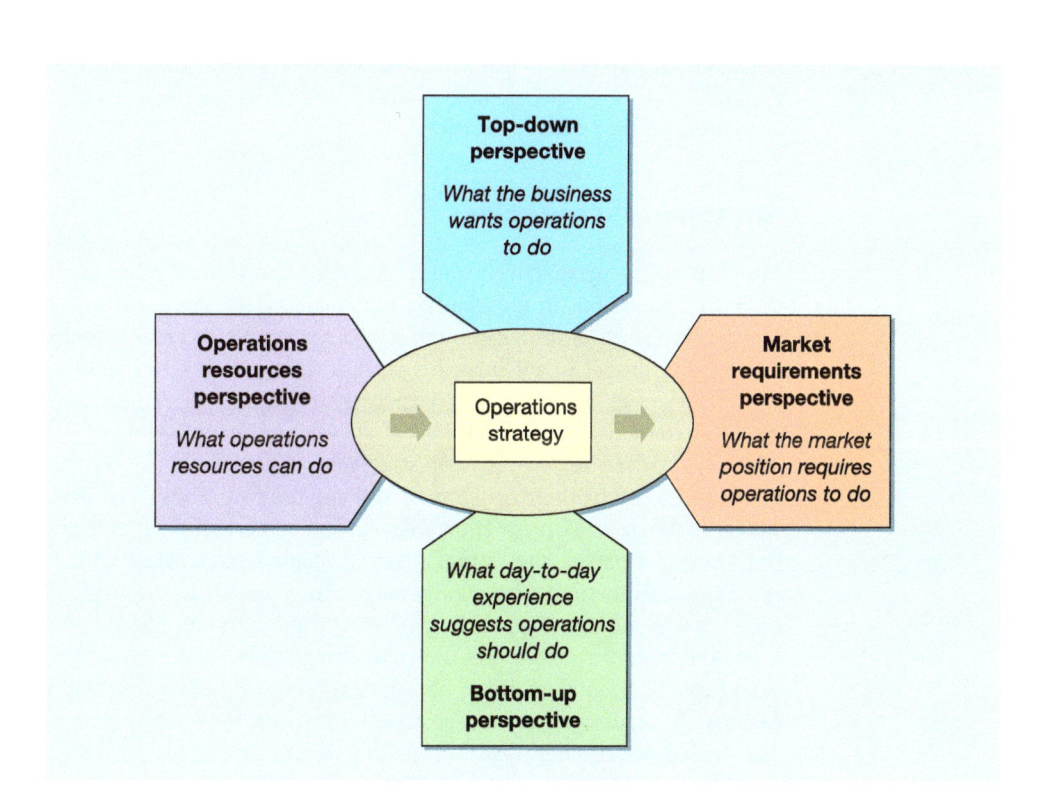

Figure 2.3 The four perspectives on operations strategy

The 'top-down' and 'bottom-up' perspectives

Top-down strategies

A large corporation will need a strategy to position itself in its global, economic, political and social environment. This will consist of decisions about what types of business the group wants to be in, what parts of the world it wants to operate in, how to allocate its cash between its various businesses, and so on. Decisions such as these form the **corporate strategy** of the corporation. Each business unit within the corporate group will also need to put together its own business strategy which sets out its individual mission and objectives. This **business strategy** guides the business in relation to its customers, markets and competitors, and also the strategy of the corporate group of which it is a part. Similarly, within the business, **functional strategies** need to consider what part each function should play in contributing to the strategic objectives of the business. The operations, marketing, product/service development and other functions will all need to consider how best they should organize themselves to support the business's objectives.

Corporate strategy

Business strategy

Functional strategy

So, one perspective on operations strategy is that it should take its place in this hierarchy of strategies. Its main influence, therefore, will be whatever the business sees as its strategic direction. For example, a printing services group has a company which prints packaging for consumer products. The group's management figures that, in the long term, only companies with significant market share will achieve substantial profitability. Its corporate objectives therefore stress market dominance. The consumer packaging company decides to achieve volume growth, even above short-term profitability or return on investment. The implication for operations strategy is that it needs to expand rapidly, investing in extra capacity (factories, equipment and labour) even if it means some excess capacity in some areas. It also needs to establish new factories in all parts of its market to offer relatively fast delivery. The important point here is that different business objectives would probably result in a very different operations strategy. The role of operations is therefore largely one of implementing or 'operationalizing' business strategy. Figure 2.4 illustrates this strategic hierarchy, with some of the decisions at each level and the main influences on the strategic decisions.

'Bottom-up' strategies

The 'top-down' perspective provides an orthodox view of how functional strategies *should* be put together. But in fact the relationship between the levels in the strategy hierarchy is more complex than this. Although it is a convenient way of thinking about strategy, this hierarchical model is not intended to represent the way strategies are always formulated. When any group is reviewing its corporate strategy, it will also take into account the circumstances, experiences and capabilities of the various businesses that form the group. Similarly, businesses, when reviewing their strategies, will consult the individual functions within the business about their constraints and capabilities. They may also incorporate the ideas which come from each function's day-to-day experience. Therefore an alternative view to the top-down perspective is that many strategic ideas emerge over time from operational experience. Sometimes companies move in a particular strategic direction because the ongoing experience of providing products and services to customers at an operational level convinces them that it is the right thing to do. There may be no high-level decisions examining alternative strategic options and choosing the one which provides the best way forward. Instead, a general consensus emerges from the operational level of the organization. The 'high-level' strategic decision-making, if it occurs at all, may confirm the consensus and provide the resources to make it happen effectively.

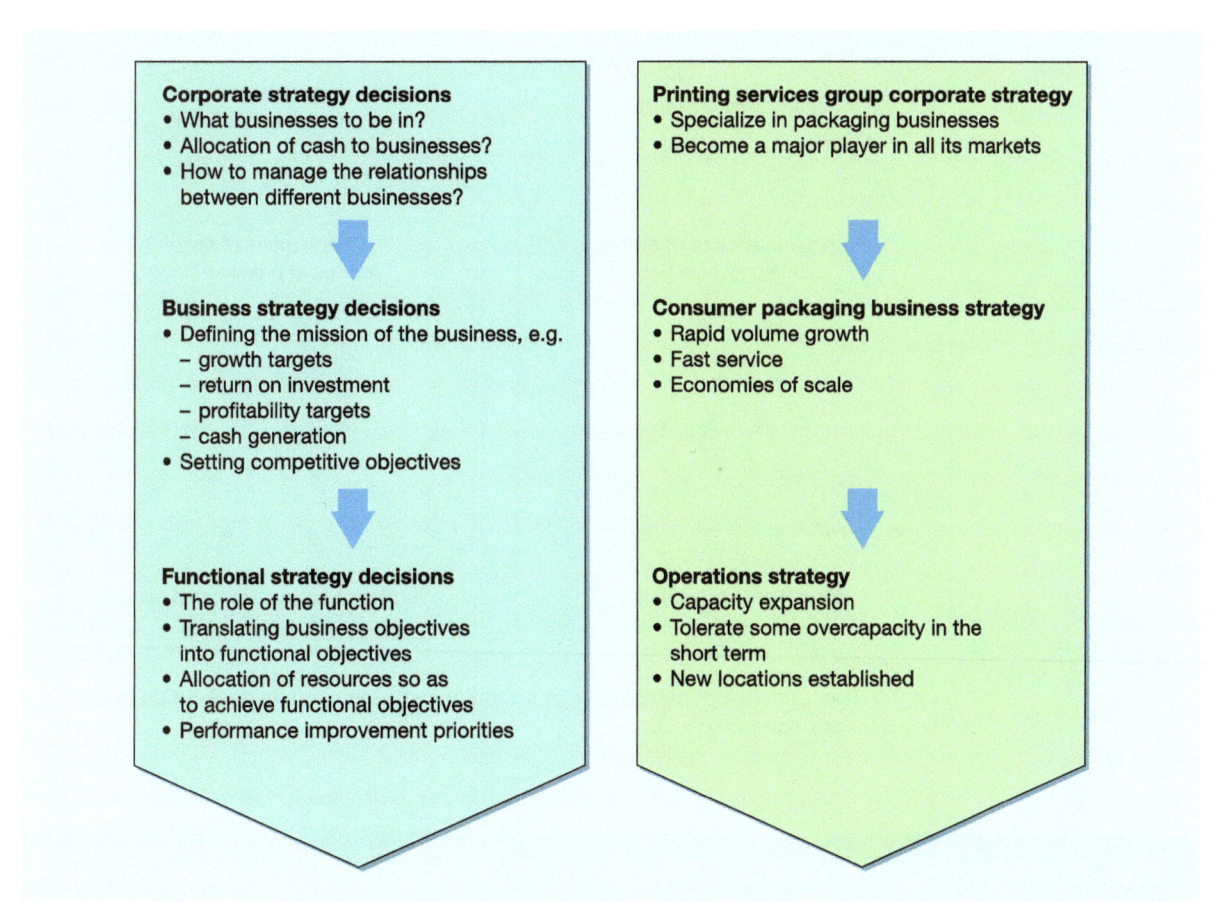

Corporate strategy decisions	Printing services group corporate strategy
• What businesses to be in? • Allocation of cash to businesses? • How to manage the relationships between different businesses?	• Specialize in packaging businesses • Become a major player in all its markets
Business strategy decisions	**Consumer packaging business strategy**

• Defining the mission of the business, e.g.
  – growth targets
  – return on investment
  – profitability targets
  – cash generation
• Setting competitive objectives
	• Rapid volume growth
	• Fast service
	• Economies of scale

Functional strategy decisions	**Operations strategy**
• The role of the function • Translating business objectives into functional objectives • Allocation of resources so as to achieve functional objectives • Performance improvement priorities	• Capacity expansion • Tolerate some overcapacity in the short term • New locations established

Figure 2.4 The top-down perspective of operations strategy and its application to the printing services group

Suppose the printing services company described previously succeeds in its expansion plans. However, in doing so it finds that having surplus capacity and a distributed network of factories allows it to offer an exceptionally fast service to customers. It also finds that some customers are willing to pay considerably higher prices for such a responsive service. Its experiences lead the company to set up a separate division dedicated to providing fast, high-margin printing services to those customers willing to pay. The strategic objectives of this new division are not concerned with high-volume growth but with high profitability.

Emergent strategies

This idea of strategy being shaped by operational level experience over time is sometimes called the concept of **emergent strategies**.[4] Strategy is gradually shaped over time and based on real-life experience rather than theoretical positioning. Indeed, strategies are often formed in a relatively unstructured and fragmented manner to reflect the fact that the future is at least partially unknown and unpredictable (see Figure 2.5). This view of operations strategy is perhaps more descriptive of how things really happen, but at first glance it seems less useful in providing a guide for specific decision-making. Yet while emergent strategies are less easy to categorize, the principle governing a bottom-up perspective is clear: shape the operation's objectives and action, at least partly, by the knowledge it gains from its day-to-day activities. The key virtues required for shaping strategy from the bottom up are an ability to learn from experience and a philosophy of continual and incremental improvement.

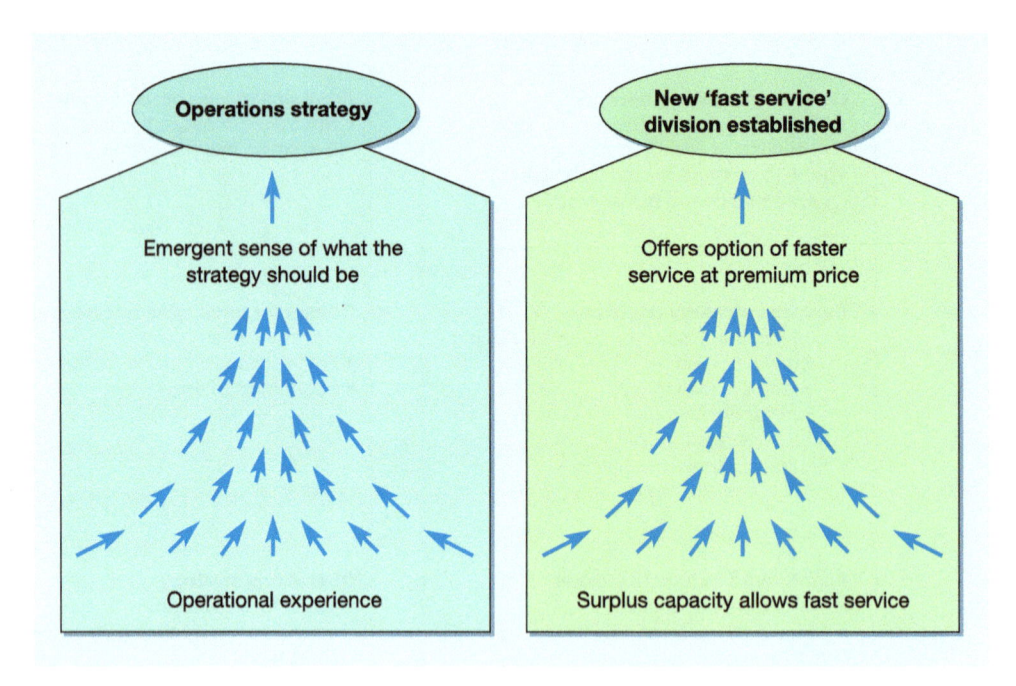

Figure 2.5 The 'bottom-up' perspective of operations strategy and its application to the printing services company

The market requirements and operations resources perspectives

Market-requirements-based strategies

One of the obvious objectives for any organization is to satisfy the requirements of its markets. No operation that continually fails to serve its markets adequately is likely to survive in the long term. Although understanding markets is usually thought of as the domain of the marketing function, it is also of importance to operations management. Without an understanding of what markets require, it is impossible to ensure that operations is achieving the right balance between its performance objectives (quality, speed, dependability, flexibility and cost). For example, the short case Giordano describes a company that designed its operations to fit what it saw as a market that was starting to prioritize quality of service.

Short case
Giordano

With a vision that explicitly states its ambition to be *'the best and the biggest world brand in apparel retailing'*, Giordano is setting its sights high. Yet it is the company that changed the rules of clothes retailing in the fast-growing markets around Hong Kong, China, Malaysia and Singapore, so industry experts take its ambitions seriously. Before Giordano, up-market shops sold high-quality products and gave good service. Cheaper clothes were piled high and sold by sales assistants more concerned with taking the cash than smiling at customers. Jimmy Lai, founder and Chief Executive of Giordano Holdings, changed all that. He saw that unpredictable quality and low levels of service offered an opportunity in the casual clothes market. Why could not value and service, together with low prices, generate better profits? His methods were radical. Overnight he raised the wages of his salespeople by between 30 and 40 per cent, all employees were told they would receive at least 60 hours of training a year and new staff would be allocated a 'big brother' or 'big sister' from among experienced staff to help them develop their service quality skills. Even more startling by the standards of his competitors, Mr Lai brought in a 'no-questions-asked' exchange policy irrespective of how long ago the garment had been purchased. Staff were trained to talk to customers and seek their opinion on products and the type of service they would like. This information would be immediately fed back to the company's designers for incorporation into their new products. How Giordano achieved the highest sales per square metre of almost any retailer in the region and its founding operations principles are summarized in its 'QKISS' list.

- Quality – do things right.
- Knowledge – update experience and share knowledge.
- Innovation – think 'outside the box'.
- Simplicity – less is more.
- Service – exceed customers' expectations.

The market influence on performance objectives

Operations seek to satisfy customers through developing their five performance objectives. For example, if customers particularly value low-priced products or services, the operation will place emphasis on its cost performance. Alternatively, a customer emphasis on fast delivery will make speed important to the operation, and so on. These factors which define the customers' requirements are called **competitive factors**.[5] Figure 2.6 shows the relationship between some of the more common competitive factors and the operations' performance objectives. This list is not exhaustive; whatever competitive factors are important to customers should influence the priority of each performance objective. Some organizations put considerable effort into bringing an idea of their customers' needs into the operation.

Competitive factors

Competitive factors If the customers value these...	Performance objectives Then the operation will need to excel at these...
Low price	Cost
High quality	Quality
Fast delivery	Speed
Reliable delivery	Dependability
Innovative products and services	Flexibility (product/service)
Wide range of products and services	Flexibility (mix)
The ability to change the timing or quantity of products and services	Flexibility (volume and/or delivery)

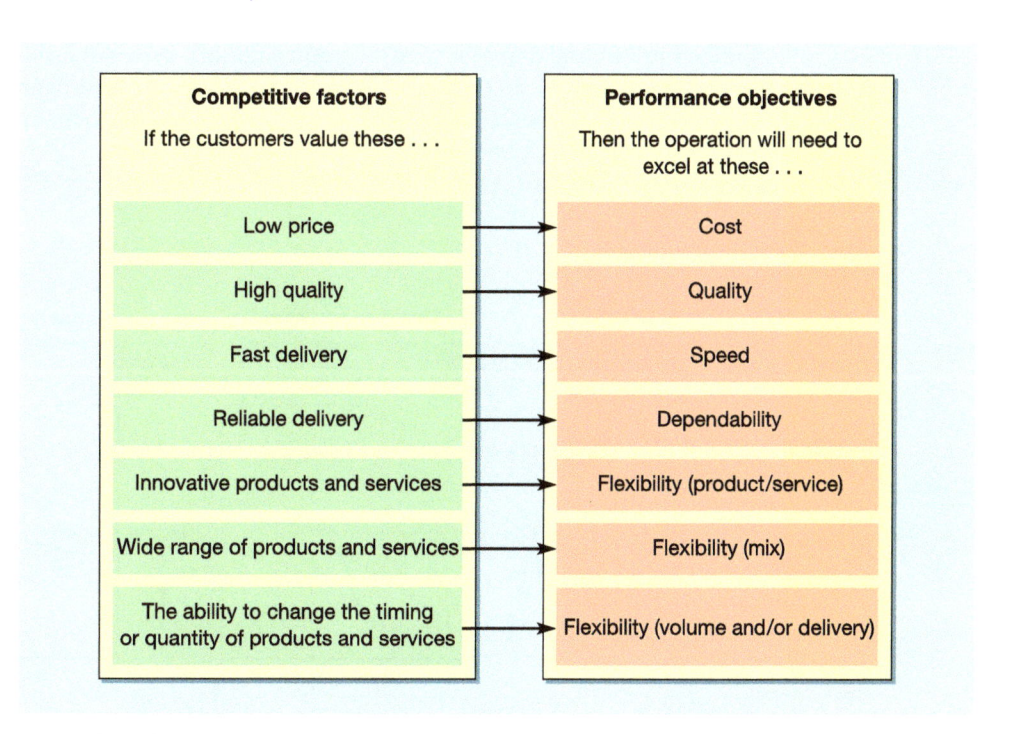

Figure 2.6 Different competitive factors imply different performance objectives

Order-winning and qualifying objectives

A particularly useful way of determining the relative importance of competitive factors is to distinguish between 'order-winning' and 'qualifying' factors.[6] **Order-winning factors** are those things which directly and significantly contribute to winning business. They are regarded by customers as key reasons for purchasing the service or product. Raising performance in an order-winning factor will either result in more business or improve the chances of gaining more business. **Qualifying factors** may not be the major competitive determinants of success, but are important in another way. They are those aspects of competitiveness where the operation's performance has to be above a particular level just to be considered by the customer. Performance below this 'qualifying' level of performance will possibly disqualify the company from being considered by many customers. However, any further improvement above the qualifying level is unlikely to gain the company much competitive benefit. To order-winning and qualifying factors can be added **less important factors** which are neither order-winning nor qualifying. They do not influence customers in any significant way. They are worth mentioning here only because they may be of importance in other parts of the operation's activities.

Figure 2.7 shows the difference between order-winning, qualifying and less important factors in terms of their utility or worth to the competitiveness of the organization. The curves illustrate the relative amount of competitiveness (or attractiveness to customers) as the operation's performance at the factor varies. Order-winning factors show a steady and significant increase in their contribution to competitiveness as the operation gets better at providing them. Qualifying factors are 'givens'; they are expected by customers and can severely disadvantage the competitive position of the operation if it cannot raise its performance above the qualifying level. Less important objectives have little impact on customers no matter how well the operation performs in them.

Different customer needs imply different objectives

If, as is likely, an operation produces goods or services for more than one customer group, it will need to determine the order-winning, qualifying and less important competitive factors for each group. For example, Table 2.1 shows two types of offerings in the banking industry. Here the distinction is drawn between the customers who are looking for banking services for their private and domestic needs (current accounts, overdraft facilities, savings accounts, mortgage loans, etc.) and those corporate customers who need banking services for their (often large) organizations. These latter services would include such things as letters of credit, cash transfer services and commercial loans.

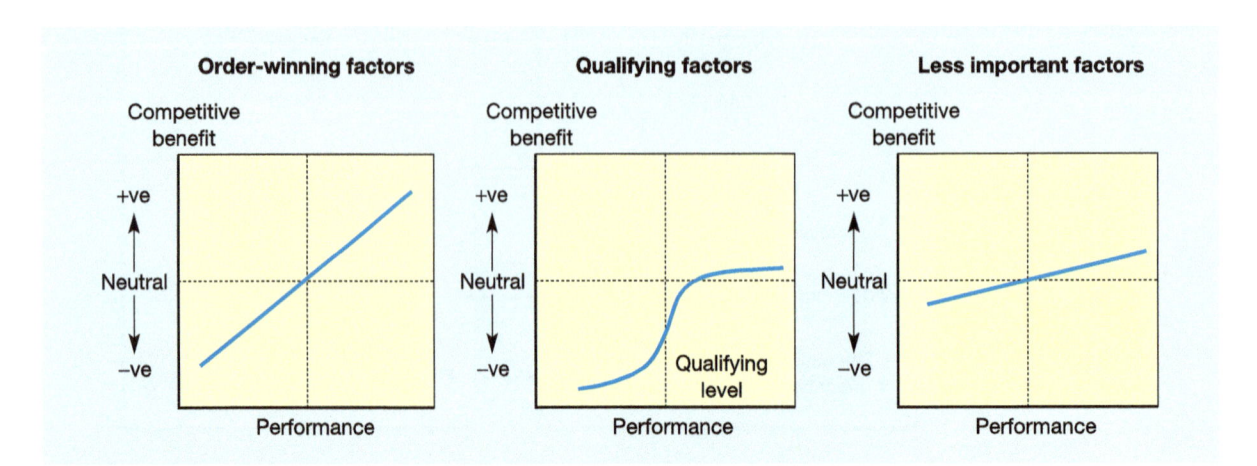

Figure 2.7 Order-winning, qualifying and less important competitive factors

Table 2.1 Different banking services require different performance objectives

	Retail banking	*Corporate banking*
Products	Personal financial services such as loans and credit cards	Special services for corporate customers
Customers	Individuals	Businesses
Product range	Medium but standardized, little need for special terms	Very wide range, many need to be customized
Design changes	Occasional	Continual
Delivery	Fast decisions	Dependable service
Quality	Means error-free transactions	Means close relationships
Volume per service type	Most services are high-volume	Most services are low-volume
Profit margins	Most are low to medium, some high	Medium to high

Competitive factors		
Order winners	Price Accessibility Speed	Customization Quality of service Reliability
Qualifiers	Quality Range	Speed Price
Less important		Accessibility

Internal performance objectives	Cost Speed Quality	Flexibility Quality Dependability

The service/product life cycle influence on performance objectives

One way of generalizing the behaviour of both customers and competitors is to link it to the life cycle of the services or products that the operation is creating. The exact form of **service/product life cycles** will vary, but generally they are shown as the sales volume passing through four stages – introduction, growth, maturity and decline. The important implication of this for operations management is that services and products will require operations strategies in each stage of their life cycle (see Figure 2.8).

Introduction stage. When a service or product is first introduced, it is likely to be offering something new in terms of its design or performance, with few competitors offering the same service or product. The needs of customers are unlikely to be well understood, so the operations management needs to develop the flexibility to cope with any changes and be able to give the quality to maintain product/service performance.

Growth stage. As volume grows, competitors may enter the growing market. Keeping up with demand could prove to be the main operations preoccupation. Rapid and dependable response to demand will help to keep demand buoyant, while quality levels must ensure that the company keeps its share of the market as competition starts to increase.

Maturity stage. Demand starts to level off. Some early competitors may have left the market and the industry will probably be dominated by a few larger companies. So operations will

Service/product life cycles

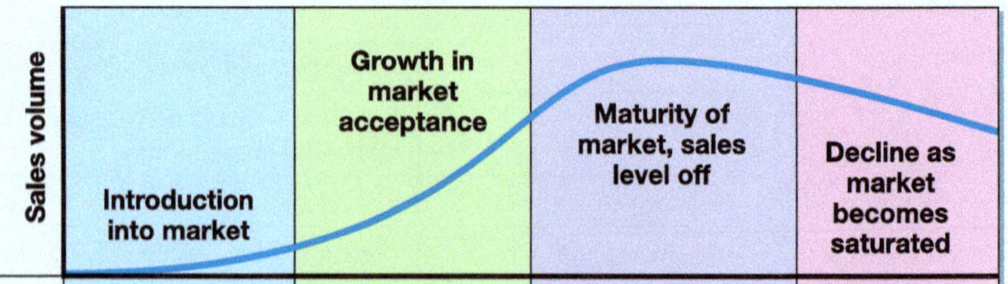

	Introduction into market	Growth in market acceptance	Maturity of market, sales level off	Decline as market becomes saturated
Customers	Innovators	Early adopters	Bulk of market	Laggards
Competitors	Few/none	Increasing numbers	Stable number	Declining number
Likely order winners	Product/service specification	Availability	Low price Dependable supply	Low price
Likely qualifiers	Quality Range	Price Range	Range Quality	Dependable supply
Dominant operations performance objectives	Flexibility Quality	Speed Dependability Quality	Cost Dependability	Cost

Figure 2.8 The effects of the life cycle on operations performance objectives

be expected to get the costs down in order to maintain profits or to allow price cutting, or both. This means that cost and productivity issues, together with dependable supply, are likely to be the operation's main concerns.

Decline stage. After time, sales will decline with more competitors dropping out of the market. There might be a residual market, but unless a shortage of capacity develops the market will continue to be dominated by price competition. Operations objectives continue to be dominated by cost.

The operations resources perspective

The fourth and final perspective we shall take on operations strategy is based on a particularly influential theory of business strategy – the **resource-based view** (RBV) of the firm.[7] Put simply, the RBV holds that firms with an 'above-average' strategic performance are likely to have gained their sustainable competitive advantage because of the core competencies (or capabilities) of their resources. This means that the way an organization inherits, or acquires, or develops its operations resources will, over the long term, have a significant impact on its strategic success. Furthermore, the impact of its 'operations resource' capabilities will be at least as great as, if not greater than, that which it gets from its market position. So understanding and developing the capabilities of operations resources, although often neglected, is a particularly important perspective on operations strategy.

Resource constraints and capabilities

No organization can merely choose which part of the market it wants to be in without considering its ability to produce products and services in a way that will satisfy that market. In other words, the constraints imposed by its operations must be taken into account. For example, a small translation company offers general translation services to a wide range of customers who wish documents such as sales brochures to be translated into another language. A small company, it operates an informal network of part-time translators who enable the company to offer translation into or from most of the major languages in the world. Some of the company's largest customers want to purchase their sales brochures on a 'one-stop shop' basis and have asked the translation company whether it is willing to offer a full service, organizing the design and production, as well as the translation, of export brochures. This is a very profitable market opportunity; however, the company does not have the resources, financial or physical, to take it up. From a market perspective, it is good business; but from an operations resource perspective, it is not feasible.

However, the operations resource perspective is not always so negative. This perspective may identify *constraints* to satisfying some markets but it can also identify *capabilities* which can be exploited in other markets. For example, the same translation company has recently employed two new translators who are particularly skilled at web site development. To exploit this, the company decides to offer a new service whereby customers can transfer documents to the company electronically, which can then be translated quickly. This new service is a 'fast response' service which has been designed specifically to exploit the capabilities within the operations resources. Here the company has chosen to be driven by its resource capabilities rather than the obvious market opportunities.

Intangible resources

An operations resource perspective must start with an understanding of the resource capabilities and constraints within the operation. It must answer the simple questions, what do we have, and what can we do? An obvious starting point here is to examine the transforming and transformed resource inputs to the operation. These, after all, are the 'building

Short case
Amazon, what exactly is your core competence?[8]

The founder and boss of Amazon, Jeff Bezos, was at a conference speaking about the company's plans. Although Amazon was generally seen as an Internet book retailer and then a more general Internet retailer, Jeff Bezos was actually pushing three of Amazon's 'utility computing' services. These were: a company that provides cheap access to online computer storage, a company that allows program developers to rent computing capacity on Amazon systems, and a service that connects firms with other firms that perform specialist tasks that are difficult to automate. The problem with online retailing, said Bezos, is its seasonality. At peak times, such as Christmas, Amazon has far more computing capacity than it needs for the rest of the year. At low points it may be using as little as 10 per cent of its total capacity. Hiring out that spare capacity is an obvious way to bring in extra revenue. In addition, Amazon had developed a search engine, a video download business, a service (Fulfilment By Amazon) that allowed other companies to use Amazon's logistics capability including the handling of returned items, and a service that provided access to Amazon's 'back-end' technology.

Amazon's apparent redefinition of its strategy was immediately criticized by some observers. 'Why not', they said, 'stick to what you know, focus on your core competence of Internet retailing?' Bezos's response was clear. 'We *are* sticking to our core competence; this is what we've been doing for the last 11 years. The only thing that's changed is that we are exposing it for [the benefit of] others.' At least for Jeff Bezos, Amazon is not so much an Internet retailer as a provider of Internet-based technology and logistics services.

blocks' of the operation. However, merely listing the type of *resources* an operation has does not give a complete picture of what it can do. Trying to understand an operation by listing its resources alone is like trying to understand an automobile by listing its component parts. To describe it more fully, we need to describe how the component parts form the internal mechanisms of the motor car. Within the operation, the equivalent of these mechanisms is its *processes*. Yet, even for an automobile, a technical explanation of its mechanisms still does not convey everything about its style or 'personality'. Something more is needed to describe these. In the same way, an operation is not just the sum of its processes. In addition, the operation has some **intangible resources**. An operation's intangible resources include such things as its relationship with suppliers, the reputation it has with its customers, its knowledge of its process technologies and the way its staff can work together in new product and service development. These intangible resources may not always be obvious within the operation, but they are important and have real value. It is these intangible resources, as well as its tangible resources, that an operation needs to deploy in order to satisfy its markets. The central issue for operations management, therefore, is to ensure that its pattern of strategic decisions really does develop appropriate capabilities within its resources and processes.

Structural and infrastructural decisions

A distinction is often drawn between the strategic decisions which determine an operation's **structure** and those which determine its **infrastructure**. An operation's structural decisions are those which we have classed as primarily influencing design activities, while infrastructural decisions are those which influence the workforce organization and the delivery (planning and control) and development (improvement) activities. This distinction in operations strategy has been compared to that between 'hardware' and 'software' in computer systems. The hardware of a computer sets limits to what it can do. In a similar way, investing in advanced technology and building more or better facilities can raise the potential of any type of operation. Within the limits which are imposed by the hardware of a computer, the software governs how effective the computer actually is in practice. The most powerful computer can only work to its full potential if its software is capable of exploiting its potential. The same principle applies with operations. The best and most costly facilities and technology will only be effective if the operation also has an appropriate infrastructure which governs the way it will work on a day-to-day basis. Table 2.2 illustrates both structural and infrastructural decision areas. The table also shows some typical questions which each strategic decision area should be addressing.

Table 2.2 Structural and infrastructural strategic decision areas

Structural strategic decisions	Typical questions which the strategy should help to answer
New service/product design	How should the operation decide which services or products to develop and how to manage the development process?
Supply network design	Should the operation expand by acquiring its suppliers or its customers? If so, what customers and suppliers should it acquire? How should it develop the capabilities of its customers and suppliers? What capacity should each operation in the network have? What number of geographically separate sites should the operation have and where should they be located? What activities and capacity should be allocated to each plant?
Process technology	What types of process technology should the operation be using? Should it be at the leading edge of technology or wait until the technology is established?

Table 2.2 *continued*

Infrastructural strategic decisions	Typical questions which the strategy should help to answer
Job design and organization	What role should the people who staff the operation play in its management? How should responsibility for the activities of the operations function be allocated between different groups in the operation? What skills should be developed in the staff of the operation?
Planning and control	How should the operation forecast and monitor the demand for its offerings? How should the operation adjust its activity levels in response to demand fluctuations? What systems should the operation use to plan and control its activities? How should the operation decide the resources to be allocated to its various activities?
Inventory	How should the operation decide how much inventory to have and where it is to be located? How should the operation control the size and composition of its inventories?
Supplier development	How should the operation choose its suppliers? How should it develop its relationship with its suppliers? How should it monitor its suppliers' performance?
Improvement	How should the operation's performance be measured? How should the operation decide whether its performance is satisfactory? How should the operation ensure that its performance is reflected in its improvement priorities? Who should be involved in the improvement process? How fast should the operation expect improvement in performance to be? How should the improvement process be managed?
Failure prevention, risk and recovery	How should the operation maintain its resources so as to prevent failure? How should the operation plan to cope with a failure if one occurs?

The process of operations strategy

The process of strategy formulation is concerned with 'how' operations strategies are put together. It is important because, although strategies will vary from organization to organization, they are usually trying to achieve some kind of alignment, or 'fit', between what the market wants, and what the operation can deliver, and how that 'alignment' can be sustained over time. So the process of operations strategy should both satisfy market requirements through appropriate operations resources, *and also* develop those resources in the long term so that they can provide competitive capabilities in the longer term that are sufficiently powerful to achieve sustainable competitive advantage.

There are many 'formulation processes' which are, or can be, used to formulate operations strategies. Most consultancy companies have developed their own frameworks, as have several academics. Typically, these formulation processes include the following elements:

- A process which formally links the total organization strategic objectives (usually a business strategy) to resource-level objectives.
- The use of competitive factors (called various things such as order winners, critical success factors, etc.) as the translation device between business strategy and operations strategy.
- A step which involves judging the relative importance of the various competitive factors in terms of customers' preferences.
- A step which includes assessing current achieved performance, usually as compared against competitor performance levels.
- An emphasis on operations strategy formulation as an iterative process.

- The concept of an 'ideal' or 'greenfield' operation against which to compare current operations. Very often the question asked is: 'If you were starting from scratch on a green-field site, how, ideally, would you design your operation to meet the needs of the market?' This can then be used to identify the differences between current operations and this ideal state.
- A 'gap-based' approach. This is a well-tried approach in all strategy formulation which involves comparing what is required of the operation by the marketplace against the levels of performance the operation is currently achieving.

What should the formulation process be trying to achieve?

So what should any operations strategy be trying to achieve? Clearly, it should provide a set of actions that, with hindsight, have provided the 'best' outcome for the organization. However, that really does not help us. What do we mean by 'the best', and what good is a judgement that can only be applied in hindsight? Yet, even if we cannot assess the 'goodness' of a strategy for certain in advance, we can check it out for some attributes that could stop it being a success. Firstly, is the operations strategy comprehensive? Secondly, is there internal coherence between the various actions it is proposing? Thirdly, do the actions being proposed as part of the operations strategy correspond to the appropriate priority for each performance objective? Fourthly, does the strategy prioritize the most critical activities or decisions?

Comprehensive

The notion of 'comprehensiveness' is a critical first step in seeking to achieve an effective operations strategy. Business history is littered with world-class companies that simply failed to notice the potential impact of, for instance, new process technology or emerging changes in their supply network. Also, many strategies have failed because operations have paid undue attention to only one key decision area.

Coherence

As a comprehensive strategy evolves over time, different tensions will emerge that threaten to pull the overall strategy in different directions. This can result in a loss of coherence. Coherence is when the choices made in each decision area do not pull the operation in different directions. For example, if new flexible technology is introduced which allows services or products to be customized to individual clients' needs, it would be 'incoherent' to devise an organizational structure which did not enable the relevant staff to exploit the technology because it would limit the effective flexibility of the operation. For the investment in flexible technology to be effective, it must be accompanied by an organizational structure which deploys the organization's skills appropriately, a performance measurement system which acknowledges that flexibility must be promoted, a new development policy which stresses appropriate types of customization, a supply network strategy which develops suppliers and customers to understand the needs of high-variety customization, a capacity strategy which deploys capacity where the customization is needed, and so on. In other words, all the decision areas complement and reinforce each other in the promotion of that particular performance objective.

Correspondence

Equally, an operation has to achieve a correspondence between the choices made against each of the decision areas and the relative priority attached to each of the performance objectives. In other words, the strategies pursued in each decision area should reflect the true priority of each performance objective. So, for example, if cost reduction is the main organizational objective for an operation, then its process technology investment decisions might err towards the purchase of 'off-the-shelf' equipment from a third-party supplier. This would reduce the capital cost of the technology and may also imply lower maintenance and running costs. Remember, however, that making such a decision will also have an impact on other performance objectives. An off-the-shelf piece of equipment may not, for example, have the flexibility that more 'made-to-order' equipment has. Also, the other decision areas must correspond with the same prioritization of objectives. If low cost is really important then one would expect to see capacity strategies which exploit natural economies of scale, supply network strategies which reduce purchasing costs, performance measurement systems which stress efficiency and productivity, continuous improvement strategies which emphasize continual cost reduction, and so on.

Criticality

In addition to the difficulties of ensuring coherence between decision areas, there is also a need to include financial and competitive priorities. Although all decisions are important and a comprehensive perspective should be maintained, in practical terms some resource or requirement intersections will be more critical than others. The judgement over exactly which intersections are particularly critical is very much a pragmatic one which must be based on the particular circumstances of an individual firm's operations strategy. It is therefore difficult to generalize as to the likelihood of any particular intersections being critical. However, in practice, one can ask revealing questions such as, 'If flexibility is important, of all the decisions we make in terms of our capacity, supply networks, process technology, or development and organization, which will have the most impact on flexibility?' This can be done for all performance objectives, with more emphasis being placed on those having the highest priority.

Short case
Sometimes any plan is better than no plan[9]

There is a famous story that illustrates the importance of having some kind of plan, even if hindsight proves it to be the wrong plan. During manoeuvres in the Alps, a detachment of Hungarian soldiers got lost. The weather was severe and the snow was deep. In these freezing conditions, after two days of wandering, the soldiers gave up hope and became reconciled to a frozen death on the mountains. Then, to their delight, one of the soldiers discovered a map in his pocket. Much cheered by this discovery, the soldiers were able to escape from the mountains. When they were safe back at their headquarters, they discovered that the map was not of the Alps at all, but of the Pyrenees. The moral of the story? A plan (or a map) may not be perfect but it gives a sense of purpose and a sense of direction. If the soldiers had waited for the right map they would have frozen to death. Yet their renewed confidence motivated them to get up and create opportunities.

Summary answers to key questions

Check and improve your understanding of this chapter using self-assessment questions and a personalized study plan, audio and video downloads, and an eBook – all at www.myomlab.com.

▶ **What is strategy and what is operations strategy?**

- Strategy is the total pattern of decisions and actions that position the organization in its environment and that are intended to achieve its long-term goals.
- Operations strategy concerns the pattern of strategic decisions and actions which set the role, objectives and activities of the operation.
- The contribution of operations to overall business strategy can range from stage 1 (holding the business back) to stage 4 (driving business strategy).

84 Operations Management

> ► **What is the difference between a 'top-down' and a 'bottom-up' view of operations strategy?**

- The 'top-down' perspective views strategic decisions at a number of levels. Corporate strategy sets the objectives for the different businesses which make up a group of businesses. Business strategy sets the objectives for each individual business and how it positions itself in its marketplace. Functional strategies set the objectives for each function's contribution to its business strategy.
- The 'bottom-up' view of operations strategy sees overall strategy as emerging from day-to-day operational experience.

> ► **What is the difference between a 'market requirements' and an 'operations resources' view of operations strategy?**

- A 'market requirements' perspective of operations strategy sees the main role of operations as satisfying markets. Operations performance objectives and operations decisions should be primarily influenced by a combination of customers' needs and competitors' actions. Both of these may be summarized in terms of the product/service life cycle.
- The 'operations resources' perspective of operations strategy is based on the resource-based view (RBV) of the firm and sees the operation's core competencies (or capabilities) as being the main influence on operations strategy. Operations capabilities are developed partly through the strategic decisions taken by the operation. Strategic decision areas in operations are usually divided into structural and infrastructural decisions. Structural decisions are those which define an operation's shape and form. Infrastructural decisions are those which influence the systems and procedures that determine how the operation will work in practice.

> ► **How can an operations strategy be put together?**

- There are many different procedures which are used by companies, consultancies and academics to formulate operations strategies. Although differing in the stages that they recommend, many of these models have similarities.
- Any operations strategy process should result in strategies that are comprehensive and coherent, provide correspondence, and prioritize the most critical activities or decisions.

Learning exercises

These problems and applications will help to improve your analysis of operations. You can find more practice problems as well as worked examples and guided solutions on MyOMLab at www.myomlab.com.

1. Explain how the four perspectives of operations strategy would apply to Ryanair and Flextronics.

2. Compare the operations strategies of Ryanair and a full-service airline such as British Airways or KLM.

3. What do you think are the qualifying or order-winning factors for IKEA described in Chapter 1?

4. Search the Internet site of Intel, the best-known microchip manufacturer, and identify what appear to be its main structural and infrastructural decisions in its operations strategy.

5 **(Advanced)** McDonald's has come to epitomize the 'fast-food' industry. Originally, McDonald's competed on low price, fast service and a totally standardized service offering. They also offered a very narrow range of items on their menu. Visit a McDonald's restaurant and deduce what you believe to be its most important performance objectives. Then try and identify two other chains which appear to compete in a slightly different way. How do these differences in the relative importance of competitive objectives influence the structural and infrastructural decisions of each chain's operations strategy?

Want to know more?

Boyer, K.K., Swink, M. and Rosenzweig, E.D. (2006) Operations strategy research in the POMS Journal, *Production and Operations Management*, vol. 14, issue 4. A survey of recent research in the area.

Hayes, R.H., Pisano, G.P., Upton, D.M. and Wheelwright, S.C. (2005) *Operations, Strategy, and Technology: Pursuing the Competitive Edge*, Wiley, Hoboken, NJ. The gospel according to the Harvard school of operations strategy. Articulate, interesting and informative.

Slack, N. and Lewis, M. (2011) *Operations Strategy*, 3rd edn, Financial Times Prentice Hall, Harlow. What can we say – just brilliant!

Useful websites

www.cranfield.ac.uk/som Look for the 'Best factory awards' link. Manufacturing, but interesting.

www.opsman.org Lots of useful stuff.

www.worldbank.org Global issues. Useful for international operations strategy research.

www.weforum.org Global issues, including some operations strategy ones.

www.ft.com Great for industry and company examples.

Now that you have finished reading this chapter, why not visit MyOMLab at www.myomlab.com where you'll find more learning resources to help you make the most of your studies and get a better grade.

Chapter 3 | Social, environmental and economic performance

Key questions

- Why is operations performance important in any organization?
- How should the operations function judge itself?
- What does top management expect from the operations function?
- What are the performance objectives of operations and what are the internal and external benefits which derive from excelling in each of them?
- How do operations performance objectives trade off against each other?

Introduction

Operations are judged by the way they perform. There are many individuals and groups doing the judging and there are many different aspects of performance on which the assessment is being made. Here, we take what is called a 'triple bottom line' approach to understand an operation's total performance. If we want to understand the strategic contribution of the operations function, it is important to understand how we can measure its performance. This chapter examines social, environmental, and economic performance before focusing on how operations can impact on the success of the whole organization. Finally, we examine how performance objectives trade off against each other. Figure 3.1 shows where this chapter fits into the overall operations model.

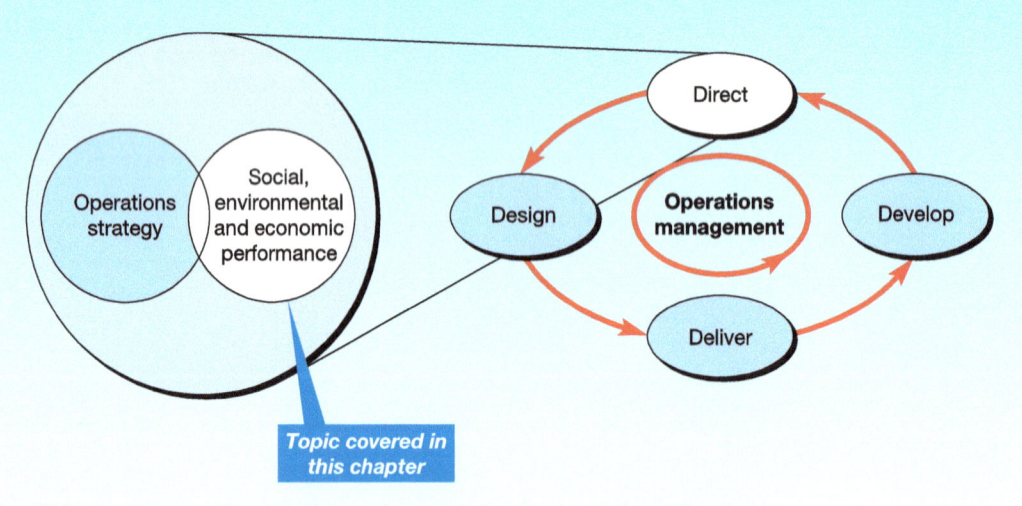

Figure 3.1 This chapter examines social, environmental and economic performance

Check and improve your understanding of this chapter using self-assessment questions and a personalized study plan, audio and video downloads, and an eBook – all at www.myomlab.com.

Operations in practice: A tale of two terminals[1]

On 15 April 2008 British Airways (BA) announced that two of its most senior executives, its director of operations and its director of customer services, would leave the company. They were paying the price for the disastrous opening of British Airways' new Terminal 5 at London's Heathrow airport. The opening of the £4.3bn terminal, said BA's boss, Willie Walsh, with magnificent understatement, 'was not the company's finest hour'. The chaos at the terminal on its opening days made news around the world and was seen by many as one of the most public failures of basic operations management in the modern history of aviation. 'It's a terrible, terrible PR nightmare to have hanging over you', said David Learmount, an aviation expert. 'Somebody who may have been a faithful customer and still not have their luggage after three weeks is not good for their [BA's] image. The one thing that's worse than having a stack of 15,000 bags is adding 5,000 a day to that heap.' According to a BA spokeswoman it needed an extra 400 volunteer staff and courier companies to wade through the backlog of late baggage. So the new terminal that had opened on 27 March could not even cope with BA's full short-haul service until 8 April (two hundred flights in and out of T5 were cancelled in its first three days). This delayed moving its long-haul operations to the new building from Terminal 4 as scheduled on 30 April, which, in turn, disrupted the operations of other airlines, many of which were scheduled to move into Terminal 4 once BA had moved its long-haul flights from there. Sharing the blame with BA was the British Airports Authority (BAA) which was already suffering criticism from passenger groups, airlines and businesses for allegedly poor performance. BAA's non-executive chairman, Sir Nigel Rudd, said he was 'bitterly disappointed' about the opening of the terminal. 'It was clearly a huge embarrassment to the company, me personally, and the board. Nothing can take away that failure. We had all believed genuinely that it would be a great opening, which clearly it wasn't.'

Yet it all should have been so different. T5 took more than six years and around 60,000 workers to build, and it's an impressive building. It is Europe's largest free-standing structure. It was also keenly anticipated by travellers and BA alike. Willie Walsh has said that the terminal 'will completely change his passengers' experience'. He was right, but not in the way he imagined! So what went wrong? As is often the case with major operations failures, it was not one thing, but several interrelated problems (all of which could have been avoided). Press reports initially blamed glitches with the state-of-the-art baggage handling system that consisted of 18 km of conveyor belts and was (theoretically) capable of transporting 12,000 bags per hour. Almost inevitably, the baggage handling system experienced problems which had not been exposed in testing. However, BAA, the airport operator, doubted that the main problem was the baggage system itself. The system had worked until it became clogged with bags that were overwhelming BA's handlers loading them onto the aircraft. Partly this may have been because staff were not sufficiently familiar with the new system and its operating processes, but handling staff had also suffered delays getting to their new (and unfamiliar) work areas, negotiating (new) security checks and finding (again, new) car parking spaces. Also, once staff were 'airside' they had problems logging in. The cumulative effect of these problems meant that the airline was unable to get ground handling staff to the correct locations for loading and unloading bags from the aircraft, so baggage could not be loaded onto aircraft fast enough, so baggage backed up, clogging the baggage handling system, which in turn meant closing baggage check-in and baggage drops, leading eventually to baggage check-in being halted.

However, not every airline underestimates the operational complexity of airport processes. During the same year that Terminal 5 at Heathrow was suffering queues, lost bags and bad publicity, Dubai International Airport's Terminal 3 opened quietly with little publicity and fewer problems. Like T5, it is also huge and designed to impress. Its new shimmering facilities are solely dedicated to Emirates Airline. Largely built underground (20 metres beneath the taxiway area) the multi-level environment reduces passenger walking by using 157 elevators, 97 escalators and 82 moving walkways. Its underground baggage handling system is the deepest and the largest of its kind in the world with 90 km of baggage belts handling around 15,000 items per hour. Also like T5 it handles about 30 million passengers a year.

A key difference between the two terminals was that Dubai's T3 could observe and learn lessons from the botched opening of Heathrow's Terminal 5. Paul Griffiths, the former head of London's Gatwick Airport, who is now Dubai Airport's chief executive, insisted that his own new terminal should not be publicly shamed in the same way. 'There was a lot of arrogance and hubris around the opening of T5, with all the . . . publicity that BA generated', Mr Griffiths says. 'The first rule of customer service is under-promise and over-deliver because that way you get their loyalty. BA was telling people that they were getting a glimpse of the future with T5, which created expectation and increased the chances of disappointment. Having watched the development of T5, it was clear that we had to make sure that everyone was on-message. We just had to bang heads together so that people realized what was at stake. We knew the world would be watching and waiting after T5 to see whether T3 was the next big terminal fiasco. We worked very hard to make sure that didn't happen.'

Paul Griffiths was also convinced that Terminal 3 should undergo a phased programme with flights added progressively, rather than a 'big bang' approach where the terminal opened for business on one day. 'We exhaustively tested the terminal systems throughout the summer . . . We continue to make sure we're putting large loads on it, week by week, improving reliability. We put a few flights in bit by bit, in waves rather than a big bang.' Prior to the opening he also said that Dubai Airports would never reveal a single opening date for its new Terminal 3 until all pre-opening test programmes had been completed. 'T3 opened so quietly', said one journalist, 'that passengers would have known that the terminal was new only if they had touched the still-drying paint.'

Operations performance is vital for any organization

Operations management is a 'make or break' activity

It is no exaggeration to view operations management as being able to either '**make or break**' any business. This is not just because the operations function is large and, in most businesses, represents the bulk of its assets and the majority of its people, but because the operations function gives the ability to compete by providing customer responsiveness and by developing the capabilities that will keep it ahead of its competitors in the future. For example, operations management principles and the performance of its operations function proved hugely important in the Heathrow T5 and Dubai T3 launches. It was a basic failure to understand the importance of operations processes that (temporarily) damaged British Airways' reputation. It was Dubai's attention to detail and thorough operational preparation that avoided similar problems.

Operations managers face many new challenges as the economic, social, political and technological environment changes. Many of these decisions and challenges seem largely economic in nature. What will be the impact on our costs of adding a new product or service feature? Can we generate an acceptable return if we invest in new technology? Other decisions have more of a 'social' aspect. How do we make sure that all our suppliers treat their staff fairly? Finally, some have an environmental impact. Are we doing enough to reduce our carbon footprint? Furthermore, the 'economic' decisions also have an environmental aspect to them. Will a new product feature make end-of-life recycling more difficult? Will the new technology increase pollution? Similarly the 'social' decisions must be made in the context of their economic consequences. Sure, we want suppliers to treat staff well, but we also need to make a profit. And this is the great dilemma. How do operations managers try to be, simultaneously, economically viable whilst being socially and environmentally responsible?

The triple bottom line

Triple bottom line

One common term that tries to capture the idea of a broader approach to assessing an organization's performance is the **'triple bottom line'** (TBL, or 3BL), also known as 'people, planet and profit'. Essentially, it is a straightforward idea, simply that organizations should measure themselves not just on the traditional economic profit that they generate for their owners, but also on the impact their operations have on society (broadly, in the sense of communities, and individually, for example in terms of their employees) and the ecological impact on the environment. The influential initiative that has come out of this triple bottom line approach is that of 'sustainability'. A sustainable business is one that creates an acceptable profit for its owners, but minimizes the damage to the environment and enhances the existence of the people with whom it has contact. In other words, it balances economic, environmental and societal interests. This gives the organization its 'license to operate' in society. The assumption underlying the triple bottom line (which is not universally accepted) is that a sustainable business is more likely to remain successful in the long-term than one which focuses on economic goals alone. Only a company that produces a balanced TBL is really accounting for the total cost of running its operations. Figure 3.2 illustrates some of the issues involved in achieving the triple bottom line.

- Recyclability of materials, energy consumption, waste material generation
- Reducing transport-related energy
- Noise pollution, fume and emission pollution
- Obsolescence and wastage
- Environmental impact of process failures
- Recovery to minimize impact of failures

Planet – The environmental account, measured by environmental impact of the operation

Sustainability

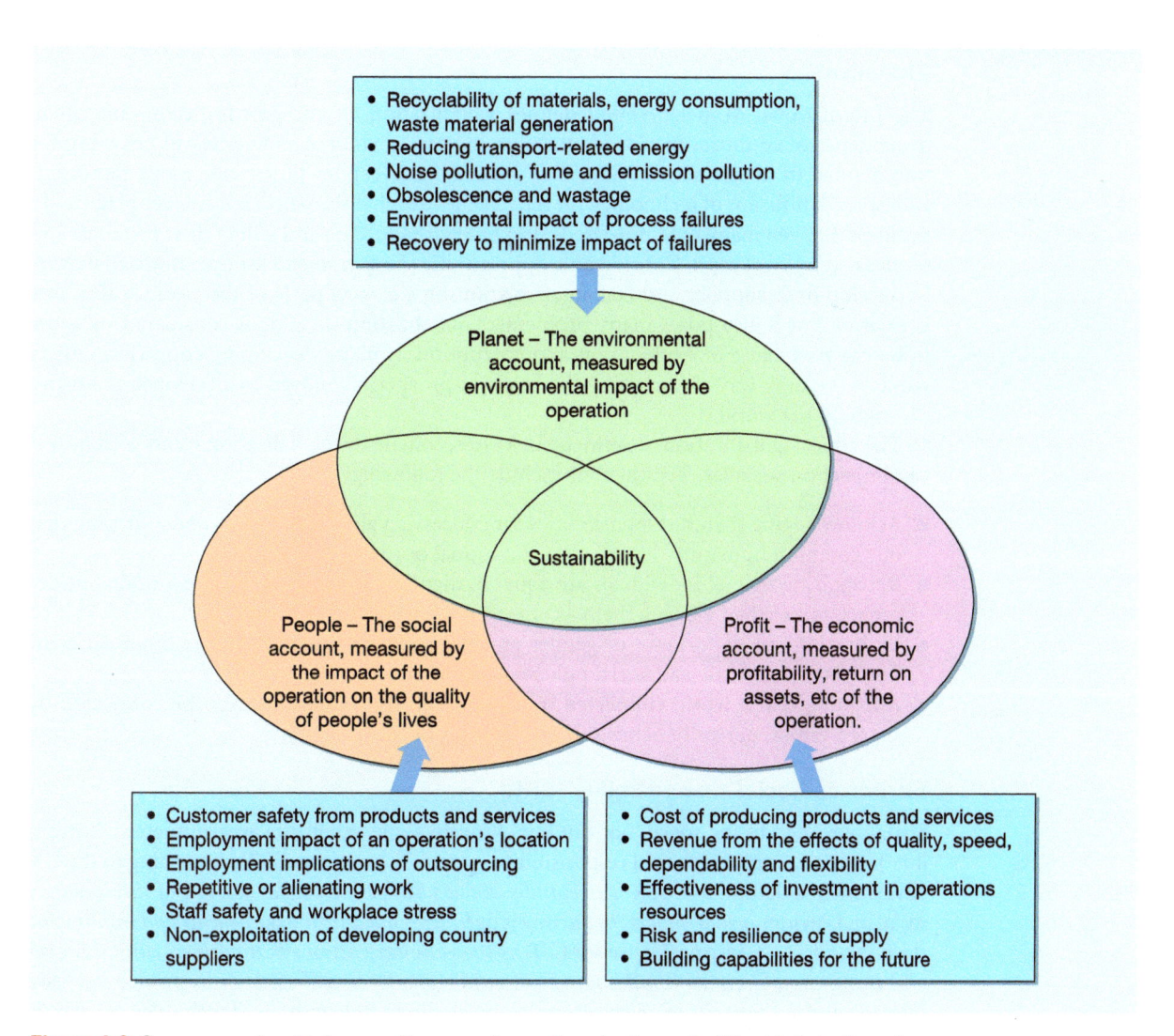

People – The social account, measured by the impact of the operation on the quality of people's lives

Profit – The economic account, measured by profitability, return on assets, etc of the operation.

- Customer safety from products and services
- Employment impact of an operation's location
- Employment implications of outsourcing
- Repetitive or alienating work
- Staff safety and workplace stress
- Non-exploitation of developing country suppliers

- Cost of producing products and services
- Revenue from the effects of quality, speed, dependability and flexibility
- Effectiveness of investment in operations resources
- Risk and resilience of supply
- Building capabilities for the future

Figure 3.2 Some ways in which operations can impact each element of the triple bottom line

The social bottom line

The fundamental idea behind the social bottom line is not simply that there is a connection between businesses and the society in which they operate (defined broadly) – that is self-evident. Rather it is that businesses should accept that they bear some responsibility for the impact they have on society and balance the external 'societal' consequences of their actions with the more direct internal consequences, such as profit.

Society is made up of organizations, groups and individuals. Each is more than a simple unit of economic exchange. Organizations have responsibility for the general well-being of society beyond short-term economic self-interest. At the level of the individual, this means devising jobs and work patterns which allow individuals to contribute their talents without undue stress. At a group level, it means recognizing and dealing honestly with employee representatives. This principle also extends beyond the boundaries of the organization. Any business has a responsibility to ensure that it does not knowingly disadvantage individuals in its suppliers or trading partners. Businesses are also a part of the larger community, often integrated into the economic and social fabric of an area. Increasingly, organizations are recognizing their responsibility to local communities by helping to promote their economic and social well-being. Of the many issues that affect society at large, arguably the one that has had the most profound effect on the way business has developed over the last few decades has been the globalization of business activity.

Globalization

The International Monetary Fund defines globalization as 'the growing economic inter-dependence of countries worldwide through increasing volume and variety of cross-border transactions in goods and services, free international capital flows, and more rapid and widespread diffusion of technology'. It reflects the idea that the world is a smaller place to do business in. Even many medium-sized companies are sourcing and selling their products and services on a global basis. Considerable opportunities have emerged for operations managers to develop both supplier and customer relationships in new parts of the world. All of this is exciting but it also poses many problems. **Globalization** of trade is considered by some to be the root cause of exploitation and corruption in many developing countries. Others see it as the only way of spreading the levels of prosperity enjoyed by developed countries throughout the world.

The ethical globalization movement seeks to reconcile the globalization trend with how it can impact on societies. Typical aims include the following:

- Acknowledging shared responsibilities for addressing global challenges and affirming that our common humanity doesn't stop at national borders.
- Recognizing that all individuals are equal in dignity and have the right to certain entitlements, rather than viewing them as objects of benevolence or charity.
- Embracing the importance of gender and the need for attention to the often different impacts of economic and social policies on women and men.
- Affirming that a world connected by technology and trade must also be connected by shared values, norms of behaviour and systems of accountability.

Corporate social responsibility (CSR)

Strongly related to the social 'bottom line' (and to some extent the environmental 'bottom line') is that of **corporate social responsibility** (generally known as CSR). According to the UK government's definition, *'CSR is essentially about how business takes account of its economic, social and environmental impacts in the way it operates – maximizing the benefits and minimizing the downsides. . . . Specifically, we see CSR as the voluntary actions that business can take, over and above compliance with minimum legal requirements, to address both its own competitive interests and the interests of wider society.'* A more direct link with the stakeholder concept is to be found in the definition used by Marks and Spencer, the UK-based retailer. *'Corporate Social Responsibility . . . is listening and responding to the needs of a company's stakeholders. This includes the requirements of sustainable development. We believe that building good relationships with employees, suppliers and wider society is the best guarantee of long-term success. This is the backbone of our approach to CSR.'* The issue of how broader social performance objectives can be included in operations management's activities is of increasing importance, from both an ethical and a commercial point of view.

The environmental bottom line

Environmental sustainability (according to the World Bank) means 'ensuring that the overall productivity of accumulated human and physical capital resulting from development actions more than compensates for the direct or indirect loss or degradation of the environment', or (according to the Brundtland Report from the United Nations) it is 'meeting the needs of the present without compromising the ability of future generations to meet their own needs'. Put more directly, it is generally taken to mean the extent to which business activity negatively impacts on the natural environment. It is clearly an important issue, not only because of the obvious impact on the immediate environment of hazardous waste, air and even noise pollution, but also because of the less obvious, but potentially far more damaging issues around global warming.

From the perspective of individual organizations, the challenging issues of dealing with sustainability are connected with the scale of the problem and the general perception of 'green' issues. Firstly, the scale issue is that cause and effect in the environmental sustainability area are judged at different levels. The effects of, and arguments for, environmentally sustainable activities are felt at a global level, while those activities themselves are essentially local. It has been argued that it is difficult to use the concept at a corporate or even at the regional level. Secondly, there is a paradox with sustainability-based decisions. It is that the more the public becomes sensitized to the benefits of firms acting in an environmentally sensitive way, the more those firms are tempted to exaggerate their environmental credentials, the so-called 'greenwashing' effect.

Environmental protection   Operations managers cannot avoid responsibility for **environmental protection** generally, or their organization's environmental performance more specifically. It is often operational failures which are at the root of pollution disasters and operations decisions (such as product design) which impact on longer-term environmental issues. The pollution-causing disasters which make the headlines seem to be the result of a whole variety of causes – oil tankers run aground, nuclear waste is misclassified, chemicals leak into a river, or gas clouds drift over industrial towns. But in fact they all have something in common. They were all the result of an operational failure. Somehow operations procedures were inadequate. Less dramatic in the short term, but perhaps more important in the long term, is the environmental impact of products which cannot be recycled and processes which consume large amounts of energy – again, both issues which are part of the operations management's broader responsibilities.

Again, it is important to understand that broad issues such as environmental responsibility are intimately connected with the day-to-day decisions of operations managers. Many of these are concerned with waste. Operations management decisions in product and service design significantly affect the utilization of materials both in the short term and in long-term recyclability. Process design influences the proportion of energy and labour that is wasted as well as materials wastage. Planning and control may affect material wastage (packaging being wasted by mistakes in purchasing, for example), but also affects energy and labour wastage. Improvement, of course, is dedicated largely to reducing wastage. Here environmental responsibility and the conventional concerns of operations management coincide. Reducing waste, in all it forms, may be environmentally sound but it also saves cost for the organization. At other times, decisions can be more difficult. Process technologies may be efficient from the operations point of view but may cause pollution, the economic and social consequences of which are borne by society at large. Such conflicts are usually resolved through regulation and legislation. Not that such mechanisms are always effective – there is evidence that just-in-time principles applied in Japan may have produced significant economic gains for the companies which adopted them, but at the price of an overcrowded and polluted road system.

The economic bottom line

An organization's top management represent the interests of the owners (or trustees, or electorate, etc.) and therefore are the direct custodians of the organization's basic purpose. They also have responsibility for translating the broad objectives of the organization into a more tangible form. Broadly they should expect all their operations managers to contribute to the economic success of the organization by **using its resources effectively**. To do this it must be creative, innovative and energetic in improving its processes, products and services. In more detail, effective operations management can give five types of advantage to the business (see Figure 3.3):

> Operations can have a significant impact on economic success

- It can reduce the **costs** of producing services and products.
- It can achieve customer satisfaction through good quality and service (and therefore **revenue** in a for-profit organization).
- It can reduce the **risk** of operational failure, because well designed and well-run operations should be less likely to fail, and if they do they should be able to recover faster and with less disruption (this is called *resilience*).
- It can reduce the amount of **investment** (sometimes called *capital employed*) that is necessary to produce the required type and quantity of products and services by increasing the effective capacity of the operation and by being innovative in how it uses its physical resources.
- It can provide the basis for *future* **innovation** by learning from its experience of operating its processes, so building a solid base of operations skills, knowledge and capability within the business.

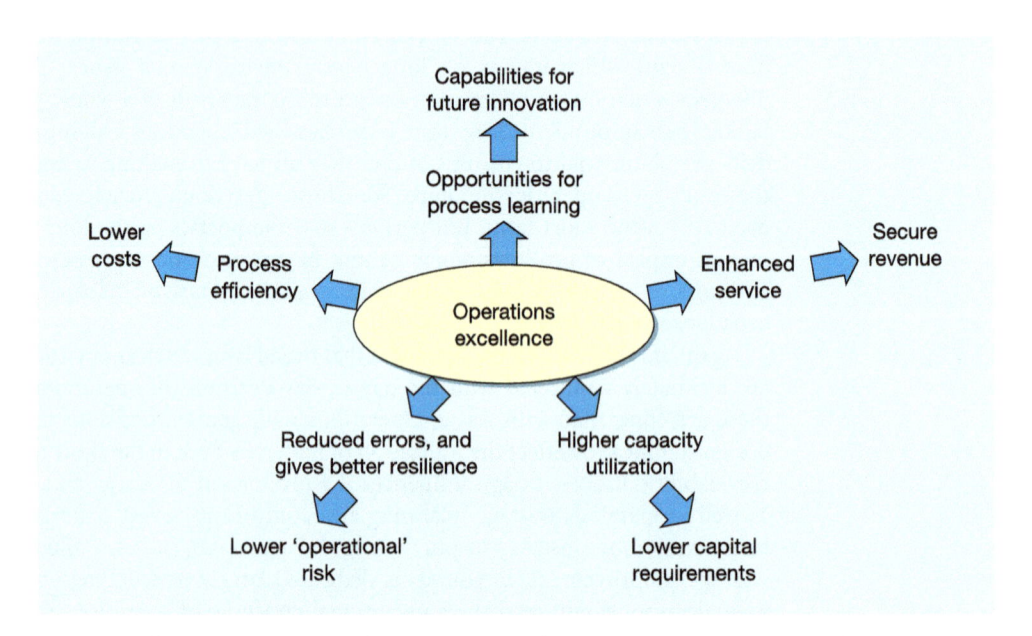

Figure 3.3 Operations can contribute to competitiveness through low costs, high levels of service (securing revenue), lower operational risk, lower capital requirements, and providing the capabilities that determine future innovation

The five operations performance objectives

Broad stakeholder objectives form the backdrop to operations decision-making, and top management's objectives provide a strategic framework, but running operations at an operational day-to-day level requires a more tightly defined set of objectives. These are the **five basic 'performance objectives'** and they apply to all types of operation. Imagine that you are an operations manager in any kind of business – a hospital administrator, for example, or a production manager at a car plant. What kind of things are you likely to want to do in order to satisfy customers and contribute to competitiveness?

Five basic 'performance objectives'

- You would want to do things right; that is, you would not want to make mistakes, and would want to satisfy your customers by providing error-free services and products which are 'fit for their purpose'. This is giving a **quality** advantage.

Quality

- You would want to do things fast, minimizing the time between a customer asking for services or products and the customer receiving them in full, thus increasing the availability of your services and products and giving a **speed** advantage.

Speed

- You would want to do things on time, so as to keep the delivery promises you have made. If the operation can do this, it is giving a **dependability** advantage.

Dependability

- You would want to be able to change what you do; that is, being able to vary or adapt the operation's activities to cope with unexpected circumstances or to give customers individual treatment. Being able to change far enough and fast enough to meet customer requirements gives a **flexibility** advantage.

Flexibility

- You would want to do things cheaply; that is, create and deliver services and products at a cost which enables them to be priced appropriately for the market while still allowing for a return to the organization; or, in a not-for-profit organization, give good value to the taxpayers or whoever is funding the operation. When the organization is managing to do this, it is giving a **cost** advantage.

Cost

The next part of this chapter examines these five performance objectives in more detail by looking at what they mean for four different operations: a general hospital, an automobile factory, a city bus company and a supermarket chain.

The quality objective

Quality is consistent conformance to customers' expectations, in other words, 'doing things right', but the things which the operation needs to do right will vary according to the kind of operation. All operations regard quality as a particularly important objective. In some ways quality is the most visible part of what an operation does. Furthermore, it is something that a customer finds relatively easy to judge about the operation. Is the service or product as it is supposed to be? Is it right or is it wrong? There is something fundamental about quality. Because of this, it is clearly **a major influence on customer satisfaction or dissatisfaction**. A customer perception of high-quality products and services means customer satisfaction and therefore the likelihood that the customer will return. Figure 3.4 illustrates how quality could be judged in four operations.

Quality is a major influence on customer satisfaction or dissatisfaction

Quality inside the operation

When quality means consistently creating and delivering services and products to specification, it not only leads to external customer satisfaction, but makes life easier inside the operation as well.

Quality reduces costs. The fewer mistakes made by each process in the operation, the less time will be needed to correct the mistakes and the less confusion and irritation will be spread. For example, if a supermarket's regional warehouse sends the wrong goods to the supermarket, it will mean staff time, and therefore cost, being used to sort out the problem.

Quality could mean . . .

Hospital
- Patients receive the most appropriate treatment
- Treatment is carried out in the correct manner
- Patients are consulted and kept informed
- Staff are courteous, friendly and helpful

Automobile plant
- All parts are made to specification
- All assembly is to specification
- The product is reliable
- The product is attractive and blemish-free

Bus company
- The buses are clean and tidy
- The buses are quiet and fume-free
- The timetable is accurate and user-friendly
- Staff are courteous, friendly and helpful

Supermarket
- Goods are in good condition
- The store is clean and tidy
- Décor is appropriate and attractive
- Staff are courteous, friendly and helpful

Figure 3.4 Quality means different things in different operations

Quality increases dependability. Increased costs are not the only consequence of poor quality. At the supermarket, poor quality could also mean that products run out on the shelves, resulting in lost revenue to the operation. Sorting the problem out could also distract the supermarket management from giving attention to the other parts of the supermarket operation. This in turn could result in further mistakes being made. So, quality (like the other performance objectives, as we shall see) has both an external impact which influences customer satisfaction and an internal impact which leads to stable and efficient processes.

Short case
Organically good quality[2]

'Organic farming means taking care and getting all the details right. It is about quality from start to finish. Not only the quality of the meat that we produce but also quality of life and quality of care for the countryside.' Nick Fuge is the farm manager at Lower Hurst Farm located within the Peak District National Park of the UK. He has day-to-day responsibility for the well-being of all the livestock and the operation of the farm on strict organic principles. The 85-hectare farm has been producing high-quality beef for almost 20 years but changed to fully organic production in 1998. Organic farming is a tough regime. No artificial fertilizers, genetically modified feedstuff or growth-promoting agents are used. All beef sold from the farm is home-bred and can be traced back to the animal from which it came.

'The quality of the herd is most important', says Nick, 'as is animal care. Our customers trust us to ensure that the cattle are organically and humanely reared, and slaughtered in a manner that minimizes any distress. If you want to

understand the difference between conventional and organic farming, look at the way we use veterinary help. Most conventional farmers use veterinarians like an emergency service to put things right when there is a problem with an animal. The amount we pay for veterinary assistance is lower because we try to avoid problems with the animals from the start. We use veterinarians as consultants to help us in preventing problems in the first place.'

Catherine Pyne runs the butchery and the mail-order meat business. *'After butchering, the cuts of meat are individually vacuum-packed, weighed and then blast-frozen. We worked extensively with the Department of Food and Nutrition at Oxford Brooks University to devise the best way to encapsulate the nutritional, textural and flavoursome characteristics of the meat in its prime state.*

So, when you defrost and cook any of our products you will have the same tasty and succulent eating qualities associated with the best fresh meat.' After freezing, the products are packed in boxes, designed and labelled for storage in a home freezer. Customers order by phone or through the Internet for next-day delivery in a special 'mini-deep-freeze' reusable container which maintains the meat in its frozen state. *'It isn't just the quality of our product which has made us a success'*, says Catherine. *'We give a personal and inclusive level of service to our customers that makes them feel close to us and maintains trust in how we produce and prepare the meat. The team of people we have here is also an important aspect of our business. We are proud of our product and feel that it is vitally important to be personally identified with it.'*

The speed objective

Speed means the elapsed time between customers requesting services or products and receiving them. Figure 3.5 illustrates what speed means for the four operations. The main benefit to the operation's (external) customers of speedy delivery of services or products is that the faster they can have the service or product, the more likely they are to buy it, or the more they will pay for it, or the greater the **benefit they receive** (see the short case 'When speed means life or death').

Speed increases value for some customers

Speed inside the operation

Inside the operation, speed is also important. Fast response to external customers is greatly helped by speedy decision-making and speedy movement of materials and information inside the operation. Speed brings other benefits too.

Speed could mean . . .

Hospital
- The time between requiring treatment and receiving treatment kept to a minimum
- The time for test results, X-rays, etc. to be returned kept to a minimum

Automobile plant
- The time between dealers requesting a vehicle of a particular specification and receiving it kept to a minimum
- The time to deliver spares to service centres kept to a minimum

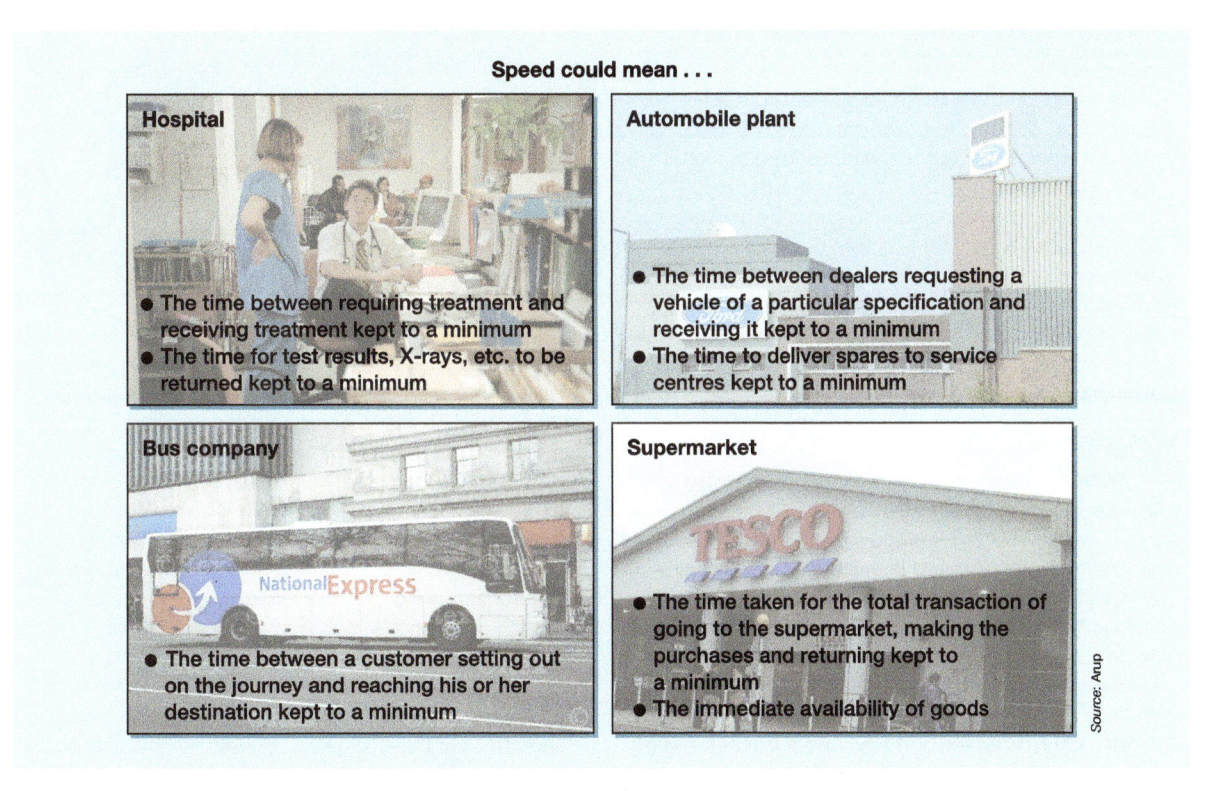

Bus company
- The time between a customer setting out on the journey and reaching his or her destination kept to a minimum

Supermarket
- The time taken for the total transaction of going to the supermarket, making the purchases and returning kept to a minimum
- The immediate availability of goods

Source: Arup

Figure 3.5 Speed means different things in different operations

Speed reduces inventories. Take, for example, the automobile plant. Steel for the vehicle's door panels is delivered to the press shop, pressed into shape, transported to the painting area, coated for colour and protection, and moved to the assembly line where it is fitted to the automobile. This is a simple three-stage process, but in practice material does not flow smoothly from one stage to the next. Firstly, the steel is delivered as part of a far larger batch containing enough steel to make possibly several hundred products. Eventually it is taken to the press area, pressed into shape, and again waits to be transported to the paint area. It then waits to be painted, only to wait once more until it is transported to the assembly line. Yet again, it waits until it is eventually fitted to the automobile. The material's journey time is far longer than the time needed to make and fit the product. It actually spends most of its time waiting as stocks (inventories) of parts and products. The longer items take to move through a process, the more time they will be waiting and the higher inventory will be.

Speed reduces risks. Forecasting tomorrow's events is far less of a risk than forecasting next year's. The further ahead companies forecast, the more likely they are to get it wrong. The faster the throughput time of a process the later forecasting can be left. Consider the automobile plant again. If the total throughput time for the door panel is six weeks, door panels are being processed through their first operation six weeks before they reach their final destination. The quantity of door panels being processed will be determined by the forecasts for demand six weeks ahead. If instead of six weeks, they take only one week to move through the plant, the door panels being processed through their first stage are intended to meet demand only one week ahead. Under these circumstances it is far more likely that the number and type of door panels being processed are the number and type which eventually will be needed.

Short case
When speed means life or death[3]

Of all the operations which have to respond quickly to customer demand, few have more need of speed than the emergency services. In responding to road accidents especially, every second is critical. The treatment you receive during the first hour after your accident (what is called the 'golden hour') can determine whether you survive and fully recover or not. Making full use of the golden hour means speeding up three elements of the total time to treatment – the time it takes for the emergency services to find out about the accident, the time it takes them to travel to the scene of the accident, and the time it takes to get the casualty to appropriate treatment.

Alerting the emergency services immediately is the idea behind Mercedes-Benz's TeleAid system. As soon as the vehicle's airbag is triggered, an on-board computer reports through the mobile phone network to a control centre (drivers can also trigger the system manually if not too badly hurt), satellite tracking allows the vehicle to be precisely located and the owner identified (if special medication is needed). Getting to the accident quickly is the next hurdle. Often the fastest method is by helicopter. When most rescues are only a couple of minutes' flying time back to the hospital speed can really saves lives.

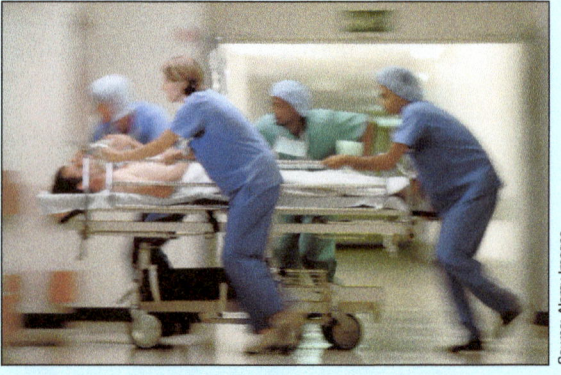

However, it is not always possible to land a helicopter safely at night (because of possible overhead wires and other hazards) so conventional ambulances will always be needed, both to get paramedics quickly to accident victims and to speed them to hospital. One increasingly common method of ensuring that ambulances arrive quickly at the accident site is to position them, not at hospitals, but close to where accidents are likely to occur. Computer analysis of previous accident data helps to select the ambulance's waiting position, and global positioning systems help controllers to mobilize the nearest unit. At all times a key requirement for fast service is effective communication between all who are involved in each stage of the emergency. Modern communications technology can play an important role in this.

Social, Environmental and Economic Performance   97

The dependability objective

Dependability means doing things in time for customers to receive their services or products exactly when they are needed, or at least when they were promised. Figure 3.6 illustrates what dependability means in the four operations. Customers might only judge the dependability of an operation after the service or product has been delivered. Initially this may not affect the likelihood that customers will select the service – they have already 'consumed' it. **Over time**, however, dependability can override all other criteria. No matter how cheap or fast a bus service is, if the service is always late (or unpredictably early) or the buses are always full, then potential passengers will be better off calling a taxi.

Dependability is judged over time

Dependability could mean . . .

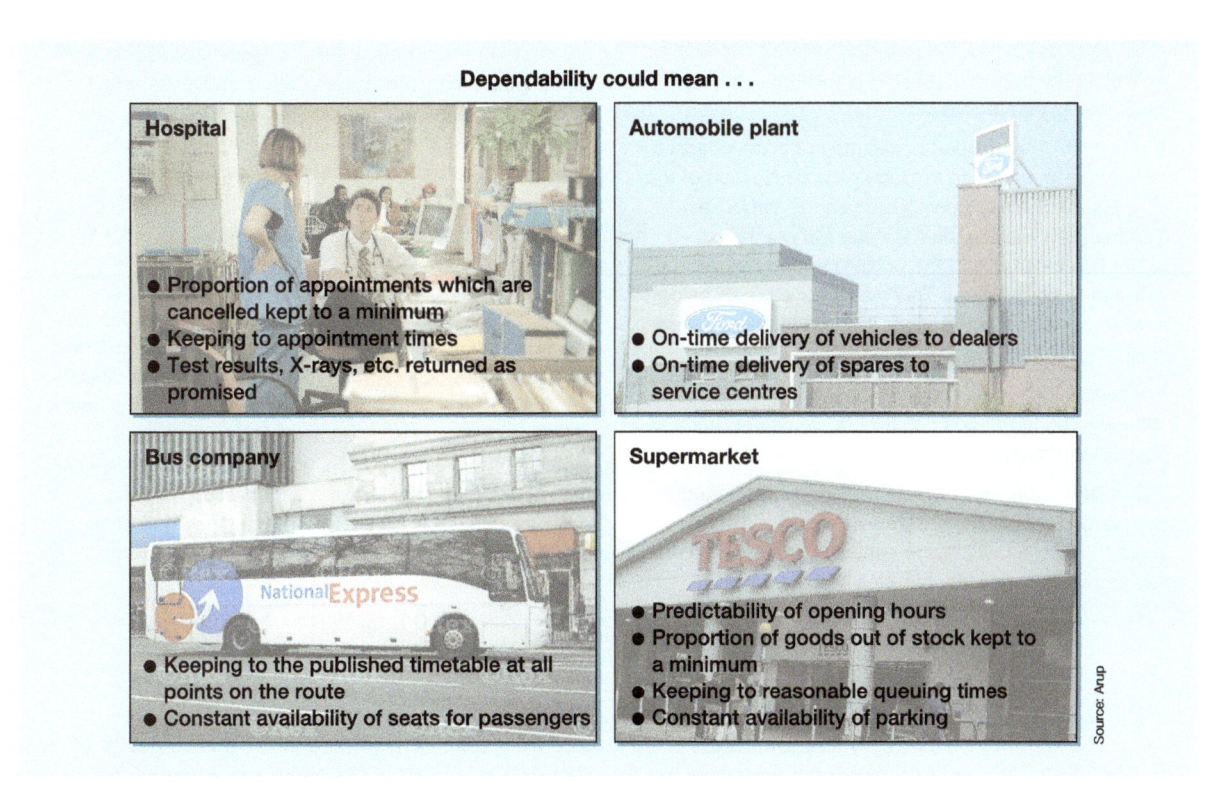

Hospital
- Proportion of appointments which are cancelled kept to a minimum
- Keeping to appointment times
- Test results, X-rays, etc. returned as promised

Automobile plant
- On-time delivery of vehicles to dealers
- On-time delivery of spares to service centres

Bus company
- Keeping to the published timetable at all points on the route
- Constant availability of seats for passengers

Supermarket
- Predictability of opening hours
- Proportion of goods out of stock kept to a minimum
- Keeping to reasonable queuing times
- Constant availability of parking

Figure 3.6 Dependability means different things in different operations

---

Short case
Dabbawalas hit 99.9999% dependability[4]

Mumbai is India's most densely populated city, and every working day its millions of commuters crowd onto packed trains for an often lengthy commute to their workplaces. Going home for lunch is not possible, so many office workers have a cooked meal sent either from their home, or from a caterer. It is Mumbai's 5,000-strong dabbawala collective that provides this service, usually for a monthly fee. The meal is cooked in the morning (by family or caterer), placed in regulation dabbas or tiffin (lunch) boxes and delivered to each individual worker's office at lunch time. After lunch the boxes are collected and returned so that they can be re-sent the next day. 'Dabbawala' means 'one who carries a box', or more colloquially, 'lunch box delivery man'. This is how the service works:

7am–9am The dabbas (boxes) are collected by dabbawalas on bicycles from nearly 200,000 suburban homes or from the dabba makers and taken to railway stations. The dabbas have distinguishing marks on them, using colours and symbols (necessary because many dabbawalas are barely literate). The dabbawala then takes them to a designated sorting place, where he and other collecting dabbawalas sort (and sometimes bundle) the lunch boxes into groups.

9am–11am The grouped boxes are put in the coaches of trains, with markings to identify the destination of the box (usually there is a designated car for the boxes). The markings include the rail station where the boxes are to be unloaded and the building address where the box has to be delivered. This may involve boxes being sorted at intermediary stations, with each single dabba changing hands up to four times.

10am–12midday Dabbas taken into Mumbai using the otherwise under-utilized capacity on commuter trains in the mid-morning.

11am–12midday Arrive downtown Mumbai where dabbas are handed over to **local dabbawalas**, who distribute them to more locations where there is more sorting and loading on to handcarts, bicycles and dabbawalas.

12midday–1pm Dabbas are delivered to appropriate office locations.

2pm Process moves into reverse, after lunch, when the empty boxes are collected from office locations and returned to suburban stations.

6pm Empty dabbas sent back to the respective houses.

The service has a remarkable record of almost flawlessly reliable delivery, even on the days of severe weather such as Mumbai's characteristic monsoons. Dabbawalas all receive the same pay and at both the receiving and the sending ends, are known to the customers personally, so are trusted by customers. Also, they are well accustomed to the local areas they collect from or deliver to, which reduces the chances of errors. Raghunath Medge, the president of the Bombay Tiffin Box Supply Charity Trust, which oversees the dabbawallas, highlights the importance of their hands-on operations management. *'Proper time management is our key to success. We do everything to keep the customer happy and they help in our marketing.'* There is no system of documentation. The success of the operation depends on teamwork and human ingenuity. Such is the dedication and commitment of the barefoot delivery men (there are only a few delivery women) that the complex logistics operation works with only three layers of management. Although the service remains essentially low-tech, with the barefoot delivery men as the prime movers, the dabbawalas now use some modern technology, for example they now allow booking for delivery through SMS and their web site, (www.mydabbawala.com).

Dependability inside the operation

Inside the operation, internal customers will judge each other's performance partly by how reliable the other processes are in delivering material or information on time. Operations where internal dependability is high are more effective than those which are not, for a number of reasons.

Dependability saves time. Take, for example, the maintenance and repair centre for the city bus company. If the centre runs out of some crucial spare parts, the manager of the centre will need to spend time trying to arrange a special delivery of the required parts and the resources allocated to service the buses will not be used as productively as they would have been without this disruption. More seriously, the fleet will be short of buses until they can be repaired and the fleet operations manager will have to spend time rescheduling services. So, entirely due to the one failure of dependability of supply, a significant part of the operation's time has been wasted coping with the disruption.

Dependability saves money. Ineffective use of time will translate into extra cost. The spare parts might cost more to be delivered at short notice and maintenance staff will expect to be paid even when there is not a bus to work on. Nor will the fixed costs of the operation, such as heating and rent, be reduced because the two buses are not being serviced. The rescheduling of buses will probably mean that some routes have inappropriately sized buses and some services could have to be cancelled. This will result in empty bus seats (if too large a bus has to be used) or a loss of revenue (if potential passengers are not transported).

Social, Environmental and Economic Performance

Dependability gives stability. The disruption caused to operations by a lack of dependability goes beyond time and cost. It affects the 'quality' of the operation's time. If everything in an operation is always perfectly dependable, a level of trust will have built up between the different parts of the operation. There will be no 'surprises' and everything will be predictable. Under such circumstances, each part of the operation can concentrate on improving its own area of responsibility without having its attention continually diverted by a lack of dependable service from the other parts.

The flexibility objective

> Flexibility means being able to change in some way

Flexibility means being able to **change** the operation in some way. This may mean changing what the operation does, how it is doing it, or when it is doing it. Specifically, customers will need the operation to change so that it can provide four types of requirement:

> Service/product flexibility

- **Service/product flexibility** – the operation's ability to introduce new or modified services and products;

> Mix flexibility

- **mix flexibility** – the operation's ability to create a wide range or mix of services and products;

> Volume flexibility

- **volume flexibility** – the operation's ability to change its level of output or activity to produce different quantities or volumes of services and products over time;

> Delivery flexibility

- **delivery flexibility** – the operation's ability to change the timing of the delivery of its services or products.

Figure 3.7 gives examples of what these different types of flexibility mean to the four different operations.

Flexibility could mean...

Hospital
- Service/product flexibility – the introduction of new types of treatment
- Mix flexibility – a wide range of available treatments
- Volume flexibility – the ability to adjust the number of patients treated
- Delivery flexibility – the ability to reschedule appointments

Automobile plant
- Service/product flexibility – the introduction of new models
- Mix flexibility – a wide range of options available
- Volume flexibility – the ability to adjust the number of vehicles manufactured
- Delivery flexibility – the ability to reschedule manufacturing priorities

Bus company
- Service/product flexibility – the introduction of new routes or excursions
- Mix flexibility – a large number of locations served
- Volume flexibility – the ability to adjust the frequency of services
- Delivery flexibility – the ability to reschedule trips

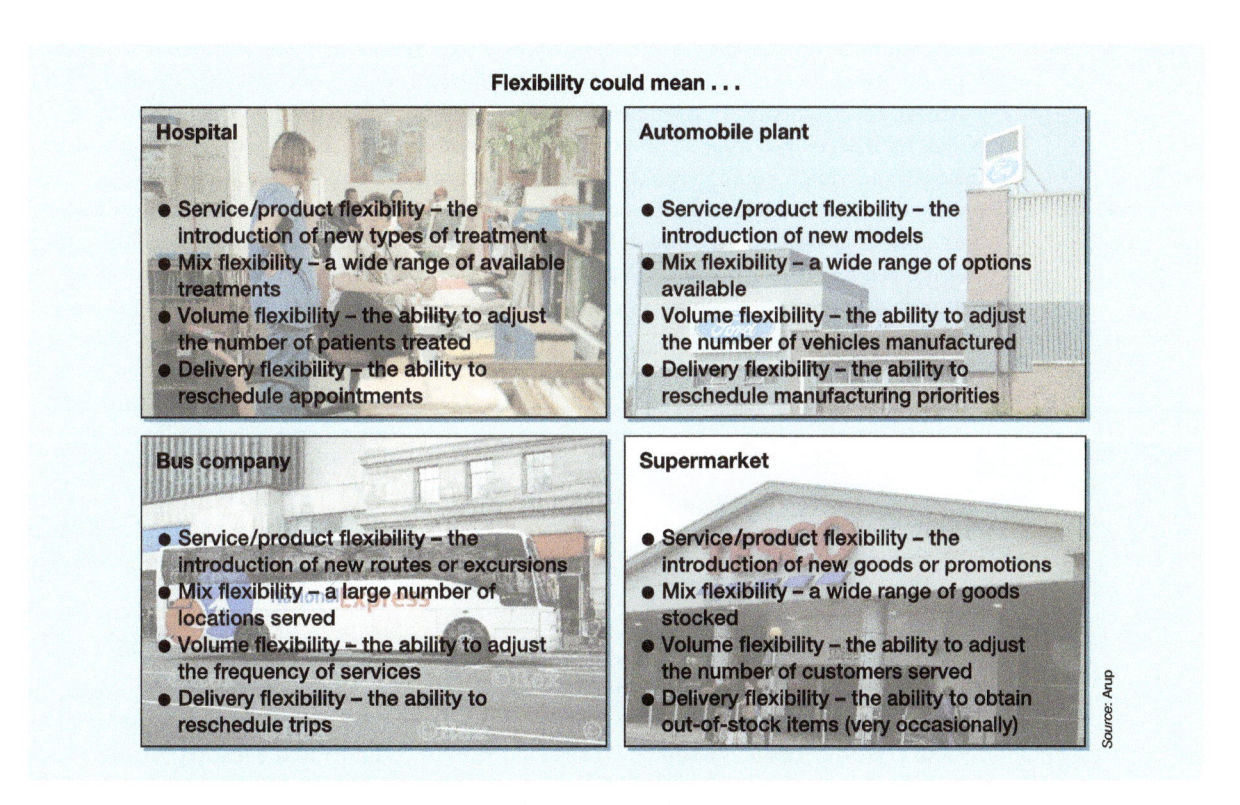

Supermarket
- Service/product flexibility – the introduction of new goods or promotions
- Mix flexibility – a wide range of goods stocked
- Volume flexibility – the ability to adjust the number of customers served
- Delivery flexibility – the ability to obtain out-of-stock items (very occasionally)

Source: Arup

Figure 3.7 Flexibility means different things in different operations

Short case
Flexibility and dependability in the newsroom[5]

Television news is big business. Satellite and cable, as well as developments in terrestrial transmission, have all helped to boost the popularity of 24-hour news services. However, news perishes fast. A daily newspaper delivered one day late is practically worthless. This is why broadcasting organizations like the BBC have to ensure that up-to-date news is delivered on time, every time. The BBC's ability to achieve high levels of dependability is made possible by the technology employed in news gathering and editing. At one time news editors would have to schedule a video-taped report to start its countdown five seconds prior to its broadcasting time. With new technology the video can be started from a freeze-frame and will broadcast the instant the command to play is given. The team have faith in the dependability of the process. In addition, technology allows them the flexibility to achieve dependability, even when news stories break just before transmission. In the hours before scheduled transmission, journalists and editors prepare an 'inventory' of news items stored electronically. The presenter will prepare his or her commentary on the autocue and each item will be timed to the second. If the team needs to make a short-term adjustment to the planned schedule, the news studio's technology allows the editors to take broadcasts live from journalists at their locations, on satellite 'takes', directly into the programme. Editors can even type news reports directly onto the autocue for the presenter to read as they are typed – nerve-racking, but it keeps the programme on time.

Mass customization

One of the beneficial external effects of flexibility is the increased ability of operations to do different things for different customers. So, high flexibility gives the ability to create a high variety of services or products. Normally high variety means high cost (see Chapter 1). Furthermore, high-variety operations do not usually produce in high volume. Some companies have developed their flexibility in such a way that products and services are customized for each individual customer. Yet they manage to produce them in a high-volume, mass-production manner which keeps costs down. This approach is called **mass customization**. Sometimes this is achieved through flexibility in design. For example, Dell is one of the largest volume producers of personal computers in the world, yet allows each customer to 'design' (albeit in a limited sense) their own configuration. Sometimes flexible technology is used to achieve the same effect. For example, Paris Miki, an up-market eyewear retailer which has the largest number of eyewear stores in the world, uses its own 'Mikissimes Design System' to capture a digital image of the customer and analyse facial characteristics. Together with a list of customers' personal preferences, the system then recommends a particular design and displays it on the image of the customer's face. In consultation with the optician the customer can adjust shapes and sizes until the final design is chosen. Within the store the frames are assembled from a range of pre-manufactured components and the lenses ground and fitted to the frames. The whole process takes around an hour.

Agility

Judging operations in terms of their **agility** has become popular. Agility is really a combination of all the five performance objectives, but particularly flexibility and speed. In addition, agility implies that an operation and the supply chain of which it is a part (supply networks are described in Chapter 7) can respond to uncertainty in the market. Agility means responding to market requirements by creating new and existing services and products fast and flexibly.

Flexibility inside the operation

Developing a flexible operation can also have advantages to the internal customers within the operation.

Flexibility speeds up response. Fast service often depends on the operation being flexible. For example, if the hospital has to cope with a sudden influx of patients from a road accident, it clearly needs to deal with injuries quickly. Under such circumstances a flexible hospital which can speedily transfer extra skilled staff and equipment to the Accident and Emergency department will provide the fast service which the patients need.

Flexibility saves time. In many parts of the hospital, staff have to treat a wide variety of complaints. Fractures, cuts or drug overdoses do not come in batches. Each patient is an individual with individual needs. The hospital staff cannot take time to 'get into the routine' of treating a particular complaint; they must have the flexibility to adapt quickly. They must also have sufficiently flexible facilities and equipment so that time is not wasted waiting for equipment to be brought to the patient. The time of the hospital's resources is being saved because they are flexible in 'changing over' from one task to the next.

Flexibility maintains dependability. Internal flexibility can also help to keep the operation on schedule when unexpected events disrupt the operation's plans. For example, if the sudden influx of patients to the hospital requires emergency surgical procedures, routine operations will be disrupted. This is likely to cause distress and considerable inconvenience. A flexible hospital might be able to minimize the disruption by possibly having reserved operating theatres for such an emergency, and being able to bring in medical staff quickly that are 'on call'.

The cost objective

To the companies which compete directly on price, cost will clearly be their major operations objective. The lower the cost of creating and delivering their services and products, the lower can be the price to their customers. Even those companies which do not compete on price will be interested in keeping costs low. Every euro or dollar removed from an operation's

Short case
Everyday low prices at Aldi[6]

Aldi is an international 'limited assortment' supermarket specializing in 'private label', mainly food products. It has carefully focused its service concept and delivery system to attract customers in a highly competitive market. The company believes that its unique approach to operations management make it 'virtually impossible for competitors to match our combination of price and quality'.

Aldi operations challenge the norms of retailing. They are deliberately simple, using basic facilities to keep down overheads. Most stores stock only a limited range of goods (typically around 700 compared with 25,000 to 30,000 stocked by conventional supermarket chains). The private label approach means that the products have been produced according to Aldi quality specifications and are only sold in Aldi stores. Without the high costs of brand marketing and advertising and with Aldi's formidable purchasing power, prices can be 30 per cent below their branded equivalents. Other cost-saving practices include open carton displays which eliminate the need for special shelving, no grocery bags to encourage reuse as well as saving costs, and using a 'cart rental' system which requires customers to return the cart to the store to get their coin deposit back.

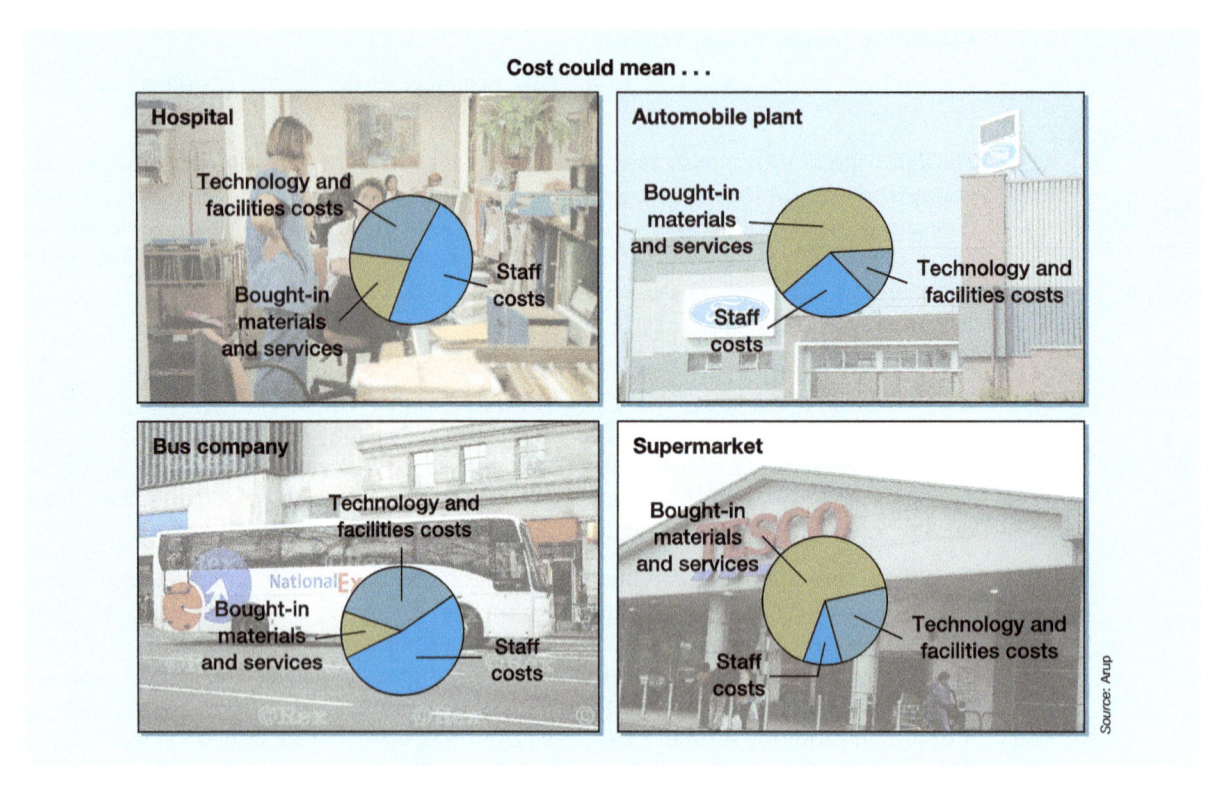

Figure 3.8 Cost means different things in different operations

---

Low cost is a universally attractive objective

cost base is a further euro or dollar added to its profits. Not surprisingly, **low cost is a universally attractive objective**. The short-case 'Everyday low prices at Aldi' describes how one retailer keeps its costs down. The ways in which operations management can influence cost will depend largely on where the operation costs are incurred. The operation will spend its money on staff (the money spent on employing people), facilities, technology and equipment (the money spent on buying, caring for, operating and replacing the operation's 'hardware') and materials (the money spent on the 'bought-in' materials consumed or transformed in the operation). Figure 3.8 shows typical cost breakdowns for the hospital, car plant, supermarket and bus company.

Cost reduction through internal effectiveness

Our previous discussion distinguished between the benefits of each performance objective to externally and internally. Each of the various performance objectives has several internal effects, but **all of them affect cost**. So, one important way to improve cost performance is to improve the performance of the other operations objectives (see Figure 3.9).

All performance objectives affect cost

- High-quality operations do not waste time or effort having to re-do things, nor are their internal customers inconvenienced by flawed service.
- Fast operations reduce the level of in-process inventory between and within processes, as well as reducing administrative overheads.
- Dependable operations do not spring any unwelcome surprises on their internal customers. They can be relied on to deliver exactly as planned. This eliminates wasteful disruption and allows the other micro-operations to operate efficiently.
- Flexible operations adapt to changing circumstances quickly and without disrupting the rest of the operation. Flexible micro-operations can also change over between tasks quickly and without wasting time and capacity.

External effects of the five performance objectives

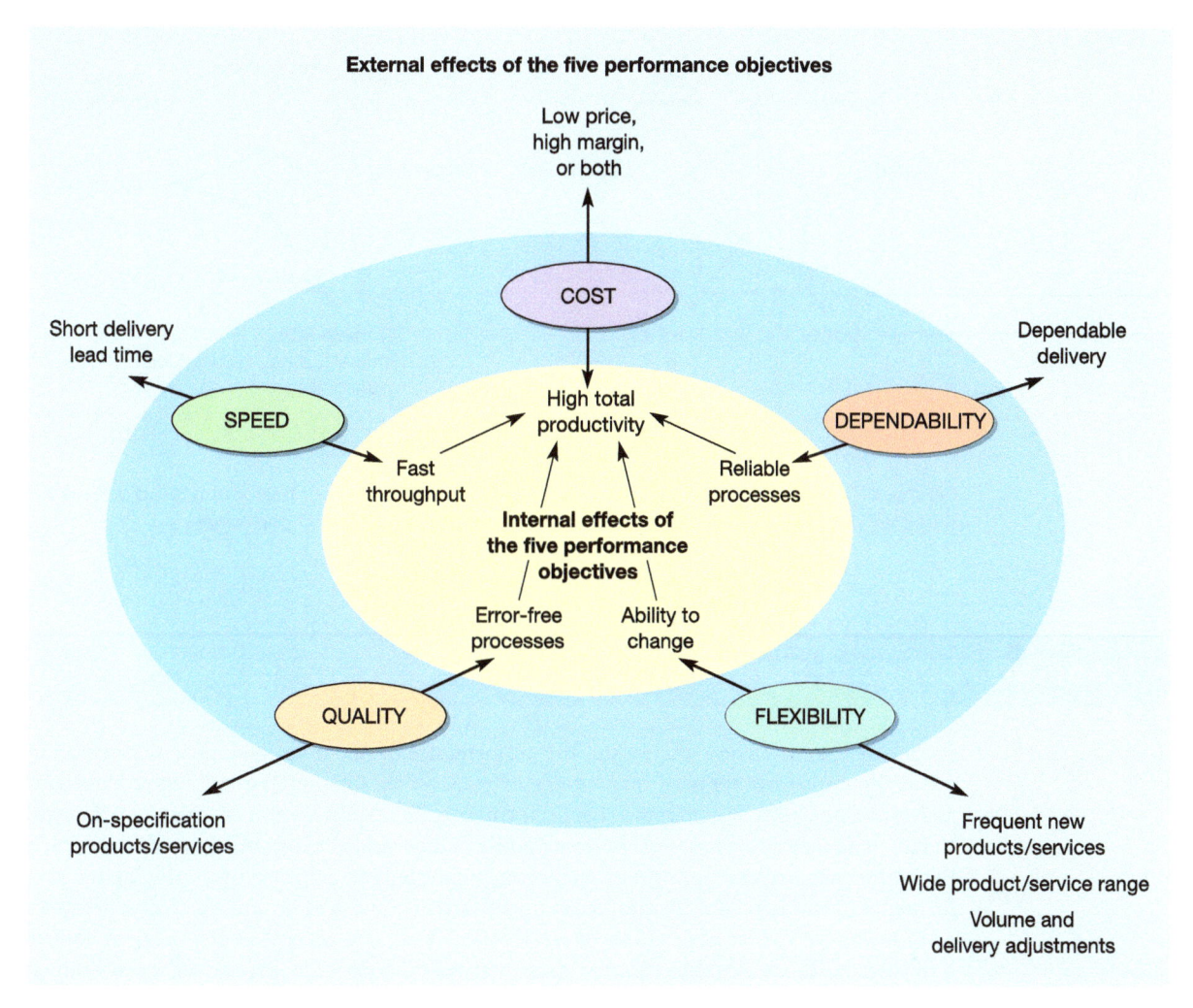

Figure 3.9 Performance objectives have both external and internal effects. Internally, cost is influenced by the other performance objectives

The polar representation of performance objectives

Polar representation

A useful way of representing the relative importance of performance objectives for a product or service is shown in Figure 3.10(a). This is called the **polar representation** because the scales which represent the importance of each performance objective have the same origin. A line describes the relative importance of each performance objective. The closer the line is to the centre, the less important is the performance objective to the operation. Two services are shown, a taxi and a bus service. Each essentially provides the same basic service, but with different objectives. The differences between the two services are clearly shown by the diagram. Of course, the polar diagram can be adapted to accommodate any number of different performance objectives. For example, Figure 3.10(b) shows a proposal for using a polar diagram to assess the relative performance of different police forces in the UK.[7] Note that this proposal uses three measures of quality (reassurance, crime reduction and crime detection), one measure of cost (economic efficiency), and one measure of how the police force develops its relationship with 'internal' customers (the criminal justice agencies). Note also that actual performance as well as required performance is marked on the diagram.

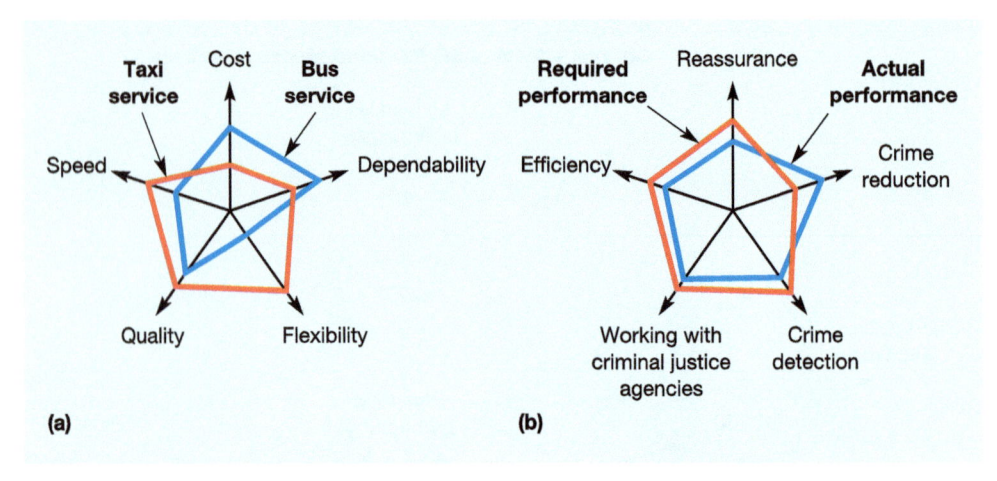

Figure 3.10 Polar representations of (a) the relative importance of performance objectives for a taxi service and a bus service, and (b) a police force targets and performance

Trade-offs between performance objectives

Earlier we examined how improving the performance of one objective inside the operation could also improve other performance objectives. Most notably, better quality, speed, dependability and flexibility can improve cost performance. But externally this is not always the case. In fact there may be a '*trade-off*' **between performance objectives**. In other words improving the performance of one performance objective might only be achieved by sacrificing the performance of another. So, for example, an operation might wish to improve its cost efficiencies by reducing the variety of products or services that it offers to its customers. '*There is no such thing as a free lunch*' could be taken as a summary of this approach. Probably the best-known summary of the trade-off idea comes from Professor Wickham Skinner, who said:

There can be a trade-off between an operation's performance objectives

> '*most managers will readily admit that there are compromises or trade-offs to be made in designing airplane or truck. In the case of an airplane, trade-offs would involve matters such as cruising speed, take-off and landing distances, initial cost, maintenance, fuel consumption, passenger comfort and cargo or passenger capacity. For instance, no one today can design a 500-passenger plane that can land on an aircraft carrier and also break the sound barrier. Much the same thing is true in [operations]*'.[8]

But there are two views of trade-offs. The first emphasizes 'repositioning' performance objectives by trading off improvements in some objectives for a reduction in performance in others. The other emphasizes increasing the 'effectiveness' of the operation by overcoming trade-offs so that improvements in one or more aspects of performance can be achieved without any reduction in the performance of others. Most businesses at some time or other will adopt both approaches. This is best illustrated through the concept of the '**efficient frontier**' of operations performance.

The efficient frontier

Trade-offs and the efficient frontier

Figure 3.11(a) shows the relative performance of several companies in the same industry in terms of their cost efficiency and the variety of products or services that they offer to their customers. Presumably all the operations would ideally like to be able to offer very high variety while still having very high levels of cost efficiency. However, the increased complexity that a high variety of product or service offerings brings will generally reduce the operation's ability to operate efficiently. Conversely, one way of improving cost efficiency is to severely

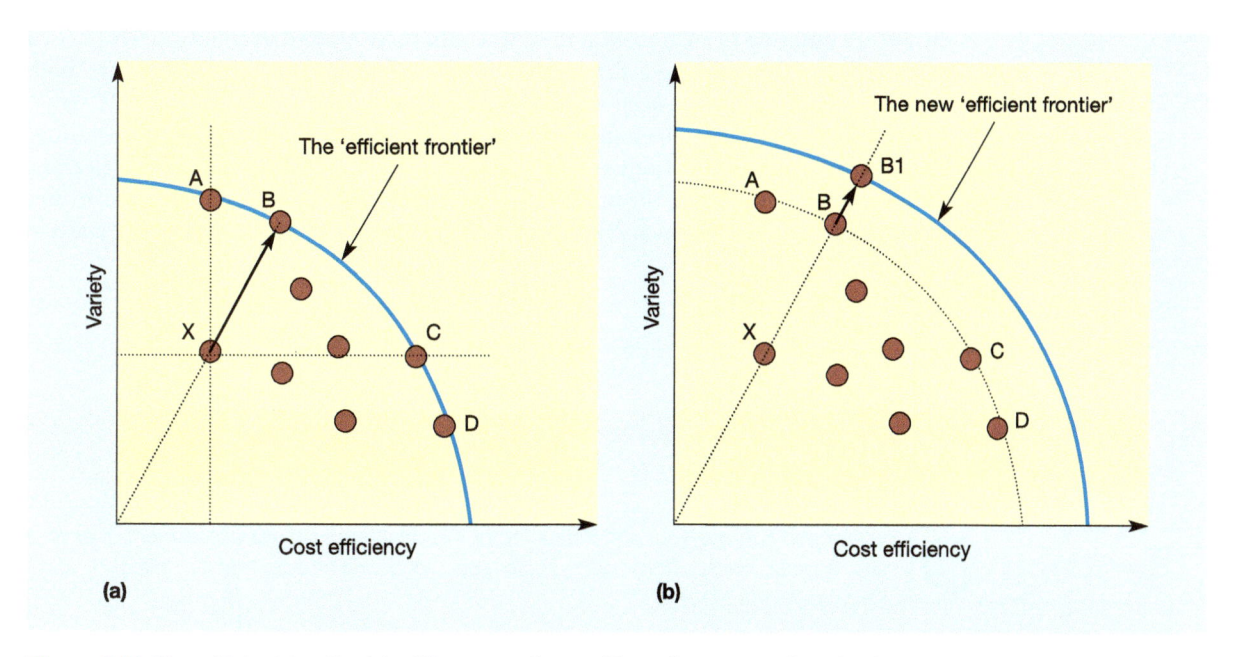

Figure 3.11 The efficient frontier identifies operations with performances that dominate other operations' performance

limit the variety on offer to customers. The spread of results in Figure 3.11(a) is typical of an exercise such as this. Operations A, B, C, D have all chosen a different balance between variety and cost efficiency. However, none is dominated by any other operation in the sense that another operation necessarily has 'superior' performance. Operation X, however, has an inferior performance because operation A is able to offer higher variety at the same level of cost efficiency and operation C offers the same variety but with better cost efficiency. The convex line on which operations A, B, C and D lie is known as the 'efficient frontier'. They may choose to position themselves differently (presumably because of different market strategies) but they cannot be criticized for being ineffective. Of course, any of these operations that lie on the efficient frontier may come to believe that the balance they have chosen between variety and cost efficiency is inappropriate. In these circumstances they may choose to reposition themselves at some other point along the efficient frontier. By contrast, operation X has also chosen to balance variety and cost efficiency in a particular way but is not doing so effectively. Operation B has the same ratio between the two performance objectives but is achieving them more effectively.

However, a strategy that emphasizes increasing effectiveness is not confined to those operations that are dominated, such as operation X. Those with a position on the efficient frontier will generally also want to improve their operations effectiveness by overcoming the trade-off that is implicit in the efficient frontier curve. For example, suppose operation B in Figure 3.11(b) wants to improve both its variety and its cost efficiency simultaneously and move to position B1. It may be able to do this, but only if it adopts operations improvements that extend the efficient frontier. For example, one of the decisions that any supermarket manager has to make is how many checkout positions to open at any time. If too many checkouts are opened then there will be times when the checkout staff do not have any customers to serve and will be idle. The customers, however, will have excellent service in terms of little or no waiting time. Conversely, if too few checkouts are opened, the staff will be working all the time but customers will have to wait in long queues. There seems to be a direct trade-off between staff utilization (and therefore cost) and customer waiting time (speed of service). Yet even the supermarket manager might, for example, allocate a number of 'core' staff to operate the checkouts but also arrange for those other staff who are performing other jobs in the supermarket to be trained and 'on call' should demand suddenly increase. If the manager on duty sees a build-up of customers at the checkouts, these other staff could quickly be used to staff checkouts. By devising a flexible system of staff allocation, the manager can both improve customer service and keep staff utilization high.

This distinction between positioning on the efficient frontier and increasing operations effectiveness by extending the frontier is an important one. Any business must make clear the extent to which it is expecting the operation to reposition itself in terms of its performance objectives and the extent to which it is expecting the operation to improve its effectiveness in several ways simultaneously.

Summary answers to key questions

Check and improve your understanding of this chapter using self-assessment questions and a personalized study plan, audio and video downloads, and an eBook – all at www.myomlab.com.

▶ Why is operations performance important in any organization?

- Operations management can either 'make or break' any business. It is large and, in most businesses, represents the bulk of its assets, but also because the operations function gives the ability to compete by providing the ability to respond to customers and by developing the capabilities that will keep it ahead of its competitors in the future.

▶ How should the operations function judge itself?

- Operations performance can be judged using the 'triple bottom line' approach. This includes social, environmental and economic performance.

▶ What does top management expect from the operations function?

- Operations can contribute to the organization as a whole by:
  - achieving customer satisfaction
  - reducing the costs
  - reducing the risk of operational failure
  - reducing the amount of investment
  - providing the basis for future innovation.

▶ What are the performance objectives of operations and what are the internal and external benefits which derive from excelling in each of them?

- By 'doing things right', operations seek to influence the quality of the company's services and products. Externally, quality is an important aspect of customer satisfaction or dissatisfaction. Internally, quality operations both reduce costs and increase dependability.
- By 'doing things fast', operations seek to influence the speed with which services and products are delivered. Externally, speed is an important aspect of customer service. Internally, speed both reduces inventories by decreasing internal throughput time and reduces risks by delaying the commitment of resources.

- By 'doing things on time', operations seek to influence the dependability of the delivery of services and products. Externally, dependability is an important aspect of customer service. Internally, dependability within operations increases operational reliability, thus saving the time and money that would otherwise be taken up in solving reliability problems and also giving stability to the operation.

- By 'changing what they do', operations seek to influence the flexibility with which the company creates its offerings. Externally, flexibility can:
  - create new offerings (service/product flexibility);
  - create a wide range or mix of offerings (mix flexibility);
  - create different quantities or volumes of offerings (volume flexibility);
  - create offerings at different times (delivery flexibility).

  Internally, flexibility can help speed up response times, save time wasted in changeovers, and maintain dependability.

- By 'doing things cheaply', operations seek to influence the cost of the company's offerings. Externally, low costs allow organizations to reduce their price in order to gain higher volumes or, alternatively, increase their profitability on existing volume levels. Internally, cost performance is helped by good performance in the other performance objectives.

> **How do operations performance objectives trade off against each other?**

- Trade-offs are the extent to which improvements in one performance objective can be achieved by sacrificing performance in others. The 'efficient frontier' concept is a useful approach to articulating trade-offs and distinguishes between repositioning performance on the efficient frontier and improving performance by overcoming trade-offs.

Learning exercises

These problems and applications will help to improve your analysis of operations. You can find more practice problems as well as worked examples and guided solutions on MyOMLab at www.myomlab.com.

1 The 'forensic science' service of a European country has traditionally been organized to provide separate forensic science laboratories for each police force around the country. In order to save costs, the government has decided to centralize this service in one large central facility close to the country's capital. What do you think are the external advantages and disadvantages of this to the stakeholders of the operation? What do you think are the internal implications to the new centralized operation that will provide this service?

2 *Step 1.* Look again at the figures in the chapter which illustrate the meaning of each performance objective for the four operations. Consider the bus company and the supermarket, and in particular consider their external customers.

Step 2. Draw the relative required performance for both operations on a polar diagram.

Step 3. Consider the internal effects of each performance objective. For both operations, identify how quality, speed, dependability and flexibility can help to reduce the cost of producing their services.

3 Visit the websites of two or three large oil companies such as Exxon, Shell, Elf, etc. Examine how they describe their policies towards their customers, suppliers, shareholders, employees and society at large. Identify areas of the company's operations where there may be conflicts between the needs of these different stakeholder groups. Discuss or reflect on how (if at all) such companies try and reconcile these conflicts.

Want to know more?

Bourne, M., Kennerley, M. and Franco, M. (2005) Managing through measures: a study of the impact on performance, *Journal of Manufacturing Technology Management*, vol. 16, issue 4, 373–95. What it says on the tin.

Kaplan, R.S. and Norton, D.P. (2005) The Balanced Scorecard: measures that drive performance, *Harvard Business Review*, Jul/Aug. The latest pronouncements on the Balanced Scorecard approach.

Pine, B.J. (1993) *Mass Customization*, Harvard Business School Press, Boston. The first substantial work on the idea of mass customization. Still a classic.

Savitz, A.W. and Weber, K. (2006) *The Triple Bottom Line: How Today's Best-Run Companies Are Achieving Economic, Social and Environmental Success – and How You Can Too*, Jossey-Bass, San Francisco, CA. An up-to-date treatment of the triple bottom line.

Waddock, S. (2003) Stakeholder performance implications of corporate responsibility, *International Journal of Business Performance Management*, vol. 5, numbers 2–3, 114–24. An introduction to stakeholder analysis.

Useful websites

www.aomonline.org General strategy site of the American Academy of Management.

www.cranfield.ac.uk/som Look for the 'Best factory awards' link. Manufacturing, but interesting.

www.opsman.org Lots of useful stuff.

www.worldbank.org Global issues. Useful for international operations strategy research.

www.weforum.org Global issues, including some operations strategy ones.

www.ft.com Great for industry and company examples.

Now that you have finished reading this chapter, why not visit MyOMLab at www.myomlab.com where you'll find more learning resources to help you make the most of your studies and get a better grade.

Chapter 4

The design of services and products

Key questions

- Why is good service and product design important?
- What are the stages in service and product design?
- Why and how should service and product design be considered interactively with process design?

Introduction

Services and products are often the first thing that customers see of a company, so they should have an impact. Whilst operations managers may not have direct responsibility for service and product design, they always have an indirect responsibility to provide the information and advice upon which successful development depends. However, operations managers are increasingly expected to take a more active part in design. Unless a service, however well conceived, can be implemented and unless a product, however well designed, can be produced to a high standard, the design can never bring its full benefits. Figure 4.1 shows where this chapter fits into the overall operations model.

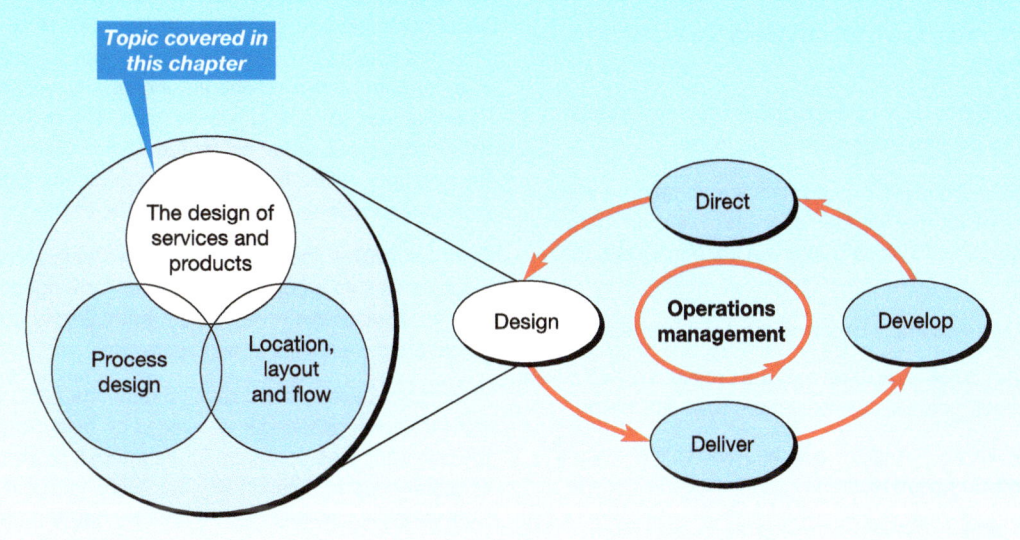

Figure 4.1 This chapter examines service and product design

Check and improve your understanding of this chapter using self-assessment questions and a personalized study plan, audio and video downloads, and an eBook – all at www.myomlab.com.

Operations in practice: The troubled history of the Airbus A380[1]

It is perhaps inevitable that a major new and complex product like a passenger aircraft will experience a few problems during its development. The history of the Airbus A380 was a long and incident-packed journey from drawing board to reality that illustrates the dangers when the design activity goes wrong. This is the story in brief.

1991 – Airbus consults with international airlines about their requirements for a super-large passenger aircraft.

January 1993 – Airbus rival Boeing says it has begun studies into 'very large' commercial aircraft.

June 1993 – Boeing decides not to go for a super-large passenger aircraft, but instead to focus on designing smaller 'jumbos'. Airbus and its partners set up the A3XX team to start the 'super-jumbo' project.

1996 – Airbus forms its 'Large Aircraft' Division. Because of the size of the aircraft, it is decided to develop specially designed engines rather than adapt existing models.

2000 – The commercial launch of the A3XX (later to be named the A380).

2002 – Work starts on manufacturing the aircraft's key components.

February 2004 – Rolls-Royce delivers the first Airbus engines to the assembly plant in Toulouse.

April 2004 – The first Airbus wings are completed in the North Wales factory. London's Heathrow airport starts to redevelop its facilities so that it can accommodate the new aircraft.

May 2004 – Assembly begins in the Toulouse plant.

December 2004 – EADS reveals the project is €1.45 billion over budget, and will now cost more than €12 billion.

January 2005 – Airbus unveils the A380 to the world's press and European leaders.

27 April 2005 – The aircraft makes its maiden flight, taking off in Toulouse and circling the Bay of Biscay for four hours before returning to Toulouse. A year of flight-testing and certification work begins.

June 2005 – Airbus announces that the plane's delivery schedule will slip by six months.

March 2006 – The plane passes important safety tests involving 850 passengers and 20 crew safely leaving the aircraft in less than 80 seconds with half the exits blocked.

July 2006 – The A380 suffers another production delay. Airbus now predicts a delay of a further six to seven months. This causes turmoil in the boardrooms of both Airbus and its parent company EADS. The company's directors are accused of suppressing the news for months before revealing it to shareholders. It leads to the resignations of Airbus' chief executive, co-chief executive, and the A380 programme manager.

October 2006 – Airbus infuriates customers by announcing yet a further delay for the A380, this time of a whole year. The first plane is now forecast to enter commercial service around twenty months later than had been originally planned. The delays will cost Airbus another estimated €4.8 billion over the next four years. The company announces a drastic cost-cutting plan to try to recoup some of the losses.

October 2007 – The super-jumbo eventually takes off in full service as a commercial airliner for Singapore Airlines. It wins rave reviews from both airlines and passengers – even if it is two years late!

So what caused the delays? Firstly, the A380 was the most complex passenger jet ever to be built. Secondly, the company was notorious for its internal rivalries, its constant need to balance work between its French and German plants so that neither country had too obvious an advantage, constant political infighting, particularly by the French and German governments, and frequent changes of management. According to one insider, 'the underlying reason for the mess we were in was the hopeless lack of integration [between the French and German sides] within the company'. Eventually it was this lack of integration between design and manufacturing processes that was the main reason for the delays to the aircraft's launch. During the early design stages the firm's French and German factories had used incompatible software to design the 500 km of wiring that each plane needs. Eventually, to resolve the cabling problems, the company had to transfer two thousand German staff from Hamburg to Toulouse. Processes that should have been streamlined had to be replaced by temporary and less efficient ones, described by one French union official as a *'do-it-yourself system'*. Feelings ran high on the shopfloor, with tension and arguments between French and German staff. *'The German staff will first have to succeed at doing the work they should have done in Germany'*, said the same official. Electricians had to resolve the complex wiring problems, with the engineers having to adjust the computer blueprints as they modified them so they could be used on future aircraft. *'Normal installation time is two to three weeks'*, said Sabine Klauke, a team leader. *'This way it is taking us four months.'* Mario Heinen, who ran the cabin and fuselage cross-border division, admitted the pressure to keep up with intense production schedules and the overcrowded conditions made things difficult. *'We have been working on these initial aircraft in a handmade way. It is not a perfectly organized industrial process.'* He claimed, there was no choice. *'We have delivered five high-quality aircraft this way. If we had left the work in Hamburg, to wait for a new wiring design, we would not have delivered one by now.'* The toll taken by these delays was high. The improvised wiring processes were far more expensive than the planned 'streamlined' processes and the delay in launching the aircraft meant two years without the revenue that the company had expected.

However, Airbus was not alone. Its great rival, Boeing, was also having problems. Engineers' strikes, supply chain problems and mistakes by its own design engineers had further delayed its '787 Dreamliner' aircraft. Specifically, fasteners used to attach the titanium floor grid to the composite 'barrel' of the fuselage had been wrongly located, resulting in 8,000 fasteners having to be replaced. By 2011 it looked as if the Boeing aircraft was also going to be two years late.

Why is good design so important?

Good design satisfies customers, communicates the purpose of the service or product to its market, and brings financial rewards to the business. The objective of good design, whether of services or products, is to satisfy customers by meeting their actual or anticipated needs and expectations. This, in turn, enhances the competitiveness of the organization. Service and product design, therefore, can be seen as starting and ending with the customer. Service designers try to put together a service which meets, or even exceeds, customer expectations. Yet at the same time the service must be within the capabilities of the operation and be delivered at reasonable cost. Product designers try to achieve aesthetically pleasing designs which meet or exceed customers' expectations. They also try to design a product which performs well and is reliable during its lifetime. Further, they should design the product so that it can be manufactured easily and quickly. In fact, the business case for putting effort into good service and product design is overwhelming according to the UK Design Council.[2] Using design throughout the business ultimately boosts the bottom line by helping create better products and services that compete on value rather than price. **Design** helps businesses connect strongly with their customers by anticipating their real needs. That in turn gives them the ability to set themselves apart in increasingly tough markets.

Good design enhances profitability

Critical commentary

Remember that not all new services and products are created in response to a clear and articulated customer need. While this is usually the case, especially for offerings that are similar to (but presumably better than) their predecessors, more radical innovations are often brought about by the innovation itself creating demand. Customers don't usually know that they need something radical. For example, in the late 1970s people were not asking for microprocessors, they did not even know what they were. They were improvised by an engineer in the USA for a Japanese customer who made calculators. Only later did they become the enabling technology for the PC and after that the innumerable devices that now dominate our lives.

What is designed in a service or product?

All services and products can be considered as having three aspects:

- a **concept**, which is the understanding of the nature, use and value of the service or product;
- a **package** of 'component' services and products that provide those benefits defined in the concept;
- the **process** defines the way in which the component services and products will be created and delivered.

The concept

Designers often talk about a 'new concept'. This might be a concept car specially created for an international show or a restaurant concept providing a different style of dining. The concept is a clear articulation of the outline specification including the nature, use and value of the product or service against which the stages of the design (see later) and the resultant product and/or service can be assessed. For example, a concept for a restaurant might be a bold and brash dining experience aimed at the early 20s market, with contemporary décor and music, providing a range of freshly made pizza and pasta dishes. Although the detailed design is important, customers are buying the particular concept. Patients consuming a pharmaceutical company's products are not particularly concerned about the ingredients contained in the drugs they are using nor about the way in which they were made, they are concerned about the notion behind them, how they will use them and the benefits they will provide for them. Thus the articulation, development and testing of the concept is a crucial stage in the design of products and services.

The package of services and products

Normally, the word 'service' implies a more intangible experience, such as an evening at a restaurant or a nightclub, and the word 'product' implies a tangible physical object, such as a car, washing machine or watch. In fact, as we discussed in Chapter 1, most, if not all, operations produce a combination of services *and* products. The purchase of a car includes the car itself and the services such as 'warranties', 'after-sales services' and 'the services of the person selling the car'. The restaurant meal includes products such as 'food' and 'drink' as well as services such as 'the delivery of the food to the table and the attentions of the waiting staff'. It is this collection of services and products that is usually referred to as the 'package' that customers buy. Some of the services or products in the package are **core**, that is they are fundamental to the purchase and could not be removed without destroying the nature of the package. Other parts will serve to enhance the core. These are **supporting services and products**. In the case of the car, the guarantees and leather trim are supporting services and products. The core good is the car itself. At the restaurant, the meal itself is the core. Its provision and preparation are important but not absolutely necessary (in some restaurants you might serve and even cook the meal yourself). By changing the core, or adding or subtracting supporting services and products, organizations can provide different packages and in so doing create quite different concepts. For instance, engineers may wish to add traction control and four-wheel drive to make the two-seater sports car more stable, but this might conflict with the concept of an 'economical' car with 'sensitive handling'.

The process

The package of components which make up a service and products, are the 'ingredients' of the design; however, designers need to design the way in which they will be created and delivered to the customer – this is process design. For the new car the assembly line has to be designed and built which will assemble the various components as the car moves down the line. The service processes of the delivery of cars to the showrooms and the sales processes have to be designed to support the concept. Likewise in the restaurant, the manufacturing processes of

Short case
Spangler, Hoover and Dyson[3]

In 1907 a janitor called Murray Spangler put together a pillowcase, a fan, an old biscuit tin and a broom handle. It was the world's first vacuum cleaner. One year later he sold his patented idea to William Hoover whose company went on to dominate the vacuum cleaner market for decades, especially in its United States homeland. Yet between 2002 and 2005, Hoover's market share dropped from 36 per cent to 13.5 per cent. Why? Because a futuristic-looking and comparatively expensive rival product, the Dyson vacuum cleaner, had jumped from nothing to over 20 per cent of the market. In fact, the Dyson product dates back to 1978 when James Dyson noticed how the air filter in the spray-finishing room of a company where he had been working was constantly clogging with powder particles (just like a vacuum cleaner bag clogs with dust). So he designed and built an industrial cyclone tower, which removed the powder particles by exerting centrifugal forces. The question intriguing him was, *'Could the same principle work in a domestic vacuum cleaner?'* Five years and five *thousand* prototypes later he had a working design, since praised for its 'uniqueness and functionality'. However, existing vacuum cleaner manufacturers were not as impressed – two rejected the design outright. So Dyson started making his new design himself. Within a few years Dyson cleaners were, in the UK, outselling the rivals that had once rejected them. The aesthetics and functionality of the design help to keep sales growing in spite of a higher retail price. To Dyson, good *'is about looking at everyday things with new eyes and working out how they can be made better. It's about challenging existing technology'*.

Dyson engineers have taken this technology one stage further and developed core separator technology to capture even more microscopic dirt. Dirt now goes through three stages of separation. Firstly, dirt is drawn into a powerful outer cyclone. Centrifugal forces fling larger debris, such as pet hair and dust particles, into the clear bin at 500 Gs (the maximum G-force the human body can take is 8 Gs). Secondly, a further cyclonic stage, the core separator, removes dust particles as small as 0.5 microns from the airflow – particles so small you could fit 200 of them on this full stop. Finally, a cluster of smaller, even faster cyclones generate centrifugal forces of up to 150,000 G – extracting particles as small as mould and bacteria.

James Dyson

food purchase, preparation and cooking need to be designed, just like the way in which the customers will be processed from reception to the bar or waiting area and to the table and the way in which the series of activities at the table will be performed in such a way as to deliver the agreed concept.

The design activity is itself a process

Producing designs for services and products is itself a process which conforms to the input–transformation–output model described in Chapter 1. It therefore has to be designed and managed like any other **process**. Figure 4.2 illustrates the design activity as an input–transformation–output diagram. The transformed resource inputs will consist mainly of information in the form of market forecasts, market preferences, technical data, and so on. Transforming resource inputs includes operations managers and specialist technical staff, design equipment and software such as computer-aided design (CAD) systems and simulation packages. One can describe the objectives of the design activity in the same way as we do any transformation process. All operations satisfy customers by producing their services and goods according to customers' desires for quality, speed, dependability, flexibility and cost. In the same way, the design activity attempts to produce designs to the same objectives.

The design activity is one of the most important operations processes

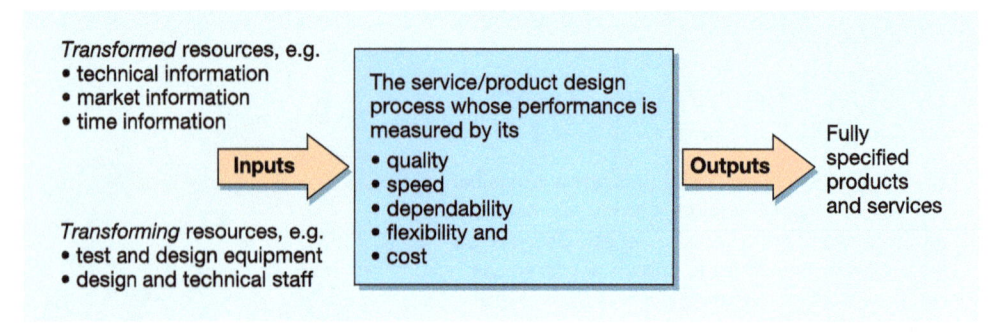

Figure 4.2 The design activity is itself a process

The stages of design – from concept to specification

Fully specified designs rarely spring, fully formed, from a designer's imagination. To get to a final design of a service or product, the design activity must pass through several key stages. These form an approximate sequence, although in practice designers will often recycle or backtrack through the stages. We will describe them in the order in which they usually occur, as shown in Figure 4.3. Firstly, comes the **concept generation** stage that develops the overall concept for the service or product. The concepts are then **screened** to try to ensure that, in broad terms, they will be a sensible addition to its portfolio and meet the concept as defined. The agreed concept has then to be turned into a **preliminary design** that then goes through a stage of **evaluation and improvement** to see if the concept can be served better, more cheaply or more easily. An agreed design may then be subjected to **prototyping and final design**.

Concept generation
Screening
Preliminary design
Evaluation and improvement
Prototyping and final design

Concept generation

The ideas for new concepts can come from sources outside the organization, such as customers or competitors, and from sources within the organization, such as staff (for example, from sales staff and front-of-house staff) or from the R&D department.

Ideas from customers. Marketing, the function generally responsible for identifying new service or product opportunities, may use many market research tools for gathering data from customers in a formal and structured way, including questionnaires and interviews. These techniques, however, usually tend to be structured in such a way as only to test out ideas or check products or services against predetermined criteria. Listening to the customer, in a less structured way, is sometimes seen as a better means of generating new ideas. **Focus groups**, for example, are one formal but unstructured way of collecting ideas and suggestions from customers. A focus group typically comprises seven to ten participants who are unfamiliar with each other but who have been selected because they have characteristics in common that

Focus groups

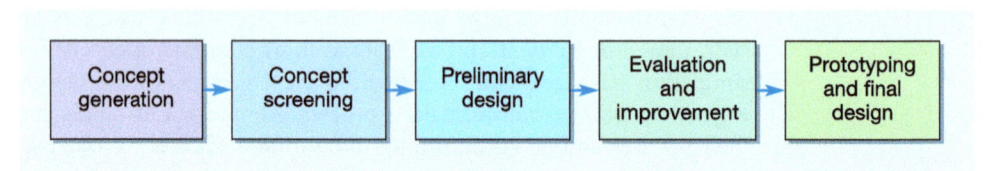

Figure 4.3 The stages of service/product design

relate to the particular topic of the focus group. Participants are invited to 'discuss' or 'share ideas with others' in a permissive environment that nurtures different perceptions and points of view, without pressurizing participants. The group discussion is conducted several times with similar types of participants in order to identify trends and patterns in perceptions. Ideas may also come from customers on a day-to-day basis. They may write to complain about a particular product or service, or make suggestions for its improvement.

Ideas from competitor activity. All market-aware organizations follow the activities of their competitors. A new idea may give a competitor an edge in the marketplace, even if it is only a temporary one, then competing organizations will have to decide whether to imitate, or alternatively to come up with a better or different idea. Sometimes this involves **reverse engineering**, that is taking apart a product to understand how a competing organization has made it. Some aspects of services may be more difficult to reverse-engineer (especially back-office services) as they are less transparent to competitors. However, by consumer-testing a service, it may be possible to make educated guesses about how it has been created. Many service organizations employ 'testers' to check out the services provided by competitors.

Ideas from staff. The contact staff in a service organization or the salesperson in a product-oriented organization could meet customers every day. These staff may have good ideas about what customers like and do not like. They may have gathered suggestions from customers or have ideas of their own as to how offerings could be developed to meet the needs of their customers more effectively.

Ideas from research and development. One formal function found in some organizations is **research and development** (R&D). As its name implies, its role is twofold. Research usually means attempting to develop new knowledge and ideas in order to solve a particular problem or to grasp an opportunity. Development is the attempt to try to utilize and operationalize the ideas that come from research. In this chapter we are mainly concerned with the 'development' part of R&D – for example, exploiting new ideas that might be afforded by new materials or new technologies. And although 'development' does not sound as exciting as 'research', it often requires as much creativity and even more persistence. Both creativity and persistence took James Dyson (see the short case earlier) from a potentially good idea to a workable technology. One product has commemorated the persistence of its development engineers in its company name. Back in 1953 the Rocket Chemical Company set out to create a rust-prevention solvent and degreaser to be used in the aerospace industry. Working in their lab in San Diego, California, it took them 40 attempts to get the water-displacing formula worked out. So that is what they called the product. WD-40 literally stands for water displacement, fortieth attempt. Originally used to protect the outer skin of the Atlas missile from rust and corrosion, the product worked so well that employees kept taking cans home to use for domestic purposes. Soon after, the product was launched, with great success, into the consumer market.

Open-sourcing – using a 'development community'[4]

Not all services or products are created by professional, employed designers for commercial purposes. Many of the software applications that we all use, for example, are developed by an open community, including the people who use the products. If you use Google, the Internet search facility, or Wikipedia, the online encyclopaedia, or shop at Amazon, you are using open-source software. The basic concept of open-source software is extremely simple. Large communities of people around the world, who have the ability to write software code, come together and produce software. The finished software is not only available to be used by anyone or any organization for free but is regularly updated to ensure it keeps pace with the necessary improvements. The production of open-source software like its commercial equivalent is continuously supported and maintained. However, unlike its commercial equivalent, it is absolutely free to use. With the maturity open-source software now has to offer, organizations have seen the benefits of using free software to drive down costs. It has been the biggest change in software development for decades and is setting new open standards in the way software is used.

The open nature of this type of development also encourages compatibility between products. BMW, for example, was reported to be developing an open-source platform for vehicle electronics. Using an open-source approach, rather than using proprietary software, BMW can allow providers of 'infotainment' services to develop compatible, plug-and-play applications. *'We were convinced we had to develop an open platform that would allow for open software since the speed in the infotainment and entertainment industry requires us to be on a much faster track'*, said Gunter Reichart, BMW vice-president of driver assistance, body electronics and electrical networks. *'We invite other OEMs to join with us, to exchange with us. We are open to exchange with others.'*

Short case
Square watermelons![5]

It sounds like a joke, but it is a genuine product innovation motivated by a market need. It's green, it's square and it originally comes from Japan. It's a square watermelon! Why square? Because Japanese grocery stores are not large and space cannot be wasted. A round watermelon does not fit into a refrigerator very conveniently and there is also the problem of trying to cut the fruit when it keeps rolling around. So an innovative farmer from Japan's south-western island of Shikoku solved the problem with the idea of making a cube-shaped watermelon which could easily be packed and stored. There is no genetic modification or clever science involved in growing watermelons. It simply involves placing the young fruit into wooden boxes with clear sides. During its growth, the fruit naturally swells to fill the surrounding shape. Now the idea has spread from Japan. *'Melons are among the most delicious and refreshing fruit around but some people find them a problem to store in their fridge or to cut because they roll around,'* said Damien Sutherland, the exotic fruit buyer from Tesco, the UK supermarket. 'We've seen samples of these watermelons and they literally stop you in their tracks because they are so eye-catching. These square melons will make it easier than ever to eat because they can be served in long strips rather than in the crescent shape.' However, not everyone liked the idea. Comments on news web sites included: *'Where will engineering everyday things for our own unreasonable convenience stop? I prefer melons to be the shape of melons!'*, *'They are probably working on straight bananas next!'*, and *'I would like to buy square sausages, then they would be easier to turn over in the frying pan.'*

Concept screening

Not all concepts which are generated will necessarily be capable of further development into services and products. Designers need to be selective as to which concepts they progress to the next design stage. The purpose of the concept-screening stage is to take the flow of concepts and evaluate them. Evaluation in design means assessing the worth or value of each design option, so that a choice can be made between them. This involves assessing each concept or option against a number of **design criteria**. While the criteria used in any particular design exercise will depend on the nature and circumstances of the exercise, it is useful to think in terms of three broad categories of design criteria:

Design criteria

The Design of Services and Products

Feasibility
- The **feasibility** of the design option – can we do it?
  - Do we have the skills (quality of resources)?
  - Do we have the organizational capacity (quantity of resources)?
  - Do we have the financial resources to cope with this option?

Acceptability
- The **acceptability** of the design option – do we want to do it?
  - Does the option satisfy the performance criteria which the design is trying to achieve? (These will differ for different designs.)
  - Will our customers want it?
  - Does the option give a satisfactory financial return?

Vulnerability
- The **vulnerability** of each design option – do we want to take the risk? That is,
  - Do we understand the full consequences of adopting the option?
  - Being pessimistic, what could go wrong if we adopt the option? What would be the consequences of everything going wrong? (This is called the 'downside risk' of an option.)

The design 'funnel'

Applying these evaluation criteria progressively reduces the number of options which will be available further along in the design activity. For example, deciding to make the outside casing of a camera case from aluminium rather than plastic limits later decisions, such as the overall size and shape of the case. This means that the uncertainty surrounding the design reduces as the number of alternative designs being considered decreases. Figure 4.4 shows what is sometimes called the **design funnel**, depicting the progressive reduction of design options from many to one. However, reducing design uncertainty also impacts on the cost of changing one's mind on some detail of the design. In most stages of design the cost of changing a decision is bound to incur some sort of rethinking and recalculation of costs. Early on in the design activity, before too many fundamental decisions have been made, the costs of change are relatively low. However, as the design progresses the interrelated and cumulative decisions already made become increasingly expensive to change.

Design funnel

> ### Critical commentary
>
> Not everyone agrees with the concept of the design funnel. For some it is just too neat and ordered an idea to reflect accurately the creativity, arguments and chaos that sometimes characterize the design activity. Firstly, they argue, managers do not start out with an infinite number of options. No one could process that amount of information – and anyway, designers often have some set solutions in their mind, looking for an opportunity to be used. Secondly, the number of options being considered often *increases* as time goes by. This may actually be a good thing, especially if the activity was unimaginatively specified in the first place. Thirdly, the real process of design often involves cycling back, often many times, as potential design solutions raise fresh questions or become dead ends. In summary, the idea of the design funnel does not describe what actually happens in the design activity. Nor does it necessarily even describe what *should* happen.

Balancing evaluation with creativity

Creativity is important in service/product design

The systematic process of evaluation is important but it must be balanced by the need for design creativity. **Creativity** is a vital ingredient in effective design. The final quality of any design of service or product will be influenced by the creativity of its designers. Increasingly, creativity is seen as an essential ingredient not just in the design of offerings, but also in the design of operations processes. Partly because of the fast-changing nature of many industries, a lack of creativity (and consequently of innovation) is seen as a major risk. For example, *'It has never been a better time to be an industry revolutionary. Conversely, it has never been a more dangerous time to be complacent . . . The dividing line between being a leader and being a laggard is today measured in months or a few days, and not in decades.'* Of course, creativity can be expensive. By its nature it involves exploring sometimes unlikely possibilities.

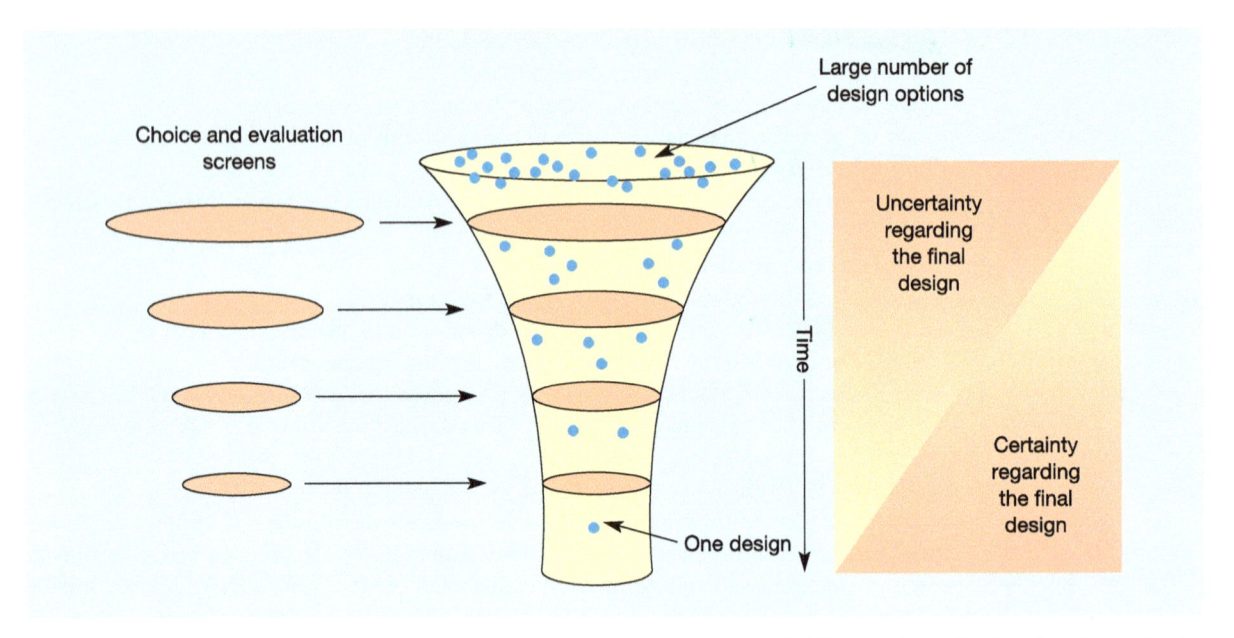

Figure 4.4 The design funnel – progressively reducing the number of possibilities until the final design is reached

Many of these will die as they are proved to be inappropriate. Yet, to some extent, the process of creativity depends on these many seemingly wasted investigations. As Art Fry, the inventor of 3M's Post-it note products, said: *'You have to kiss a lot of frogs to find the prince. But remember, one prince can pay for a lot of frogs.'*

Short case
The Daniel Hersheson Blowdry Bar at Topshop[6]

Even at the chic and stylish end of the hairdressing business, close as it is to the world of changing fashion trends, true innovation and genuinely novel new services are a relative rarity. Yet real service innovation can reap significant rewards as Daniel and Luke Hersheson, the father and son team behind the Daniel Hersheson salons, fully understand. The Hersheson brand has successfully bridged the gaps between salon, photo session and fashion catwalk. The team first put themselves on the fashion map with a salon in London's Mayfair followed by a salon and spa in Harvey Nichols's flagship London store.

Their latest innovation is the 'Blowdry Bar at Topshop'. This is a unique concept that is aimed at customers who want fashionable and catwalk quality styling at an affordable price without the full 'cut and blow-dry' treatment. The Hersheson Blowdry Bar was launched in December 2006 to ecstatic press coverage in Topshop's flagship Oxford Circus store. The four-seater pink pod within the Topshop store is a scissors-free zone dedicated to styling on the go. Originally seen as a walk-in, no-appointment-necessary format, demand has proved to be so high that an appointment system has been implemented to avoid disappointing customers. Once in the pod, customers can choose from a tailor-made picture menu of nine fashion styles with names like 'The Super Straight', 'The Classic Big and Bouncy' and 'Wavy Gravy'. Typically, the wash and blow-dry takes around 30 minutes. *'It's just perfect for a client who wants to look that bit special for a big night out but who doesn't want a full cut'*, says Ryan Wilkes, one of the stylists at the Blowdry Bar. *'Some clients will "graduate" to become regular customers at the main Daniel Hersheson salons. I have clients who started out using the Blowdry Bar but now also get their hair cut with me in the salon.'*

<mark>Partnering with Topshop is an important element in the design of the service,</mark> says Daniel Hersheson, 'We are delighted to be opening the UK's first blow-dry bar at Topshop. Our philosophy of constantly relating hair back to fashion means we will be perfectly at home in the most creative store on the British high street.' Topshop also recognizes the fit. *'The Daniel Hersheson Blowdry Bar is a really exciting service addition to our Oxford Circus flagship and offers the perfect finishing touch to a great shopping experience at Topshop'.*

The new service has not just been a success in the market; it also has advantages for the operation itself.

'It's a great opportunity for young stylists not only to develop their styling skills, but also to develop the confidence that it takes to interact with clients', says George Northwood, Manager of Daniel Hersheson's Mayfair salon. *'You can see a real difference after a trainee stylist has worked in the Blowdry Bar. They learn how to talk to clients, to understand their needs, and to advise them. It's the confidence that they gain that is so important in helping them to become fully qualified and successful stylists in their own right.'*

Preliminary design

Having generated an acceptable, feasible and viable concept the next stage is to create a preliminary design. The objective of this stage is to have a first attempt at both specifying the component products and services in the *package*, and defining the *processes* to create the package.

Specify the components of the package

The first task in this stage of design is to define exactly what will go into the service or product: that is, specifying the components of the package. This will require the collection of information about such things as the *constituent component parts* which make up the package and the **component structure**, the order in which the components of the package have to be put together. For example, the components for a remote mouse for a computer may include, upper and lower casings, a control unit and packaging, which are themselves made up of other components. The product structure shows how these components fit together to make the mouse (see Figure 4.5).

Component structure

Reducing design complexity

Simplicity is usually seen as a virtue amongst designers. The most elegant design solutions are often the simplest. However, when an operation produces a variety of services or products, the range considered as a whole can become complex, which, in turn, increases costs. Designers

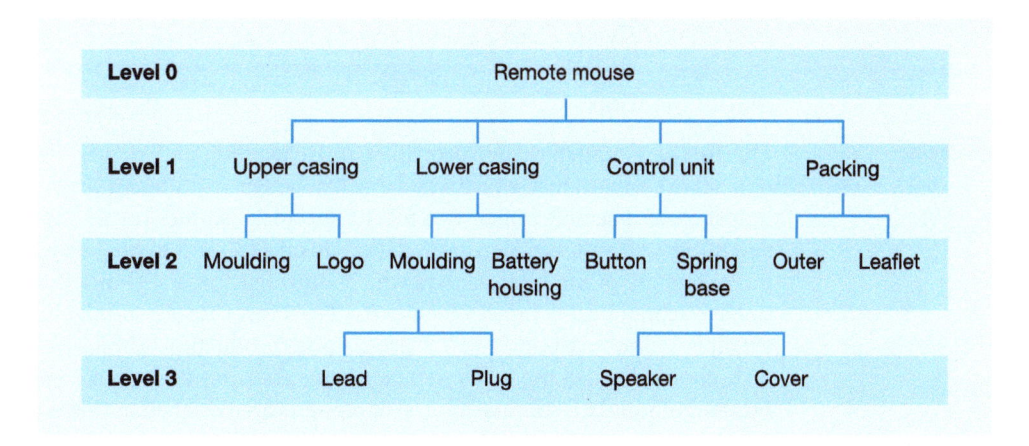

Figure 4.5 The component structure of a remote mouse

adopt a number of approaches to reducing the inherent complexity in the design of their range. Here we describe three common approaches to complexity reduction – standardization, commonality and modularization.

Standardization

Operations sometimes attempt to overcome the cost penalties of high variety by **standardizing** their services, products, or processes. This allows them to restrict variety to that which has real value for the end-customer. Often it is the operation's outputs which are standardized. Examples of this are fast-food restaurants, discount supermarkets and telephone-based insurance companies. Perhaps the most common example of standardization is the clothes which most of us buy. Although everybody's body shape is different, garment manufacturers produce clothes in only a limited number of sizes. The range of sizes is chosen to give a reasonable fit for most body shapes. To suit all their potential customers and/or to ensure a perfect fit, garment manufacturers would have to provide an infeasibly large range of sizes. Alternatively, they would need to provide a customized service. Both solutions would have a significant impact on cost. This control of variety is an important issue with most companies. A danger facing established operations is that they allow variety to grow excessively. They are then faced with the task of *variety reduction*, often by assessing the real profit or contribution of each service or product. Many organizations have significantly improved their profitability by careful variety reduction. In order to overcome loss of business, customers may be offered alternative services or products which provide similar value.

Commonality

Using common service or product elements can also simplify design complexity. The more that different services and products can be based on common components, the less complex it is to produce them. For example, the European aircraft maker Airbus has designed its new generation of jetliners with a high degree of **commonality**. Airbus developed full design and operational commonality with the introduction of fly-by-wire technology on its civil aircraft in the late 1980s. This meant that ten aircraft models ranging from the 100-seat A318 through to the world's largest aircraft, the 555-seat A380, feature virtually identical flight decks, common systems and similar handling characteristics. In some cases, such as the entire A320 family, the aircraft even share the same 'pilot-type rating', which enables pilots with a single licence to fly any of them. The advantages of commonality for the airline operators include a much shorter training time for pilots and engineers when they move from one aircraft to another. This offers pilots the possibility of flying a wide range of routes from short-haul to ultra-long-haul and leads to greater efficiencies because common maintenance procedures can be designed with maintenance teams capable of servicing any aircraft in the same family. Also, when up to 90 per cent of all parts are common within a range of aircraft, there is a reduced need to carry a wide range of spare parts.

Modularization

The use of **modular** design principles involves designing standardized 'sub-components' of a service or product which can be put together in different ways. The package holiday industry can assemble holidays to meet a specific customer requirement, from pre-designed and purchased air travel, accommodation, insurance, and so on. In education also there is an increasing use of modular courses which allow 'customers' choice but permit each module to have economical volumes of students. The short case 'Customizing for kids' describes an example of modularization in TV programme production. Similarly, it is possible to create wide choice through the fully interchangeable assembly of various combinations of a smaller number of standard sub-assemblies; computers are designed in this way, for example. These standardized modules, or sub-assemblies, can be produced in higher volume, thereby reducing their cost.

Short case
Customizing for kids[7]

Reducing design complexity is a principle that applies just as much to service as to manufactured products. For example, television programmes are made increasingly with a worldwide market in mind. However, most television audiences around the world have a distinct preference for programmes which respect their regional tastes, culture and of course language. The challenge facing global programme makers therefore is to try and achieve the economies which come as a result of high volume production while allowing programmes to be customized for different markets. For example, take the programme *Art Attack!* made for the Disney Channel, a children's TV channel shown around the world. In 2001 two hundred and sixteen episodes of the show were made in six different language versions. About 60 per cent of each show is common across all versions. Shots without speaking or where the presenter's face is not visible are shot separately. For example, if a simple cardboard model is being made all versions will share the scenes where the presenter's hands only are visible. Commentary in the appropriate language is over-dubbed onto the scenes which are edited seamlessly with other shots of the appropriate presenter. The final product will have the head and shoulders of Brazilian, French, Italian, German, or Spanish presenters flawlessly mixed with the same pair of (British) hands constructing the model. The result is that local viewers in each market see the show as their own. Even though presenters are flown into the UK production studies, the cost of making each episode is only about one third of producing separate programmes for each market.

Define the process to create the package

The component structure specifies what goes into a product or service. It is around this stage in the design process where it is necessary to examine how a process could put together the various components to create the final service or product. At one time this activity would have been delayed until the very end of the design process. However, this can cause problems if the designed service or product cannot be created or delivered to the required quality and cost constraints. For now, what is important to understand is that processes should at least be examined in outline well before any design is finalized.

Design evaluation and improvement

The purpose of this stage in the design activity is to take the preliminary design and see if it can be improved before the offering is tested in the market. There are a number of techniques that can be employed at this stage to evaluate and improve the preliminary design. Here we discuss two which have proved particularly useful:

- Quality function deployment (QFD)
- Value engineering (VE)

Quality function deployment

Quality function deployment

The key purpose of **quality function deployment** (QFD) is to try to ensure that the eventual service or product actually meets the needs of its customers. Customers may not have been considered explicitly since the concept generation stage, and therefore it is appropriate to check that what is being proposed for the design of the product or service will meet their needs. It is also known as the 'house of quality' (because of its shape) and the 'voice of the customer' (because of its purpose). The technique tries to capture *what* the customer needs and *how* it might be achieved. Figure 4.6 shows an example of quality function deployment being used in the design of a new information system. The QFD matrix is a formal articulation of how the company sees the relationship between the requirements of the customer (the *whats*) and the design characteristics of the new product (the *hows*). The matrix contains various sections, as explained below:

- The *whats*, or 'customer requirements', is the list of competitive factors which customers find significant. Their relative importance is scored, in this case on a 10-point scale, with *accurate* scoring the highest.

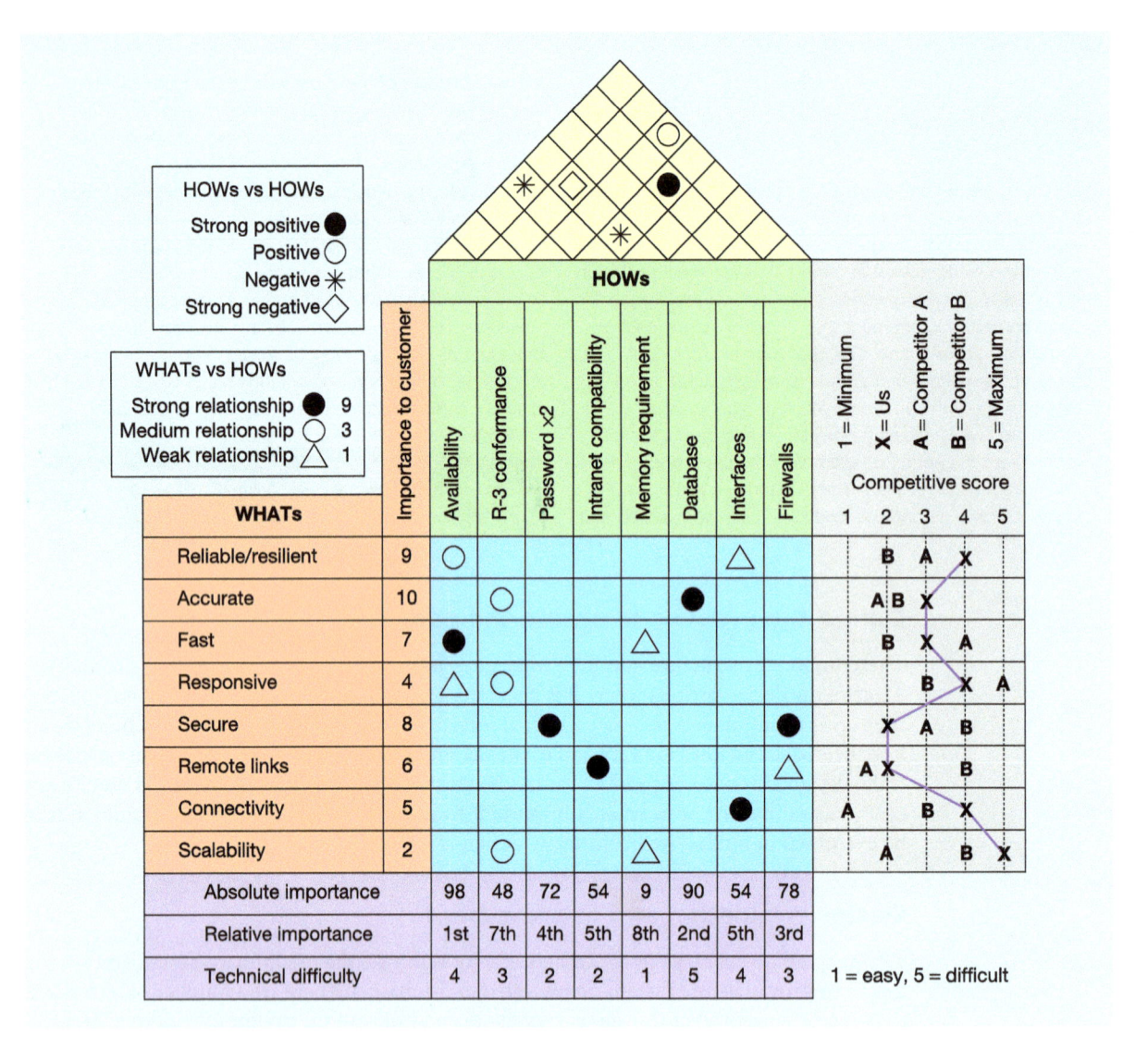

Figure 4.6 A QFD matrix for an information system product

- The competitive scores indicate the relative performance of the product, in this case on a 1 to 5 scale. Also indicated are the performances of two competitor offerings.
- The *hows*, or 'design characteristics' of the product, are the various 'dimensions' of the design which will operationalize customer requirements within the service or product.
- The central matrix (sometimes called the 'relationship matrix') represents a view of the interrelationship between the *whats* and the *hows*. This is often based on value judgements made by the design team. The symbols indicate the strength of the relationship – for example, the relationship between the ability to link remotely to the system and the intranet compatibility of the product is strong. All the relationships are studied, but in many cases, where the cell of the matrix is blank, there is none.
- The bottom box of the matrix is a technical assessment of the product. This contains the absolute importance of each design characteristic. (For example, the design characteristic 'interfaces' has a relative importance of $(9 \times 5) + (1 \times 9) = 54$.) This is also translated into a ranked relative importance. In addition, the degree of technical difficulty to achieve high levels of performance in each design characteristic is indicated on a 1 to 5 scale.
- The triangular 'roof' of the 'house' captures any information the team has about the correlations (positive or negative) between the various design characteristics.

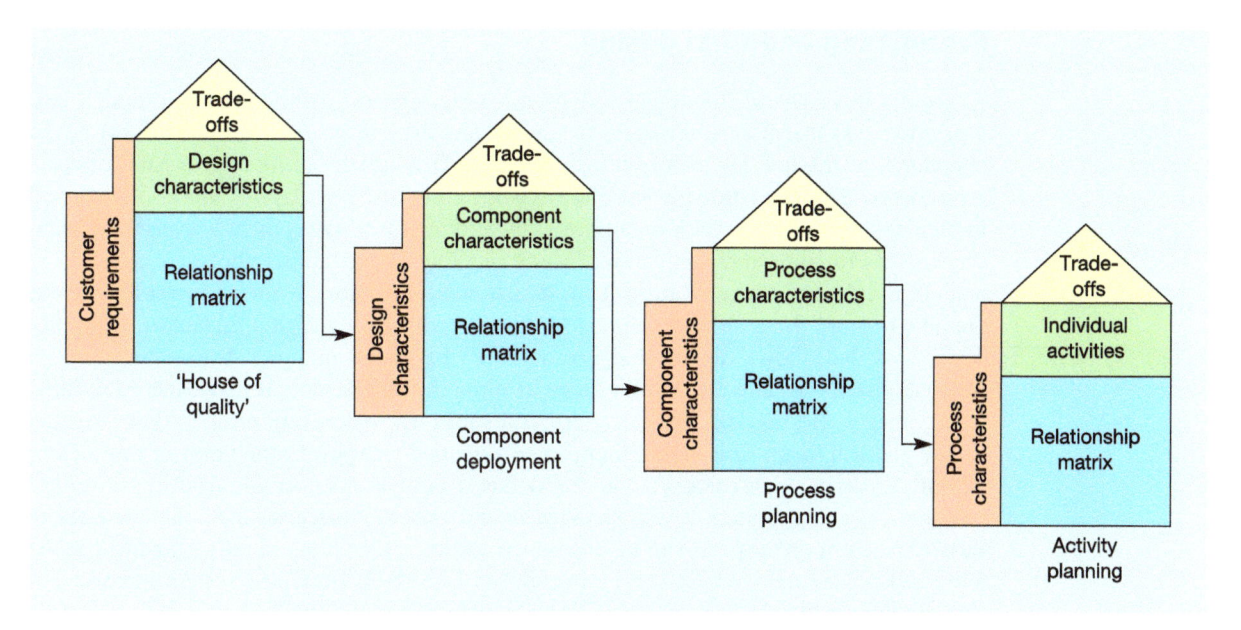

Figure 4.7 QFD matrices can be linked with the 'hows' of one matrix forming the 'whats' of the next

Although the details of QFD may vary between its different variants, the principle is generally common, namely to identify the customer requirements for a service or product (together with their relative importance) and to relate them to the design characteristics which translate those requirements into practice. In fact, this principle can be continued by making the *hows* from one stage become the *whats* of the next. Some experienced users of QFD have up to four linked matrices in this way (see Figure 4.7). If engineering or process trade-offs need to be made at a later stage, the interrelated houses enable the effect on customer requirements to be determined.

Value engineering

The purpose of **value engineering** is to try to reduce costs, and prevent any unnecessary costs, before creating the service or product. Simply put, it tries to eliminate any costs that do not contribute to the value and performance of the service or product. ('Value analysis' is the name given to the same process when it is concerned with cost reduction after the product or service has been introduced.) Value-engineering programmes are usually conducted by project teams consisting of designers, purchasing specialists, operations managers and financial analysts. The chosen elements of the package are subject to rigorous scrutiny, by analysing their function and cost, then trying to find any similar components that could simplify processes do the same job at lower cost. The team may attempt to simplify the service delivery process, reduce the number of components, or use cheaper materials. For example, Motorola used value engineering to reduce the number of parts in its mobile phones from 'thousands' down to 'hundreds' and even less, with a drastic reduction in processing time and cost.

Value engineering requires innovative and critical thinking, but it is also carried out using a formal procedure. The procedure examines the purpose of the service or product, its basic functions and its secondary functions. Taking the example of the remote mouse used previously:

- The **purpose** of the remote mouse is to communicate with the computer.
- The **basic function** is to control presentation slide shows.
- The **secondary function** is to be plug-and-play-compatible with any system.

Team members would then propose ways to improve the secondary functions by combining, revising or eliminating them. All ideas would then be checked for feasibility, acceptability, vulnerability and their contribution to the value and purpose of the service or product.

Prototyping and final design

At around this stage in the design activity it is necessary to turn the improved design into a prototype so that it can be tested. It may be too risky to go into full production of the telephone, or the holiday, before testing it out, so it is usually more appropriate to create a prototype. Service prototypes may also include computer simulations but also the actual implementation of the service on a pilot basis. Product prototypes include everything from clay models to computer simulations. Many retailing organizations pilot new offerings in a small number of stores in order to test customers' reaction to them. Increasingly, it is possible to store the data that define a service or product in a digital format on computer systems, which allows this **virtual prototype** to be tested in much the same way as a physical prototype. This is a familiar idea in some industries such as magazine publishing, where images and text can be rearranged and subjected to scrutiny prior to them existing in any physical form. This allows them to be amended right up to the point of production without incurring high costs. Virtual-reality-based simulations now allow businesses to test new services and products as well as visualize and plan the processes that will create them. Individual component parts can be positioned together virtually and tested for fit or interference. Even virtual workers can be introduced into the prototyping system to check for ease of operating.

Computer-aided design (CAD)

CAD systems provide the computer-aided ability to create and modify designs. These systems allow conventionally used shapes such as points, lines, arcs, circles and text, to be added to a computer-based representation of the design. Once incorporated into the design, these entities can be copied, moved about, rotated through angles, magnified or deleted. The designs thus created can be saved in the memory of the system and retrieved for later use. This enables a library of standardized drawings of parts and components to be built up. The most obvious advantage of CAD systems is that their ability to store and retrieve design data quickly, as well as their ability to manipulate design details, can considerably increase the productivity of the design activity. In addition to this, however, because changes can be made rapidly to designs, CAD systems can considerably enhance the flexibility of the design activity, enabling modifications to be made much more rapidly. Further, the use of standardized libraries of shapes and entities can reduce the possibility of errors in the design.

Skunkworks[8]

Encouraging creativity in design, while at the same time recognizing the constraints of everyday business life, has always been one of the great challenges of industrial design. One well-known approach to releasing the design and development creativity of a group has been called a 'Skunkworks'. This is usually taken to mean a small team who are taken out of their normal work environment and granted freedom from their normal management activities and constraints. It was an idea that originated in the Lockheed aircraft company in the 1940s, where designers were set up outside the normal organizational structure and given the task of designing a high-speed fighter plane. The experiment was so successful that the company continued with it to develop other innovative products.

Since that time many other companies have used a similar approach, although 'Skunkworks' is a registered trademark of Lockheed Martin Corporation. Motorola's mobile phone 'Razr' was designed and developed in a Skunkworks-like special laboratory that the company set up, well away from its main Research and Development site in Illinois. Even the décor and layout of the laboratory were different: open-plan and with lots of bright colours. Something similar is reportedly used by Malaysia Airlines to tackle wider business issues, not just 'design' assignments.

The benefits of interactive design

Earlier we made the point that in practice it is a mistake to separate the design of services and products from the design of the processes which will create them. Operations managers should have some involvement from the initial evaluation of the concept right through to its introduction to the market. Merging the design of services/products and the processes which create them is sometimes called **interactive design**. Its benefits come from the reduction in the elapsed time for the whole design activity, from concept through to market introduction. This is often called the **time to market** (TTM). The argument in favour of reducing time to market is that doing so gives increased competitive advantage. For example, if it takes a company five years to develop a service from concept to market, with a given set of resources, it can introduce a new service only once every five years. If its rival can develop a service in three years, it can introduce its new service, together with its (presumably) improved performance, once every three years. This means that the rival company does not have to make such radical improvements in performance each time it introduces a new service, because it is introducing its new services more frequently. In other words, shorter TTM means that companies get more opportunities to improve the performance of their services or products.

If the development process takes longer than expected (or even worse, longer than competitors') two effects are likely to show. The first is that the costs of development will increase. Having to use development resources, such as designers, technicians, subcontractors, and so on, for a longer development period usually increases the costs of development. Perhaps more seriously, the late introduction of the product or service will delay the revenue from its sale (and possibly reduce the total revenue substantially if competitors have already got to the market with their own services or products). The net effect of this could be not only a considerable reduction in sales but also reduced profitability – an outcome which could considerably extend the time before the company breaks even on its investment in the new service or product. This is illustrated in Figure 4.8.

Interactive design
Interactive design can shorten time to market

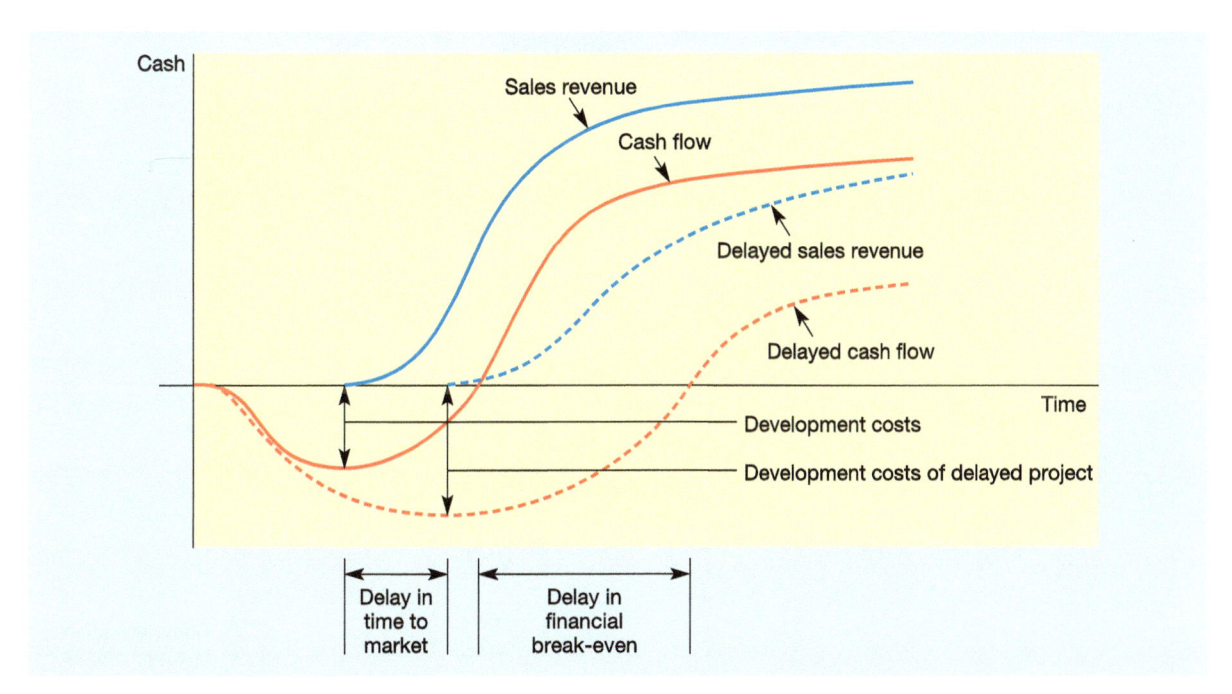

Figure 4.8 Delay in the time to market of new services and products not only reduces and delays revenues, it also increases the costs of development. The combination of both these effects usually delays the financial break-even point far more than the delay in the time to market

A number of factors have been suggested which can significantly reduce time to market for a service or product, including the following:

- simultaneous development of the various stages in the overall process;
- an early resolution of design conflict and uncertainty;
- an organizational structure which reflects the development project.

Simultaneous development

Earlier in the chapter we described the design process as essentially a set of individual, predetermined stages. Sometimes one stage is completed before the next one commences. This step-by-step, or **sequential**, approach has traditionally been the typical form of development. It has some advantages. It is easy to manage and control design projects organized in this way, since each stage is clearly defined. In addition, each stage is completed before the next stage is begun, so each stage can focus its skills and expertise on a limited set of tasks. The main problem of the sequential approach is that it is both time-consuming and costly. When each stage is separate, with a clearly defined set of tasks, any difficulties encountered during the design at one stage might necessitate the design being halted while responsibility moves back to the previous stage. This sequential approach is shown in Figure 4.9(a).

Yet often there is really little need to wait until the absolute finalization of one stage before starting the next. For example, perhaps while generating the concept, the evaluation activity of screening and selection could be started. It is likely that some concepts could be judged as

Sequential approach to design

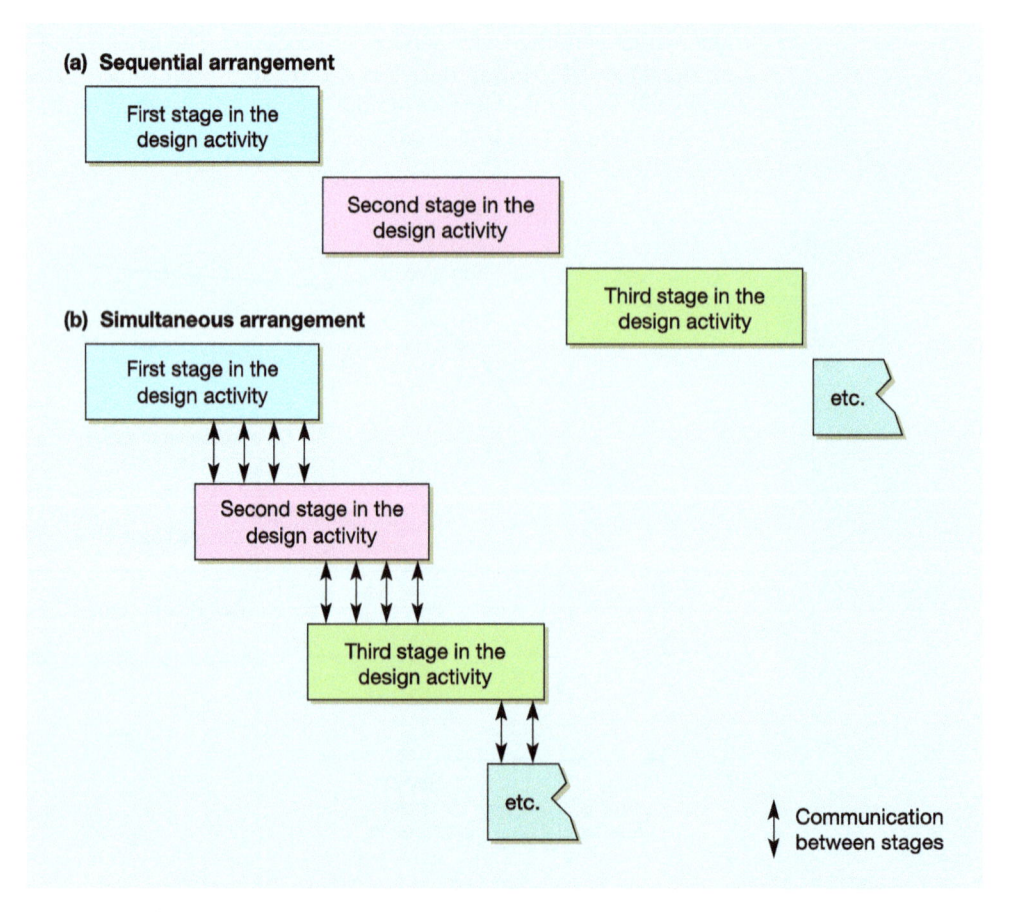

Figure 4.9 (a) Sequential arrangement of the stages in the design activity; (b) simultaneous arrangement of the stages in the design activity

Simultaneous or concurrent approach to design

'non-starters' relatively early on in the process of idea generation. Similarly, during the screening stage, it is likely that some aspects of the design will become obvious before the phase is finally complete. Therefore, the preliminary work on these parts of the design could be commenced at that point. This principle can be taken right through all the stages, one stage commencing before the previous one has finished, so there is **simultaneous or concurrent** work on the stages (see Figure 4.9(b)).

Early conflict resolution

Characterizing the design activity as a whole series of decisions is a useful way of thinking about design. However, a decision, once made, need not totally and utterly commit the organization. For example, if a design team is designing a new vacuum cleaner, the decision to adopt a particular style and type of electric motor might have seemed sensible at the time the decision was made but might have to be changed later, in the light of new information. It could be that a new electric motor becomes available which is clearly superior to the one initially selected. Under those circumstances the designers might very well want to change their decision.

There are other, more avoidable, reasons for designers changing their minds during the design activity, however. Perhaps one of the initial design decisions was made without sufficient discussion among those in the organization who have a valid contribution to make. It may even be that when the decision was made there was insufficient agreement to formalize it, and the design team decided to carry on without formally making the decision. Yet subsequent decisions might be made as though the decision had been formalized. For example, suppose the company could not agree on the correct size of electric motor to put into its vacuum cleaner. It might well carry on with the rest of the design work while further discussions and investigations take place on what kind of electric motor to incorporate in the design. Yet much of the rest of the product's design is likely to depend on the choice of the electric motor. Failure to resolve these conflicts and/or decisions early on in the process can prolong the degree of uncertainty in the total design activity. In addition, if a decision is made (even implicitly) and then changed later on in the process, the costs of that change can be very large. However, if the design team manages to resolve conflict early in the design activity, this will reduce the degree of uncertainty within the project and reduce the extra cost and, most significantly, time associated with either managing this uncertainty or changing decisions already made. Figure 4.10 illustrates two patterns of design changes through the life of the total design, which imply different time-to-market performances.

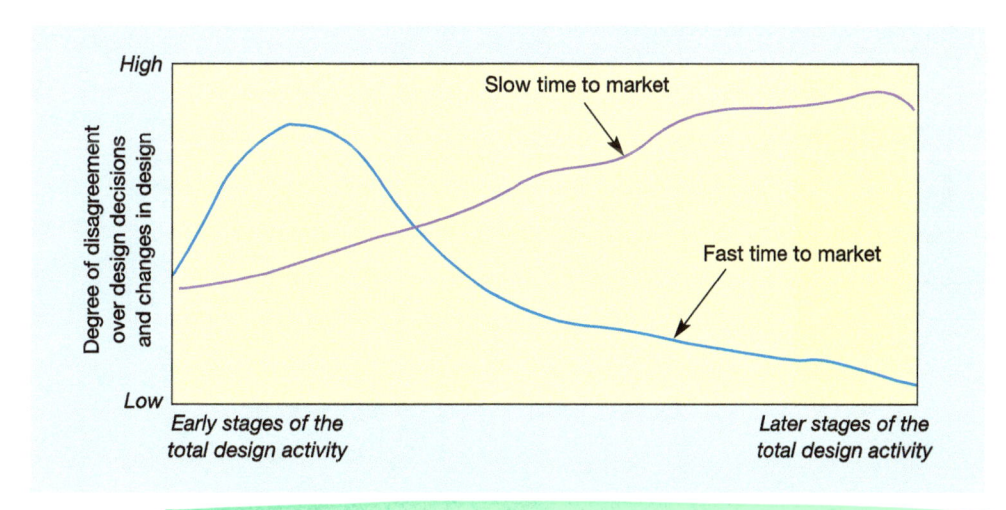

Figure 4.10 Sorting out problems early saves greater disruption later in the design activity

Project-based organization structures

The total process of developing concepts through to market will almost certainly involve personnel from several different areas of the organization. To continue the vacuum cleaner example, it is likely that the vacuum cleaner company would involve staff from its research and development department, engineering, production management, marketing and finance. All these different functions will have some part to play in making the decisions which will shape the final design. Yet any design project will also have an existence of its own. It will have a project name, an individual manager or group of staff who are championing the project, a budget and, hopefully, a clear strategic purpose in the organization. The organizational question is which of these two ideas – the various organizational functions which contribute to the design or the design project itself – should dominate the way in which the design activity is managed?

Before answering this, it is useful to look at the range of organizational structures which are available – from **pure functional** to **pure project** forms. In a pure functional organization, all staff associated with the design project are based unambiguously in their functional groups. There is no project-based group at all. They may be working full-time on the project but all communications and liaison are carried out through their functional manager. The project exists because of agreement between these functional managers. At the other extreme, all the individual members of staff from each function who are involved in the project could be moved out of their functions and perhaps even physically relocated to a **task force** dedicated

Functional design organization
Project design organization

Task force

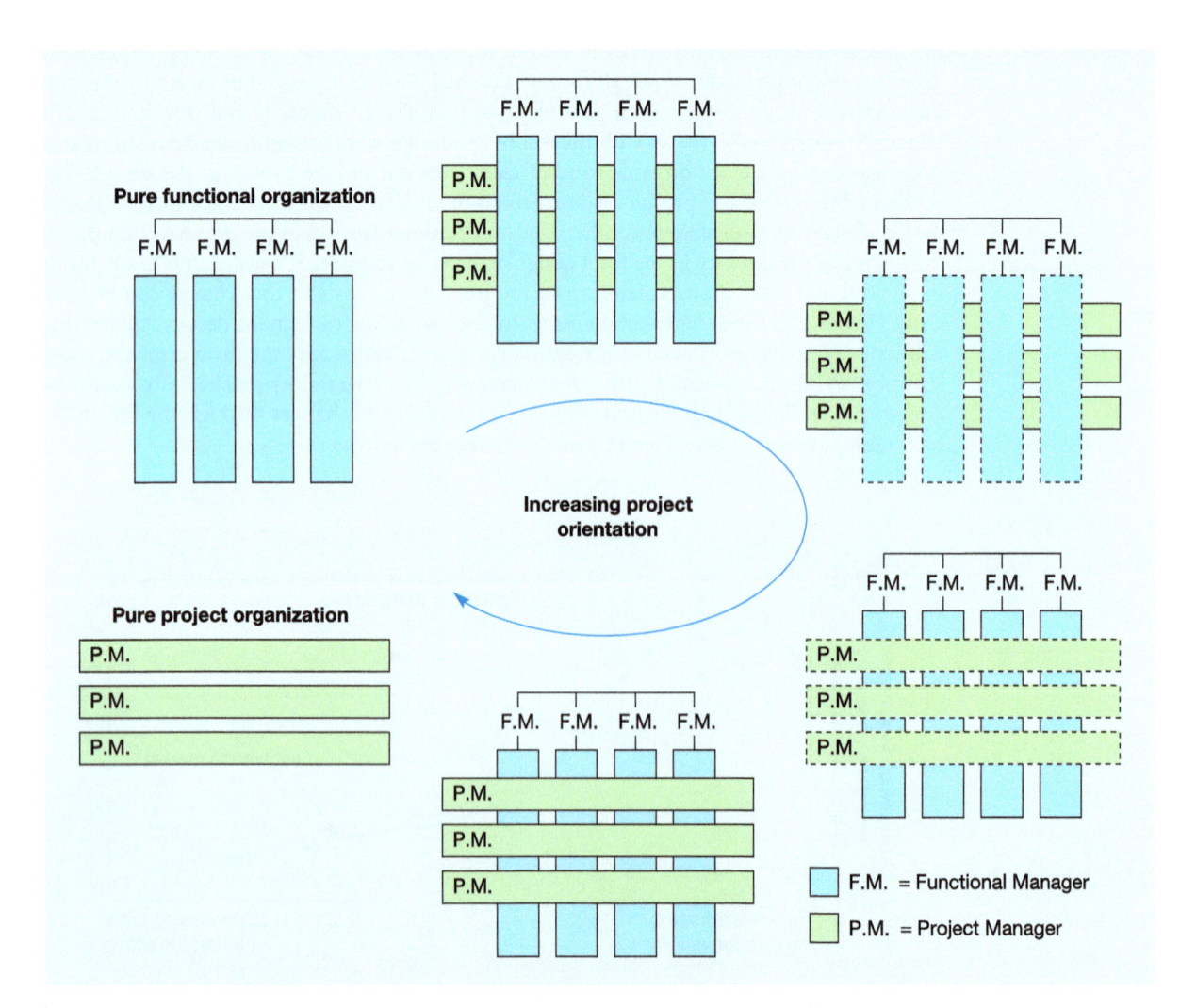

Figure 4.11 Organization structures for the design activity

solely to the project. The task force could be led by a project manager who might hold all the budget allocated to the design project. Not all members of the task force necessarily have to stay in the team throughout the development period, but a substantial core might see the project through from start to finish. Some members of a design team may even be from other companies. In between these two extremes there are various types of **matrix organization** with varying emphasis on these two aspects of the organization (see Figure 4.11). Although the 'task force' type of organization, especially for small projects, can sometimes be a little cumbersome, it seems to be generally agreed that, for substantial projects at least, it is more effective at reducing overall time to market.[9]

Summary answers to key questions

Check and improve your understanding of this chapter using self-assessment questions and a personalized study plan, audio and video downloads, and an eBook – all at www.myomlab.com.

➤ Why is good service and product design important?

- Good design makes good business sense because it translates customer needs into the shape and form of the product or service and so enhances profitability.
- Design includes formalizing three particularly important issues: the concept, package and process implied by the design.
- Design is a process that itself must be designed according to the process design principles described in the previous chapter.

➤ What are the stages in service and product design?

- *Concept generation* transforms an idea for a service or product into a concept which captures the nature of the product or service and provides an overall specification for its design.
- *Screening* the concept involves examining its feasibility, acceptability and vulnerability in broad terms to ensure that it is a sensible addition to the company's portfolio.
- *Preliminary design* involves the identification of all the component parts of the service or product and the way they fit together. Typical tools used during this phase include component structures and flow charts.
- *Design evaluation and improvement* involve re-examining the design to see if it can be done in a better way, more cheaply or more easily. Typical techniques used here include quality function deployment and value engineering.
- *Prototyping and final design* involve providing the final details which allow the offering to be delivered or created. The outcome of this stage is a fully developed specification for the package of services and products, as well as a specification for the processes that will make and deliver them to customers.

➤ Why and how should service and product design be considered interactively with process design?

- Quality of the service or product and of the process can be improved by looking at them in parallel rather than in sequence. It helps a design 'break even' on its investment earlier than would otherwise have been the case.

- Employ *simultaneous development* where design decisions are taken as early as they can be, without necessarily waiting for a whole design phase to be completed.
- Ensure *early conflict resolution* which allows contentious decisions to be resolved early in the design process, thereby not allowing them to cause far more delay and confusion if they emerge later in the process.
- Use a *project-based organizational structure* which can ensure that a focused and coherent team of designers is dedicated to a single design or group of design projects.

Learning exercises

These problems and applications will help to improve your analysis of operations. You can find more practice problems as well as worked examples and guided solutions on MyOMLab at www.myomlab.com.

1. A company is developing a new web site that will allow customers to track the progress of their orders. The website developers charge €10,000 for every development week and it is estimated that the design will take 10 weeks from the start of the design project to the launch of the web site. Once launched, it is estimated that the new site will attract extra business that will generate profits of €5,000 per week. However, if the web site is delayed by more than 5 weeks, the extra profit generated would reduce to €2,000 per week. How will a delay of 5 weeks affect the time when the design will break even in terms of cash flow?

2. How can the concept of modularization be applied to package holidays sold through an online travel agent?

3. One product where a very wide range of product types is valued by customers is that of domestic paint. Most people like to express their creativity in the choice of paints and other home-decorating products that they use in their homes. Clearly, offering a wide range of paint must have serious cost implications for the companies which manufacture, distribute and sell the product. Visit a store which sells paint and get an idea of the range of products available on the market. How do you think paint manufacturers and retailers manage to design their products and services so as to maintain high variety but keep costs under control?

4. Design becomes particularly important at the interface between services or products and the people that use them. This is especially true for internet-based services. Consider two types of website:
    (a) those which are trying to sell something such as Amazon.com, and
    (b) those which are primarily concerned with giving information, for example bbc.co.uk.

    For each of these categories, what seems to constitute 'good design'? Find examples of particularly good and particularly poor web design and explain what makes them good or bad.

Want to know more?

Bangle, C. (2001) The ultimate creativity machine: how BMW turns art into profit, *Harvard Business Review*, Jan, 47–55. A good description of how good aesthetic design translates into business success.

Bruce, M. and Bessant, J. (2002) *Design in Business: Strategic Innovation through Design*, Financial Times Prentice Hall and The Design Council. Probably one of the best overviews of design in a business context available today.

Goldstein, S.M., Johnston, R., Duffy, J. and Raod, J. (2002) The service concept: the missing link in service design research? *Journal of Operations Management*, volume 20, issue 2, April, 121–34. Readable.

The Industrial Designers Society of America (2003) *Design Secrets: Products: 50 Real-Life Projects Uncovered (Design Secrets)*, Rockport Publishers Inc, Gloucester, MA. Very much a practitioner book with some great examples.

Useful websites

www.cfsd.org.uk The Centre for Sustainable Design's site. Some useful resources, but obviously largely confined to sustainability issues.

www.conceptcar.co.uk A site devoted to automotive design. Fun if you like new car designs!

www.betterproductdesign.net A site that acts as a resource for good design practice. Set up by Cambridge University and the Royal College of Art. Some good material that supports all aspects of design.

www.ocw.mit.edu/courses/sloan-school-of-management Good source of open courseware from MIT.

www.design-council.org.uk Site of the UK's Design Council. One of the best sites in the world for design-related issues.

www.nathan.com/ed/glossary/#ED

www.opsman.org Lots of useful stuff.

Now that you have finished reading this chapter, why not visit MyOMLab at www.myomlab.com where you'll find more learning resources to help you make the most of your studies and get a better grade.

Chapter 5

Process design

Key questions
- What is process design?
- How do volume and variety affect process design?
- How are processes designed in detail?
- What are the human implications for process design?

Introduction

Say you are a 'designer' and most people will assume that you are someone who is concerned with how a product looks. However, the design activity is much broader than that and while there is no universally recognized definition of 'design'. We take it to mean 'the process by which some functional requirement of people is satisfied through the shaping or configuration of the resources and/or activities that compose a service, a product, or the transformation process that creates and delivers them'. All operations managers are designers. When they purchase or rearrange the position of a piece of equipment, or when they change the way of working within a process, it is a design decision because it affects the physical shape and nature of their processes. This chapter examines the design of processes. Figure 5.1 shows where this chapter fits within the overall model of operations management.

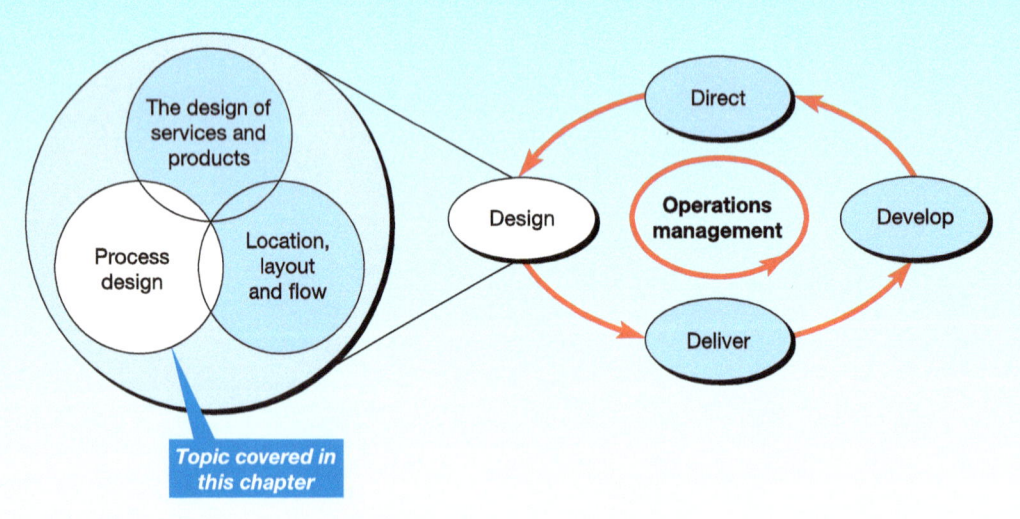

Figure 5.1 This chapter examines process design

Check and improve your understanding of this chapter using self-assessment questions and a personalized study plan, audio and video downloads, and an eBook – all at www.myomlab.com.

Operations in practice: Fast-food drive-throughs[1]

The quick-service restaurant (QSR) industry reckons that the very first drive-through dates back to 1928 when Royce Hailey first promoted the drive-through service at his Pig Stand restaurant in Los Angeles. Customers would simply drive by the back door of the restaurant where the chef would come out and deliver the restaurant's famous 'Barbequed Pig' sandwiches. Today, drive-through processes are slicker and faster. They are also more common. In 1975, McDonald's did not have any drive-throughs, but now more than 90 per cent of its US restaurants incorporate a drive-through process. In fact 80 per cent of recent fast-food growth has come through the growing number of drive-throughs. Says one industry specialist, *'There are a growing number of customers for whom fast-food is not fast enough. They want to cut waiting time to the very minimum without even getting out of their car. Meeting their needs depends on how smooth we can get the process.'*

The competition to design the fastest and most reliable drive-through process is fierce. Starbucks' drive-throughs have strategically placed cameras at the order boards so that servers can recognize regular customers and start making their order even before it's placed. Burger King has experimented with sophisticated sound systems, simpler menu boards and see-through food bags to ensure greater accuracy (no point in being fast if you don't deliver what the customer ordered). These details matter. McDonald's reckon that their sales increase one per cent for every six seconds saved at a drive-through, while a single Burger King restaurant calculated that its takings increased by 15,000 dollars a year each time it reduced queuing time by one second.

Menu items must be easy to read and understand. Designing 'combo meals' (burger, fries and a cola), for example, saves time at the ordering stage. Perhaps the most remarkable experiment in making drive-through process times slicker is being carried out by McDonald's in the USA. On California's central coast 150 miles from Los Angeles, a call centre takes orders remotely from 40 McDonald's outlets around the country. The orders are then sent back to the restaurants through the Internet and the food is assembled only a few metres from where the order was placed. It may only save a few seconds on each order, but that can add up to extra sales at busy times of the day. However, not everyone is thrilled by the boom in drive-throughs. People living in the vicinity may complain of the extra traffic they attract and the unhealthy image of fast food combined with a process that does not even make customers get out of their car, is, for some, a step too far.

Source: Getty Images

What is process design?

Design happens before creation

To 'design' is to conceive the looks, arrangement, and workings of something *before it is created*. In that sense it is a conceptual exercise. Yet it is one which must deliver a solution that will work in practice. Design is also an activity that can be approached at different levels of detail. One may envisage the general shape and intention of something before getting down to defining its details. This is certainly true for process design. At the start of the process design activity it is important to understand the design objectives, especially at first, when the overall shape and nature of the process is being decided. The most common way of doing this is by positioning it according to its volume and variety characteristics. Eventually the details of the process must be analysed to ensure that it fulfils its objectives effectively. Yet, it is often only through getting to grips with the detail of a design that the feasibility of

What objectives should process design have?

The whole point of process design is to make sure that the performance of the process is appropriate for whatever it is trying to achieve. For example, if an operation competed primarily on its ability to respond quickly to customer requests, its processes would need to be designed to give fast throughput times. This would minimize the time between customers requesting a service or product and their receiving it. Similarly, if an operation competed on low price, cost-related objectives would dominate its process design. Some kind of logic should link what the operation as a whole is attempting to achieve and the **performance objectives** of its individual processes. This is illustrated in Table 5.1.

Process design should reflect process objectives

Operations performance objectives translate directly to process design objectives as shown in Table 5.1. As processes are managed at a very operational level, process design also needs to consider a more 'micro' and detailed set of objectives. These are largely concerned with flow through the process. When whatever are being 'processed' enter a process, they will progress through a series of activities where they are 'transformed' in some way. Between these activities they may dwell for some time in inventories, waiting to be transformed by the next activity. This means that the time that a unit spends in the process (its throughput time) will be longer than the sum of all the transforming activities that it passes through. Also the resources that perform the processes activities may not be used all the time because not all units will necessarily require the same activities and the capacity of each resource may not match the demand placed upon it. So neither the units moving through the process, nor the resources performing the activities may be fully utilized.

Table 5.1 The impact of strategic performance objectives on process design objectives and performance

Operations performance objective	Typical process design objectives	Some benefits of good process design
Quality	• Provide appropriate resources, capable of achieving the services or product specification • Error-free processing	• Products and services produced 'on-specification' • Less recycling and wasted effort within the process
Speed	• Minimum throughput time • Output rate appropriate for demand	• Short customer waiting time • Low in-process inventory
Dependability	• Provide dependable process resources • Reliable process output timing and volume	• On-time deliveries of products and services • Less disruption, confusion and rescheduling within the process
Flexibility	• Provide resources with an appropriate range of capabilities • Change easily between processing states (what, how, or how much is being processed)	• Ability to process a wide range of products and services • Low cost/fast product and service change • Low cost/fast volume and timing changes • Ability to cope with unexpected events (e.g. supply or a processing failure)

Cost	• Appropriate capacity to meet demand
	• Eliminate process waste in terms of
	  – excess capacity
	  – excess process capability
	  – in-process delays
	  – in-process errors
	  – inappropriate process inputs
		• Low processing costs
		• Low resource costs (capital costs)
		• Low delay and inventory costs (working capital costs)

Because of this the way that units leave the process is unlikely to be exactly the same as the way they arrive at the process. It is common for more 'micro' performance flow objectives to be used that describe process flow performance. For example:

Throughput rate

- **Throughput rate** (or flow rate) is the rate at which units emerge from the process, i.e. the number of units passing through the process per unit of time.

Throughput time

- **Throughput time** is the average elapsed time taken for inputs to move through the process and become outputs.

Work in process

- The number of units in the process (also called the '**work in process**' or in-process inventory), as an average over a period of time.

Utilization

- The **utilization** of process resources is the proportion of available time that the resources within the process are performing useful work.

Environmentally sensitive design

With the issues of environmental protection becoming more important, both process and service/product designers have to take account of 'green' issues. In many developed countries, legislation has already provided some basic standards which restrict the use of toxic materials, limit discharges to air and water, and protect employees and the public from immediate and long-term harm. Interest has focused on some fundamental issues:

Short case
Ecologically smart[2]

When Daimler-Chrysler started to examine the feasibility of the Smart town car, the challenge was not just to examine the economic feasibility of the product but also to build in environmental sensitivity to the design of the product and the process that was to make it. This is why environmental protection is now a fundamental part of all production activities in its 'Smartville' plant at Hambach near France's border with Germany. The product itself is designed on environmentally compatible principles. Even before assembly starts, the product's disassembly must be considered. In fact the modular construction of the Smart car helps to guarantee economical dismantling at the end of its life. This also helps with the recycling of materials. Over 85 per cent of the Smart's components are recyclable and recycled material is used in its initial construction. For example, the Smart's instrument panel comprises 12 per cent recycled plastic material. Similarly, production processes are designed to be ecologically sustainable. The plant's environmentally friendly painting technique allows less paint to be used while maintaining a high quality of protection. It also involves no solvent emission and no hazardous waste, as well as the recycling of surplus material. It is not only the use of new technology that contributes to the plant's ecological credentials. Ensuring a smooth and efficient movement of materials within the plant also saves time, effort and, above all, energy. So, traffic flow outside and through the building has been optimized, buildings are made accessible to suppliers delivering to the plant, and conveyor systems are designed to be loaded equally in both directions so as to avoid empty runs. The company even claims that the buildings themselves are a model for ecological compatibility. No construction materials contain formaldehyde or CFCs and the outside of the buildings are lined with 'TRESPA', a raw material made from European timber that is quick to regenerate.

- *The sources of inputs* to a service or product. (Will they damage rainforests? Will they use up scarce minerals? Will they exploit the poor or use child labour?)
- *Quantities and sources of energy* consumed in the process. (Do plastic beverage bottles use more energy than glass ones? Should waste heat be recovered and used in fish farming?)
- *The amounts and type of waste material* that are created in the processes. (Can this waste be recycled efficiently, or must it be burnt or buried in landfill sites? Will the waste have a long-term impact on the environment as it decomposes and escapes?)
- *The life of the product itself.* It is argued that if a product has a useful life of, say, twenty years, it will consume fewer resources than one that only lasts five years, which must therefore be replaced four times in the same period. However, the long-life product may require more initial inputs, and may prove to be inefficient in the latter part of its use, when the latest products use less energy or maintenance to run.
- *The end-of-life of the product.* (Will the redundant product be difficult to dispose of in an environmentally friendly way? Could it be recycled or used as a source of energy? Could it still be useful in third-world conditions? Could it be used to benefit the environment, such as old cars being used to make artificial reefs for sea life?)

Designers are faced with complex trade-offs between these factors, although it is not always easy to obtain all the information that is needed to make the 'best' choices. For example, it is relatively straightforward to design a long-life product, using strong material, over-designed components, ample corrosion protection, and so on. However, its production might use more materials and energy and it could create more waste on disposal. To help make more rational decisions in the design activity, some industries are experimenting with **life cycle analysis**. This technique analyses all the production inputs, the life-cycle use of the product and its final disposal, in terms of total energy used (and more recently, of all the emitted wastes such as carbon dioxide, sulphurous and nitrous gases, organic solvents, solid waste, etc.). The inputs and wastes are evaluated at *every* stage in its creation, beginning with the extraction or farming of the basic raw materials. The short case 'Ecologically smart' demonstrates that it is possible to include ecological considerations in all aspects of product and process design.

Life cycle analysis

Process types – the volume–variety effect on process design

In Chapter 1 we saw how processes in operations can range from creating a very high volume of products or services (for example, a food canning factory) to a very low volume (for example, major project consulting engineers). Also they can range from producing a very low variety of products or services (for example, in an electricity utility) to a very high variety (as, for example, in an architects' practice). Usually the two dimensions of volume and variety go together. Low-volume operations processes often have a high variety of services and products, and high-volume operations processes often have a narrow variety of services and products. Thus there is a continuum from low volume and high variety through to high volume and low variety, on which we can position operations. Different operations, even those in the same operation, may adopt different types of processes. In a medical service, compare the approach taken during mass medical treatments, such as large-scale immunization programmes, with that taken for a transplant operation where the treatment is designed specifically to meet the needs of one person. These differences go well beyond their differing technologies or the processing requirements of their products or services. They are explained by the fact that no one type of process design is best for all types of operation in all circumstances. The differences are because of the different **volume–variety positions** of the operations.

Volume–variety positions

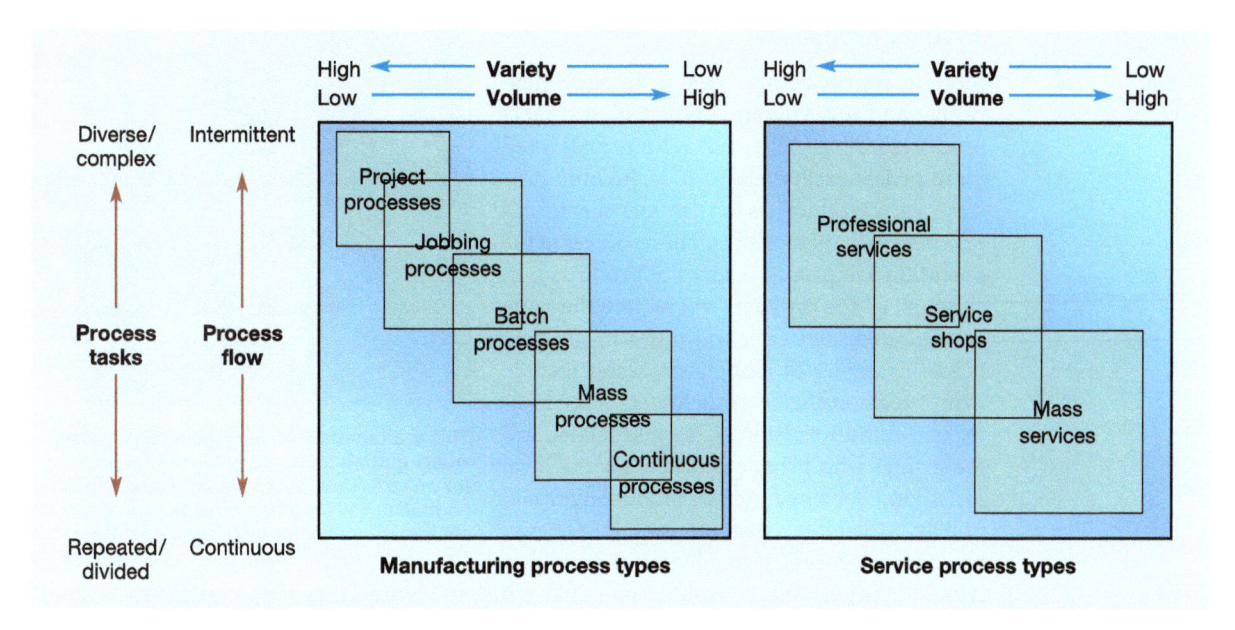

Figure 5.2 Different process types imply different volume–variety characteristics for the process

Process types

The position of a process on the volume–variety continuum shapes its overall design and the general approach to managing its activities. These 'general approaches' to designing and managing processes are called **process types**. Different terms are sometimes used to identify process types depending on whether they are predominantly manufacturing or service processes, and there is some variation in the terms used. For example, it is not uncommon to find the 'manufacturing' terms used in service industries. Figure 5.2 illustrates how these 'process types' are used to describe different positions on the volume–variety spectrum.

Project processes

Project processes are those which deal with discrete, usually highly customized products. Often the timescale of making the product or service is relatively long, as is the interval between the completion of each product or service. So low volume and high variety are characteristics of project processes. The activities involved in making the product can be ill-defined and uncertain, sometimes changing during the production process itself. Examples of project processes include shipbuilding, most construction companies, movie production companies, large fabrication operations such as those manufacturing turbo generators, and installing a computer system. The essence of project processes is that each job has a well-defined start and finish, the time interval between starting different jobs is relatively long and the transforming resources which make the product will probably have been organized especially for each product. The process map for project processes will almost certainly be complex. This is partly because each unit of output is so large with many activities occurring at the same time and partly because the activities in such processes often involve significant discretion to act according to professional judgement.

The major construction site shown in this picture is a project process. Each 'product' (project) is different and poses different challenges to those running the process (civil engineers).

Jobbing processes

Jobbing processes

Jobbing processes also deal with very high variety and low volumes. Whereas in project processes each product has resources devoted more or less exclusively to it, in jobbing processes each product has to share the operation's resources with many others. The resources of the operation will process a series of products but, although all the products will require the same kind of attention, each will differ in its exact needs. Examples of jobbing processes include many precision engineers such as specialist toolmakers, furniture restorers, bespoke tailors, and the printer who produces tickets for the local social event. Jobbing processes produce more and usually smaller items than project processes but, like project processes, the degree of repetition

This craftsperson is using general purpose wood-cutting technology to make a product for an individual customer. The next product he makes will be different (although it may be similar), possibly for a different customer.

is low. Many jobs will probably be 'one-offs'. Again, any process map for a jobbing process could be relatively complex for similar reasons to project processes. However, jobbing processes usually produce physically smaller products and, although sometimes involving considerable skill, such processes often involve fewer unpredictable circumstances.

Batch processes

Batch processes

Batch processes can often look like jobbing processes, but batch does not have quite the degree of variety associated with jobbing. As the name implies, each time batch processes produce a product they produce more than one. So each part of the operation has periods when it is repeating itself, at least while the 'batch' is being processed. The size of the batch could be just two or three, in which case the batch process will differ little from jobbing, especially if each batch is a totally novel product. Conversely, if the batches are large, and especially if the products are familiar to the

In this kitchen, food is being prepared in batches. All batches go through the same sequence (preparation, cooking, storing), but each batch is a different dish.

operation, batch processes can be fairly repetitive. Because of this, the batch type of process can be found over a wide range of volume and variety levels. Examples of batch processes include machine tool manufacturing, the production of some special gourmet frozen foods, and the manufacture of most of the component parts which go into mass-produced assemblies such as automobiles.

Mass processes

Mass processes

Mass processes are those which produce goods in high volume and relatively narrow variety – narrow, that is, in terms of the fundamentals of the product design. An automobile plant, for example, might produce several thousand variants of car if every option of engine size, colour, extra equipment, etc. is taken into account. Yet essentially it is a mass operation because the different variants of its product do not affect

This automobile plant is everyone's idea of a mass process. Each product is almost (but not quite) the same, and is made in large quantities.

the basic process of production. The activities in the automobile plant, like all mass operations, are essentially repetitive and largely predictable. Examples of mass processes include the automobile plant, a television factory, most food processes and DVD production. Several variants of a product could be produced on a mass process such as an assembly line, but the process itself is unaffected. The equipment used at each stage of the process can be designed to handle several different types of components loaded into the assembly equipment. So, provided the sequence of components in the equipment is synchronized with the sequence of models moving through the process, the process seems to be almost totally repetitive.

Continuous processes

Continuous processes

Continuous processes are one step beyond mass processes insomuch as they operate at even higher volume and often have even lower variety. They also usually operate for longer periods of time. Sometimes they are literally continuous in that their products are inseparable, being produced in an endless flow. Continuous processes are often associated with relatively inflexible, capital-intensive technologies with highly predictable flow. Examples of continuous processes include petrochemical refineries, electricity utilities, steel making and some paper making. There are often few elements of discretion in this type of process and although products may be stored during the process, the predominant characteristic of most continuous

This continuous water treatment process almost never stops (it only stops for maintenance) and performs a narrow range of tasks (filters impurities). Often we only notice the process if it goes wrong!

processes is of smooth flow from one part of the process to another. Inspections are likely to form part of the process, although the control applied as a consequence of those inspections is often automatic rather than requiring human discretion.

Professional services

Professional services

Professional services are defined as high-contact organizations where customers spend a considerable time in the service process. Such services provide high levels of customization, the service process being highly adaptable in order to meet individual customer needs. A great deal of staff time is spent in the front office and contact staff are given considerable discretion in servicing customers. Professional services tend to be people-based rather than equipment-based, with emphasis placed on the process (how the service is delivered) rather than the 'product' (what is delivered). Professional services include management consultants, lawyers' practices, architects, doctors' surgeries, auditors, health and safety inspectors and some computer field service operations. A typical example would be OEE, a consultancy that sells the problem-solving

Here consultants are preparing to start a consultancy assignment. They are discussing how they might approach the various stages of the assignment, from understanding the real nature of the problem through to the implementation of their recommended solutions. This is a process map, although a very high level one. It guides the nature and sequence of the consultants' activities.

expertise of its skilled staff to tackle clients' problems. Typically, the problem will first be discussed with clients and the boundaries of the project defined. Each 'product' is different, and a high proportion of work takes place at the client's premises, with frequent contact between consultants and the client.

Service shops

Service shops are characterized by levels of customer contact, customization, volumes of customers and staff discretion, which position them between the extremes of professional and mass services (see next paragraph). Service is provided via mixes of front- and back-office activities. Service shops include banks, high-street shops, holiday tour operators, car rental companies, schools, most restaurants, hotels and travel agents. For example, an equipment hire and sales organization may have a range of products displayed in front-office outlets, while back-office operations look after purchasing and administration. The front-office staff have some technical training and can advise customers during the process of selling the product. Essentially the customer is buying a fairly standardized product but will be influenced by the process of the sale which is customized to the customer's individual needs.

The health club shown in the picture has front-office staff who can give advice on exercise programmes and other treatments. To maintain a dependable service the staff need to follow defined processes every day.

Mass services

Mass services have many customer transactions, involving limited contact time and little customization. Such services may be equipment-based and 'product'-oriented, with most value added in the back office and relatively little judgement applied by front-office staff. Staff are likely to have a closely defined division of labour and to follow set procedures. Mass services include supermarkets, a national rail network, an airport, telecommunications services and libraries. For example, rail services such as SNCF in France all move a large number of passengers with a variety of rolling stock on an immense infrastructure of railways. Passengers pick a journey from the range offered. One of the most common types of mass service is the call centres used by almost all companies that deal directly with consumers. Coping with a very high volume of enquiries requires some kind of structuring of the process of communicating with customers. This is often achieved by using a carefully designed enquiry process (sometimes known as a 'script').

This is an account management centre for a large retail bank. It deals with thousands of customer requests every day. Although each customer request is different, they are all of the same type – involving customers' accounts.

Critical commentary

Although the idea of process types is useful insomuch as it reinforces the, sometimes important, distinctions between different types of process, it is in many ways simplistic. In reality there is no clear boundary between process types. For example, a specialist camera retailer would normally be categorized as a service shop, yet it also will give, sometimes very specialized, technical advice to customers. It is not a professional service like a consultancy of course, but it does have elements of a professional service process within its design. This is why the volume and variety characteristics of a process are sometimes seen as being a more realistic way of describing processes. The product–process matrix described next adopts this approach.

The product–process matrix

Making comparisons between different processes along a spectrum which goes, for example, from shipbuilding at one extreme to electricity generation at the other has limited value. No one grumbles that yachts are so much more expensive than electricity. The real point is that because the different process types overlap, organizations often have a choice of what type of process to employ. This choice will have consequences to the operation, especially in terms of its cost and flexibility. The classic representation of how cost and flexibility vary with process choice is the **product–process matrix** that comes from Professors Hayes and Wheelwright of Harvard University.[3] They represent process choices on a matrix with the volume–variety as one dimension, and process types as the other (our matrix has been updated to incorporate both product and service operations). Figure 5.3 shows their matrix adapted to fit with the terminology used here. Most operations stick to **the 'natural' diagonal** of the matrix, and few, if any, are found in the extreme corners of the matrix. However, because there is some overlap between the various process types, operations might be positioned slightly off the diagonal.

The diagonal of the matrix shown in Figure 5.3 represents a 'natural' lowest cost position for an operation. Operations which are on the right of the 'natural' diagonal have processes which would normally be associated with lower volumes and higher variety. This means that their processes are likely to be more flexible than seems to be warranted by their actual volume–variety position. Put another way, they are not taking advantage of their ability to standardize their processes. Therefore, their costs are likely to be higher than they would be with a process that was closer to the diagonal. Conversely, operations that are on the left of the diagonal have adopted processes which would normally be used in a higher-volume and lower-variety situation. Their processes will therefore be 'over-standardized' and probably too inflexible for their volume–variety position. This lack of flexibility can also lead to high costs because the process will not be able to change from one activity to another as efficiently as a more flexible process.

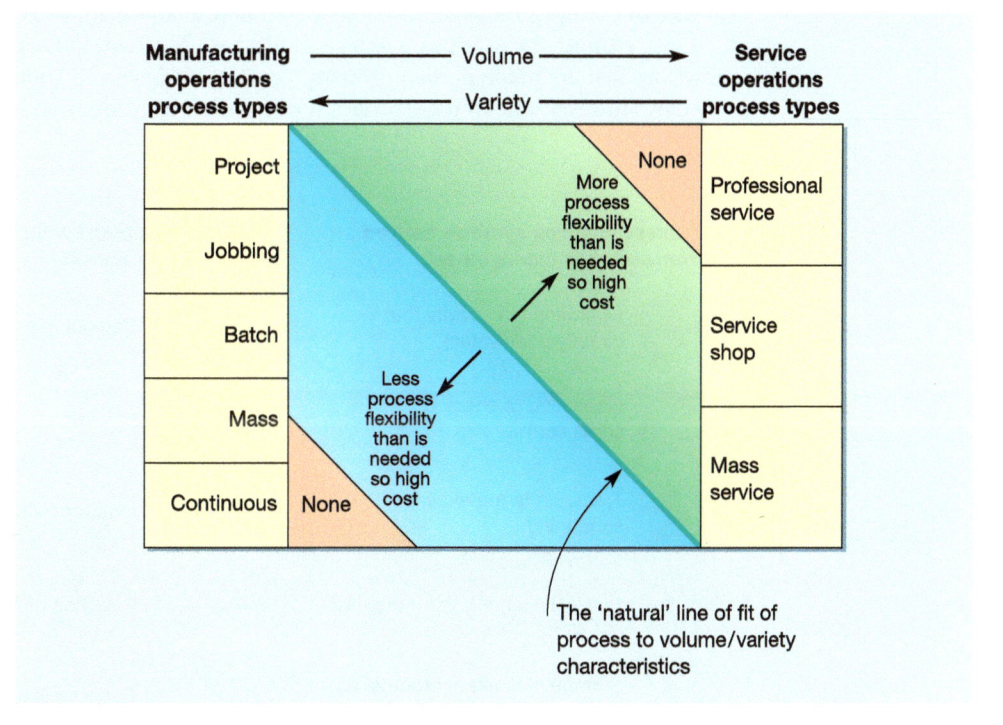

Figure 5.3 Deviating from the 'natural' diagonal on the product–process matrix has consequences for cost and flexibility

Source: Based on Hayes and Wheelwright[4]

Detailed process design

After the overall design of a process has been determined, its individual activities must be configured. At its simplest this detailed design of a process involves identifying all the individual activities that are needed to fulfil the objectives of the process and deciding on the sequence in which these activities are to be performed and who is going to do them. There will, of course, be some constraints on this. Some activities must be carried out before others and some activities can only be done by certain people or machines. Nevertheless, for a process of any reasonable size, the number of alternative process designs is usually large. This means that process design is often done using some simple visual approach such as **process mapping**.

Process mapping

Process mapping simply involves describing processes in terms of how the activities within the process relate to each other. There are many techniques which can be used for *process mapping* (or **process blueprinting**, or **process analysis**, as it is sometimes called). However, all the techniques identify the different *types of* activity that take place during the process and show the flow of materials or people or information through the process.

Process mapping symbols

Process mapping symbols are used to classify different types of activity. And although there is no universal set of symbols used all over the world for any type of process, there are some that are commonly used. Most of these derive either from the early days of 'scientific' management around a century ago or, more recently, from information system flowcharting. Figure 5.4 shows the symbols we shall use here.

These symbols can be arranged in order, and in series or in parallel, to describe any process. For example, the retail catering operation of a large campus university has a number of outlets around the campus selling sandwiches. Most of these outlets sell 'standard' sandwiches that are made in the university's central kitchens and transported to each outlet every day. However, one of these outlets is different; it is a kiosk that makes more expensive

Process mapping symbols derived from scientific management

- ○ Operation (an activity that directly adds value)
- ▢ Inspection (a check of some sort)
- ⇨ Transport (a movement of something)
- D Delay (a wait, e.g. for materials)
- ▽ Storage (deliberate storage, as opposed to a delay)

Process mapping symbols derived from system analysis

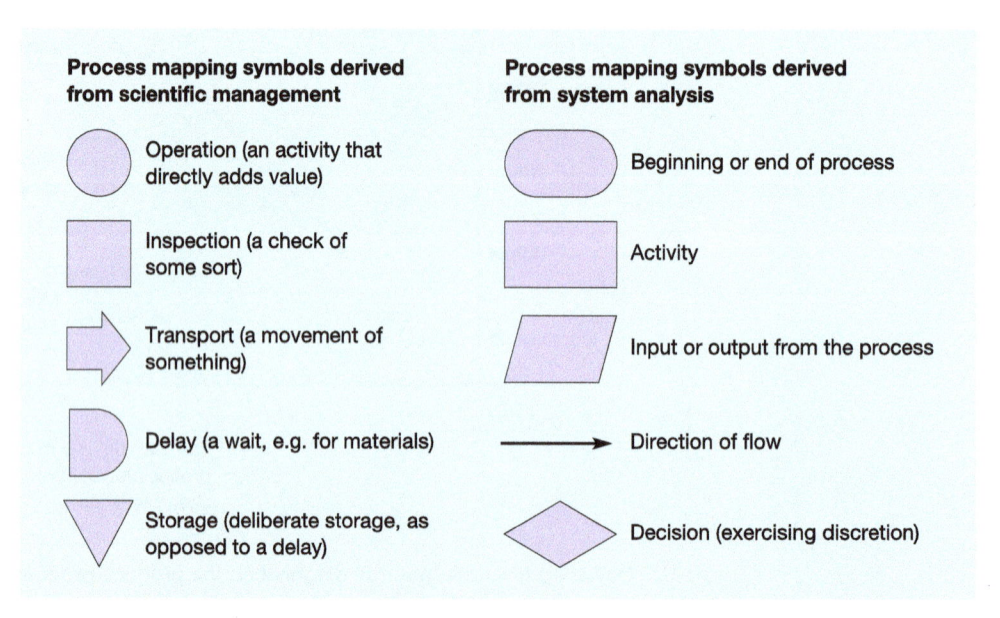

- ⬭ Beginning or end of process
- ▢ Activity
- ▱ Input or output from the process
- → Direction of flow
- ◇ Decision (exercising discretion)

Figure 5.4 Some common process mapping symbols

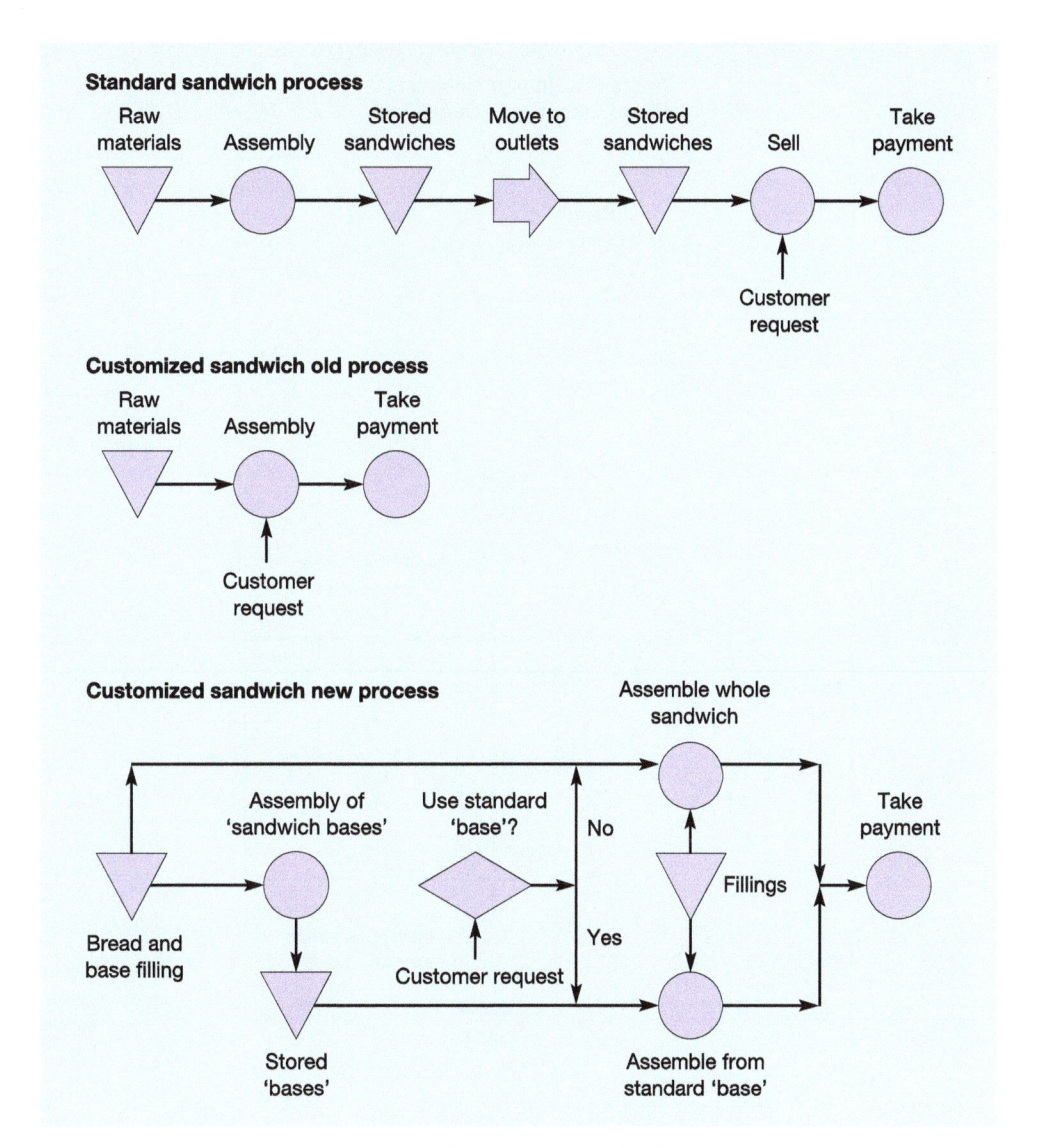

Figure 5.5 Process maps for three sandwich making and selling processes

'customized' sandwiches to order. Customers can specify the type of bread they want and choose from a very wide combination of different fillings. As queues for this customized service are becoming excessive, the catering manager is considering redesigning the process to speed it up. This new process design is based on the findings from a recent student study of the current process which proved that 95 per cent of all customers ordered only two types of bread (soft roll and Italian bread) and three types of protein filling (cheese, ham and chicken). Therefore the six 'sandwich bases' (2 types of bread × 3 protein fillings) could be prepared in advance and customized with salad, mayonnaise, etc. as customers ordered them. The process maps for making and selling the standard sandwiches, the current customized sandwiches and the new customized process are shown in Figure 5.5.

Note how the introduction of some degree of discretion in the new process makes it more complex to map at this detailed level. This is one reason why processes are often mapped at a more aggregated level, called **high-level process mapping**, before more detailed maps are drawn. Figure 5.6 illustrates this for the new customized sandwich operation. At the highest level the process can be drawn simply as an input–transformation–output process with sandwich materials and customers as its input resources and satisfied

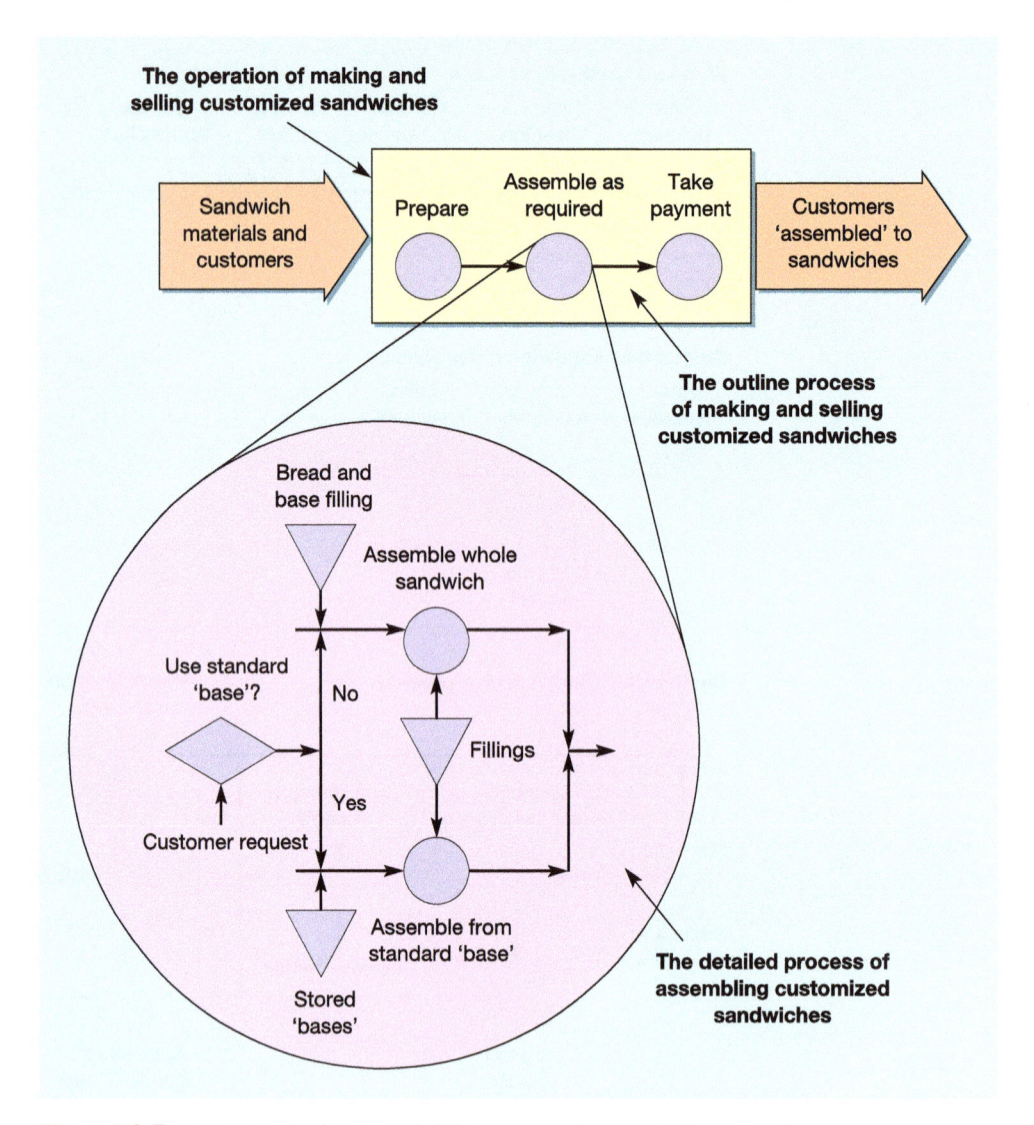

Figure 5.6 The new customized sandwich process mapped at three levels

customers with 'assembled' sandwiches as outputs. No details of how inputs are transformed into outputs are included. At a slightly lower, or more detailed level, what is sometimes called an **outline process map** (or chart) identifies the sequence of activities but only in a general way. So the activity of finding out what type of sandwich a customer wants, deciding if it can be assembled from a sandwich 'base' and then assembling it to meet the customer's request, is all contained in the general activity 'assemble as required'. At the more detailed level, all the activities are shown (we have shown the activities within 'assemble as required').

Outline process map

Using process maps to improve processes

One significant advantage of mapping processes is that each activity can be systematically challenged in an attempt to improve the process. For example, Figure 5.7 shows the flow process chart which Intel Corporation, the computer chip company, drew to describe its method of processing expense reports (claims forms). It also shows the process chart for the same process after critically examining and improving the process. The new process cut the number

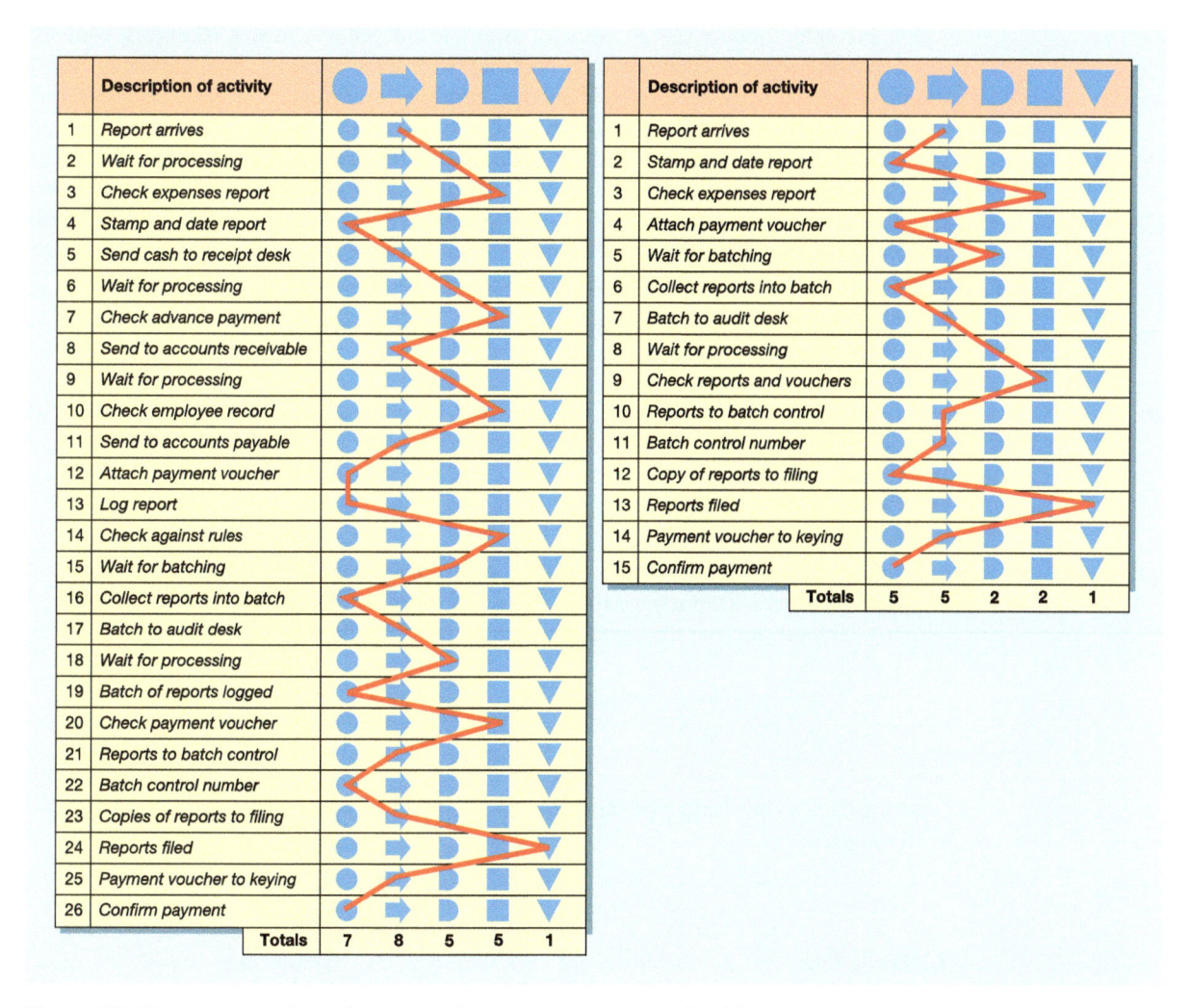

	Description of activity	●	➡	D	■	▼
1	Report arrives					
2	Wait for processing					
3	Check expenses report					
4	Stamp and date report					
5	Send cash to receipt desk					
6	Wait for processing					
7	Check advance payment					
8	Send to accounts receivable					
9	Wait for processing					
10	Check employee record					
11	Send to accounts payable					
12	Attach payment voucher					
13	Log report					
14	Check against rules					
15	Wait for batching					
16	Collect reports into batch					
17	Batch to audit desk					
18	Wait for processing					
19	Batch of reports logged					
20	Check payment voucher					
21	Reports to batch control					
22	Batch control number					
23	Copies of reports to filing					
24	Reports filed					
25	Payment voucher to keying					
26	Confirm payment					
	Totals	7	8	5	5	1

	Description of activity	●	➡	D	■	▼
1	Report arrives					
2	Stamp and date report					
3	Check expenses report					
4	Attach payment voucher					
5	Wait for batching					
6	Collect reports into batch					
7	Batch to audit desk					
8	Wait for processing					
9	Check reports and vouchers					
10	Reports to batch control					
11	Batch control number					
12	Copy of reports to filing					
13	Reports filed					
14	Payment voucher to keying					
15	Confirm payment					
	Totals	5	5	2	2	1

Figure 5.7 Flow process charts for processing expense reports at Intel before and after improving the process

of activities from 26 down to 15. The accounts payable's activities were combined with the cash-receipt's activities of checking employees' past expense accounts (activities 8, 10 and 11) which also eliminated activities 5 and 7. After consideration, it was decided to eliminate the activity of checking items against company rules, because it seemed '*more trouble than it was worth*'. Also, logging the batches was deemed unnecessary. All this combination and elimination of activities had the effect of removing several 'delays' from the process. The end-result was a much-simplified process which reduced the staff time needed to do the job by 28 per cent and considerably speeded up the whole process.

Throughput, cycle time and work-in-process

The new customized sandwich process has one indisputable advantage over the old process: it is faster in the sense that customers spend less time in the process. The additional benefit this brings is a reduction in cost per customer served (because more customers can be served without increasing resources). Note, however, that the total amount of work needed to make and sell a sandwich has not reduced. All the new process has done is to move some of the work to a less busy time. So the **work content** (the total amount of work required to produce a unit of output) has not changed but customer **throughput time** (the time for a unit to move through the process) has improved.

Work content
Throughput time

Cycle time

Work-in-process

For example, suppose that the time to assemble and sell a sandwich (the work content) using the old process was two minutes and that two people were staffing the process during the busy period. Each person could serve a customer every two minutes, therefore every two minutes two customers were being served, so on average a customer is emerging from the process every minute. This is called the **cycle time** of the process, the average time between units of output emerging from the process. When customers join the queue in the process they become **work-in-process** (or work-in-progress) sometimes written as WIP. If the queue is ten people long (including that customer) when the customer joins it, he or she will have to wait ten minutes to emerge from the process. Put more succinctly:

$$\text{Throughput time} = \text{Work-in-process} \times \text{Cycle time}$$

In this case,

$$10 \text{ minutes wait} = 10 \text{ people in the system} \times 1 \text{ minute per person}$$

Worked example

Suppose the regional back-office operation of a large bank is designing an operation which will process its mortgage applications. The number of applications to be processed is 160 per week and the time available to process the applications is 40 hours per week.

$$\text{Cycle time for the process} = \frac{\text{time available}}{\text{number to be processed}} = \frac{40}{160} = \frac{1}{4} \text{ hour}$$

$$= 15 \text{ minutes}$$

So the bank's layout must be capable of processing a completed application once every 15 minutes.

Little's law

Little's law

This mathematical relationship (throughput time = work-in-process × cycle time) is called **Little's law**. It is simple but very useful, and it works for any stable process. For example, suppose it is decided that, when the new process is introduced, the average number of customers in the process should be limited to around ten and the maximum time a customer is in the process should be on average four minutes. If the time to assemble and sell a sandwich (from customer request to the customer leaving the process) in the new process has reduced to 1.2 minutes, how many staff should be serving?

Putting this into Little's law:

$$\text{Throughput time} = 4 \text{ minutes}$$

and

$$\text{Work-in-progress, WIP} = 10$$

So, since

$$\text{Throughput time} = \text{WIP} \times \text{Cycle time}$$

$$\text{Cycle time} = \frac{\text{Throughput time}}{\text{WIP}}$$

$$\text{Cycle time for the process} = \frac{4}{10} = 0.4 \text{ minute}$$

That is, a customer should emerge from the process every 0.4 minute, on average.

Given that an individual can be served in 1.2 minutes,

$$\text{Number of servers required} = \frac{1.2}{0.4} = 3$$

In other words, three servers would serve three customers in 1.2 minutes. Or one customer in 0.4 minute.

Worked example

Mike was totally confident in his judgement, *'You'll never get them back in time'*, he said. *'They aren't just wasting time, the process won't allow them to all have their coffee and get back for 11 o'clock.'* Looking outside the lecture theatre, Mike and his colleague Silvia were watching the 20 business people who were attending the seminar queuing to be served coffee and biscuits. The time was 10.45 and Silvia knew that unless they were all back in the lecture theatre at 11 o'clock there was no hope of finishing his presentation before lunch. *'I'm not sure why you're so pessimistic'*, said Silvia. *'They seem to be interested in what I have to say and I think they will want to get back to hear how operations management will change their lives.'* Mike shook his head. *'I'm not questioning their motivation'*, he said, *'I'm questioning the ability of the process out there to get through them all in time. I have been timing how long it takes to serve the coffee and biscuits. Each coffee is being made fresh and the time between the server asking each customer what they want and them walking away with their coffee and biscuits is taking 48 seconds. Remember that, according to Little's law, throughput equals work-in-process multiplied by cycle time. If the work-in-process is the 20 managers in the queue and cycle time is 48 seconds, the total throughput time is going to be 20 multiplied by 0.8 minute which equals 16 minutes. Add to that sufficient time for the last person to drink their coffee and you must expect a total throughput time of a bit over 20 minutes. You just haven't allowed long enough for the process.'* Silvia was impressed. *'Err . . . what did you say that law was called again?' 'Little's law'*, said Mike.

Worked example

Every year it was the same. All the workstations in the building had to be renovated (tested, new software installed, etc.) and there was only one week in which to do it. The one week fell in the middle of the August vacation period when the renovation process would cause minimum disruption to normal working. Last year the company's 500 workstations had all been renovated within one working week (40 hours). Each renovation last year took on average 2 hours and 25 technicians had completed the process within the week. This year there would be 530 workstations to renovate but the company's IT support unit had devised a faster testing and renovation routine that would only take on average 1½ hours instead of 2 hours. How many technicians will be needed this year to complete the renovation processes within the week?

Last year:

$$\text{Work-in-progress (WIP)} = 500 \text{ workstations}$$
$$\text{Time available } (T_t) = 40 \text{ hours}$$
$$\text{Average time to renovate} = 2 \text{ hours}$$
$$\text{Therefore throughput rate } (T_r) = \tfrac{1}{2} \text{ hour per technician}$$
$$= 0.5N$$

where $N = $ Number of technicians

Little's law:

$$WIP = T_t \times T_r$$
$$500 = 40 \times 0.5N$$
$$N = \frac{500}{40 \times 0.5}$$
$$= 25 \text{ technicians}$$

This year:

Work-in-progress (WIP) = 530 workstations
Time available = 40 hours
Average time to renovate = 1.5 hours
Throughput rate $(T_r) = 1/1.5$ per technician
$= 0.67N$

where N = Number of technicians

Little's law:

$$WIP = T_t \times T_r$$
$$530 = 40 \times 0.67N$$
$$N = \frac{530}{40 \times 0.67}$$
$$= 19.88 \text{ technicians}$$
$$\approx 20 \text{ technicians}$$

Balancing and bottlenecks

Balancing

One of the most important design decisions in layout is that of **balancing**. Perfect balancing would mean that work content is allocated equally to each stage in the process. This is nearly always impossible to achieve in practice and some imbalance in the work allocation results. Inevitably this will increase the effective cycle time of the process. If it becomes greater than the required cycle time, it may be necessary to devote extra resources, in the shape of a further stage, to compensate for the imbalance. The effectiveness of the balancing activity is measured by **balancing loss**. This is the time wasted through the unequal allocation of work as a percentage of the total time invested in processing the product or service. The longest stage in the process is called a '**bottleneck**'. It will govern the flow of items through the whole process.

Balancing loss

Bottleneck

Worked example

In Figure 5.8 the work allocations in a four-stage process are illustrated. The total amount of time invested in creating each service or product is four times the cycle time because, for every unit produced, all four stages have been working for the cycle time. When the work is equally allocated between the stages, the total time invested in each service or product is $4 \times 2.5 = 10$ minutes. However, when work is unequally allocated, as illustrated, the time invested is $3.0 \times 4 = 12$ minutes, i.e. 2.0 minutes of time, 16.67 per cent of the total, is wasted.

Figure 5.8 Balancing loss is that proportion of the time invested in processing the product or service which is not used productively

Calculating balancing loss:

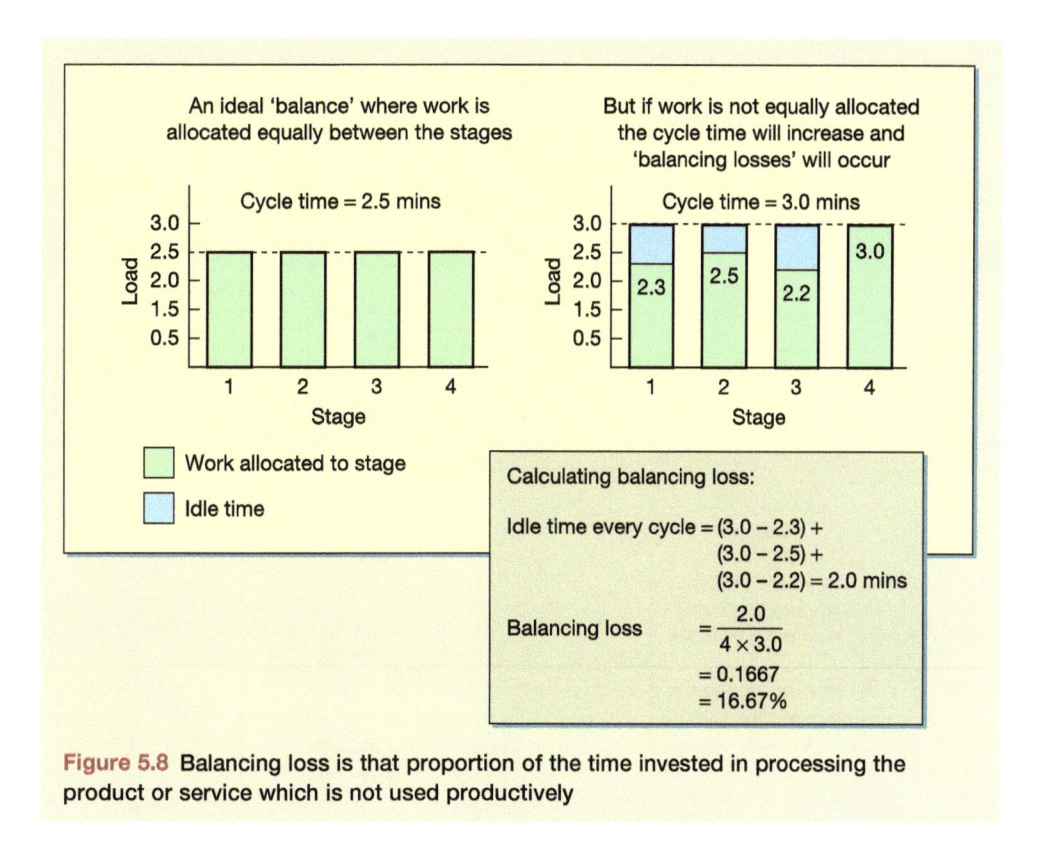

Idle time every cycle = (3.0 − 2.3) + (3.0 − 2.5) + (3.0 − 2.2) = 2.0 mins

Balancing loss $= \dfrac{2.0}{4 \times 3.0}$
$= 0.1667$
$= 16.67\%$

'Long thin' on 'short fat' processes

Return to the mortgage-processing process in the earlier worked example. It requires four stages working on the task to maintain a cycle time of one processed application every 15 minutes. The conventional arrangement of the four stages would be to lay them out in one line, each stage having 15 minutes' worth of work. However, nominally, the same output rate could also be achieved by arranging the four stages as two shorter lines, each of two stages with 30 minutes' worth of work each. Alternatively, following this logic to its ultimate conclusion, the stages could be arranged as four parallel stages, each responsible for the whole work content. Figure 5.9 shows these options.

This may be a simplified example, but it represents a genuine issue. Should the process be arranged as a single **long thin** line, as several **short fat** parallel lines, or somewhere in between? (Note that 'long' refers to the number of stages and 'fat' to the amount of work allocated to each stage.) In any particular situation there are usually technical constraints which limit either how 'long and thin' or how 'short and fat' the process can be, but there is usually a range of possible options within which a choice needs to be made.

The advantages of long thin processes include:

- *Controlled flow of materials or customers* – which is easy to manage.
- *Simple materials handling* – especially if a product being manufactured is heavy, large or difficult to move.
- *Lower capital requirements*. If a specialist piece of equipment is needed for one element in the job, only one piece of equipment would need to be purchased; on short fat arrangements every stage would need one.
- *More efficient operation*. If each stage is only performing a small part of the total job, the person at the stage will have a higher proportion of direct productive work as opposed to the non-productive parts of the job, such as picking up tools and materials.

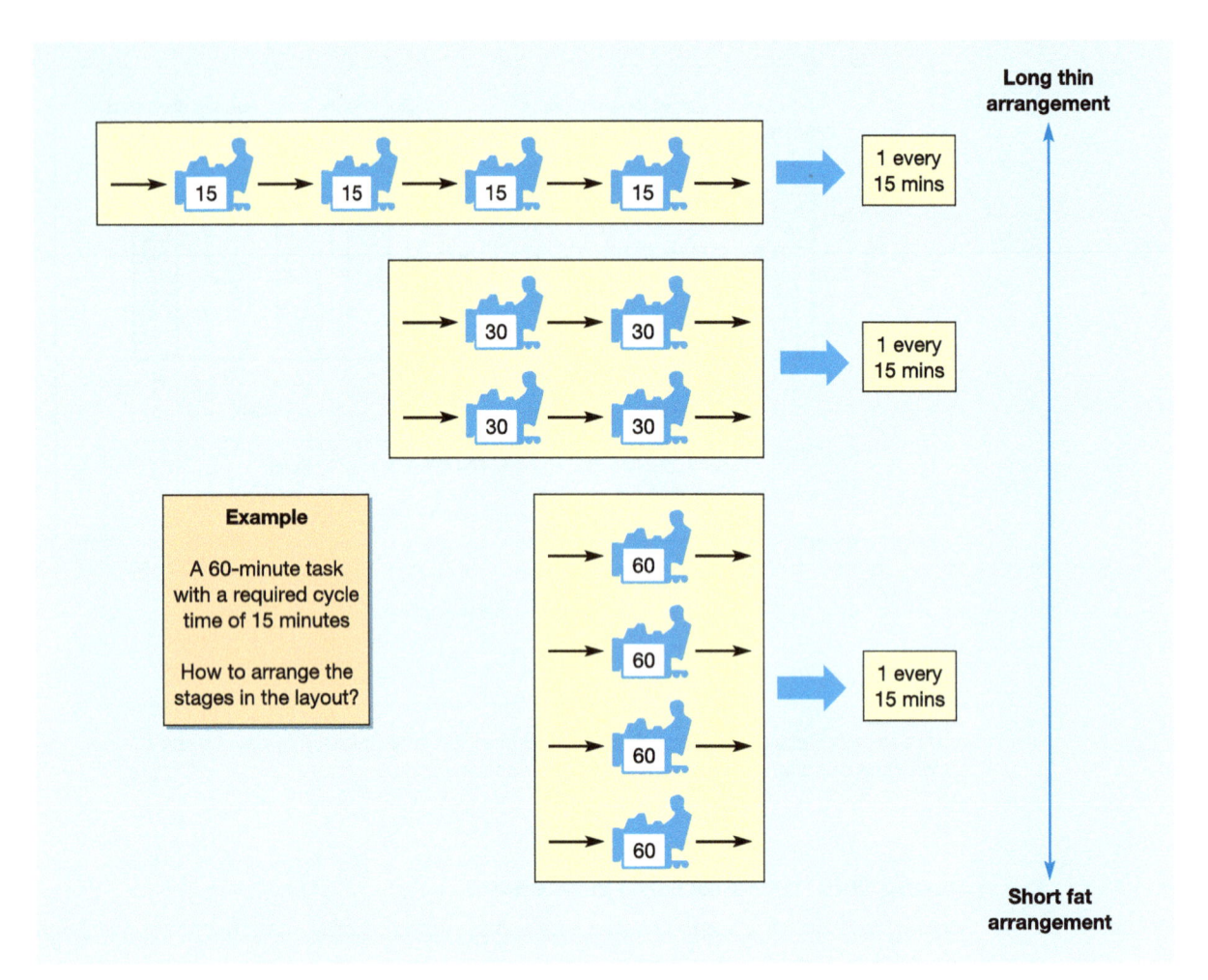

Figure 5.9 The arrangement of stages in product layout can be described on a spectrum from 'long thin' to 'short fat'

The advantages of the short fat processes include:

- *Higher mix flexibility*. If the layout needs to process several types of product or service, each stage or line could specialize in different types.
- *Higher volume flexibility*. As volume varies, stages can simply be closed down or started up as required; long thin processes would need rebalancing each time the cycle time changed.
- *Higher robustness*. If one stage breaks down or ceases operation in some way, the other parallel stages are unaffected; a long thin process would cease operating completely.
- *Less monotonous work*. In the mortgage example, the staff in the short fat arrangement are repeating their tasks only every hour; in the long thin arrangement it is every 15 minutes.

Throughput efficiency

This idea that the throughput time of a process is different from the work content of whatever it is processing has important implications. What it means is that for significant amounts of time no useful work is being done to the materials, information or customers that are progressing through the process. In the case of the simple example of the sandwich process described earlier, customer throughput time is restricted to 4 minutes, but the work content of the task (serving the customer) is only 1.2 minutes. So, the item being processed (the customer) is only being 'worked on' for 1.2/4 = 30 per cent of its time. This is called the **throughput efficiency** of the process.

$$\text{Percentage throughput efficiency} = \frac{\text{Work content}}{\text{Throughput time}} \times 100$$

In this case the throughput efficiency is very high, relative to most processes, perhaps because the 'items' being processed are customers who react badly to waiting. In most material and information transforming processes, throughput efficiency is far lower, usually in single percentage figures.

Worked example

A vehicle licensing centre receives application documents, keys in details, checks the information provided on the application, classifies the application according to the type of licence required, confirms payment and then issues and mails the licence. It is currently processing an average of 5,000 licences every 8-hour day. A recent spot check found 15,000 applications that were 'in progress' or waiting to be processed. The sum of all activities that are required to process an application is 25 minutes. What is the throughput efficiency of the process?

$$\text{Work-in-progress} = 15{,}000 \text{ applications}$$

$$\text{Cycle time} = \frac{\text{Time producing}}{\text{Number produced}} = \frac{8 \text{ hours}}{5{,}000} = \frac{480 \text{ minutes}}{5{,}000} = 0.096 \text{ minute}$$

From Little's law,

$$\text{Throughput time} = \text{WIP} \times \text{Cycle time}$$

$$\text{Throughput time} = 15{,}000 \times 0.096$$

$$= 1{,}440 \text{ minutes}$$

$$\text{Throughput efficiency} = \frac{\text{Work content}}{\text{Throughput time}} = \frac{25}{1{,}440} = 1.74 \text{ per cent}$$

Although the process is achieving a throughput time of 24 hours (which seems reasonable for this kind of process) the applications are only being worked on for 1.74 per cent of the time they are in the process.

Value-added throughput efficiency

The approach to calculating throughput efficiency that is described above assumes that all the 'work content' is actually needed. Yet we have already seen from the Intel expense report example that changing a process can significantly reduce the time that is needed to complete the task. Therefore, work content is actually dependent upon the methods and technology used to perform the task. It may be also that individual elements of a task may not be considered 'value-added'. In the Intel expense report example the new method eliminated some steps because they were 'not worth it', that is, they were not seen as adding value. So, **value-added throughput efficiency** restricts the concept of work content to only those tasks that are actually adding value to whatever is being processed. This often eliminates activities such as movement, delays and some inspections.

For example, if in the licensing worked example, of the 25 minutes of work content only 20 minutes were actually adding value, then

$$\text{Value-added throughput efficiency} = \frac{20}{1{,}440} = 1.39 \text{ per cent}$$

Workflow[5]

When the transformed resource in a process is information (or documents containing information), and when information technology is used to move, store and manage the information, process design is sometimes called 'workflow' or 'workflow management'. It is defined as 'the automation of procedures where documents, information or tasks are passed between participants according to a defined set of rules to achieve, or contribute to, an overall business goal'. Although workflow may be managed manually, it is almost always managed using an IT system. More specifically, workflow is concerned with the following:

- analysis, modelling, definition and subsequent operational implementation of business processes;
- the technology that supports the processes;
- the procedural (decision) rules that move information or documents through processes;
- defining the process in terms of the sequence of work activities, the human skills needed to perform each activity and the appropriate IT resources.

The effects of process variability

So far in our treatment of process design we have assumed that there is no significant variability either in the demand to which the process is expected to respond or in the time taken for the process to perform its various activities. Clearly, this is not the case in reality. So, it is important to take account of variability in process design.

There are many reasons why **variability** occurs in processes. These can include: the late or early arrival of material, information or customers, a temporary malfunction or breakdown of process technology within a stage of the process, the recycling of 'mis-processed' materials, information or customers to an earlier stage in the process, and variation in the requirements of items being processed. All these sources of variation interact with each other, but result in two fundamental types of variability.

- Variability in the demand for processing at an individual stage within the process, usually expressed in terms of variation in the inter-arrival times of units to be processed.
- Variation in the time taken to perform the activities (i.e. process a unit) at each stage.

To understand the effect of arrival variability on process performance, it is first useful to examine what happens to process performance in a very simple process as arrival time changes under conditions of no variability. For example, the simple process shown in Figure 5.10 is composed of one stage that performs exactly 10 minutes of work. Units arrive at the process at a constant and predictable rate. If the arrival rate is one unit every 30 minutes, then the process will be utilized for only 33.33% of the time, and the units will never have to wait to be processed. This is shown as point A on Figure 5.10. If the arrival rate increases to one arrival every 20 minutes, the utilization increases to 50%, and again the units will not have to wait to be processed. This is point B on Figure 5.10. If the arrival rate increases to one arrival every 10 minutes, the process is now fully utilized, but, because a unit arrives just as the previous one has finished being processed, no unit has to wait. This is point C on Figure 5.10. However, if the arrival rate ever exceeded one unit every 10 minutes, the waiting line in front of the process activity would build up indefinitely, as is shown as point D in Figure 5.10. So, in a perfectly constant and predictable world, the relationship between process waiting time and utilization is a rectangular function as shown by the red dotted line in Figure 5.10.

However, when arrival and process times are variable, then sometimes the process will have units waiting to be processed, while at other times the process will be idle, waiting for units to arrive. Therefore the process will have both a 'non-zero' average queue and be under-utilized in the same period. So, a more realistic point is that shown as point X in Figure 5.10. If the average arrival time were to be changed with the same variability, the blue line in Figure 5.10 would show **the relationship between average waiting time and process utilization**. As the process moves closer to 100% utilization the higher the average waiting time will become. To put it another way, the only way to guarantee very low waiting times for the units is to suffer low process utilization.

Process Design 153

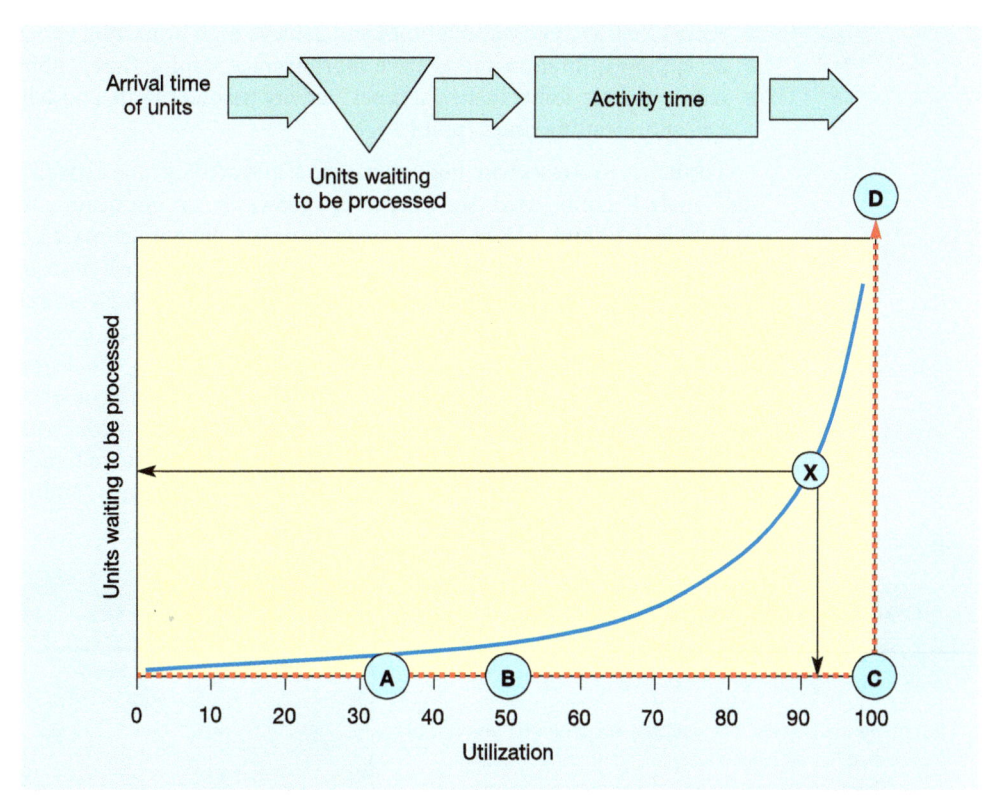

Figure 5.10 The relationship between process utilization and number of units waiting to be processed for constant, and variable, arrival and process times

The greater the variability in the process, the more the waiting time utilization deviates from the simple rectangular function of the 'no variability' conditions that was shown in Figure 5.10. A set of curves for a typical process is shown in Figure 5.11(a). This phenomenon has important implications for the design of processes. In effect it presents three options to process designers wishing to improve the waiting time or utilization performance of their processes, as shown in Figure 5.11(b):

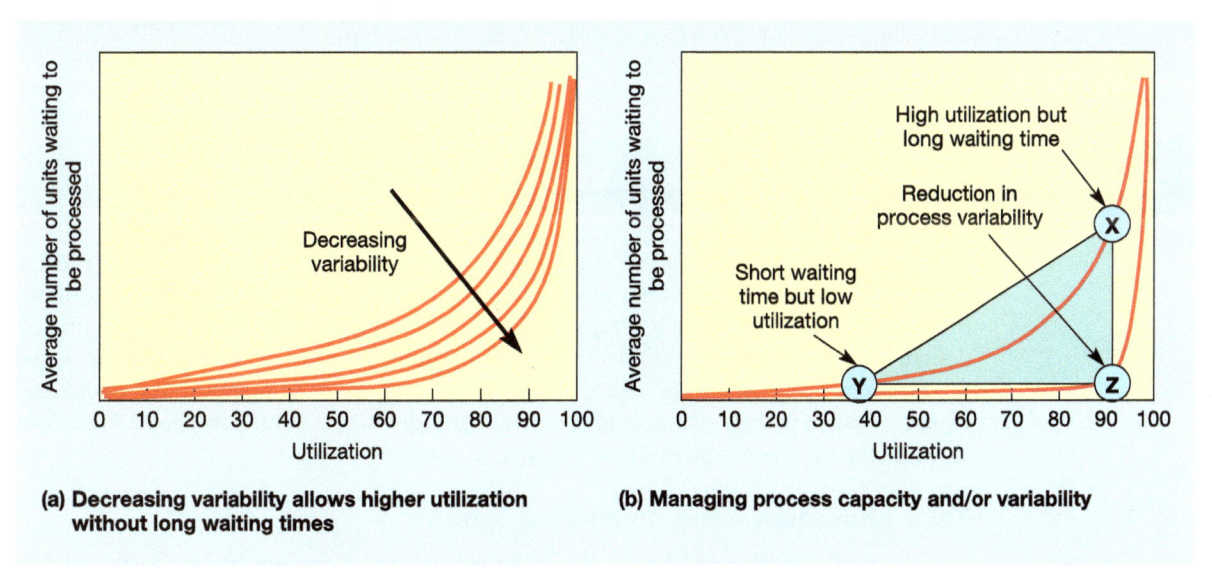

(a) Decreasing variability allows higher utilization without long waiting times

(b) Managing process capacity and/or variability

Figure 5.11 The relationship between process utilization and number of units waiting to be processed for variable arrival and activity times

- accept long average waiting times and achieve high utilization (point X);
- accept low utilization and achieve short average waiting times (point Y); or
- reduce the variability in arrival times, activity times, or both, and achieve higher utilization and short waiting times (point Z).

To analyse processes with both inter-arrival and activity time variability, queuing or 'waiting line' analysis can be used (see Chapter 8). However, do not dismiss the relationship shown in Figures 5.10 and 5.11 as some minor technical phenomenon. It is far more than this. It identifies an important choice in process design that could have strategic implications. Which is more important to a business, fast throughput time or high utilization of its resources? The only way to have both of these simultaneously is to reduce variability in its processes, which may itself require strategic decisions such as limiting the degree of customization of products or services, or imposing stricter limits on how products or services can be delivered to customers, and so on. It also demonstrates an important point concerned with the day-to-day management of processes – the only way to absolutely guarantee a hundred per cent utilization of resources is to accept an infinite amount of work-in-progress and/or waiting time.

Short case
Heathrow delays caused by capacity utilization[6]

It may be the busiest international airport in the world, but it is unlikely to win any prizes for being the most loved. Long delays, overcrowding and a shortage of capacity has meant that Heathrow is often a cause of frustration to harassed passengers. Yet to the airlines it is an attractive hub. Its size and location give it powerful 'network effects'. This means that it can match incoming passengers with outgoing flights to hundreds of different cities. Actually it is its attractiveness to the airlines that is one of its main problems. Heathrow's runways are in such demand that they are almost always operating at, or close to, their maximum capacity. In fact, its runways operate at 99% of capacity. This compares with about 70% at most other large airports. This means that the slightest variability (bad weather or an unscheduled landing such as a plane having to turn back with engine trouble) causes delays, which in turn cause more delays. (See Figure 5.11 for the theoretical explanation of this effect.) The result is that 33% of all flights at Heathrow are delayed by at least 15 minutes. This is poor when compared with other large European airports such as Amsterdam and Frankfurt, which have 21% and 24% of flights delayed respectively.

Human implications for process design

Although we are here dealing with the human implications of process design as the last topic of this chapter, this does not mean that it should be seen as secondary, or unimportant in any way. On the contrary, it is regarded by many as by far the dominant issue of process design. However, there is a whole other field of study – organizational behaviour – that specialises in these issues. Yet, it is included in this chapter in recognition that operations managers are, in practice, the ones who have a significant influence on how people's reactions to their jobs are accommodated in the design of processes.

Task allocation – the division of labour

Division of labour

The idea of the **division of labour** – dividing the total task down into smaller parts, was first formalized as a concept by the economist Adam Smith in his *Wealth of Nations* in 1746.

Perhaps the epitome of the division of labour is the assembly line, where products move along a single path and are built up by operators continually repeating a single task. This is the predominant model of job design in most mass-produced products and in some mass-produced services (fast food, for example). There are some *real advantages* in division of labour:

- *It promotes faster learning.* It is obviously easier to learn how to do a relatively short and simple task than a long and complex one.
- *Automation becomes easier.* Dividing a total task into small parts raises the possibility of automating some of those small tasks.
- *Reduced non-productive work.* This is probably the most important benefit of division of labour. In large, complex tasks the proportion of time spent picking up tools and materials, putting them down again and generally finding, positioning and searching can be very high indeed (called non-productive elements of work). But in shorter, divided, tasks non-productive work can be considerably reduced, which would be very significant to the costs of the operation.

There are also serious drawbacks to highly divided jobs:

- *Monotony.* The shorter the task, the more often operators will need to repeat it. Repeating the same task, for example every 30 seconds, eight hours a day and five days a week, can hardly be called a fulfilling job. As well as any ethical objections, there are other, more obviously practical objections. These include the increased likelihood of absenteeism and staff turnover and the increased likelihood of error.
- *Physical injury.* The continued repetition of a very narrow range of movements can, in extreme cases, lead to physical injury. The over-use of some parts of the body (especially the arms, hands and wrists) can result in pain and a reduction in physical capability. This is sometimes called repetitive strain injury (RSI).
- *Low flexibility.* Dividing a task up into many small parts often gives the job design a rigidity which is difficult to change under changing circumstances.
- *Poor robustness.* Highly divided jobs imply customers, materials or information passing between several stages. If one of these stages is not working correctly, for example because some equipment is faulty, the whole operation is affected.

Scientific management

Related to the division of labour are the ideas of 'scientific' management. The term **scientific management** became established in 1911 with the publication of the book of the same name by Fredrick Taylor (this whole approach to job design is sometimes referred to, pejoratively, as **Taylorism**). In this work he identified what he saw as the basic tenets of scientific management:[7]

- All aspects of work should be investigated on a scientific basis to establish the laws, rules and formulae governing the best methods of working.
- Such an investigative approach to the study of work is necessary to establish what constitutes a 'fair day's work'.
- Workers should be selected, trained and developed methodically to perform their tasks.
- Managers should act as the planners of the work (analysing jobs and standardizing the best method of doing the job) while workers should be responsible for carrying out the jobs to the standards laid down.
- Cooperation should be achieved between management and workers based on the 'maximum prosperity' of both.

The important thing to remember about scientific management is that it is not 'scientific' as such, although it certainly does take an 'investigative' approach to improving operations. Perhaps a better term for it would be 'systematic management'. It gave birth to two separate, but related, fields of study, **method study**, which determines the methods and activities to be included in jobs, and **work measurement**, which is concerned with measuring the time that should be taken for performing jobs. Together, these two fields are often referred to as **work study**.

> ### Critical commentary
>
> Even in 1915, criticisms of the scientific management approach were being voiced.[8] In a submission to the United States Commission on Industrial Relations, scientific management is described as:
>
> - being in 'spirit and essence a cunningly devised speeding up and sweating system';
> - intensifying the 'modern tendency towards specialization of the work and the task';
> - condemning 'the worker to a monotonous routine';
> - putting 'into the hands of employers an immense mass of information and methods that may be used unscrupulously to the detriment of workers';
> - tending to 'transfer to the management all the traditional knowledge, the judgement and skills of workers';
> - greatly intensifying 'unnecessary managerial dictation and discipline';
> - tending to 'emphasize quantity of product at the expense of quality'.

Designing the human interface – ergonomic workplace design

Ergonomics

Human factors engineering

Ergonomics is concerned primarily with the physiological aspects of job design. Physiology is about the way the body functions. It involves two aspects: firstly, how a person interfaces with his or her immediate working area; secondly, how people react to environmental conditions. Ergonomics is sometimes referred to as **human factors engineering** or just 'human factors'. Both aspects are linked by two common ideas:

- There must be a fit between people and the jobs they do. To achieve this fit there are only two alternatives. Either the job can be made to fit the people who are doing it, or, alternatively, the people can be made (or perhaps less radically, recruited) to fit the job. Ergonomics addresses the former alternative.
- It is important to take a 'scientific' approach to job design, for example collecting data to indicate how people react under different job design conditions and trying to find the best set of conditions for comfort and performance.

We will explain further some of the aspects of ergonomics in Chapter 6.

Job commitment – behavioural approaches to job design

Behavioural approach

Processes which are designed purely on division of labour, scientific management or even purely ergonomic principles can alienate the people performing them. Process design should also take into account the desire of individuals to fulfil their needs for self-esteem and personal development. This is where motivation theory and its contribution to the **behavioural approach** to process design is important. This achieves two important objectives. Firstly, it provides jobs which have an intrinsically higher quality of working life – an ethically desirable end in itself. Secondly, because of the higher levels of motivation it engenders, it is instrumental in achieving better performance for the operation, in terms of both the quality and the quantity of output.[9] This approach to job design involves two conceptual steps: firstly, exploring how the various characteristics of the job affect people's motivation; secondly, exploring how individuals' motivation towards the job affects their performance at that job.

Some of the job characteristics that are held to have a positive effect on job satisfaction are as follows.

Job rotation

Job rotation

If increasing the number of related tasks in the job is constrained in some way, for example by the technology of the process, one approach may be to encourage **job rotation**. This means moving individuals periodically between different sets of tasks to provide some variety in their activities. When successful, job rotation can increase skill flexibility and make a small contribution to reducing monotony. However, it is not viewed as universally beneficial either by management (because it can disrupt the smooth flow of work) or by the people performing the jobs (because it can interfere with their rhythm of work).

Job enlargement

The most obvious method of achieving at least some of the objectives of behavioural job design is by allocating a larger number of tasks to individuals. If these extra tasks are broadly of the same type as those in the original job, the change is called **job enlargement**. This may not involve more demanding or fulfilling tasks, but it may provide a more complete and therefore slightly more meaningful job. If nothing else, people performing an enlarged job will not repeat themselves as often, which could make the job less monotonous.

Job enrichment

Job enrichment, not only means increasing the number of tasks, but also allocating extra tasks which involve more decision making, greater autonomy and greater control over the job. For example, the extra tasks could include maintenance, planning and control, or monitoring quality levels. The effect is both to reduce repetition in the job and to increase autonomy and personal development. So, in the assembly-line example, each operator, as well as being allocated a job which is twice as long as that previously performed could also be allocated responsibility for carrying out routine maintenance and such tasks as record-keeping and managing the supply of materials.

Empowerment

Empowerment is usually taken to mean more than simple autonomy. Whereas autonomy means giving staff the *ability* to change how they do their jobs, empowerment means giving staff the *authority* to make changes to the job itself, as well as how it is performed. This can be designed into jobs to different degrees.[10] At a minimum, staff could be asked to contribute their suggestions for how the operation might be improved. Going further, staff could be empowered to redesign their jobs. Further still, staff could be included in the strategic direction and performance of the whole organization. The *benefits* of empowerment are generally seen as providing fast responses to customer needs, employees who feel better about their jobs and who will interact with customers with more enthusiasm, promoting 'word-of-mouth' advertising and customer retention. However, there are *costs* associated with empowerment, including higher selection and training costs, perceived inequity of service and the possibility of poor decisions being made by employees.

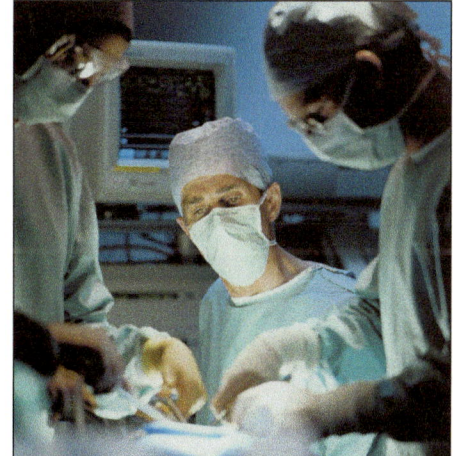

Team-working

A development in job design which is closely linked to the empowerment concept is that of **team-based work organization** (sometimes called self-managed work teams). This is where staff, often with overlapping skills, collectively perform a defined task and have a high degree of discretion over how they actually perform the task. The team would typically control such things as task allocation between members, scheduling work, quality measurement and improvement, and sometimes the hiring of staff. To some extent most work has always been a group-based activity. The concept of teamwork, however, is more prescriptive and assumes a shared set of objectives and responsibilities. Groups are described as teams when the virtues of working together are being emphasized, such as the ability to make use of the various skills within the team. Teams may also be used to compensate for other organizational changes such as the move towards flatter organizational structures. When organizations have fewer managerial levels, each manager will have a wider span of activities to control. Teams which are capable of autonomous decision-making have a clear advantage in these circumstances.

Summary answers to key questions

Check and improve your understanding of this chapter using self-assessment questions and a personalized study plan, audio and video downloads, and an eBook – all at www.myomlab.com.

▶ What is process design?

- Process design is the activity which shapes the physical form and purpose of the processes that create and deliver services and products.
- The overall purpose of process design is to meet the needs of customers through achieving appropriate levels of quality, speed, dependability, flexibility and cost.
- The design activity must also take account of environmental issues. These include examination of the source and suitability of materials, the sources and quantities of energy consumed, the amount and type of waste material, the life of the product itself, and the end-of-life state of the product.

▶ How do volume and variety affect process design?

- The overall nature of any process is strongly influenced by the volume and variety of what it has to process.
- The concept of process types summarizes how volume and variety affect overall process design.
- In manufacturing, these process types are (in order of increasing volume and decreasing variety) project, jobbing, batch, mass and continuous processes. In service operations, the terms often used (again in order of increasing volume and decreasing variety) are professional services, service shops and mass services.

▶ How are processes designed in detail?

- Processes are designed initially by breaking them down into their individual activities. Often common symbols are used to represent types of activity. The sequence of activities in a process is then indicated by the sequence of symbols representing activities. This is called 'process mapping'. Alternative process designs can be compared using process maps and improved processes considered in terms of their operations performance objectives.
- Process performance in terms of throughput time, work-in-progress, and cycle time are related by a formula known as Little's law: throughput time equals work-in-progress multiplied by cycle time.
- Variability has a significant effect on the performance of processes, particularly the relationship between waiting time and utilization.

▶ What are the human implications for process design?

- There are many ideas (and a whole field of study – organizational behaviour) that should be taken into account when designing processes. These include the division of labour, ergonomics and more behavioural approaches such as job rotation, job enlargement, job enrichment, empowerment and team-working.

Learning exercises

These problems and applications will help to improve your analysis of operations. You can find more practice problems as well as worked examples and guided solutions on MyOMLab at www.myomlab.com.

1 Read again the description of fast-food drive-through processes at the beginning of this chapter. (a) Draw a process map that reflects the types of process described. (b) What advantage do you think is given to McDonald's through its decision to establish a call centre for remote order-taking for some of its outlets?

2 A regional government office that deals with passport applications is designing a process that will check applications and issue the documents. The number of applications to be processed is 1,600 per week and the time available to process the applications is 40 hours per week. What is the required cycle time for the process?

3 For the passport office, described above, the total work content of all the activities that make up the total task of checking, processing and issuing a passport is, on average, 30 minutes. How many people will be needed to meet demand?

4 The same passport office has a 'clear desk' policy that means that all desks must be clear of work by the end of the day. How many applications should be loaded onto the process in the morning in order to ensure that every one is completed and desks are clear by the end of the day? (Assume a 7.5-hour (450-minute) working day.)

Want to know more?

Chopra, S., Anupindi, R., Deshmukh, S.D., Van Mieghem, J.A. and Zemel, E. (2006) *Managing Business Process Flows*, Prentice-Hall, Englewood Cliffs, NJ. An excellent, although mathematical, approach to process design in general.

Hammer, M. (1990) Reengineering work: don't automate, obliterate, *Harvard Business Review*, July–August. This is the paper that launched the whole idea of business processes and process management in general to a wider managerial audience. Slightly dated but worth reading.

Hopp, W.J. and Spearman, M.L. (2001) *Factory Physics*, 2nd edn, McGraw-Hill, New York. Very technical so don't bother with it if you aren't prepared to get into the maths. However, there is some fascinating analysis, especially concerning Little's law.

Smith, H. and Fingar, P. (2003) *Business Process Management: The Third Wave*, Meghan-Kiffer Press, Tampa, Fl. A popular book on process management from a business process re-engineering perspective.

Useful websites

www.bpmi.org Site of the Business Process Management Initiative. Some good resources including papers and articles.

www.bptrends.com News site for trends in business process management generally. Some interesting articles.

www.bls.gov/oes/ US Department of Labor employment statistics.

www.fedee.com Federation of European Employers guide to employment and job trends in Europe.

www.iienet.org The Global Association of Productivity and Efficiency Professionals site. This is an important professional body for process design and related topics.

www.opsman.org Lots of useful stuff.

www.waria.com A Workflow and Reengineering Association web site. Some useful topics.

Now that you have finished reading this chapter, why not visit MyOMLab at www.myomlab.com where you'll find more learning resources to help you make the most of your studies and get a better grade.

Chapter 6

Location, layout and flow

Key questions

- Where should operations be located?
- What is 'layout' and what are the types used in operations?
- What type of layout should an operation choose?
- How should items be positioned in a workplace?

Introduction

This chapter is about where you put things or, more formally, how operations resources are positioned relative to each other. We shall examine this positioning at three levels from macro to micro. Firstly, we look at how operations locate their sites geographically. Secondly (and this constitutes the majority of the chapter), we look at the layout of resources within operations and processes. Finally, we briefly examine how equipment is positioned within individuals' work areas. This positioning decision is important because it determines the way transformed resources flow through supply networks, operations and processes. Relatively small changes in the position of products in a supermarket, or changing rooms in a sports centre, or the position of a machine in a factory, can affect the flow through the operation which, in turn, affects the costs and general effectiveness of the operation. Figure 6.1 shows where this chapter fits into the overall operations model.

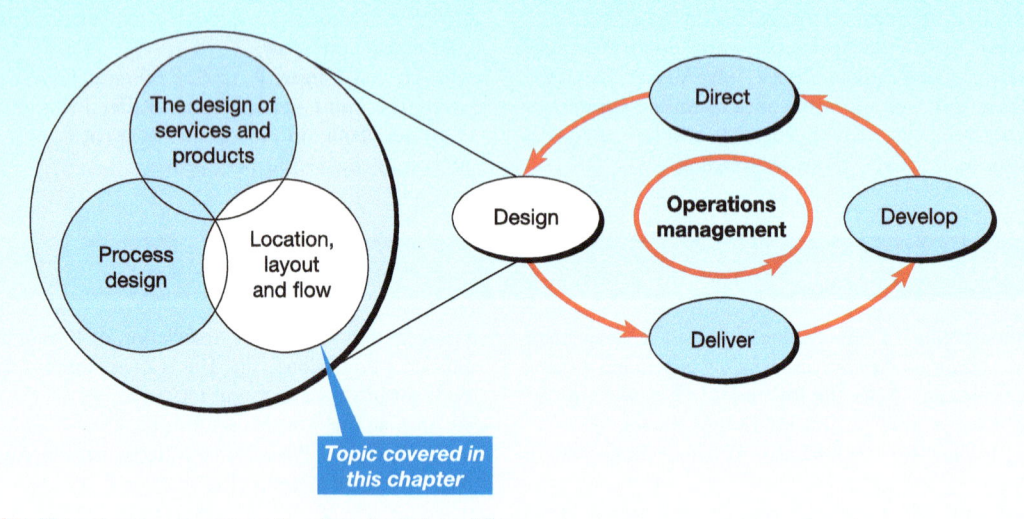

Figure 6.1 This chapter examines location, layout and flow

Check and improve your understanding of this chapter using self-assessment questions and a personalized study plan, audio and video downloads, and an eBook – all at www.myomlab.com.

Operations in practice: Tesco's store flow processes[1]

Finding, purchasing and developing the sites for its retail stores is a major (and controversial) part of Tesco's activities. In its UK market, the main issue is obtaining permission from local government authorities. The UK's planning regime, once relatively relaxed to encourage retail development and stimulate economic growth, is now far stricter, more complicated and takes longer. Frequently there are local objections to supermarket development. Some are from smaller retailers who fear loss of business, some are from residents wary of traffic congestion, and some from people who dislike the dominance of firms like Tesco. To go through all this effort, Tesco must be convinced that any potential location represents a sound business investment. Location (or, more accurately, layout) within their stores is equally important.

Successful supermarkets like Tesco also know that the design of their stores has a huge impact on profitability. They must maximize their revenue per square metre and minimize the costs of operating the store, while keeping customers happy. At a basic level, supermarkets have to get the amount of space allocated to the different areas right. Tesco's 'One in front' campaign, for example, tries to avoid long waiting times by opening additional tills if more than one customer is waiting at a checkout. Tesco also uses technology to understand exactly how customers flow through their stores. The 'Smartlane' system from Irisys, a specialist in intelligent infrared technologies, counts the number and type of customers entering the store (in family or other groups known as 'shopping units'), tracks their movement using infrared sensors, and predicts the likely demand at the checkouts up to an hour in advance. The circulation of customers through the store must be right and the right layout can make customers buy more. Some supermarkets put their entrance on the left-hand side of a building with a layout designed to take customers in a clockwise direction around the store. Aisles are made wide to ensure a relatively slow flow of trolleys so that customers pay more attention to the products on display (and buy more). However, wide aisles can come at the expense of reduced shelf space that would allow a wider range of products to be stocked.

The actual location of all the products is a critical decision, directly affecting the convenience to customers, their level of spontaneous purchase and the cost of filling the shelves. Although the majority of supermarket sales are packaged, tinned or frozen goods, the displays of fruit and vegetables are usually located adjacent to the main entrance, as a signal of freshness and wholesomeness, providing an attractive and welcoming point of entry. Basic products that figure on most people's shopping lists, such as flour, sugar and bread, may be located at the back of the store and apart from each other so that customers have to pass higher-margin items as they search. High-margin items are usually put at eye level on shelves (where they are more likely to be seen) and low-margin products lower down or higher up. Some customers also go a few paces up an aisle before they start looking for what they need. Some supermarkets call the shelves occupying the first metre of an aisle 'dead space' – not a place to put impulse-bought goods. The prime site in a supermarket is the 'gondola-end', the shelves at the end of the aisle. Moving products to this location can increase sales 200 or 300 per cent. It's not surprising that suppliers are willing to pay for their products to be located here. The supermarkets themselves are keen to point out that, although they obviously lay out their stores with customers' buying behaviour in mind, it is counterproductive to be too manipulative. Some commonly held beliefs about supermarket layout are not always true. They deny that they periodically change the location of foodstuffs in order to jolt customers out of their habitual shopping patterns so that they are more attentive to other products and end up buying more. Occasionally layouts are changed, they say mainly to accommodate changing tastes and new ranges. At a more micro-level, Tesco will be concerned to make its checkout areas safe and convenient for its staff and customers. Similarly the design of self checkout equipment must be conveniently designed. So positioning, whether it is location, store layout, or workstation design, will have an impact on Tesco's performance.

The location of operations

It was reputedly Lord Sieff, one-time boss of Marks and Spencer, the UK-based retail organization, who said, '*There are three important things in retailing – location, location and location*', and any retailing operation knows exactly what he meant. Get the location wrong and it can have a significant impact on profits. For example, mislocating a fire service station can slow down the average journey time of the fire crews in getting to the fires; locating a factory where there is difficulty attracting labour with appropriate skills will affect the effectiveness of the factory's operations. Location decisions will usually have an effect on an operation's costs as well as its ability to serve its customers (and therefore its revenues). Also, location decisions, once taken, are difficult to undo. The costs of moving an operation can be hugely expensive and the risks of inconveniencing customers very high. No operation wants to move very often.

Reasons for location decisions

Whilst the location of some operations is largely historical, they are implicitly making a decision not to move. Presumably their assumption is that the cost and disruption involved in changing location would outweigh any potential benefits of a new location. Two stimuli often cause organizations to change locations: changes in demand for their services and products, and changes in supply of their inputs.

Changes in demand. A change in location may be prompted by customer demand shifting. For example, as garment manufacturers moved from Europe to Asia, suppliers of zips, threads, etc. started to follow them. Changes in the volume of demand can also prompt relocation. To meet higher demand, an operation could expand its existing site, choose a larger site in another location, or keep its existing location and find a second location for an additional operation; the last two options will involve a location decision. High-visibility operations may not have the choice of expanding on the same site to meet rising demand. A dry cleaning service may attract only marginally more business by expanding an existing site because it offers a local, and therefore convenient, service. Finding a new location for an additional operation is probably its only option for expansion.

Changes in supply. The other stimulus for relocation is changes in the cost or availability of supply of inputs to the operation. For example, a mining or oil company will need to relocate as the minerals it is extracting become depleted. A manufacturing company might choose to relocate its operations to a part of the world where labour costs are low, because the equivalent resources (people) in its original location have become relatively expensive. Sometimes a business might choose to relocate to release funds if the value of the land it occupies is worth more than an alternative, equally good, location.

The objectives of the location decision

The aim of the location decision is to achieve an appropriate balance between three related objectives:

Spatially variable costs

- the **spatially variable costs** of the operation (spatially variable means that something changes with geographical location);
- the service the operation is able to provide to its customers;
- the revenue potential of the operation.

In for-profit organizations the last two objectives are related. The assumption is that the better the service the operation can provide to its customers, the better will be its potential to attract custom and therefore generate revenue. In not-for-profit organizations, revenue

Short case
The Tata Nano finds a new home[2]

Finding a suitable site for any operation can be a political as well as an economic problem. It certainly was when Tata, the Indian company, unveiled its plans for the Nano in 2007. Named the '1 lakh car' (in India one lakh means 100,000), it would be the cheapest car in the world, with the basic model priced at 100,000 rupees, or $2,500, excluding taxes. The price was about half of existing low-cost cars. The site chosen by Tata was equally bold. It was to be made at Singur, in the Indian state of West Bengal, a populous state with Calcutta (now called Kolkata) as its capital. Although the Communist Party had ruled the state for four decades, the West Bengal government was keen to encourage the Nano plant. It would bring much-needed jobs and send a message that the state welcomed inward investment. In fact, it had won the plant against stiff competition from rival states.

Controversially, the state government had expropriated land for the factory using an old law dating from 1894, which requires private owners to sell land for a 'public purpose'. The government justified this action by pointing out that over 13,000 people had some kind of claim to parts of the land required for the new plant. Tata could not be expected to negotiate, one by one, with all of them. Also financial compensation was offered at significantly above market rates. Unfortunately about 2,250 people refused to accept the offered compensation. The political opposition organized mass protests in support of the farmers who did not want to move. They blocked roads, threatened staff and even assaulted an employee of a Tata supplier. In response, Ratan Tata, chairman of the Tata group, threatened to move the Nano plant from the state if the company really was not wanted, even though the company had already invested 15 billion rupees in the project. Eventually, exasperated with being caught in the 'political crossfire', Tata said it would abandon its factory in the state. Instead, the company selected a location in Gujarat, one of India's most industrialized states, which quickly approved even more land than the West Bengal site.

potential might not be a relevant objective and so cost and customer service are often taken as the twin objectives of location. In making decisions about where to locate an operation, operations managers are concerned with minimizing spatially variable costs and maximizing revenue and customer service. Location affects both of these but not equally for all types of operation. For example, with most products, customers may not care very much where they were made. Location is unlikely to affect the operation's revenues significantly. However, the costs of the operation will probably be very greatly affected by location. Services, on the other hand, often have both costs and revenues affected by location. The location decision for any operation is determined by the relative strength of supply-side and demand-side factors (see Figure 6.2).

Supply-side factors
Which vary to influence costs as location varies.
For example ...
- labour costs
- land costs
- energy costs
- transportation costs
- community factors

→ The operation →

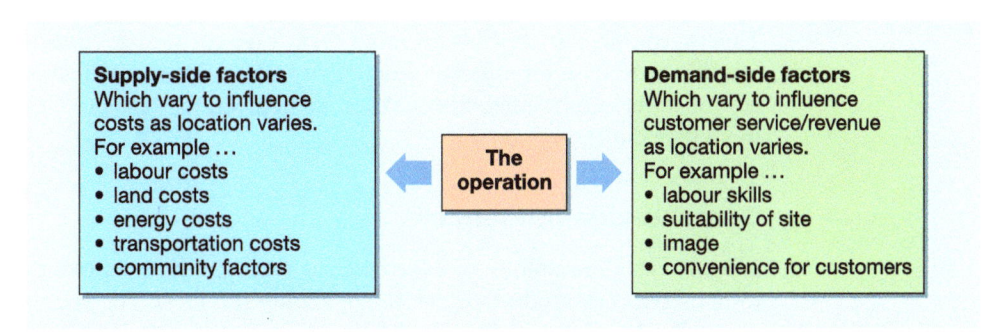

Demand-side factors
Which vary to influence customer service/revenue as location varies.
For example ...
- labour skills
- suitability of site
- image
- convenience for customers

Figure 6.2 Supply-side and demand-side factors in location decisions

Supply-side influences

Labour costs. The costs of employing people with particular skills can vary between different areas in any country, but are likely to be more significant when international comparisons are made. Labour costs can be expressed in two ways. The 'hourly cost' is what firms have to pay workers on average per hour. However, the 'unit cost' is an indication of the labour cost per unit of production. This includes the effects both of productivity differences between countries and of differing currency exchange rates. Exchange rate variation can cause unit costs to change dramatically over time. Yet, labour costs exert a major influence on the location decision, especially in some industries such as clothing, where labour costs as a proportion of total costs are relatively high.

Land costs. The cost of acquiring the site itself is sometimes a relevant factor in choosing a location. Land and rental costs vary between countries and cities. At a more local level, land costs are also important. A retail operation, when choosing 'high-street' sites, will pay a particular level of rent only if it believes it can generate a certain level of revenue from the site.

Energy costs. Operations which use large amounts of energy, such as aluminium smelters, can be influenced in their location decisions by the availability of relatively inexpensive energy. This may be direct, as in the availability of hydroelectric generation in an area, or indirect, such as low-cost coal which can be used to generate inexpensive electricity.

Transportation costs. Transportation costs include both the cost of transporting inputs from their source to the site of the operation, and the cost of transporting goods from the site to customers. Whereas almost all operations are concerned to some extent with the former, not all operations transport goods to customers; rather, customers come to them (for example, hotels). Even for operations that do transport their goods to customers (most manufacturers, for example), we consider transportation as a supply-side factor because as location changes, transportation costs also change. Proximity to sources of *supply* dominates the location decision where the cost of transporting input materials is high or difficult. Food processing and other agriculture-based activities, for example, are often carried out close to growing areas. Conversely, transportation to *customers* dominates location decisions where this is expensive or difficult. Civil engineering projects, for example, are constructed mainly where they will be needed.

Community factors. Community factors are those influences on an operation's costs which derive from the social, political and economic environment of its site. These include:

- local tax rates
- government financial and planning assistance
- political stability, and local attitudes to 'inward investment'
- language
- availability of support services
- history of labour relations and behaviour
- environmental restrictions and waste disposal.

A major influence in where businesses locate is the cost of operating at different locations. Total operating cost depends on more than wage costs, or even total labour costs (which includes allowances for different productivity rates). Figure 6.3 illustrates what makes up the cost of shirts sold in different countries. Remember, the retailer will often sell the item for more than double the cost.[3]

Demand-side influences

Labour skills. The abilities of a local labour force can have an effect on customer reaction to the services or products which the operation produces. For example, 'science parks' are usually located close to universities because they hope to attract companies that are interested in using the skills available at the university.

The cost of a shirt

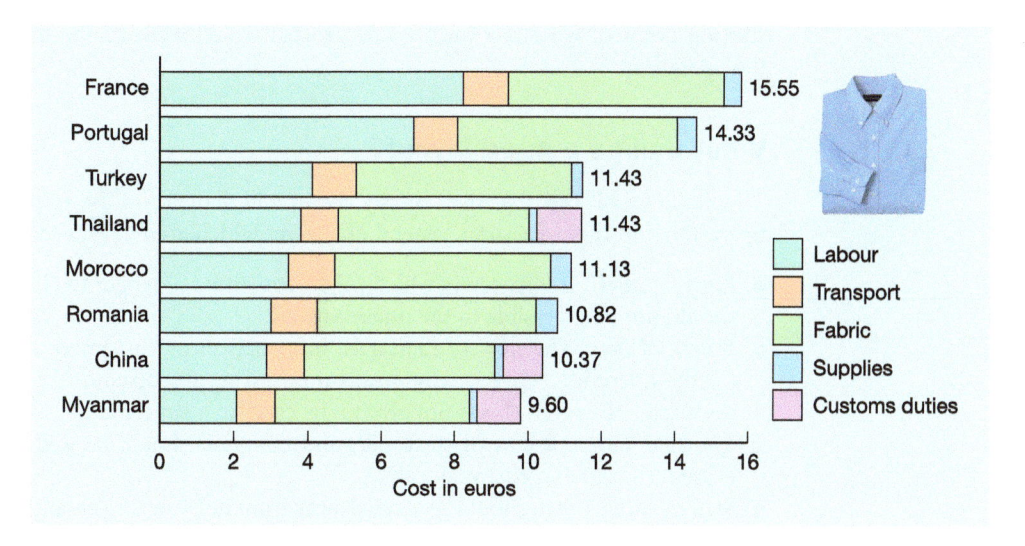

Country	Cost in euros
France	15.55
Portugal	14.33
Turkey	11.43
Thailand	11.43
Morocco	11.13
Romania	10.82
China	10.37
Myanmar	9.60

Components: Labour, Transport, Fabric, Supplies, Customs duties

Figure 6.3 The cost of a shirt

The suitability of the site itself. Different sites are likely to have different intrinsic characteristics which can affect an operation's ability to serve customers and generate revenue. For example, the location of a luxury resort hotel which offers up-market holiday accommodation is very largely dependent on the intrinsic characteristics of the site. Located next to the beach, surrounded by waving palm trees and overlooking a picturesque bay, the hotel is very attractive to its customers. Move it a few kilometres away into the centre of an industrial estate and it rapidly loses its attraction.

Image of the location. Some locations are firmly associated in customers' minds with a particular image. Suits from Savile Row (the centre of the up-market bespoke tailoring district in London) may be no better than high-quality suits made elsewhere but, by locating its operation there, a tailor has probably enhanced its reputation and therefore its revenue. The product and fashion design houses of Milan and the financial services in the City of London also enjoy a reputation shaped partly by that of their location.

Convenience for customers. Of all the demand-side factors, this is, for many operations, the most important. Locating a general hospital, for instance, in the middle of the countryside may have many advantages for its staff, and even perhaps for its costs, but it clearly would be very inconvenient to its customers. Those visiting the hospital would need to travel long distances. This means that general hospitals are located close to centres of demand. Similarly with other public services and restaurants, stores, banks, petrol filling stations etc., location determines the effort to which customers have to go in order to use the operation.

What is layout and what are the types used in operations?

The 'layout' of an operation or process means how its transformed resources are positioned relative to each other and how its various tasks are allocated to these transforming resources. Together these two decisions will dictate the pattern of flow for transformed resources as they progress through the operation or process. It is an important decision because, if the layout proves wrong, it can lead to over-long or confused flow patterns, customer queues, long process times, inflexible operations, unpredictable flow and high cost. Also, re-laying out an existing operation can cause disruption, leading to customer dissatisfaction or lost operating time. So, because the **layout decision** can be difficult and expensive, operations managers are reluctant to do it too often. Therefore layout must start with a full appreciation of the objectives that the layout should be trying to achieve. However, this is only the

The layout decision is relatively infrequent but important

starting point of what is a multi-stage process which leads to the final physical layout of the operation.

What makes a good layout?

To a large extent the objectives of any layout will depend on the strategic objectives of the operation, but there are some general objectives which are relevant to all operations:

- *Inherent safety*. All processes which might constitute a danger to either staff or customers should not be accessible to the unauthorized.
- *Length of flow*. The flow of materials, information or customers should be appropriate for the operation. This usually means minimizing the distance travelled by transformed resources. However, this is not always the case (in a supermarket, for example).
- *Clarity of flow*. All flow of customers and materials should be well signposted, clear and evident to staff and customers alike.
- *Staff conditions*. Staff should be located away from noisy or unpleasant parts of the operation.
- *Management coordination*. Supervision and communication should be assisted by the location of staff and communication devices.
- *Accessibility*. All machines and facilities should be accessible for proper cleaning and maintenance.
- *Use of space*. All layouts should use space appropriately. This usually means minimizing the space used, but sometimes can mean achieving an impression of spacious luxury, as in the entrance lobby of a high-class hotel.
- *Long-term flexibility*. Layouts need to be changed periodically. A good layout will have been devised with the possible future needs of the operation in mind.

The basic layout types

Most practical layouts are derived from only four **basic layout types**. These are:

- **fixed-position layout**
- **functional layout**
- **cell layout**
- **line layout (also called product layout)**

Which type of layout is used will (partly) depend on which type of process is being used. Process 'types' (described in Chapter 5) represent the broad approaches to the organization of processes and activities. Layout is a narrower, but related concept. It is the physical manifestation of a process type, but there is often some overlap between **process types** and the layouts that they could use. As Table 6.1 indicates, a process type does not necessarily imply only one particular basic layout.

Fixed-position layout

Fixed-position layout is in some ways a contradiction in terms, since the transformed resources do not move between the transforming resources. Instead of materials, information or customers flowing through an operation, the recipient of the processing is stationary and the equipment, machinery, plant and people who do the processing move as necessary. This could be because the product or the recipient of the service is too large to be moved conveniently, or it might be too delicate to move, or perhaps it could object to being moved; for example:

- *Motorway construction* – the product is too large to move.
- *Open-heart surgery* – patients are too delicate to move.
- *High-class service restaurant* – customers would object to being moved to where food is prepared.

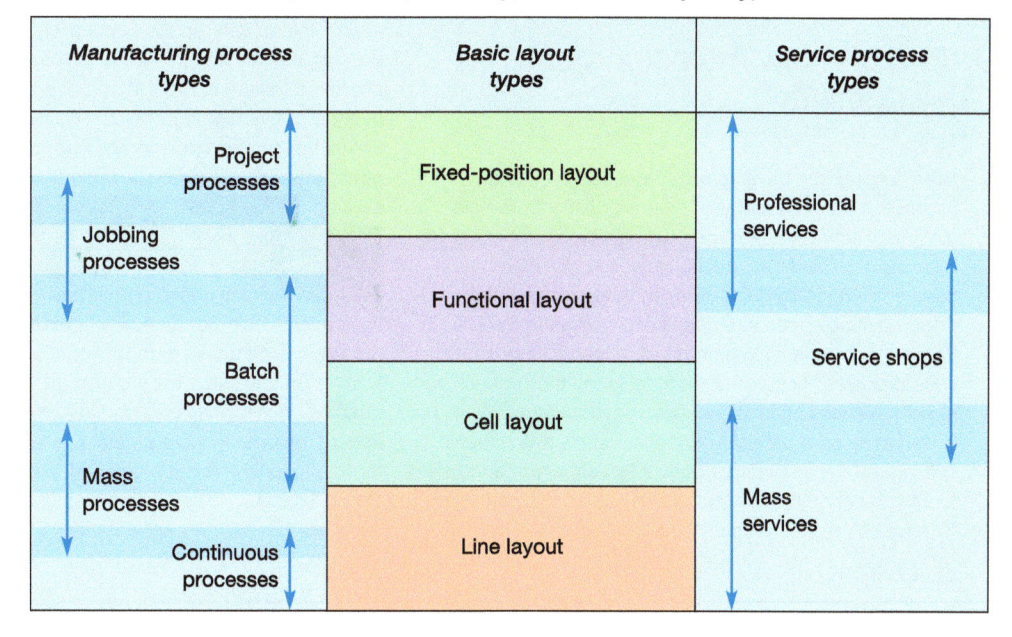

Table 6.1 The relationship between process types and basic layout types

Manufacturing process types	Basic layout types	Service process types
Project processes	Fixed-position layout	Professional services
Jobbing processes	Functional layout	
Batch processes	Cell layout	Service shops
Mass processes		
Continuous processes	Line layout	Mass services

- *Mainframe computer maintenance* – the product is too big and probably also too delicate to move, and the customer might object to bringing it in for repair.

A construction site is typical of a fixed-position layout in that there is a limited amount of space which must be allocated to the various transforming resources. The main problem in designing this layout will be to allocate areas of the site to the various contractors so that they have adequate space, they can receive and store their deliveries of materials, they can have access to their parts of the project without interfering with each other's movements, they minimize movement, and so on.

Functional layout

Functional layout is so called because it conforms to the needs and convenience of the functions performed by the transforming resources within the processes. (Confusingly, functional layout is also referred to as 'process layout' but this term is being superseded.) In functional layout, similar resources or processes are located together. This may be because it is convenient to group them together, or that the utilization of transforming resources is improved. It means that when materials, information or customers flow through the operation, their route is determined according to their needs. Different customers or products will have different needs and therefore take different routes. Usually this makes the flow pattern in the operation very complex. Examples of functional layouts include:

- *Hospital* – some processes (e.g. X-ray machines and laboratories) are required by several types of patient; some processes (e.g. general wards) can achieve high staff- and bed-utilization.
- *Machining the parts which go into aircraft engines* – some processes (e.g. heat treatment) need specialist support (heat and fume extraction); some processes (e.g. machining centres) require the same technical support from specialist setter–operators; some processes (e.g. grinding machines) get high machine utilization as all parts which need grinding pass through a single grinding section.
- *Supermarket* – some products, such as tinned goods, are convenient to restock if grouped together. Some areas, such as those holding frozen vegetables, need the common technology of freezer cabinets. Others, such as the areas holding fresh vegetables, might be together because that way they can be made to look attractive to customers (see the opening short case).

Short case
'Factory flow' helps surgery productivity[4]

Even surgery can be seen as a process, and like any process, it can be improved. Normally patients remain stationary with surgeons and other theatre staff performing their tasks around the patient. However, this idea has been challenged by John Petri, an Italian consultant orthopaedic surgeon at a hospital in Norfolk in the UK. Frustrated by spending time drinking tea while patients were prepared for surgery, he redesigned the process so now he moves continually between two theatres. While he is operating on a patient in one theatre, his anaesthetist colleagues are preparing a patient for surgery in another theatre. After finishing with the first patient, the surgeon 'scrubs up', moves to the second operating theatre, and begins the surgery on the second patient. While he is doing this the first patient is moved out of the first operating theatre and the third patient is prepared. This method of overlapping operations in different theatres allows the surgeon to work for five hours at a time rather than the previous standard three-and-a-half-hour session. *'If you were running a factory'*, says the surgeon, *'you wouldn't allow your most important and most expensive machine to stand idle. The same is true in a hospital.'* Currently used on hip and knee replacements, this layout would not be suitable for all surgical procedures. Since its introduction the surgeon's waiting list has fallen to zero and his productivity has doubled. *'For a small increase in running costs we are able to treat many more patients'*, said a spokesperson for the hospital management. *'What is important is that clinicians . . . produce innovative ideas and we demonstrate that they are effective.'*

Assembly line surgery

① **7.20am** Anaesthetist prepares patient for surgery in theatre one

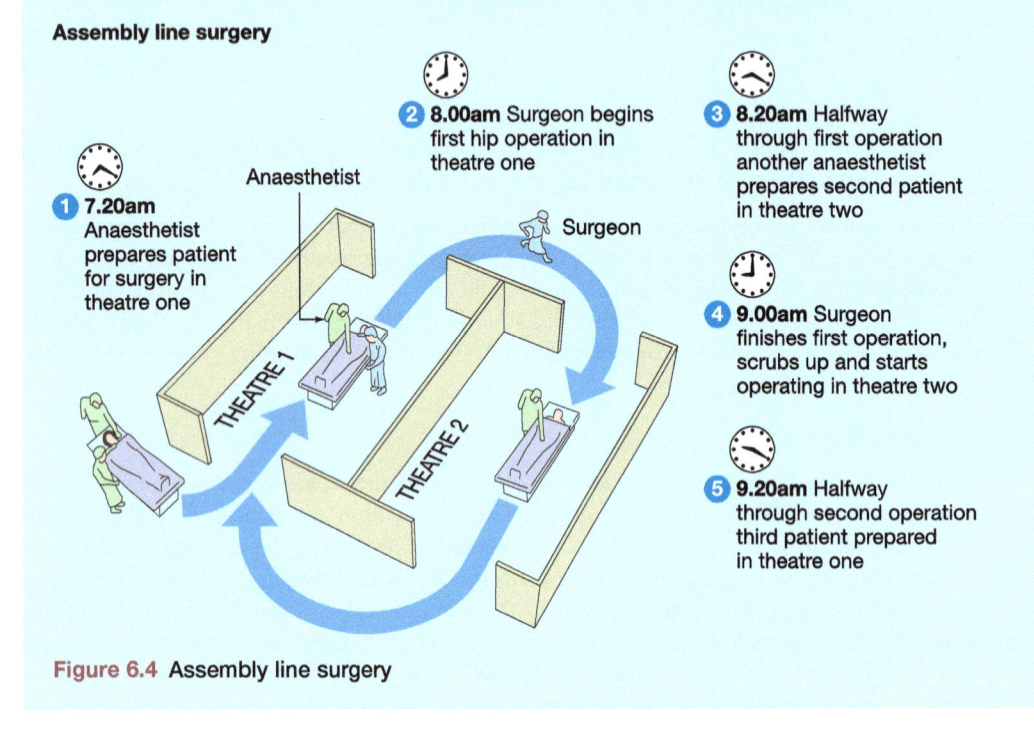

② **8.00am** Surgeon begins first hip operation in theatre one

③ **8.20am** Halfway through first operation another anaesthetist prepares second patient in theatre two

④ **9.00am** Surgeon finishes first operation, scrubs up and starts operating in theatre two

⑤ **9.20am** Halfway through second operation third patient prepared in theatre one

Figure 6.4 Assembly line surgery

Figure 6.5 shows a functional layout in a university library. The various areas – reference books, enquiry desk, journals, and so on – are located in different parts of the operation. The customer is free to move between the areas depending on his or her requirements. The figure also shows the route taken by one customer on one visit to the library. If the routes for the customers were superimposed on the plan, the pattern of the traffic between the various parts of the operation would be revealed. The density of this traffic flow is an important piece of information in the detailed design of this type of layout. Changing the location of the various areas in the library will change the pattern of flow for the library as a whole.

The detailed design of functional layouts is complex, as is flow in this type of layout. Chief among the factors which lead to this complexity is the very large number of different options. For example, in the very simplest case of just two work centres, there are only two ways of arranging these *relative to each other*. But there are six ways of arranging three centres and 120 ways of arranging five centres. This relationship is a factorial one. For N centres there are factorial N ($N!$) different ways of arranging the centres, where:

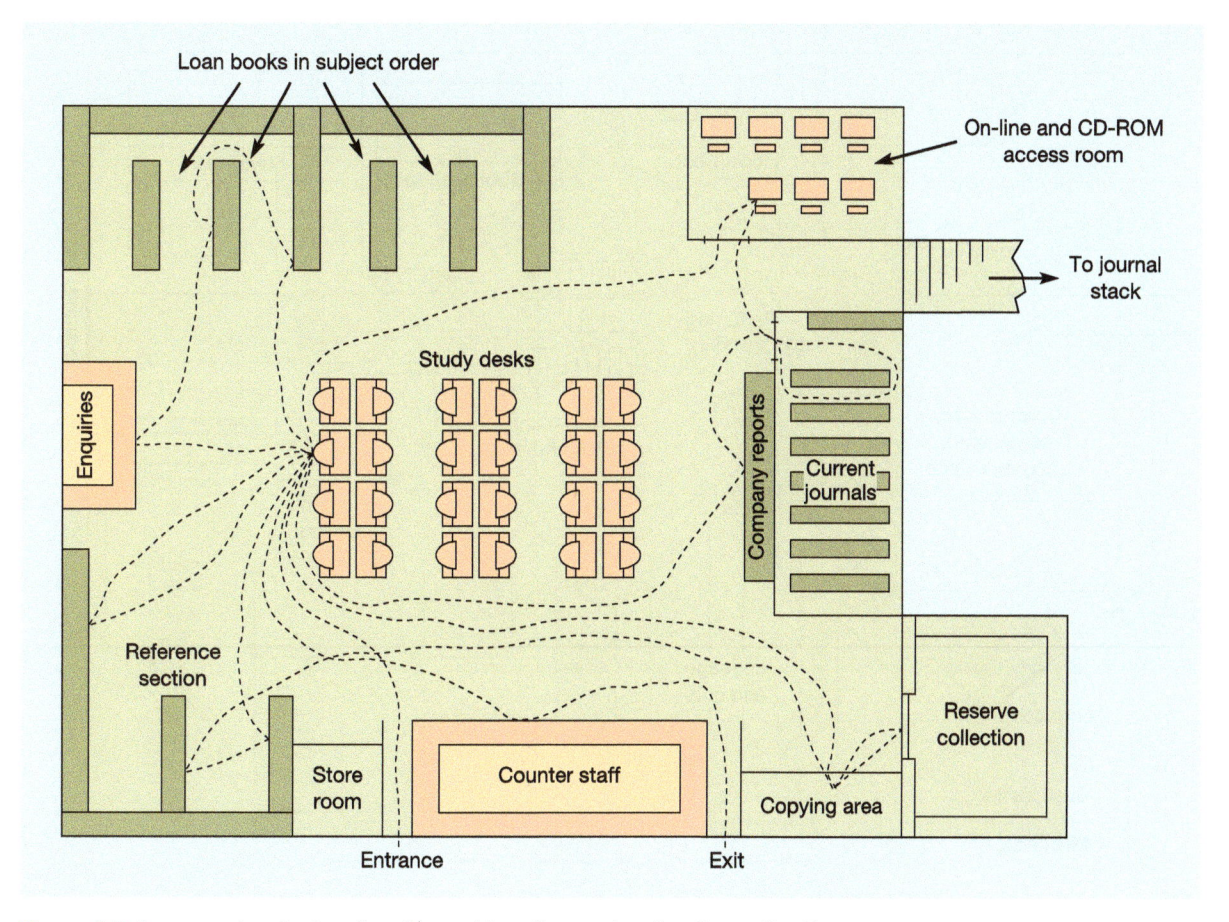

Figure 6.5 An example of a functional layout in a library showing the path of just one customer

$$N! = N \times (N-1) \times (N-2) \times \ldots \times (1)$$

Combinatorial complexity

So for a relatively simple functional layout with, say, 20 work centres, there are $20! = 2.433 \times 10^{18}$ ways of arranging the operation. This **combinatorial complexity** of functional layouts makes optimal solutions difficult to achieve in practice. Most functional layouts are designed by a combination of intuition, common sense and systematic trial and error.

Cell layout

A cell layout is one where the transformed resources entering the operation are pre-selected (or pre-select themselves) to move to one part of the operation (or cell) in which all the transforming resources, to meet their immediate processing needs, are located. After being processed in the cell, the transformed resources may go on to another cell. In effect, cell layout is an attempt to bring some order to the complexity of flow which characterizes functional layout. Examples of cell layouts include:

- *Maternity unit in a hospital* – customers needing maternity attention are a well-defined group who can be treated together and who are unlikely to need the other facilities of the hospital at the same time that they need the maternity unit.
- *Some laptop assembly* – within a contract manufacturer's factory, the assembly of different laptop brands may be done in a special area dedicated to that one brand that has special requirements such as particularly high quality levels.
- *'Lunch' products area in a supermarket* – some customers use the supermarket just to purchase sandwiches, savoury snacks, etc. for their lunch. These products may be located together so that these customers do not have to search around the store.

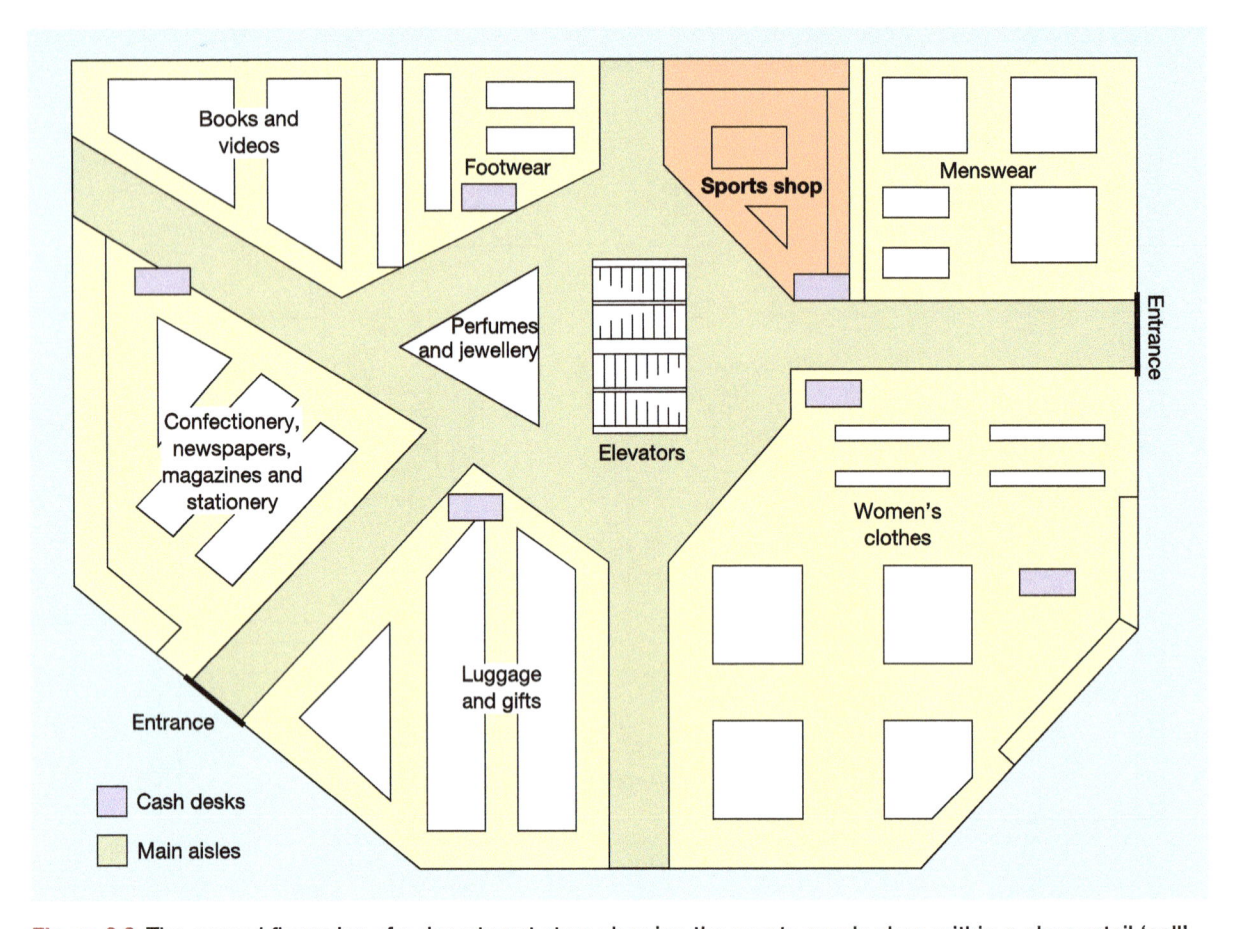

Figure 6.6 The ground floor plan of a department store showing the sports goods shop-within-a-shop retail 'cell'

Shop-within-a-shop

In Figure 6.6 the ground floor of a department store is shown, comprising displays of various types of goods in different parts of the store. In this sense the predominant layout of the store is a functional layout. However, some 'themed' products may be put together, such as in the sports shop. This area is a **shop-within-a-shop** which will stock sports clothes, sports shoes, sports bags, sports books and DVDs, sports equipment and energy drinks, which are also located elsewhere in the store. They have been located in the 'cell' not because they are similar goods (shoes, books and drinks would not usually be located together) but because they are needed to satisfy the needs of a particular type of customer. Enough customers come to the store to buy 'sports goods' in particular to devote an area specifically for them. Also, customers intending to buy sports shoes might also be persuaded to buy other sports goods if they are placed in the same area.

Line layout

Line layout

Line layout (also called product layout) involves locating the transforming resources entirely for the convenience of the transformed resources. Customers, products or pieces of information follow a prearranged route in which the sequence of activities that are required matches the sequence in which the processes have been located. The transformed resources 'flow' as in a 'line' through the process. Flow is predictable and therefore relatively easy to control. Examples of line layout include:

- *Loan application processing* – all applications require the same sequence of clerical and decision-making activities.
- *Self-service cafeteria* – generally the sequence of customer requirements (starter, main course, dessert, drink) is common to all customers, but layout also helps control customer flow.

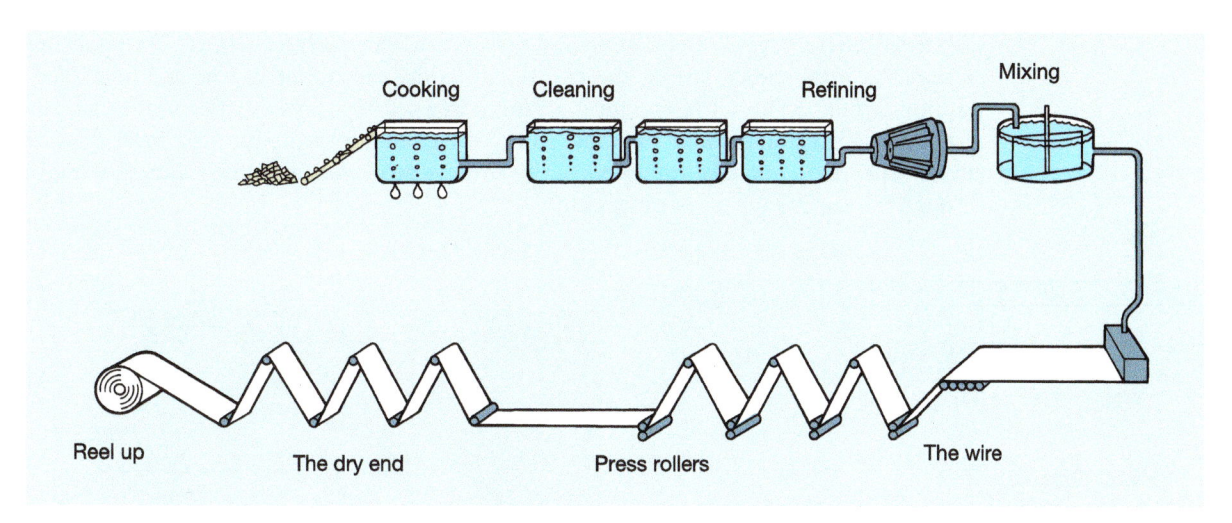

Figure 6.7 The sequence of processes in paper-making; each process will be laid out in the same sequence

- *Automobile assembly* – almost all variants of the same model require the same sequence of processes.

Figure 6.7 shows the sequence of processes in a paper-making operation. Such an operation would use product layout. Gone are the complexities of flow which characterized functional layouts, and to a lesser extent cell layouts, and although different types of paper are produced in this operation, all types have the same processing requirements.

Mixed layouts

Many operations either design themselves hybrid layouts which combine elements of some or all of the basic layout types, or use the 'pure' basic layout types in different parts of the operation. For example, a hospital would normally be arranged on functional-layout principles, each department representing a particular type of process (the X-ray department, the surgical theatres, the blood-processing laboratory, and so on). Yet within each department, quite different layouts are used. The X-ray department is probably arranged in a functional layout, the surgical theatres in a fixed-position layout, and the blood-processing laboratory in a line layout. Another example is shown in Figure 6.8. Here a restaurant complex is shown

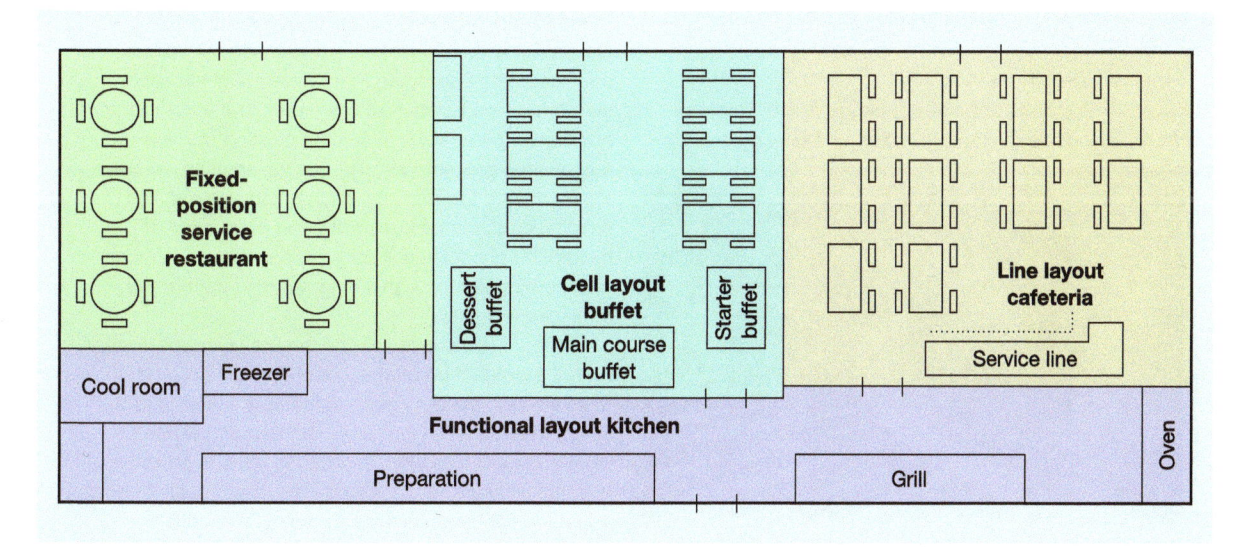

Figure 6.8 A restaurant complex with all four basic layout types

with three different types of restaurant and the kitchen which serves them all. The kitchen is arranged in a functional layout, the traditional service restaurant is arranged in a fixed-position layout, the buffet restaurant is arranged in a cell-type layout, while in the cafeteria restaurant, all customers take the same route when being served with their meal – a line layout. They may not take the opportunity to be served with every dish but they move through the same sequence of processes.

Short case
Chocolate and customers flow through Cadbury's[5]

Flow of chocolate
In the famous Cadbury's chocolate factory at Bourneville, on the outskirts of Birmingham, UK, chocolate products are manufactured to a high degree of consistency and efficiency. Production processes are based on a *product layout*. This has allowed Cadbury's engineers to develop and procure machinery to meet the technical and capacity requirements of each stage of the process. Consider, for example, the production of Cadbury's Dairy Milk bars. First, the standard liquid chocolate is prepared from cocoa beans, fresh milk and sugar using specialized equipment, connected together with pipes and conveyors. These processes operate continuously, day and night, to ensure consistency of both the chocolate itself and the rate of output. Next, the liquid is pumped through heated pipework to the moulding department, where it is automatically dispensed into a moving line of precision-made plastic moulds which form the chocolate bars and vibrate them to remove any trapped air bubbles. The moulds are continuously conveyed into a large refrigerator, allowing sufficient time for the chocolate to harden. The next stage inverts the moulds and shakes out the moulded bars. These then pass directly to a set of highly automated wrapping and packing machines, from where they go to the warehouse.

Flow of customers
Cadbury also has a large visitor centre called 'Cadbury World' alongside the factory (linked to a viewing area

Customers being processed

Chocolate being processed

which looks onto the packaging area described above). Cadbury World is a permanent exhibition devoted entirely to chocolate and the part Cadbury has played in its fascinating history. As most of the attractions are indoors, with limited circulation space, the main exhibition and demonstration areas are designed to allow a smooth flow of customers, where possible avoiding bottlenecks and delays. The design is also a line layout with a single route for all customers. Entry to the Exhibition Area is by timed ticket, to ensure a constant flow of input customers, who are free to walk around at their preferred speed, but are constrained to keep to the single track through the sequence of displays. On leaving this section, they are directed upstairs to the Chocolate Packaging Plant, where a guide escorts standard-sized batches of customers to the appropriate positions where they can see the packing processes and a video presentation. The groups are then led down to and around the Demonstration Area, where skilled employees demonstrate small-scale production of handmade chocolates. Finally, visitors are free to roam unaccompanied through a long, winding path of the remaining exhibits.

Cadbury has chosen to use the line layout design for both the production of chocolates and the processing of its visitors. In both cases, volumes are large and the variety offered is limited. Sufficient demand exists for each standard 'product', and the operations objective is to achieve consistent high quality at low cost. Neither operation has much volume flexibility, and both are expensive to change.

What is layout and what are the types used in operations?

The volume and variety characteristics of an operation will influence its layout

The importance of flow to an operation will depend on its **volume and variety characteristics**. When volume is very low and variety is relatively high, 'flow' is not a major issue. For example, in telecommunications satellite manufacture, a fixed-position layout is likely to be appropriate because each product is different and because products 'flow' through the operation very infrequently, so it is just not worth arranging facilities to minimize the flow of parts through the operation. With higher volume and lower variety, flow becomes an issue. If the variety is still high, however, an entirely flow-dominated arrangement is difficult because there will be different flow patterns. For example, the library in Figure 6.5 will arrange its different categories of books and its other services partly to minimize the average distance its customers have to 'flow' through the operation. But, because its customers' needs vary, it will arrange its layout to satisfy the majority of its customers (but perhaps inconvenience a minority). When the variety of products or services reduces to the point where a distinct 'category' with similar requirements becomes evident but variety is still not small, cell layout could become appropriate, as in the sports goods cell in Figure 6.6. When variety is relatively small and volume is high, flow can become regularized and a line layout is likely to be appropriate (see Figure 6.7).

Selecting a layout type

The volume–variety characteristics of the operation will, to a large extent, narrow the choice down to one or two layout options. The decision as to which layout type to adopt will be influenced by an understanding of their relative advantages and disadvantages. Table 6.2 shows some of the more significant advantages and disadvantages associated with each layout

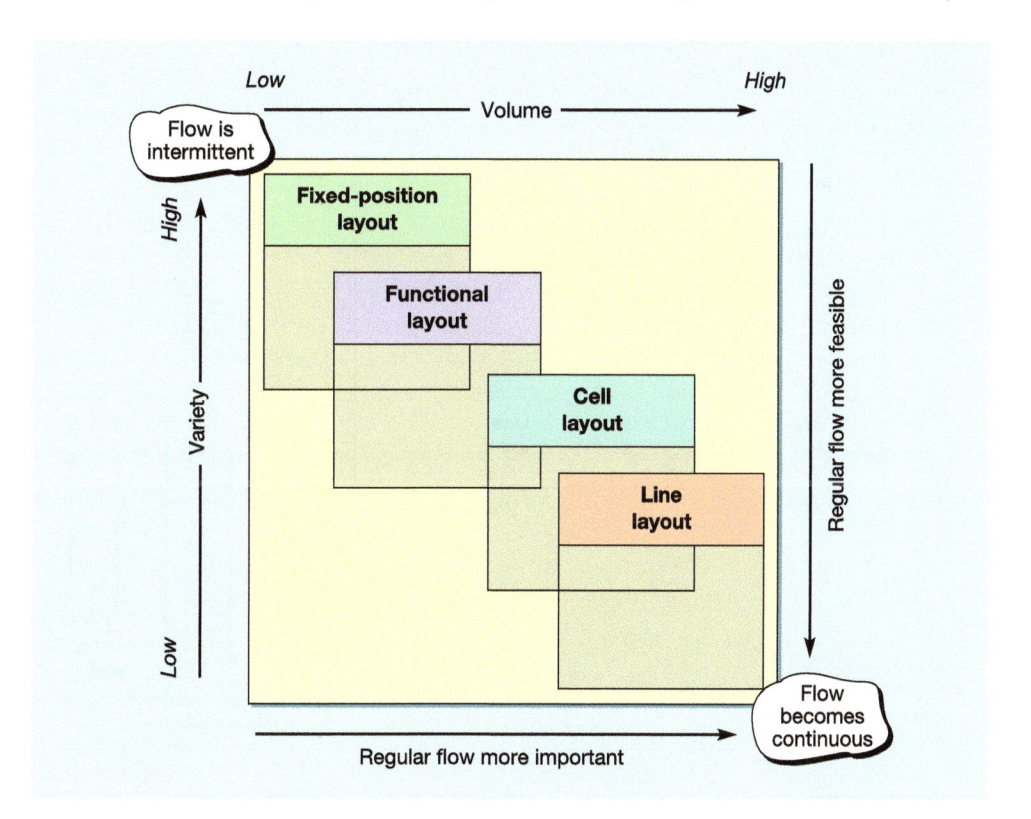

Figure 6.9 The volume–variety process position of an operation influences its layout and, in turn, the flow of transformed resources

Table 6.2 The advantages and disadvantages of the basic layout types

	Advantages	Disadvantages
Fixed-position	Very high mix and product flexibility Product or customer not moved or disturbed High variety of tasks for staff	Very high unit costs Scheduling of space and activities can be difficult Can mean much movement of plant and staff
Functional	High mix and product flexibility Relatively robust in the case of disruptions Relatively easy supervision of equipment or plant	Low facilities utilization Can have very high work-in-progress or customer queuing Complex flow can be difficult to control
Cell	Can give a good compromise between cost and flexibility for relatively high-variety operations Fast throughput Group work can result in good motivation	Can be costly to rearrange existing layout Can need more plant and equipment Can give lower plant utilization
Line	Low unit costs for high volume Gives opportunities for specialization of equipment Materials or customer movement is convenient	Can have low mix flexibility Not very robust if there is disruption Work can be very repetitive

type. It should be stressed, however, that the type of operation will influence their relative importance. For example, a high-volume television manufacturer may find the low-cost characteristics of a line layout attractive, but an amusement theme park may adopt the same layout type primarily because of the way it 'controls' customer flow.

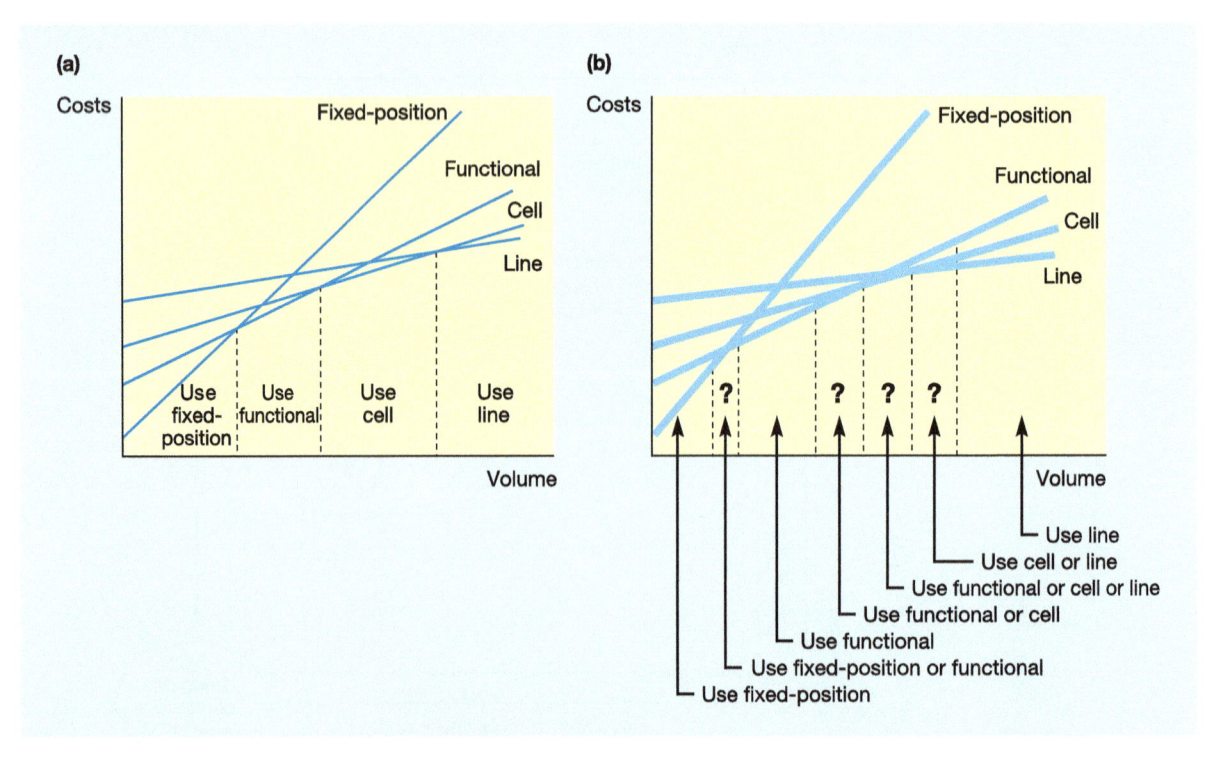

Figure 6.10 (a) The basic layout types have different fixed- and variable-cost characteristics which seem to determine which one to use. (b) In practice the uncertainty about the exact fixed and variable costs of each layout means the decision can rarely be made on cost alone

Of all the characteristics of the various layout types, perhaps the most generally significant are the unit cost implications of layout choice. This is best understood by distinguishing between the fixed- and variable-cost elements of adopting each layout type. For any particular product or service, the fixed costs of physically constructing a fixed-position layout are relatively small compared with any other way of producing the same product or service. However, the variable costs of producing each individual product or service are relatively high compared to the alternative layout types. Fixed costs then tend to increase as one moves from fixed-position, through functional and cell, to line layout. Variable costs per product or service tend to decrease, however. The total costs for each layout type will depend on the volume of products or services produced and are shown in Figure 6.10(a). This seems to show that for any volume there is a lowest-cost basic layout. However, in practice, the cost analysis of layout selection is rarely as clear as this. The exact cost of operating the layout is difficult to forecast and will probably depend on many often-difficult-to-predict factors. Rather than use lines to represent the cost of layout as volume increases, broad bands, within which the real cost is likely to lie, are probably more appropriate (see Figure 6.10(b)). The discrimination between the different layout types is now far less clear. There are ranges of volume for which any of two or three layout types might provide the lowest operating cost. The less certainty there is over the costs, the broader the cost 'bands' will be, and the less clear the choice will be. The probable costs of adopting a particular layout need to be set in the broader context of advantages and disadvantages in Table 6.2.

Workplace layout

At a micro and detailed level, the 'positioning' of equipment has the same purpose as the positioning of operations geographically or the positioning of resources within the operation; this is to minimize cost and maximize some combination of safety, quality, speed, dependability and flexibility. In the workplace, this usually translates to mean minimizing human effort, promoting good-quality work and preventing injury. This may mean positioning equipment so that it does not place undue physical demands on staff, providing mechanical assistance where required and ensuring that items are placed clearly and conveniently. The subject of ergonomics that we mentioned in the process design chapter can help in achieving these aims.

Anthropometric aspects

Anthropometric data

Many ergonomic improvements are primarily concerned with what are called the anthropometric aspects of jobs – that is, the aspects related to people's size, shape and other physical abilities. The design of an assembly task, for example, should be governed partly by the size and strength of the operators who do the job. The data which ergonomists use when doing this is called **anthropometric data**. Because we all vary in our size and capabilities, ergonomists are particularly interested in our range of capabilities, which is why anthropometric data is usually expressed in percentile terms. Figure 6.11 illustrates this idea. This shows the idea of size (in this case height) variation. Only 5 per cent of the population are smaller than the person on the extreme left (5th percentile), whereas 95 per cent of the population are smaller than the person on the extreme right (95th percentile). When this principle is applied to other dimensions of the body, for example arm length, it can be used to design work areas. Figure 6.11 also shows the normal and maximum work areas derived from anthropometric data. It would be inadvisable, for example, to place frequently used components or tools outside the maximum work area derived from the 5th percentile dimensions of human reach.

176 Operations Management

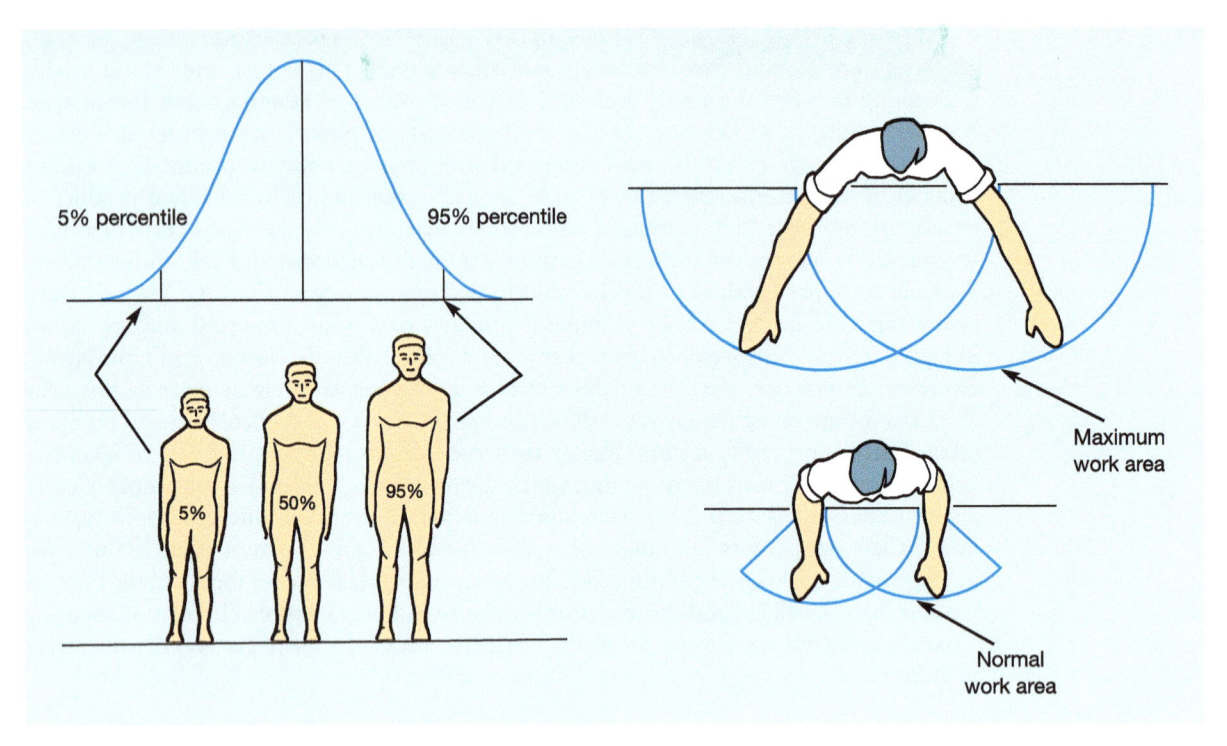

Figure 6.11 The use of anthropometric data in job design

Summary answers to key questions

Check and improve your understanding of this chapter using self-assessment questions and a personalized study plan, audio and video downloads, and an eBook – all at www.myomlab.com.

▶ Where should operations be located?

- The stimuli which act on an organization during the location decision can be divided into supply-side and demand-side influences. Supply-side influences are the factors such as labour, land and utility costs which change as location changes. Demand-side influences include such things as the image of the location, its convenience for customers and the suitability of the site itself.

▶ What is layout and what are the types used in operations?

- The 'layout' of an operation or process means how its transformed resources are positioned relative to each other and how its various tasks are allocated to these transforming resources.
- There are four basic layout types. They are fixed-position layout, functional layout, cell layout and line layout.

▶ What type of layout should an operation choose?

- Partly this is influenced by the nature of the process type, which in turn depends on the volume–variety characteristics of the operation. Partly also the decision will depend on the objectives of the operation. Cost and flexibility are particularly affected by the layout decision.

- The fixed and variable costs implied by each layout differ such that, in theory, one particular layout will have the minimum costs for a particular volume level. However, in practice, uncertainty over the real costs involved in layout makes it difficult to be precise on which is the minimum-cost layout.

> **How should items be positioned in a workplace?**

- Usually workplace design involves positioning equipment to minimize effort, minimize the risk of injury, and maximize quality of work.

Learning exercises

These problems and applications will help to improve your analysis of operations. You can find more practice problems as well as worked examples and guided solutions on MyOMLab at www.myomlab.com.

1. Sketch the layout of your local shop, coffee bar or sports hall reception area. Observe the area and draw onto your sketch the movements of people through the area over a sufficient period of time to get over 20 observations. Assess the flow in terms of volume, variety and type of layout.

2. Revisit the opening short case in this chapter that examines some of the principles behind supermarket layout. Then visit a supermarket and observe people's behaviour. You may wish to try and observe which areas they move slowly past and which areas they seem to move past without paying attention to the products. (You may have to exercise some discretion when doing this; people generally don't like to be stalked round the supermarket too obviously.) Try and verify, as far as you can, some of the principles that were outlined in the opening short case. If you were to redesign the supermarket what would you recommend?

3. Draw a rough plan of your (or someone else's) kitchen. Note (or observe) movements around the kitchen during food preparation and cleaning. How could its layout be improved?

Want to know more?

This is a relatively technical chapter and, as you would expect, most books on the subject are technical. Here are a few of the more accessible.

Karlsson, C. (1996) Radically new production systems, *International Journal of Operations and Production Management*, vol. 16, no. 11. An interesting paper because it traces the development of Volvo's factory layouts over the years.

Meyers, F.E. and Stephens, M.P. (2000) *Manufacturing Facilities Design and Material Handling*, Prentice-Hall, Upper Saddle River, NJ. Exactly what it says, thorough.

Meller, R.D. and Kai-Yin Gau (1996) The facility layout problem: recent and emerging trends and perspectives, *Journal of Manufacturing Systems*, vol. 15, issue 5, 351–66. A review of the literature in the area.

Useful websites

www.bpmi.org Site of the Business Process Management Initiative. Some good resources including papers and articles.

www.bptrends.com News site for trends in business process management generally. Some interesting articles.

www.iienet.org The Global Association of Productivity and Efficiency Professionals site. They are an important professional body for process design and related topics.

www.waria.com A Workflow and Reengineering Association website. Some useful topics.

www.opsman.org Lots of useful stuff.

Now that you have finished reading this chapter, why not visit MyOMLab at www.myomlab.com where you'll find more learning resources to help you make the most of your studies and get a better grade.

Chapter 7 | Supply network management

Key questions

- Why should an organization take a supply network perspective?
- What is involved in managing supply networks?
- What is involved in designing a supply network?
- What are the types of relationships between operations in supply networks?
- What is the 'natural' dynamic of a supply network?
- How can supply networks be improved?

Introduction

No operation exists in isolation. Every operation is part of a larger and interconnected *supply network*. These networks not only include suppliers and customers, but also suppliers' suppliers and customers' customers, and so on. As operations outsource many of their activities, the way they manage the supply of services and products is hugely important. At a strategic level, operations managers are involved in 'designing' the shape of their network and determining what to do and what to buy. At a more operational level, operations managers must consider the type of relationships they wish to develop with suppliers, understand the dynamics of their network, and improve their supply networks in order to ultimately satisfy end customers. Figure 7.1 shows where this chapter fits into the overall operations model.

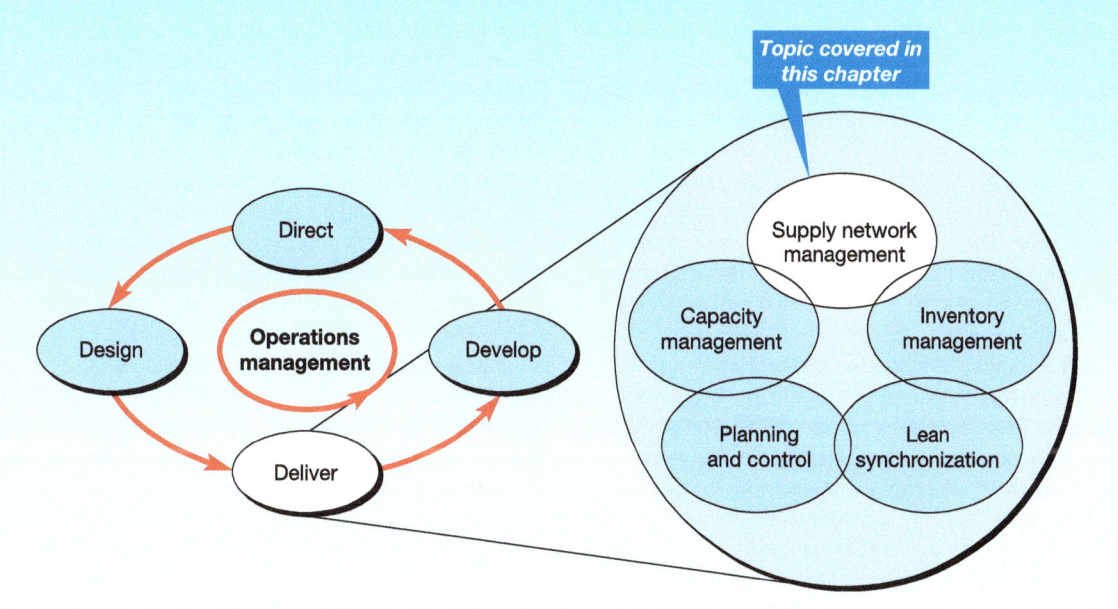

Figure 7.1 This chapter examines supply network management

Check and improve your understanding of this chapter using self-assessment questions and a personalized study plan, audio and video downloads, and an eBook – all at www.myomlab.com.

Operations in practice: Dell: no operating model lasts forever[1]

When he was a student at the University of Texas at Austin, Michael Dell's sideline of buying unused stock of PCs from local dealers, adding components, and re-selling the now higher-specification machines to local businesses was so successful that he quit university and founded a computer company which was to revolutionize the industry's supply network management. His fledgling company was just too small to make its own components. Better, he figured to learn how to manage a network of committed specialist component manufacturers and take the best of what was available in the market. Dell says that his commitment to outsourcing was always done for the most positive of reasons. '*We focus on how we can coordinate our activities to create the most value for customers*'. Yet Dell still faced a cost disadvantage against its far bigger competitors, so they decided to sell its computers direct to its customers, bypassing retailers. This allowed the company to cut out the retailer's (often considerable) margin, which in turn allowed Dell to offer lower prices. Dell also realized that cutting out the link in the supply network between them and the customer also provided them with significant learning opportunities to get to know their customers' needs far more intimately. Most importantly it allowed Dell to learn how to run its supply chain so that products could move through the supply chain to the end-customer in a fast and efficient manner, reducing Dell's level of inventory and giving Dell a significant cost advantage.

However, what is right at one time may become a liability later on. Two decades later Dell's growth started to slow down. The irony of this is that, what had been one of the company's main advantages, its direct sales model using the Internet and its market power to squeeze price reductions from suppliers, were starting to be seen as disadvantages. Although the market had changed, Dell's operating model had not. Some commentators questioned Dell's size. How could a $56 billion company remain lean, sharp, and alert? Other commentators pointed out that Dell's rivals had also now learnt to run efficient supply networks. However, one of the main factors was seen as the shift in the nature of the market itself. Sales of PCs to business users had become largely a commodity business with wafer-thin margins, and this part of the market was growing slowly compared to the sale of computers to individuals. Selling computers to individuals provided slightly better margins than the corporate market, but they increasingly wanted up-to-date computers with a high design value, and most significantly, they wanted to see, touch and feel the products before buying them. This was clearly a problem for a company like Dell which had spent 20 years investing in its telephone- and later, internet-based sales channels. What all commentators agreed on was that in the fast-moving and cut-throat computer business, where market requirements could change overnight, operations resources must constantly develop appropriate new capabilities.

However, Michael Dell said it could regain its spot as the world's number one PC maker by switching its focus to consumers and the developing world. He also conceded that the company had missed out on the boom in supplying computers to home users – who make up just 15% of its revenues – because it was focused on supplying businesses. '*Let's say you wanted to buy a Dell computer in a store nine months ago – you'd have searched a long time and not found one. Now we have over 10,000 stores that sell our products*.' He rejected the idea that design was not important to his company, though he accepted that it had not been a top priority when all the focus was on business customers. '*As we've gone to the consumer we've been paying quite a bit more attention to design, fashion, colors, textures and materials.*'

The supply network perspective

Supply network

Supply side
First-tier suppliers
Second-tier suppliers
Demand side

A **supply network** perspective means setting an operation in the context of all the customers and suppliers that interact with it. Materials, parts, information, ideas and people may all flow through the supply network. On its **supply side**, an operation has its suppliers of materials, information or services. These are often called **first-tier suppliers**. These suppliers themselves have their own **second-tier suppliers** who in turn could also have suppliers, and so on. On the **demand side** the operation has customers. These customers might not be the final consumers of the operation's services or products; they might have their own set of customers. 'First-tier' customers are the main customer group for the operation, who in turn supply 'second-tier' customers.

Figure 7.2 illustrates the simplified supply network for two operations. First is a plastic homeware (kitchen bowls, food containers, etc.) manufacturer. Note that on the demand side the homeware manufacturer supplies some of its basic products to wholesalers which supply retail outlets. However, it also supplies some retailers directly with 'made-to-order' products. The second example, an enclosed shopping mall, also has suppliers and customers that themselves have their own suppliers and customers. Along with the flow of services and products in the network, each link in the network will feed back orders and information to its suppliers. It is a two-way process with goods flowing one way and information flowing the other.

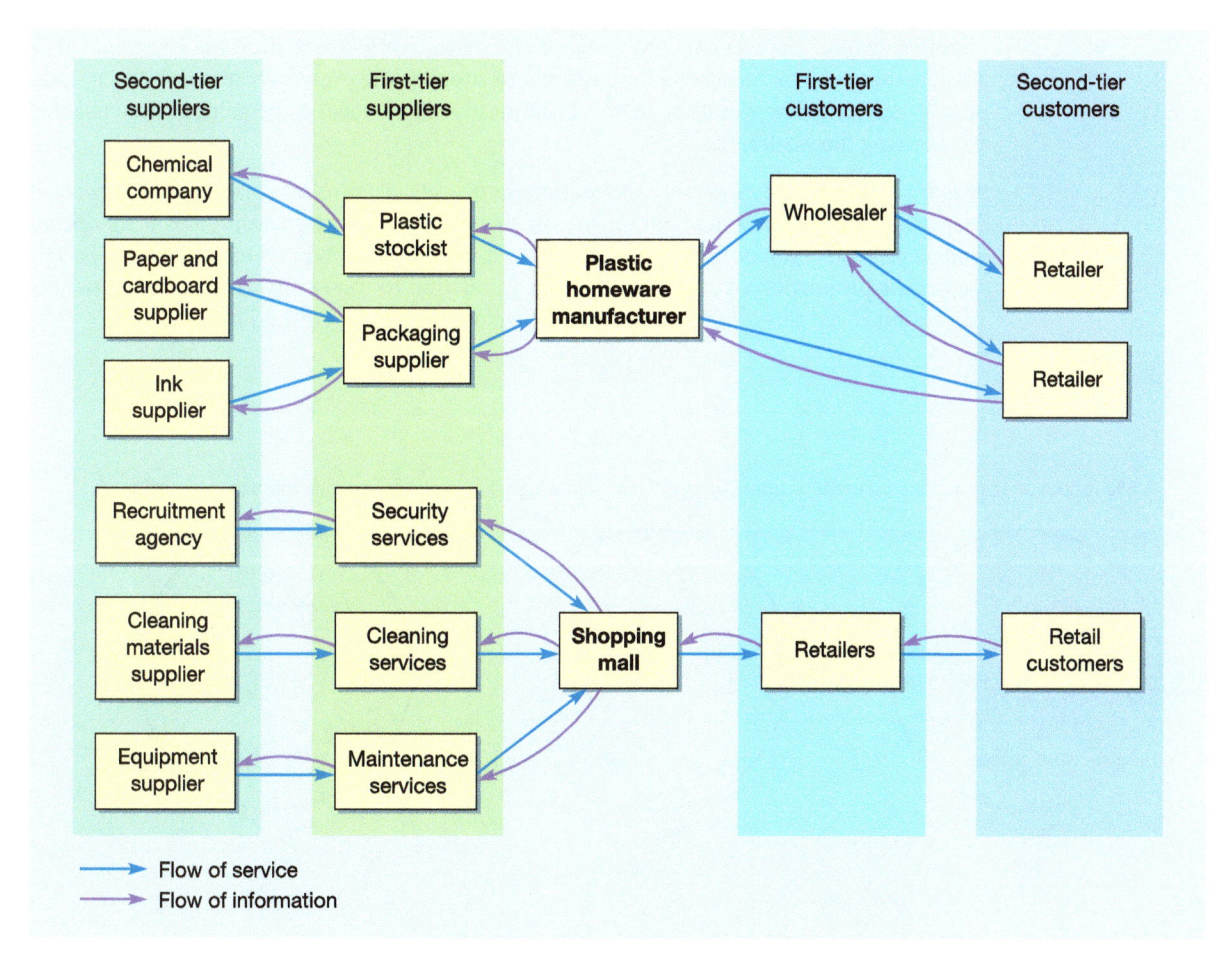

Figure 7.2 Operations network for a plastic homeware company and a shopping mall

Why consider the whole supply network?

There are a number of important reasons for taking a supply network perspective:

It helps an understanding of competitiveness. Immediate customers and immediate suppliers, quite understandably, are the main concern to competitively minded companies. Yet sometimes they need to look beyond these immediate contacts to understand why customers and suppliers act as they do. If it wants to understand its ultimate customers' needs at the end of the network, an operation can and should rely on the intermediate links in the network between itself and its end customers.

It helps identify significant links in the network. The key to understanding supply networks lies in identifying the parts of the network which contribute to those performance objectives valued by end-customers. Any analysis of networks must start, therefore, by understanding the **downstream** end of the network. After this, the **upstream** parts of the network which contribute most to end-customer service will need to be identified. For example, the important end-customers for domestic plumbing appliances are the installers and service companies that deal directly with domestic consumers. They are supplied by 'stock holders' which must have all parts in stock and deliver them fast. Suppliers of parts to the stock holders can best contribute to their end-customers' competitiveness partly by offering a short delivery lead time but mainly through dependable delivery. The key players in this example are the stock holders. The best way of winning end-customer business in this case is to give the stock holder prompt delivery which helps keep costs down while providing high availability of parts.

It helps focus on long-term issues. There are times when circumstances render parts of a supply network weaker than its adjacent links. A major machine breakdown, for example, or a labour dispute might disrupt a whole network. Should its immediate customers and suppliers exploit the weakness to enhance their own competitive position, or should they tolerate the problems, and hope the customer or supplier will eventually recover? A long-term supply-network view would be to weigh the relative advantages to be gained from assisting or replacing the weak link.

It helps focus on cost. Typically the volume and value of purchased goods and services is increasing as organizations concentrate on their 'core tasks'. **Purchasing has a significant impact on total organizational costs**, thus increasing the impact on an operation's costs. The higher the proportion of procurement costs in relation to total costs, the more profitability can be improved through reduction in procurement costs. Figure 7.3 illustrates this.

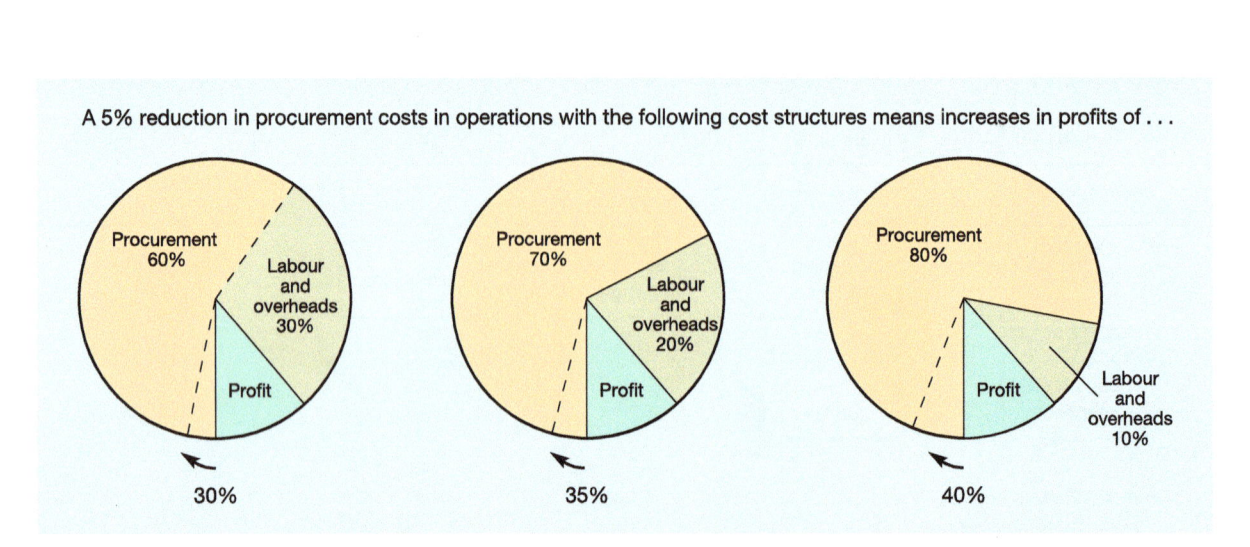

A 5% reduction in procurement costs in operations with the following cost structures means increases in profits of . . .

- Procurement 60%, Labour and overheads 30%, Profit → 30%
- Procurement 70%, Labour and overheads 20%, Profit → 35%
- Procurement 80%, Labour and overheads 10%, Profit → 40%

Figure 7.3 Impact of reduced procurement costs on total costs and profit

Designing and managing supply networks

A supply network is all the operations linked together to provide services and products through to the end-customers

A supply chain is a strand of linked operations

Designing and managing **supply networks** is a holistic approach to managing the interconnection of organizations that combine to produce value to the ultimate consumer in the form of services and products. Within supply networks, there can be many hundreds of strands of linked operations, commonly referred to as **supply chains**. An analogy often used to describe supply chains is that of the 'pipeline'. Just as liquids flow through a pipeline, so services and products flow down a supply chain. Long pipelines will, of course, contain more liquid than short ones, so the time taken for liquid to flow all the way through a long pipeline will be longer.

Some of the terms used in supply network management are not universally applied. Furthermore, some of the concepts behind the terminology overlap in the sense that they refer to common parts of the total supply network (Figure 7.4). *Supply network management* (also called supply chain management) coordinates all the operations on the supply side and the demand side. *Purchasing and supply management* deals with the operation's interface with its supply markets. *Physical distribution management* may mean supplying immediate customers, while *logistics* is an extension that often refers to materials and information flow down through a distribution channel, to the retail store or consumers (increasingly common because of the growth of internet-based retailing). The term *third-party logistics* (TPL) indicates outsourcing to a specialist logistics company. *Materials management* is a more limited term and refers to the flow of materials and information only through the immediate supply network.

Performance objectives of supply networks

The key objective in managing supply networks is the satisfaction of the end-customer. All parts of the network must consider the final customer, no matter how far an individual operation is from them. When customers decide to make a purchase, they trigger action across the whole network. All the businesses in the supply network pass on portions of

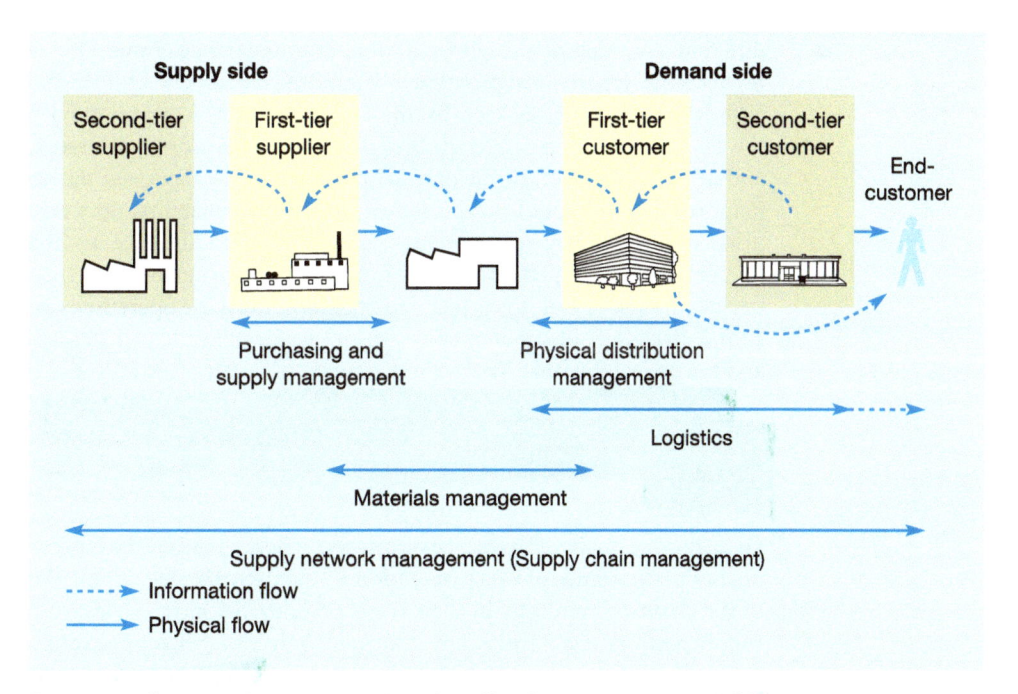

Figure 7.4 Some of the terms used to describe the management of different parts of the supply network

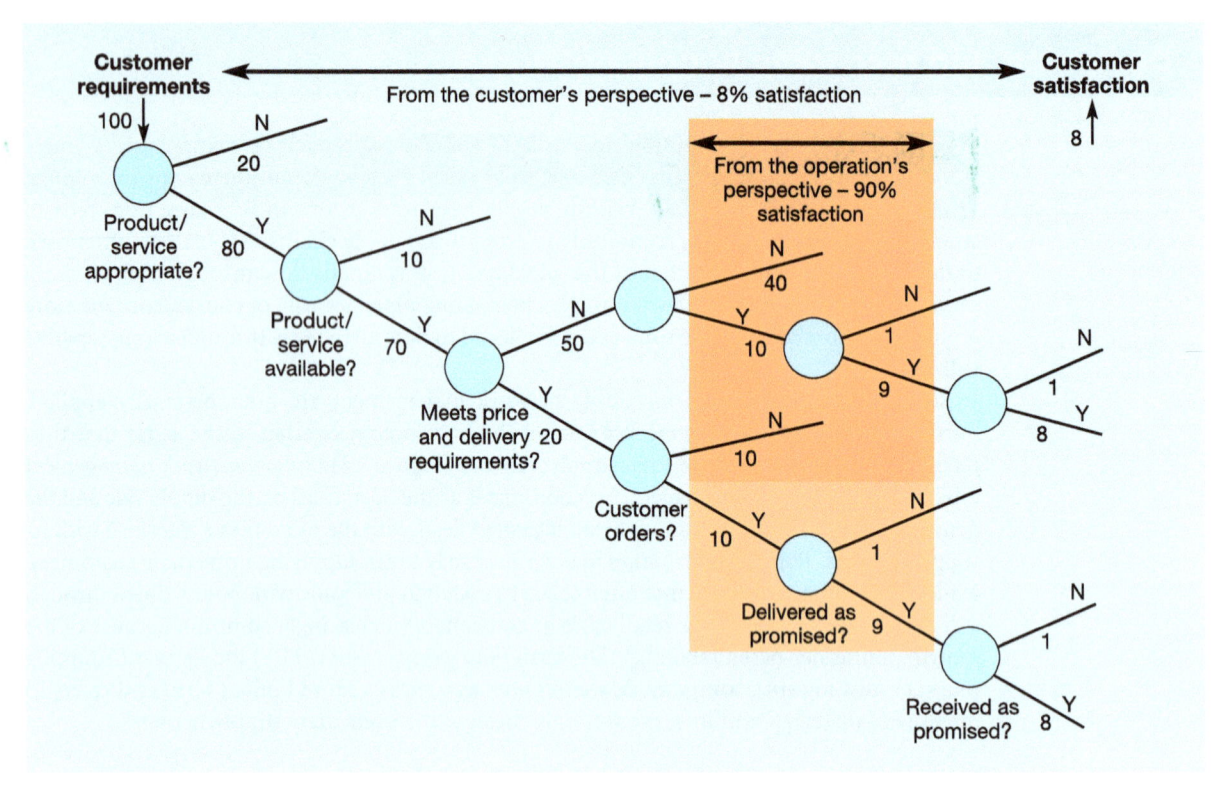

Figure 7.5 Taking a customer perspective of supply network performance can lead to very different conclusions

that end-customer's money to each other, each retaining a margin for the value it has added. Each operation in the network should be satisfying its own customer, but also making sure that eventually the end-customer is satisfied.

For a demonstration of how end-customer perceptions of supply satisfaction can be very different from that of a single operation, examine the customer 'decision tree' in Figure 7.5. It charts the hypothetical progress of a hundred customers requiring service from a business. Supply performance, as seen by the core operation, is represented by the shaded part of the diagram. It has received 20 orders, 18 of which were delivered as promised (on time, and in full). However, of the original customers who requested the service, 20 found it was inappropriate, 10 could not be served due to unavailability, 50 were not satisfied with the price and/or delivery requirements (though 10 did still place an order). So what seems a 90 per cent supply performance is in fact an 8 per cent performance from the customer's perspective. Note that this is just one operation from the operation's perspective. Include the cumulative effect of similar reductions in performance for all the operations in a network, and the probability that the end-customer is adequately served could become remote.

The point here is that the performance both of the supply network as a whole, and its constituent operations, should be judged in terms of how end-customer needs are satisfied, in terms of the five operations performance objectives: quality, speed, dependability, flexibility and cost.

Quality – the quality of a service or product when it reaches the customer is a function of the quality performance of every operation in the network that supplied it. Errors in each stage of the chain can multiply in their effect on end-customer service, so if each of 7 stages in a supply network has a 1 per cent error rate, only 93.2 per cent of services or products will be of good quality on reaching the end-customer. This is why, only by every stage taking some responsibility for its own *and its suppliers'* performance, can a supply network achieve high end-customer quality.

Speed has two meanings in a supply network context. The first is how fast customers can be served. However, fast customer response can be achieved simply by over-resourcing or over-stocking within the network. For example, an accounting firm may be able to respond quickly to customer demand by having a large number of accountants on standby waiting for demand that may (or may not) occur. An alternative perspective on speed is the time taken for services and products to move through the network. So, for example, products that move quickly across a supply network will spend little time as inventory, which in turn reduces inventory-related costs in the network.

Dependability – like speed, one can almost guarantee 'on-time' delivery by keeping excessive resources, such as inventory, within the network. However, dependability of throughput time is a much more desirable aim because it reduces uncertainty. If individual operations do not deliver as promised, there will be a tendency for customers to over-order, or order early, in order to provide some kind of insurance against late delivery. This is why delivery dependability is often measured as 'on time, in full' in supply networks.

Flexibility – in a supply network context, flexibility is usually taken to mean the ability to cope with changes and disturbances. Very often this is referred to as agility. The concept of agility includes previously discussed issues such as focusing on the end-customer and ensuring fast throughput and responsiveness to customer needs. But, in addition, agile supply networks are sufficiently flexible to cope with changes, either in the nature of customer demand or in the supply capabilities of operations within the network.

Cost – in addition to the costs incurred within each operation, the supply network as a whole incurs additional costs that derive from operations doing business with each other. These may include such things as the costs of finding appropriate suppliers, setting up contractual agreements, monitoring supply performance, transporting products between operations, holding inventories, and so on. Many developments in supply network management, such as partnership agreements or reducing the number of suppliers, are attempts to minimize transaction costs.

Short case
Ford Motors' team value management[2]

Purchasing managers are a vital link between an operation and its suppliers. They work best when teamed up with mainstream operations managers who know what the operation really needs, especially if, between them, they take a role that challenges previous assumptions. That is the basis behind Ford Motor Company's 'team value management' (TVM) approach. Reputedly, it all started when Ford's Head of Global Purchasing, David Thursfield, discovered that a roof rack designed for one of Ford's smaller cars was made of plastic-coated aluminium and capable of bearing a 100 kg load. This prompted the questions, *'Why is this rack covered in plastic? Why would anyone want to put 100 kg on the roof of a car that small?'* He found that no one had ever questioned the original specification. When Ford switched to using steel roof racks capable of bearing a smaller weight, they halved the cost. *'It is important'*, he says, *'to check whether the company is getting the best price for parts and raw material that provide the appropriate level of performance without being too expensive.'* The savings in a large company such as Ford can be huge. Often in multinationals, each part of the business makes sourcing and design decisions independently and does not exploit opportunities for cross-usage of components. The TVM approach is designed to bring together engineering and purchasing staff and identify where cost can be taken out of purchased parts and where there is opportunity for parts commonality (see Chapter 4) between different models. When a company's global purchasing budget is $75bn like Ford's, the potential for cost savings is significant.

Supply network design

Taking a supply network perspective is useful because it prompts a number of important design decisions. These combine to determine how a supply network can operate and its ability to deliver value to customers. These decisions include:

1. Who should do what in the network? How many steps should there be in the network? What is the role of customers, suppliers, complementors and competitors? This is called the network shape decision.
2. How much of the network should the operation own? This is called the do-or-buy, outsourcing or vertical integration decision.
3. How should supply networks be configured when operations compete in different ways in different markets? This is called the supply network matching decision.

The network shape decision

Supply base reduction

Reconfiguring a supply network sometimes involves parts of the operation being merged – not necessarily in the sense of a change of ownership of any parts of an operation, but rather in the way responsibility is allocated for carrying out activities. The most common example of network reconfiguration has come through the many companies that have recently reduced the number of direct suppliers. The complexity of dealing with many thousands of suppliers may both be expensive for an operation and (sometimes more important) prevent the operation from developing a close relationship with a supplier. It is not easy to be close to so many different suppliers.

Disintermediation

Another trend in some supply networks is that of companies within a network bypassing customers or suppliers to make contact directly with customers' customers or suppliers' suppliers. 'Cutting out the middlemen' in this way is called **disintermediation**. An obvious example of this is the way the Internet has allowed some suppliers to 'disintermediate' traditional retailers in supplying services and products to consumers. So, for example, many services in the travel industry that used to be sold through retail outlets (travel agents) are now also available direct from the suppliers. The option of purchasing the individual components of a vacation through the websites of the airline, hotel, car hire company, etc., is now easier for consumers. Of course, they may still wish to purchase an 'assembled' product from retail travel agents which can have the advantage of convenience.

Co-opetition

One approach to thinking about supply networks sees any business as being surrounded by four types of players: suppliers, customers, competitors and complementors. Complementors enable one's services or products to be valued more by customers because they can also have the complementor's products or services, as opposed to when they have yours alone. Competitors are the opposite: they make customers value your service or product less when they can have their product or service, rather than yours alone. Competitors can also be complementors and vice versa. For example, adjacent restaurants may see themselves as competitors for customers' business. A customer standing outside and wanting a meal will choose between the two of them. Yet, in another way they are complementors. Would that customer have come to this part of town unless there was more than one restaurant to choose from? Restaurants, theatres, art galleries and tourist attractions generally, all cluster together in a form of cooperation to increase the total size of their joint market. It is important to distinguish between the way companies cooperate in increasing the total size of a market and the way in which they then compete for a share of that market. In the long term it creates value for the total network to find ways of increasing value for suppliers and well as customers. All the players in the supply network, whether they are customers, suppliers, competitors or complementors, can be both friends and enemies at different times. The term used to capture this idea is '**co-opetition**'.[3]

The do-or-buy decision

No single business does everything that is required to deliver its services and products. Bakers do not grow wheat or even mill it into flour. Banks do not usually do their own credit checking: they retain the services of specialist agencies that have the information systems and expertise to do it better. Although most companies have always outsourced some of their activities, a larger proportion of direct activities are now being bought from suppliers. In addition, many indirect processes are also being outsourced, often referred to as '**business process outsourcing**' (**BPO**). Financial service companies in particular are starting to outsource some of their more routine back-office processes. In a similar way many processes within the human resource function, from payroll services through to more complex training and development processes, are being outsourced to specialist companies. The processes may still be physically located where they were before, but the staff and technology are managed by the outsourcing service provider. The reason for doing this is often primarily to reduce cost. However, there can also be significant gains in the quality and flexibility of service offered. Deciding what to do itself in-house and what to outsource is often called the 'do or buy' decision, when individual components or activities are being considered, or the 'vertical integration decision' when it is the ownership of whole operations that is being decided. Vertical integration can be defined in terms of three factors.[4]

1 *The direction of vertical integration.* Should an operation expand by buying one of its suppliers or by buying one of its customers? The strategy of expanding on the supply side of the network is sometimes called 'backward' or 'upstream' vertical integration, and expanding on the demand side is sometimes called 'forward' or 'downstream' vertical integration.
2 *The extent of vertical integration.* How far should an operation take the extent of its vertical integration? Some organizations deliberately choose not to integrate far, if at all, from their original part of the network. Alternatively, some organizations choose to become very vertically integrated.
3 *The balance among stages.* How exclusive should the relationship be between operations? A totally balanced network relationship is one where an operation produces only for the next stage in the network and totally satisfies its requirements. Less than full balance allows each operation to sell its output to other companies or to buy in some of its supplies from other companies.

Making the do-or-buy decision

Whether it is referred to as the do-or-buy, vertical integration or the outsourcing decision, the choice facing operations is rarely simple. Organizations in different circumstances with different objectives are likely to take different decisions. Yet the question itself is relatively simple, even if the decision itself is not: 'Does in-house or outsourced supply in a particular set of circumstances give the appropriate performance objectives that it requires to compete more effectively in its markets?' For example, if the main performance objectives for an operation are dependable delivery and meeting short-term changes in customers' delivery requirements, the key question should be: 'How does in-house or outsourcing give better dependability and delivery flexibility performance?' Table 7.1 summarizes some arguments for in-house supply and outsourcing in terms of each performance objective.

Although the effect of outsourcing on the operation's performance objective is important, there are other factors that companies take into account when deciding if outsourcing an activity is a sensible option. If an activity has long-term **strategic importance** to a company,

Table 7.1 How in-house and outsourced supply may affect an operation's performance objectives

Performance objective	'Do it yourself' in-house supply	'Buy it in' outsourced supply
Quality	The origins of any quality problems are usually easier to trace in-house and improvement can be more immediate but there can be some risk of complacency.	Supplier may have specialized knowledge and more experience, also may be motivated through market pressures, but communication more difficult.
Speed	Can mean synchronized schedules which speeds throughput of materials and information, but if the operation has external customers, internal customers may be low-priority.	Speed of response can be built into the supply contract where commercial pressures will encourage good performance, but there may be significant transport/delivery delays.
Dependability	Easier communications can help dependability, but, if the operation also has external customers, internal customers may be low priority.	Late-delivery penalties in the supply contract can encourage good delivery performance, but organizational barriers may inhibit in communication.
Flexibility	Closeness to real business needs can alert the in-house operation to required changes, but the ability to respond may be limited by the scale and scope of internal operations.	Outsourced suppliers may be larger with wider capabilities and have more ability to respond to changes, but may have to balance conflicting needs of different customers.
Cost	In-house operations do not have to make the margin required by outside suppliers so the business can capture the profits which would otherwise be given to the supplier, but relatively low volumes may mean that it is difficult to gain economies of scale or the benefits of process innovation.	Probably the main reason why outsourcing is so popular. Outsourced companies can achieve economies of scale and they are motivated to reduce their own costs because it directly impacts on their profits, but costs of communication and coordination with supplier need to be taken into account.

it is unlikely to outsource it. For example, a retailer might choose to keep the design and development of its website in-house even though specialists could perform the activity at less cost because it plans to move into web-based retailing at some point in the future. Nor would a company usually outsource an activity where it had specialized skills or knowledge. For example, a company making laser printers may have built up specialized knowledge in the production of sophisticated laser drives. This capability may allow it to introduce product or process innovations in the future. It would be foolish to 'give away' such capability. After these two more strategic factors have been considered, the company's operations performance can be taken into account. Obviously if its operations performance is already superior to any potential supplier, it would be unlikely to outsource the activity. Even if its performance was currently below that of potential suppliers, it may not outsource the activity if it feels that it could significantly improve its performance. Figure 7.6 illustrates this decision logic.

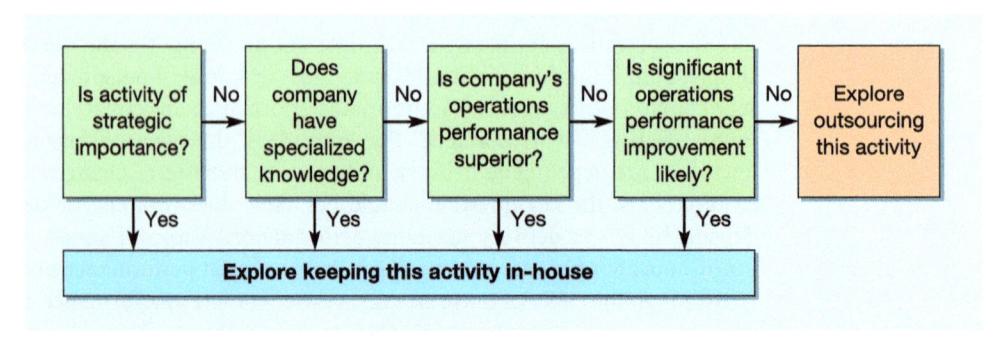

Figure 7.6 The decision logic of outsourcing

Short case
Behind the brand names[5]

The market for notebook computers is a fast-evolving and competitive one. Yet few who buy these products know that the majority of the world's notebooks are made by a small number of Taiwanese and Korean manufacturers. Taiwanese firms alone make around 60 per cent of all notebooks in the world, including most of Dell, Compaq and Apple machines. In a market with unremitting technological innovation and fierce price competition, it makes sense to outsource production to companies that can achieve the economies that come with high-volume manufacture as well as develop the expertise which enables new designs to be put into production without the usual cost overruns and delays. However, the big brand names are keen to defend their products' performance. Dell, for example, admits that a major driver of its outsourcing policy is the requirement to keep costs at a competitive level, but says that it can ensure product quality and performance through its relationship with its suppliers. *'The production lines are set up by Dell and managed by Dell'*, says Tony Bonadero, Director of Product Marketing for Dell's laptop range. Dell also imposes strict quality control and manages the overall design of the product.

Supply network alignment

An important question for supply managers to consider is 'How should supply networks be configured when operations compete in different ways in different markets?' One answer, proposed by Professor Marshall Fisher of Wharton Business School, is to organize the supply network serving those individual markets in different ways.[6] He points out that many companies have seemingly similar products which, in fact, compete in different ways. Shoe manufacturers may produce classics which change little over the years, as well as fashions which last only one or two seasons. Chocolate manufacturers have stable lines which have been sold for 50 years, but also create 'specials' associated with an event or film release, maybe selling only for a few months. Demand for the former products will be relatively stable and predictable, but demand for the latter will be far more uncertain. Also, the profit margin commanded by the innovative product will probably be higher than that of the more functional product. However, the price (and therefore the margin) of the innovative product may drop rapidly once it has become unfashionable in the market.

The supply network policies which are seen to be appropriate for functional services and products and innovative services and products are termed by Fisher **efficient supply network** policies and **responsive supply network** policies, respectively. Efficient supply network policies include keeping inventories low, especially in the downstream parts of the network, so as to maintain fast throughput and reduce the amount of working capital tied up in the inventory. What inventory there is in the network is concentrated mainly in the manufacturing operation, where it can keep utilization high and therefore manufacturing costs low. Information must flow quickly up and down the chain from retail outlets back up to the manufacturer so that schedules can be given the maximum amount of time to adjust efficiently. The network is then managed to make sure that products flow as quickly as possible down the chain to replenish what few stocks are kept in the network. By contrast, responsive supply policies stress high service levels and responsive supply to the end-customer. The inventory in the network will be deployed as closely as possible to the customer. In this way, the network can still supply even when dramatic changes occur in customer demand. Fast throughput from the upstream parts of the network will still be needed to replenish downstream stocks. But

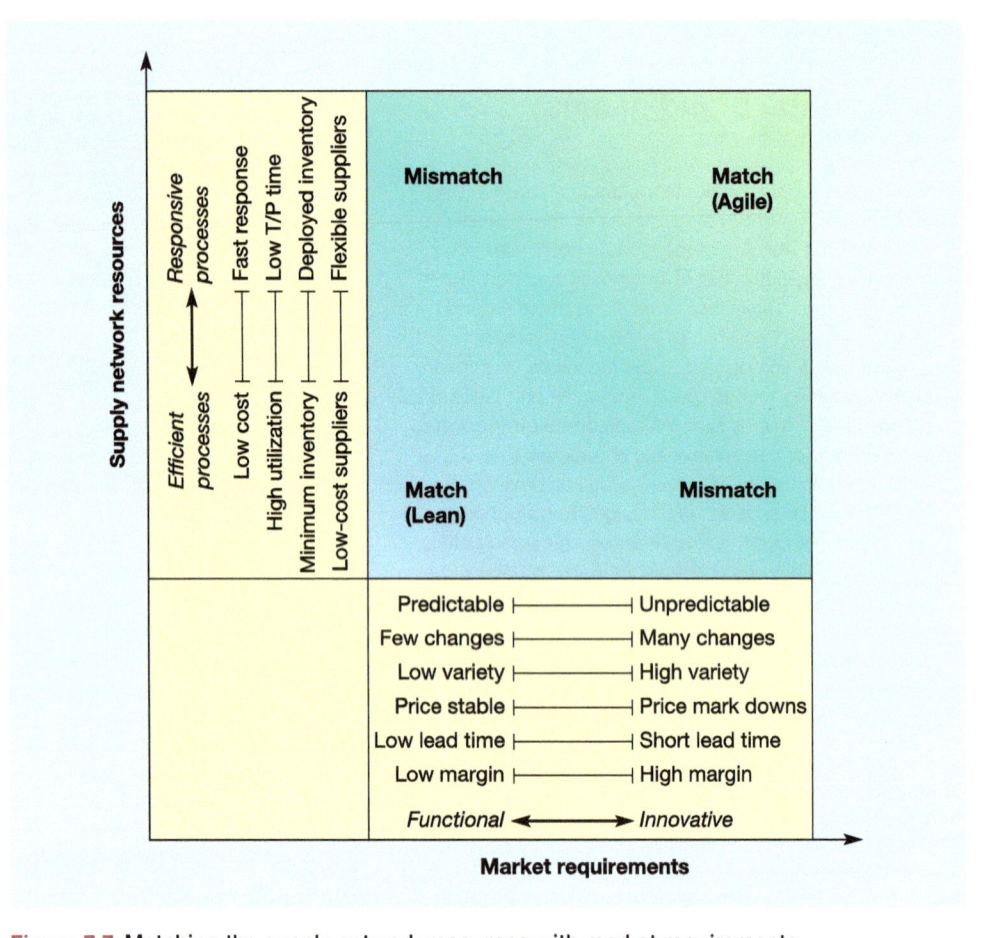

Figure 7.7 Matching the supply network resources with market requirements

Source: Adapted from Fisher, M.C. (1997) What is the right supply chain for your product? *Harvard Business Review*, March–April, 105–16.

those downstream stocks are needed to ensure high levels of availability to end-customers. Figure 7.7 illustrates how the different supply network policies match the different market requirements implied by functional and innovative products.

Types of relationships in supply networks

One of the key issues within a supply network is how relationships with suppliers and customers should be managed. The behaviour of the supply network as a whole is, after all, made up of the relationships which are formed between individual pairs of operations. It is important, therefore, to have some framework which helps us to understand the different ways in which supply relationships can be developed.

Business or consumer relationships?

We can distinguish between relationships that are the final link in the supply network, involving the ultimate consumer, and those involving two commercial businesses (Figure 7.8). So, **business-to-business** (B2B) relationships are by far the most common in a supply network context. **Business-to-consumer** (B2C) relationships include both 'bricks and mortar' retailers

Business to business
Business to consumer

		Relationship – to . . .	
		Business	Consumer (Peer)
Relationship – from . . .	Business	**B2B** *Relationship* • Most common, all but the last link in the supply network *E-commerce examples* • Electronic marketplaces • e.g. b2b Index	**B2C** *Relationship* • Retail operations • Comparison web sites *E-commerce examples* • Online retailers • e.g. Amazon.com
	Consumer (Peer)	**C2B** *Relationship* • Consumers offer, business responds *E-commerce examples* • Usually focused on specialist area • e.g. Google Adsense	**C2C (P2P)** *Relationship* • Originally one of the driving forces behind the modern Internet (ARPANET) *E-commerce examples* • File sharing networks (legal and illegal) • e.g. Napster, Gnutella

Figure 7.8 The business–consumer relationship matrix

Consumer to business

Customer to customer

and online retailers. **Consumer-to-business** (C2B) relationships involve consumers posting their needs on the web (sometimes stating the price they are willing to pay), and companies then deciding whether to offer. **Customer-to-customer** (C2C) or peer-to-peer (P2P) relationships include the online exchange and auction services and file-sharing services. In this chapter we deal almost exclusively with B2B relationships.

Types of business-to-business relationship

A convenient way of categorizing supply relationships is to examine the extent and nature of what a company chooses to buy in from suppliers. Two dimensions are particularly important – *what* the company chooses to outsource, and *who* it chooses to supply it. In terms of what is outsourced, a key question is, 'how many activities are outsourced?' from doing everything in-house at one extreme, to outsourcing everything at the other extreme. In terms of who is chosen to supply products and services, two questions are important, 'how many suppliers will be used by the operation?' and 'how close are the relationships?' Figure 7.9 illustrates this way of characterizing relationships. It also identifies some of the more common types of relationship and shows some of the trends in how supply relationships have moved.

Traditional market supply relationships

Short-term transactional relationships

The very opposite of performing an operation in-house is to purchase services and products from outside in a 'pure' market fashion, often seeking the 'best' supplier every time it is necessary to purchase. Each transaction effectively becomes a separate decision. The **relationship** between buyer and seller, therefore, can be very short-term. Once the services or products are delivered and payment is made, there may be no further trading between the parties. Short-term relationships may be used on a trial basis when new companies are being considered as more regular suppliers. Also, many purchases which are made by operations are

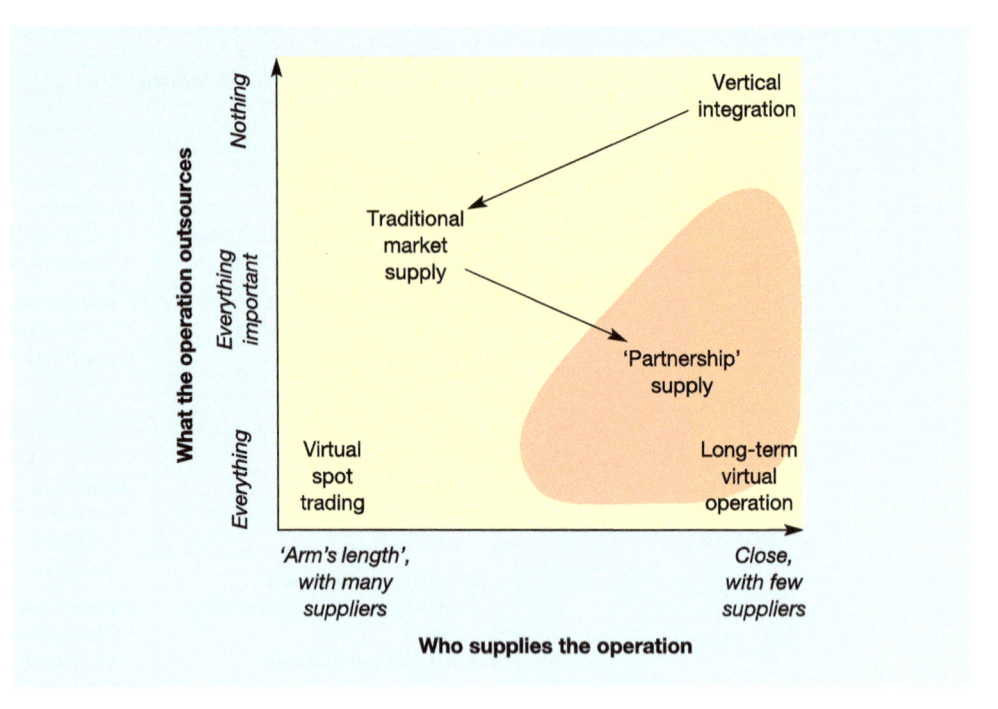

Figure 7.9 Types of supply chain relationship

one-off or very irregular. The advantages of traditional market supplier relationships are usually seen as follows:

- They maintain competition between alternative suppliers. This promotes a constant drive between suppliers to provide best value.
- A supplier specializing in a small number of services or products, but supplying them to many customers, can gain natural economies of scale. This enables the supplier to offer the products and services at a lower price than would be obtained if customers performed the activities themselves.
- There is inherent flexibility in outsourced supplies. If demand changes, customers can simply change the number and type of suppliers. This is a far faster and simpler alternative to having to redirect internal activities.
- Innovations can be exploited no matter where they originate. Specialist suppliers are more likely to come up with innovative products and services which can be bought in faster and cheaper than would be the case if the company were itself trying to innovate.
- They help operations to concentrate on their core activities. One business cannot be good at everything. It is sensible therefore to concentrate on the important activities and outsource the rest.

There are, however, disadvantages in buying in a totally 'free market' manner:

- There may be supply uncertainties. Once an order has been placed, it is difficult to maintain control over how that order is fulfilled. This is a particular problem if the buyer is small relative to the supplier, so lacks power to influence their behaviour.
- Choosing who to buy from takes time and effort. Gathering sufficient information and making decisions continually are, in themselves, activities which need to be resourced.
- There are strategic risks in subcontracting activities to other businesses. An over-reliance on outsourcing can 'hollow out' the company, leaving it with few internal capabilities to exploit in its markets.
- Short-term, price-oriented types of relationship can have a downside in terms of ongoing support and reliability. This may mean that a short-term 'least-cost' purchase decision will lead to long-term high cost.

Short case
Northern Foods wins a slice of the in-flight meals business[7]

The companies that provide airline catering services are in a tough business. Meals must be of a quality that is appropriate for the class and type of flight, yet the airlines that are their customers are always looking to keep costs as low as possible, menus must change frequently and the airlines must respond promptly to customer feedback. If this were not enough, forecasting passenger numbers is difficult. Catering suppliers are advised of the likely numbers of passengers for each flight several days in advance, but the actual minimum number of passengers for each class is only fixed six hours before take-off. Also, flight arrivals are sometimes delayed, putting pressure on everyone to reduce the turnaround time, and upsetting work schedules. Even when a flight lands on time no more than 40 minutes are allowed before the flight is ready for take-off again, so complete preparation and a well-ordered sequence of working is essential. It is a specialized business, and in order to maintain a fast, responsive and agile service, airline caterers have traditionally produced food on, or near, airport sites using their own chefs and staff to cook and tray-set meals. The catering companies' suppliers are also usually airline specialists who themselves are located near the caterers so that they can offer very short response times.

The companies that provide catering services may also provide related services. For example, LSG Sky Chefs (a subsidiary of Deutsche Lufthansa AG) is a provider of tailor-made in-flight services for all types of airlines around the world. Their main areas of service are Airline Catering, In-flight Equipment and Logistics and In-flight Management. They are also large, employing 30,000 people at 200 customer service centres in 49 countries. In 2007 they produced 418 million meals for more than 300 airlines, representing more than 30 per cent of the global airline catering market.

The airline sector has over recent years suffered a series of shocks including 9/11, oil price volatility, financial crises and world recession. This has meant that airlines are reviewing their catering supply solutions. In December 2008 Gate Gourmet, the world's largest independent provider of airline catering lost the contract to supply British Airways' short-haul flights out of Heathrow to new entrants into the airline catering market, a consortium of Northern Foods, a leading food producer, whose normal business is supplying retailers with own-label and branded food, and DHL, a subsidiary of Deutsche Post and the market-leading international express and logistics company. DHL is already a large supplier to 'airside' caterers at Heathrow and already has its own premises at the airport. Northern Foods will make the food at its existing factories and deliver it to DHL, which will assemble onto airline catering trays and transfer them onto aircraft. The new contract is the first time that Northern Foods, whose biggest customer is Marks and Spencer, the UK retail chain, has developed new business outside its normal supermarket customer base.

Specialized companies have developed that prepare food in specialized factories, often for several airlines.

Source: Virgin Atlantic

'Partnership' supply relationships

Partnership relationships

Partnership relationships in supply networks are sometimes seen as a compromise between vertical integration on the one hand (owning the resources which supply you) and pure market relationships on the other (having only a transactional relationship with those who supply you). Although to some extent this is true, partnership relationships are not only a simple mixture of vertical integration and market trading, although they do attempt to achieve some of the closeness and coordination efficiencies of vertical integration, but at the same time attempt to achieve a relationship that has a constant incentive to improve. Partnership relationships are defined as: *'relatively enduring inter-firm cooperative agreements, involving flows and linkages that use resources and/or governance structures from autonomous organizations, for the joint accomplishment of individual goals linked to the corporate mission of each* *sponsoring firm*'.[8] What this means is that suppliers and customers are expected to cooperate, even to the extent of sharing skills and resources, to achieve joint benefits beyond those they could have achieved by acting alone. At the heart of the concept of partnership lies the issue of the *closeness* of the relationship. Partnerships are close relationships, the degree of which is influenced by a number of factors:

- *Sharing success*. An attitude of shared success means that both partners work together in order to increase the total amount of joint benefit they receive, rather than manoeuvring to maximize their own individual contribution.
- *Long-term expectations*. Partnership relationships imply relatively long-term commitments, but not necessarily permanent ones.
- *Multiple points of contact*. Communication between partners is not only through formal channels, but may take place between many individuals in both organizations.
- *Joint learning*. Partners in a relationship are committed to learn from each other's experience and perceptions of the other operations in the chain.
- *Few relationships*. Although partnership relationships do not necessarily imply single sourcing by customers, they do imply a commitment on the part of both parties to limit the number of customers or suppliers with whom they do business. It is difficult to maintain close relationships with many different trading partners.
- *Joint coordination of activities*. As there are fewer relationships, it becomes possible jointly to coordinate activities such as the flow of materials or service, payment, and so on.
- *Information transparency*. An open and efficient information exchange is seen as a key element in partnerships because it helps to build confidence between the partners.
- *Joint problem-solving*. Although partnerships do not always run smoothly, jointly approaching problems can increase closeness over time.
- *Trust*. This is probably the key element in partnership relationships. In this context, trust means the willingness of one party to relate to the other on the understanding that the relationship will be beneficial to both, even though that cannot be guaranteed. Trust is widely held to be both the key issue in successful partnerships, but also, by far, the most difficult element to develop and maintain.

Virtual operations

Virtual operation

An extreme form of outsourcing operational activities is that of the **virtual operation**. Virtual operations do relatively little themselves, but rely on a network of suppliers that can provide services and products on demand. A network may be formed for only one project and then disbanded once that project ends. For example, some software and Internet companies are virtual in the sense that they buy in all the services needed for a particular development. This may include not only the specific software development skills but also such things as project management, testing, applications prototyping, marketing, physical production, and so on. Much of the Hollywood film industry also operates in this way. A production company may buy and develop an idea for a movie, but it is created, edited and distributed by a loose network of agents, actors, technicians, studios and distribution companies. The advantage of virtual operations is their flexibility and the fact that the risks of investing in production facilities are far lower than in a conventional operation. However, without any solid base of resources, a company may find it difficult to hold onto and develop a unique core of technical expertise. The resources used by virtual companies will almost certainly be available to competitors. In effect, the core competence of a virtual operation lies in the way it is able to manage its supply network.

Selecting suppliers

Choosing appropriate suppliers should involve trading off alternative attributes. Rarely are potential suppliers so clearly superior to their competitors that the decision is self-evident.

Table 7.2 Factors for rating alternative suppliers

Short-term ability to supply	Longer-term ability to supply
Range of services or products provided	Potential for innovation
Quality of services or products	Ease of doing business
Responsiveness	Willingness to share risk
Dependability of supply	Long-term commitment to supply
Delivery and volume flexibility	Ability to transfer knowledge as well as products and services
Total cost of being supplied	Technical capability
Ability to supply in the required quantity	Operations capability
	Financial capability
	Managerial capability

Most businesses find it best to adopt some kind of supplier 'scoring' or assessment procedure. This should be capable of rating alternative suppliers in terms of factors such as those in Table 7.2.

Selecting suppliers should involve evaluating the relative importance of all these factors. So, for example, a business might choose a supplier that, although more expensive than alternative suppliers, has an excellent reputation for on-time delivery, or because the high level of supply dependability allows the business to hold lower stock levels. Other trade-offs may be more difficult to calculate. For example, a potential supplier may have high levels of technical capability, but may be financially weak, with a small but finite risk of going out of business. Other suppliers may have little track record of supplying the products or services required, but show the managerial talent and energy for potential customers to view developing a supply relationship as an investment in future capability.

Worked example

A hotel chain has decided to change its supplier of cleaning supplies because its current supplier has become unreliable in its delivery performance. The two alternative suppliers that it is considering have been evaluated, on a 1–10 scale, against the criteria shown in Table 7.3. That also shows the relative importance of each criterion, also on a 1–10 scale. Based on this evaluation, Supplier B has the superior overall score.

Table 7.3 Weighted supplier selection criteria for the hotel chain

Factor	Weight	Supplier A score	Supplier B score
Cost performance	10	8 (8 × 10 = 80)	5 (5 × 10 = 50)
Quality record	10	7 (7 × 10 = 70)	9 (9 × 10 = 90)
Delivery speed promised	7	5 (5 × 7 = 35)	5 (5 × 7 = 35)
Delivery speed achieved	7	4 (4 × 7 = 28)	8 (8 × 7 = 56)
Dependability record	8	6 (6 × 8 = 48)	8 (8 × 8 = 64)
Range provided	5	8 (8 × 5 = 40)	5 (5 × 5 = 25)
Innovation capability	4	6 (6 × 4 = 24)	9 (9 × 4 = 36)
Total weighted score		325	356

An important decision facing most purchasing managers is whether to source each individual product or service from one or more than one supplier, known, respectively, as **single-sourcing** and **multi-sourcing**. Some of the advantages and disadvantages of single- and multi-sourcing are shown in Table 7.4.

Table 7.4 Advantages and disadvantages of single- and multi-sourcing

	Single-sourcing	Multi-sourcing
Advantages	• Potentially better quality because more supplier quality assurance possibilities • Strong relationships which are more durable • Greater dependency encourages more commitment and effort • Better communication • Easier to cooperate on new innovation • More scale economies • Higher confidentiality	• Purchaser can drive price down by competitive tendering • Reduces dependency on individual suppliers • Can switch sources in case of supply failure • Wide sources of knowledge and expertise to tap
Disadvantages	• More vulnerable to disruption if a failure to supply occurs • Individual supplier more affected by volume fluctuations • Supplier might exert upward pressure on prices if no alternative supplier is available	• Difficult to encourage commitment by supplier • Less easy to develop effective SQA • More effort needed to communicate • Suppliers less likely to invest in new processes • More difficult to obtain scale economies

It may seem as though companies that multi-source do so exclusively for their own short-term benefit. However, this is not always the case: multi-sourcing can bring benefits to both supplier and purchaser in the long term. For example, Robert Bosch GmbH, the German automotive components business, required that subcontractors do no more than 20 per cent of their total business with them. This was to prevent suppliers becoming too dependent and allow volumes to be fluctuated without pushing the supplier into bankruptcy. However, there has been a trend for purchasing functions to reduce the number of companies supplying any one part or service.

Dual sourcing or **parallel sourcing** is often seen as a way to balance the relative merits of single and multi-sourcing. This involves using two suppliers for similar goods or services. Whilst dual suppliers are usually required to cooperate, an element of competition may also be encouraged by adjusting the percentage of the contract awarded to each supplier based on previous performance.

Global sourcing

One of the major developments of recent years has been the expansion in the proportion of services and products which businesses source from outside their home country; this is called **global sourcing**. Traditionally, even companies that exported their goods and services all over the world (that is, they were international on their demand side) still sourced the majority of their supplies locally. There are a number of factors promoting global sourcing:

- The formation of trading blocs in different parts of the world has lowered tariff barriers, at least within those blocs. For example, the single market developments within the European Union (EU), the North American Free Trade Agreement (NAFTA) and the South American Trade Group (MERCOSUR) have all made it easier to trade internationally within the regions.
- Transportation infrastructures are considerably more sophisticated and cheaper than they once were. Super-efficient port operations in Rotterdam and Singapore, for example, integrated road–rail systems, jointly developed autoroute systems, and cheaper air freight have all reduced some of the cost barriers to international trade.
- Perhaps most significantly, far tougher world competition has forced companies to look to reducing their total costs. Given that in many industries bought-in items are the largest single part of operations costs, an obvious strategy is to source from wherever is cheapest.

Supply Network Management   **197**

There are, of course, challenges to global sourcing. Suppliers that are further away need to transport their products across long distances. The risks of delays and hold-ups can be far greater than when sourcing locally. Also, negotiating with suppliers whose native language is different from one's own makes communication more difficult and can lead to misunderstandings over contract terms. Therefore global sourcing decisions require businesses to balance cost, performance, service and risk factors, not all of which are obvious. These factors are important in global sourcing because of non-price or 'hidden' cost factors such as cross-border freight and handling fees, complex inventory stocking and handling requirements, more complex administrative, documentation and regulatory requirements, and increased operational risk caused by geopolitical factors.

Supply network dynamics

The bullwhip effect

The 'bullwhip effect' is used to describe how a small disturbance at the downstream end of a supply network causes increasingly large disturbances, errors, inaccuracies and volatility as it works its way upstream. Its main cause is an understandable desire by the different links in the supply network to manage their production rates and inventory levels sensibly. To demonstrate this, examine the production rate and stock levels for the supply network shown in Table 7.5. This is a four-stage supply network where the focal operation is served by three tiers of suppliers. The demand from the market has been running at a rate of 100 items per period, but in period 2 demand reduces to 95 items. All stages in the supply chain work on the principle that they will keep in stock one period's demand (a simplification but not a gross one). The 'stock' column shows the starting stock at the beginning, and the finish stock at the end, of the period. At the beginning of period 2, the focal operation has

Table 7.5 Fluctuations of production levels along supply chain in response to small change in end-customer demand

Period	Third-tier supplier Prodn.	Third-tier supplier Stock	Second-tier supplier Prodn.	Second-tier supplier Stock	First-tier supplier Prodn.	First-tier supplier Stock	Focal operation Prodn.	Focal operation Stock	Demand
1	100	100 100	100	100 100	100	100 100	100	100 100	100
2	20	100 60	60	100 80	80	100 90	90	100 95	95
3	180	60 120	120	80 100	100	90 95	95	95 95	95
4	60	120 90	90	100 95	95	95 95	95	95 95	95
5	100	90 95	95	95 95	95	95 95	95	95 95	95
6	95	95 95	95	95 95	95	95 95	95	95 95	95

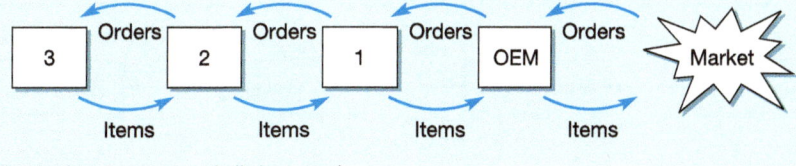

[3] ← Orders → [2] ← Orders → [1] ← Orders → [OEM] ← Orders → Market
       ← Items →   ← Items →   ← Items →   ← Items →

(Note all operations keep one period's inventory.)

100 units in stock. Demand in period 2 is 95 and the operation must produce enough to finish up at the end of the period with 95 in stock (this being the new demand rate). To do this, it need only manufacture 90 items; these, together with 5 items taken out of the starting stock, will supply demand and leave a finished stock of 95 items. Note, however, that a change in demand of only 5 items has produced a fluctuation of 10 items in the operation's production rate.

Now carry this same logic through to the first-tier supplier. At the beginning of period 2, the second-tier supplier has 100 items in stock. The demand which it has to supply in period 2 is derived from the production rate of the focal operation. This has dropped down to 90 in period 2. The first-tier supplier therefore has to produce enough to supply the demand of 90 and leave one month's demand (now 90 items) as its finished stock. A production rate of 80 items per month will achieve this. It will therefore start period 3 with an opening stock of 90 items, but the demand from its customers has now risen to 95 items. It therefore has to produce sufficient to fulfil this demand of 95 items and leave 95 items in stock. To do this, it must produce 100 items in period 3. This logic can be extended right back to the third-tier supplier. The further back up the supply chain an operation is placed, the more drastic are the fluctuations caused by the relatively small change in demand from the final customer. The decision of how much to produce each month is governed by the following relationship:

Total available for sale in any period = Total required in the same period
Starting stock + Production rate = Demand + Closing stock
Starting stock + Production rate = 2 × Demand (because closing stock must be equal to demand)
Production rate = 2 × Demand − Starting stock

Causes of the bullwhip effect

Whenever two operations in a supply network arrange for one to provide services or products to the other, there is the potential for misunderstanding and miscommunication. This may be caused simply by not being sufficiently clear about what a customer expects or what a supplier is capable of delivering. Other causes of the bullwhip effect include errors in forecasting, long or variable lead times, order batching, volatility in demand caused by price fluctuations or promotions, panic ordering (shortage gaming), and the perceived risk of other's bounded rationality within a supply network. Figure 7.10 shows the bullwhip effect in a typical supply network, with relatively small fluctuations in the market causing increasing volatility further back in the network.

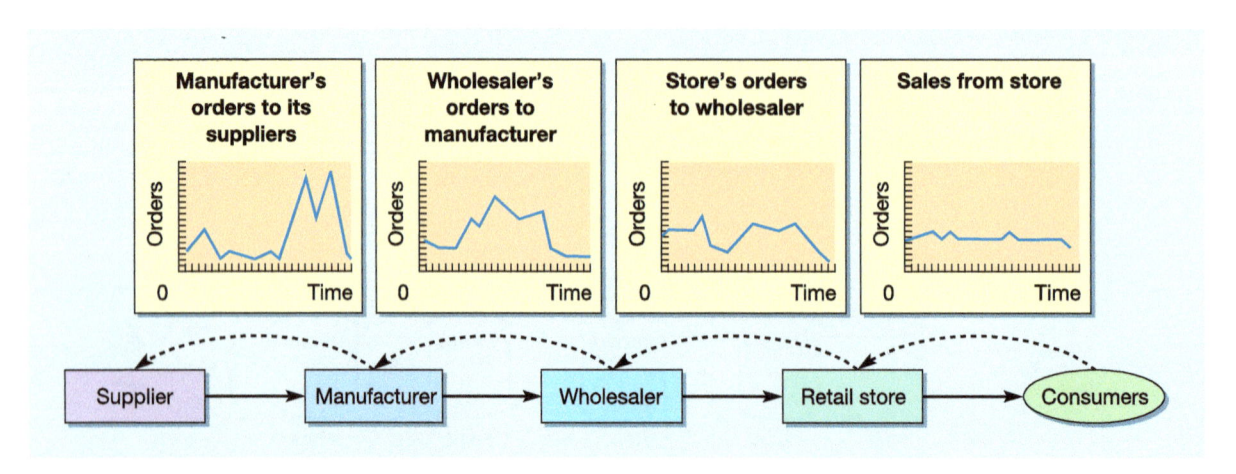

Figure 7.10 Typical supply chain dynamics

Improving supply networks

Increasingly important for operations managers are attempts to improve performance of supply networks. These are usually attempts to either coordinate activities throughout the network or to better understand the complexity of supply processes.

Operational efficiency

Operational efficiency helps improve supply network performance

'Operational efficiency' means the efforts that each operation in the network can make to reduce its own complexity, reduce the cost of doing business with other operations and increase throughput time. The cumulative effect of these individual activities is to simplify the whole **network**. For example, imagine a network of operations whose performance level is relatively poor: quality defects are frequent, the lead time to order products and services is long, and delivery is unreliable and so on. The behaviour of the network would be a continual sequence of errors and effort wasted in replanning to compensate for the errors. Poor quality would mean extra and unplanned orders being placed, and unreliable delivery and slow delivery lead times would mean high safety stocks. Just as important, most operations managers' time would be spent coping with the inefficiency. By contrast, a network whose operations had high levels of operations performance would be more predictable and have faster throughput, both of which would help to minimize supply chain fluctuations.

Supply network time compression

One of the most important approaches to improving the operational efficiency of supply networks is known as **time compression**. This means speeding up the flow of materials and information through the network. The bullwhip effect we observed in Table 7.5 and Figure 7.10 was due partly to the slowness of information moving back up the chain. Figure 7.11 illustrates the advantages of time compression in terms of its overall impact on profitability.[9]

The use of e-business to improve supply networks

New information technology applications combined with internet-based e-business have transformed supply networks. Without appropriate information, supply managers cannot make the decisions that coordinate activities and flows through the network. To some extent, they are 'driving blind' and have to rely on the most obvious of mismatches between the activities of different stages in the network (such as excess inventory) to inform their decisions. Conversely, with accurate and 'near real-time' information, integration is possible and can benefit the network and, eventually, the end-customer. Just as importantly, the collection, analysis and distribution of information using e-business technologies is far less expensive to arrange than previous, less automated methods. Table 7.6 summarizes some of the effects of

Table 7.6 Some effects of e-business on supply chain management practice

	Market/sales information flow	*Product/service flow*	*Cash flow*
Supply-chain-related activities	Understanding customers' needs Designing appropriate services/products Demand forecasting	Purchasing Inventory management Throughput / waiting times Distribution	Supplier payments Customer invoicing Customer receipts
Beneficial effects of e-business practices	Better customer relationship management Monitoring real-time demand On-line customization Ability to coordinate output with demand	Lower purchasing administration costs Better purchasing deals Reduced bullwhip effect Reduced inventory More efficient distribution	Faster movement of cash Automated cash movement Integration of financial information with sales and operations activities

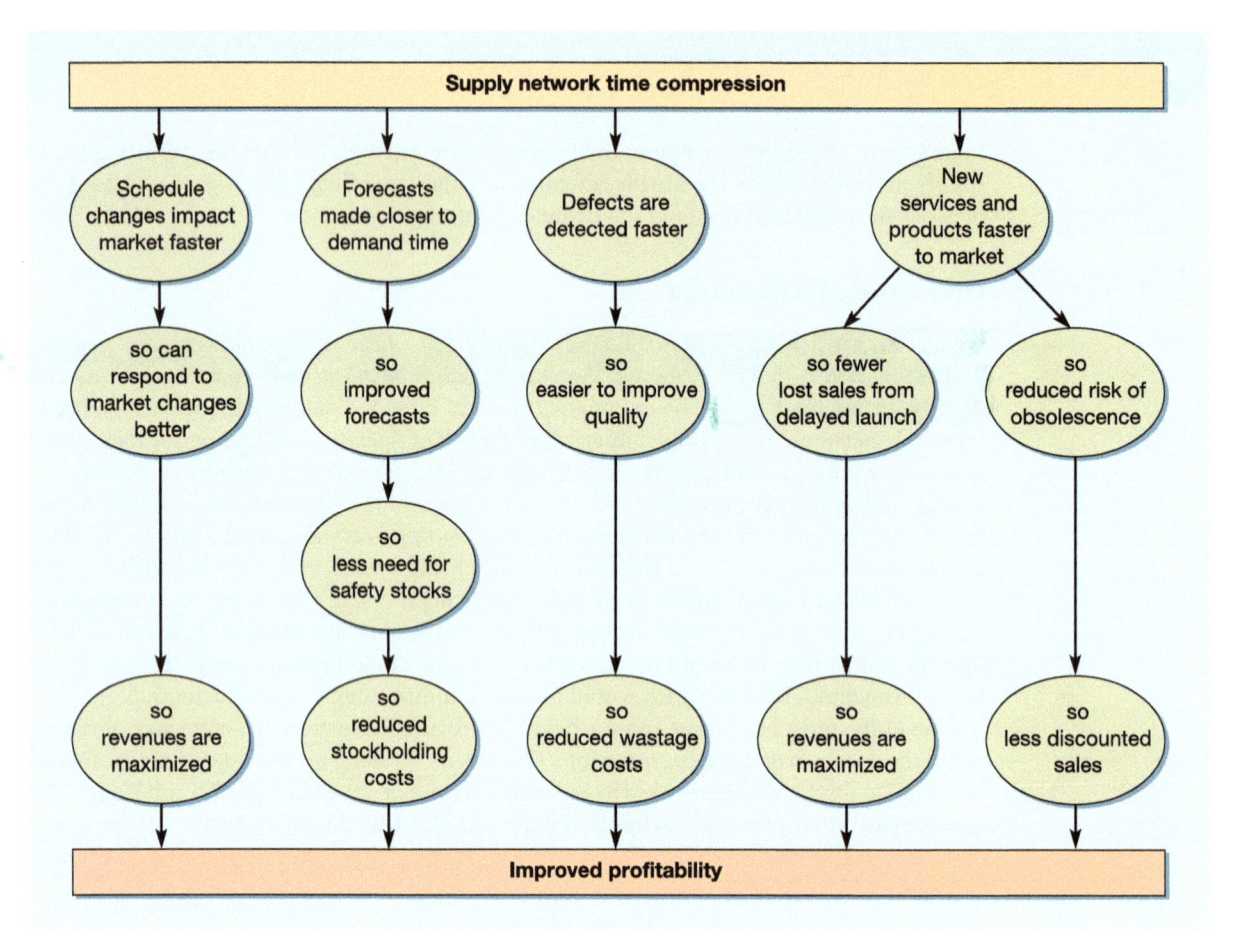

Figure 7.11 Supply network time compression can both reduce costs and increase revenues
Source: Based on Towill

e-business on three important aspects of supply network management – business and market information flow, product and service flow, and the cash flow.

E-procurement

E-procurement
E-procurement is the generic term used to describe the use of electronic methods in every stage of the purchasing process from identification of requirement through to payment, and potentially to contract management.[10] For some years, electronic means have been used by businesses to confirm purchased orders and ensure payment to suppliers. The rapid development of the Internet, however, opened up the potential for far more fundamental changes in purchasing behaviour. Partly this was as the result of supplier information made available through the Internet. By making it easier to search for alternative suppliers, the Internet has changed the economies of the search process and offers the potential for wider searches. It also changed the economies of scale in purchasing. For example, purchasers requiring relatively low volumes find it easier to group together in order to create orders of sufficient size to warrant lower prices. However, whilst the cost savings from purchased goods and services may be the most visible advantage of e-procurement, some managers say that it is just the tip of the iceberg. It can also be far more efficient because purchasing staff are no longer chasing purchase orders and performing routine administrative tasks. Much of the advantage and time savings comes from the decreased need to re-enter information, from streamlining the interaction with suppliers and from having a central repository for data with everything contained in one system. Purchasing staff can negotiate with vendors faster and

more effectively. Online auctions can compress negotiations from months to one or two hours, or even minutes.

E-procurement has grown largely because of the development over the last ten years of electronic marketplaces (also sometimes called infomediaries or cybermediaries). These intermediaries allow buyers and sellers in a B2B context to exchange information about prices and offerings. They can be categorized as consortium, private or third party.

- A private e-marketplace is where buyers or sellers conduct business in the market only with their partners and suppliers by previous arrangement.
- The consortium e-marketplace is where several large businesses combine to create an e-marketplace controlled by the consortium.
- A third-party e-marketplace is where an independent party creates an unbiased, market-driven e-marketplace for buyers and sellers in an industry.

The Internet is an important source of purchasing information, even if the purchase itself is made using more traditional methods. Also, even though many businesses have gained advantages by using e-procurement, it does not mean that everything should be bought electronically. When businesses purchase very large amounts of strategically important products or services, they will negotiate multimillion-euro deals, which involve months of discussion, arranging for deliveries up to a year ahead. In such environments, e-procurement may add little value.

Logistics and the Internet

In supply networks dealing with physical assets, transportation is required. Internet communications in this area of supply management have had two major effects. The first is to make information more readily available along the **distribution chain**. This means that the transport companies, warehouses, suppliers and customers that make up the network can share knowledge of where things are at any given time. This allows the operations within the network to coordinate their activities more readily, with potentially significant cost savings. For example, an important issue for transportation companies is **back-loading**. When the company is contracted to transport goods from A to B, its vehicles may have to return from B to A empty. Back-loading means finding a potential customer that wants their goods transported from B to A in the right time frame. Companies which can fill their vehicles on both the outward and return journeys will have significantly lower costs per distance travelled than those whose vehicles are empty for half the total journey.

The second impact of the Internet on logistics has been in the 'business to consumer' part of the supply network. While the last few years have seen an increase in the number of goods bought by consumers online, most goods still have to be physically transported to the customer. Often early e-retailers ran into major problems in the **order fulfilment** task of actually supplying their customers. Partly this was because many traditional warehouse and distribution operations were not designed for e-commerce fulfilment. Supplying a conventional retail operation requires relatively large vehicles to move relatively large quantities of goods from warehouses to shops. Distributing to individual customers requires a large number of smaller deliveries.

Information-sharing

One of the reasons for the fluctuations in output described in the bullwhip example earlier was that each operation in the network reacted to the orders placed by its immediate customer. None of the operations had an overview of what was happening throughout the chain. If information had been available and **shared throughout the chain**, it is unlikely that such wild fluctuations would have occurred. It is sensible therefore to try to transmit information throughout the chain so that all the operations can monitor true demand, free of these distortions. An obvious improvement is to make information on end-customer demand

Short case
TDG serving the whole supply chain[11]

TDG are specialists in providing *third-party* logistics services to the growing number of manufacturers and retailers that choose not to do their own distribution. Instead they outsource to companies like TDG, which have operations spread across 250 sites that cover the UK, Ireland, France, Spain, Poland and Holland, employ 8,000 people and use 1,600 vehicles.

'There are a number of different types of company providing distribution services', says David Garman, Chief Executive Officer of TDG, 'each with different propositions for the market. At the simplest level, there are the "haulage" and "storage" businesses. These companies either move goods around or they store them in warehouses. Clients plan what has to be done and it is done to order. One level up from the haulage or storage operations are the physical distribution companies, who bring haulage and storage together. These companies collect clients' products, put them into storage facilities and deliver them to the end-customer as and when required. After that there are the companies who offer contract logistics. As a contract logistics service provider, you are likely to be dealing with the more sophisticated clients who are looking for better quality facilities and management and the capability to deal with more complex operations. One level further up is the market for supply chain management services. To do this you have to be able to manage supply chains from end to end, or at least some significant part of the whole chain. Doing this requires a much greater degree of analytical and modelling capability, business process reengineering and consultancy skills.'

TDG, along with other prominent logistics companies, describes itself as a 'lead logistics provider'. This means that they can provide the consultancy-led, analytical and strategic services integrated with a sound base of practical experience in running successful 'on-the-road' operations. 'In 1999 TDG was a UK distribution company', says David Garman, 'now we are a European contract logistics provider with a vision to becoming a full supply chain management company. Providing such services requires sophisticated operations capability, especially in terms of information technology and management dynamism. Because our sites are physically dispersed with our vehicles at any time spread around the motorways of Europe, IT is fundamental to this industry. It gives you visibility of your operation. We need the best operations managers, supported by the best IT.'

Source: TDG Logistics

---

available to upstream operations. Electronic point-of-sale (EPOS) systems used by many retailers attempt to do this. Sales data from checkouts or cash registers are consolidated and transmitted to the warehouses, transportation companies and supplier manufacturing operations that form their supply network. Similarly, electronic data interchange (EDI) helps to share information (see the short case on Seven-Eleven Japan). EDI can also affect the economic order quantities shipped between operations in the supply chain.

Channel alignment

> Channel alignment focuses on harmonizing the network

Channel alignment means the adjustment of scheduling, material movements, stock levels, pricing and other sales strategies so as to bring all the operations in the network into line with each other. This goes beyond the provision of information. It means that the systems and methods of planning and control decision-making are harmonized through the network. For example, even when using the same information, differences in forecasing methods or purchasing practices can lead to fluctuations in orders between operations in the chain. One way of avoiding this is to allow an upstream supplier to manage the inventories of its downstream customer. This is known as **vendor-managed inventory** (VMI). So, for example, a packaging supplier could take responsibility for the stocks of packaging materials held by a food manufacturing customer. In turn, the food manufacturer takes responsibility for the stocks of its products which are held in its customer's, the supermarket's warehouses.

> Vendor-managed inventory

Short case
Seven-Eleven Japan's agile supply chain[12]

Seven-Eleven Japan (SEJ) is Japan's largest and most successful retailer. The average amount of stock in an SEJ store is between 7 and 8.4 days of demand, a remarkably fast stock turnover for any retailer. Industry analysts see SEJ's agile supply management as being the driving force behind its success. It is an agility that is supported by a fully integrated information system that provides visibility of the whole supply network and ensures fast replenishment of goods in its stores customized exactly to the needs of individual stores. As a customer comes to the checkout counter the assistant first keys in the customer's gender and approximate age and then scans the bar codes of the purchased goods. This sales data is transmitted to the Seven-Eleven headquarters through its own high-speed lines. Simultaneously, the store's own computer system records and analyzes the information so that store managers and headquarters have immediate point-of-sale information. This allows both store managers and headquarters to, hour by hour, analyze sales trends, any stock-outs, types of customer buying certain products, and so on. The headquarter's computer aggregates all this data by region, product and time so that all parts of the supply network, from suppliers through to the stores, have the information by the next morning. Every Monday, the company chairman and top executives review all performance information for the previous week and develop plans for the up-coming week. These plans are presented on Tuesday morning to SEJ's 'operations field counsellors' each of which is responsible for facilitating performance improvement in around eight stores. On Tuesday afternoon the field counsellors for each region meet to decide how they will implement the overall plans for their region. On Tuesday night the counsellors fly back to their regions and by next morning are visiting their stores to deliver the messages developed at headquarters which will help the stores implement their plans. SEJ's physical distribution is also organized on an agile basis. The distribution company maintains radio communications with all drivers and SEJ's headquarters keeps track of all delivery activities. Delivery times and routes are planned in great detail and published in the form of a delivery time-table. On average each delivery takes only one and a half minutes at each store, and drivers are expected to make their deliveries within ten minutes of scheduled time. If a delivery is late by more than thirty minutes the distribution company has to pay the store a fine equivalent to the gross profit on the goods being delivered. The agility of the whole supply system also allows SEJ headquarters and the distribution company to respond to disruptions. For example, on the day of the Kobe earthquake, SEJ used 7 helicopters and 125 motor cycles to rush through a delivery of 64,000 rice balls to earthquake victims.

The SCOR model

The Supply Chain Operations Reference model (SCOR) is a broad, but highly structured and systematic, framework for improving supply networks. The framework uses a methodology, diagnostic and benchmarking tools that are increasingly widely accepted for evaluating and comparing supply activities and their performance. Just as important, the SCOR model allows its users to improve, and communicate management practices within and between all interested parties in their supply network by using a standard language and a set of structured definitions. Companies that have used the model include BP, AstraZeneca, Shell, SAP AG, Siemens AG and Bayer. Claimed benefits from using the SCOR model include improved process understanding and performance, improved supply network performance, increased customer satisfaction and retention, a decrease in required capital, better profitability and return on investment, and increased productivity. The model uses three individual techniques turned into an integrated approach. These are:

- Business process modelling.
- Benchmarking performance.
- Best practice analysis.

Business process modelling

SCOR does not represent organizations or functions, but rather processes. Each basic 'link' in the supply network is made up of five types of process, each process being a 'supplier–customer' relationship, see Figure 7.12.

- 'Source' is the procurement, delivery, receipt and transfer of raw material items, sub-assemblies, and/or services.
- 'Make' is the transformation process of adding value to products and services through mixing operations processes.
- 'Deliver' processes perform all customer-facing order management and fulfilment activities including outbound logistics.
- 'Plan' processes manage each of these customer–supplier links and balance the activity of the supply network. They are the supply and demand reconciliation process, which includes prioritization when needed.
- 'Return' processes look after the reverse logistics flow of moving material back from end-customers upstream in the supply chain because of product defects, post-delivery customer support, or recycling (end-of-life reverse supply).

All these processes are modelled at increasingly detailed levels from level 1 through to level 3.

Benchmarking performance

Performance metrics in the SCOR model are also structured by level. Level 1 metrics are the yardsticks by which an organization can measure how successful it is in achieving its desired positioning within the competitive environment, as measured by the performance of a particular supply chain. These level 1 metrics are the key performance indicators (KPIs) of the chain and are created from lower-level diagnostic metrics (called level 2 and level 3 metrics) which are calculated on the performance of lower-level processes.

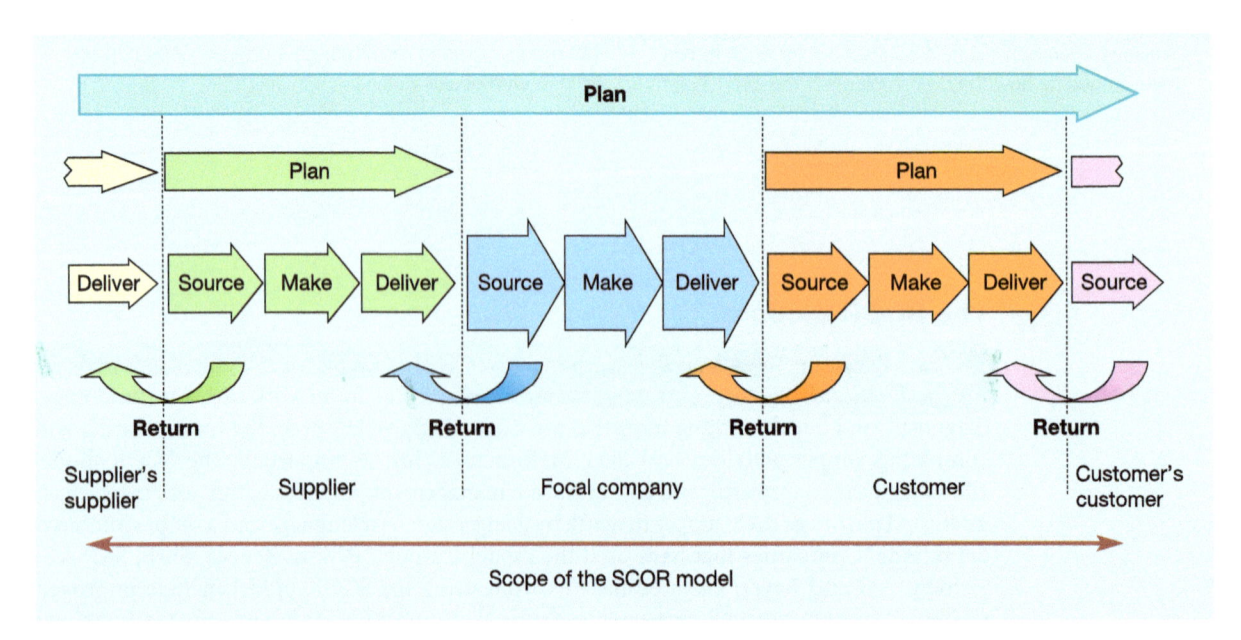

Figure 7.12 Matching the operations resources in the supply network with market requirements

Best practice analysis

Best practice analysis follows the benchmarking activity that should have measured the performance of the supply network processes and identified the main performance gaps. Best practice analysis identifies the activities that need to be performed to close the gaps. The definition of a 'best practice' in the SCOR model is one that:

- Is current – neither untested (emerging) nor outdated.
- Is structured – it has clearly defined goals, scope and processes.
- Is proven – there has been some clearly demonstrated success.
- Is repeatable – it has been demonstrated to be effective in various contexts.
- Has an unambiguous method – the practice can be connected to business processes, operations strategy, technology, supply relationships, and information or knowledge management systems.
- Has a positive impact on results – operations improvement can be linked to KPIs.

The SCOR roadmap

The SCOR model can be implemented by using a five-phase project 'roadmap'. Within this roadmap lies a collection of tools and techniques that both help to implement and support the SCOR framework. In fact many of these tools are commonly used management decision tools such as Pareto charts, cause–effect diagrams, maps of material flow and brainstorming.

Phase 1: Discover – Involves supply-network definition and prioritization where a 'Project Charter' sets the scope for the project. This identifies logic groupings of supply network within the scope of the project. The priorities, based on a weighted rating method, determine which supply network should be dealt with first. This phase also identifies the resources that are required, identified and secured through business process owners or actors.

Phase 2: Analyse – Using data from benchmarking and competitive analysis, the appropriate level of performance metrics are identified; that will define the strategic requirements of each supply network.

Phase 3: Material flow design – In this phase the project teams have their first go at creating a common understanding of how processes can be developed. The current state of processes is identified and an initial analysis attempts to see where there are opportunities for improvement.

Phase 4: Work and information flow design – The project teams collect and analyse the work involved in all relevant processes (plan, source, make, deliver and return) and map the productivity and yield of all transactions.

Phase 5: Implementation planning – This is the final and preparation phase for communicating the findings of the project. Its purpose is to transfer the knowledge of the SCOR team(s) to individual implementation or deployment teams.

Summary answers to key questions

Check and improve your understanding of this chapter using self-assessment questions and a personalized study plan, audio and video downloads, and an eBook – all at www.myomlab.com.

► Why should an organization take a supply network perspective?

- The main advantage is that it helps any operation to understand how it can compete effectively within the network. This is because a supply network approach requires operations managers to think about their suppliers and their customers *as operations*. It can also help to identify particularly significant links within the network and hence identify long-term strategic changes which will affect the operation.

► What is involved in managing supply networks?

- Managing supply networks involves understanding and influencing the various linkages between upstream and downstream operations with the objective of delivering better performance to the end-customer.
- Key activities include designing the supply network, determining the type of supply relationships, understanding supply dynamics and improving supply networks.

► What is involved in designing a supply network?

- Deciding the 'shape' of the supply network: This may involve reducing the number of suppliers to the operation so as to develop closer relationships, bypassing or disintermediating operations in the network, and co-opetition.
- Deciding what to do and what to buy: This concerns the nature of the ownership of the operations within a supply network. The direction of vertical integration refers to whether an organization wants to own operations on its supply side or demand side (backwards or forwards integration). The extent of vertical integration relates to whether an organization wants to own a wide span of the supply network. The balance of integration refers to whether operations can trade with only their vertically integrated partners or with organizations as well.
- Deciding how to align supply and demand in the network: Marshall Fisher distinguishes between functional markets and innovative markets. He argues that functional markets, which are relatively predictable, require efficient supply networks, whereas innovative markets, which are less predictable, require responsive supply networks.

► What are the types of relationship between operations in supply networks?

- Supply networks are made up of individual pairs of buyer–supplier relationships. Business-to-business (B2B) relationships are of the most interest to operations managers. They can be characterized on two dimensions – what is outsourced to a supplier, and the number and closeness of the relationships.
- Traditional market supplier relationships are where a purchaser chooses suppliers on an individual periodic basis. No long-term relationship is usually implied by such 'transactional' relationships, but it makes it difficult to build internal capabilities.
- Partnership supplier relationships involve customers forming long-term relationships with suppliers. In return for the stability of demand, suppliers are expected to commit to high levels of service. True partnerships are difficult to sustain and rely heavily on the degree of trust which is allowed to build up between partners.

- Virtual operations are an extreme form of outsourcing where an operation does relatively little itself and subcontracts almost all its activities.
- Selecting suppliers involves deciding whether to source from one (single), two (dual or parallel) or many (multi) suppliers. One must then consider the relative merits of alternative suppliers.

➤ What is the 'natural' dynamic of a supply network?

- Supply networks exhibit a dynamic behaviour known as the 'bullwhip' effect. This shows how small changes at the demand end of a supply chain are progressively amplified for operations further back in the network.
- Common causes of the bullwhip effect include errors in forecasting, long and variable lead-times, order batching, demand volatility, panic ordering, and bounded rationality.

➤ How can supply networks be improved?

- To reduce the 'bullwhip' effect, operations can adopt some mixture of coordination strategies:
  - operational efficiency: this means eliminating sources of inefficiency or ineffectiveness in the network; of particular importance is 'time compression', which attempts to increase the throughput speed of the operations in the network;
  - e-business: new IT applications have transformed supply networks, enabling improvements in flows of services, information, and products;
  - information-sharing: the efficient distribution of information throughout the chain can reduce demand fluctuations along the chain by linking all operations to the source of demand;
  - channel alignment: this means adopting the same or similar decision-making processes throughout the chain to coordinate how and when decisions are made.
- The Supply Chain Operations Reference model (SCOR) is a highly structured framework for supply network improvement using business process modelling, benchmarking and best practice analysis in an integrated approach.

Learning exercises

These problems and applications will help to improve your analysis of operations. You can find more practice problems as well as worked examples and guided solutions on MyOMLab at www.myomlab.com.

1. Visit sites on the Internet that offer (legal) downloadable music using MP3 or other compression formats. Consider the music business supply network, **(a)** for the recordings of a well-known popular music artist, and **(b)** for a less well-known (or even largely unknown) artist struggling to gain recognition. How might the transmission of music over the Internet affect each of these artists' sales? What implications does electronic music transmission have for record shops?

2. 'Look, why should we waste our time dealing with suppliers who can merely deliver good product, on time, and in full? There are any number of suppliers who can do that. What we are interested in is developing a set of suppliers who will be able to supply us with suitable components for the generation of products that comes after the next products we launch. It's the underlying capability of suppliers that we are really interested in.'

   (a) Devise a set of criteria that this manager could use to evaluate alternative suppliers.
   (b) Suggest ways in which she could determine how to weight each criterion.

3. The example of the bullwhip effect shown in Table 7.5 shows how a simple 5 per cent reduction in demand at the end of the supply network causes fluctuations that increase in severity the further back an operation is placed in the chain.

   (a) Using the same logic and the same rules (i.e. all operations keep one period's inventory), what would the effect on the chain be if demand fluctuated period by period between 100 and 95? That is, period 1 has a demand of 100, period 2 has a demand of 95, period 3 a demand of 100, period 4 a demand of 95, and so on?

   (b) What happens if all operations in the supply network decided to keep only half of the period's demand as inventory?

4. Visit a C2C auction site (for example eBay) and analyse the function of the site in terms of the way it facilitates transactions. What does such a site have to get right to be successful?

Want to know more?

Carmel, E. and Tjia, P. (2005) *Offshoring Information Technology: Sourcing and Outsourcing to a Global Workforce*, Cambridge University Press, Cambridge. An academic book on outsourcing.

Chopra, S. and Meindl, P. (2001) *Supply Chain Management: Strategy, Planning and Operations*, Prentice Hall, Upper Saddle River, NJ. A good textbook that covers both strategic and operations issues.

Fisher, M.L. (1997) What is the right supply chain for your product?, *Harvard Business Review*, vol. 75, no. 2. A particularly influential article that explores the issue of how supply networks are not all the same.

Harrison, A. and van Hoek, R. (2002) *Logistics Management and Strategy*, Financial Times Prentice Hall, Harlow. A short but readable book that explains many of the modern ideas in supply network management including lean supply networks and agile supply networks.

Vashistha, A. and Vashistha, A. (2006) *The Offshore Nation: Strategies for Success in Global Outsourcing and Offshoring*, McGraw-Hill Higher Education. A topical book on outsourcing.

Useful websites

www.cio.com/topic/3207/supply_chain_management Site of CIO's Supply Chain Management Research Center. Topics include procurement and fulfilment, with case studies.

www.gsb.stanford.edu/scforum/ Stanford University's supply chain forum. Interesting debate.

www.rfidc.com/ Site of the RFID Centre that contains RFID demonstrations and articles to download.

www.spychips.com/ Vehemently anti-RFID site. If you want to understand the nature of some activists' concern over RFID, this site provides the arguments.

www.cips.org/ The Chartered Institute of Purchasing and Supply (CIPS) is an international organization, serving the purchasing and supply profession and dedicated to promoting best practice. Some good links.

www.opsman.org Lots of useful stuff.

Now that you have finished reading this chapter, why not visit MyOMLab at www.myomlab.com where you'll find more learning resources to help you make the most of your studies and get a better grade.

Chapter 8

Capacity management

Key questions

- What is capacity management?
- How are demand and capacity measured?
- What are the alternative ways of coping with demand fluctuation?
- How can operations manage their capacity level?
- How can queuing theory be used to plan capacity?

Introduction

Providing the capability to satisfy current and future demand is a fundamental responsibility of operations management. Get the balance between capacity and demand right and the operation can satisfy its customers cost-effectively. Get it wrong and it will fail to satisfy demand, and have excessive costs. Capacity management is also sometimes referred to as *aggregate planning*. This is because, at this level, demand and capacity calculations are usually performed on an aggregated basis which does not discriminate between the different services and products that an operation might offer. The essence of the task is to reconcile, at a general and aggregated level, the supply of capacity with the level of demand which it must satisfy. Figure 8.1 shows where this chapter fits into the overall operations model.

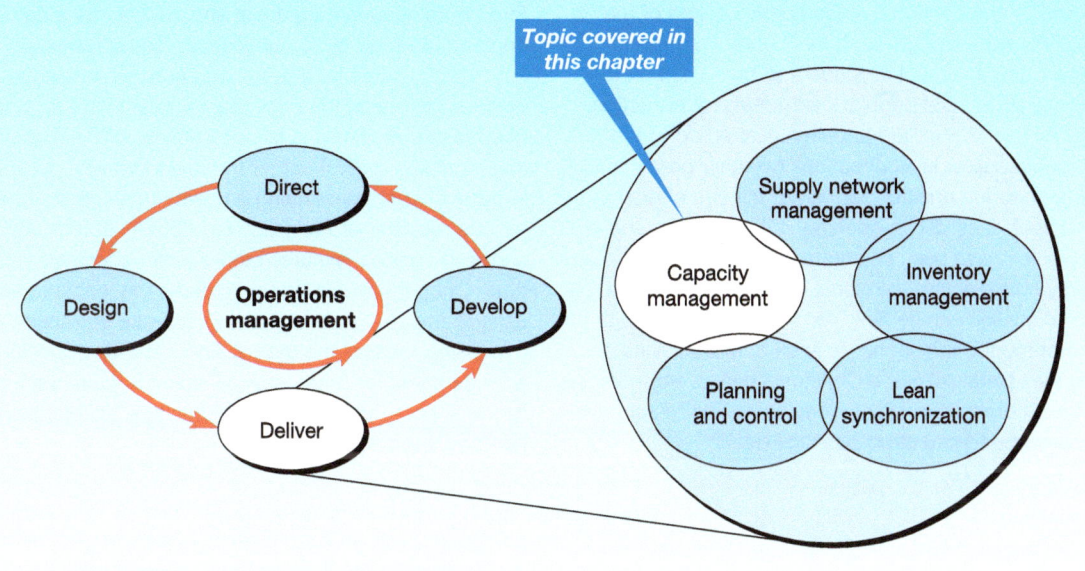

Figure 8.1 This chapter examines capacity management

Check and improve your understanding of this chapter using self-assessment questions and a personalized study plan, audio and video downloads, and an eBook – all at www.myomlab.com.

Operations in practice: The London Eye

The British Airways London Eye is the world's largest observation wheel and one of the UK's most spectacular tourist attractions. The 32 passenger capsules each hold 25 people. The wheel rotates continuously, so entry requires customers to step into the capsules which are moving at 0.26 metres per second, which is a quarter of normal walking speed. One complete 360 degree rotation takes 30 minutes, at the end of which the doors open and passengers disembark. Boarding and disembarkation are separated on the specially designed platform which is built out over the river. The attraction has a 'timed admissions booking system' (TABS) for both individual and group bookings. This allocates requests for 'flights' on the basis of half-hour time slots. At the time of writing, the BA London Eye is open every day except Christmas Day. Admission is from 10.00 am to 9.30 pm in the summer, from the beginning of April to mid-September. For the rest of the year, the winter season, admission begins at 10.00 am, and last admissions are for the 5.30 to 6.00 pm slot.

When opened, in 2000, the London Eye was known as the Millennium Wheel. At that time, British Airways was the main sponsor. Today, the London Eye is operated by the London Eye Company Limited of the Merlin Entertainment group. It has become an iconic landmark and a symbol of modern Britain. The London Eye is the UK's most popular paid-for visitor attraction, visited by over 3.5 million people a year enjoying the 40 kilometres view in all directions (weather permitting!). In addition to the spectacular views, the Eye offers many other possibilities. Since opening, 433 weddings and civil partnerships have been celebrated 'on board'. New Year's Eve fireworks displays are also a regular feature. For a fee, private capsules can be hired for up to 25 guests, with the option of food, champagne, or even a 'Mulled Wine and Mince Pies Capsule' in the Christmas period. Partnerships with local hotels, river cruise companies and restaurants also allow the Eye to offer 'package deals'.

To 'fly' on the Eye, customers must first buy their (timed) tickets in the Ticket Hall then queue to board the wheel itself. And because The Eye is extremely popular (especially in summer) queues can last up to four hours although, on a wet and cold winter's day, demand (and therefore queues) can be far lower. Fast Track tickets (at a premium price) will avoid the queues. However, the best way for customers to avoid queues at busy times is to book tickets online, but this means risking poor weather the day of your 'flight'. Groups of customers hiring a private capsule are asked for one member of the group to check-in at a priority check-in desk 15 minutes before their scheduled flight time. Once the whole group is ready, the 'capsule host' escorts the group through the Fast Track entrance bypassing most of the queue. There are also special arrangements for other 'special' ticket holders such as schools' bookings, disabled tickets, flexi tickets, flexi fast-track and so on.

Source: British Airways London Eye

What is capacity management?

The most common use of the word capacity is in the static, physical sense of the fixed *volume* of a container, or the space in a building. This meaning of the word is also sometimes used by operations managers. For example, a pharmaceutical manufacturer may invest in new 1,000-litre capacity reactor vessels, a property company purchases a 500-vehicle capacity city-centre car park, and a 'multiplex' cinema is built with 10 screens and a total capacity of 2,500 seats. Although these capacity measures describe the **scale** of these operations, they do not reflect the processing capacities of these investments. To do this we must incorporate a **time** dimension appropriate to the use of assets. So the pharmaceutical company will be concerned with the level of output that can be achieved using the 1,000-litre reactor vessel. If a batch of standard products can be produced every hour, the planned processing capacity could be as high as 24,000 litres per day. If the reaction takes four hours, and two hours are used for cleaning between batches, the vessel may only produce 4,000 litres per day. Similarly, the car park may be fully occupied by office workers during the working day, 'processing' only 500 cars per day. Alternatively, it may be used for shoppers staying on average only one hour, and theatre-goers occupying spaces for three hours in the evening. The processing capacity would then be up to 5,000 cars per day. Thus the definition of the capacity of an operation is the **maximum level of value-added activity over a period of time** that the process can achieve under normal operating conditions.

Capacity considers scale and time dimensions

Capacity is the maximum level of activity over a time period

Capacity constraints

Many organizations operate at below their maximum processing capacity, either because there is insufficient demand to completely 'fill' their capacity, or as a deliberate policy, so that the operation can respond quickly to extra demand. Often organizations find themselves with some parts of their operation operating below their capacity while other parts are at their capacity 'ceiling'. It is the parts of the operation that are operating at their capacity ceiling which are the **capacity constraint** for the whole operation. For example, a retail superstore might offer a gift-wrapping service which at normal times can cope with all requests for its services without delaying customers unduly. At Christmas, however, the demand for gift wrapping might increase proportionally far more than the overall increase in custom for the store as a whole. Unless extra resources are provided to increase the capacity of this micro-operation, it could constrain the capacity of the whole store.

Capacity constraint

Managing capacity

Capacity management is the task of setting the effective capacity of the operation so that it can respond to the demands placed upon it. This usually means deciding how the operation should react to fluctuations in demand. Long-term changes in demand and the alternative capacity strategies for dealing with the changes is usually concerned with introducing (or deleting) major increments of capacity. We called this task **long-term capacity strategy**. In this chapter we are treating the shorter timescale where capacity decisions are being made largely within the constraints of the capacity limits set by the operation's long-term capacity strategy.

Long-term capacity strategy

Medium- and short-term capacity

Having established long-term capacity, operations managers must decide how to adjust the capacity of the operation in the **medium term**. This usually involves an assessment of the demand forecasts over a period of 2–18 months ahead, during which time planned output can be varied, for example, by changing the number of hours the equipment is used. In practice, however, few forecasts are accurate, and most operations also need to respond to changes in

Medium-term capacity management

demand which occur over a shorter timescale. Hotels and restaurants have unexpected and apparently random changes in demand from night to night, but also know from experience that certain days are on average busier than others. So operations managers also have to make **short-term capacity** adjustments, which enable them to flex output for a short period, either on a predicted basis (for example, bank checkouts are always busy at lunchtimes) or at short notice (for example, a sunny day at a theme park).

Short-term capacity management

Aggregate demand and capacity

Aggregate capacity management

The important characteristic of capacity management, as we are treating it here, is that it is concerned with setting capacity levels over the medium and short terms in **aggregated** terms. This means making broad capacity decisions without concern for all of the detail of the individual services and products offered. This may mean some degree of approximation, especially if the mix of offerings varies significantly (as we shall see later in this chapter). Nevertheless, as a first step in capacity management, aggregation is necessary. For example, a hotel might think of demand and capacity in terms of 'room nights per month', which ignores the number of guests in each room and their individual requirements, but is a good first approximation. A woollen knitwear factory might measure demand and capacity in the number of garments it is capable of making per month, ignoring size, colour or style variations. Aluminium producers could use tonnes per month, ignoring types of alloy, gauge and batch size variation. The ultimate aggregation measure is money. For example, retail stores, which sell an exceptionally wide variety of services and products, use revenue per month, ignoring variation in spend, number of items bought, the gross margin of each item and the number of items per customer transaction. If all this seems very approximate, remember that most operations have sufficient experience of dealing with aggregated data to find it useful.

The objectives of capacity management

The decisions taken by operations managers in devising their capacity plans will affect several different aspects of performance:

- *Quality* of services or products might be affected by a capacity plan which involves large fluctuations in capacity levels, by hiring temporary staff for example. The disruption to the routine working of the operation could increase the probability of errors.
- *Speed* of response to customer demand could be enhanced, either by the build-up of inventories or by the deliberate provision of surplus capacity to avoid queuing.
- *Dependability* of supply will also be affected by how close demand levels are to capacity. The closer demand gets to the operation's capacity ceiling, the less able it is to cope with any unexpected disruptions.
- *Flexibility*, especially volume flexibility, will be enhanced by surplus capacity, which allows the operation to respond to any unexpected increase in demand.
- *Costs* will be affected by the balance between capacity and demand. Capacity levels in excess of demand could mean under-utilization of capacity and therefore high unit cost.
- *Revenues* will also be affected by the balance between capacity and demand, but in the opposite way. Capacity levels equal to or higher than demand at any point in time will ensure that all demand is satisfied and no revenue lost.
- *Working capital* will be affected if an operation decides to build up finished goods inventory prior to demand. This might allow demand to be satisfied, but the organization will have to fund the inventory until it can be sold.

The steps of capacity management

The sequence of capacity management decisions which need to be taken by operations managers is illustrated in Figure 8.2. Typically, operations managers are faced with a forecast of demand which is unlikely to be either certain or constant. They will also have some idea of their own ability to meet this demand. Nevertheless, before any further decisions are

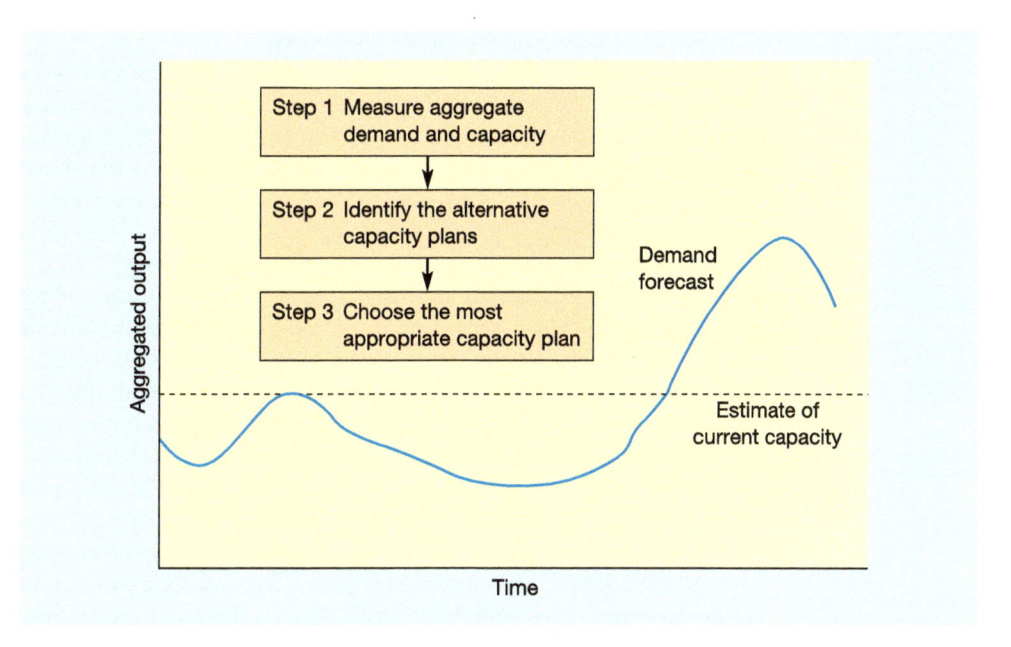

Figure 8.2 The steps in capacity management

taken, they must have quantitative data on both capacity and demand. So the first step will be to measure the aggregate demand and capacity levels for the planning period. The second step will be to identify the alternative capacity plans which could be adopted in response to the demand fluctuations. The third step will be to choose the most appropriate capacity plan for their circumstances.

Measuring demand and capacity

Forecasting demand fluctuations

Forecasting is a key input to capacity management

Although **demand forecasting** is usually the responsibility of the sales and/or marketing functions, it is a very important input into capacity management decisions, and is therefore of interest to operations managers. After all, without an estimate of future demand it is not possible to plan effectively for future events, only to react to them. It is therefore important to understand the basis and rationale for these demand forecasts. As far as capacity management is concerned, there are three requirements from a demand forecast.

It is expressed in terms which are useful for capacity management
If forecasts are expressed only in money terms and give no indication of the demands that will be placed on an operation's capacity, they will need to be translated into realistic expectations of demand, expressed in the same units as the capacity (for example, operatives required, space needed, machine hours per year, etc.).

It is as accurate as possible
In capacity management, the accuracy of a forecast is important because, whereas demand can change instantaneously, there is a lag between deciding to change capacity and the change taking effect. Thus, many operations managers are faced with a dilemma. In order to attempt to meet demand, they must often decide output in advance, based on a forecast which might change before the demand occurs, or worse, prove not to reflect actual demand at all.

It gives an indication of relative uncertainty

Decisions to operate extra hours and recruit extra staff are usually based on forecast levels of demand, which could in practice differ considerably from actual demand, leading to unnecessary costs or unsatisfactory customer service. For example, a forecast of demand levels in a supermarket may show initially slow business that builds up to a lunchtime rush. After this, demand slows, only to build up again for the early evening rush, and it finally falls again at the end of trading. The supermarket manager can use this forecast to adjust checkout capacity throughout the day. But although this may be an accurate average demand forecast, no single day will exactly conform to this pattern. Of equal importance is an estimate of how much actual demand could differ from the average. This can be found by examining demand statistics to build up a distribution of demand at each point in the day. The importance of this is that the manager now has an understanding of when it will be important to have reserve staff, perhaps filling shelves, but on call to staff the checkouts should demand warrant it. Generally, the advantage of probabilistic forecasts such as this is that it allows operations managers to make a judgement between possible plans that would virtually guarantee the operation's ability to meet actual demand, and plans that minimize costs. Ideally, this judgement should be influenced by the nature of the way the business wins orders: price-sensitive markets may require a risk-avoiding cost minimization plan that does not always satisfy peak demand, whereas markets that value responsiveness and service quality may justify a more generous provision of operational capacity.

Seasonality of demand

Demand seasonality
Supply seasonality

In many organizations, capacity management is concerned largely with coping with seasonal demand fluctuations. Almost all services and products have some **demand seasonality** and some also have **supply seasonality**, usually where the inputs are seasonal agricultural products – for example, in processing frozen vegetables. These fluctuations in demand or supply may be reasonably forecastable, but some are usually also affected by unexpected variations in the weather and by changing economic conditions. Figure 8.3 gives some examples of seasonality, and the short case 'Operating while the sun shines' discusses the sometimes unexpected link between weather conditions and demand levels.

Consider the four different types of operation described previously: a city hotel, a wool knitwear factory, a supermarket and an aluminium producer. Their demand patterns are shown in Figure 8.4. The city hotel and the woollen knitwear business both have seasonal

Causes of seasonality

Climatic | Festive | Behavioural | Political | Financial | Social

Some seasonal services and products
- Travel services
- Holidays
- Tax processing
- Doctors (influenza epidemic)
- Sports services
- Education services
- Construction materials
- Beverages (beer, cola)
- Foods (ice-cream, Christmas cakes)
- Clothing (swimwear, shoes)
- Gardening items (seeds, fertilizer)
- Fireworks

Figure 8.3 Many types of operation have to cope with seasonal demand

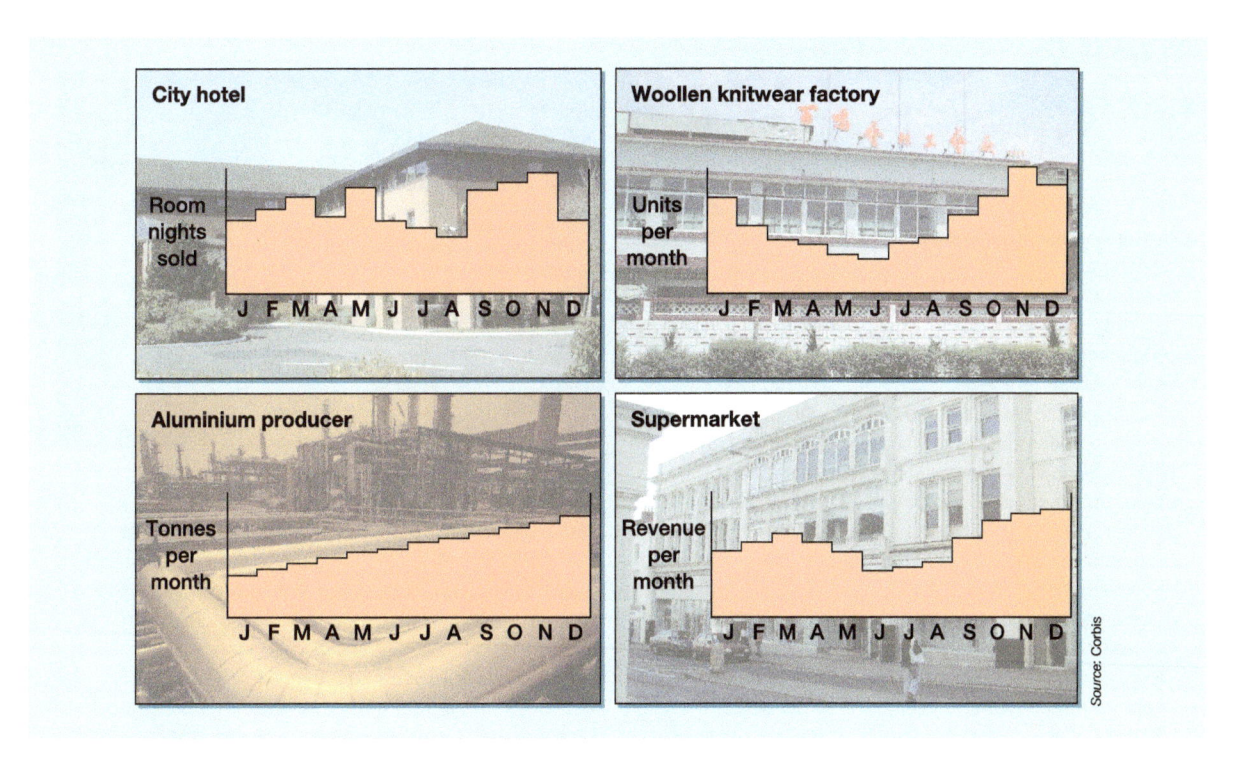

Figure 8.4 Aggregate demand fluctuations for four organizations

sales demand patterns, but for different reasons: the woollen knitwear business because of climatic patterns (cold winters, warm summers) and the hotel because of demand from business people, who take vacations from work at Christmas and in the summer. The retail supermarket is a little less seasonal, but is affected by pre-vacation peaks and reduced sales during vacation periods. The aluminium producer shows virtually no seasonality, but is showing a steady growth in sales over the forecast period.

Weekly and daily demand fluctuations

Seasonality of demand occurs over a year, but similar predictable variations in demand can also occur for some services and products on a shorter cycle. The daily and weekly demand patterns of a supermarket will fluctuate, with some degree of predictability. Demand might be low in the morning, higher in the afternoon, with peaks at lunchtime and after work in the evening. Demand might be low on Monday and Tuesday, build up during the latter part of the week and reach a peak on Friday and Saturday. Banks, public offices, telephone sales organizations and electricity utilities all have weekly and daily, or even hourly, demand patterns which require capacity adjustment. The extent to which an operation will have to cope with very short-term demand fluctuations is partly determined by how long its customers are prepared to wait for their services. An operation whose customers are incapable of, or unwilling to, wait will have to plan for very short-term demand fluctuations. Emergency services, for example, will need to understand the hourly variation in the demand for their services and plan capacity accordingly.

Measuring capacity

The main problem with measuring capacity is the complexity of most operations. Only when the operation is highly standardized and repetitive is capacity easy to define unambiguously. A government office, for example, may have the capacity to print and post 500,000 tax forms

Short case
Operating while the sun shines[1]

The sales of many operations are profoundly affected by the weather. Sunglasses, sunscreen, waterproof clothing and ice cream are all obvious examples. Yet the range of operations interested in weather forecasting has expanded significantly. Energy utilities, soft drink producers and retailers are all keen to purchase the latest weather forecasts. But so are operations such as banking call centres and mobile phone operators. It would appear that the demand for telephone banking falls dramatically when the sun shines, as does the use of mobile phones. A motorway catering group was surprised to find that their sales of hot meals fell predictably by €110,000 per day for each degree temperature rise above 20 °C. Similarly, insurance companies have found it wise to sell their offerings when the weather is poor and likely customers are trapped indoors rather than relaxing outside in the sun, refusing to worry about the future. In the not-for-profit sector, new understanding is being developed on the link between various illnesses and temperature. Here temperature is often used as a predictor of demand. So, for example, coronary thrombosis cases peak two days after a drop in temperature, for strokes the delay is around five days, while deaths from respiratory infections peak twelve days from a temperature drop. Knowing this, hospital managers can plan for changes in their demand.

Because of this, meteorological services around the world now sell increasingly sophisticated forecasts to a wide range of companies. In the UK, the Meteorological Office offers an internet-based service for its customers. It is also used to help insurance specialists price insurance policies to provide compensation against weather-related risk. Complex financial products called 'weather derivates' are now available to compensate for weather-related uncertainty. So, for example, an energy company could buy a financial option before winter where the seller pays the company a guaranteed sum of money if the temperature rises above a certain level. If the weather is mild and energy sales are low, the company gets compensation. If the weather is cold, the company loses the premium it has paid to the seller but makes up for it by selling more power at higher prices. However, as meteorologists point out, it is up to the individual businesses to use the information wisely. Only they have the experience to assess the full impact of weather on their operation. So, for example, supermarkets know that a rise in temperature will impact on the sales of cottage cheese, whereas, unaccountably, the sales of cottage cheese with pineapple chunks are not affected!

Source: Alamy/Medical-on-line

---

per week. A fast ride at a theme park might be designed to process batches of 60 people every three minutes – a capacity to convey 1,200 people per hour. In each case, an **output capacity measure** is the most appropriate measure because the output from the operation does not vary in its nature. For many operations, however, the definition of capacity is not so obvious. When a much wider range of outputs places varying demands on the process, for instance, output measures of capacity are less useful. Here **input capacity measures** are frequently used to define capacity. Almost every type of operation could use a mixture of both input and output measures, but in practice, most choose to use one or the other (see Table 8.1).

Output capacity measure

Input capacity measures

Capacity depends on activity mix

The hospital measures its capacity in terms of its resources, partly because there is not a clear relationship between the number of beds it has and the number of patients it treats. If all its patients required relatively minor treatment with only short stays in hospital, it could treat many people per week. Alternatively, if most of its patients required long periods of observation or recuperation, it could treat far fewer. Output depends on the mix of activities in which the hospital is engaged and, because most hospitals perform many different types of activities, output is difficult to predict. Certainly it is difficult to compare directly the capacity of hospitals which have very different activities.

Capacity Management

Table 8.1 Input and output capacity measures for different operations

Operation	Input measure of capacity	Output measure of capacity
Hospital	**Beds available**	Number of patients treated per week
Theatre	**Number of seats**	Number of customers entertained per week
University	**Number of students**	Students graduated per year
Retail store	**Sales floor area**	Number of items sold per day
Airline	**Number of seats available on the sector**	Number of passengers per week
Air-conditioner plant	Machine hours available	**Number of units per week**
Electricity company	Generator size	**Megawatts of electricity generated**
Brewery	Volume of fermentation tanks	**Litres per week**

Note: The most commonly used measure is shown in bold.

Worked example

Suppose an air-conditioner factory produces three different models of air-conditioner unit: the de luxe, the standard and the economy. The de luxe model can be assembled in 1.5 hours, the standard in 1 hour and the economy in 0.75 hour. The assembly area in the factory has 800 staff hours of assembly time available each week.

If demand for de luxe, standard and economy units is in the ratio 2:3:2, the time needed to assemble 2 + 3 + 2 = 7 units is:

$$(2 \times 1.5) + (3 \times 1) + (2 \times 0.75) = 7.5 \text{ hours}$$

The number of units produced per week is:

$$\frac{800}{7.5} \times 7 = 746.7 \text{ units}$$

If demand changes to a ratio of de luxe, economy, standard units of 1:2:4, the time needed to assemble 1 + 2 + 4 = 7 units is:

$$(1 \times 1.5) + (2 \times 1) + (4 \times 0.75) = 6.5 \text{ hours}$$

Now the number of units produced per week is:

$$\frac{800}{6.5} \times 7 = 861.5 \text{ units}$$

Overall equipment effectiveness[2]

The **overall equipment effectiveness** (OEE) measure is an increasingly popular method of judging the effectiveness of operations equipment. It is based on three aspects of performance:

- *the time* that equipment is available to operate;
- *the quality* of the product or service it creates;
- *the speed*, or throughput rate, of the equipment.

Overall equipment effectiveness is calculated by multiplying an availability rate by a performance (or speed) rate multiplied by a quality rate. Some of the reduction in available capacity of a piece of equipment (or any process) is caused by time losses such as set-up and changeover losses (when the equipment or process is being prepared for its next activity), and breakdown failures when the machine is being repaired. Some capacity is lost through speed losses such as when equipment is idling (for example when it is temporarily waiting for work from another process) and when equipment is being run below its optimum work rate.

Operations Management

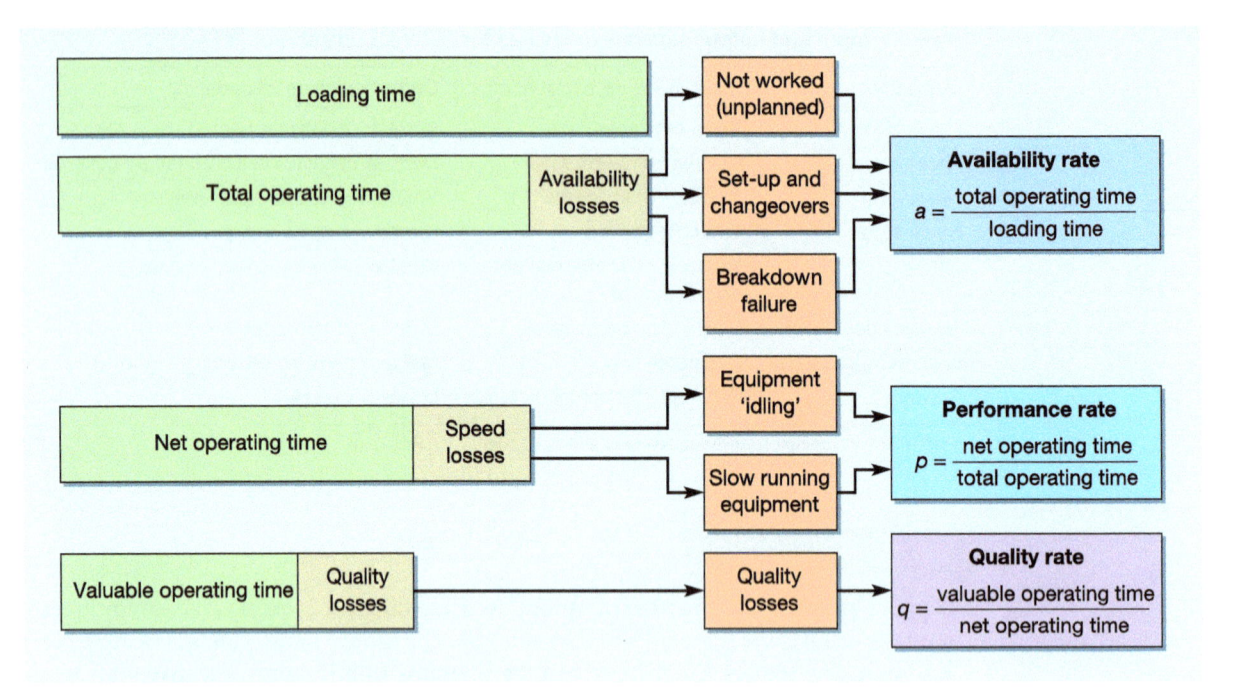

Figure 8.5 Operating equipment effectiveness

Finally, not everything processed by a piece of equipment will be error-free. So some capacity is lost through quality losses (see Figure 8.5).

Taking the notation in Figure 8.5,

$$\text{OEE} = a \times p \times q$$

For equipment to operate effectively, it needs to achieve high levels of performance against all three of these dimensions. Viewed in isolation, these individual metrics are important indicators of performance, but they do not give a complete picture of *overall* effectiveness. This can only be understood by looking at the combined effect of the three measures, calculated by multiplying the three individual metrics together. All these losses to the OEE performance can be expressed in terms of units of time – the design cycle time to deliver one unit. In effect, this means that an OEE represents the valuable operating time as a percentage of the design capacity.

Worked example

In a typical 7-day period, the planning department programmes a particular machine to work for 150 hours – its loading time. Changeovers and set-ups take an average of 10 hours and breakdown failures average 5 hours every 7 days. The time when the machine cannot work because it is waiting for material to be delivered from other parts of the process is 5 hours on average and during the period when the machine is running, it averages 90 per cent of its rated speed. Three per cent of the parts processed by the machine are subsequently found to be defective in some way.

$$\text{Maximum time available} = 7 \times 24 \text{ hours}$$
$$= 168 \text{ hours}$$

$$\text{Loading time} = 150 \text{ hours}$$

$$\text{Availability losses} = 10 \text{ hours (set-ups)} + 5 \text{ hrs (breakdowns)}$$
$$= 15 \text{ hours}$$

So, Total operating time = Loading time − Availability
= 150 hours − 15 hours
= 135 hours

Speed losses = 5 hours (idling) + ((135 − 5) × 0.1)(10% of remaining time)
= 18 hours

So, Net operating time = Total operating time − Speed losses
= 135 − 18
= 117 hours

Quality losses = 117 (Net operating time) × 0.03 (Error rate)
= 3.51 hours

So, Valuable operating time = Net operating time − Quality losses
= 117 − 3.51
= 113.49 hours

Therefore, availability rate $= a = \dfrac{\text{Total operating time}}{\text{Loading time}}$

$= \dfrac{135}{150} = 90\%$

and, performance rate $= p = \dfrac{\text{Net operating time}}{\text{Total operating time}}$

$= \dfrac{117}{135} = 86.67$

and quality rate $= q = \dfrac{\text{Valuable operating time}}{\text{Net operating time}}$

$= \dfrac{113.49}{117} = 97\%$

OEE $(a \times p \times q) = 75.6\%$

The alternative capacity plans

With an understanding of both demand and capacity, the next step is to consider the alternative methods of responding to demand fluctuations. There are three 'pure' options available for coping with such variation:

Level capacity plan
Chase demand plan
Demand management

- Ignore the fluctuations and keep activity levels constant (**level capacity plan**).
- Adjust capacity to reflect the fluctuations in demand (**chase demand plan**).
- Attempt to change demand to fit capacity availability (**demand management**).

In practice, most organizations will use a mixture of all of these 'pure' plans, although often one plan might dominate. The Short case 'Seasonal salads' describes how one operation pursues some of these options.

Level capacity plan

In a level capacity plan, the processing capacity is set at a uniform level throughout the planning period, regardless of the fluctuations in forecast demand. This means that the same

Short case
Seasonal salads

Lettuce is an all-year-round ingredient for most salads, but both the harvesting of the crop and its demand are seasonal. Lettuces are perishable and must be kept in cold stores and transported in refrigerated vehicles. Even then the product only stays fresh for a maximum of a week. In most north European countries, demand continues throughout the winter at around half the summer levels, but outdoor crops cannot be grown during the winter months. Glasshouse cultivation is possible but expensive.

One of Europe's largest lettuce growers is G's Fresh Salads. Their supermarket customers require fresh produce to be delivered 364 days a year, but because of the limitations of the English growing season, the company has developed other sources of supply in Europe. It acquired a farm and packhouse in the Murcia region of south-eastern Spain, which provides the bulk of salad crops during the winter, transported daily to the UK by a fleet of refrigerated trucks. Further top-up produce is imported by air from around the world.

Sales forecasts are agreed with the individual supermarkets well in advance, allowing the planting and growing programmes to be matched to the anticipated level of sales. However, the programme is only a rough guide. The supermarkets may change their orders right up to the afternoon of the preceding day. Weather is a dominant factor. First, it determines supply – how well the crop grows and how easy it is to harvest. Second, it influences sales – cold, wet periods during the summer discourage the eating of salads, whereas hot spells boost demand greatly.

The fluctuating nature of the actual sales is the result of a combination of weather-related availability and supermarket demand. These do not always match. When demand is higher than expected, the picking rigs and their crews continue to work into the middle of night, under floodlights. Another capacity problem is the operation's staffing levels. It relies on temporary seasonal harvesting and packing staff to supplement the full-time employees for both the English and Spanish seasons. Since most of the crop is transported to the UK in bulk, a large permanent staff is maintained for packing and distribution in the UK. The majority of the Spanish workforce is temporary, with only a small number retained during the extremely hot summer to grow and harvest other crops such as melons.

The specialist lettuce harvesting machines (the 'rigs') are shipped over to Spain every year at the end of the English season, so that the company can achieve maximum utilization from all this expensive capital equipment. These rigs not only enable very high productivity of the pickers, but also ensure the best possible conditions for quality packing and rapid transportation to the cold stores.

---

number of staff operate the same processes and should therefore be capable of delivering the same aggregate output in each period. Where non-perishable materials are processed, but not immediately sold, they can be transferred to finished goods inventory in anticipation of sales at a later time. Thus this plan is feasible (but not necessarily desirable) for our examples of the woollen knitwear company and the aluminium producer (see Figure 8.6).

Level capacity plans of this type can achieve the objectives of stable employment patterns, high process utilization, and usually also high productivity with low unit costs. Unfortunately, they can also create considerable inventory which has to be financed and stored. Perhaps the biggest problem, however, is that decisions have to be taken as to what to produce for inventory rather than for immediate sale. Will green woollen sweaters knitted in July still be fashionable in October? Could a particular aluminium alloy in a specific sectional shape still be sold months after it has been produced? Most firms operating this plan, therefore, give priority to only creating inventory where future sales are relatively certain and unlikely to be affected by changes in fashion or design. Clearly, such plans are not suitable for 'perishable' products, such as foods and some pharmaceuticals, for products where fashion changes rapidly and unpredictably (for example, popular music CDs, fashion garments), or for customized products.

A level capacity plan could also be used by the hotel and supermarket, although this would not be the usual approach of such organizations, because it usually results in a waste of staff

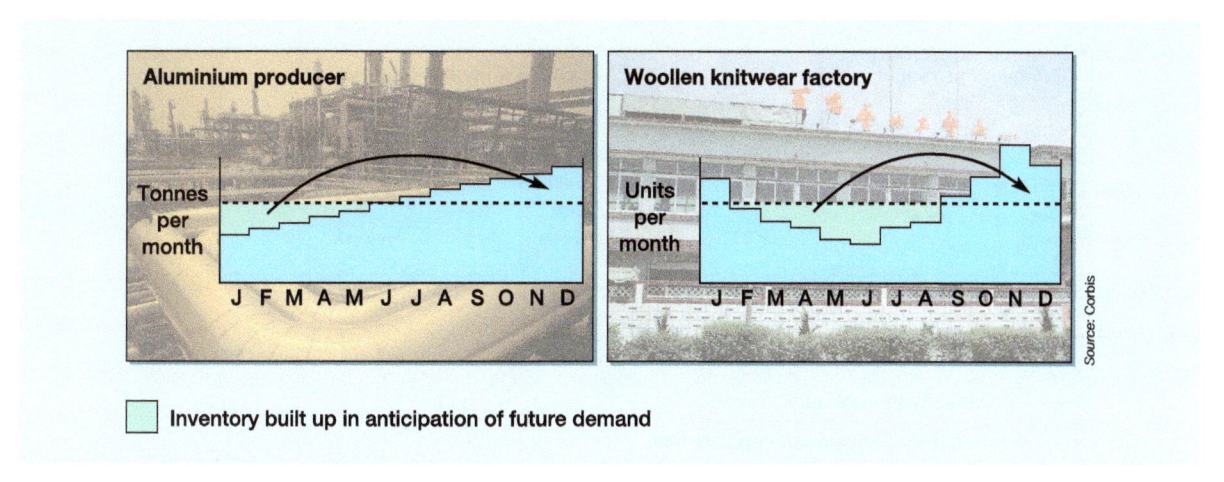

Figure 8.6 Level capacity plans which use anticipation inventory to supply future demand

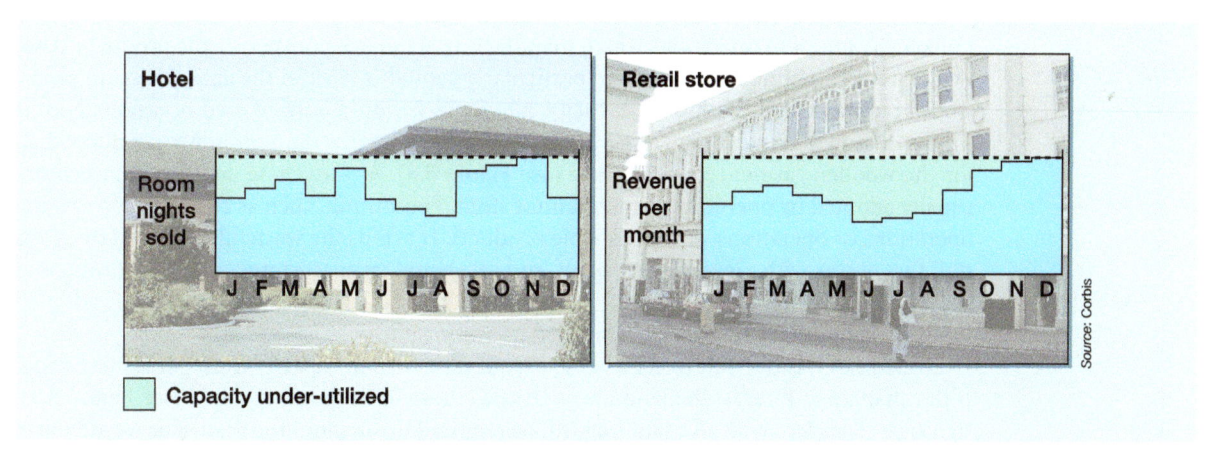

Figure 8.7 Level capacity plans with under-utilization of capacity

resources, reflected in low productivity. Because service cannot be stored as inventory, a level capacity plan would involve running the operation at a uniformly high level of capacity availability. The hotel would employ sufficient staff to service all the rooms, to run a full restaurant, and to staff the reception even in months when demand was expected to be well below capacity. Similarly, the supermarket would plan to staff all the checkouts, warehousing operations, and so on, even in quiet periods (see Figure 8.7).

Low utilization can make level capacity plans prohibitively expensive in many service operations, but may be considered appropriate where the opportunity costs of individual lost sales are very high. For example, in the high-margin retailing of jewellery and in (real) estate agents. It is also possible to set the capacity somewhat below the forecast peak demand level in order to reduce the degree of under-utilization. However, in the periods where demand is expected to exceed planned capacity, customer service may deteriorate. Customers may have to queue for long periods or may be 'processed' faster and less sensitively. While this is obviously far from ideal, the benefits to the organization of stability and productivity may outweigh the disadvantages of upsetting some customers.

Chase demand plan

The opposite of a level capacity plan is one which attempts to match capacity closely to the varying levels of forecast demand. This is much more difficult to achieve than a level capacity plan, as different numbers of staff, different working hours, and even different amounts of equipment may be necessary in each period. For this reason, pure chase demand plans are

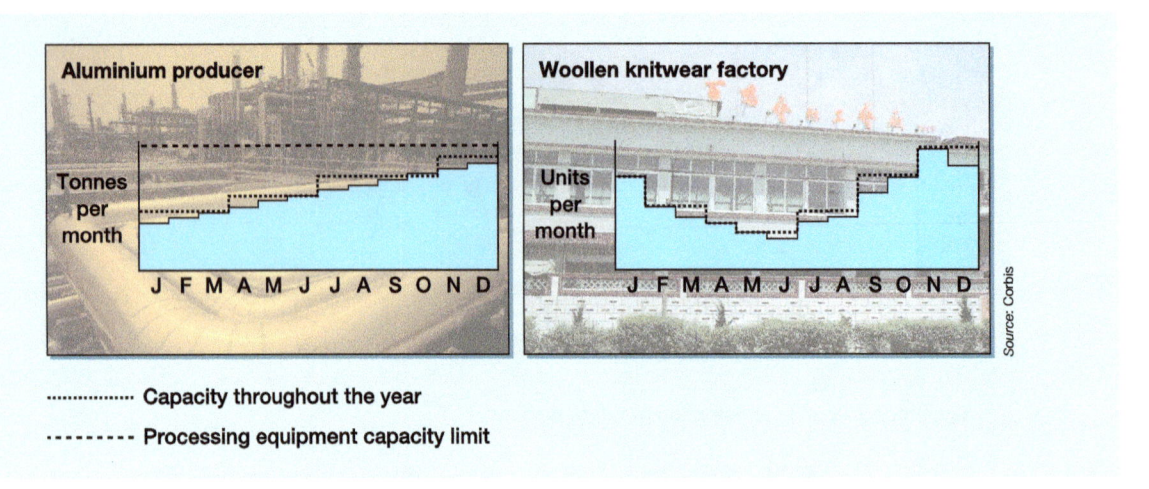

Figure 8.8 Chase demand capacity plans with changes in capacity which reflect changes in demand

unlikely to appeal to operations which manufacture standard, non-perishable products. Also, where manufacturing operations are particularly capital-intensive, the chase demand policy would require a level of physical capacity, all of which would only be used occasionally. It is for this reason that such a plan is less likely to be appropriate for the aluminium producer than for the woollen garment manufacturer (see Figure 8.8). A pure chase demand plan is more usually adopted by operations which cannot store their output, such as customer-processing operations or operations with perishable products. It avoids the wasteful provision of excess staff that occurs with a level capacity plan, and yet should satisfy customer demand throughout the planned period. Where output can be stored, the chase demand policy might be adopted in order to minimize or eliminate finished goods inventory.

Sometimes it is difficult to achieve very large variations in capacity from period to period. If the changes in forecast demand are as large as those in the hotel example (see Figure 8.9), significantly different levels of staffing will be required throughout the year. This would mean employing part-time and temporary staff, requiring permanent employees to work longer hours, or even bringing in contract labour. The operations managers will then have the difficult task of ensuring that quality standards and safety procedures are still adhered to, and that the customer service levels are maintained.

Methods of adjusting capacity

The chase demand approach requires that capacity is adjusted by some means. There are a number of different methods for achieving this, although they may not all be feasible for all types of operation. Some of these methods are now discussed.

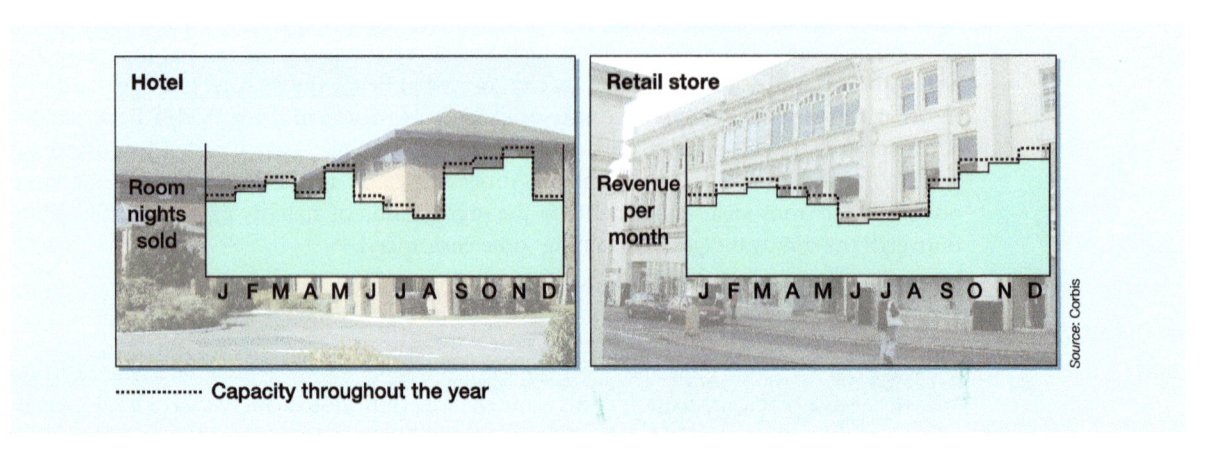

Figure 8.9 Chase demand capacity plans with changes in capacity which reflect changes in demand

Overtime and idle time

Often the quickest and most convenient method of adjusting capacity is by varying the number of productive hours worked by the staff in the operation. When demand is higher than nominal capacity, **overtime** is worked, and when demand is lower than nominal capacity the amount of time spent by staff on productive work can be reduced. In the latter case, it may be possible for staff to engage in some other activity such as cleaning or maintenance. This method is only useful if the timing of the extra productive capacity matches that of the demand. For example, there is little to be gained in asking a retail operation's staff to work extra hours in the evening if all the extra demand is occurring during their normal working period. The costs associated with this method are either the extra payment which is normally necessary to secure the agreement of staff to work overtime, or in the case of **idle time**, the costs of paying staff who are not engaged in direct productive work. Further, there might be costs associated with the fixed costs of keeping the operation heated, lit and secure over the extra period staff are working. There is also a limit to the amount of extra working time which any workforce can deliver before productivity levels decrease. **Annualized hours** approaches, as described below in the Short case 'Working by the year', are one way of flexing working hours without excessive extra costs.

Varying the size of the workforce

If capacity is largely governed by workforce size, one way to adjust it is to adjust the size of the workforce. This is done by hiring extra staff during periods of high demand and laying them off as demand falls, or **hire and fire**. However, there are cost and ethical implications to be taken into account before adopting such a method. The costs of hiring extra staff include those associated with recruitment, as well as the costs of low productivity while new staff go through the learning curve. The costs of lay-off may include possible severance payments, but might also include the loss of morale in the operation and loss of goodwill in the local labour market. At a micro-operation level, one method of coping with peaks in demand in one area of an operation is to build sufficient flexibility into job design and job demarcation so that staff can transfer across from less busy parts of the operation. For example, the French hotel chain Novotel has trained some of its kitchen staff to escort customers from the reception area up to their rooms. The peak times for registering new customers coincide with the least busy times in the kitchen and restaurant areas.

Using part-time staff

A variation on the previous strategy is to recruit **part-time staff**, that is, for less than the normal working day. This method is extensively used in service operations such as supermarkets and fast-food restaurants but is also used by some manufacturers to staff an evening shift after the normal working day. However, if the fixed costs of employment for each employee, irrespective of how long he or she works, are high then using this method may not be worthwhile.

Subcontracting

In periods of high demand, an operation might buy capacity from other organizations, called **subcontracting**. This might enable the operation to meet its own demand without the extra expense of investing in capacity which will not be needed after the peak in demand has passed. Again, there are costs associated with this method. The most obvious one is that subcontracting can be very expensive. The subcontractor will also want to make sufficient margin out of the business. A subcontractor may not be as motivated to deliver on time or to the desired levels of quality. Finally, there is the risk that the subcontractors might decide to enter the same market themselves.

Manage demand plan

The most obvious mechanism of **demand management** is to **change demand** through price. Although this is probably the most widely applied approach in demand management, it is more common for services than for products. For example, some city hotels offer low-cost

> **Critical commentary**
>
> To many, the idea of fluctuating the workforce to match demand, either by using part-time staff or by hiring and firing, is more than just controversial. It is regarded as unethical. It is any business's responsibility, they argue, to engage in a set of activities which are capable of sustaining employment at a steady level. Hiring and firing merely for seasonal fluctuations, which can be predicted in advance, is treating human beings in a totally unacceptable manner. Even hiring people on a short-term contract, in practice, leads to them being offered poorer conditions of service and leads to a state of permanent anxiety as to whether they will keep their jobs. On a more practical note, it is pointed out that, in an increasingly global business world where companies may have sites in different countries, those countries that allow hiring and firing are more likely to have their plants 'downsized' than those where legislation makes this difficult.

'city break' vacation packages in the months when fewer business visitors are expected. Skiing and camping holidays are cheapest at the beginning and end of the season and are particularly expensive during school vacations. Discounts are given by photo-processing firms during winter periods, but never around summer holidays. Ice cream is 'on offer' in many supermarkets during the winter. The objective is invariably to stimulate off-peak demand and to constrain peak demand, in order to smooth demand as much as possible. Organizations can also attempt to increase demand in low periods by appropriate advertising. For example, turkey growers in the UK and the USA make vigorous attempts to promote their products at times other than Christmas and Thanksgiving.

Short case
Working by the year[3]

One method of fluctuating capacity as demand varies throughout the year without many of the costs associated with overtime or hiring temporary staff is called the Annual Hours Work Plan. This involves staff contracting to work a set number of hours per year rather than a set number of hours per week. The advantage of this is that the amount of staff time available to an organization can be varied throughout the year to reflect the real state of demand. Annual hours plans can also be useful when supply varies throughout the year. For example, a UK cheese factory of Express Foods, like all cheese factories, must cope with processing very different quantities of milk at different times of the year. In spring and during early summer, cows produce large quantities of milk, but in late summer and autumn the supply of milk slows to a trickle. Before the introduction of annualized hours, the factory had relied on overtime and hiring temporary workers during the busy season. Now the staff are contracted to work a set number of hours a year with rotas agreed more than a year in advance and after consultation with the union. This means that at the end of July staff broadly know what days and hours they will be working up to September of the following year. If an emergency should arise, the company can call in people from a group of 'super crew' who work more flexible hours in return for higher pay but can do any job in the factory.

However, not all experiments with annualized hours have been as successful as that at Express Foods. In cases where demand is very unpredictable, staff can be asked to come in to work at very short notice. This can cause considerable disruption to social and family life. For example, at one news-broadcasting company, the scheme caused problems. Journalists and camera crew who went to cover a foreign crisis found that they had worked so many hours they were asked to take the whole of one month off to compensate. Since they had no holiday plans, many would have preferred to work.

Alternative offerings

Sometimes, a more radical approach is required to fill periods of low demand such as developing offerings which can be delivered using existing processes, but have different demand patterns throughout the year (see the Short case 'Getting the message' for an example of this approach). Most universities fill their accommodation and lecture theatres with conferences and company meetings during vacations. Ski resorts provide organized mountain activity holidays in the summer. Some garden tractor companies in the US now make snow movers in the autumn and winter. The apparent benefits of filling capacity in this way must be weighted against the risks of damaging the core service or product, and the operation must be fully capable of serving both markets. Some universities have been criticized for providing sub-standard, badly decorated accommodation which met the needs of impecunious undergraduates, but which failed to impress executives at a trade conference.

Mixed plans

Each of the three 'pure' plans is applied only where its advantages strongly outweigh its disadvantages. For many organizations, however, these 'pure' approaches do not match their required combination of competitive and operational objectives. Most operations managers are required simultaneously to reduce costs and inventory, to minimize capital investment, and yet to provide a responsive and customer-oriented approach at all times. For this reason, most choose to follow a mixture of the three approaches. This can be best illustrated by the woollen knitwear company example (see Figure 8.10). Here some of the peak demand has been brought forward by the company offering discounts to selected retail customers (manage demand plan). Capacity has also been adjusted at two points in the year to reflect the broad changes in demand (chase demand plan). Yet the adjustment in capacity is not sufficient to totally avoid the build-up of inventories (level capacity plan).

Yield management

Yield management

In operations which have relatively fixed capacities, such as airlines and hotels, it is important to use the capacity of the operation for generating revenue to its full potential. One approach used by such operations is called **yield management**.[4] This is really a collection of methods, some of which we have already discussed, which can be used to ensure that an operation maximizes its potential to generate profit. Yield management is especially useful where:

- capacity is relatively fixed;
- the market can be fairly clearly segmented;
- the service cannot be stored in any way;

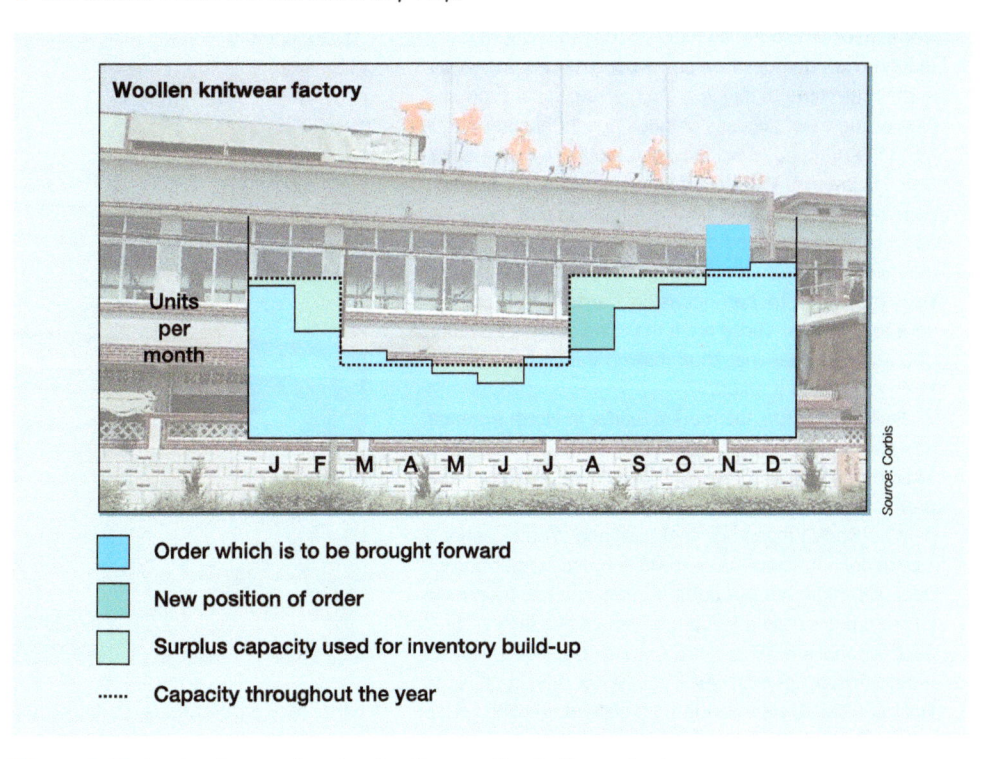

Figure 8.10 A mixed capacity plan for the woollen knitwear factory

- the services are sold in advance;
- the marginal cost of making a sale is relatively low.

Airlines, for example, fit all these criteria. They adopt a collection of methods to try to maximize the yield (i.e. profit) from their capacity. These include the following:

- *Over-booking capacity.* Not every passenger who has booked a place on a flight will actually show up for the flight. If the airline did not fill this seat it would lose the revenue from it. Because of this, airlines regularly book more passengers onto flights than the capacity of the aircraft can cope with. If they over-book by the exact number of passengers who fail to show up, they have maximized their revenue under the circumstances. Of course, if more passengers show up than they expect, the airline will have a number of upset passengers to deal with (although they may be able to offer financial inducements for the passengers to take another flight). If they fail to over-book sufficiently, they will have empty seats. By studying past data on flight demand, airlines try to balance the risks of over-booking and under-booking.
- *Price discounting.* At quiet times, when demand is unlikely to fill capacity, airlines will also sell heavily discounted tickets to agents who themselves take the risk of finding customers for them. In effect, this is using the price mechanism to affect demand.
- *Varying service types.* Discounting and other methods of affecting demand are also adjusted depending on the demand for particular types of service. For example, the relative demand for first-, business- and economy-class seats varies throughout the year. There is no point discounting tickets in a class for which demand will be high. Yield management also tries to adjust the availability of the different classes of seat to reflect their demand. They will also vary the number of seats available in each class by upgrading or even changing the configuration of airline seats.

Short case
Getting the message[5]

Companies which traditionally operate in seasonal markets can demonstrate some considerable ingenuity in their attempts to develop counter-seasonal products. One of the most successful industries in this respect has been the greetings card industry. Mother's Day, Father's Day, Halloween, Valentine's Day and other occasions have all been promoted as times to send (and buy) appropriately designed cards. Now, having run out of occasions to promote, greetings card manufacturers have moved on to 'non-occasion' cards, which can be sent at any time. These have the considerable advantage of being less seasonal, thus making the companies' seasonality less marked.

Hallmark Cards, the market leader in North America, has been the pioneer in developing non-occasion cards. Their cards include those intended to be sent from a parent to a child with messages such as 'Would a hug help?', 'Sorry I made you feel bad' and 'You're perfectly wonderful – it's your room that's a mess'. Other cards deal with more serious adult themes such as friendship ('You're more than a friend, you're just like family') or even alcoholism ('This is hard to say, but I think you're a much neater person when you're not drinking'). Now Hallmark Cards has founded a 'loyalty marketing group' that 'helps companies communicate with their customers at an emotional level'. It promotes the use of greetings cards for corporate use, to show that customers and employees are valued. Whatever else these products may be, they are not seasonal!

Choosing a capacity management approach

Before an operation can decide which of the capacity plans to adopt, it must be aware of the consequences of adopting each plan in its own set of circumstances. Two methods are particularly useful in helping to assess the consequences of adopting particular capacity plans:

Cumulative representations
Queuing theory

- **cumulative representations** of demand and capacity;
- **queuing theory**.

Cumulative representations

Figure 8.11 shows the forecast aggregated demand for a chocolate factory which makes confectionery products. Demand for its products in the shops is greatest at Christmas. To meet this demand and allow time for the products to work their way through the distribution system, the factory must supply a demand which peaks in September, as shown. One method of assessing whether a particular level of capacity can satisfy the demand would be to calculate the degree of over-capacity below the graph which represents the capacity levels (areas A and C) and the degree of under-capacity above the graph (area B). If the total over-capacity is greater than the total under-capacity for a particular level of capacity, then that capacity could be regarded as adequate to satisfy demand fully, the assumption being that inventory has been accumulated in the periods of over-capacity. However, there are two problems with this approach. The first is that each month shown in Figure 8.11 may not have the same amount of productive time. Some months (August, for example) may contain vacation periods which reduce the availability of capacity. The second problem is that a capacity level which seems adequate may only be able to supply products *after* the demand for them has occurred. For example, if the period of under-capacity occurred at the beginning of the year, no inventory could have accumulated to meet demand. A far superior way of assessing capacity plans is first to plot demand on a *cumulative* basis. This is shown as the blue line in Figure 8.12.

The cumulative representation of demand immediately reveals more information. First, it shows that although total demand peaks in September, because of the restricted number of available productive days, the peak demand per productive day occurs a month earlier in August. Second, it shows that the fluctuation in demand over the year is even greater than it seemed. The ratio of monthly peak demand to monthly lowest demand is 6.5:1, but the ratio of peak to lowest demand per productive day is 10:1. Demand per productive day is more relevant to operations managers, because productive days represent the time element of capacity.

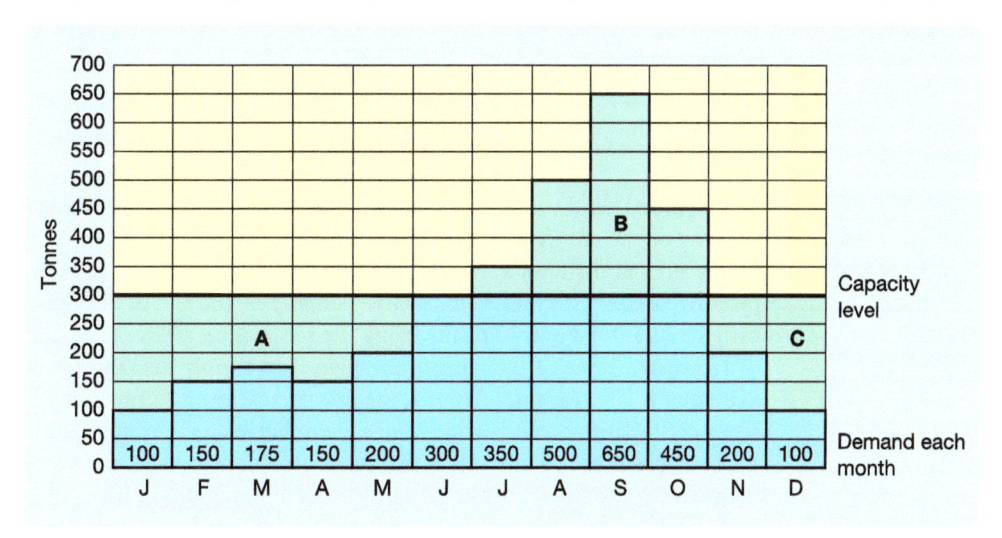

Figure 8.11 If the over-capacity areas (A+C) are greater than the under-capacity area (B), the capacity level seems adequate to meet demand. This may not necessarily be the case, however

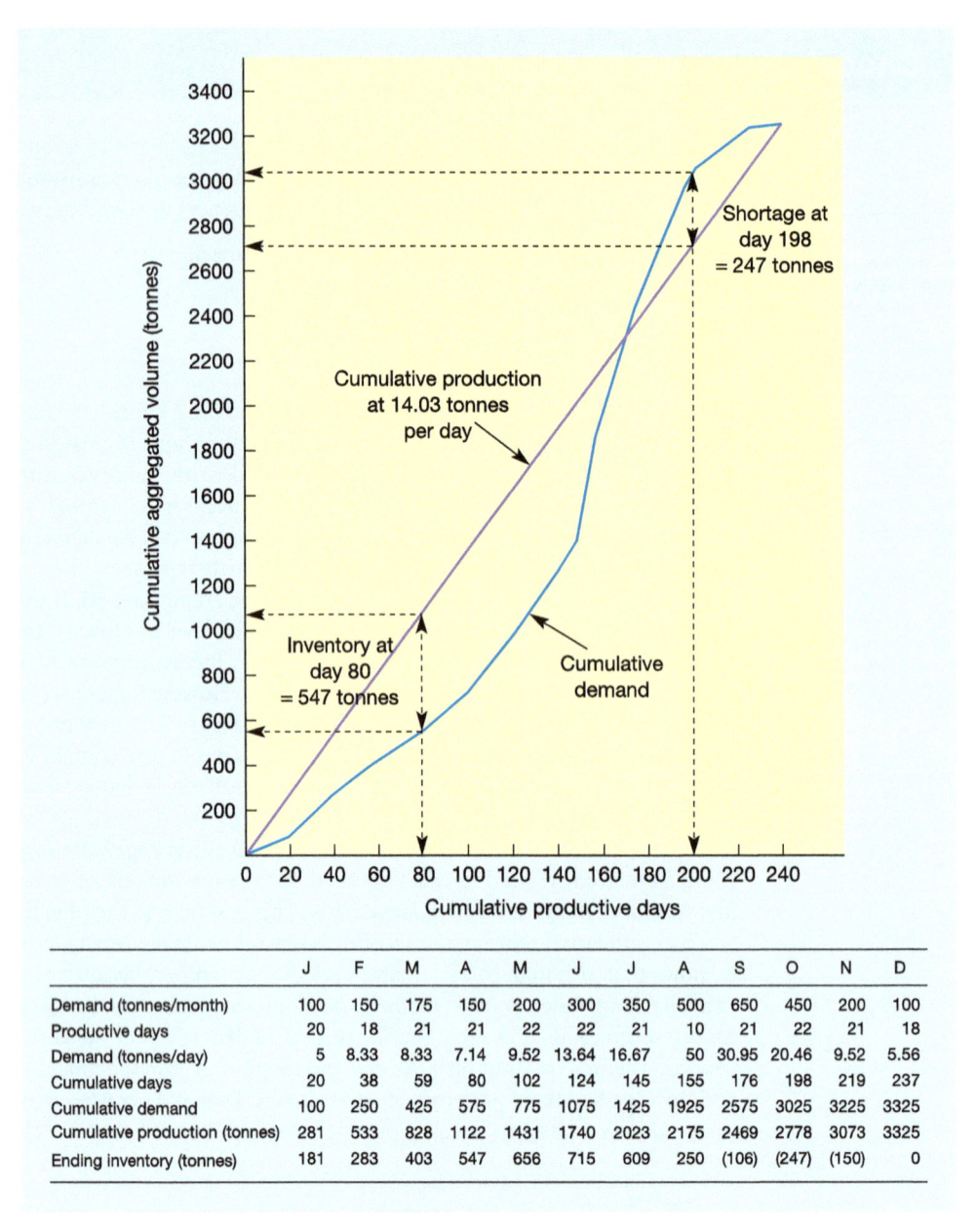

	J	F	M	A	M	J	J	A	S	O	N	D
Demand (tonnes/month)	100	150	175	150	200	300	350	500	650	450	200	100
Productive days	20	18	21	21	22	22	21	10	21	22	21	18
Demand (tonnes/day)	5	8.33	8.33	7.14	9.52	13.64	16.67	50	30.95	20.46	9.52	5.56
Cumulative days	20	38	59	80	102	124	145	155	176	198	219	237
Cumulative demand	100	250	425	575	775	1075	1425	1925	2575	3025	3225	3325
Cumulative production (tonnes)	281	533	828	1122	1431	1740	2023	2175	2469	2778	3073	3325
Ending inventory (tonnes)	181	283	403	547	656	715	609	250	(106)	(247)	(150)	0

Figure 8.12 A level capacity plan which produces shortages in spite of meeting demand at the end of the year

The most useful consequence of plotting demand on a cumulative basis is that, by plotting capacity on the same graph, the feasibility and consequences of a capacity plan can be assessed. Figure 8.12 also shows a level capacity plan which produces at a rate of 14.03 tonnes per productive day. This meets cumulative demand by the end of the year. It would also pass our earlier test of total over-capacity being the same as or greater than under-capacity.

However, if one of the aims of the plan is to supply demand when it occurs, the plan is inadequate. Up to around day 168, the line representing cumulative production is above that representing cumulative demand. This means that at any time during this period, more product has been produced by the factory than has been demanded from it. In fact the vertical distance between the two lines is the level of inventory at that point in time. So by day 80, 1,122 tonnes have been produced but only 575 tonnes have been demanded. The surplus of production above demand, or inventory, is therefore 547 tonnes. When the cumulative demand line lies above the cumulative production line, the reverse is true. The vertical distance between the two lines now indicates the shortage, or lack of supply. So by day 198, 3,025 tonnes have been demanded but only 2,778 tonnes produced. The shortage is therefore 247 tonnes.

For any capacity plan to meet demand as it occurs, its cumulative production line must always lie above the cumulative demand line. This makes it a straightforward task to judge the adequacy of a plan, simply by looking at its cumulative representation. An impression of the inventory implications can also be gained from a cumulative representation by judging the area between the cumulative production and demand curves. This represents the amount of inventory carried over the period. Figure 8.13 illustrates an adequate level capacity plan for the chocolate manufacturer, together with the costs of carrying inventory. It is assumed that

	J	F	M	A	M	J	J	A	S	O	N	D
Demand (tonnes/month)	100	150	175	150	200	300	350	500	650	450	200	100
Productive days	20	18	21	21	22	22	21	10	21	22	21	18
Demand (tonnes/day)	5	8.33	8.33	7.14	9.52	13.64	16.67	50	30.95	20.46	9.52	5.56
Cumulative days	20	38	59	80	102	124	145	155	176	198	219	237
Cumulative demand	100	250	425	575	775	1075	1425	1925	2575	3025	3225	3325
Cumulative production (tonnes)	306	581	902	1222	1559	1895	2216	2368	2689	3025	3346	3621
Ending inventory (tonnes)	206	331	477	647	784	820	791	443	114	0	121	296
Average inventory (tonnes)	103	270	404	562	716	802	806	617	279	57	61	209
Inventory cost for month (£)	4120	9720	16,968	23,604	31,504	35,288	33,852	12,340	11,718	2508	2562	7524

Total inventory cost for year = £191,608

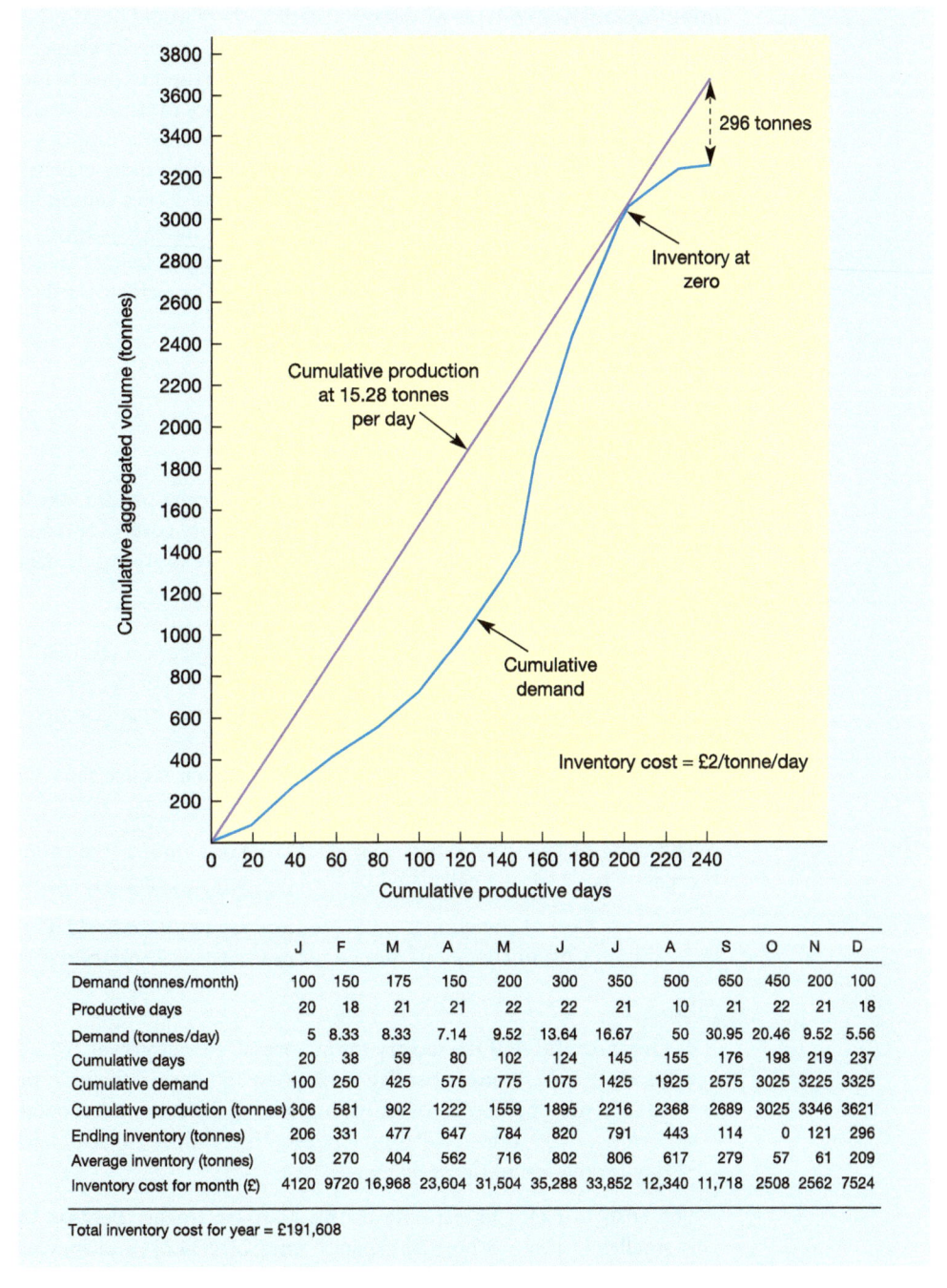

Figure 8.13 A level capacity plan which meets demand at all times during the year

inventory costs £2 per tonne per day to keep in storage. The average inventory each month is taken to be the average of the beginning- and end-of-month inventory levels, and the inventory-carrying cost each month is the product of the average inventory, the inventory cost per day per tonne and the number of days in the month.

Comparing plans on a cumulative basis

Chase demand plans can also be illustrated on a cumulative representation. Rather than the cumulative production line having a constant gradient, it would have a varying gradient representing the output rate at any point in time. If a pure demand chase plan was adopted, the cumulative production line would match the cumulative demand line. The gap between the two lines would be zero and hence inventory would be zero. Although this would eliminate inventory-carrying costs, as we discussed earlier, there would be costs associated with changing capacity levels. Usually, the marginal cost of making a capacity change increases with the size of the change. For example, if the chocolate manufacturer wishes to increase capacity by 5 per cent, this can be achieved by requesting its staff to work overtime – a simple, fast and relatively inexpensive option. If the change is 15 per cent, overtime cannot provide sufficient extra capacity and temporary staff will need to be employed – a more expensive solution which also would take more time. Increases in capacity of above 15 per cent might only be achieved by subcontracting some work out. This would be even more expensive. The cost of the change will also be affected by the point from which the change is being made, as well as the direction of the change. Usually, it is less expensive to change capacity towards what is regarded as the 'normal' capacity level than away from it.

Worked example

Suppose the chocolate manufacturer, which has been operating the level capacity plan as shown in Figure 8.13, is unhappy with the inventory costs of this approach. It decides to explore two alternative plans, both involving some degree of demand chasing.

Plan 1

- Organize and staff the factory for a 'normal' capacity level of 8.7 tonnes per day.
- Produce at 8.7 tonnes per day for the first 124 days of the year, then increase capacity to 29 tonnes per day by heavy use of overtime, hiring temporary staff and some subcontracting.
- Produce at 29 tonnes per day until day 194, then reduce capacity back to 8.7 tonnes per day for the rest of the year.

The costs of changing capacity by such a large amount (the ratio of peak to normal capacity is 3.33:1) are calculated by the company as being:

Cost of changing from 8.7 tonnes/day to 29 tonnes/day = £110,000
Cost of changing from 29 tonnes/day to 8.7 tonnes/day = £60,000

Plan 2

- Organize and staff the factory for a 'normal' capacity level of 12.4 tonnes per day.
- Produce at 12.4 tonnes per day for the first 150 days of the year, then increase capacity to 29 tonnes per day by overtime and hiring some temporary staff.
- Produce at 29 tonnes/day until day 190, then reduce capacity back to 12.4 tonnes per day for the rest of the year.

The costs of changing capacity in this plan are smaller because the degree of change is smaller (a peak to normal capacity ratio of 2.34:1), and they are calculated by the company as being:

Cost of changing from 12.4 tonnes/day to 29 tonnes/day = £35,000
Cost of changing from 29 tonnes/day to 12.4 tonnes/day = £15,000

Figure 8.14 illustrates both plans on a cumulative basis. Plan 1, which envisaged two drastic changes in capacity, has high capacity change costs but, because its production levels are close to demand levels, it has low inventory carrying costs. Plan 2 sacrifices some of the inventory cost advantage of Plan 1 but saves more in terms of capacity change costs.

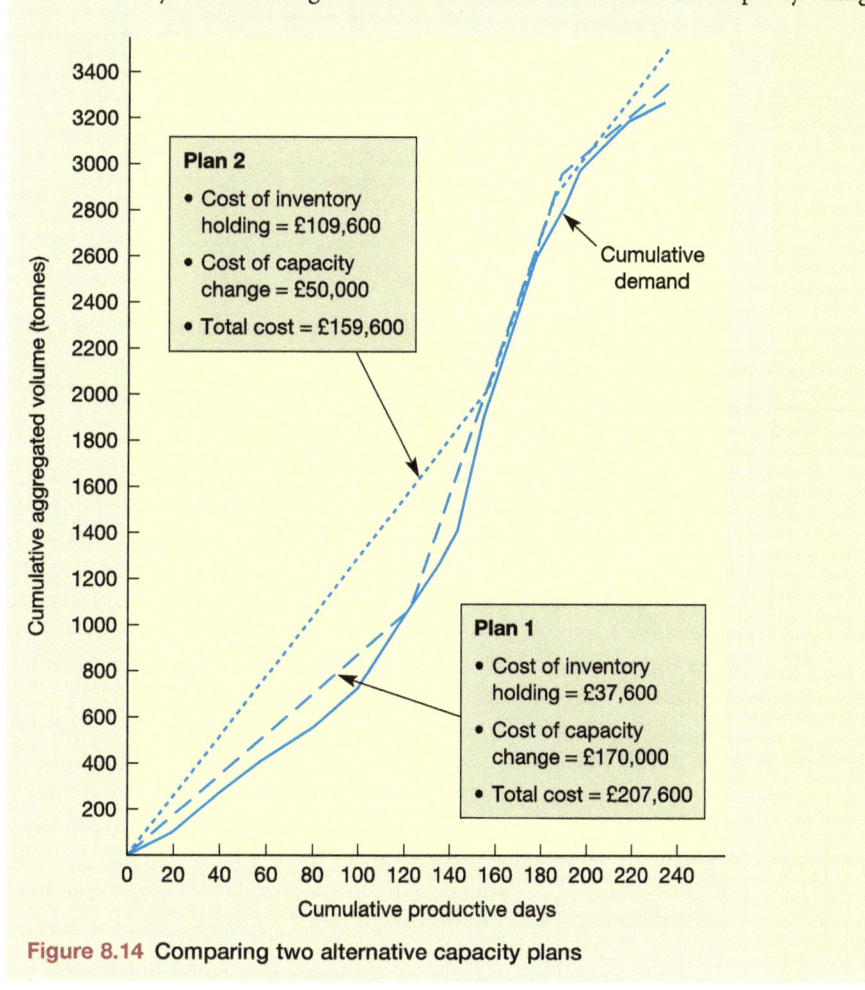

Plan 2
- Cost of inventory holding = £109,600
- Cost of capacity change = £50,000
- Total cost = £159,600

Plan 1
- Cost of inventory holding = £37,600
- Cost of capacity change = £170,000
- Total cost = £207,600

Figure 8.14 Comparing two alternative capacity plans

Capacity planning as a queuing problem

Cumulative representations of capacity plans are useful where the operation has the ability to store its finished goods as inventory. However, for operations where it is not possible to produce products and services *before* demand for them has occurred, a cumulative representation would tell us relatively little. The cumulative 'production' could never be above the cumulative demand line. At best, it could show when an operation failed to meets its demand. So the vertical gap between the cumulative demand and production lines would indicate the amount of demand unsatisfied. Some of this demand would look elsewhere to be satisfied, but some would wait. This is why, for operations which, by their nature, cannot store their output, such as most service operations, capacity planning and control is best considered using waiting or **queuing theory**.

Queuing theory

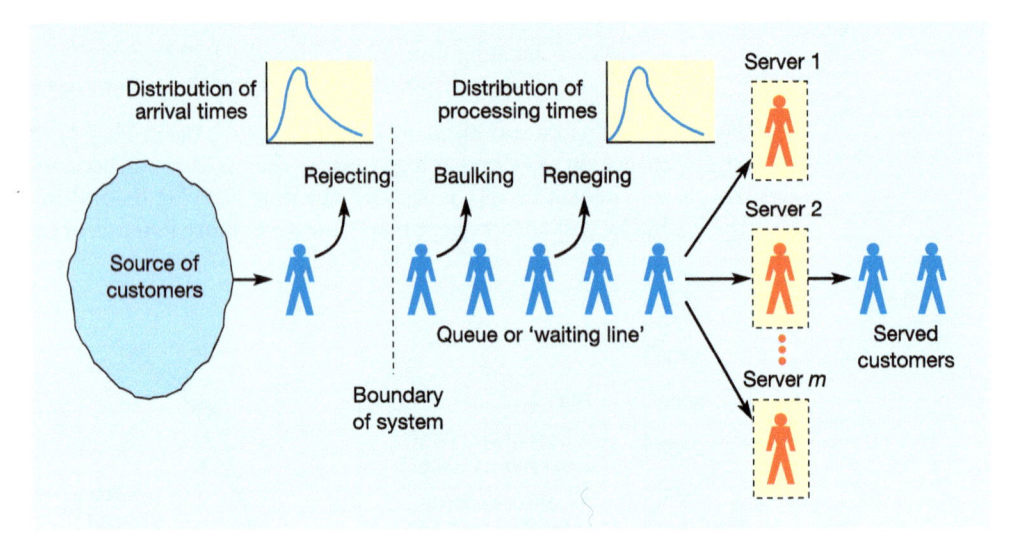

Figure 8.15 The general form of the capacity decision in queuing systems

Queuing or 'waiting line' management

When we were illustrating the use of cumulative representations for capacity planning and control, our assumption was that, generally, any production plan should aim to meet demand at any point in time (the cumulative production line must be above the cumulative demand line). Looking at the issue as a queuing problem (in many parts of the world queuing concepts are referred to as 'waiting line' concepts) accepts that, while sometime demand may be satisfied instantly, at other times customers may have to wait. This is particularly true when the arrival of individual demands on an operation are difficult to predict, or the time to produce a service or product is uncertain, or both. These circumstances make providing adequate capacity at all points in time particularly difficult. Figure 8.15 shows the general form of this capacity issue. Customers arrive according to some probability distribution and wait to be processed (unless part of the operation is idle); when they have reached the front of the queue, they are processed by one of the *n* parallel 'servers' (their processing time also being described by a probability distribution), after which they leave the operation. There are many examples of this kind of system. Table 8.2 illustrates some of these. All of these examples can be described by a common set of elements that define their queuing behaviour.

The source of customers – sometimes called the **calling population** – is the source of supply of customers. In queue management 'customers' are not always human. 'Customers' could for example be trucks arriving at a weighbridge, orders arriving to be processed or machines waiting to be serviced, etc. The source of customers for queuing system can be either *finite*

Table 8.2 Examples of operations which have parallel processors

Operation	Arrivals	Processing capacity
Bank	Customers	Tellers
Supermarket	Shoppers	Checkouts
Hospital clinic	Patients	Doctors
Graphic artist	Commissions	Artists
Custom cake decorators	Orders	Cake decorators
Ambulance service	Emergencies	Ambulances with crews
Telephone switchboard	Calls	Telephonists
Maintenance department	Breakdowns	Maintenance staff

or *infinite*. A finite source has a known number of possible customers. For example, if one maintenance person serves four assembly lines, the number of customers for the maintenance person is known, i.e. four. There will be a certain probability that one of the assembly lines will break down and need repairing. However, if one line really does break down the probability of another line needing repair is reduced because there are now only three lines to break down. So, with a finite source of customers the probability of a customer arriving depends on the number of customers already being serviced. By contrast, an infinite customer source assumes that there is a large number of potential customers so that it is always possible for another customer to arrive no matter how many are being serviced. Most queuing systems that deal with outside markets have infinite, or 'close-to-infinite', customer sources.

Balancing capacity and demand

The dilemma in managing the capacity of a queuing system is how many servers to have available at any point in time in order to avoid unacceptably long queuing times or unacceptably low utilization of the servers. Because of the probabilistic arrival and processing times, only rarely will the arrival of customers match the ability of the operation to cope with them. Sometimes, if several customers arrive in quick succession and require longer-than-average processing times, queues will build up in front of the operation. At other times, when customers arrive less frequently than average and also require shorter-than-average processing times, some of the servers in the system will be idle. So even when the average capacity (processing capability) of the operation matches the average demand (arrival rate) on the system, both queues and idle time will occur.

If the operation has too few servers (that is, capacity is set at too low a level), queues will build up to a level where customers become dissatisfied with the time they are having to wait, although the utilization level of the servers will be high. If too many servers are in place (that is, capacity is set at too high a level), the time which customers can expect to wait will not be long but the utilization of the servers will be low. This is why the capacity management problem for this type of operation is often presented as a trade-off between customer waiting time and system utilization. What is certainly important in making capacity decisions is being able to predict both of these factors for a given operation.

Variability in demand or supply

Variability reduces effective capacity

The variability, either in demand or capacity, as discussed above, will reduce the ability of an operation to process its inputs. That is, it will **reduce its effective capacity**. This effect was explained in Chapter 5 when the consequences of variability in individual processes were discussed. As a reminder, the greater the variability in arrival time or activity time at a process the more the process will suffer both high throughput times and reduced utilization. This principle holds true for whole operations, and because long throughput times mean that queues will build up in the operation, high variability also affects inventory levels. This is illustrated in Figure 8.16. The implication of this is that the greater the variability, the more extra capacity will need to be provided to compensate for the reduced utilization of available capacity. Therefore, operations with high levels of variability will tend to set their base level of capacity relatively high in order to provide this extra capacity.

Customer perceptions of queuing

If the 'customers' waiting in a queue are real human customers, an important aspect of how they judge the service they receive from a queuing system is how they perceive the time spent queuing. It is well known that if you are told that you'll be waiting in a queue for fifteen minutes and you are actually serviced in ten minutes, your perception of the queuing experience will be more positive than if you were told that you would be waiting five minutes but the queue actually took ten minutes. Because of this, the management of queuing systems

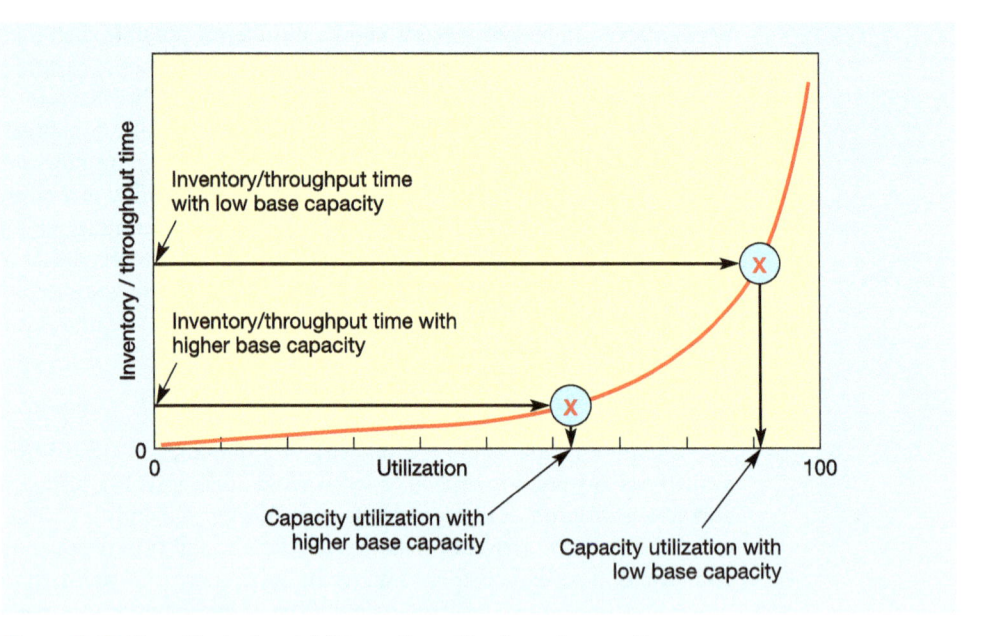

Figure 8.16 The effect of variability on the utilization of capacity

usually involves attempting to manage customers' perceptions and expectations in some way (see the Short case on Madame Tussaud's for an example of this). There are a number of principles that influence how customers perceive waiting times:[6]

Short case
Managing queues at Madame Tussaud's, Amsterdam

A short holiday in Amsterdam would not be complete without a visit to Madame Tussaud's, located on four upper floors of the city's most prominent department store in Dam Square. With 600,000 visitors each year, this is one of the most popular tourist attractions in Amsterdam. On busy days in the summer, the centre can just manage to handle 5,000 visitors. On a wet day in January, however, there may only be 300 visitors throughout the whole day. The centre is open for admission, seven days a week, from 10.00 am to 5.30 pm. In the streets outside, orderly queues of expectant tourists snake along the pavement, looking in at the displays in the store windows. In this public open space, Tussaud's can do little to entertain the visitors, but entrepreneurial buskers and street artists are quick to capitalize on a captive market. On reaching the entrance lobby, individuals, families and groups purchase their admission tickets. The lobby is in the shape of a large horseshoe, with the ticket sales booth in the centre. On winter days or at quiet spells, there will only be one sales assistant, but on busier days, visitors can pay at either side of the ticket booth, to speed up the process. Having paid, the visitors assemble in the lobby outside the two lifts. While waiting in this area, a photographer wanders around offering to take photos of the visitors standing next to life-sized wax figures of famous people. They may also be entertained by living look-alikes of famous personalities who act as guides to groups of visitors in batches of around 25 customers (the capacity of each of the two lifts which takes visitors up to the facility). The lifts arrive every four minutes and customers simultaneously disembark, forming one group of about 50 customers, who stay together throughout the session.

- Time spent idle is perceived as longer than time spent occupied.
- The wait before a service starts is perceived as more tedious than a wait within the process.
- Anxiety and/or uncertainty heightens the perception that time spent waiting is long.
- A wait of unknown duration is perceived as more tedious than a wait of known duration.
- An unexplained wait is perceived as more tedious than a wait that is explained.
- The higher the value of the service for the customer, the longer the waiting tolerance.
- Waiting on one's own is more tedious than waiting in a group (unless you really don't like the others in the group).

Summary answers to key questions

Check and improve your understanding of this chapter using self-assessment questions and a personalized study plan, audio and video downloads, and an eBook – all at www.myomlab.com.

▶ What is capacity management?

- It is the way operations organize the level of value-added activity which they can achieve under normal operating conditions over a period of time.
- It is usual to distinguish between long-, medium- and short-term capacity decisions. Medium- and short-term capacity management, where the capacity level of the organization is adjusted within the fixed limits which are set by long-term capacity decisions, is sometimes called aggregate planning and control.
- Almost all operations have some kind of fluctuation in demand (or seasonality) caused by some combination of climatic, festive, behavioural, political, financial or social factors.

▶ How are demand and capacity measured?

- Either by the availability of its input resources or by the output which is created. Which of these measures is used partly depends on how stable the mix of outputs is. If it is difficult to aggregate the different types of output from an operation, input measures are usually preferred.
- The usage of capacity can be measured by overall equipment effectiveness (OEE).

▶ What are the alternative ways of coping with demand fluctuation?

- Output can be kept level, in effect ignoring demand fluctuations. This will result in under-utilization of capacity where outputs cannot be stored, or the build-up of inventories where output can be stored or queues when they can't be stored.
- Output can chase demand by fluctuating the output level through some combination of overtime, varying the size of the workforce, using part-time staff and subcontracting.
- Demand can be changed, either by influencing the market through such measures as advertising and promotion, or by developing alternative products with a counter-seasonal demand pattern.
- Most operations use a mix of all these three 'pure' strategies.

> **How can operations manage their capacity level?**

- Representing demand and output in the form of cumulative representations allows the feasibility of alternative capacity plans to be assessed.
- In many operations, especially service operations, a queuing approach can be used to explore capacity strategies.

> **How can queuing theory be used to plan capacity?**

- By considering the capacity decision as a dynamic decision which periodically updates the decisions and assumptions upon which decisions are based.

Learning exercises

These problems and applications will help to improve your analysis of operations. You can find more practice problems as well as worked examples and guided solutions on MyOMLab at www.myomlab.com.

1. A local government office issues hunting licences. Demand for these licences is relatively slow in the first part of the year but then increases after the middle of the year before slowing down again towards the end of the year. The department works a 220-day year on a 5-days-a-week basis. Between working days 0 and 100, demand is 25 per cent of demand during the peak period which lasts between day 100 and day 150. After 150 demand reduces to about 12 per cent of the demand during the peak period. In total, the department processes 10,000 applications per year. The department has 2 permanent members of staff who are capable of processing 15 licence applications per day. If an untrained temporary member of staff can only process 10 licences per day, how many temporary staff should the department recruit between days 100 and 150?

2. In the example above, if a new computer system is installed that allows experienced staff to increase their work rate to 20 applications per day, and untrained staff to 15 applications per day, (a) does the department still need 2 permanent staff, and (b) how many temporary members of staff will be needed between days 100 and 150?

3. A field service organization repairs and maintains printing equipment for a large number of customers. It offers one level of service to all its customers and employs 30 staff. The operation's marketing vice-president has decided that in future the company will offer 3 standards of service, platinum, gold and silver. It is estimated that platinum-service customers will require 50 per cent more time from the company's field service engineers than the current service. The current service is to be called 'the gold service'. The silver service is likely to require about 80 per cent of the time of the gold service. If future demand is estimated to be 20 per cent platinum, 70 per cent gold and 10 per cent silver service, how many staff will be needed to fulfil demand?

4. Look again at the principles which govern customers' perceptions of the queuing experience. For the following operations, apply the principles to minimize the perceived negative effects of queuing.

    (a) A cinema
    (b) A doctor's surgery
    (c) Waiting to board an aircraft.

Want to know more?

Hopp, W.J. and Spearman, M.L. (2000) *Factory Physics*, 2nd edn, McGraw-Hill, New York, NY. Very mathematical indeed, but includes some interesting maths on queuing theory.

Olhager, J., Rudberg, M. and Wikner, J. (2001) Long-term capacity management: linking the perspectives from manufacturing strategy and sales and operations planning, *International Journal of Production Economics*, vol. 69, issue 2, 215–25. Academic article, but interesting.

Vollmann, T., Berry, W., Whybark, D.C. and Jacobs, F.R. (2004) *Manufacturing Planning and Control Systems for Supply Chain Management: The Definitive Guide for Professionals*, McGraw-Hill Higher Education, New York. The latest version of the 'bible' of manufacturing planning and control. It's exhaustive in its coverage of all aspects of planning and control including aggregate planning.

Useful websites

www.bis.gov.uk/employment Website which has developed a framework for employers and employees to promote a skilled and flexible labour market founded on principles of partnership.

www.worksmart.org.uk/index.php This site is from the Trades Union Congress. Its aim is 'to help today's working people get the best out of the world of work'.

www.opsman.org Lots of useful stuff.

www.equalityhumanrights.com This web site aims to provide a resource for legal advisers and representatives who are conducting claims on behalf of applicants in sex discrimination and equal pay cases in England and Wales. This site covers employment-related sex discrimination only.

www.dol.gov/index.htm US Department of Labor's site with information regarding using part-time employees.

www.downtimecentral.com/ Lots of information on operational equipment efficiency (OEE).

Now that you have finished reading this chapter, why not visit MyOMLab at www.myomlab.com where you'll find more learning resources to help you make the most of your studies and get a better grade.

Chapter 9

Inventory management

Key questions

- What is inventory?
- What are the reasons for holding inventory and what are the disadvantages?
- How much inventory should an operation hold?
- When should an operation replenish its inventory?
- How can inventory be managed?

Introduction

Operations managers often have an ambivalent attitude towards inventories. On the one hand, they are costly, sometimes tying up considerable amounts of working capital. They are also risky because items held in stock could deteriorate, become obsolete or just get lost, and, furthermore, they take up valuable space in the operation. This risk is also seen when inventory is in the form of customers who rarely enjoy waiting. On the other hand, inventories provide some security in an uncertain environment that one can deliver items in stock or work on customers in process should demand materialize. This is the dilemma of inventory management: in spite of the cost and the other disadvantages associated with inventories, they do facilitate the smoothing of supply and demand. In fact they only exist because supply and demand are not exactly in harmony with each other. Figure 9.1 shows where this chapter fits into the overall operations model.

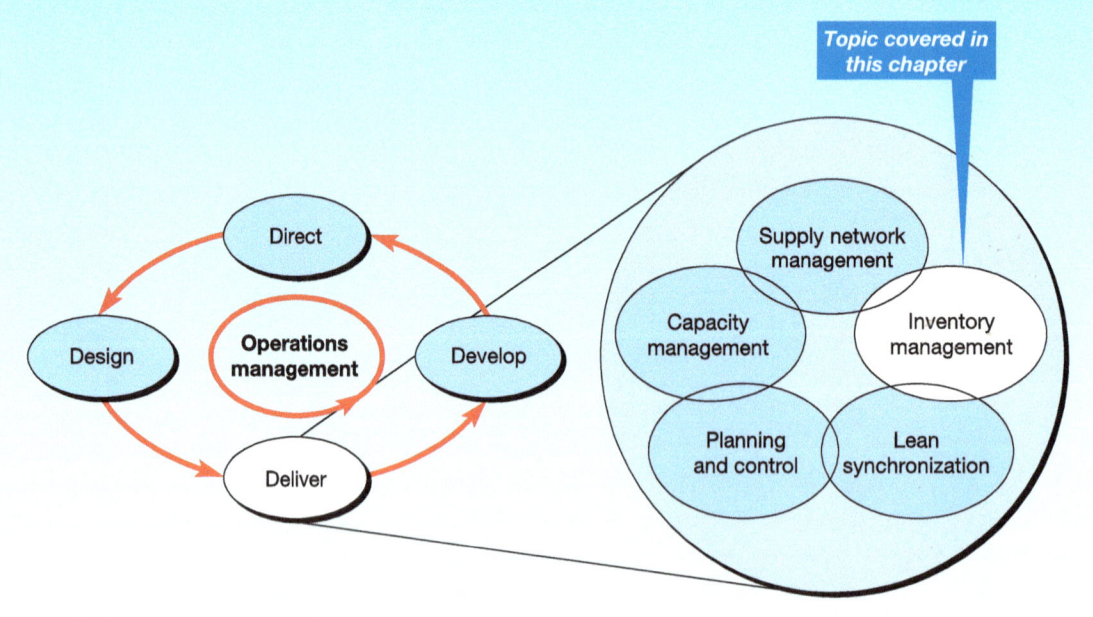

Figure 9.1 This chapter examines inventory management

Check and improve your understanding of this chapter using self-assessment questions and a personalized study plan, audio and video downloads, and an eBook – all at www.myomlab.com.

Operations in practice: The UK's National Blood Service[1]

No inventory manager likes to run out of stock. But for blood services, such as the UK's National Blood Service (NBS) the consequences of running out of stock can be particularly serious. Many people owe their lives to transfusions that were made possible by the efficient management of blood, stocked in a supply network that stretches from donation centres through to hospital blood banks. The NBS supply chain has three main stages:

1 *Collection*, which involves recruiting and retaining blood donors, encouraging them to attend donor sessions (at mobile or fixed locations) and transporting the donated blood to their local blood centre.
2 *Processing*, which breaks blood down into its constituent parts (red cells, platelets and plasma) as well over twenty other blood-based 'products'.
3 *Distribution*, which transports blood from blood centres to hospitals in response to both routine and emergency requests. Of the Service's 200,000 deliveries a year, about 2,500 are emergency deliveries.

Inventory accumulates at all three stages, and in individual hospitals' blood banks. Within the supply chain, around 11.5 per cent of donated red blood cells donated are lost. Much of this is due to losses in processing, but around 5 per cent is not used because it has 'become unavailable', mainly because it has been stored for too long. Part of the Service's inventory control task is to keep this 'time-expired' loss to a minimum. In fact, only small losses occur within the NBS, most blood being lost when it is stored in hospital blood banks that are outside its direct control. However, it does attempt to provide advice and support to hospitals to enable them to use blood efficiently.

Blood components and products need to be stored under a variety of conditions, but will deteriorate over time. This varies depending on the component; platelets have a shelf life of only five days and demand can fluctuate significantly. This makes stock control particularly difficult. Even red blood cells that have a shelf life of 35 days may not be acceptable to hospitals if they are close to their 'use-by date'. Stock accuracy is crucial. Giving a patient the wrong type of blood can be fatal.

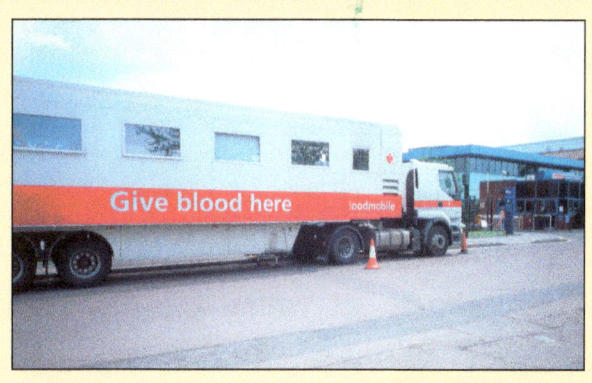

At a local level demand can be affected significantly by accidents. For example, one serious accident involving a cyclist used 750 units of blood, which completely exhausted the available supply (miraculously, he survived). Large-scale accidents usually generate a surge of offers from donors wishing to make immediate donations. There is also a more predictable seasonality to the donating of blood, however, with a low period during the summer vacation. Yet there is always an unavoidable tension between maintaining sufficient stocks to provide a very high level of supply dependability to hospitals and minimizing wastage. Unless blood stocks are controlled carefully, they can easily go past the 'use-by date' and be wasted. But avoiding outdated blood products is not the only inventory objective at NBS. It also measures the percentage of requests that it was able to meet in full, the percentage emergency requests delivered within two hours, the percentage of units banked to donors bled, the number of new donors enrolled, and the number of donors waiting longer than 30 minutes before they are able to donate. The traceability of donated blood is also increasingly important. Should any problems with a blood product arise, its source can be traced back to the original donor.

Source: Alamy/Van Hilversum

What is inventory?

Inventory

Inventory, or 'stock' as it is more commonly called in some countries, is defined here as the *stored accumulation of resources in a transformation system*. Sometimes the term 'inventory' is also used to describe any capital-transforming resource, such as rooms in a hotel, or cars in a vehicle-hire firm, but we will not use that definition here. Usually the term refers only to *transformed resources*. So a manufacturing company will hold stocks of materials, a tax office will hold stocks of information, and a theme park will hold stocks of customers. Note that when it is customers who are being processed we normally refer to these 'stocks' as 'queues'. This chapter will deal particularly with inventories of materials.

Revisiting operations objectives; the roles of inventory

Inventory can influence all performance objectives

Most of us are accustomed to keeping inventory for use in our personal lives, but often we don't think about it. For example, most families have some stocks of food and drinks, so that they don't have to go out to the shops before every meal. Holding a variety of food ingredients in stock in the kitchen cupboard or freezer gives us the ability to respond quickly (with *speed*) in preparing a meal whenever unexpected guests arrive. It also allows us the *flexibility* to choose a range of menu options without having to go to the time and trouble of purchasing further ingredients. We may purchase some items because we have found something of exceptional *quality*, but intend to save it for a special occasion. Many people buy multiple packs to achieve lower *costs* for a wide range of goods. In general, our inventory planning protects us from critical stock-outs; so this approach gives a level of *dependability* of supplies.

It is, however, entirely possible to manage our inventory differently. For example, some people are short of available cash and/or space, and so cannot 'invest' in large inventories of goods. They may shop locally for much smaller quantities. They forfeit the cost benefits of bulk-buying, but do not have to transport heavy or bulky supplies. They also reduce the risk of forgetting an item in the cupboard and letting it go out of date. Essentially, they purchase against specific known requirements (the next meal). However, they may find that the local shop is temporarily out of stock of a particular item, forcing them, for example, to drink coffee without their usual milk. How we control our own supplies is therefore a matter of choice which can affect their quality (e.g. freshness), availability or speed of response, dependability of supply, flexibility of choice, and cost. It is the same for most organizations. Significant levels of inventory can be held for a range of sensible and pragmatic reasons but it must also be tightly controlled for other equally good reasons.

Why is inventory necessary?

No matter what is being stored as inventory, or where it is positioned in the operation, it will be there because there is a difference in the timing or rate of supply and demand. If the supply of any item occurred exactly when it was demanded, the item would never be stored. A common analogy is the water tank shown in Figure 9.2. If, over time, the rate of supply of water to the tank differs from the rate at which it is demanded, a tank of water (inventory) will be needed if supply is to be maintained. When the rate of supply exceeds the rate of demand, inventory increases; when the rate of demand exceeds the rate of supply, inventory decreases. So if an operation can match supply and demand rates, it will also succeed in reducing its inventory levels.

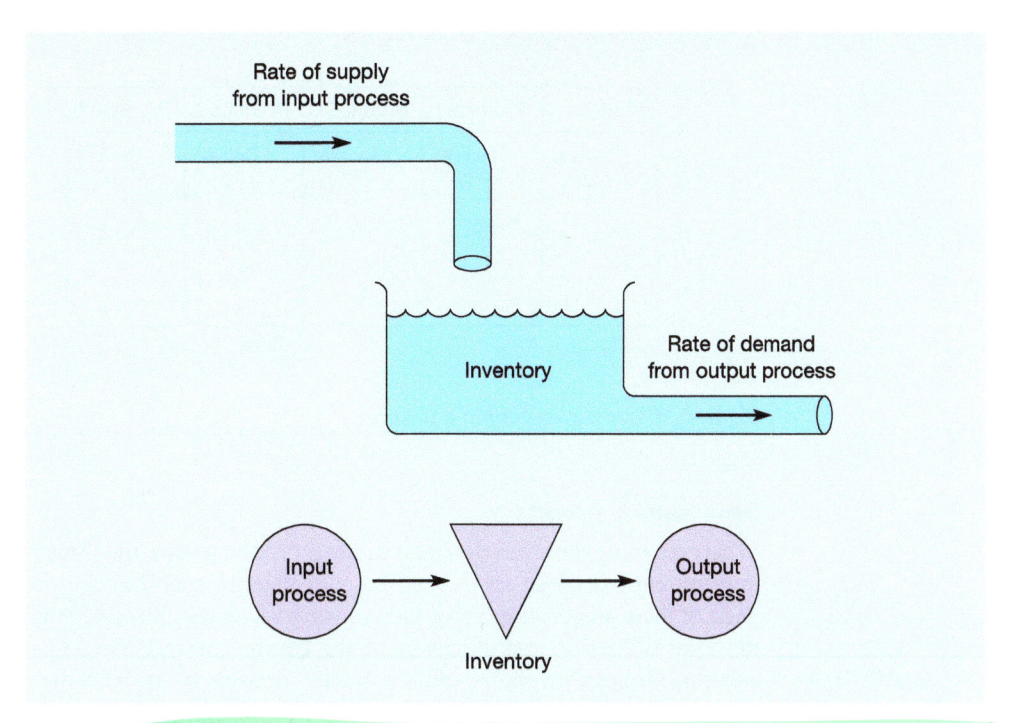

Figure 9.2 Inventory is created to compensate for the differences in timing between supply and demand

Types of inventory

The various reasons for an imbalance between the rates of supply and demand at different points in any supply network lead to the different types of inventory. There are five of these: buffer inventory, cycle inventory, de-coupling inventory, anticipation inventory and pipeline inventory.

Buffer inventory

Buffer inventory
Safety inventory

Buffer inventory is also called **safety inventory**. Its purpose is to compensate for the unexpected fluctuations in supply and demand. For example, a retail operation can never forecast demand perfectly, even when it has a good idea of the most likely demand level. It will order goods from its suppliers such that there is always a certain amount of most items in stock. This minimum level of inventory is there to cover against the possibility that demand will be greater than expected during the time taken to deliver the goods. It can also compensate for the uncertainties in the process of the supply of goods into the store, perhaps because of the unreliability of certain suppliers or transport firms.

Cycle inventory

Cycle inventory

Cycle inventory occurs because one or more stages in the process cannot supply all the items it produces simultaneously. For example, suppose a baker makes three types of bread, each of which is equally popular with its customers. Because of the nature of the mixing and baking process, only one kind of bread can be produced at any time. The baker would have to produce each type of bread in batches as shown in Figure 9.3. The batches must be large enough to satisfy the demand for each kind of bread between the times when each batch is ready for sale. So even when demand is steady and predictable, there will always be some inventory to compensate for the intermittent supply of each type of bread. Cycle inventory only results from the need to produce products in batches, and the amount of it depends on volume decisions which are described in a later section of this chapter.

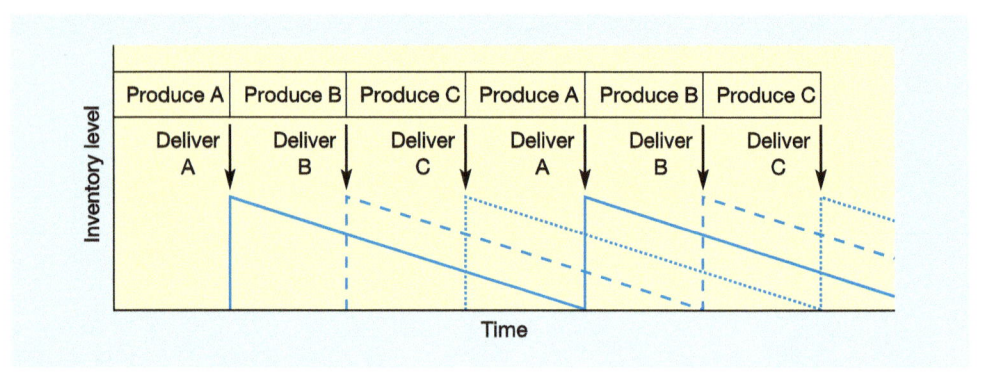

Figure 9.3 Cycle inventory in a bakery

De-coupling inventory

Wherever an operation is designed to use a process layout, the transformed resources move intermittently between specialized areas or departments that comprise similar operations. Each of these areas can be scheduled to work relatively independently in order to maximize the local utilization and efficiency of the equipment and staff. As a result, each batch of work-in-progress inventory joins a queue, awaiting its turn in the schedule for the next processing stage. This also allows each operation to be set to the optimum processing speed (cycle time), regardless of the speed of the steps before and after. Thus **de-coupling inventory** creates the opportunity for independent scheduling and processing speeds between process stages.

Anticipation inventory

In Chapter 8 we saw how anticipation inventory can be used to cope with seasonal demand. Rather than trying to make the product (such as chocolate) only when it was needed, it was produced throughout the year ahead of demand and put into inventory until it was needed. **Anticipation inventory** is most commonly used when demand fluctuations are large but relatively predictable. It might also be used when supply variations are significant, such as in the canning or freezing of seasonal foods.

Pipeline inventory

Pipeline inventory exists because material cannot be transported instantaneously between the point of supply and the point of demand. If a retail store orders a consignment of items from one of its suppliers, the supplier will allocate the stock to the retail store in its own warehouse, pack it, load it onto its truck, transport it to its destination, and unload it into the retailer's inventory. From the time that stock is allocated (and therefore it is unavailable to any other customer) to the time it becomes available for the retail store, it is pipeline inventory. Pipeline inventory also exists within processes where the layout is geographically spread out. For example, a large European manufacturer of specialized steel regularly moves cargoes of part-finished materials between its two mills in the UK and Scandinavia using a dedicated vessel that shuttles between the two countries every week. All the thousands of tonnes of material in transit are pipeline inventory.

The position of inventory

Not only are there several reasons for supply–demand imbalance, there could also be several points where such imbalance exists between different stages in the operation. Perhaps the simplest level is the single-stage inventory system, such as a retail store, which will have only one stock of goods to manage. An automotive parts distribution operation will have a central depot and various local distribution points which contain inventories. In many manufacturers of standard items, there are three types of inventory. The **raw material** and **components inventories** (sometimes called input inventories) receive goods from the operation's suppliers; the raw materials and components work their way through the various stages of the production process but spend considerable amounts of time as **work-in-progress** (or work-in-process) (WIP) before finally reaching the **finished goods inventory**.

Some disadvantages of holding inventory

Although inventory plays an important role in many operations performance, there are a number of negative aspects of inventory:

- Inventory ties up money, in the form of working capital, which is therefore unavailable for other uses, such as reducing borrowings or making investment in productive fixed assets.
- Inventory incurs storage costs (leasing space, maintaining appropriate conditions, etc.).
- Inventory may become obsolete as alternatives become available.
- Inventory can be damaged, or deteriorate.
- Inventory could be lost, or be expensive to retrieve, as it gets hidden amongst other inventory.
- Inventory might be hazardous to store (for example flammable solvents, explosives, chemicals and drugs), requiring special facilities and systems for safe handling.
- Inventory uses space that could be used to add value.
- Inventory involves administrative and insurance costs.

Day-to-day inventory decisions

At each point in the inventory system, operations managers need to manage the day-to-day tasks of running the system. Orders will be received from internal or external customers; these will be dispatched and demand will gradually deplete the inventory. Orders will need to be placed for replenishment of the stocks; deliveries will arrive and require storing. In managing the system, operations managers are involved in three major types of decision:

- *How much to order.* Every time a replenishment order is placed, how big should it be (sometimes called the *volume decision*)?
- *When to order.* At what point in time, or at what level of stock, should the replenishment order be placed (sometimes called the *timing decision*)?
- *How to control the system.* What procedures and routines should be installed to help make these decisions? Should different priorities be allocated to different stock items? How should stock information be stored?

The rest of this chapter examines the three key decisions.

The volume decision – how much to order

To illustrate this decision, consider again the example of the food and drinks we keep at our home. In managing this inventory we implicitly make decisions on *order quantity*, which is how much to purchase at one time. In making this decision we are balancing two sets of costs: the costs associated with going out to purchase the food items and the costs associated with holding the stocks. The option of holding very little or no inventory of food and purchasing each item only when it is needed has the advantage that it requires little money since purchases are made only when needed. However, it would involve purchasing provisions several times a day, which is inconvenient. At the very opposite extreme, making one journey to the local superstore every few months and purchasing all the provisions we would need until our next visit reduces the time and costs incurred in making the purchase but requires a very large amount of money each time the trip is made – money which could otherwise be in the bank and earning interest. We might also have to invest in extra cupboard units and a very large freezer. Somewhere between these extremes there will lie an ordering strategy which will minimize the total costs and effort involved in the purchase of food.

Inventory costs

The same principles apply in commercial order-quantity decisions as in the domestic situation. In making a decision on how much to purchase, operations managers must try to identify the costs which will be affected by their decision. Several types of costs are directly associated with order size.

Cost of placing an order

1 *Cost of placing the order*. Every time that an order is placed to replenish stock, a number of transactions are needed which incur costs to the company. These include the clerical tasks of preparing the order and all the documentation associated with it, arranging for the delivery to be made, arranging to pay the supplier for the delivery, and the general costs of keeping all the information which allows us to do this. Also, if we are placing an 'internal order' on part of our own operation, there are still likely to be the same types of transaction concerned with internal administration. In addition, there could also be a 'changeover' cost incurred by the part of the operation which is to supply the items, caused by the need to change from producing one type of item to another.

Price discounts

2 *Price discount costs*. In many industries suppliers offer discounts on the normal purchase price for large quantities; alternatively they might impose extra costs for small orders.

3 *Stock-out costs*. If we misjudge the order-quantity decision and we run out of stock, there will be costs to us incurred by failing to supply our customers. If the customers are external, they may take their business elsewhere; if internal, stock-outs could lead to idle time at the next process, inefficiencies and disatisfaction.

Working capital

4 *Working capital costs*. Soon after we receive a replenishment order, the supplier will demand payment for their goods. Eventually, when (or after) we supply our own customers, we in turn will receive payment. However, there will probably be a lag between paying our suppliers and receiving payment from our customers. During this time we will have to fund the costs of inventory. This is called the *working capital* of inventory. The costs associated with it are the interest we pay the bank for borrowing it, or the opportunity costs of not investing it elsewhere.

Storage costs

5 *Storage costs*. These are the costs associated with physically storing the inventories. Renting, heating and lighting the warehouse, as well as insuring the inventory, can be expensive, especially when special conditions are required such as low temperature or high security.

Obsolescence costs

6 *Obsolescence costs*. When we order large quantities, this usually results in stocked items spending a long time stored in inventory. Then there is a risk that the items might either become obsolete (in the case of a change in fashion, for example) or deteriorate with age (in the case of most foodstuffs, for example).

Operating inefficiencies

7 *Operating inefficiency costs*. According to lean synchronization philosophies, high inventory levels prevent us seeing the full extent of problems within the operation. This argument is fully explored in Chapter 11.

There are two points to be made about this list of costs. The first is that some of the costs will decrease as order size is increased; the first three costs are like this, whereas the other costs generally increase as order size is increased. The second point is that it may not be the same organization that incurs the costs. For example, sometimes suppliers agree to hold **consignment stock**. This means that they deliver large quantities of inventory to their customers to store but will only charge for the goods as and when they are used. In the meantime they remain the supplier's property so do not have to be financed by the customer, who does, however, provide storage facilities.

Consignment stock

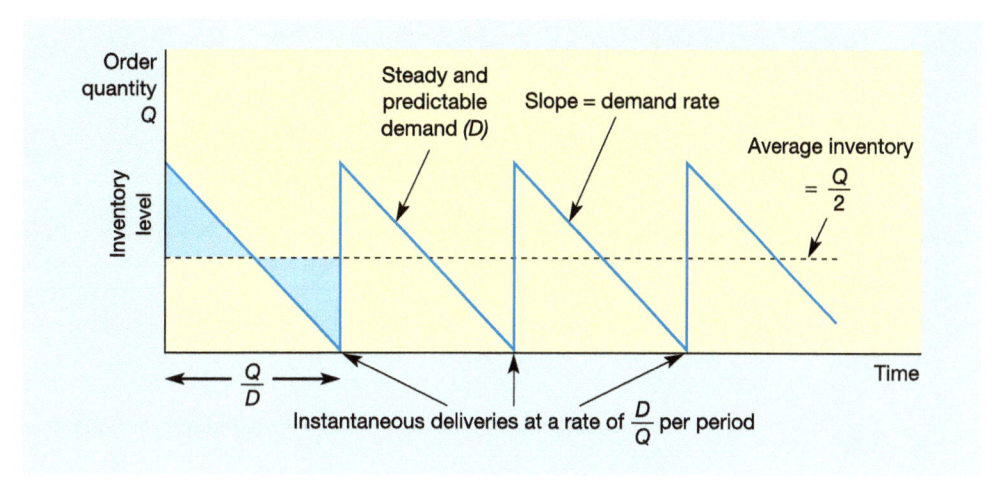

Figure 9.4 Inventory profiles chart the variation in inventory level

Inventory profiles

An inventory profile is a visual representation of the inventory level over time. Figure 9.4 shows a simplified inventory profile for one particular stock item in a retail operation. Every time an order is placed, Q items are ordered. The replenishment order arrives in one batch instantaneously. Demand for the item is then steady and perfectly predictable at a rate of D units per month. When demand has depleted the stock of the items entirely, another order of Q items instantaneously arrives, and so on. Under these circumstances:

The average inventory $= \dfrac{Q}{2}$ (because the two shaded areas in Figure 9.4 are equal)

The time interval between deliveries $= \dfrac{Q}{D}$

The frequency of deliveries = the reciprocal of the time interval $= \dfrac{D}{Q}$

The economic order quantity (EOQ) formula

Economic order quantity

The most common approach to deciding how much of any particular item to order when stock needs replenishing is called the **economic order quantity** (EOQ) approach. This approach attempts to find the best balance between the advantages and disadvantages of holding stock. For example, Figure 9.5 shows two alternative order-quantity policies for an item. Plan A, represented by the unbroken line, involves ordering in quantities of 400 at a time. Demand in this case is running at 1,000 units per year. Plan B, represented by the dotted line, uses smaller but more frequent replenishment orders. This time only 100 are ordered at a time, with orders being placed four times as often. However, the average inventory for plan B is one-quarter of that for plan A.

To find out whether either of these plans, or some other plan, minimizes the total cost of stocking the item, we need some further information, namely the total cost of holding one unit in stock for a period of time (C_h) and the total costs of placing an order (C_o). Generally, holding costs are taken into account by including:

- working capital costs
- storage costs
- obsolescence risk costs.

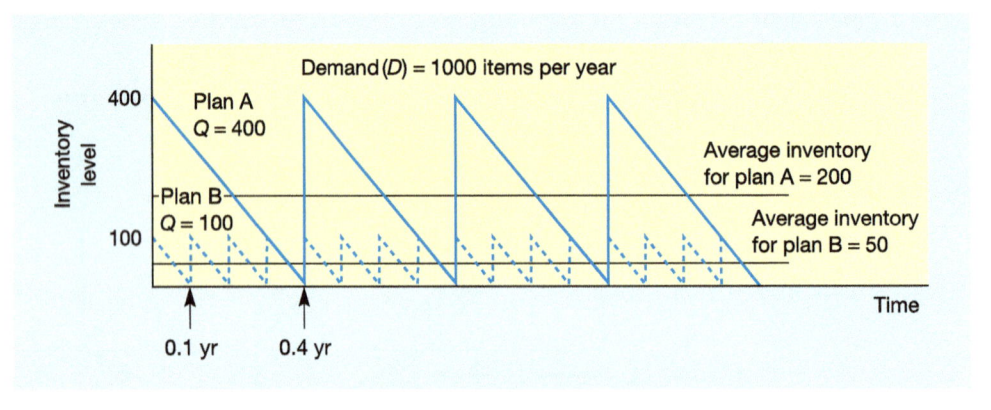

Figure 9.5 Two alternative inventory plans with different order quantities (Q)

Order costs are calculated by taking into account:

- cost of placing the order (including transportation of items from suppliers if relevant);
- price discount costs.

In this case the cost of holding stocks is calculated at £1 per item per year and the cost of placing an order is calculated at £20 per order.

We can now calculate total holding costs and ordering costs for any particular ordering plan as follows:

$$\text{Holding costs} = \text{holding cost/unit} \times \text{average inventory}$$

$$= C_h \times \frac{Q}{2}$$

$$\text{Ordering costs} = \text{ordering cost} \times \text{number of orders per period}$$

$$= C_o \times \frac{D}{Q}$$

$$\text{So, total cost, } C_t = \frac{C_h Q}{2} + \frac{C_o D}{Q}$$

We can now calculate the costs of adopting plans with different order quantities. These are illustrated in Table 9.1. As we would expect with low values of Q, holding costs are low but the costs of placing orders are high because orders have to be placed very frequently. As Q increases, the holding costs increase but the costs of placing orders decrease. Initially

Table 9.1 Costs of adoption of plans with different order quantities

Demand (D) = 1,000 units per year Holding costs (C_h) = £1 per item per year
Order costs (C_o) = £20 per order

Order quantity (Q)	Holding costs (0.5Q × C_h)	+	Order costs ((D/Q) × C_o)	=	Total costs
50	25		20 × 20 = 400		425
100	50		10 × 20 = 200		250
150	75		6.7 × 20 = 134		209
200	100		5 × 20 = 100		200*
250	125		4 × 20 = 80		205
300	150		3.3 × 20 = 66		216
350	175		2.9 × 20 = 58		233
400	200		2.5 × 20 = 50		250

*Minimum total cost.

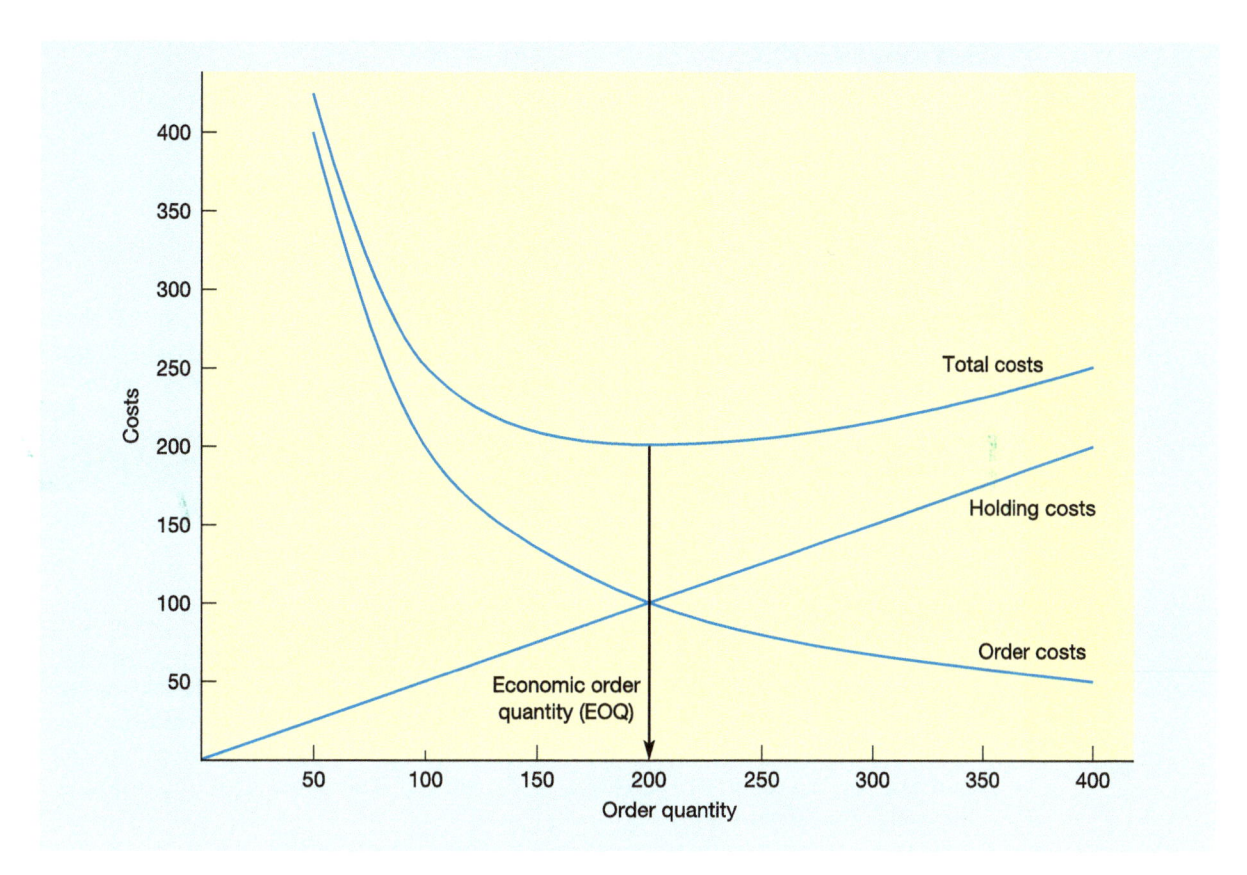

Figure 9.6 Graphical representation of the economic order quantity

the decrease in ordering costs is greater than the increase in holding costs and the total cost falls. After a point, however, the decrease in ordering costs slows, whereas the increase in holding costs remains constant and the total cost starts to increase. In this case the order quantity, Q, which minimizes the sum of holding and order costs, is 200. This 'optimum' order quantity is called the *economic order quantity* (*EOQ*). This is illustrated graphically in Figure 9.6.

A more elegant method of finding the EOQ is to derive its general expression. This can be done using simple differential calculus as follows. From before:

$$\text{Total cost} = \text{holding cost} + \text{order cost}$$

$$C_t = \frac{C_h Q}{2} + \frac{C_o D}{Q}$$

The rate of change of total cost is given by the first differential of C_t with respect to Q:

$$\frac{dC_t}{dQ} = \frac{C_h}{2} - \frac{C_o D}{Q^2}$$

The lowest cost will occur when $dC_t/dQ = 0$, that is:

$$0 = \frac{C_h}{2} - \frac{C_o D}{Q_o^2}$$

where Q_o = the EOQ. Rearranging this expression gives:

$$Q_o = \text{EOQ} = \sqrt{\frac{2C_o D}{C_h}}$$

When using the EOQ:

$$\text{Time between orders} = \frac{\text{EOQ}}{D}$$

$$\text{Order frequency} = \frac{D}{\text{EOQ}} \text{ per period}$$

Sensitivity of the EOQ

Examination of the graphical representation of the total cost curve in Figure 9.6 shows that, although there is a single value of Q which minimizes total costs, any relatively small deviation from the EOQ will not increase total costs significantly. In other words, costs will be near-optimum provided a value of Q which is reasonably close to the EOQ is chosen. Put another way, small errors in estimating either holding costs or order costs will not result in a significant deviation from the EOQ. This is a particularly convenient phenomenon because, in practice, both holding and order costs are not easy to estimate accurately.

> **Worked example**
>
> A building materials supplier obtains its bagged cement from a single supplier. Demand is reasonably constant throughout the year, and last year the company sold 2,000 tonnes of this product. It estimates the costs of placing an order at around £25 each time an order is placed, and calculates that the annual cost of holding inventory is 20 per cent of purchase cost. The company purchases the cement at £60 per tonne. How much should the company order at a time?
>
> $$\text{EOQ for cement} = \sqrt{\frac{2C_o D}{C_h}}$$
>
> $$= \sqrt{\frac{2 \times 25 \times 2{,}000}{0.2 \times 60}}$$
>
> $$= \sqrt{\frac{100{,}000}{12}}$$
>
> $$= 91.287 \text{ tonnes}$$
>
> After calculating the EOQ the operations manager feels that placing an order for 91.287 tonnes *exactly* seems somewhat over-precise. Why not order a convenient 100 tonnes?
>
> *Total cost of ordering plan for $Q = 91.287$:*
>
> $$= \frac{C_h Q}{2} + \frac{C_o D}{Q}$$
>
> $$= \frac{(0.2 \times 60) \times 91.287}{2} + \frac{25 \times 2{,}000}{91.287}$$
>
> $$= £1{,}095.454$$
>
> *Total cost of ordering plan for $Q = 100$:*
>
> $$= \frac{(0.2 \times 60) \times 100}{2} + \frac{25 \times 2{,}000}{100}$$
>
> $$= £1{,}100$$
>
> The extra cost of ordering 100 tonnes at a time is £1,100 − £1,095.45 = £4.55. The operations manager therefore should feel confident in using the more convenient order quantity.

Inventory Management

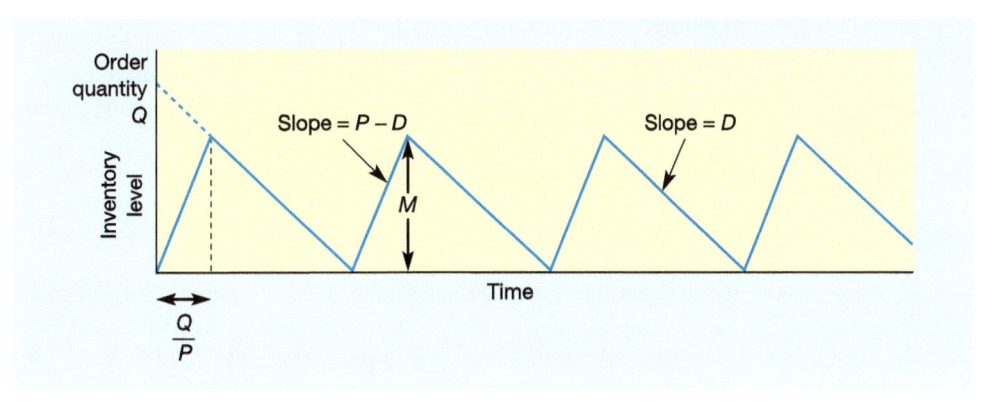

Figure 9.7 Inventory profile for gradual replacement of inventory

Gradual replacement – the economic batch quantity (EBQ) model

Although the simple inventory profile shown in Figure 9.4 made some simplifying assumptions, it is broadly applicable in most situations where each complete replacement order arrives at one point in time. In many cases, however, replenishment occurs over a time period rather than in one lot. A typical example of this is where an internal order is placed for a batch of parts to be produced on a machine. The machine will start to produce the parts and ship them in a more or less continuous stream into inventory, but at the same time demand is continuing to remove parts from the inventory. Provided the rate at which parts are being made and put into the inventory (P) is higher than the rate at which demand is depleting the inventory (D), then the size of the inventory will increase. After the batch has been completed the machine will be reset (to produce some other part), and demand will continue to deplete the inventory level until production of the next batch begins. The resulting profile is shown in Figure 9.7. Such a profile is typical for cycle inventories supplied by batch processes, where items are produced internally and intermittently. For this reason the minimum-cost batch quantity for this profile is called the **economic batch quantity** (EBQ). It is also sometimes known as the economic manufacturing quantity (EMQ), or the production order quantity (POQ). It is derived as follows:

Economic batch quantity

$$\text{Maximum stock level} = M$$

$$\text{Slope of inventory build-up} = P - D$$

Also, as is clear from Figure 9.7:

$$\text{Slope of inventory build-up} = M \div \frac{Q}{P}$$

$$= \frac{MP}{Q}$$

So,

$$\frac{MP}{Q} = P - D$$

$$M = \frac{Q(P - D)}{P}$$

$$\text{Average inventory level} = \frac{M}{2}$$

$$= \frac{Q(P - D)}{2P}$$

As before:

$$\text{Total cost} = \text{holding cost} + \text{order cost}$$

$$C_t = \frac{C_h Q(P-D)}{2P} + \frac{C_o D}{Q}$$

$$\frac{dC_t}{dQ} = \frac{C_h(P-D)}{2P} - \frac{C_o D}{Q^2}$$

Again, equating to zero and solving Q gives the minimum-cost order quantity EBQ:

$$\text{EBQ} = \sqrt{\frac{2C_o D}{C_h(1 - (D/P))}}$$

Worked example

The manager of a bottle-filling plant which bottles soft drinks needs to decide how long a 'run' of each type of drink to process. Demand for each type of drink is reasonably constant at 80,000 per month (a month has 160 production hours). The bottling lines fill at a rate of 3,000 bottles per hour, but take an hour to clean and reset between different drinks. The cost (of labour and lost production capacity) of each of these changeovers has been calculated at £100 per hour. Stock-holding costs are counted at £0.1 per bottle per month.

$$D = 80,000 \text{ per month}$$
$$= 500 \text{ per hour}$$

$$\text{EBQ} = \sqrt{\frac{2C_o D}{C_h(1 - (D/P))}}$$

$$= \sqrt{\frac{2 \times 100 \times 80,000}{0.1(1 - (500/3,000))}}$$

$$\text{EBQ} = 13,856$$

The staff who operate the lines have devised a method of reducing the changeover time from 1 hour to 30 minutes. How would that change the EBQ?

New C_o = £50

$$\text{New EBQ} = \sqrt{\frac{2 \times 50 \times 80,000}{0.1(1 - (500/3,000))}}$$

$$= 9,798$$

Critical commentary

The approach to determining order quantity which involves optimizing costs of holding stock against costs of ordering stock, typified by the EOQ and EBQ models, has always been subject to criticisms. Originally these concerned the validity of some of the assumptions of the model; more recently they have involved the underlying rationale of the approach itself. The criticisms fall into four broad categories, all of which we shall examine further:

- The assumptions included in the EOQ models are simplistic.
- The real costs of stock in operations are not as assumed in EOQ models.
- The models are really descriptive, and should not be used as prescriptive devices.
- Cost minimization is not an appropriate objective for inventory management.

Responding to the criticisms of EOQ

In order to keep EOQ-type models relatively straightforward, it was necessary to make assumptions. These concerned such things as the stability of demand, the existence of a fixed and identifiable ordering cost, that the cost of stock holding can be expressed by a linear function, shortage costs which were identifiable, and so on. While these assumptions are rarely strictly true, most of them can approximate to reality. Furthermore, the shape of the total cost curve has a relatively flat optimum point which means that small errors will not significantly affect the total cost of a near-optimum order quantity. However, at times the assumptions do pose severe limitations to the models. For example, the assumption of steady demand is untrue for a wide range of inventory problems.

Cost of stock

Other questions surround some of the assumptions made concerning the nature of stock-related costs. For example, placing an order with a supplier as part of a regular and multi-item order might be relatively inexpensive, whereas asking for a special one-off delivery of an item could prove far more costly. Similarly with stock-holding costs – although many companies make a standard percentage charge on the purchase price of stock items, this might not be appropriate. The marginal costs of increasing stock-holding levels might be merely the cost of the working capital involved. On the other hand, it might necessitate the lease of a whole new stock-holding facility such as a warehouse. Operations managers using an EOQ-type approach must check that the decisions implied by the use of the formulae do not exceed the boundaries within which the cost assumptions apply. And it is useful at this stage to examine the effect on an EOQ approach of regarding inventory as being more costly than previously believed. Increasing the slope of the holding cost line increases the level of total costs of *any* order quantity, but more significantly, shifts the minimum cost point substantially to the left, in favour of a lower economic order quantity. In other words, the less willing an operation is to hold stock on the grounds of cost, the more it should move towards smaller, more frequent ordering.

Using EOQ models as prescriptions

Perhaps the most fundamental criticism of the EOQ approach comes from the 'lean' and JIT philosophies. The EOQ tries to optimize order decisions. Implicitly the costs involved are taken as fixed, in the sense that the task of operations managers is to find out what are the true costs rather than to change them in any way. EOQ is essentially a reactive approach. Some critics would argue that it fails to ask the right question. Rather than asking the EOQ question of 'What is the optimum order quantity?', operations managers should really be asking, 'How can I change the operation in some way so as to reduce the overall level of inventory I need to hold?' The EOQ approach may be a reasonable description of stock-holding costs but should not necessarily be taken as a strict prescription over what decisions to take. For example, many organizations have made considerable efforts to reduce the effective cost of placing an order. Often they have done this by working to reduce changeover times on machines. This means that less time is taken changing over from one product to the other, and therefore less operating capacity is lost, which in turn reduces the cost of the changeover. Under these circumstances, the order cost curve in the EOQ formula reduces and, in turn, reduces the effective economic order quantity. Figure 9.8 shows the EOQ formula represented graphically with increased holding costs (*see* the previous discussion) and reduced order costs. The net effect of this is to significantly reduce the value of the EOQ.

Should the cost of inventory be minimized?

Many organizations (such as supermarkets and wholesalers) make the most of their revenue and profits simply by holding and supplying inventory. Because their main investment is in the inventory it is critical that they make a good return on this capital, by ensuring that it has the highest possible 'stock turn' (defined later in this chapter) and/or gross profit

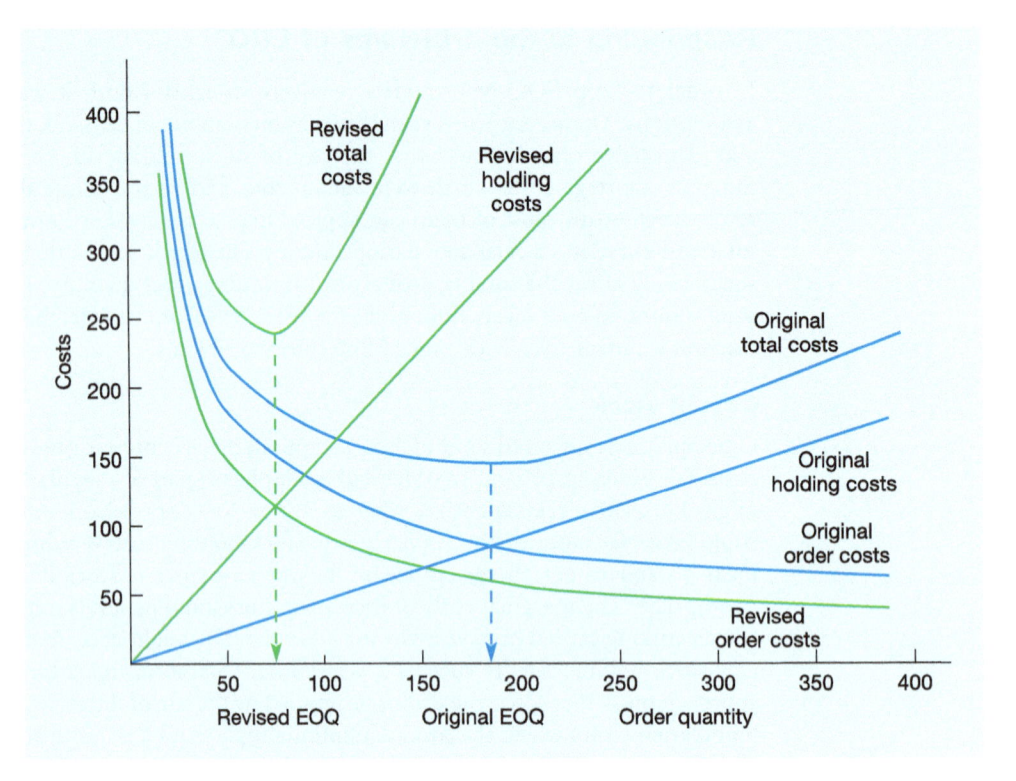

Figure 9.8 If the true costs of stock holding are taken into account, and if the cost of ordering (or changeover) is reduced, the economic order quantity (EOQ) is much smaller

Short case
Howard Smith Paper Group[2]

The Howard Smith Paper Group operates the most advanced warehousing operation within the European paper merchanting sector, delivering over 120,000 tonnes of paper annually. The function of a paper merchant is to provide the link between the paper mills and the printers or converters. This is illustrated in Figure 9.9. It is a sales- and service-driven business, so the role of the operation function is to deliver whatever the salesperson has promised to the customer. Usually, this means precisely the right product at the right time at the right place and in the right quantity. The company's operations are divided into two areas, 'logistics' which combines all warehousing and logistics tasks, and 'supply side' which includes inventory planning, purchasing and merchandizing decisions. Its main stocks are held at the national distribution centre, which was chosen because it is at the centre of the company's main customer location and also because it has good access to motorways. The key to any efficient merchanting operation lies in its ability to do three things well. Firstly, it must efficiently store the desired volume of required inventory. Secondly, it must have a 'goods inward' programme that sources the

Dispatch activity at Howard Smith Paper Group

required volume of desired inventory. Thirdly, it must be able to fulfil customer orders by 'picking' the desired goods fast and accurately from its warehouse. The warehouse is operational 24 hours per day, 5 days per week. A total of 52 staff are employed in the warehouse, including maintenance and cleaning staff. Skill sets are not an issue, since all pickers are trained for all tasks. This facilitates easier capacity management, since pickers can be deployed where most urgently needed. Contract labour is used on occasions, although this is less effective because the staff tend to be less motivated, and have to learn the job.

Inventory Management   **253**

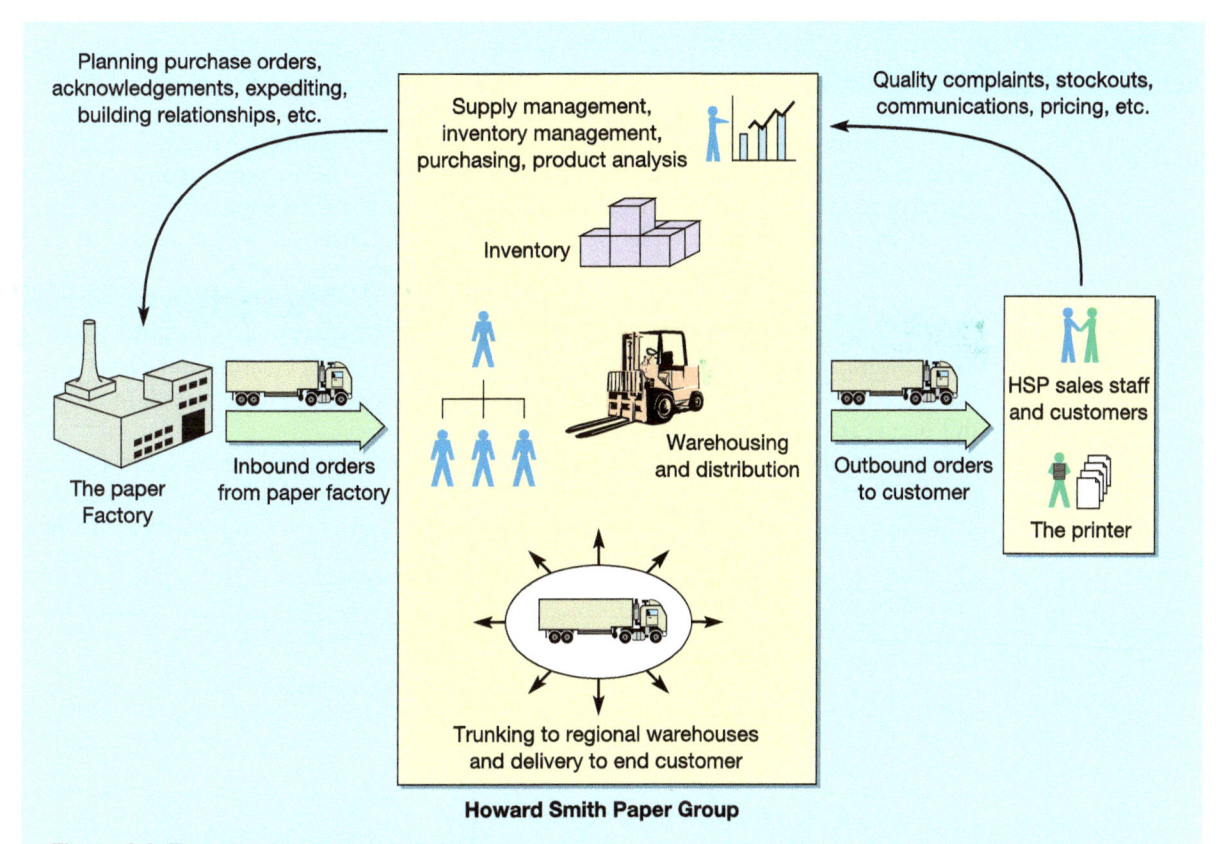

Figure 9.9 The role of the paper merchant

At the heart of the company's operations is a warehouse known as a 'dark warehouse'. All picking and movement within the dark warehouse is fully automatic and there is no need for any person to enter the high-bay stores and picking area. The important difference with this warehouse operation is that pallets are brought to the pickers. Conventional paper merchants send pickers with handling equipment into the warehouse aisles for stock. A warehouse computer system (WCS) controls the whole operation without the need for human input. It manages pallet location and retrieval, robotic crane missions, automatic conveyors, bar-code label production and scanning, and all picking routines and priorities. It also calculates operator activity and productivity measures, as well as issuing documentation and planning transportation schedules. The fact that all products are identified by a unique bar code means that accuracy is guaranteed. The unique user log-on ensures that any picking errors can be traced back to the name of the picker, to ensure further errors do not occur. The WCS is linked to the company's ERP system such that once the order has been placed by a customer, computers manage the whole process from order placement to order dispatch.

margin. Alternatively, they may also be concerned to maximize the use of space by seeking to maximize the profit earned per square metre. The EOQ model does not address these objectives. Similarly for products that deteriorate or go out of fashion, the EOQ model can result in excess inventory of slower-moving items. In fact, the EOQ model is rarely used in such organizations, and there is more likely to be a system of periodic review (described later) for regular ordering of replenishment inventory. For example, a typical builders' supply merchant might carry around 50,000 different items of stock (SKUs – stock-keeping units). However, most of these cluster into larger families of items such as paints, sanitaryware or metal fixings. Single orders are placed at regular intervals for all the required replenishments in the supplier's range, and these are then delivered together at one time. For example, if such deliveries were made weekly, then on average, the individual item order quantities will be for only one week's usage. Less popular items, or ones with erratic demand patterns, can be individually ordered at the same time, or (when urgent) can be delivered the next day by carrier.

The timing decision – when to place an order

When we assumed that orders arrived instantaneously and demand was steady and predictable, the decision on when to place a replenishment order was self-evident. An order would be placed as soon as the stock level reached zero. This would arrive instantaneously and prevent any stock-out occurring. If replenishment orders do not arrive instantaneously, but have a lag between the order being placed and it arriving in the inventory, we can calculate the timing of a replacement order as shown in Figure 9.10. In this case, the lead time for an order to arrive is two weeks, so the **re-order point** (ROP) is the point at which stock will fall to zero minus the order lead time. Alternatively, we can define the point in terms of the level which the inventory will have reached when a replenishment order needs to be placed. In this case this occurs at a **re-order level** (ROL) of 200 items.

However, this assumes that both the demand and the order lead time are perfectly predictable. In most cases, of course, this is not so. Both demand and the order lead time are likely to vary to produce a profile which looks something like that in Figure 9.11. In these

Re-order point

Re-order level

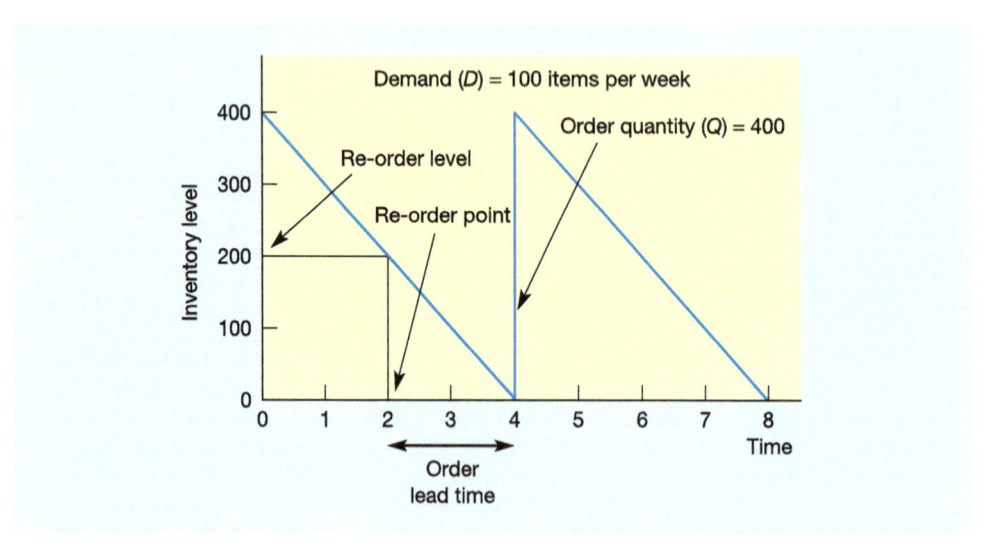

Figure 9.10 Re-order level (ROL) and re-order point (ROP) are derived from the order lead time and demand rate

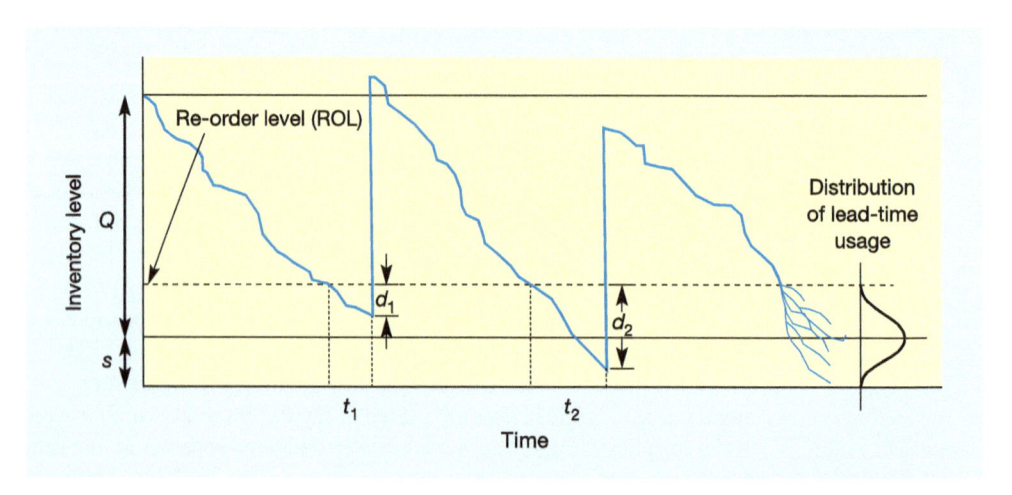

Figure 9.11 Safety stock (s) helps to avoid stock-outs when demand and/or order lead time are uncertain

circumstances it is necessary to make the replenishment order somewhat earlier than would be the case in a purely deterministic situation. This will result in, on average, some stock still being in the inventory when the replenishment order arrives. This is buffer (safety) stock. The earlier the replenishment order is placed, the higher will be the expected level of safety stock (s) when the replenishment order arrives. But because of the variability of both lead time (t) and demand rate (d), there will sometimes be a higher-than-average level of safety stock and sometimes lower. The main consideration in setting safety stock is not so much the average level of stock when a replenishment order arrives but rather the probability that the stock will not have run out before the replenishment order arrives.

Worked example

A company which imports running shoes for sale in its sports shops can never be certain of how long, after placing an order, the delivery will take. Examination of previous orders reveals that out of ten orders: one took one week, two took two weeks, four took three weeks, two took four weeks and one took five weeks. The rate of demand for the shoes also varies between 110 pairs per week and 140 pairs per week. There is a 0.2 probability of the demand rate being either 110 or 140 pairs per week, and a 0.3 chance of demand being either 120 or 130 pairs per week. The company needs to decide when it should place replenishment orders if the probability of a stock-out is to be less than 10 per cent.

Both lead time and the demand rate during the lead time will contribute to the lead-time usage. So the distributions which describe each will need to be combined. Figure 9.12 and Table 9.2 show how this can be done. Taking lead time to be one, two, three, four or five weeks, and demand rate to be 110, 120, 130 or 140 pairs per week, and also assuming the two variables to be independent, the distributions can be combined as shown in Table 9.2. Each element in the matrix shows a possible lead-time usage with the probability of its occurrence. So if the lead time is one week and the demand rate is 110 pairs per week, the actual lead-time usage will be $1 \times 110 = 110$ pairs. Since there is a 0.1 chance of the lead time being one week, and a 0.2 chance of demand rate being 110 pairs per week, the probability of both these events occurring is $0.1 \times 0.2 = 0.02$.

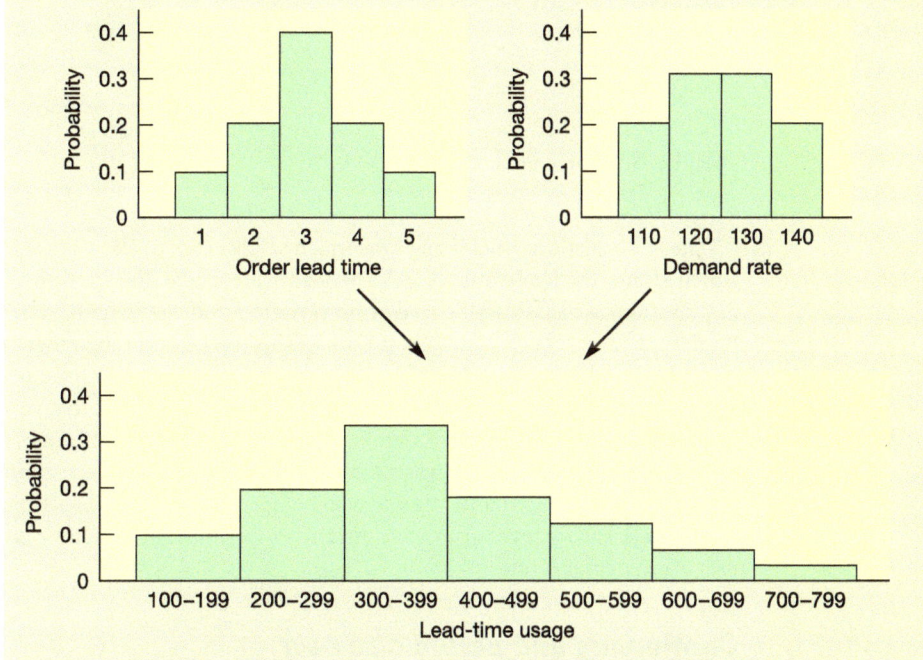

Figure 9.12 The probability distributions for order lead time and demand rate combine to give the lead-time usage distribution

Table 9.2 Matrix of lead-time and demand-rate probabilities

			Lead-time probabilities				
			1 0.1	2 0.2	3 0.4	4 0.2	5 0.1
Demand-rate probabilities	110	0.2	110 (0.02)	220 (0.04)	330 (0.08)	440 (0.04)	550 (0.02)
	120	0.3	120 (0.03)	240 (0.06)	360 (0.12)	480 (0.06)	600 (0.03)
	130	0.3	130 (0.03)	260 (0.06)	390 (0.12)	520 (0.06)	650 (0.03)
	140	0.2	140 (0.02)	280 (0.04)	420 (0.08)	560 (0.04)	700 (0.02)

We can now classify the possible lead-time usages into histogram form. For example, summing the probabilities of all the lead-time usages which fall within the range 100–199 (all the first column) gives a combined probability of 0.1. Repeating this for subsequent intervals results in Table 9.3.

Table 9.3 Combined probabilities

Lead-time usage	100–199	200–299	300–399	400–499	500–599	600–699	700–799
Probability	0.1	0.2	0.32	0.18	0.12	0.06	0.02

This shows the probability of each possible range of lead-time usage occurring, but it is the cumulative probabilities that are needed to predict the likelihood of stock-out (see Table 9.4).

Table 9.4 Combined probabilities

Lead-time usage X	100	200	300	400	500	600	700	800
Probability of usage being greater than X	1.0	0.9	0.7	0.38	0.2	0.08	0.02	0

Setting the re-order level at 600 would mean that there is only a 0.08 chance of usage being greater than available inventory during the lead time, i.e. there is a less than 10 per cent chance of a stock-out occurring.

Lead-time usage

The key statistic in calculating how much safety stock to allow is the probability distribution which shows the **lead-time usage**. The lead-time usage distribution is a combination of the distributions which describe lead-time variation and the demand rate during the lead time. If safety stock is set below the lower limit of this distribution then there will be shortages every single replenishment cycle. If safety stock is set above the upper limit of the distribution, there is no chance of stock-outs occurring. Usually, safety stock is set to give a predetermined likelihood that stock-outs will not occur. Figure 9.11 shows that, in this case, the first replenishment order arrived after t_1, resulting in a lead-time usage of d_1. The second replenishment order took longer, t_2, and demand rate was also higher, resulting in a lead-time usage of d_2. The third order cycle shows several possible inventory profiles for different conditions of lead-time usage and demand rate.

Continuous and periodic review

Continuous review

The approach we have described to making the replenishment timing decision is often called the **continuous review** approach. This is because, to make the decision in this way, there must

Inventory Management

be a process to review the stock level of each item continuously and then place an order when the stock level reaches its re-order level. The virtue of this approach is that, although the timing of orders may be irregular (depending on the variation in demand rate), the order size (Q) is constant and can be set at the optimum economic order quantity. Such continual checking on inventory levels can be time-consuming, especially when there are many stock withdrawals compared with the average level of stock, but in an environment where all inventory records are computerized, this should not be a problem unless the records are inaccurate.

Periodic review

An alternative and far simpler approach, but one which sacrifices the use of a fixed (and therefore possibly optimum) order quantity, is called the **periodic review** approach. Here, rather than ordering at a predetermined re-order level, the periodic approach orders at a fixed and regular time interval. So the stock level of an item could be found, for example, at the end of every month and a replenishment order placed to bring the stock up to a predetermined level. This level is calculated to cover demand between the replenishment order being placed and the following replenishment order arriving. Figure 9.13 illustrates the parameters for the periodic review approach.

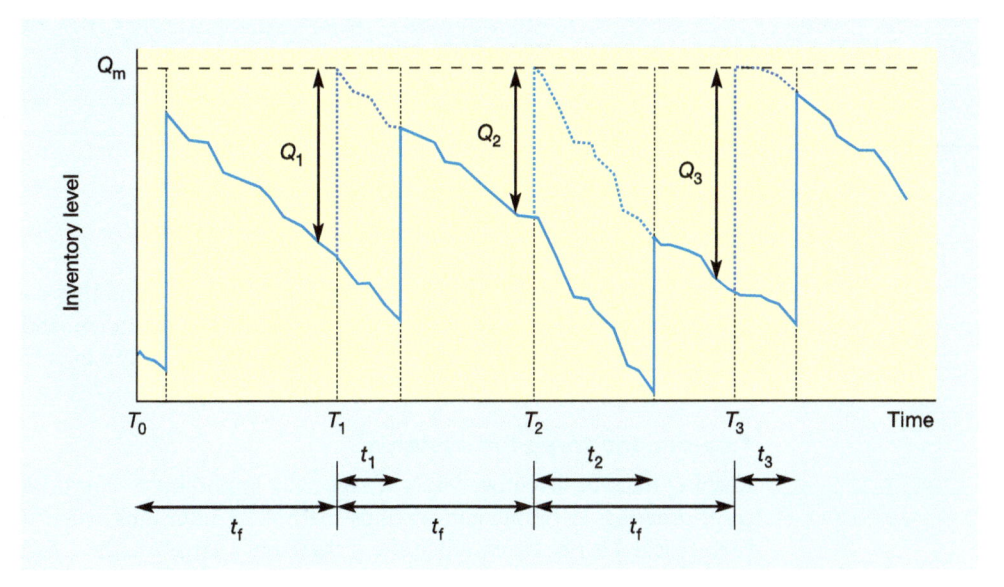

Figure 9.13 A periodic review approach to order timing with probabilistic demand and lead time

At time T_1 in Figure 9.13 the inventory manager would examine the stock level and order sufficient to bring it up to some maximum, Q_m. However, that order of Q_1 items will not arrive until a further time of t_1 has passed, during which demand continues to deplete the stocks. Again, both demand and lead time are uncertain. The Q_1 items will arrive and bring the stock up to some level lower than Q_m (unless there has been no demand during t_1). Demand then continues until T_2, when again an order Q_2 is placed which is the difference between the current stock at T_2 and Q_m. This order arrives after t_2, by which time demand has depleted the stocks further. Thus the replenishment order placed at T_1 must be able to cover for the demand which occurs until T_2 and t_2. Safety stocks will need to be calculated, in a similar manner to before, based on the distribution of usage over this period.

The time interval

The interval between placing orders, t_1, is usually calculated on a deterministic basis, and derived from the EOQ. So, for example, if the demand for an item is 2,000 per year, the cost of placing an order £25, and the cost of holding stock £0.5 per item per year:

$$\text{EOQ} = \sqrt{\frac{2C_o D}{C_h}} = \sqrt{\frac{2 \times 2{,}000 \times 25}{0.5}} = 447$$

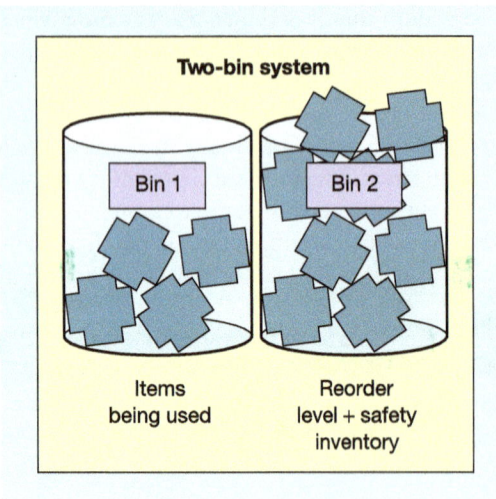

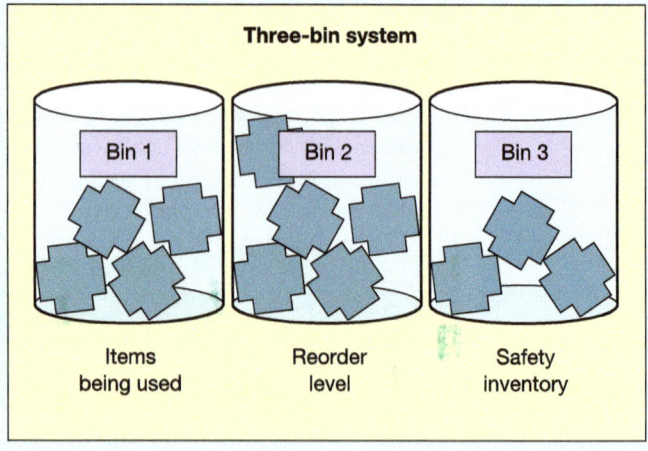

Figure 9.14 The two-bin and three-bin systems of re-ordering

The optimum time interval between orders, t_f, is therefore:

$$t_f = \frac{\text{EOQ}}{D} = \frac{447}{2{,}000} \text{ years}$$

$$= 2.68 \text{ months}$$

It may seem paradoxical to calculate the time interval assuming constant demand when demand is, in fact, uncertain. However, uncertainties in both demand and lead time can be allowed for by setting Q_m to allow for the desired probability of stock-out based on usage during the period t_f + lead time.

Two-bin and three-bin systems

Keeping track of inventory levels is especially important in continuous review approaches to re-ordering. A simple and obvious method of indicating when the re-order point has been reached is necessary, especially if there are a large number of items to be monitored. The two- and three-bin systems illustrated in Figure 9.14 are such methods. The simple **two-bin system** involves storing the re-order point quantity plus the safety inventory quantity in the second bin and using parts from the first bin. When the first bin empties, that is the signal to order the next re-order quantity. Sometimes the safety inventory is stored in a third bin (the **three-bin system**), so it is clear when demand is exceeding that which was expected. Different 'bins' are not always necessary to operate this type of system. For example, a common practice in retail operations is to store the second 'bin' quantity upside-down behind or under the first 'bin' quantity. Orders are then placed when the upside-down items are reached.

Inventory analysis and control systems

The models we have described, even the ones which take a probabilistic view of demand and lead time, are still simplified compared with the complexity of real stock management. Coping with many thousands of stocked items, supplied by many hundreds of different suppliers, with possibly tens of thousands of individual customers, makes for a complex and dynamic operations task. In order to control such complexity, operations managers have to do two things. First, they have to discriminate between different stocked items, so that they

Inventory priorities – the ABC system

In any inventory which contains more than one stocked item, some items will be more important to the organization than others. Some, for example, might have a very high usage rate, so if they ran out many customers would be disappointed. Other items might be of particularly high value, so excessively high inventory levels would be particularly expensive. One common way of discriminating between different stock items is to rank them by the **usage value** (their usage rate multiplied by their individual value). Items with a particularly high usage value are deemed to warrant the most careful control, whereas those with low usage values need not be controlled quite so rigorously. Generally, a relatively small proportion of the total range of items contained in an inventory will account for a large proportion of the total usage value. This phenomenon is known as the **Pareto law** (after the person who described it), sometimes referred to as the 80/20 rule. It is called this because, typically, 80 per cent of an operation's sales are accounted for by only 20 per cent of all stocked item types. The relationship can be used to classify the different types of items kept in an inventory by their usage value. **ABC inventory control** allows inventory managers to concentrate their efforts on controlling the more significant items of stock.

Usage value

Pareto law

ABC inventory control

Worked example

Table 9.5 shows all the parts stored by an electrical wholesaler. The 20 different items stored vary in terms of both their usage per year and cost per item as shown. However, the wholesaler has ranked the stock items by their usage value per year. The total usage value per year is £5,569,000. From this it is possible to calculate the usage value per year of each item as a percentage of the total usage value, and from that a running cumulative

Table 9.5 Warehouse items ranked by usage value

Stock no.	Usage (items/year)	Cost (£/item)	Usage value (£000/year)	% of total value	Cumulative % of total value
A/703	700	20.00	1,400	25.14	25.14
D/012	450	2.75	1,238	22.23	47.37
A/135	1,000	0.90	900	16.16	63.53
C/732	95	8.50	808	14.51	78.04
C/375	520	0.54	281	5.05	83.09
A/500	73	2.30	168	3.02	86.11
D/111	520	0.22	114	2.05	88.16
D/231	170	0.65	111	1.99	90.15
E/781	250	0.34	85	1.53	91.68
A/138	250	0.30	75	1.34	93.02
D/175	400	0.14	56	1.01	94.03
E/001	80	0.63	50	0.89	94.92
C/150	230	0.21	48	0.86	95.78
F/030	400	0.12	48	0.86	96.64
D/703	500	0.09	45	0.81	97.45
D/535	50	0.88	44	0.79	98.24
C/541	70	0.57	40	0.71	98.95
A/260	50	0.64	32	0.57	99.52
B/141	50	0.32	16	0.28	99.80
D/021	20	0.50	10	0.20	100.00
Total			5,569	100.00	

total of the usage value as shown. The wholesaler can then plot the cumulative percentage of all stocked items against the cumulative percentage of their value. So, for example, the part with stock number A/703 is the highest-value part and accounts for 25.14 per cent of the total inventory value. As a part, however, it is only one-twentieth or 5 per cent of the total number of items stocked. This item together with the next highest value item (D/012) accounts for only 10 per cent of the total number of items stocked, yet accounts for 47.37 per cent of the value of the stock, and so on.

This is shown graphically in Figure 9.15. Here the wholesaler has classified the first four part numbers (20 per cent of the range) as Class A items and will monitor the usage and ordering of these items very closely and frequently. A few improvements in order quantities or safety stocks for these items could bring significant savings. The six next, part numbers C/375 through to A/138 (30 per cent of the range), are to be treated as Class B items with slightly less effort devoted to their control. All other items are classed as Class C items whose stocking policy is reviewed only occasionally.

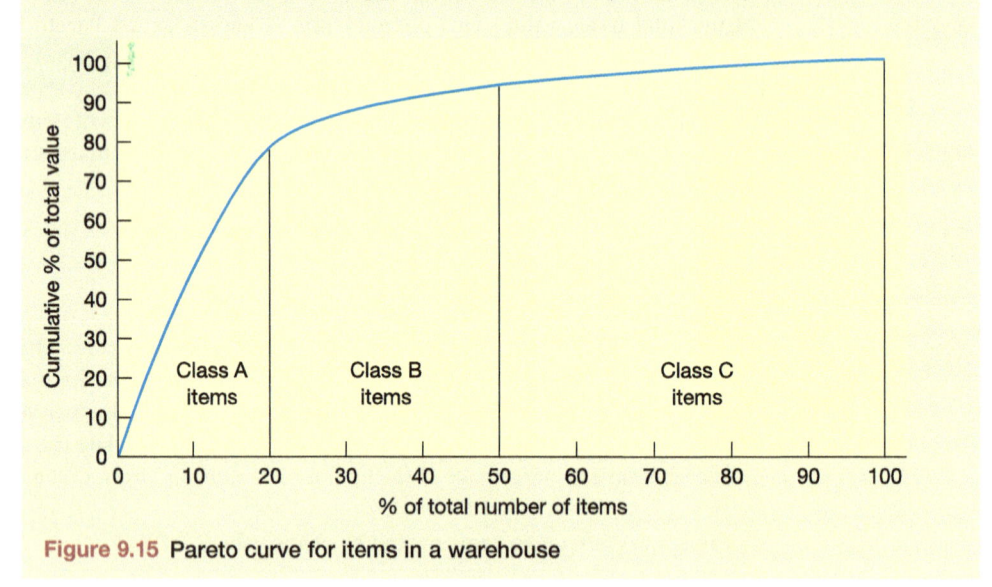

Figure 9.15 Pareto curve for items in a warehouse

- *Class A items* are those 20 per cent or so of high-usage-value items which account for around 80 per cent of the total usage value.
- *Class B items* are those of medium usage value, usually the next 30 per cent of items which often account for around 10 per cent of the total usage value.
- *Class C items* are those low-usage-value items which, although comprising around 50 per cent of the total types of items stocked, probably only account for around 10 per cent of the total usage value of the operation.

Although annual usage and value are the two criteria most commonly used to determine a stock classification system, other criteria might also contribute towards the (higher) classification of an item:

- *Consequence of stock-out*. High priority might be given to those items which would seriously delay or disrupt other operations, or the customers, if they were not in stock.
- *Uncertainty of supply*. Some items, although low value, might warrant more attention if their supply is erratic or uncertain.
- *High obsolescence or deterioration risk*. Items which could lose their value through obsolescence or deterioration might need extra attention and monitoring.

Some more complex stock classification systems might include these criteria by classifying on an A, B, C basis for each. For example, a part might be classed as A/B/A meaning it is an

A category item by value, a class B item by consequence of stock-out and a class A item by obsolescence risk.

> ### Critical commentary
>
> This approach to inventory classification can sometimes be misleading. Many professional inventory managers point out that the Pareto law is often misquoted. It does not say that 80 per cent of the SKUs (stock-keeping units) account for only 20 per cent inventory value. It accounts for 80 per cent of inventory 'usage' or throughput value, in other words sales value. In fact it is the slow-moving items (the C category items) that often pose the greatest challenge in inventory management. Often these slow-moving items, although only accounting for 20 per cent of sales, require a large part (typically between one-half and two-thirds) of the total investment in stock. This is why slow-moving items are a real problem. Moreover, if errors in forecasting or ordering result in excess stock in 'A class' fast-moving items, it is relatively unimportant in the sense that excess stock can be sold quickly. However, excess stock in a slow-moving C item will be there a long time. According to some inventory managers, it is the A items that can be left to look after themselves, it is the B and even more the C items that need controlling.

Measuring inventory

In our example of ABC classifications we used the monetary value of the annual usage of each item as a measure of inventory usage. Monetary value can also be used to measure the absolute level of inventory at any point in time. This would involve taking the number of each item in stock, multiplying it by its value (usually the cost of purchasing the item) and summing the value of all the individual items stored. This is a useful measure of the investment that an operation has in its inventories but gives no indication of how large that investment is relative to the total throughput of the operation. To do this we must compare the total number of items in stock against their rate of usage. There are two ways of doing this. The first is to calculate the amount of time the inventory would last, subject to normal demand, if it were not replenished. This is sometimes called the number of weeks' (or days', months', years', etc.) *cover* of the stock. The second method is to calculate how often the stock is used up in a period, usually one year. This is called the **stock turn** or turnover of stock and is the reciprocal of the stock-cover figure.

Stock cover
Stock turn

Inventory information systems

Most inventories of any significant size are managed by computerized systems. The many relatively routine calculations involved in stock control lend themselves to computerized support. This is especially so since data capture has been made more convenient through the use of bar-code readers, radio-frequency identification (RFID), and the point-of-sale recording of sales transactions. Many commercial systems of stock control are available, although they tend to share certain common functions.

Updating stock records

Every time a transaction takes place (such as the sale of an item, the movement of an item from a warehouse into a truck, or the delivery of an item into a warehouse) the position, status and possibly value of the stock will have changed. This information must be recorded so that operations managers can determine their current inventory status at any time.

Generating orders

The two major decisions we have described previously, namely how much to order and when to order, can both be made by a computerized stock control system. The first decision, setting the value of how much to order (Q), is likely to be taken only at relatively infrequent intervals. Originally almost all computer systems automatically calculated order quantities by using the EOQ formulae covered earlier. Now more sophisticated algorithms are used, often using probabilistic data and based on examining the marginal return on investing in stock. The system will hold all the information which goes into the ordering algorithm but might periodically check to see if demand or order lead times, or any of the other parameters, have changed significantly and recalculate Q accordingly. The decision on when to order, on the other hand, is a far more routine affair which computer systems make according to whatever decision rules operations managers have chosen to adopt: either continuous review or periodic review. Furthermore, the systems can automatically generate whatever documentation is required, or even transmit the re-ordering information electronically through an electronic data interchange (EDI) system.

Generating inventory reports

Inventory control systems can generate regular reports of stock value for the different items stored, which can help management monitor its inventory control performance. Similarly, customer service performance, such as the number of stock-outs or the number of incomplete orders, can be regularly monitored. Some reports may be generated on an exception basis. That is, the report is only generated if some performance measure deviates from acceptable limits.

Summary answers to key questions

Check and improve your understanding of this chapter using self-assessment questions and a personalized study plan, audio and video downloads, and an eBook – all at www.myomlab.com.

➤ What is inventory?

- Inventory, or stock, is the stored accumulation of the transformed resources in an operation. Sometimes the words 'stock' and 'inventory' are also used to describe transforming resources, but the terms *stock control* and *inventory control* are nearly always used in connection with transformed resources.
- Almost all operations keep some kind of inventory, most usually of materials but also of information and customers (customer inventories are normally called 'queues').

➤ What are the reasons for holding inventory and what are the disadvantages?

- Inventory occurs in operations because the timing of supply and the timing of demand do not always match. Inventories are needed, therefore, to smooth the differences between supply and demand.
- There are five main reasons for keeping inventory:
    - to cope with random or unexpected interruptions in supply or demand (buffer inventory);
    - to cope with an operation's inability to make all products simultaneously (cycle inventory);
    - to allow different stages of processing to operate at different speeds and with different schedules (de-coupling inventory);
    - to cope with planned fluctuations in supply or demand (anticipation inventory);
    - to cope with transportation delays in the supply network (pipeline inventory).

Inventory Management

- There are a number of disadvantages of holding inventory:
  - Inventory is often a major part of working capital, tying up money which could be used more productively elsewhere.
  - If inventory is not used quickly, there is an increasing risk of damage, loss, deterioration, or obsolescence.
  - Inventory invariably takes up space and has to be managed, stored in appropriate conditions, insured and physically handled when transactions occur. It therefore contributes to overhead costs.

➤ How much inventory should an operation hold?

- This depends on balancing the costs associated with holding stocks against the costs associated with placing an order. The main stock-holding costs are usually related to working capital, whereas the main order costs are usually associated with the transactions necessary to generate the information to place an order.
- The best-known approach to determining the amount of inventory to order is the economic order quantity (EOQ) formula. The EOQ formula can be adapted to different types of inventory profile using different stock behaviour assumptions.
- The EOQ approach, however, has been subject to a number of criticisms regarding the true cost of holding stock, the real cost of placing an order, and the use of EOQ models as prescriptive devices.

➤ When should an operation replenish its inventory?

- Partly this depends on the uncertainty of demand. Orders are usually timed to leave a certain level of average safety stock when the order arrives. The level of safety stock is influenced by the variability of both demand and the lead time of supply. These two variables are usually combined into a lead-time usage distribution.
- Using re-order level as a trigger for placing replenishment orders necessitates the continual review of inventory levels. This can be time-consuming and expensive. An alternative approach is to make replenishment orders of varying size but at fixed time periods.

➤ How can inventory be managed?

- The key issue here is how managers discriminate between the levels of control they apply to different stock items. The most common way of doing this is by what is known as the ABC classification of stock. This uses the Pareto principle to distinguish between the different values of, or significance placed on, types of stock.
- Inventory is usually managed through sophisticated computer-based information systems which have a number of functions: the updating of stock records, the generation of orders, the generation of inventory status reports and demand forecasts. These systems critically depend on maintaining accurate inventory records.

Learning exercises

These problems and applications will help to improve your analysis of operations. You can find more practice problems as well as worked examples and guided solutions on MyOMLab at www.myomlab.com.

1. An electronics circuit supplier buys microchips from a large manufacturer. Last year the company supplied 2,000 specialist D/35 chips to customers. The cost of placing an order is $50 and the annual holding cost is estimated to be $2.4 per chip per year. How much should the company order at a time, and what is the total cost of carrying inventory of this product?

2. Supermedicosupplies.com works a 44-week year. If the lead time between placing an order for stethoscopes and receiving them is two weeks, what is the re-order point for the Thunderer stethoscopes?

3. The Super Pea Canning Company produces canned peas. It uses 10,000 litres of green dye per month. Because of the hazardous nature of this product it needs special transport; therefore the cost of placing an order is €2,000. If the storage costs of holding the dye are €5 per litre per month, how much dye should be ordered at a time?

4. In the example above, if the storage costs of keeping the dye reduce to €3 per litre per month, how much will inventory costs reduce?

Want to know more?

DeHoratius, N. and Raman, Ananth (2008) Inventory Record Inaccuracy: An Empirical Analysis, University of Chicago, http://faculty.chicagobooth.edu/nicole.dehoratius/research.

Viale, J.D. (1997) *The Basics of Inventory Management*, Crisp Publications, Menlo Park, CA. Very much 'the basics', but that is exactly what most people need.

Waters, D. (2003) *Inventory Control and Management*, John Wiley and Sons Ltd, Chichester. Conventional but useful coverage of the topic.

Wild, T. (2002) *Best Practice in Inventory Management*, Elsevier Science, Oxford. A straightforward and readable practice-based approach to the subject.

Useful websites

www.inventoryops.com/dictionary.htm A great source for information on inventory management and warehouse operations.

www.apics.org Site of APICS: a US 'educational society for resource managers'.

www.inventorymanagement.com Site of the Centre for Inventory Management. Cases and links.

www.opsman.org Lots of useful stuff.

Now that you have finished reading this chapter, why not visit MyOMLab at www.myomlab.com where you'll find more learning resources to help you make the most of your studies and get a better grade.

Chapter 10

Planning and control

Key questions

- What is planning and control?
- How do supply and demand affect planning and control?
- What are the activities of planning and control?
- How can enterprise resource planning (ERP) help planning and control?

Introduction

Within the constraints imposed by its design, an operation has to be run on an ongoing basis. 'Planning and control' is concerned with managing the ongoing activities of the operation so as to satisfy customer demand. All operations require plans and require controlling, although the degree of formality and detail may vary. This chapter introduces and provides an overview of some of the principles and methods of planning and control. We also examine information technology (IT), in the form of ERP (enterprise resources planning) systems. The different aspects of planning and control can be viewed as representing the reconciliation of supply with demand. Figure 10.1 shows where this chapter fits into the overall operations model.

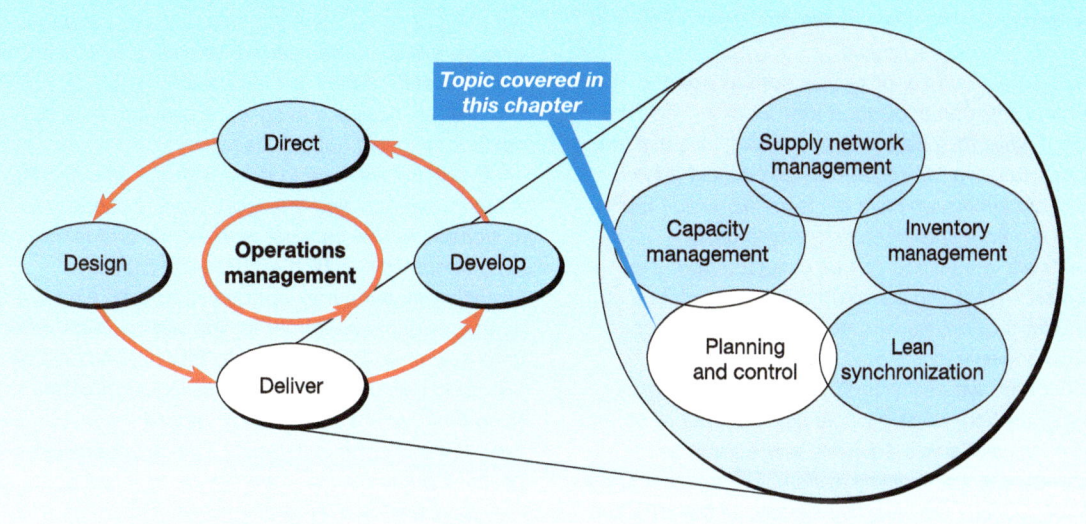

Figure 10.1 This chapter examines planning and control

Check and improve your understanding of this chapter using self-assessment questions and a personalized study plan, audio and video downloads, and an eBook – all at www.myomlab.com.

Operations in practice: Joanne manages the schedule[1]

Joanne Cheung is the Senior Service Adviser at a premier BMW dealership. She and her team act as the interface between customers who want their cars serviced and repaired, and the 16 technicians who carry out the work in their state-of-the-art workshop. 'There are three types of work that we have to organize', says Joanne. 'The first is performing repairs on customers' vehicles. They usually want this doing as soon as possible. The second type of job is routine servicing. It is usually not urgent so customers are generally willing to negotiate a time for this. The remainder of our work involves working on the pre-owned cars which our buyer has bought-in to sell on to customers. Before any of these cars can be sold they have to undergo extensive checks. To some extent we treat these categories of work slightly differently. We have to give good service to our internal car buyers, but there is some flexibility in planning these jobs. At the other extreme, emergency repair work for customers has to be fitted into our schedule as quickly as possible. If someone is desperate to have their car repaired at very short notice, we sometimes ask them to drop their car in as early as they can and pick it up as late as possible. This gives us the maximum amount of time to fit it into the schedule.

'There are a number of service options open to customers. We can book short jobs in for a fixed time and do it while they wait. Most commonly, we ask the customer to leave the car with us and collect it later. To help customers we have ten loan cars which are booked out on a first-come first-served basis. Alternatively, the vehicle can be collected from the customer's home and delivered back there when it is ready. Our four drivers who do this are able to cope with up to twelve jobs a day.

'Most days we deal with fifty to eighty jobs, taking from half-an-hour up to a whole day. To enter a job into our process all Service Advisers have access to the computer-based scheduling system. On-screen it shows the total capacity we have day-by-day, all the jobs that are booked in, the amount of free capacity still available, the number of loan cars available, and so on. We use this to see when we have the capacity to book a customer in, and then enter all the customer's details. BMW have

Joanne has to balance the needs of customers and the constraints of the workshop

issued "standard times" for all the major jobs. However, you have to modify these standard times a bit to take account of circumstances. That is where the Service Adviser's experience comes in.

'We keep all the most commonly used parts in stock, but if a repair needs a part which is not in stock, we can usually get it from the BMW parts distributors within a day. Every evening our planning system prints out the jobs to be done the next day and the parts which are likely to be needed for each job. This allows the parts staff to pick out the parts for each job so that the technicians can collect them first thing the next morning without any delay.

'Every day we have to cope with the unexpected. A technician may find that extra work is needed, customers may want extra work doing, and technicians are sometimes ill, which reduces our capacity. Occasionally parts may not be available so we have to arrange with the customer for the vehicle to be rebooked for a later time. Every day up to four or five customers just don't turn up. Usually they have just forgotten to bring their car in so we have to rebook them in at a later time. We can cope with most of these uncertainties because our technicians are flexible in terms of the skills they have and also are willing to work overtime when needed. Also, it is important to manage customers' expectations. If there is a chance that the vehicle may not be ready for them, it shouldn't come as a surprise when they try and collect it.'

What is planning and control?

Planning and control reconciles supply and demand

Planning and control is concerned with the reconciliation between what the market requires and what the operation's resources can deliver. **Planning and control** activities provide the systems, procedures and decisions which bring different aspects of supply and demand together. The purpose is always the same – to make a connection between supply and demand that will ensure that the operation's processes run effectively and efficiently and produce products and services as required by customers. Consider, for example, the way in which routine surgery is organized in a hospital. When a patient arrives and is admitted to the hospital, much of the planning for the surgery will already have happened. The operating theatre will have been reserved, and the doctors and nurses who staff the operating theatre will have been provided with all the information regarding the patient's condition. Appropriate preoperative and postoperative care will have been organized. All this will involve staff and facilities in different parts of the hospital. All must be given the same information and their activities coordinated. Soon after the patient arrives, he or she will be checked to make sure that their condition is as expected. Blood, if required, will be cross-matched and reserved, and any medication will be made ready. Any last-minute changes may require some degree of replanning. For example, if the patient shows unexpected symptoms, observation may be necessary before the surgery can take place. Not only will this affect the patient's own treatment, but other patients' treatment may also have to be rescheduled. All these activities of scheduling, coordination and organization are concerned with the planning and control of the hospital.

The difference between planning and control

Planning concerns what should happen in the future

Control copes with changes

We have chosen to treat planning and control together. This is because the division between planning and control is not always clear. However, there are some general features that help to distinguish between the two. **Planning** is a formalization of what is intended to happen at some time in the future. But a plan does not guarantee that an event will actually happen. Customers change their minds about what they want and when they want it. Suppliers may not always deliver on time, machines may fail, or staff may be absent through illness. **Control** is the process of coping with changes. It may mean that plans need to be redrawn. It may also mean that an 'intervention' will need to be made in the operation to bring it back 'on track' – for example, finding a new supplier that can deliver quickly, repairing the machine which failed, or moving staff from another part of the operation to cover for the absentees. Control makes the adjustments which allow the operation to achieve the objectives that the plan has set, even when the assumptions on which the plan was based do not hold true.

Long-, medium- and short-term planning and control

The nature of planning and control activities changes over time. In the very long term, operations managers make plans concerning what they intend to do, what resources they need, and what objectives they hope to achieve. The emphasis is on planning rather than control, because there is little to control as such. They will use forecasts of likely demand which are described in aggregated terms. For example, a hospital will make plans for '2,000 patients' without necessarily going into the details of the individual needs of those patients. Similarly, the hospital might plan to have 100 nurses and 20 doctors but again without deciding on the specific attributes of the staff. Operations managers will be concerned mainly to achieve financial targets. Budgets will be put in place which identify its costs and revenue targets.

Medium-term planning and control is more detailed. It looks ahead to assess the overall demand which the operation must meet in a partially disaggregated manner. By this time, for example, the hospital must distinguish between different types of demand. The number of patients coming as accident and emergency cases will need to be distinguished from those requiring routine operations. Similarly, different categories of staff will have been identified

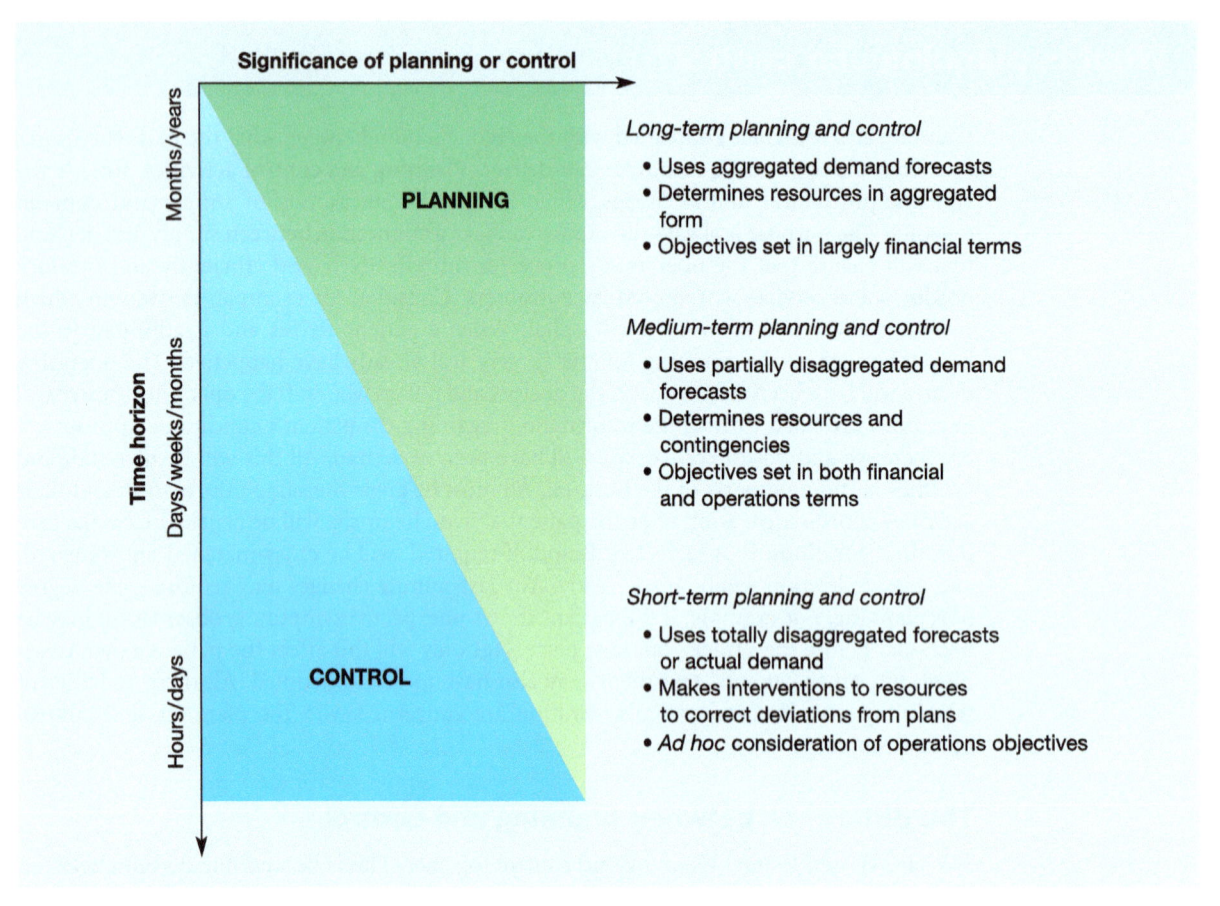

Figure 10.2 The balance between planning and control activities changes in the long, medium and short term

and broad staffing levels in each category set. Just as important, contingencies will have been put in place which allow for slight deviations from the plans.

In short-term planning and control, many of the resources will have been set and it will be difficult to make large changes. However, short-term interventions are possible if things are not going to plan. By this time, demand will be assessed on a totally disaggregated basis, with all types of surgical procedures treated as individual activities. More importantly, individual patients will have been identified by name, and specific time slots booked for their treatment. In making short-term interventions and changes to the plan, operations managers will be attempting to balance the quality, speed, dependability, flexibility and costs of their operation on an *ad hoc* basis. It is unlikely that they will have the time to carry out detailed calculations of the effects of their short-term planning and control decisions on all these objectives, but a general understanding of priorities will form the background to their decision making. Figure 10.2 shows how the control aspects of planning and control increase in significance closer to the date of the event.

Supply and demand effects on planning and control

If planning and control is the process of reconciling demand with supply, then the nature of the decisions taken to plan and control an operation will depend on both the nature of demand and the nature of supply in that operation. In this section, we examine some differences in

Short case
Operations control at Air France[2]

'In many ways a major airline can be viewed as one large planning problem which is usually approached as many independent, smaller (but still difficult) planning problems. The list of things which need planning seems endless: crews, reservation agents, luggage, flights, through trips, maintenance, gates, inventory, equipment purchases. Each planning problem has its own considerations, its own complexities, its own set of time horizons, its own objectives, but all are interrelated.'

Air France has eighty flight planners working 24-hour shifts in their flight planning office at Roissy, Charles de Gaulle. Their job is to establish the optimum flight routes, anticipate any problems such as weather changes, and minimize fuel consumption. Overall the goals of the flight planning activity are first, and most important, safety followed by economy and passenger comfort. Increasingly powerful computer programs process the mountain of data necessary to plan the flights, but in the end many decisions still rely on human judgement. Even the most sophisticated expert systems only serve as support for the flight planners. Planning Air France's schedule is a massive job. Just some of the considerations which need to be taken into account include the following.

- *Frequency* – for each airport how many separate services should the airline provide?
- *Fleet assignment* – which type of plane should be used on each leg of a flight?
- *Banks* – at any airline hub where passengers arrive and may transfer to other flights to continue their journey, airlines like to organize flights into 'banks' of several planes which arrive close together, pause to let passengers change planes, and all depart close together. So, how many banks should there be and when should they occur?
- *Block times* – a block time is the elapsed time between a plane leaving the departure gate at an airport and arriving at its gate in the arrival airport. The longer the allowed block time the more likely a plane will be to keep to schedule even if it suffers minor delays. However, longer block times also mean fewer flights can be scheduled.
- *Planned maintenance* – any schedule must allow time for planes to have time at a maintenance base.
- *Crew planning* – pilot and cabin crew must be scheduled to allocate pilots to fly planes on which they are licensed and to keep within maximum 'on duty' times for all staff.
- *Gate plotting* – if many planes are on the ground at the same time there may be problems in loading and unloading them simultaneously.
- *Recovery* – many things can cause deviations from any plan in the airline industry. Allowances must be built in to allow for recovery.

For flights within and between Air France's 12 geographic zones, the planners construct a flight plan that will form the basis of the actual flight only a few hours later. All planning documents need to be ready for the flight crew who arrive two hours before the scheduled departure time. Being responsible for passenger safety and comfort, the captain always has the final say and, when satisfied, co-signs the flight plan together with the planning officer.

demand and supply which can affect the way in which operations managers plan and control their activities.

Uncertainty in supply and demand

Uncertainty makes both planning and control more difficult. Local village carnivals, for example, rarely work to plan. Events take longer than expected, some of the acts scheduled in the programme may be delayed *en route*, and some traders may not arrive. The event requires a good compère to keep it moving, keep the crowd amused, and in effect control the event. Demand may also be unpredictable. A fast-food outlet inside a shopping centre does not know how many people will arrive, when they will arrive and what they will order. It may be possible to predict certain patterns, such as an increase in demand over the lunch and tea-time periods, but a sudden rainstorm that drives shoppers indoors into the centre could significantly increase demand. Conversely, other operations are reasonably predictable, and the need for control is minimal. For example, cable TV services provide programmes to a schedule into subscribers' homes. It is rare to change the programme plan. Demand may also be predictable. In a school, for example, once classes are fixed and the term or semester has started, a teacher knows how many pupils are in the class. A combination of uncertainty in the operation's ability to supply, and in the demand for its products and services, is particularly difficult to plan and control.

Dependent and independent demand

Some operations can predict demand with more certainty than others. For example, consider an operation providing professional decorating and refurbishment services which has as its customers a number of large hotel chains. Most of these customers plan the refurbishment and decoration of their hotels months or even years in advance. Because of this, the decoration company can itself plan its activities in advance. Its own demand is dependent upon the relatively predictable activities of its customers. By contrast, a small painter and decorator serves the domestic and small business market. Some business also comes from house construction companies, but only when their own painters and decorators are fully occupied. In this case, demand on the painting and decorating company is relatively unpredictable. To some extent, there is a random element in demand which is virtually independent of any factors obvious to the company.

Dependent demand

Dependent demand, then, is demand which is relatively predictable because it is dependent upon some factor which is known. For example, the manager who is in charge of ensuring that there are sufficient tyres in an automobile factory will not treat the demand for tyres as a totally random variable. He or she will not be totally surprised by the exact quantity of tyres which are required by the plant every day. The process of demand forecasting is relatively straightforward. It will consist of examining the manufacturing schedules in the car plant and deriving the demand for tyres from these. If 200 cars are to be manufactured on a particular day, then it is simple to calculate that 1,000 tyres will be demanded by the car plant (each car has five tyres) – demand is dependent on a known factor, the number of cars to be manufactured. Because of this, the tyres can be ordered from the tyre manufacturer to a delivery schedule which is closely in line with the demand for tyres from the plant (as in Figure 10.3). In fact, the demand for every part of the car plant will be derived from the assembly schedule for the finished cars. Manufacturing instructions and purchasing requests will all be dependent upon this figure.

Independent demand

Some operations are subject to **independent demand**. They will supply demand without having any firm forward visibility of customer orders. For example, customers do not have to inform a supermarket when they are arriving and what they will buy. The supermarket takes its planning and control decisions based on its experience and understanding of the market, independent of what may actually happen. They run the risk of being out of stock of items when demand does not match their expectations. For example, the Ace Tyre Company, which operates a drive-in tyre replacement service, will need to manage a stock of tyres. In that sense it is exactly the same task that faced the manager of tyre stocks in the car plant. However, demand is very different for Ace Tyre. It cannot predict either the volume or the specific needs of customers. It must make decisions on how many and what type of tyres to stock, based on demand forecasts and in the light of the risks it is prepared to run of being out of stock. This is the nature of *independent demand planning and control*. It makes 'best guesses' concerning future demand, attempts to put the resources in place which can satisfy this demand, and attempts to respond quickly if actual demand does not match the forecast.

Responding to demand

In conditions of dependent demand, an operation will only start the process of producing goods or services when it needs to. Each order triggers the planning and control activities to

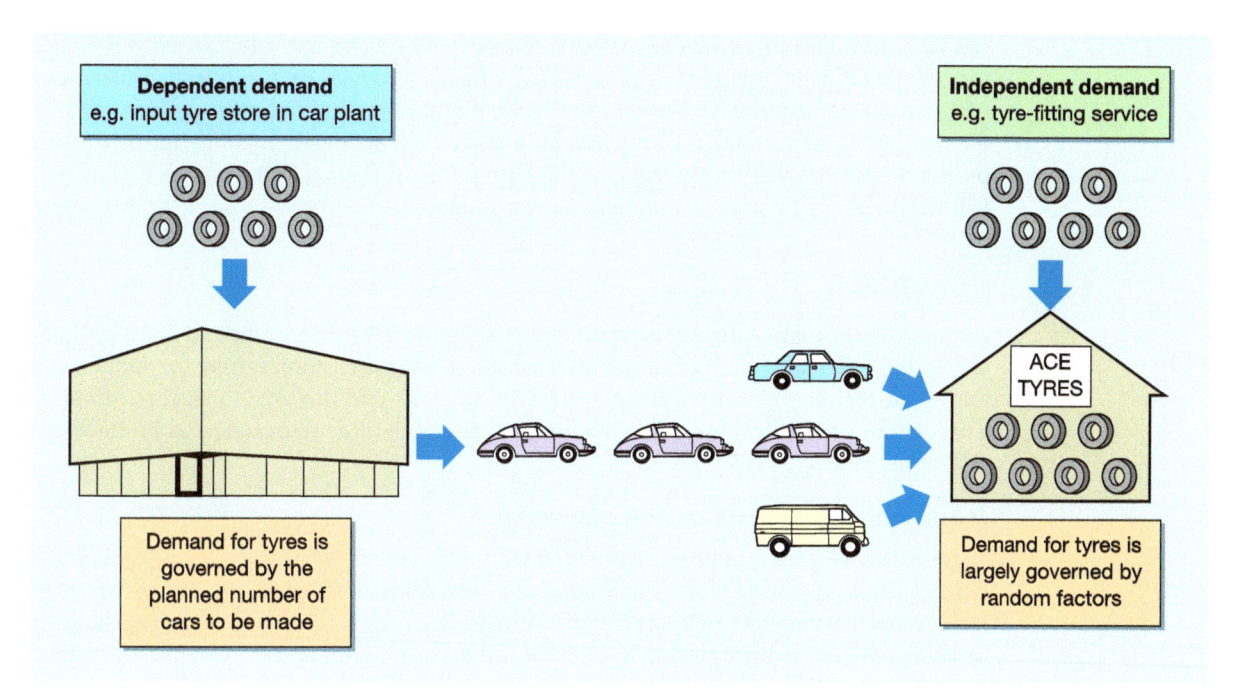

Figure 10.3 Dependent demand is derived from the demand for something else; independent demand is more random

organize their production. For example, a specialist housebuilder might only start the process of planning and controlling the construction of a house when requested to do so by the customer. The builder might not even have the resources to start building before the order is received. The material that will be necessary to build the house will be purchased only when the timing and nature of the house are certain. The staff and the construction equipment might also be 'purchased' only when the nature of demand is clear. In a similar way, a specialist conference organizer will start planning for an event only when specifically requested to do so by the clients. A venue will be booked, speakers organized, meals arranged and the delegates contacted only when the nature of the service is clear. The planning and control necessary for this kind of operation can be called **resource-to-order** planning and control.

Resource-to-order

Other operations might be sufficiently confident of the nature of demand, if not its volume and timing, to keep 'in stock' most of the resources it requires to satisfy its customers. Certainly it will keep its transforming resources, if not its transformed resources. However, it would still make the actual product or service only to a firm customer order. For example, a house builder who has standard designs might choose to build each house only when a customer places a firm order. Because the design of the house is relatively standard, suppliers of materials will have been identified, even if the building operation does not keep the items in stock itself. The equivalent in the conference business would be a conference centre which has its own 'stored' permanent resources (the building, staff, etc.) but only starts planning a conference when it has a firm booking. In both cases, the operations would need **create-to-order or make-to-order** planning and control.

Create-to-order and make-to-order

Some operations produce services or products ahead of any firm orders 'to stock'. For example, some builders will construct pre-designed standard houses or apartments ahead of any firm demand for them. This will be done either because it is less expensive to do so or because it is difficult to create the goods or services on a one-off basis (it is difficult to make each apartment only when a customer chooses to buy one). If demand is high, customers may place requests for houses before they are started or during their construction. In this case, the customer will form a backlog of demand and must wait. The builder is also taking the risk, however, of holding a stock of unsold houses if buyers do not come along before they are finished. In fact, it is difficult for small builders to operate in this way, but less so for (say) a bottled cola manufacturer or other mass producer. The equivalent in the conference market would be a conference centre which schedules a series of events and conferences, programmed in advance and open to individual customers to book into or even turn up on the day. Cinemas and theatres usually work in this manner. Their performances are produced and supplied irrespective of the level of actual demand. Operations of this type will require **make-to-stock** planning and control.

P:D ratios[3]

Another way of characterizing the graduation between resource-to-order and make-to-stock is by using a *P:D ratio*. This contrasts the total length of time customers have to wait between asking for the service and receiving it, demand time, D, and the total throughput time, P. Throughput time is how long the operation takes to obtain the resources, and produce and deliver the service.

P and D times depend on the operation

Make-to-stock operations produce their services and products in advance of any demand. For example, in an operation making consumer durables, demand time, D, is the sum of the times for transmitting the order to the company's warehouse or stock point, picking and packing the order and physically transporting it to the customer. Behind this visible order cycle, however, lie other cycles. Reduction in the finished goods stock will eventually trigger the decision to manufacture a replenishment batch. This 'produce' cycle involves scheduling work in the manufacturing process. Behind the 'produce' cycle lies the 'obtain resources' cycle – the time for obtaining the input stocks. So, for this type of operation, the 'demand' time which the customer sees is very short compared with the total 'throughput' cycle. Contrast this with a resource-to-order operation. Here, D is the same as P. Both include the 'obtain resources', 'produce' and 'delivery' cycles. The produce-to-order operation lies in between these two (see Figure 10.4).

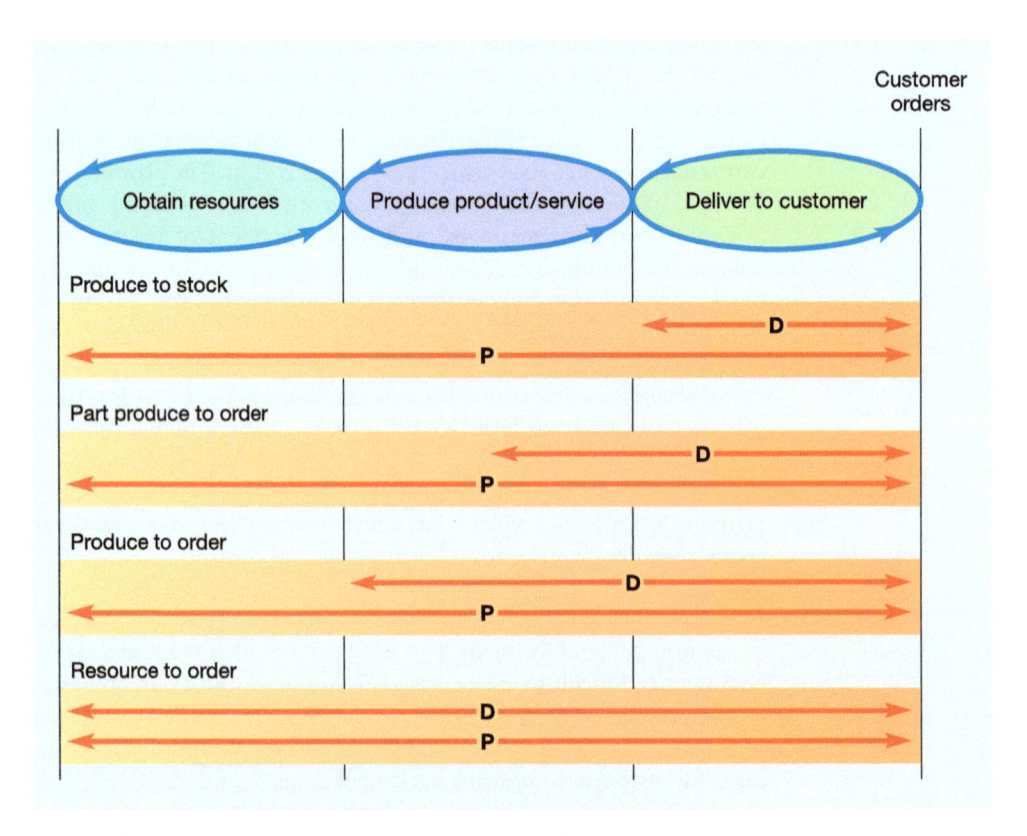

Figure 10.4 *P* and *D* for the different types of planning and control

P:D ratios indicate the degree of speculation

Reducing total throughput time *P* will have varying effects on the time the customer has to wait for demand to be filled. In resource-to-order operations, *P* and *D* are the same. Speeding up any part of *P* will reduce customer's waiting time, *D*. On the other hand, in 'produce-to-stock' operations, customers would only see reduced *D* time if the 'deliver' part of *P* were reduced. Also, in Figure 10.4, *D* is always shown as being smaller than *P*, which is the case for most companies. How much smaller *D* is than *P* is important because it indicates the proportion of the operation's activities which are speculative, that is, carried out on the expectation of eventually receiving a firm order for its efforts. The larger *P* is compared with *D*, the higher the proportion of speculative activity in the operation and the greater the risk the operation carries. The speculative element in the operation is there because demand cannot be forecast perfectly. With exact or close to exact forecasts, risk would be non-existent or very low, no matter how much bigger *P* was than *D*. Expressed another way: when *P* and *D* are equal, no matter how inaccurate the forecasts are, speculation is eliminated because everything is resourced and made to a firm order (although bad forecasting will lead to other problems). Reducing the *P:D* ratio becomes, in effect, a way of taking some of the risk out of operations planning and control.

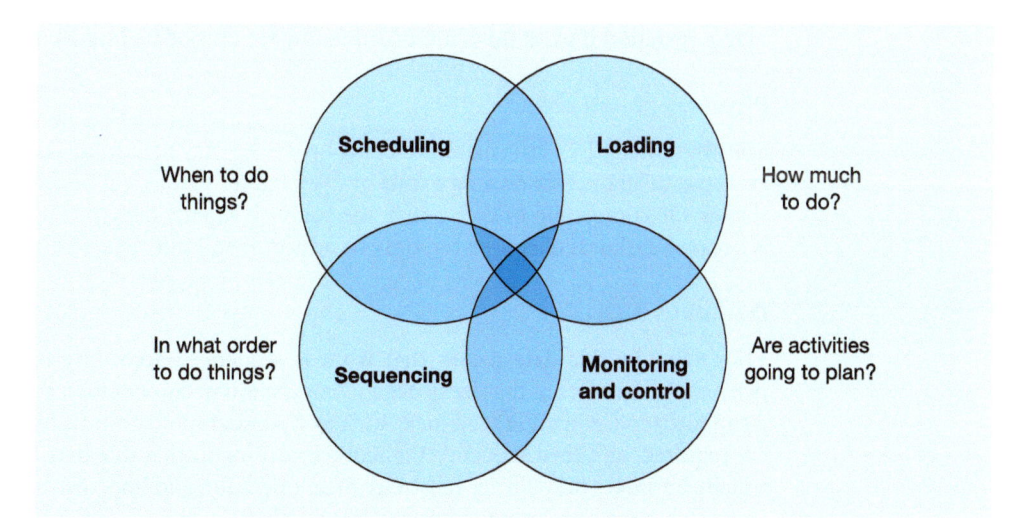

Planning and control activities

There are four overlapping activities: loading, sequencing, scheduling, and monitoring and control that together form the planning and control task (see Figure 10.5). Some caution is needed when using these terms. Different organizations may use them in different ways, and even textbooks in the area adopt different definitions. For example, some authorities describe what we have called 'planning and control' as 'operations scheduling'. However, the terminology of planning and control is less important than understanding the basic ideas.

Loading

Loading is the amount of work that is allocated to a part of an operation. For example, a machine on the shop floor of a manufacturing business is available, in theory, 168 hours

Figure 10.5 Planning and control activities

a week. However, this does not necessarily mean that 168 hours of work can be loaded onto that machine. For some periods the machine cannot be worked; for example, it may not be available on statutory holidays and weekends. Therefore, the load put onto the machine must take this into account. Of the time that the machine is available for work, other losses further reduce the available time. For example, time may be lost while changing over from making one component to another. If the machine breaks down, it will not be available. If there is machine reliability data available, this must also be taken into account. Sometimes the machine may be waiting for parts to arrive or be 'idling' for some other reason. Other losses could include an allowance for the machine being run below its optimum speed (for example, because it has not been maintained properly) and an allowance for the 'quality losses' or defects which the machine may produce. Likewise, in a service-dominant operation it may not be appropriate to schedule workers for 8 hours per day. Loading will need to take into account rest breaks, idle time, changing from one task to another, and boredom reducing actual time available, for example. Of course, many of these losses should be small or non-existent in a well-managed operation. However, the **valuable operating time** available for productive working, even in the best operations, can be significantly below the maximum time available.

Sequencing

When work arrives at any part of an operation decisions must be taken on the order in which the work will be tackled. This activity is termed **sequencing**. The priorities given to work in an operation are often determined by some predefined set of rules, some of which are summarized below.

Customer priority

Operations will sometimes use **customer priority sequencing**, which allows an important or aggrieved customer (or item) to be 'processed' prior to others, irrespective of the order of arrival. This approach is typically used by operations whose customer base is skewed, containing a mass of small customers and a few large, very important customers. Some banks, for example, give priority to important customers. The emergency services often have to use their judgement in prioritizing the urgency of requests for service. For example, in the priority system used by police forces the operators receiving emergency and other calls are trained to grade the calls into priority categories. The response by the police is then organized to match the level of priority. The triage system in hospitals operates in a similar way (see short case). However, customer priority sequencing, although giving a high level of service to some customers, may erode the service given to many others. This may lower the overall performance of the operation if work flows are disrupted to accommodate important customers.

Physical constraints

The physical nature of the materials being processed may determine the priority of work. For example, in an operation using paints or dyes, lighter shades will be sequenced before darker shades. On completion of each batch, the colour is slightly darkened for the next batch. This is because darkness of colour can only be added to and not removed from the colour mix.

Due date (DD)

Prioritizing by due date means that work is sequenced according to when it is 'due' for delivery, irrespective of the size of each job or the importance of each customer. For example, a support service in an office block, such as a reprographic unit, will often ask when copies are required, and then sequence the work according to that due date. **Due date sequencing** usually improves the delivery reliability of an operation and improves average delivery speed. However, it may not provide optimal productivity, as a more efficient sequencing of work may reduce total costs.

Short case
The hospital triage system[4]

One of the hospital environments that is most difficult to sequence is the Accident and Emergency department, where patients arrive at random, without any prior warning, throughout the day. It is up to the hospital's reception and the medical staff to devise very rapidly a schedule which meets most of the necessary criteria. In particular, patients who arrive having had very serious accidents, or presenting symptoms of a serious illness, need to be attended to urgently. Therefore, the hospital will sequence these cases first. Less urgent cases – perhaps patients who are in some discomfort, but whose injuries or illnesses are not life-threatening – will have to wait until the urgent cases are treated. Routine non-urgent cases will have the lowest priority of all. In many circumstances, these patients will have to wait for the longest time, which may be many hours, especially if the hospital is busy. Sometimes these non-urgent cases may even be turned away if the hospital is too busy with more important cases. In situations where hospitals expect sudden influxes of patients, they have developed what is known as a triage system, whereby medical staff hurriedly sort through the patients who have arrived to determine which category of urgency each patient fits into. In this way a suitable schedule for the various treatments can be devised in a short period of time.

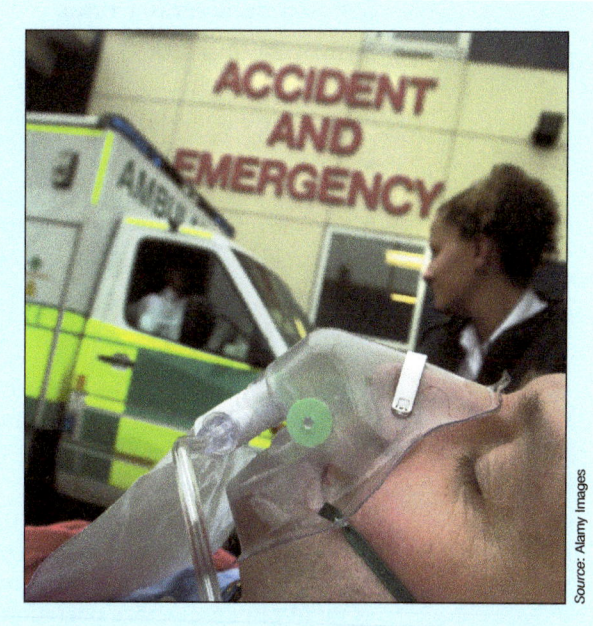

Last-in first-out (LIFO)

Last-in first-out sequencing

Last-in first-out (LIFO) is a method of sequencing usually selected for practical reasons. For example, unloading an elevator is more convenient on a LIFO basis, as there is only one entrance and exit. However, it is not an equitable approach. Patients at hospital clinics may be infuriated if they see newly arrived patients examined first.

First-in first-out (FIFO)

First-in first-out sequencing

Some operations serve customers in exactly the sequence they arrive in. This is called **first-in first-out sequencing** (FIFO), or sometimes 'first come, first served' (FCFS). For example, passport offices receive mail, and sort it according to the day when it arrived. They work through the mail, opening it in sequence, and process the passport applications in order of arrival.

Longest operation time (LOT)

Longest operation time sequencing

Operations may feel obliged to sequence their longest jobs first in the system called **longest operation time sequencing**. This has the advantage of occupying work centres for long periods. By contrast, relatively small jobs progressing through an operation will take up time at each work centre because of the need to change over from one job to the next. However, although longest operation time sequencing keeps utilization high, this rule does not take into account delivery speed, reliability or flexibility.

Shortest operation time first (SOT)

Shortest operation time sequencing

Most operations at some stage become cash-constrained. Larger jobs that take more time will not enable the business to invoice as quickly. In these situations, the sequencing rules may be adjusted to tackle short jobs first in the system, called **shortest operation time sequencing**. These jobs can then be invoiced and payment received to ease cash-flow problems. This has an effect of improving delivery performance, if the unit of measurement is delivery of jobs. However, it may adversely affect total productivity and can damage service to larger customers.

Judging sequencing rules

All five performance objectives, or some variant of them, could be used to judge the effectiveness of sequencing rules. However, the objectives of dependability, speed and cost are particularly important. So, for example, the following performance objectives are often used:

- Meeting 'due date' promised to customer (dependability);
- Minimizing the time the job spends in the process, also known as 'flow time' (speed);
- Minimizing work-in-progress inventory (an element of cost);
- Minimizing idle time of work centres (another element of cost).

Scheduling

Having determined the sequence that work is to be tackled in, some operations require a detailed timetable showing at what time or date jobs should start and when they should end – this is **scheduling**. Schedules are familiar statements of volume and timing in many consumer environments. For example, a bus schedule shows that more buses are put on routes at more frequent intervals during rush-hour periods. The bus schedule shows the time each bus is due to arrive at each stage of the route. Schedules of work are used in operations where some planning is required to ensure that customer demand is met. Other operations, such as rapid-response service operations where customers arrive in an unplanned way, cannot schedule the operation in a short-term sense. They can only respond at the time demand is placed upon them.

The complexity of scheduling[5]

The scheduling activity is one of the most complex tasks in operations management. Firstly, schedulers must deal with several different types of resource simultaneously. Machines will have different capabilities and capacities; staff will have different skills. More importantly, the number of possible schedules increases rapidly as the number of activities and processes increases. For example, suppose one machine has five different jobs to process. Any of the five jobs could be processed first and, following that, any one of the remaining four jobs, and so on. This means that there are:

$$5 \times 4 \times 3 \times 2 = 120 \text{ different schedules possible}$$

More generally, for n jobs there are $n!$ (factorial n) different ways of scheduling the jobs through a single process. We can now consider what impact there would be if, in the same situation, there was more than one type of machine. If we were trying to minimize the number of set-ups on two machines, there is no reason why the sequence on machine 1 would be the same as the sequence on machine 2. If we consider the two sequencing tasks to be independent of each other, for two machines there would be:

$$120 \times 120 = 14{,}400 \text{ possible schedules of the two machines and five jobs.}$$

A general formula can be devised to calculate the number of possible schedules in any given situation, as follows:

$$\text{Number of possible schedules} = (n!)m$$

where n is the number of jobs and m is the number of machines. In practical terms, this means that there are often many millions of feasible schedules, even for relatively small operations. This is why scheduling rarely attempts to provide an 'optimal' solution but rather satisfies itself with an 'acceptable' feasible one.

Forward and backward scheduling

Forward scheduling involves starting work as soon as it arrives. **Backward scheduling** involves starting jobs at the last possible moment to prevent them from being late. For example, assume that it takes six hours for a contract laundry to wash, dry and press a batch of overalls. If the work is collected at 8.00 am and is due to be picked up at 4.00 pm, there are more than six hours available to do it. Table 10.1 shows the different start times of each job, depending on whether they are forward- or backward-scheduled.

Table 10.1 The effects of forward and backward scheduling

Task	Duration	Start time (backwards)	Start time (forwards)
Press	1 hour	3.00 pm	1.00 pm
Dry	2 hours	1.00 pm	11.00 am
Wash	3 hours	10.00 am	8.00 am

The choice of backward or forward scheduling depends largely upon the circumstances. Table 10.2 lists some advantages and disadvantages of the two approaches.

Table 10.2 Advantages of forward and backward scheduling

Advantages of forward scheduling	Advantages of backward scheduling
High labour utilization – workers always start work to keep busy	Lower material costs – materials are not used until they have to be, therefore delaying added value until the last moment
Flexible – the time slack in the system allows unexpected work to be loaded	Less exposed to risk in case of schedule change by the customer Tends to focus the operation on customer due dates

Gantt charts

Gantt chart

The most common method of scheduling is by use of the **Gantt chart**. This is a simple device which represents time as a bar, or channel, on a chart. The start and finish times for activities can be indicated on the chart and sometimes the actual progress of the job is also indicated. The advantages of Gantt charts are that they provide a simple visual representation both of what should be happening and of what actually is happening in the operation. Furthermore, they can be used to 'test out' alternative schedules. It is a relatively simple task to represent alternative schedules (even if it is a far from simple task to find a schedule which fits all the resources satisfactorily). Figure 10.6 illustrates a Gantt chart for a specialist software developer. It indicates the progress of several jobs as they are expected to progress through five stages of the process. Gantt charts are not an optimizing tool, they merely facilitate the development of alternative schedules by communicating them effectively.

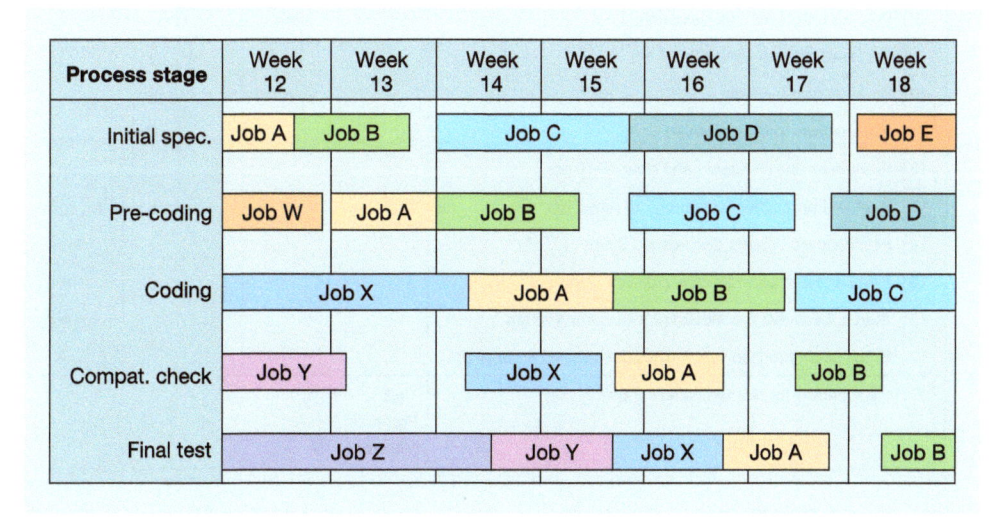

Figure 10.6 Gantt chart showing the schedule for jobs at each process stage

Short case
The life and times of a chicken salad sandwich[6]

Pre-packed sandwiches are a growth product around the world as consumers put convenience and speed above relaxation and cost. But if you have recently consumed a pre-packed sandwich, think about the schedule of events which has gone into its making. For example, take a chicken salad sandwich. Less than 5 days ago, the chicken was on the farm unaware that it would never see another weekend. The Gantt chart schedule shown in Figure 10.7 tells the story of the sandwich, and (posthumously), of the chicken.

From the forecast, orders for non-perishable items are placed for goods to arrive up to a week in advance of their use. Orders for perishable items will be placed daily, a day or two before the items are required. Tomatoes, cucumbers and lettuces have a three-day shelf life so may be received up to three days before production. Stock is held on a strict first-in-first-out (FIFO) basis. If today is Wednesday, vegetables are processed that have been received during the last three days. This morning the bread arrived from a local bakery and the chicken arrived fresh, cooked and in strips ready to be placed directly in the sandwich during assembly. Yesterday (Tuesday) it had been killed, cooked, prepared and sent on its journey to the factory. By midday orders for tonight's production will have been received on the Internet. From 2.00 pm until 10.00 pm the production lines are closed down for maintenance and a very thorough cleaning. During this time the production planning team is busy planning the night's production run. Production for delivery to customers furthest away from the factory will have to be scheduled first. By 10 pm production is ready to start. Sandwiches are made on production lines. The bread is loaded onto a conveyor belt by hand and butter is spread automatically by a machine. Next the various fillings are applied at each stage according to the specified sandwich 'design', see Figure 10.8. After the filling has been assembled the top slice of bread is placed on the sandwich and machine-chopped into two triangles, packed and sealed by machine. It is now early Thursday morning and by 2.00 am the first refrigerated lorries are already departing on their journeys to various customers. Production continues through until 2.00 pm on the Thursday, after which once again the maintenance and cleaning teams move in. The last sandwiches are dispatched by 4.00 pm on the Thursday. There is no finished goods stock.

ID	Task name
1	Orders for tomorrow's fresh deliveries
2	Packaging for tonight's production arrives
3	Tomatoes arrive – whole
4	Cucumbers arrive – whole
5	Lettuces arrive – whole
6	Preparation (slice/wash/dry/portion)
7	Chickens killed
8	Prepared chicken meat despatched
9	Prepared chicken arrives 9–12 am
10	Bread arrives 9–12 am
11	EDI customer orders received
12	Production line shutdown and clean 2–10 pm
13	Start first production (assembly) 10 pm–2 am
14	First sandwich orders despatched 2 am
15	First sandwich order travels to distant depots
16	Start subsequent production runs (assembly) 2 am
17	Subsequent prod'ion sandwiches despatched 8 am–4 pm

Outline schedule for chicken salad sandwich

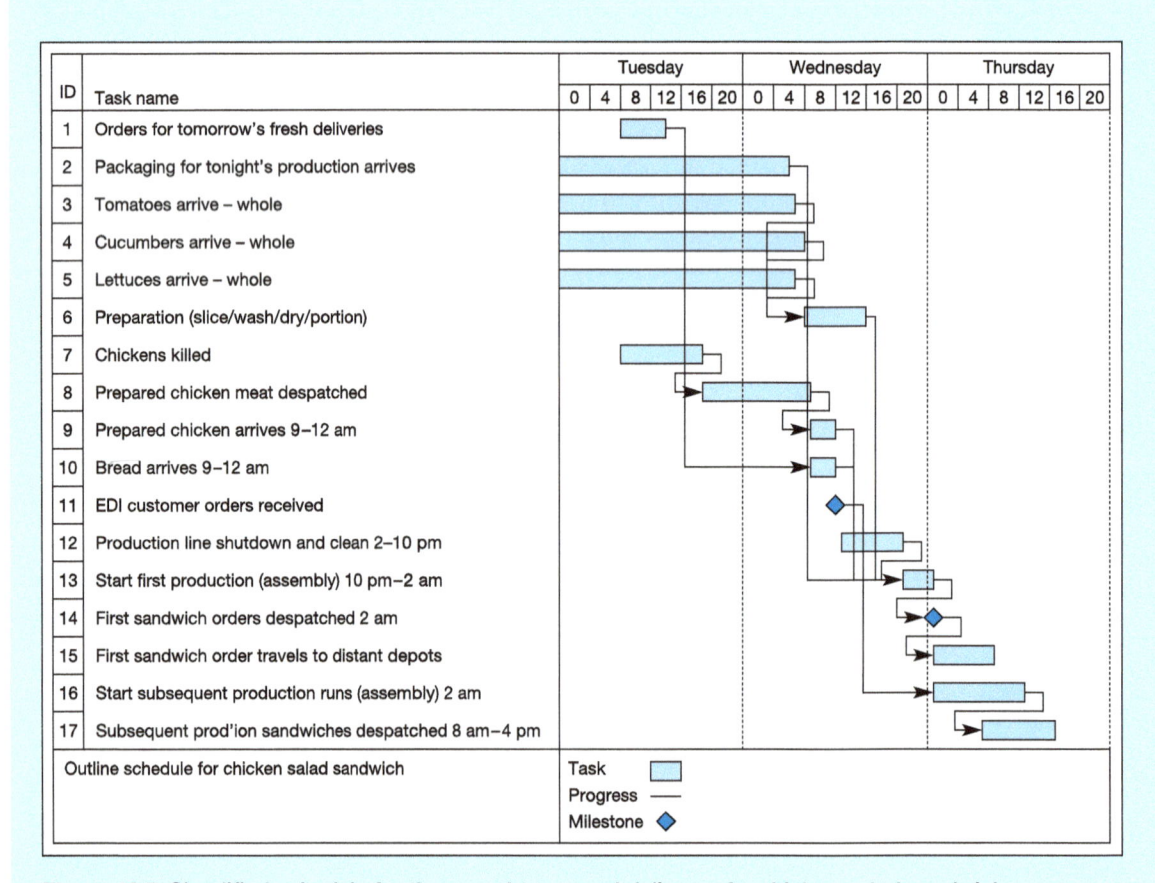

Figure 10.7 Simplified schedule for the manufacture and delivery of a chicken salad sandwich

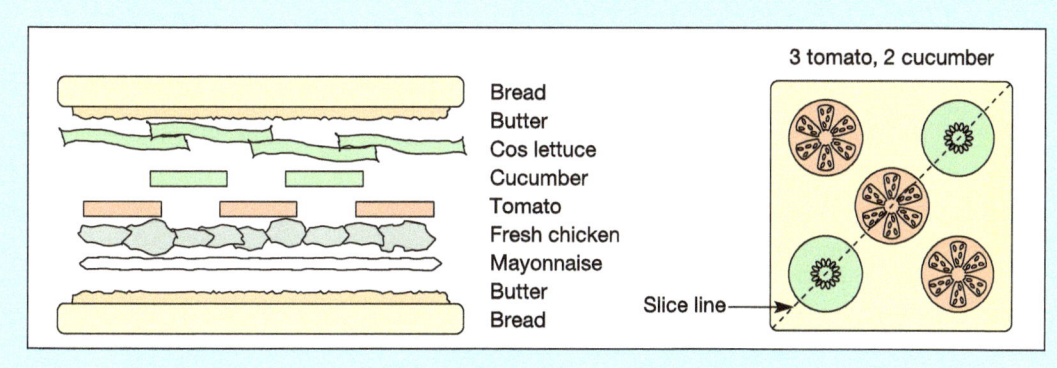

Figure 10.8 Design for a chicken salad sandwich

Scheduling work patterns

Where the dominant resource in an operation is its staff, then the schedule of work times effectively determines the capacity of the operation itself. The main task of scheduling, therefore, is to make sure that sufficient numbers of people are working at any point in time to provide a capacity appropriate for the level of demand at that point in time. This is often called **staff rostering**. Operations such as call centres, postal delivery, policing, holiday couriers, retail shops and hospitals will all need to schedule the working hours of their staff with demand in mind. This is a direct consequence of these operations having relatively high 'visibility'. Such operations cannot store their outputs in inventories and so must respond directly to customer demand. For example, Figure 10.9 shows the scheduling of shifts for a small technical 'hot line' support service for a small software company. It gives advice to customers on their technical problems. Its service times are 04.00 hrs to 20.00 hrs on Monday, 04.00 hrs to 22.00 hrs Tuesday to Friday, 06.00 hrs to 22.00 hrs on Saturday, and 10.00 hrs to 20.00 hrs on Sunday. Demand is heaviest Tuesday to Thursday, starts to decrease on Friday, is low over the weekend and starts to increase again on Monday.

The scheduling task for this kind of problem can be considered over different timescales, two of which are shown in Figure 10.9. During the day, working hours need to be agreed with individual staff members. During the week, days off need to be agreed. During the year, vacations, training periods and other blocks of time where staff are unavailable need to be agreed. All this has to be scheduled such that:

- capacity matches demand;
- the length of each shift is neither excessively long nor too short to be attractive to staff;

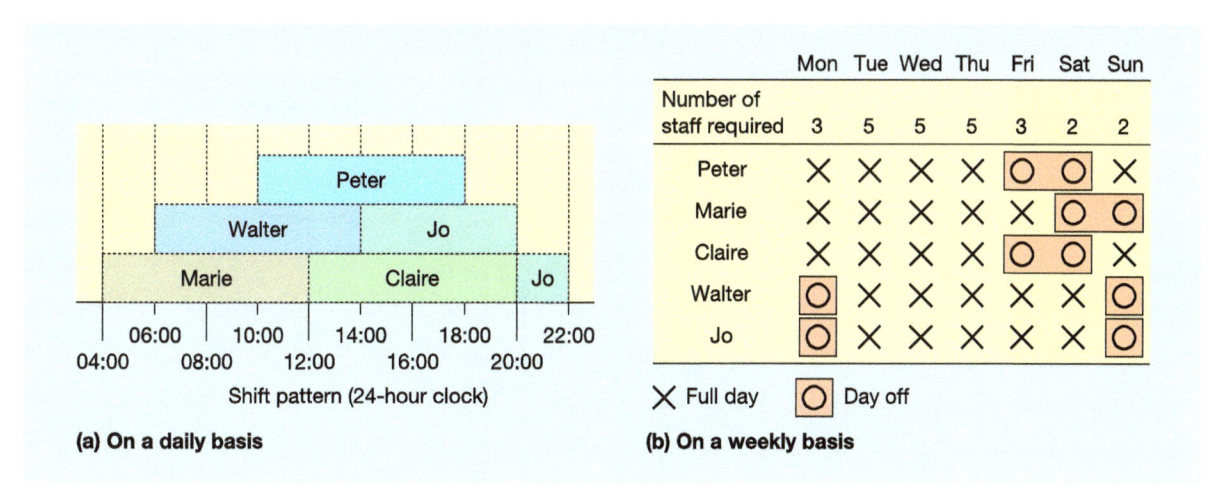

(a) On a daily basis

(b) On a weekly basis

Figure 10.9 Shift scheduling in a home-banking enquiry service

- working at unsocial hours is minimized;
- days off match agreed staff conditions (for example) in this example – staff prefer two consecutive days off every week;
- vacation and other 'time-off' blocks are accommodated;
- sufficient flexibility is built into the schedule to cover for unexpected changes in supply (staff illness) and demand (surge in customer calls).

Scheduling staff times is one of the most complex of scheduling problems. In the relatively simple example shown in Figure 10.9 we have assumed that all staff have the same level and type of skill. In very large operations with many types of skill to schedule and uncertain demand (for example a large hospital) the scheduling problem becomes extremely complex. Some mathematical techniques are available but most scheduling of this type is, in practice, solved using heuristics (rules of thumb), some of which are incorporated into commercially available software packages.

Monitoring and controlling the operation

Having created a plan for the operation through loading, sequencing and scheduling, each part of the operation has to be monitored to ensure that planned activities are indeed happening. Any deviation from the plans can then be rectified through some kind of intervention in the operation, which itself will probably involve some replanning. Figure 10.10 illustrates a simple view of control. The output from a work centre is monitored and compared with the plan which indicates what the work centre is supposed to be doing. Deviations from this plan are taken into account through a replanning activity and the necessary interventions made to the work centre which will ensure that the new plan is carried out. Eventually, some further deviation from planned activity will be detected and the cycle is repeated.

Push and pull control

One element of control is periodic intervention into the activities of the operation. An important decision is how this intervention takes place. The key distinction is between intervention signals which **push** work through the processes within the operation and those which **pull** work only when it is required. In a push system of control, activities are scheduled by means of a central system and completed in line with central instructions, such as an ERP system (see later). Each work centre pushes out work without considering whether the succeeding work centre can make use of it. Work centres are coordinated by means of the

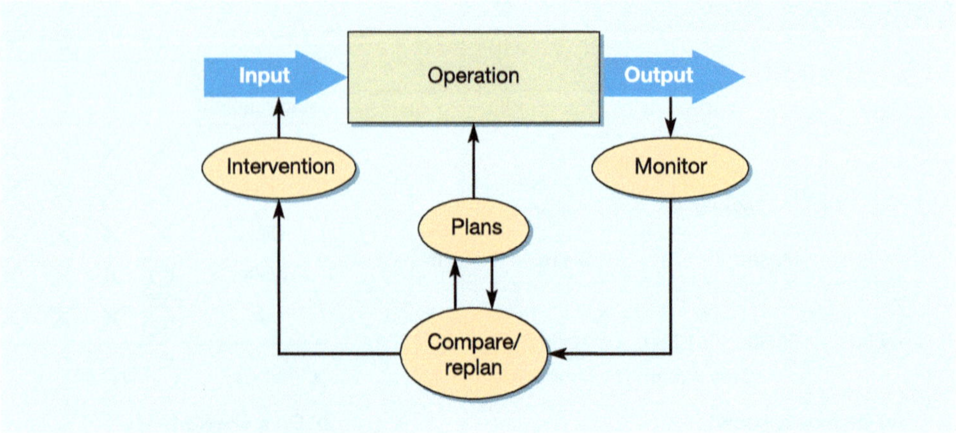

Figure 10.10 A simple model of control

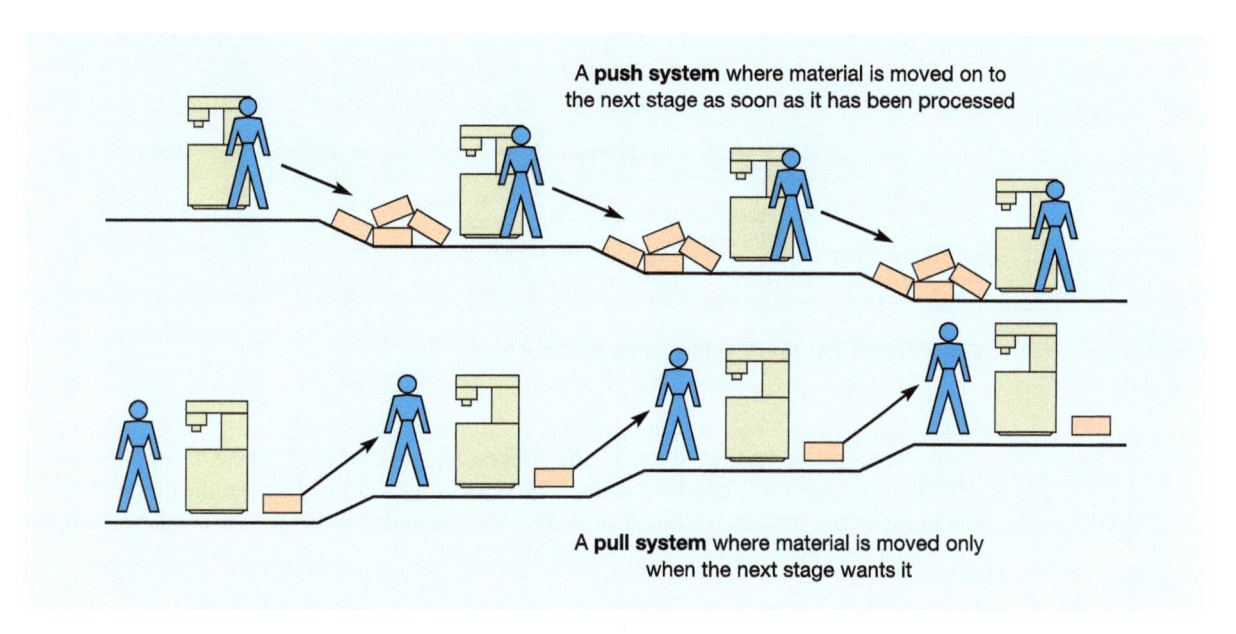

A push system where material is moved on to the next stage as soon as it has been processed

A pull system where material is moved only when the next stage wants it

Figure 10.11 Push versus pull: the gravity analogy

central operations planning and control system. In practice, however, there are many reasons why actual conditions differ from those planned. As a consequence, idle time, queues and inventory often characterize push systems. By contrast, in a pull system of control, the pace and specification of what is done are set by the 'customer' workstation, which 'pulls' work from the preceding (supplier) workstation. The customer acts as the only 'trigger' for movement. If a request is not passed back from the customer to the supplier, the supplier cannot do anything. A request from a customer not only triggers activity at the supplying stage, but also prompts the supplying stage to request a further delivery from its own suppliers. In this way, demand is transmitted back through the stages from the original point of demand by the original customer.

Understanding the differing principles of push and pull is important because they have different effects in terms of their propensities to accumulate inventory in the operation. Pull systems are far less likely to result in inventory build-up and are therefore favoured by lean operations (see Chapter 11).

Drum, buffer, rope

Drum, buffer, rope
Theory of constraints

The **drum, buffer, rope** concept comes from the **theory of constraints** (TOC) originally described by Eli Goldratt in his novel *The Goal*.[7] It is an idea that helps to decide exactly *where* in a process control should occur. Most operations do not have the same amount of work loaded onto each separate work centre (that is, they are not perfectly balanced). This means there is likely to be a part of the process which is acting as a bottleneck on the work flowing through the process. Goldratt argued that the bottleneck in the process should be the control point of the whole process. It is called the *drum* because it sets the 'beat' for the rest of the process to follow. Because it does not have sufficient capacity, a bottleneck is (or should be) working all the time. Therefore, it is sensible to keep a *buffer* of inventory in front of it to make sure that it always has something to work on. Because it constrains the output of the whole process, any time lost at the bottleneck will affect the output from the whole process. Therefore, it is not worthwhile for the parts of the process before the bottleneck to work to their full capacity. All they would do is produce work which

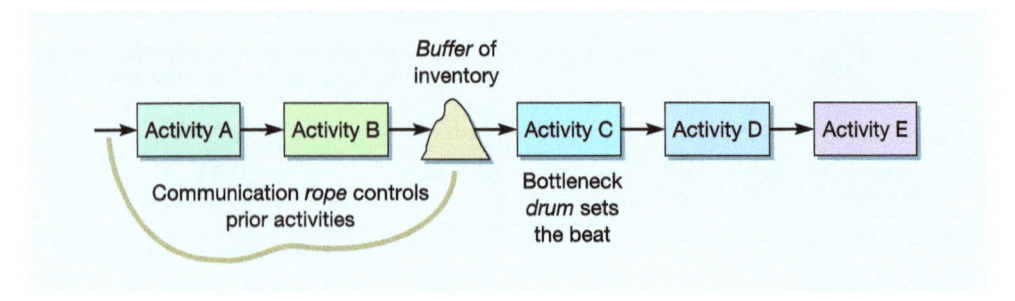

Figure 10.12 The drum, buffer, rope concept

would accumulate further along in the process up to the point where the bottleneck is constraining the flow. Therefore, some form of communication between the bottleneck and the input to the process is needed to make sure that activities before the bottleneck do not overproduce. This is called the *rope* (see Figure 10.12).

> ### Critical commentary
>
> Most of the perspectives on control taken in this chapter are simplifications of a far more messy reality. They are based on models used to understand mechanical systems such as car engines. But anyone who has worked in real organizations knows that organizations are not machines. They are social systems, full of complex and ambiguous interactions. Simple models such as these assume that operations objectives are always clear and agreed, yet organizations are political entities where different and often conflicting objectives compete. Local government operations, for example, are overtly political. Furthermore, the outputs from operations are not always easily measured. A university may be able to measure the number and qualifications of its students, for example, but it cannot measure the full impact of its education on their future happiness. Also, even if it is possible to work out an appropriate intervention to bring an operation back into 'control', most operations cannot perfectly predict what effect the intervention will have. Even the largest burger bar chain does not know *exactly* how a new shift allocation system will affect performance. Also, some operations never do the same thing more than once anyway. Most of the work done by construction operations is one-offs. If every output is different, how can 'controllers' ever know what is supposed to happen? Their plans themselves are mere speculation.

Enterprise resource planning (ERP)

One of the most important issues in planning and controlling operations is managing the sometimes vast amounts of information generated by the activity. It is not just the operations function that is the author and recipient of this information – almost every other function of a business will be involved. So, it is important that all relevant information that is spread throughout the organization is brought together. Then it can inform planning and control decisions such as when activities should take place, where they should happen, who should be doing them, how much capacity will be needed, and so on. This is what enterprise resource planning (ERP) does.

What is ERP?

Enterprise resource planning

An easy way of thinking about **enterprise resource planning** (ERP) is to imagine that you have decided to hold a party in two weeks' time and expect about 40 people to attend. As well as drinks, you decide to provide sandwiches and snacks. You will probably do some simple calculations, estimating guests' preferences and how much people are likely to drink and eat. You may already have some food and drink in the house which you will use, so you will take that into account when making your shopping list. If any of the food is to be cooked from a recipe, you may have to multiply up the ingredients to cater for 40 people. Also, you may also wish to take into account the fact that you will prepare some of the food the week before and freeze it, while you will leave the rest to either the day before or the day of the party. So, you will need to decide when each item is required so that you can shop in time. In fact, planning a party requires a series of interrelated decisions about the volume (quantity) and timing of the *materials* needed. This is the basis of the foundation concept for ERP called

Materials requirement planning

materials requirement planning (MRP). It is a process that helps companies make volume and timing calculations (similar to those in the party, but on a much larger scale, and with a greater degree of complexity). But your planning may extend beyond 'materials'. You may want to hire in a sound system from a local supplier – you will have to plan for this. The party also has financial implications. You may have to agree a temporary increase to your credit card limit. Again, this requires some forward planning and calculations of how much it is going to cost, and how much extra credit you require. Both the equipment and financial implications may vary if you increase the number of guests. But, if you postpone the party for a month, these arrangements will change. Also, there are also other implications of organizing the party. You will need to give friends, who are helping with the organization, an idea of when they should come and for how long. This will depend on the timing of the various tasks to be done (making sandwiches etc.).

So, even for this relatively simple activity, the key to successful planning is how we generate, integrate and organize all the information on which planning and control depends. Of course, in business operations it is more complex than this. Companies usually sell many different services and products to many hundreds of customers with constantly changing demands. This is a bit like organizing 200 parties one week, 250 the next and 225 the following week, all for different groups of guests with different requirements who keep changing their minds about what they want to eat and drink. This is what ERP does, it helps companies 'forward-plan' these types of decisions and understand all the implications of any changes to the plan.

How did ERP develop?

Enterprise resource planning is the latest, and the most significant, development of the original materials requirements planning (MRP) philosophy. The large companies which have grown almost exclusively on the basis of providing ERP systems include SAP and Oracle. Yet to understand ERP, it is important to understand the various stages in its development, summarized in Figure 10.13. The original MRP became popular during the 1970s, although the planning and control logic that underlies it had, by then, been known for some time. What popularized MRP was the availability of computer power to drive the basic planning and control mathematics.

Manufacturing Resource Planning

Manufacturing Resource Planning (MRP II) expanded out of MRP during the 1980s. Again, it was a technology innovation that allowed the development. Local-area networks (LANs), together with increasingly powerful desktop computers, allowed a much higher degree of processing power and communication between different parts of a business. Also MRP II's extra sophistication allowed the forward modelling of 'what-if' scenarios. The strength of MRP and MRP II lay always in the fact that it could explore the *consequences* of any changes to what an operation was required to do. So, if demand changed, the MRP system would calculate all the 'knock-on' effects and issue instructions accordingly. This

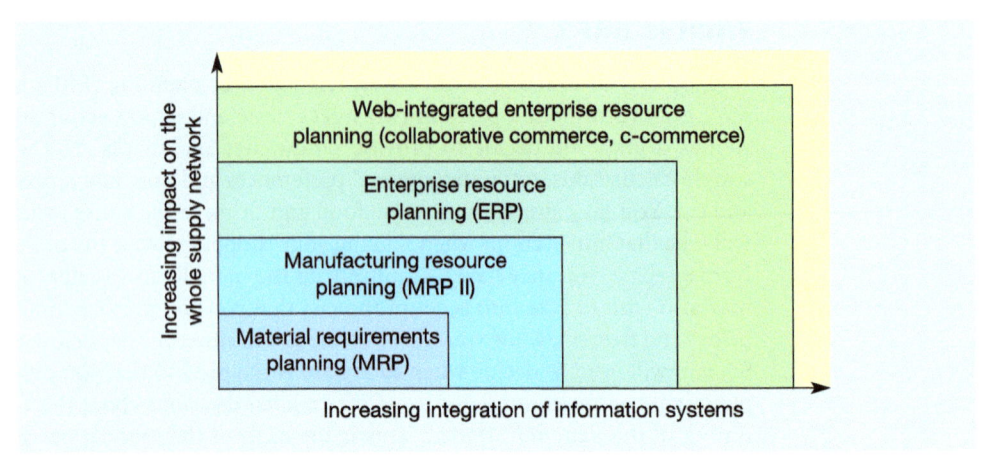

Figure 10.13 The development of ERP

Enterprise resource planning

same principle also applies to ERP, but on a much wider basis. **Enterprise resource planning** (ERP) has been defined as,

> '*a complete enterprise wide business solution. The ERP system consists of software support modules such as: marketing and sales, field service, product design and development, production and inventory control, procurement, distribution, industrial facilities management, process design and development, manufacturing, quality, human resources, finance and accounting, and information services. Integration between the modules is stressed without the duplication of information.*'[8]

So, ERP systems allow decisions and databases from all parts of the organization to be integrated so that the consequences of decisions in one part of the organization are reflected in the planning and control systems of the rest of the organization (see Figure 10.14). ERP is the equivalent of the organization's central nervous system, sensing information about the condition of different parts of the business and relaying the information to other parts of

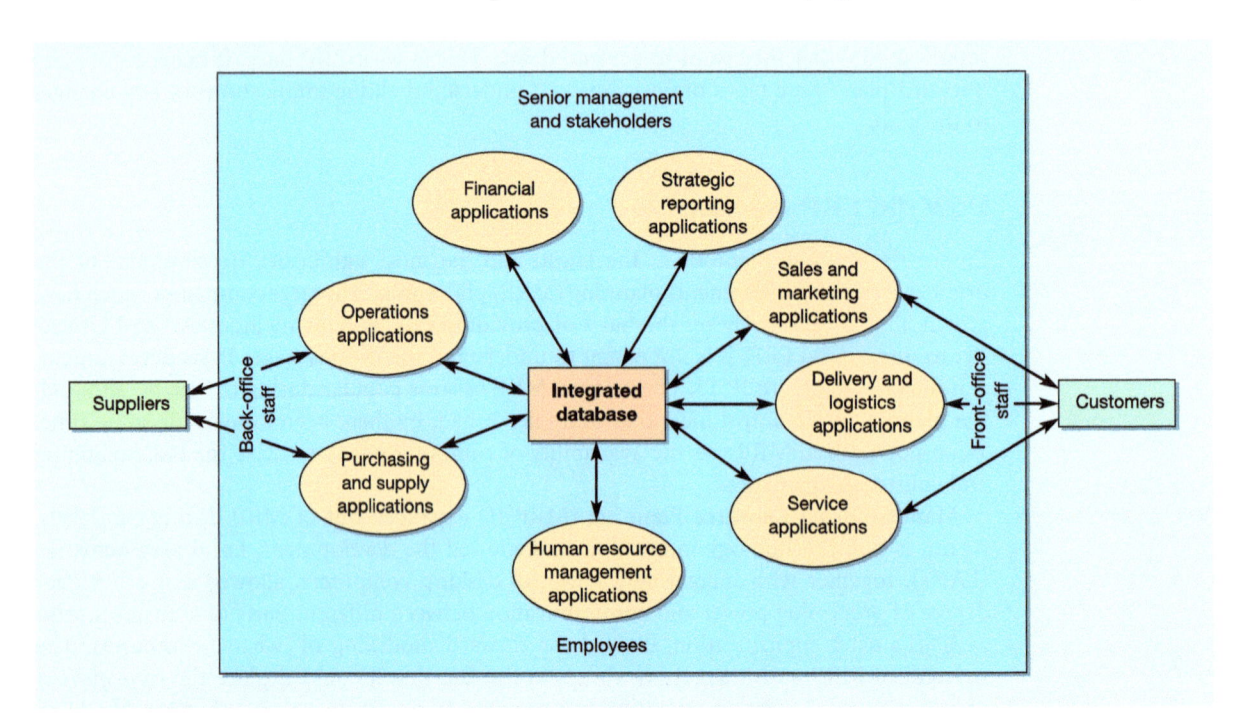

Figure 10.14 ERP integrates information from all parts of the organization

the business that need it. The information is updated in real time by those who use it and yet is always available to everyone connected to the ERP system.

Also, the potential of web-based communication has provided a further boost to ERP development. Many companies have suppliers, customers and other businesses with whom they collaborate who themselves have ERP-type systems. An obvious development is to allow these systems to communicate across supply networks. However, the technical, as well as organizational and strategic consequences of this can be formidable. Nevertheless, many authorities believe that the true value of ERP systems is only fully exploited when such **web-integrated ERP** (known by some people as 'collaborative commerce', or c-commerce) becomes widely implemented.

Web-integrated ERP

Summary answers to key questions

Check and improve your understanding of this chapter using self-assessment questions and a personalized study plan, audio and video downloads, and an eBook – all at www.myomlab.com.

▶ What is planning and control?

- Planning and control is the reconciliation of the potential of the operation to supply services and products, with the demands of its customers on the operation. It is the set of day-to-day activities that run the operation.
- A plan is a formalization of what is intended to happen at some time in the future. Control is the process of coping with changes to the plan and the operation to which it relates. Although planning and control are theoretically separable, they are usually treated together.
- The balance between planning and control changes over time. Planning dominates in the long term and is usually done on an aggregated basis. At the other extreme, in the short term, control usually operates within the resource constraints of the operation but makes interventions into the operation in order to cope with short-term changes in circumstances.

▶ How do supply and demand affect planning and control?

- The degree of uncertainty in demand affects the balance between planning and control. The greater the uncertainty, the more difficult it is to plan, and greater emphasis must be placed on control.
- This idea of uncertainty is linked with the concepts of dependent and independent demand. Dependent demand is relatively predictable because it is dependent on some known factor. Independent demand is less predictable because it depends on the chances of the market or customer behaviour.
- The different ways of responding to demand can be characterized by differences in the *P:D* ratio of the operation. The *P:D* ratio is the ratio of total throughput time of goods or services to demand time.

▶ What are the activities of planning and control?

- In planning and controlling the volume and timing of activity in operations, four distinct activities are necessary:
    - loading, which dictates the amount of work that is allocated to each part of the operation;
    - sequencing, which decides the order in which work is tackled within the operation;

- scheduling, which determines the detailed timetable of activities and when activities are started and finished;
- monitoring and control, which involve detecting what is happening in the operation, replanning if necessary, and intervening in order to impose new plans. Two important types are 'pull' and 'push' control. Pull control is a system whereby demand is triggered by requests from a work centre's (internal) customer. Push control is a centralized system whereby decisions are issued to work centres which are then required to perform the task and supply the next workstation.

> **How can enterprise resource planning (ERP) help planning and control?**

- ERP is an enterprise-wide information system that integrates all the information from many functions, that is needed for planning and controlling operations activities. This integration around a common database allows for transparency.
- ERP can be seen as the latest development from the original planning and control approach known as materials requirements planning (MRP).
- Although ERP is becoming increasingly competent at the integration of internal systems and databases, there is the even more significant potential of integration with other organizations' ERP (and equivalent) systems.

Learning exercises

These problems and applications will help to improve your analysis of operations. You can find more practice problems as well as worked examples and guided solutions on MyOMLab at www.myomlab.com.

1. Re-read the 'operations management in practice' at the beginning of the chapter, 'Joanne manages the schedule', and also the short case on Air France. What are the differences and what are the similarities between the planning and control tasks in these two operations?

2. A specialist sandwich retailer must order sandwiches at least 8 hours before they are delivered. When they arrive in the shop, they are immediately displayed in a temperature-controlled cabinet. The average time that the sandwiches spend in the cabinet is 6 hours. What is the *P:D* ratio for this retail operation?

3. *Step 1* – Make a list of all the jobs you have to do in the next week. Include in this list jobs relating to your work and/or study, jobs relating to your domestic life, in fact all the things you have to do.

   Step 2 – Prioritize all these jobs on a 'most important' to 'least important' basis.

   Step 3 – Draw up an outline schedule of exactly when you will do each of these jobs.

   Step 4 – At the end of the week compare what your schedule said you *would* do with what you actually *have* done. If there is a discrepancy, why did it occur?

   Step 5 – Draw up your own list of planning and control rules from your experience in this exercise in personal planning and control.

4. From your own experience of making appointments at your general practitioner's surgery, or by visiting whoever provides you with primary medical care, reflect on how patients are scheduled to see a doctor or nurse.

    (a) What do you think planning and control objectives are for a general practitioner's surgery?
    (b) How could your own medical practice be improved?

Want to know more?

Goldratt, E.Y. and Cox, J. (1984) *The Goal*, North River Press, Great Barrington, MA. Don't read this if you like good novels but do read it if you want an enjoyable way of understanding some of the complexities of scheduling. It particularly applies to the drum, buffer, rope concept described in this chapter.

Kehoe, D.F. and Boughton, N.J. (2001) New paradigms in planning and control across manufacturing supply chains – the utilization of Internet technologies, *International Journal of Operations and Production Management*, vol. 21, issue 5/6, 582–93.

Vollmann, T., Berry, W., Whybark, D.C. and Jacobs, F.R. (2004) *Manufacturing Planning and Control Systems for Supply Chain Management: The Definitive Guide for Professionals*, McGraw-Hill Higher Education, New York. The latest version of the 'bible' of planning and control.

Useful websites

www.bpic.co.uk/ Some useful information on general planning and control topics.

www.apics.org The American professional and education body that has its roots in planning and control activities.

www.opsman.org Lots of useful stuff.

Now that you have finished reading this chapter, why not visit MyOMLab at www.myomlab.com where you'll find more learning resources to help you make the most of your studies and get a better grade.

Chapter 11

Lean synchronization

Key questions

➤ What is lean synchronization?
➤ How does lean synchronization eliminate waste?
➤ How does lean synchronization apply throughout the supply network?

Introduction

This chapter examines an approach that we call 'lean synchronization' or just 'lean'. It was originally called 'just-in-time' (JIT) when it started to be adopted outside its birthplace, Japan. It is both a philosophy and a method of operations planning and control. Lean synchronization aims to meet demand instantaneously, with perfect quality and no waste. This involves supplying services and products in perfect synchronization with the demand for them. These principles were once a radical departure from traditional operations practice, but have now become orthodox in promoting the synchronization of flow through processes, operations and supply networks. Although we will focus on planning and control issues, in practice the 'lean' concept has much wider implications for improving operations performance. Figure 11.1 shows where this chapter fits into the overall operations model.

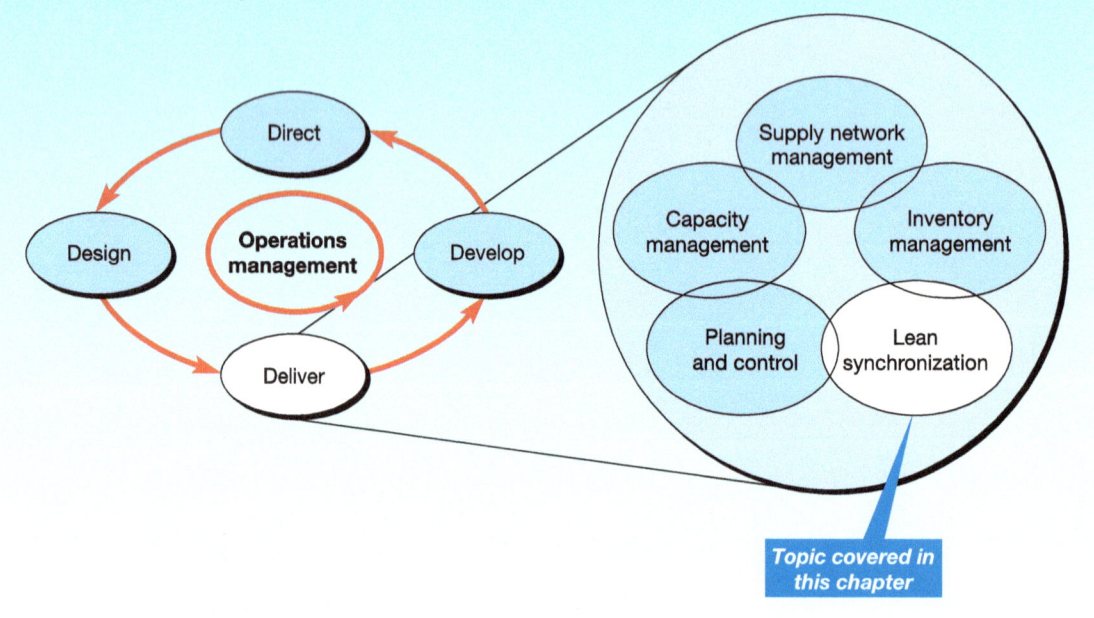

Figure 11.1 This chapter examines lean synchronization

Check and improve your understanding of this chapter using self-assessment questions and a personalized study plan, audio and video downloads, and an eBook – all at www.myomlab.com.

Operations in practice: Toyota

Seen as the leading practitioner and the main originator of the lean approach, the Toyota Motor Company has progressively synchronized all its processes simultaneously to give high-quality, fast throughput and exceptional productivity. It has done this by developing a set of practices that has largely shaped what we now call 'lean' or 'just-in-time' but which Toyota calls the Toyota Production System (TPS). The TPS has two themes, 'just-in-time' and 'jidoka'. Just-in-time is defined as the rapid and coordinated movement of parts throughout the production system and supply network to meet customer demand. It is operationalized by means of *heijunka* (levelling and smoothing the flow of items), *kanban* (signalling to the preceding process that more parts are needed) and *nagare* (laying out processes to achieve smoother flow of parts throughout the production process). *Jidoka* is described as 'humanizing the interface between operator and machine'. Toyota's philosophy is that the machine is there to serve the operator's purpose. The operator should be left free to exercise his or her judgement. Jidoka is operationalized by means of fail-safeing (or machine jidoka), line-stop authority (or human jidoka) and visual control (at-a-glance status of production processes and visibility of process standards).

Toyota believes that both just-in-time and jidoka should be applied ruthlessly to the elimination of waste, where waste is defined as 'anything other than the minimum amount of equipment, items, parts and workers that are absolutely essential to production'. Fujio Cho of Toyota identified seven types of waste that must be eliminated from all operations processes. They are: waste from over-production, waste from waiting time, transportation waste, inventory waste, processing waste, waste of motion and waste from product defects. Beyond this, authorities on Toyota claim that its strength lies in understanding the differences between the tools and practices used with Toyota operations and the overall philosophy of their approach to lean synchronization. This is what some have called the apparent paradox of the Toyota production system: 'namely, that activities, connections and production flows in a Toyota factory are rigidly scripted, yet at the same time Toyota's operations are enormously flexible and adaptable. Activities and processes are constantly being challenged and pushed to a higher level of performance, enabling the company to continually innovate and improve.'

One influential study of Toyota identified four rules that guide the design, delivery, and development activities within the company.[1]

- *Rule one* – all work shall be highly specified as to content, sequence, timing, and outcome.
- *Rule two* – every customer–supplier connection must be direct and there must be an unambiguous yes or no method of sending requests and receiving responses.
- *Rule three* – the route for every product and service must be simple and direct.
- *Rule four* – any improvement must be made in accordance with the scientific method, under the guidance of a teacher, and at the lowest possible level in the organization.

What is lean synchronization?

Synchronization

Synchronization means that the flow of products and services always delivers exactly what customers want (perfect quality), in exact quantities (neither too much nor too little), exactly when needed (not too early or too late), and exactly where required (not to the wrong location). *Lean* synchronization is to do all this at the lowest possible cost. It results in items flowing rapidly and smoothly through processes, operations and supply networks.

The benefits of synchronized flow

Lean
Just-in-time

When first introduced, the lean synchronization (or '**lean**' or '**just-in-time**') approach was relatively radical, even for large and sophisticated companies. Now the lean, just-in-time approach is being adopted outside its traditional automotive, high-volume and manufacturing roots. But wherever it is applied, the principles remain the same. The best way to understand how lean synchronization differs from more traditional approaches to managing flow is to contrast the two simple processes in Figure 11.2. The traditional approach assumes that each stage in the process will place its output in an inventory that 'buffers' that stage from the next one downstream in the process. The next stage down will then take outputs from the inventory, process them, and pass them through to the next buffer inventory. These buffers are there to insulate each stage from its neighbours, making each stage relatively independent so that if, for example, stage A stops operating for some reason, stage B can continue, at least for a time. The larger the buffer inventory, the greater the degree of insulation between the stages. This insulation has to be paid for in terms of inventory and slow throughput times because items will spend time waiting in the buffer inventories.

But, the main argument against this traditional approach lies in the very conditions it seeks to promote, namely the insulation of the stages from one another. When a problem occurs at one stage, the problem will not immediately be apparent elsewhere in the system. The responsibility for solving the problem will be centred largely on the people within that stage, and the consequences of the problem will be prevented from spreading to the whole system. However, contrast this with the pure lean synchronized process illustrated in Figure 11.2b.

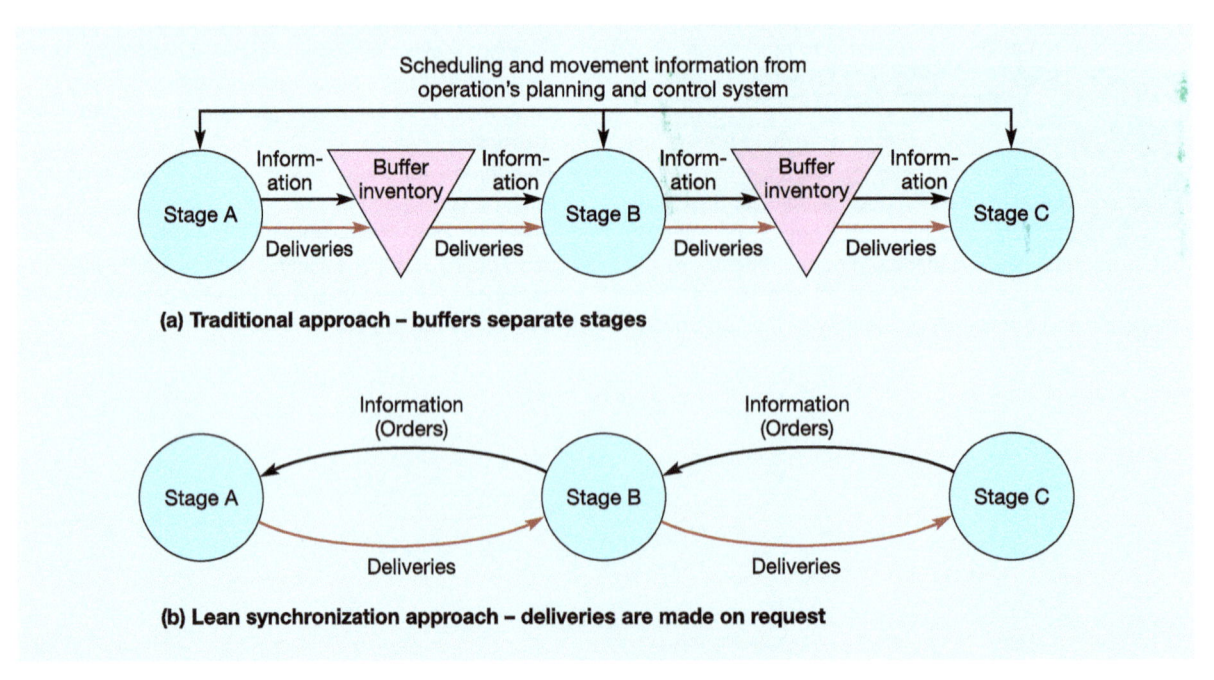

Figure 11.2 (a) Traditional and (b) lean synchronized flow between stages

Here items are processed and then passed directly to the next stage 'just-in-time' for them to be processed further. Problems at any stage have a very different effect in such a system. Now if stage A stops processing, stage B will notice immediately and stage C very soon after. Stage A's problem is now quickly exposed to the whole process, which is immediately affected by the problem. This means that the responsibility for solving the problem is no longer confined to the staff at stage A. It is now shared by everyone, considerably improving the chances of the problem being solved, if only because it is now too important to be ignored. In other words, by preventing items accumulating between stages, the operation has increased the chances of the intrinsic efficiency of the plant being improved.

Non-synchronized approaches seek to encourage efficiency by protecting each part of the process from disruption. The lean synchronized approach takes the opposite view. Exposure of the system to problems can both make them more evident and change the 'motivation structure' of the whole system towards solving the problems. Lean synchronization sees accumulations of inventory as a 'blanket of obscurity' that lies over the system and prevents problems being noticed. This same argument can be applied when, instead of queues of material, or information, an operation has to deal with queues of customers. Table 11.1 shows how certain aspects of inventory are analogous to certain aspects of queues.

Table 11.1 Inventories of materials, information or customers have similar characteristics

	Inventory		
	Of material (queue of material)	Of information (queue of information)	Of customers (queue of people)
Cost	Ties up working capital	Less current information and so worth less	Wastes customers' time
Space	Needs storage space	Needs memory capacity	Needs waiting area
Quality	Defects hidden, possible damage	Defects hidden, possible data corruption	Gives negative perception
De-coupling	Makes stages independent	Makes stages independent	Promotes job specialization/ fragmentation
Utilization	Stages kept busy by work-in-progress	Stages kept busy by work in data queues	Servers kept busy by waiting customers
Coordination	Avoids need for synchronization	Avoids need for straight-through processing	Avoids having to match supply and demand

Source: Adapted from Fitzsimmons, J.A. (1990) Making continual improvement: a competitive strategy for service firms, in Bowen, D.E., Chase, R.B., Cummings, T.G. and Associates (eds) *Service Management Effectiveness*, Copyright © 1990 Jossey-Bass. Reproduced with permission of John Wiley & Sons Inc.

The river and rocks analogy

The idea of obscuring effects of inventory is often illustrated diagrammatically, as in Figure 11.3. The many problems of the operation are shown as rocks in a river bed that cannot be seen because of the depth of the water. The water in this analogy represents the inventory in the operation. Yet, even though the rocks cannot be seen, they slow the progress of the river's flow and cause turbulence. Gradually reducing the depth of the water (inventory) exposes the worst of the problems which can be resolved, after which the water is lowered further, exposing more problems, and so on. The same argument will also apply for the flow between whole processes, or whole operations. For example, stages A, B and C in Figure 11.2 could be a supplier operation, a focal operation and a customer's operation, respectively.

Synchronization, 'lean' and 'just-in-time'

Different terms are used to describe what here we call 'lean synchronization'. Our definition – *'lean synchronization aims to meet demand instantaneously, with perfect quality and no*

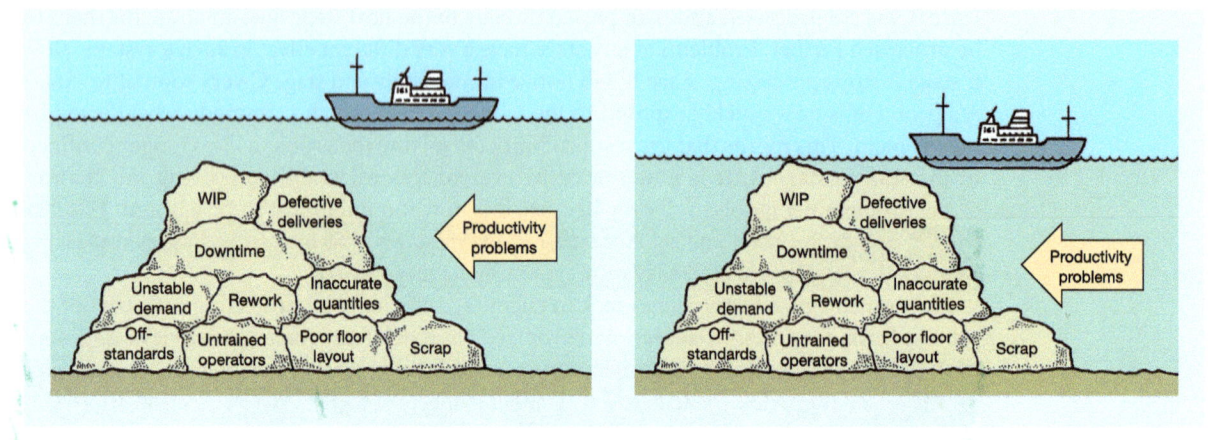

Figure 11.3 Reducing the level of inventory (water) allows operations management (the ship) to see the problems in the operation (the rocks) and work to reduce them

waste' – could also be used to describe the general concept of 'lean', or 'just-in-time' (JIT). The concept of 'lean' stresses the elimination of waste, while 'just-in-time' emphasizes the idea of producing items only when they are needed. But all three concepts overlap to a large degree, and no definition fully conveys the full implications for operations practice. Here we use the term 'lean synchronization' because it best describes the impact of these ideas on flow and delivery.

Lean synchronization and capacity utilization

Lean synchronization has many benefits but these come at the cost of capacity utilization. Return to the process shown in Figure 11.2. When stoppages occur in the traditional system, the buffers allow each stage to continue working and thus achieve high-capacity utilization. The high utilization does not necessarily make the process as a whole produce more. Often extra 'production' goes into buffer inventories. In a lean process, any stoppage will affect the whole process. This will necessarily lead to lower-capacity utilization, at least in the short term. However, there is no point in producing output just for its own sake. Unless the output is useful and allows the operation as a whole to produce saleable products or to process customers satisfactorily, there is no point in doing it anyway. In fact, working just to keep utilization high is not only pointless, it is counter-productive, because the extra inventory produced (or queues created in the case of customer-processing operations) merely serves to make improvements less likely. Figure 11.4 illustrates the two approaches to capacity utilization.

The lean philosophy

Lean synchronization can be viewed in different ways: as a broad philosophy of operations management, as a set of useful prescriptions of how to manage day-to-day operations, or a collection of tools and techniques for improving operations performance. Some of these tools and techniques are well known outside the lean sphere and relate to activities covered in other chapters of this book. As a philosophy, lean synchronization is founded on smoothing flow through processes by doing all the simple things well, on gradually doing them better and (above all) on squeezing out waste every step of the way. Three key issues define the lean philosophy: the involvement of staff in the operation, the drive for continuous improvement, and the elimination of waste. We will look at the first two issues briefly, but devote a whole section to the central idea of the elimination of waste.

The involvement of everyone

Lean philosophy is often put forward as a 'total' system. Its aim is to provide guidelines which embrace everyone and every process in the organization. An organization's culture is seen

Lean Synchronization   **293**

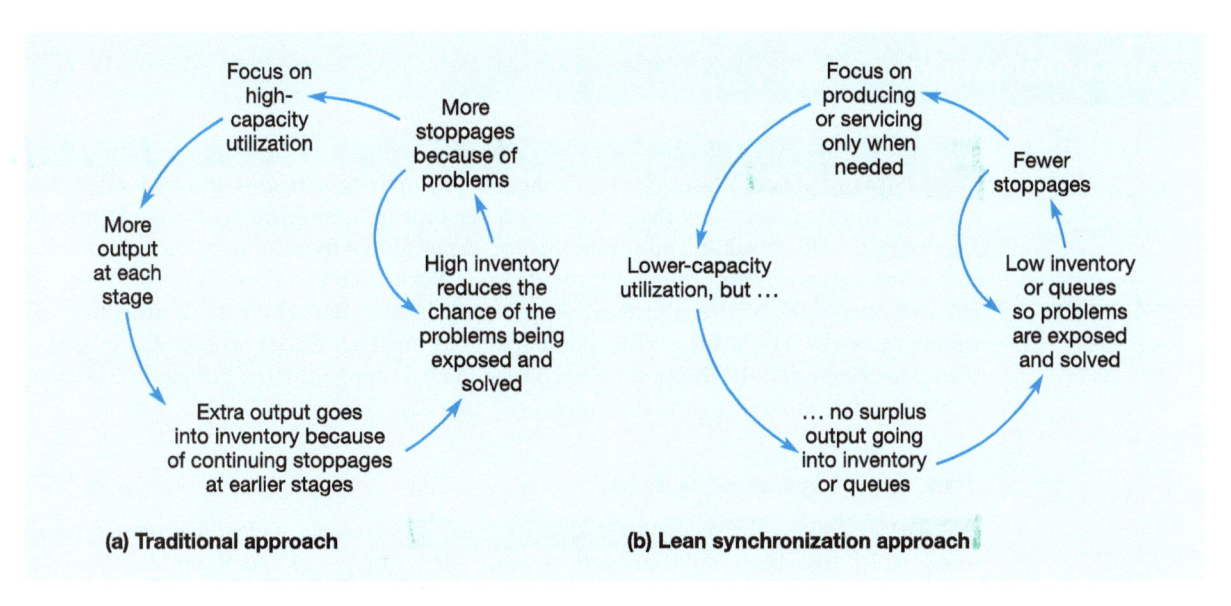

Figure 11.4 The different views of capacity utilization in (a) traditional and (b) JIT approaches to operations

as being important in supporting these objectives through an emphasis on involving all of the organization's staff. This culture is sometimes seen as synonymous with 'total quality' and is discussed in detail in Chapter 12. The lean approach to people management has also been called the **respect-for-humans** system. It encourages (and often requires) team-based problem-solving, job enrichment (by including maintenance and set-up tasks in operators' jobs), job rotation and multi-skilling. The intention is to encourage a high degree of personal responsibility, engagement and 'ownership' of the job.

Respect for humans

> ### Critical commentary
>
> Not all commentators see JIT-influenced people-management practices as entirely positive. The JIT approach to people management can be viewed as patronizing. It may be, to some extent, less autocratic than some Japanese management practice dating from earlier times. However, it is certainly not in line with some of the job design philosophies which place a high emphasis on contribution and commitment. Even in Japan the approach of JIT is not without its critics. Kamata wrote an autobiographical description of life as an employee at a Toyota plant called *Japan in the Passing Lane*.[2] His account speaks of 'the inhumanity and the unquestioning adherence' of working under such a system. Similar criticisms have been voiced by some trade union representatives.

Continuous improvement

Lean objectives are often expressed as ideals, such as our definition: 'to meet demand instantaneously with perfect quality and no waste'. While any operation's current performance may be far removed from such ideals, a fundamental lean belief is that it is possible to get closer to them over time. Without such beliefs to drive progress, lean proponents claim improvement is more likely to be transitory than continuous. This is why the concept of continuous improvement is such an important part of the lean philosophy. If its aims are set in terms of ideals which individual organizations may never fully achieve, then the emphasis must be on the way in which an organization moves closer to the ideal state. The Japanese word for continuous improvement is **kaizen**, and it is a key part of the lean philosophy. It is explained fully in Chapter 13.

Kaizen

The elimination of waste

The elimination of waste is central to lean approaches

Arguably the most significant part of the lean philosophy is its focus on the **elimination of all forms of waste.** Waste can be defined as any activity that does not add value. For example, studies often show that as little as 5 per cent of total throughput time is actually spent directly adding value. This means that for 95 per cent of its time, an operation is adding cost to the service or product, but not adding value. Such calculations can alert even relatively efficient operations to the enormous waste which is dormant within their processes and supply networks. This same phenomenon applies as much to service processes as it does to manufacturing ones. Relatively simple requests, such as applying for a driving licence, may only take a few minutes to actually process, yet take days or weeks to be returned.

The seven types of waste

The seven types of waste

Identifying waste is the first step towards eliminating it. Toyota have identified **seven types of waste**, which have been found to apply in many different types of operations – both service and production – and which form the core of lean philosophy:

1 *Over-production.* Producing more than is immediately needed by the next process in the operation is the greatest source of waste according to Toyota.
2 *Waiting time.* Equipment efficiency and labour efficiency are two popular measures which are widely used to measure equipment and labour waiting time, respectively. Less obvious is the amount of waiting time of items, disguised by operators who are kept busy doing things that are not needed at the time.
3 *Transport.* Moving items or customers around the operation often does not add value. Layout changes which bring processes closer together, improvements in transport methods and workplace organization can all reduce waste.
4 *Process.* The process itself may be a source of waste. Some operations may only exist because of poor product or service design, or poor maintenance, and so could be eliminated.
5 *Inventory.* All inventory should become a target for elimination. However, it is only by tackling the causes of inventory that it can be reduced.
6 *Motion.* An operator may look busy but sometimes no value is being added by the work. Simplification of work is a rich source of reduction in the waste of motion.
7 *Defectives.* Quality waste is often very significant in operations. Total costs of quality are much greater than has traditionally been considered, and it is therefore more important to attack the causes of such costs. This is discussed further in Chapter 12.

Between them, these seven types of waste contribute to four barriers to any operation achieving lean synchronization. They are: waste from irregular (non-streamlined) flow, waste from inexact supply, waste from inflexible response, and waste from variability. We will examine each of these barriers to achieving lean synchronization.

Eliminate waste through streamlined flow

The smooth flow of materials, information and people in the operation is a central idea of lean synchronization. Long process routes provide opportunities for delay and inventory build-up, add no value, and slow down throughput time. So, the first contribution any operation can make to streamlining flow is to reconsider the basic layout of its processes. Primarily, reconfiguring the layout of a process to aid lean synchronization involves moving it down the 'natural diagonal' of process design that was discussed in Chapter 5. Broadly speaking, this means moving from functional layouts towards cell-based layouts, or from cell-based layouts towards line layouts. Either way, it is necessary to move towards a layout that brings more systematization and control to the process flow. At a more detailed level, typical layout techniques include: placing workstations close together so that inventory of materials or customers just cannot build up because there is no space for it to do so, and arranging workstations in such a way that all those who contribute to a common activity are in sight of each other and can provide mutual help, for example by facilitating movement between workstations to balance capacity.

Examine all elements of throughput time

Throughput time is often taken as a surrogate measure for waste in a process. The longer that items being processed are held in inventory, moved, checked, or subject to anything else that does not add value, the longer they take to progress through the process. So, looking at exactly what happens to items within a process is an excellent method of identifying sources of waste.

Value stream mapping **Value stream mapping** (also known as 'end-to-end' system mapping) is a simple but effective approach to understanding the flow of material, customers and information as value is added as it progresses through a process, operation, or supply network. It visually maps a product or services path from start to finish. In doing so it records, not only the direct activities of creating products and services, but also the 'indirect' information systems that support the direct process. It is called 'value stream' mapping because it focuses on value-adding activities and distinguishes between value-adding and non-value-adding activities. It is similar to process mapping (see Chapter 5) but different in four ways:

- It uses a broader range of information than most process maps.
- It is usually at a higher level (5–10 activities) than most process maps.
- It often has a wider scope, frequently spanning the whole supply network.
- It can be used to identify where to focus future improvement activities.

A value stream perspective involves working on and improving the 'big picture', rather than just optimizing individual processes. Value stream mapping is seen by many practitioners as a starting point to help recognize waste and identify its causes. It is a four-step technique that identifies waste and suggests ways in which activities can be streamlined. Firstly, it involves identifying the value stream (the process, operation or supply chain) to map. Secondly, it involves physically mapping a process, then above it mapping the information flow that enables the process to occur. This is the so-called 'current state' map. Thirdly, problems are diagnosed and changes suggested, making a future state map that represents the improved process, operation or supply chain. Finally, the changes are implemented. Figure 11.5 shows a value stream map for an air conditioning installation service. The service process itself is broken down into five relatively large stages and various items of data for each stage are marked on the chart. The type of data collected here does vary, but all types of value stream map compare the total throughput time with the amount of value-added time within the larger process. In this case, only 8 of the 258 hours of the process is value-adding.

Worked example[3]

An ordinary flight, just a trip to Amsterdam for two or three days. Breakfast was a little rushed but left the house at 6.15. Had to return a few minutes later, forgot my passport. Managed to find it and leave (again) by 6.30. Arrived at the airport 7.00, dropped Angela off with bags at terminal and went to the long-term car park. Eventually found a parking space after 10 minutes. Waited 8 minutes for the courtesy bus. Six minute journey back to the terminal, we start queuing at the check-in counters by 7.24. Twenty minute wait. Eventually get to check-in and find that we have been allocated seats at different ends of the plane. Staff helpful but takes 8 minutes to sort it out. Wait in queue for security checks for 10 minutes. Security decide I look suspicious and search bags for 3 minutes. Waiting in lounge by 8.05. Spend 1 hour and 5 minutes in lounge reading computer magazine and looking at small plastic souvenirs. Hurrah, flight is called 9.10, takes 2 minutes to rush to the gate and queue for further 5 minutes at gate. Through the gate and on to air bridge

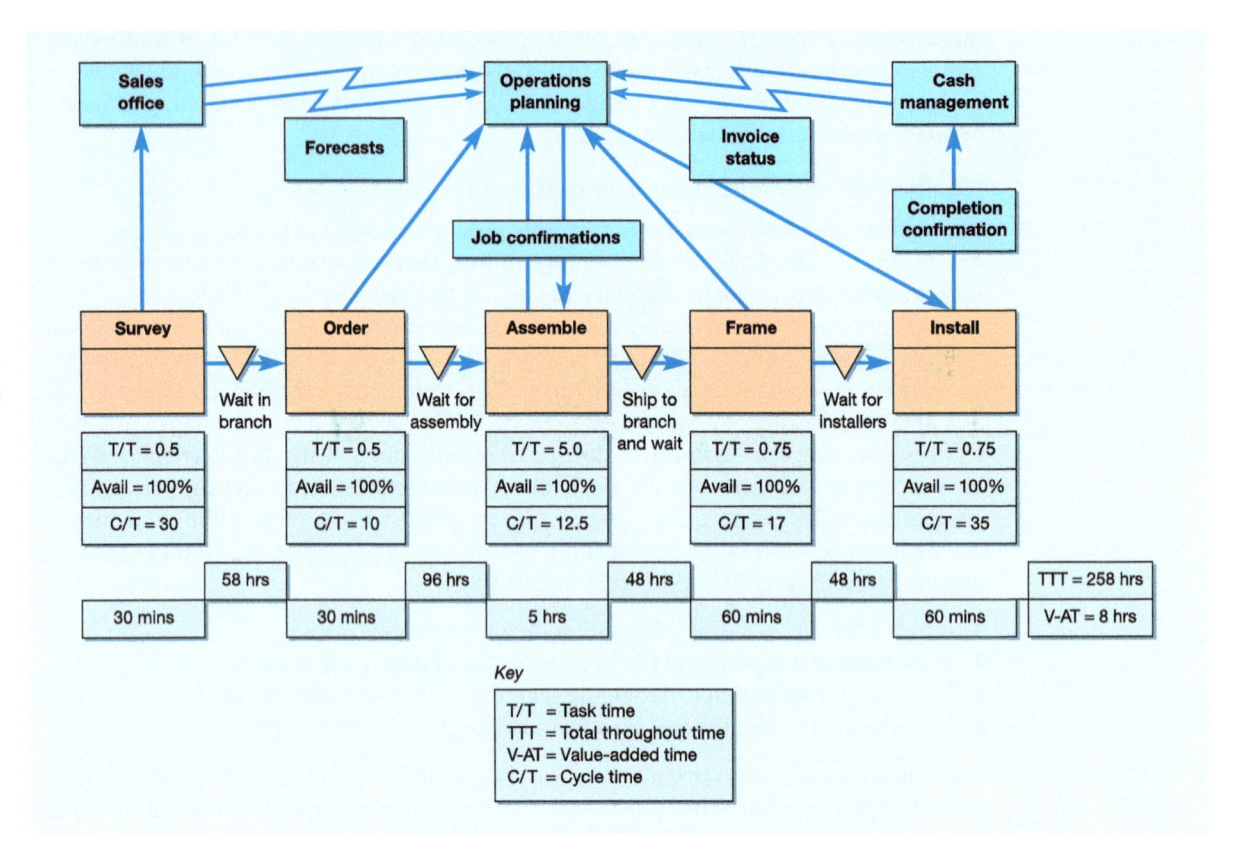

Figure 11.5 Value stream map for an industrial air conditioning installation service

which is continuous queue going onto plane, takes 4 minutes but finally in seats by 9.21. Wait for plane to fill up with other passengers for 14 minutes. Plane starts to taxi to runway at 9.35. Plane queues to take-off for 10 minutes. Plan takes off 9.45. Smooth flight to Amsterdam, 55 minutes. Stacked in queue of planes waiting to land for 10 minutes. Touch down at Schipol Airport 10.50. Taxi to terminal and wait 15 minutes to disembark. Disembark at 11.05 and walk to luggage collection (calling at lavatory on way), arrive luggage collection 11.15. Wait for luggage 8 minutes. Through customs (not searched by Netherlands security who decide I look trustworthy) and to taxi rank by 11.26. Wait for taxi 4 minutes. In to taxi by 11.30, 30 minutes ride into Amsterdam. Arrive hotel 12.00.

Analysis

How much of all this time was value-added? The total elapsed time, or throughput time, for the whole process was between 6.15 and 12.00, i.e. 5 hours 45 minutes. A detailed analysis of what was happening to the items being processed (Angela and me) indicates the following breakdown.

Time waiting in queue for check-in, luggage, etc. = 59 minutes
Time being 'served' at end of queue = 11 minutes
Waiting in lounge/plane etc. = 1 hour 55 minutes
Generally non-value-added moving about in airports, car parks etc. = 31 minutes
Quality error because I forgot my passport = 15 minutes
Value-added travelling time in car + plane + taxi = 1 hour 55 minutes.

So, only 1 hour 55 minutes of a total throughput time of 5 hours 45 minutes was spent in value-added activity. That is, 33.3 per cent value-added. Note, this was a smooth flight with no appreciable problems or delays.

Ensure visibility

Visibility

Appropriate layout also includes the extent to which all movement is transparent to everyone within the process. High **visibility** of flow makes it easier to recognize potential improvements to flow. It also promotes quality within a process because the more transparent the operation or process, the easier it is for all staff to share in its management and improvement. Problems are more easily detectable and information becomes simple, fast and visual. Visibility measures include the following.

- Clearly indicated process routes using signage.
- Performance measures clearly displayed in the workplace.
- Coloured lights used to indicate stoppages.
- An area is devoted to displaying samples of one's own and competitors' process outputs, together with samples of good and defective output.
- Visual control systems (e.g. kanbans, discussed later).

An important technique used to ensure flow visibility is the use of simple, but highly visual signals to indicate that a problem has occurred, together with operational authority to stop the process. For example, on an assembly line, if an employee detects some kind of quality problem, he or she could activate a signal that illuminates a light (called an 'andon' light) above the workstation and stops the line. Although this may seem to reduce the efficiency of the line, the idea is that this loss of efficiency in the short term is less than the accumulated losses of allowing defects to continue on in the process. Unless problems are tackled immediately, they may never be corrected.

Use small-scale simple process technology

Several small units instead of one large unit

There may also be possibilities to encourage smooth streamlined flow through the use of small-scale technologies. That is, using several small units of process technology rather than one large unit. Small machines have several advantages over large ones. First, they can process different products and services simultaneously. For example, in Figure 11.6 one large machine produces a batch of A, followed by a batch of B, and followed by a batch of C. However, if three smaller machines are used they can each produce A, B or C simultaneously. The system is also more robust. If one large machine breaks down, the whole system ceases to operate. If one of the three smaller machines breaks down, it is still operating at two-thirds effectiveness. Small machines are also easily moved, so that layout flexibility is enhanced, and the risks of making errors in investment decisions are reduced. However, investment in capacity may increase in total because parallel facilities are needed, so utilization may be lower.

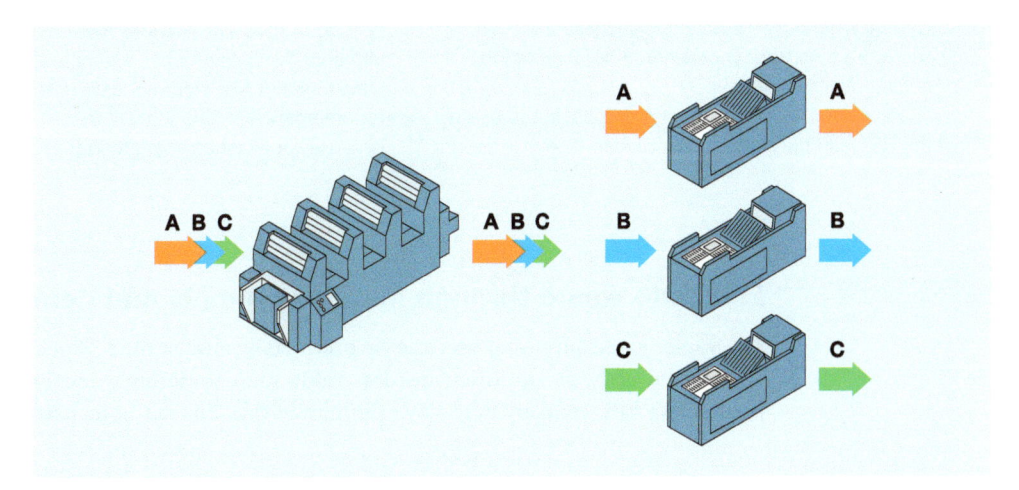

Figure 11.6 Using several small machines rather than one large one, allows simultaneous processing, is more robust, and is more flexible

Short case
Lean hospitals[4]

One of the increasing number of health-care services to adopt lean principles, the Bolton Hospitals National Health Service Trust in the north of England, has reduced its hospitals' mortality rate in one injury by more than a third. David Fillingham, chief executive of Bolton Hospitals NHS Trust said, '*We had far more people dying from fractured hips than should have been dying.*' Then the trust greatly reduced its mortality rate for fractured neck of femur by redesigning the patient's stay in hospital to reduce or remove the waits between 'useful activity'. The mortality rate fell from 22.9% to 14.6%, which is the equivalent of 14 more patients surviving every six months. At the same time, average length of stay fell by a third from 34.6 days to 23.5 days. The trust held five 'rapid improvement events', involving employees from across the organization who spent several days examining processes and identifying alternative ways to improve them. Some management consultants were also used but strictly in an advisory role. In addition third-party experts were brought in. These included staff from the Royal Air Force, who had been applying lean principles to running aircraft carriers. The value of these outsiders was not only their expertise, '*They asked all sorts of innocent, naïve questions*', said Mr Fillingham, '*to which, often, no member of staff has an answer.*' Other lean-based improvement initiatives included examining the patient's whole experience from start to finish so that delays (some of which could prove fatal) could be removed on their journey to the operating theatre, speeding up the radiology process and eliminating unnecessary paperwork. Cutting the length of stay and reducing process complications should also start to reduce costs, although Mr Fillingham says that it could take several years for the savings to become substantial. Not only that, but staff are also said to be helped by the changes because they can spend more time helping patients rather than doing non-value-added activities.

Meanwhile at Salisbury district hospital in the south of the UK, lean principles have reduced delays in waiting for the results of tests from the ultrasound department. Waiting lists have been reduced from 12 weeks to between 2 weeks and zero after an investigation showed that 67% of demand was coming from just 5% of possible ultrasound tests: abdominal, gynaecological and urological. So all work was streamed into routine 'green' streams and complex 'red' ones. This is like having different traffic lanes on a motorway dedicated to different types of traffic with fast cars in one lane and slow trucks in another. Mixing both types of work is like mixing fast cars and slow-moving trucks in all lanes. The department then concentrated on doing the routine 'green' work more efficiently. For example, the initial date scan used to check the age of a foetus took only two minutes, so a series of five-minute slots were allocated just for these. '*The secret is to get the steady stream of high-volume, low-variety chugging down the ultrasound motorway*', says Kate Hobson, who runs the department. Streaming routine work in this way has left more time to deal with the more complex jobs, yet staff are not overloaded. They are more likely to leave work on time and also believe that the department is doing a better job, all of which has improved morale, says Kate Hobson, '*I think people feel their day is more structured now. It's not that madness, opening the doors and people coming at you.*' Nor has this more disciplined approach impaired the department's ability to treat really urgent jobs. In fact it has stopped leaving space in its schedule for emergencies – the, now standard, short waiting time is usually sufficient for urgent jobs.

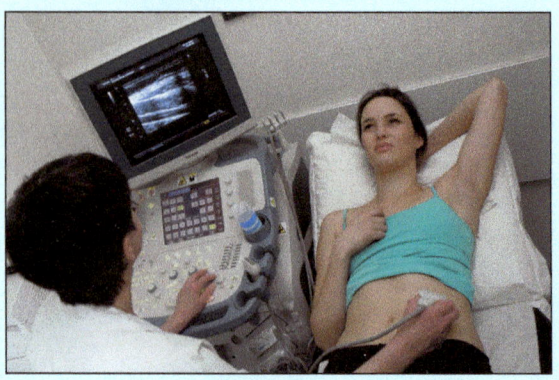

Eliminate waste through matching supply and demand exactly

The value of the supply of services or products is always time-dependent. Something that is delivered early or late often has less value than something delivered exactly when it is needed. We can see many everyday examples of this. For example, parcel delivery companies charge more for guaranteed faster delivery. This is because our real need for the delivery is often for it to be as fast as possible. The closer to instantaneous delivery we can get the more value the delivery has for us and the more we are willing to pay for it. In fact delivery of information earlier than it is required can be even more harmful than late delivery because it results in information inventories that serve to confuse flow through the process. For example, an Australian tax office used to receive applications by mail, open the mail and send it through to the relevant department which, after processing it, sent it to the next department. This led to piles of unprocessed applications building up within its processes, causing problems in tracing applications, and losing them, sorting through and prioritizing applications, and worst of all, long throughput times. Now they only open mail when the stages in front can process it. Each department requests more work only when they have processed previous work.

Pull control

The exact matching of supply and demand is often best served by using 'pull control' wherever possible (discussed in Chapter 10). At its simplest, consider how some fast-food restaurants cook and assemble food and place it in the warm area only when the customer-facing server has sold an item. Production is being triggered only by real customer demand. Similarly supermarkets usually replenish their shelves only when customers have taken sufficient products off the shelf. The movement of goods from the 'back-office' store to the shelf is triggered only by the 'empty-shelf' demand signal. Some construction companies make it a rule to call for material deliveries to their sites, only the day before those items are actually needed. This not only reduces clutter and the chances of theft, it speeds up throughput time and reduces confusion and inventories. The essence of pull control is to let the downstream stage in a process, operation, or supply network, pull items through the system rather than have them 'pushed' to them by the supplying stage. As Richard Hall, an authority on lean operations put it, *'Don't send nothing nowhere, make 'em come and get it.'*[5]

Kanbans

Kanbans

The use of kanbans is one method of operationalizing pull control. **Kanban** is the Japanese for card or signal. It is sometimes called the 'invisible conveyor' that controls the transfer of items between the stages of an operation. In its simplest form, it is a card used by a customer stage to instruct its supplier stage to send more items. Kanbans can also take other forms. In some Japanese companies, they are solid plastic markers or even coloured ping-pong balls. Whichever kind of kanban is being used, the principle is always the same: the receipt of a kanban triggers the movement, production or supply of one unit. If two kanbans are received, this triggers the movement, production or supply of two units and so on. Kanbans are the only means by which movement, production or supply can be authorized. Some companies use 'kanban squares'. These are marked spaces on the shop floor or bench that are drawn to fit one or more work pieces or containers. Only the existence of an empty square triggers production at the stage that supplies the square. As one would expect, at Toyota the key control tool is its kanban system. The kanban is seen as serving three purposes:

- It is an instruction for the preceding process to send more work.
- It is a visual control tool to show up areas of over-production and lack of synchronization.
- It is a tool for kaizen (continuous improvement). Toyota's rules state that 'the number of kanbans should be reduced over time'.

> ### Critical commentary
>
> Just-in-time principles can be taken to an extreme. When lean ideas first started to have an impact on operations practice in the West, some authorities advocated the reduction of between-process inventories to zero. While in the long term this provides the ultimate in motivation for operations managers to ensure the efficiency and reliability of each process stage, it does not admit the possibility of some processes always being intrinsically less than totally reliable. An alternative view is to allow inventories (albeit small ones) around process stages with higher than average uncertainty. This at least allows some protection for the rest of the system. The same ideas apply to just-in-time delivery between factories. The Toyota Motor Corp., often seen as the epitome of lean, has suffered from its low inter-plant inventory policies. Both the Kobe earthquake and fires in supplier plants have caused production at Toyota's main factories to close down for several days because of a shortage of key parts. Even in the best-regulated networks, one cannot always account for such events.

Eliminate waste through flexible processes

Responding exactly and instantaneously to customer demand implies that operations resources need to be sufficiently flexible to change both what they do and how much they do of it without incurring high cost or long delays. In fact, flexible processes (often with flexible technologies) can significantly enhance smooth and synchronized flow. For example, new publishing technologies allow professors to assemble printed and e-learning course material customized to the needs of individual courses or even individual students. In this case flexibility is allowing customized, small batches to be delivered 'to order'. In another example, a firm of lawyers used to take ten days to prepare its bills for customers. This meant that customers were not asked to pay until ten days after the work had been done. Now they use a system that, every day, updates each customer's account. So, when a bill is sent it includes all work up to the day before the billing date. The principle here is that process inflexibility also delays cash flow.

Reduce set-up times

For many technologies, increasing process flexibility, means reducing set-up times; defined as the time taken to change over the process from one activity to the next. Compare the time it takes you to change the tyre on your car with the time taken by a Formula 1 team. **Set-up reduction** can be achieved by a variety of methods such as cutting out time taken to search for tools and equipment, the pre-preparation of tasks which delay changeovers, and the constant practice of set-up routines. The other common approach to set-up time reduction is to convert work which was previously performed while the machine was stopped (called internal work) to work that is performed while the machine is running (called external work). There are three major methods of achieving the transfer of internal set-up work to external work:[6]

- Pre-prepare equipment instead of having to do it while the process is stopped. Preferably, all adjustment should be carried out externally.
- Make equipment capable of performing all required tasks so that changeovers become a simple adjustment.
- Facilitate the change of equipment, for example by using simple devices such as roller conveyors.

Fast changeovers are particularly important for airlines because they can't make money from aircraft that are sitting idle on the ground. It is called 'running the aircraft hot' in the industry. For many smaller airlines, the biggest barrier to running hot is that their markets are not large enough to justify passenger flights during the day and night. So, in order to avoid

Set-up time reduction

aircraft being idle over night, they must be used in some other way. That was the motive behind Boeing's 737 'Quick Change' (QC) aircraft. With it, airlines have the flexibility to use it for passenger flights during the day and, with less than a one-hour changeover (set-up) time, use it as a cargo aircraft throughout the night. Boeing engineers designed frames that hold entire rows of seats that could smoothly glide on and off the aircraft, allowing twelve seats to be rolled into place at once. When used for cargo, the seats are simply rolled out and replaced by special cargo containers designed to fit the curve of the fuselage and prevent damage to the interior. Before reinstalling the seats the sidewalls are thoroughly cleaned so that, once the seats are in place, passengers cannot tell the difference between a QC aircraft and a normal 737. Some airlines particularly value the aircraft's flexibility. It allows them to provide frequent reliable services in both passenger and cargo markets.

Eliminate waste through minimizing variability

One of the biggest causes of the variability that will disrupt flow and prevent lean synchronization is variation in the quality of items. This is why a discussion of lean synchronization should always include an evaluation of how quality conformance is ensured within processes. In particular, the principles of statistical process control (SPC) can be used to understand quality variability. Chapter 12 examines this subject, so in this section we shall focus on other causes of variability. The first of these is variability in the mix of products and services moving through processes, operations, or supply networks.

Level schedules as much as possible

Heijunka

Levelled scheduling (or **heijunka**) means keeping the mix and volume of flow between stages even over time. For example, instead of producing 500 parts in one batch, which would cover the needs for the next three months, levelled scheduling would require the process to make only one piece per hour regularly. Thus, the principle of levelled scheduling is very straightforward. However, the requirements to put it into practice are quite severe. The move from conventional to levelled scheduling is illustrated in Figure 11.7. Conventionally, if a mix of products were required in a time period (usually a month), a batch size would be calculated for each product and the batches produced in some sequence. Figure 11.7(a) shows three products that are produced in a 20-day time period in a production unit.

Quantity of product A required = 3,000
Quantity of product B required = 1,000
Quantity of product C required = 1,000

Batch size of product A = 600
Batch size of product B = 200
Batch size of product C = 200

Starting at day 1, the unit commences producing product A. During day 3, the batch of 600 As is finished and dispatched to the next stage. The batch of Bs is started but is not finished until day 4. The remainder of day 4 is spent making the batch of Cs and both batches are dispatched at the end of that day. The cycle then repeats itself. The consequence of using large batches is, first, that relatively large amounts of inventory accumulate within and between the units, and second, that most days are different from one another in terms of what they are expected to produce (in more complex circumstances, no two days would be the same).

Now suppose that the flexibility of the unit could be increased to the point where the batch sizes for the products were reduced to a quarter of their previous levels without loss of capacity (see Fig. 11.7(b)):

Batch size of product A = 150
Batch size of product B = 50
Batch size of product C = 50

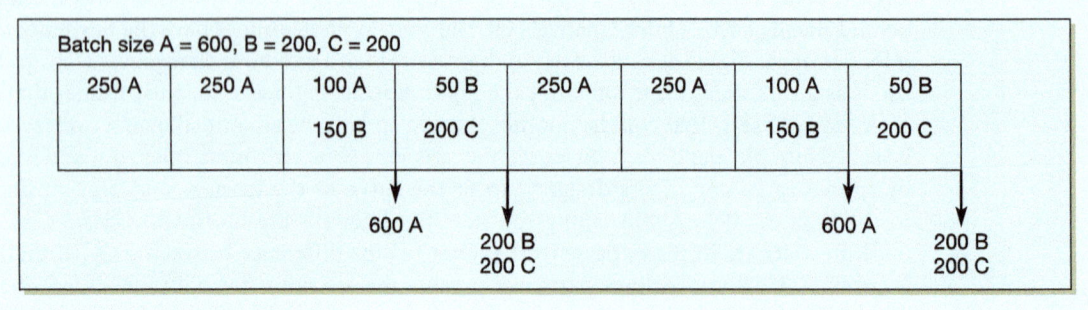

(a) Scheduling in large batches

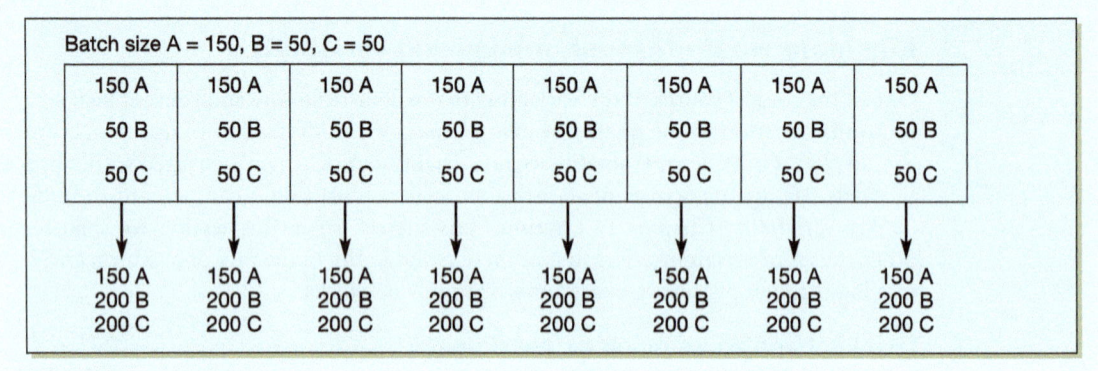

Batch size A = 600, B = 200, C = 200							
250 A	250 A	100 A 150 B	50 B 200 C	250 A	250 A	100 A 150 B	50 B 200 C

↓ 600 A   ↓ 200 B / 200 C   ↓ 600 A   ↓ 200 B / 200 C

(b) Levelled scheduling

Batch size A = 150, B = 50, C = 50							
150 A 50 B 50 C	150 A 50 B 50 C	150 A 50 B 50 C	150 A 50 B 50 C	150 A 50 B 50 C	150 A 50 B 50 C	150 A 50 B 50 C	150 A 50 B 50 C

↓ 150 A / 200 B / 200 C (×8)

Figure 11.7 Levelled scheduling equalizes the mix of products made each day

A batch of each product can now be completed in a single day, at the end of which the three batches are dispatched to their next stage. Smaller batches of inventory are moving between each stage, which will reduce the overall level of work-in-progress in the operation. Just as significant, however, is the effect on the regularity and rhythm of production at the unit. Now every day in the month is the same in terms of what needs to be produced. This makes planning and control of each stage in the operation much easier. For example, if on day 1 of the month the daily batch of As was finished by 11.00 am, and all the batches were successfully completed in the day, then the following day the unit will know that, if it again completes all the As by 11.00 am, it is on schedule. When every day is different, the simple question 'Are we on schedule to complete our production today?' requires some investigation before it can be answered. However, when every day is the same, everyone in the unit can tell whether production is on target by looking at the clock. Control becomes visible and transparent to all, and the advantages of regular, daily schedules can be passed to upstream suppliers.

Level delivery schedules

A similar concept to levelled scheduling can be applied to many transportation processes. For example, a chain of convenience stores may need to make deliveries of all the different types of products it sells every week. Traditionally it may have dispatched a truck loaded with one particular product around all its stores so that each store received the appropriate amount of the product that would last them for one week. This is equivalent to the large batches discussed in the previous example. An alternative would be to dispatch smaller quantities of all products in a single truck more frequently. Then, each store would receive smaller deliveries more frequently, inventory levels would be lower and the system could respond to trends in demand more readily because more deliveries means more opportunity to change the quantity delivered to a store. This is illustrated in Figure 11.8.

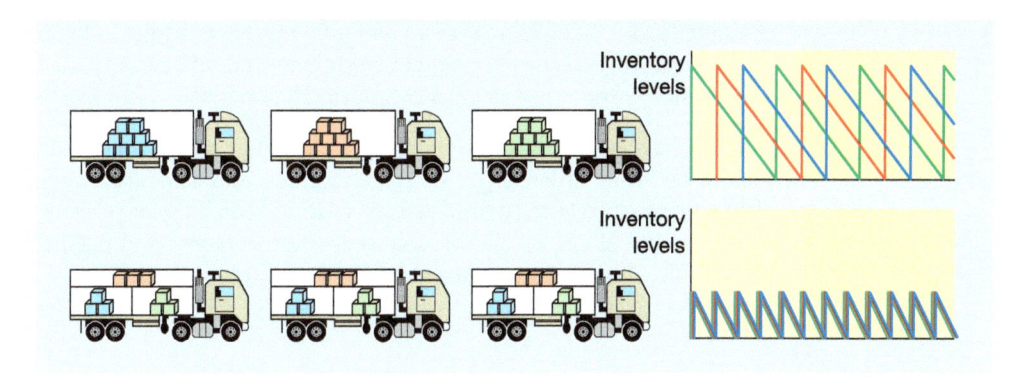

Figure 11.8 Delivering smaller quantities more often can reduce inventory levels

Adopt mixed modelling where possible

The principle of levelled scheduling can be taken further to give mixed modelling; that is, a repeated mix of outputs. Suppose that the machines in the production unit can be made so flexible that they achieve the JIT ideal of a batch size of one. The sequence of individual products emerging from the unit could be reduced progressively as illustrated in Figure 11.9. This would produce a steady stream of each product flowing continuously from the unit. However, the sequence of products does not always fall as conveniently as in Figure 11.9. The unit production times for each product are not usually identical and the ratios of required volumes are less convenient. For example, if a process is required to produce products A, B and C in the ratio 8:5:4, it could produce 800 of A, followed by 500 of B, followed by 400 of A, or 80A, 50B, and 40C. But ideally, sequencing the products as smoothly as possible, it would produce in the order . . . BACABACABACABACAB . . . repeated . . . repeated . . . etc. Doing this achieves relatively smooth flow (but does rely on significant process flexibility).

Keep things simple – the 5 Ss

The **5-S terminology** came originally from Japan, and although the translation into English is approximate, they are generally taken to represent the following.

1 **Sort** (*Seiri*) – eliminate what is not needed and keep what is needed.
2 **Straighten** (*Seiton*) – position things in such a way that they can be easily reached whenever they are needed.

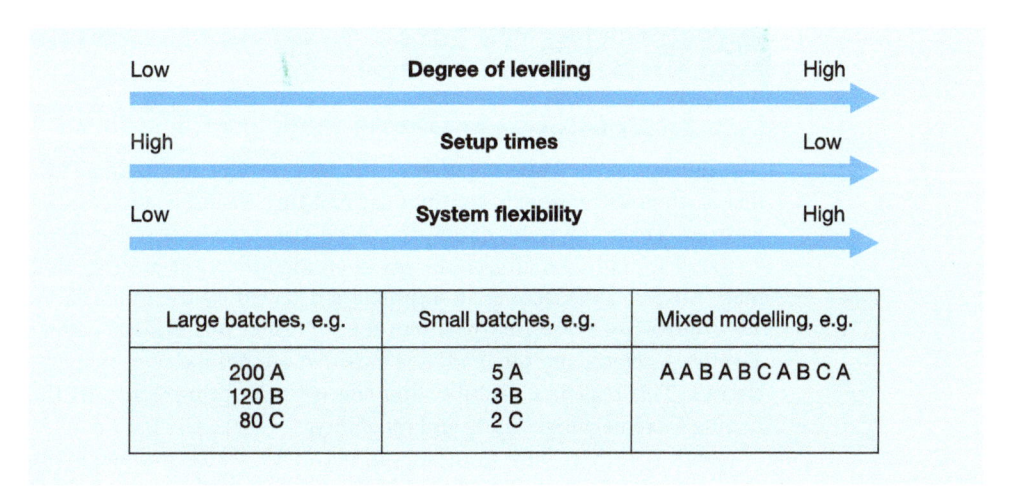

Large batches, e.g.	Small batches, e.g.	Mixed modelling, e.g.
200 A 120 B 80 C	5 A 3 B 2 C	A A B A B C A B C A

Figure 11.9 Levelled scheduling and mixed modelling: mixed modelling becomes possible as the batch size approaches one

3 **Shine** (*Seiso*) – keep things clean and tidy; no refuse or dirt in the work area.
4 **Standardize** (*Seiketsu*) – maintain cleanliness and order – perpetual neatness.
5 **Sustain** (*Shitsuke*) – develop a commitment and pride in keeping to standards.

The 5 Ss can be thought of as a simple housekeeping methodology to organize work areas that focuses on visual order, organization, cleanliness and standardization. It helps to eliminate all types of waste relating to uncertainty, waiting, searching for relevant information, creating variation, and so on. By eliminating what is unnecessary, and making everything clear and predictable, clutter is reduced, needed items are always in the same place and work is made easier and faster.

Lean synchronization applied throughout the supply network

Although most of the concepts and techniques discussed in this chapter are devoted to the management of stages *within* processes and processes *within* an operation, the same principles can apply to the whole supply network. In this context, the stages in a process are the whole businesses, operations or processes between which services and products flow. And as any business starts to approach lean synchronization it will eventually come up against the constraints imposed by the lack of lean synchronization of the other operations in its supply network. So, achieving further gains must involve trying to spread lean synchronization practice outward to its partners in the network; a far more demanding task than doing the same within a single process. And it becomes more complex as more of the supply network embraces the lean philosophy. The nature of the interaction between whole operations is far more complex than between individual stages within a process. To make a **supply network lean** means more than making each operation lean. A collection of localized lean operations rarely leads to an overall lean network. Rather one needs to apply the lean synchronization philosophy to the supply network as a whole. And essentially the principles of lean synchronization are the same for a supply network as they are for a process. Fast throughput throughout the whole supply network is still valuable and will save cost. Lower levels of inventory will still make it easier to achieve lean synchronization. Waste is just as evident (and even larger) at the level of the supply network and reducing waste is still a worthwhile task. Streamline flow, exact matching of supply and demand, enhanced flexibility, and minimizing variability are all still tasks that will benefit the whole network. The principles of pull control can work between whole operations in the same way as they can between stages within a single process. In fact, the principles and the techniques of lean synchronization are essentially the same no matter what level of analysis is being used.

Lean supply networks

Lean supply networks are like air traffic control systems[7]

The concept of the lean supply network has been likened to an air traffic control system, in that it attempts to provide continuous, 'real-time visibility and control' to all elements in the network. This is the secret of how the world's busiest airports handle thousands of departures and arrivals daily. All aircraft are given an identification number that shows up on a radar map. Aircraft approaching an airport are detected by the radar and contacted using radio. The control tower precisely positions the aircraft in an approach pattern which it coordinates. The radar detects any small adjustments that are necessary, which are communicated to the aircraft. This real-time visibility and control can optimize airport throughput while maintaining extremely high safety and reliability.

Contrast this to how most supply networks are coordinated. Information is captured only periodically, probably once a day, and any adjustments to logistics, output levels at the various operations in the supply network are adjusted, and plans rearranged. But imagine what would happen if this was how the airport operated, with only a 'radar snapshot' once a day. Coordinating aircraft with sufficient tolerance to arrange take-offs and landings every two minutes would be out of the question. Aircraft would be jeopardized, or alternatively, if aircraft were spaced further apart to maintain safety, throughput would be drastically reduced. Yet this is how most supply networks have traditionally operated. They use a daily 'snapshot' from their ERP systems (see Chapter 10 for an explanation of ERP). This limited visibility means operations must either space their work out to avoid 'collisions' (i.e. missed customer orders) thereby reducing output, or they must 'fly blind' thereby jeopardizing reliability.

Lean service

Any attempt to consider how lean ideas apply throughout a whole supply network must also confront the fact that these networks include service operations. So how can lean principles be applied in these parts of the network? The idea of lean factory operations is relatively easy to understand. Waste is evident in over-stocked inventories, excess scrap, badly sited machines and so on. In services it is less obvious, inefficiencies are more difficult to see. Yet most of the principles and techniques of lean synchronization, although often described in the context of manufacturing operations, are also applicable to service settings. In fact, some of the philosophical underpinning to lean synchronization can also be seen as having its equivalent in the service sector. Take, for example, the role of inventory. The comparison between manufacturing systems that hold large stocks of inventory between stages and those that did not centred on the effect which inventory had on improvement and problem-solving. Exactly the same argument can be applied when, instead of queues of material (inventory), an operation has to deal with queues of information or customers. With its customer focus, standardization, continuous quality improvement, smooth flow and efficiency, lean thinking has direct application in all operations, manufacturing or service. Bradley Staats and David Upton of Harvard Business School[8] have studied how lean ideas can be applied in service operations. They make three main points:

1. In terms of operations and improvements, the service industries in general are a long way behind manufacturing.
2. Not all lean manufacturing ideas translate from factory floor to office cubicle. For example, tools such as empowering manufacturing workers to 'stop the line' when they encounter a problem is not directly replicable when there is no line to stop.
3. Adopting lean operations principles alters the way a company learns through changes in problem solving, coordination through connections, and pathways and standardization.

Examples of lean service

Many of the examples of lean philosophy and lean techniques in service industries are directly analogous to those found in manufacturing industries because physical items are being moved or processed in some way. Consider the following examples.

- Supermarkets usually replenish their shelves only when customers have taken sufficient products off the shelf. The movement of goods from the 'back-office' store to the shelf is triggered only by the 'empty-shelf' demand signal. *Principle: pull control.*
- An Australian tax office used to receive applications by mail, open the mail and send it through to the relevant department which, after processing it, sent it to the next department. Now they only open mail when the stages in front can process it. Each department requests more work only when they have processed previous work. *Principle: don't let inventories build up, use pull control.*
- One construction company makes a rule of only calling for material deliveries to its sites the day before materials are needed. This reduces clutter and the chances of theft. *Principle: pull control reduces confusion.*

- Many fast-food restaurants cook and assemble food and place it in the warm area only when the customer-facing server has sold an item. *Principle: pull control reduces throughput time.*

Other examples of lean concepts and methods apply even when most of the service elements are intangible.

- Some web sites allow customers to register for a reminder service that automatically e-mails reminders for action to be taken, for example, the day before a partner's birthday, in time to prepare for a meeting, etc. *Principle: the value of delivered information, like delivered items, can be time-dependent; too early and it deteriorates (you forget it), too late and it's useless (because it's too late).*
- A firm of lawyers used to take ten days to prepare its bills for customers. This meant that customers were not asked to pay until ten days after the work had been done. Now they use a system that, every day, updates each customer's account. So, when a bill is sent it includes all work up to the day before the billing date. *Principle: process delays also delay cash flow, fast throughput improves cash flow.*
- New publishing technologies allow professors to assemble printed and e-learning course material customized to the needs of individual courses or even individual students. *Principle: flexibility allows customization and small batch sizes delivered 'to order'.*

Summary answers to key questions

Check and improve your understanding of this chapter using self-assessment questions and a personalized study plan, audio and video downloads, and an eBook – all at www.myomlab.com.

▶ What is lean synchronization?

- Lean synchronization is an approach to operations which tries to meet demand instantaneously with perfect quality and no waste. It is an approach which differs from traditional operations practices insomuch as it stresses waste elimination and fast throughput, both of which contribute to low inventories.
- The ability to deliver just-in-time not only saves working capital (through reducing inventory levels) but also has a significant impact on the ability of an operation to improve its intrinsic efficiency.
- The lean synchronization philosophy can be summarized as concerning three overlapping elements, (a) the elimination of waste in all its forms, (b) the inclusion of all staff of the operation in its improvement, and (c) the idea that all improvement should be on a continuous basis.

▶ How does lean synchronization eliminate waste?

- The most significant part of the lean philosophy is its focus on the elimination of all forms of waste, defined as any activity that does not add value.
- Lean synchronization identifies seven types of waste that, together, form four barriers to achieving lean synchronization. They are: waste from irregular (non-streamlined) flow, waste from inexact supply, waste from inflexible response, and waste from variability.

> **How does lean synchronization apply throughout the supply network?**
> - Most of the concepts and techniques of lean synchronization, although usually described as applying to individual processes and operations, also apply to the whole supply networks.
> - The concept of the lean supply network has been likened to an air traffic control system, in that it attempts to provide continuous, 'real-time visibility and control' to all elements in the network.
> - Most of the ideas of lean synchronization are directly applicable to all the service operations in the supply network.

Learning exercises

These problems and applications will help to improve your analysis of operations. You can find more practice problems as well as worked examples and guided solutions on MyOMLab at www.myomlab.com.

1. Revisit the worked example earlier in the chapter that analysed a journey in terms of value-added time (actually going somewhere) and non-value-added time (the time spent queuing etc.). Calculate the value-added time for a recent journey that you have taken.

2. A production process is required to produce 1,400 of product X, 840 of product Y and 420 of product Z in a 4-week period. If the process works 7 hours per day and 5 days per week, devise a mixed model schedule in terms of the number of each products required to be produced every hour, that would satisfy demand.

3. Revisit the 'Operations in action' at the beginning of this chapter, and (a) list all the different techniques and practices which Toyota adopts. (b) How are operations objectives (quality, speed, dependability, flexibility, cost) influenced by the practices which Toyota adopts?

4. Consider how set-up reduction principles can be used on the following:
   (a) changing a tyre at the side of the road (following a puncture);
   (b) cleaning out an aircraft and preparing it for the next flight between an aircraft on its inbound flight landing and disembarking its passengers, and the same aircraft being ready to take-off on its outbound flight;
   (c) the time between the finish of one surgical procedure in a hospital's operating theatre, and the start of the next one;
   (d) the 'pitstop' activities during a Formula One race (how does this compare to (a) above?).

Want to know more?

Ahlstrom, P. (2004) Lean service operations: translating lean production principles to service operations, *International Journal of Services, Technology and Management*, vol. 5, nos 5/6. Explains how lean can be used in services.

Bicheno, J. and Holweg, M. (2009) *The Lean Toolbox: The Essential Guide to Lean Transformation*, 4th edn, Piscie Press, Buckingham. A manual of lean techniques, very much a 'how to do it' book, and none the worse for it.

Holweg, M. (2007) The genealogy of lean production, *Journal of Operations Management*, vol. 25, 420–37. An excellent overview of how lean ideas developed.

Spear, S. and Bowen, H.K. (1999) Decoding the DNA of the Toyota Production System, *Harvard Business Review*, September–October. Revisits the leading company as regards JIT practice and re-evaluates the underlying philosophy behind the way it manages its operations. Recommended.

Womack, J.P. and Jones, D.T. (1996) *Lean Thinking: Banish Waste and Create Wealth in Your Corporation*, Simon and Schuster, New York. Some of the lessons from *The Machine that Changed the World* but applied in a broader context.

Womack, J.P., Jones, D.T. and Roos, D. (1990) *The Machine that Changed the World*, Rawson Associates, New York. Arguably the most influential book on operations management practice of the last fifty years. Firmly rooted in the automotive sector but did much to establish lean.

Useful websites

www.lean.org/ Site of the lean enterprise unit, set up by one of the founders of the lean thinking movement.

www.theiet.org/index.cfm The site of the Institution Electrical Engineers (which includes manufacturing engineers surprisingly) has material on this and related topics as well as other issues covered in this book.

www.mfgeng.com The manufacturing engineering site.

www.opsman.org Lots of useful stuff.

Now that you have finished reading this chapter, why not visit MyOMLab at www.myomlab.com where you'll find more learning resources to help you make the most of your studies and get a better grade.

Index

Note: Locators followed by 'b', 'f' and 't' refer to box, figure and table

A
ABC system, 259–261
Accuracy, 213
Aggregation level, 212
Agility, 100
Alignment policies, supply network management, 189–190, 190f

B
Balancing demand, 233
Balancing layout, 148–149, 149f
Benchmarking, 204
Bottom-up strategies, 72–74, 74f
B2B services, 53
B2C services, 54
Buffer, 241
Bullwhip effect, 197–198, 197f
Business process re-engineering (BPR), 16

C
Capacity management
    aggregation level, 212
    balancing demand, 233
    case studies, 210b, 220b, 226b, 234b
    chase demand plan, 221–223
    constraints, 211
    cumulative representation, 227–231
    defined, 211
    demand and supply variability, 233–235, 234f
    demand forecasting, 214–215
    level plans, 219–221
    long-term strategy, 211
    measuring, 215–219
    medium-term strategy, 211–212
    mixed plans, 225, 225f
    objectives, 212
    planning demand, 223–225
    queuing problem, 231, 231f
    short-term strategy, 211–212
    steps, 212–213, 213f
    waiting line, 232–233
    See also Yield management
Capacity management, alternative plans
    adjustment methods, 222
    chase demand plan, 221–222
    demand, managing and changing of, 223–224
    different demand patterns, 225–226
    idle time, 223
    level capacity plan, 219–221
    overtime, 223
    part-time staff, 223
    steps, 213–214, 214f
    subcontracting, 223
    workforce's size, 223
Computer-aided design (CAD), 124
Concept generation, services and products design
    from competitors, 115
    from customers, 114–115
    from R&D (research and development), 115
    from staff, 115
Concept screening, services and products design
    acceptability, 117
    creativity evaluation, 117–118
    design funnel, 117
    feasibility, 117
    vulnerability, 117
Control management
    vs planning, 267–268, 268f
    See also Planning and control
Core function, operation management, 3–5
Corporate social responsibility (CSR), 90–91
Cumulative representation, capacity management
    comparing plans, 230, 231f
    examples, 230–231
    levels of capacity, 227–229, 227f, 228f, 229f
Customer
    -dominant logic perspective, 28–29
    defined, 26–27
    service outcomes, 29

D
Demand forecasting, capacity management
    accuracy, 213
    daily fluctuation, 215
    expressions, 213
    importance of, 213
    seasonality, 214–215, 214f, 215f
    uncertainty indication, 214
    weekly fluctuation, 215
Dependability objectives
    money, 98
    stability, 98
    time, 98
Division of labour
    advantages, 155
    disadvantages, 155
    process design, 156
    scientific management, 155
    task allocation, 154–155
Downstream supply network, 182, 182f
Due date (DD), 274

E
E-business, 199–200, 199t
Economic batch quantity (EBQ), 249
Economic manufacturing quantity (EMQ), 249
Economic order quantity (EOQ), inventory management
    criticisms, 250–253, 252f
    defined, 247
    differential calculus method, 247–248
    economic batch quantity (EBQ), 249
    economic manufacturing quantity (EMQ), 249
    example, 248, 250
    gradual replacement model, 249–250, 249f

graphical representation, 247
holding cost, 245
order cost, 246
production order quantity (POQ), 249
sensitivity issues, 248
Enterprise resource planning (ERP)
   defined, 283–284
   development of, 283–284, 284f
   integration, 284f
   manufacturing requirement planning (MRP), 283
   materials requirement planning (MRP), 283
   web-integrated, 285
Environmentally sensitive design
   end of product life, 136
   energy source and quantities, 136
   input sources, 136
   product life, 136
   waste materials, amount and type, 136

F

First-in-first-out (FIFO), 275
5Ss, 303–304, waste elimination
Flexibility objectives
   delivery, 99
   mix of services, 99
   services and products, 99
   volume, 99
Flow, *see* Line layout

G

Globalization
   business environment, effect on, 9t
   IMF definition, 90
   social bottom line and, 90

H

Hayes and Wheelwright's model
   external neutrality and supportive stage, 70
   internal neutrality and supportive stage, 69
Hierarchy
   examples, 14t
   internal customer, 13
   internal supplier, 13
   operation process, 9–10, 14t, 15f
   process, defined, 13
   supply network, 14t
Human implications, process design
   division of labour, 154–155
   scientific management, 155
   Taylorism, 155

I

Information system, inventory management
   order generation, 261–262
   reports generation (inventory), 262
   stock records, updating, 261
Input resources
   customers, 11

facilities, 11
information, 11
materials, 11
operation process, 9
staff, 11
transforming resources, 11
Inventory cost
   for consignment, 244
   obsolescence, 244
   operating inefficiencies, 244
   order placement, 244
   price discount, 244
   for storage, 244
   working capital, 244
Inventory management
   ABC system, 259–261
   analysis and control system, 258–259
   anticipation, 242
   buffer, 241
   case studies, 239b, 252b–253b
   components, 243
   continuous review, 256–258
   costing, 244
   cycle, 241, 242f
   day-to-day decisions, 243
   de-coupling, 242
   defined, 240
   different plans, 246f, 246t
   economic order quantity (EOQ) formula, 245–253
   finished goods, 243
   information system, 261–262
   need for, 240, 241f
   negative aspects, 243
   periodic review, 256–258
   pipeline, 242
   profiles, 245
   raw material, 243
   role in operations, 240
   stock cover, 261
   stock turn, 261
   timing decisions, 254–256
   volume decisions, 243–244
   work-in progress, 243
Inventory priorities
   ABC system, 259–261
   example, 259–260
   Pareto law, 259, 260f
   usage value, 259

J

Job design, behavioral approaches
   commitment, 156
   empowerment, 157
   enlargement, 157
   enrichment, 157
   rotation, 156–157
   team working, 157

K

Kanbans, 299

L

Last-in-first-out (LIFO), 275
Layout
   case studies, 168b, 172f
   cell, 169–170, 170f
   decision, 165–166
   defined, 173
   fixed-position, 166–167, 167t
   functional, 167–169, 169f
   general objectives, 166
   line, 170–171, 171f
   mixed, 171–172
   operations type, 173
   selection, 173–175
   types, advantages and disadvantages, 174f, 174t
   volume and variety characteristics, 173, 173f
   workplace, 175–176, 176f
Lean synchronization
   as total system, 292–293, 293f
   benefits, 290–291, 290f
   case studies, 289b, 298b
   characteristics of inventories, 291t
   continuous improvement, 293
   defined, 290
   just-in-time, 291, 292f
   philosophy of, 292
   river and rocks analogy, 291
   service operation of, 305–306
   supply network, 304–305
   terminology, 291–292
   waste elimination, 293–304
Line layout, 170–171, 171f
Little's law, process design, 146–148
Location
   case studies, 161b, 163b
   decisions, 162
   demand side influences, 163f, 164–165, 165f
   objectives, 162–163
   operation, 162
   supply side influences, 163f, 164
Longest operation time (LOT), 275

M

Manufacturing requirement planning (MRP), 283
Market-requirements-based strategies
   case studies, 74b–75b
   customer needs, 76–77, 76f, 77t
   performance objectives, 75, 75f
   qualifying factors, 76
   resources perspectives, 74
   service/product life cycle, 77–78
Materials requirement planning (MRP), 283
Micro performance, process design
   throughput rate/time, 135
   utilization, 135
   work in process, 135

N

Negative aspects, 243
   inventory, 243
   natural environment, 91
   QFD, 122
Neutrality and supportive stage, competitive strategy, 70
Not-for-profit service, 55

O

Operation control
   push and pull, 280–281, 281f
   See also Planning and controlling
Operation process
   business process re-engineering (BPR), 16
   end-to-end' business process, 16
   example, 20
   hierarchy, 9–10
   input resources, 9
   output of services and products, 9–10
   transformation process model, 9
   typology, 20f
   variation dimension, 17–18
   variety dimension, 17
   visibility dimension, 17–18
   volume dimension, 17
Operation strategy
   bottom-up strategies, 72–74, 74f
   case studies, 68b–69b
   formulation, 82–83
   Hayes and Wheelwright's four stage model, 69–70
   perspectives, 71
   process, 81–82
   strategy comparison with, 69
   top-down startegies, 72, 73f
Operations function
   core function, 3–5
   defined, 3–4
   process, 16
   support function and, 4, 5f
   vs non-operations function, 16f
Operations management
   activities, 21–22
   case studies, 2b–3b, 7b, 8b–9b, 13b, 18b–19b
   characteristics, 17–20
   customer's perspective, 47–50
   defined, 3–4
   in not-for-profit organizations, 8
   in smaller organization, 6–7
   input process, 10
   input-transformations-output process, 9–13
   model, 21, 22f
   modern business, impact on, 9
   multiple customers, 50
   responsibility, 16, 21, 34
   service concept, understanding, 53
   strategy, implementation of, 45–46
   tactical and operations management, 44–45
   types of organizations, 5–9
Operations managers
   business case making, 47
   customer management, 50–51
Organization structure, services and products
   functional design, 128

matrix, 129
project design, 128
task force, 128
Output of services and products
　example, 12
　facilitating products and services, 12
　operation process, 9–10, 12f
　pure products and services, 12

P

Pareto law, 259, 260f
Performance objectives supply network
　cost, 185
　dependability, 185
　flexibility, 185
　quality, 184
　speed, 185
Performance objectives
　agility, 100
　case studies, 87b–88b, 94b–95b, 96b, 97b–98b, 100b
　corporate social responsibility (CSR), 90–91
　cost efficiency, 101–103, 102f, 103f
　dependability, 97–99
　economic bottom line, 92
　efficient frontier, 104–106, 105f
　environmental bottom line, 91–92
　flexibility in, 99–101
　make or break activities, 88
　mass customization, 100
　polar representation, 103–104, 104f
　quality, 93–95, 94f
　social bottom line, 90
　speed, 95–96, 95f
　trade-offs, 104–106
　triple bottom line, 89, 89f
Planning and controlling
　case studies, 266b, 269b, 275b, 278b–279f
　defined, 267
　demand effects, 268–272
　drum, buffer, rope concept, 281–282
　level of complexity, 276
　loading, 273–274
　long term, 267–268
　medium term, 267–268
　monitoring, 280–281
　scheduling, 276–280
　sequencing, 274–276
　short term, 267–268
　supply effects, 268–270
　theory of constraints (TOC), 281
　work pattern, 279–280
Planning management
　vs control, 267–268, 268f
　See also Planning and controlling
Process design
　balancing layout, 148–149, 149f
　batch, 138
　case studies, 133b, 154b
　continuous, 139
　cycle time, 145–146
　defined, 133–134
　environmentally sensitive, 135–136
　ergonomic principles, 156
　examples, 146–148, 148, 151
　flow chart, expense reports, 145f
　human implications, 154–156
　jobbing, 138
　life cycle analysis, 136
　Little's law, 146–148
　long-thin on short fat, 149, 150f
　mapping symbols, 142–145, 142f, 143f, 144f
　mass, 138–140
　micro performance, 135
　natural diagonal, 141, 141f
　objectives, 134–135
　product-process matrix, 141
　professional services, 139
　project, 136
　service shops, 139
　strategic performance, 134t
　throughput efficiency, 145–146, 150–152
　variability effects, 152–154, 153f
　volume-variety positions, 136, 137f
Production order quantity (POQ), 249
Public services (G2C), 54–55

Q

Quality function deployment (QFD), 121–123, 122f, 123f
Quality, performance objectives
　cost reduction, 93
　dependability, increase of, 94
Queuing problem, capacity management
　calling population, 232
　customer perception, 233–234
　demand utilization level, 233
　finite or infinite source, customers, 232–233
　individual process, variability, 233
　parallel processors, examples, 232t
Queuing theory, 231
　See also Queuing problem, capacity management

R

R&D (research and development), 11
Real time services, 51
Re-order level (ROL), 254, 254f
Re-order point (ROP), 254, 254f
River and rocks analogy, 291
Rotation, job design, 156–157

S

Scheduling
　backward, 276–277
　forward, 276–277
　Gantt chart, 277–278
　staff rostering, 279

Index

SCOR model, Supply network management
  benchmarking, 204
  benefits, 203–204
  best practices, 204
  business process, 204
  road map, 204
Sequencing
  customer priority, 274
  due date (DD), 274
  first-in-first-out (FIFO), 275
  judging rules, 276
  last-in-first-out (LIFO), 275
  longest operation time (LOT), 275
  physical constraints, 274
  shortest operation time (SOT), 275
Service operations management
  case studies, 30b, 31b–32b, 34b–35b, 45b–46b
  challenges, 60–61
  co-production, 33
  customers in, 26–30, 36
  defined, 26, 33–34
  economic contribution, 37
  operation's perspective, 27–28, 28f
  organizational benefit, 36–37
  principles, overview, 25–26
  products and values, 31–32
  real time services, 51
  staff, better experience, 36
  types, 26–27
Service operations manager
  case studies, 63b–64b
  challenges, 37, 44, 47, 52, 57, 60
  co-ordination, 51–52
  customer management, 50–51
  customer perspectives, 47–49, 49t
  key tasks, 50
  multiple customer management, 50
  responsibility, 34
  success tips, 36
  time management, 51
  See also Operations managers
Service processes
  capability (low volume and high variety), 58–59
  challenges, 57–58
  commodity (high volume and low variety), 58
  complexity (high volume and high variety), 59–60
  simplicity (low volume and low variety), 59
  types, 58f
Services
  business case for, 47
  case studies, 49b–50b, 55b–56b
  challenges, 52–53, 53t
  concept, defined, 47
  internal, 54
  not-for-profit, 55
  public services (G2C), 54–55
  types of processes, 57–58
  within sectors, 56–57, 56t

Services and products design
  activities, 126f, 128f
  aspects, 112
  case studies, 110b–111b, 113b, 116b, 118b–119b, 121b
  commonality, 120
  complexity, reduction of, 119–120
  component structure, 119, 119f
  computer-aided design (CAD), 124
  concept, 112
  conflict resolution, 127
  creativity, evaluation of, 117–118
  criteria, 116–117
  funnel concept of, 117
  generation of concept, 114–115
  good design, objectives, 111
  interactive design, benefits of, 125–126
  modularization, 120
  open sourcing, 115–116
  organization structure, 128–129
  packages, 112
  preliminary stages, 119
  process, 112–114, 114f, 121
  quality function deployment (QFD), 121–123, 122f, 123f
  sequential approach, 126–127, 126f
  simultaneous development, 126–127, 126f
  Skunkworks, 124
  stages, 114f
  standardization, 120
  time to market delays, 125f
  value engineering, 123
  virtual prototyping, 124
Shortest operation time (SOT), 275
Speed, performance objectives
  inventories, reduction of, 96
  risk reduction, 96
Strategy formulation
  case studies, 83b
  coherence, 82
  comprehensive, 82
  correspondence, 82–83
  criticality, 83
Supply Chain Operations Reference model (SCOR), *see* SCOR model, Supply network management
Supply network management
  alignment policies, 189–190, 190f
  alternative suppliers, rating of, 195t
  bullwhip effect, 197–198, 197f
  business or consumer relationship, 190–191, 191f
  business to business relationship, 191
  case studies, 180b, 185b, 189b, 193b, 202b, 203b
  channel alignment, 202
  co-opetition, 186–187
  customer perspectives, 184f
  defined, 181
  demand and supply side, 181
  design, 183

disintermediation, 186
do-or-buy decision, 187–189
dynamics, 198f
e-business, 199–200, 199t
e-procurement, 200–201
example, 195
first and second tier suppliers, 181
global sourcing, 196–197
in-house vs outsourcing, 188t
information sharing, 201–202
Internet and, 201
logistics, 201
market requirements, 190f, 204f
multi sourcing, advantages and disadvantages, 196t
operation perspectives, 181, 181f
operational efficiency, 199
outsourcing, 188f
partnership, 193–194
performance objectives, 182–185, 182f
reconfiguration, 186
relationship, types, 192f
SCOR model, 203–205
selecting suppliers, 194–196
single sourcing, advantages and disadvantages, 196t
terminology, 183f
time compression, 200f
traditional market, 191–192
upstream and downstream end, 182, 182f
virtual operations, 194
Support function and operations function, 4, 5f

T
Taylorism, 155
Theory of constraints (TOC), 281
Throughput efficiency
example, 151
process, 150–151
value-added, 151
workflow, 152
Timing decision, inventory management
example, 255–256
lead-time usage, 256

re-order level (ROL), 254, 254f
re-order point (ROP), 254, 254f
safety stock, 254f

U
Uncertainty indication, 214
Upstream supply network, 182, 182f

V
Value engineering, 123
Virtual prototyping, 124

W
Waste elimination
case studies, 298
delivery schedules, 302, 303f
example, 295–296
5Ss, 303–304
kanbans, 299
level schedules, 301–302, 302f
mixed modeling, adoption, 303, 303f
pull control, 299
set-up time, reduction of, 300–301
small scale technologies, 297, 297f
streamlined flow, 294–295
supply and demand processes, 298–299
throughput time, 295–296, 296f
types, 294
visibility measures, 297
Workplace layout
anthropometric aspects, 175–176, 176f
ergonomics design, 156

Y
Yield management
fixed capacities, 225–226
over-booking capacity, 226
price discounting, 226
service types, 226